W9-COJ-270

MODERN ARCHITECTURE IN EUROPE

A GUIDE TO BUILDINGS
SINCE THE INDUSTRIAL REVOLUTION

Dennis J. De Witt is an architectural consultant based in Boston, Massachusetts. He holds two graduate degrees in architecture, has served on the faculty of the Graduate School of Design at Harvard University, and has been head of the History Department of the Boston Architectural Center. His partner and navigator Elizabeth R. De Witt, an interested lay observer of architecture, heads a small public charitable foundation. The De Witts travelled 55,000 miles and visited 1,500 buildings during the preparation of this book.

To Jean-Bernard AT 40.
HAPPY BIRTHDAY.
Love, FRED

MODERN ARCHITECTURE IN EUROPE

A GUIDE TO BUILDINGS
SINCE THE INDUSTRIAL REVOLUTION

DENNIS J. DE WITT & **ELIZABETH R. DE WITT**

E. P. DUTTON   NEW YORK

To our mothers
And the memory of our fathers

Copyright © 1987 by Dennis J. De Witt and Elizabeth R. De Witt
All rights reserved. Printed in Great Britain.

No part of this publication may reproduced or transmitted in any
form or by any means, electronic or mechanical, including photocopy,
recording, or any information storage and retrieval system
now known or to be invented, without permission in writing from the
publisher, except by a reviewer who wishes to quote brief
passages in connection with a review written for inclusion in a magazine,
newspaper, or broadcast.

Published in the United States by E. P. Dutton,
a division of NAL Penguin Inc.,
2 Park Avenue, New York, N.Y. 10016.

Published simultaneously in Canada by Fitzhenry & Whiteside Limited, Toronto.

Library of Congress Catalog Card Number: 86–71614.

ISBN: 0–525–24415–8 (cloth)
ISBN: 0–525–48216–4 (DP)

COBE

Designed by Helen Lewis

Printed and bound in Great Britain by
Butler & Tanner Ltd. Frome and London

10 9 8 7 6 5 4 3 2 1
First American Edition

Maps and plans drawn by Technical Arts Services.
The maps for Vienna, Brussels, Berlin, Copenhagen, Barcelona, Paris, Rome, Milan, Amsterdam, The
Hague, Rotterdam, Stockholm and Helsinki are drawn from Falk Plans by kind permission of Falk-
Verlag GmbH. Falk Plans are available in bookshops.

CONTENTS

ACKNOWLEDGEMENTS

We must gratefully acknowledge all those without whom. . . .

Bob Venturi, who first showed us architecture's difficulty and richness, and who first encouraged an improbable undertaking; all our predecessors in this quest to experience, first hand, the *reality* of buildings and of places, especially G. E. Kidder Smith who demonstrated that it could be done with perception on a continental scale, and Ian Nairn, who breathed life and passion into what previously had too often been the preserve of opinionless organizers of dry facts; the RIBA in whose library so many of these buildings first came to our attention; Harvard University's Graduate School of Design which, through a four-year research appointment to its faculty, greatly assisted the process of organizing, verifying and generally putting into perspective the vast amount of material gathered during thirty-two months of European travel, and all the local institutions, architects and historians, who gave so freely of their time, knowledge and hospitality: the Norwegian Architects' Association; Asko Salokorpi and the Finnish Architecture Museum; Bengt Johansson of the Swedish Architecture Museum; Jørgen Sestoft of the Archive for Modern Danish Architecture; the Association of Catalan Architects; David Mackay (Catalonia); Carlos Flores (Spain); Dick van Woerkom (Netherlands); Dennis Sharp (Britain); Nuno Portas (Portugal); Marc Emery (France); Ralph Culpepper (Paris); Leonardo Benevolo (Italy); Vittorio Gregotti (Milan); Karl and Eva Mang (Austria); Julius Posner (Germany); Rolf and Jan Rave (Berlin); Wend Fischer (Munich); and especially Francis Strauven (Belgium), whose notes and encyclopedic knowledge of Europe's modern architecture contributed much to what we hope is a sense of completeness and balance; as well as Peter Blake, Dick Chafee and Don Grinberg, who read portions of the manuscript. Nor can we fail to acknowledge our great debt to three sometime mentor-colleagues at Harvard – Eduard Sekler, Stani von Moos and Neil Levine. Through friendly criticism and by example they deepened our appreciation of many of the problems we faced and set standards against which we have tried to judge our own efforts. Finally, we cannot omit Cyril Nelson and our US publisher E. P. Dutton, who first had the faith to take on this project; Michael Dover and our UK publisher, Weidenfeld & Nicolson, who accepted the difficult task of producing the book; and Martha Caute, our editor at Weidenfeld & Nicolson, who has patiently and graciously dealt with the inevitable conflicts of such a transatlantic production and whose meticulous double-checking of thousands of details is reflected throughout the book.

But for all of these individuals and institutions this guide would be both poorer and thinner. We alone, however, must be responsible for all judgements, errors and omissions.

PREFACE

Some years ago, when planning a long-anticipated architectural pilgrimage, we were surprised and frustrated to discover that there existed no comprehensive guide to modern European architecture. Although we found architectural guide-maps and books for individual cities and countries, or covering limited periods of time, it would have been impossible to collect or carry them all. So, perhaps naively, we decided to compile one ourselves: a guide that might be as interesting and useful to the inquisitive but uninitiated traveller as to the professional architect or student.

Since that innocent beginning, we have discovered why this book had not been written before. Eventually, we spent two and a half years travelling (twice as long as originally planned), covered 55,000 miles and visited 1500 buildings. This guide, which was to have been a by-product of our journey, had become its *raison d'être*.

Before we could begin, however, we had to set limits to our task.

HOW WERE THE BUILDINGS CHOSEN?

The buildings in this book reflect selection standards that vary somewhat according to their period and place.

In practice, our recognition of the mid-eighteenth-century origins of modern architecture (see Introduction) has not led to the inclusion of many pre-Art Nouveau buildings. Earlier buildings of significance to the development of modern architecture were never numerous, and many have not survived.

Some of the buildings in this book have been included because they helped shape the canons of modern architecture. Generally, these are to be found where important avant-garde theorists lived: that is, Britain, France, Holland and Germany. (Such 'canonical' buildings also form the bulk of the pre-Art Nouveau entries.) Readers who are well versed in the history of modern architecture may notice the occasional omission of such a building even though it still exists. Usually this is either because it has been so modified that visiting it would not be worthwhile for the average person, or because it cannot be seen without intruding on the occupants' privacy. Two examples of the latter sort are Alvar Aalto's Villa Mairea and Hugo Häring's experimental farm, Gut Garkau.

A majority of the selections have been made not for their place in the genealogy of modern architecture but because of their aesthetic or design quality. This is especially true of the post-Second World War listings. While the selection of these buildings has also been more subjective, an effort has been made to reflect the variety of postwar movements.

A few additional entries were chosen because they were the only accessible works by architects whose best-known buildings are now lost (F-16b, GB-43), were never built (F-53), or are not in Western Europe (B-8, D-37, GB-6).

Finally, there are some items that fall outside the narrowest definitions of architecture, but which are too important or interesting to ignore. These include urban designs (F-5), bridges (F-58, GB-59), structures (F-16, SF-15), and landscapes (E-12, P-2b, S-21), as well as some constructions that are best described as follies (F-57).

OTHER NOTED BUILDINGS

Many of the entries are accompanied by short notes mentioning related buildings which, although of interest, do not merit a separate listing. In addition to buildings by the same architect or in a similar style, these can also include works that are programmatically or ideologically similar, or simply buildings that are near by.

THE BUILDING REFERENCE NUMBERS

For ease of access and cross-reference, each entry in the book has been assigned a unique reference number – or, more precisely, a number preceded by a national identification letter or letters (e.g. GB-22). Originally devised for motor licence identification purposes, these letters determine the order in which the countries are listed. There is a separate numerical sequence for each country. The letters and the countries to which they refer are:

A	Austria (Österreich)	**GB**	Great Britain
B	Belgium (Belgie/Belgique)	**I**	Italy (Italia)
CH	Switzerland (Confederatio	**IRL**	Ireland (Eire)
	Helvetica/Schweiz/Suisse/	**N**	Norway (Norge)
	Svizzera)	**NL**	Netherlands (Nederland)
D	Germany (Deutschland)	**P**	Portugal
DK	Denmark (Danmark)	**S**	Sweden (Sverige)
E	Spain (España)	**SF**	Finland (Suomi)
F	France		

The first entry for each country usually consists of some brief comments about the country and its role in the history of modern architecture. Additional comments about major cities or about particular groups of buildings are also treated as separate entries.

A building mentioned in a 'note' accompanying an entry is identified by the entry's reference number plus the noted building's own lower case identification letter (e.g. D-70b).

HOW TO FIND THE BUILDINGS

The easiest, probably the only, way to see all these buildings is by car: one hotel (S-30) is seventy miles up a dirt road. But most urban buildings, and many of the rural ones, can be reached by some form of public transport.

Although there are 'metros' (subways/undergrounds) in a number of the larger cities (London, Paris, Berlin, Stockholm, Milan, Barcelona, Munich, Rome, etc.), stations are given only where the systems are complete enough to be of real use. Instructions are not given for other forms of public transport because they are too subject to schedule and routeing changes. Complete local transport information can always be obtained from tourist offices.

For the most important cities, as well as in certain other exceptional situations, maps showing the locations of the listed and noted buildings have been provided. Precise directions from some easy-to-find place or road explain how to reach those buildings not marked on a map.

To keep the directions from occupying a disproportionate amount of space, the following terms, abbreviations, and symbols have been used:

CENTRUM	= a word or name in capitals is to be found on a sign		m	= metres
→	= 'follow the sign indicated', or 'toward the place indicated' (e.g. → CENTRUM)		mi	= miles
			M123 (M with a number, no hyphen)	= in Britain, a motorway or expressway
⇨	= 'which becomes' – indicates that a road changes names, possibly more than once (e.g. av Gabriel ⇨ rue de Rivoli ⇨ rue St Antoine)		Map SF-19	= marked on indicated map, in this case the map that accompanies SF-19
			(Map GB-2 →)	= continue, following the directions, along the route marked with an arrow and the building's reference number at the edge of the indicated map – here the map that accompanies GB-2
A123 (A with a number, no hyphen)	= in Britain and Denmark, a main highway; in France and Italy, a motorway or expressway			
abt	= about			
av	= avenue, *avenida*, etc.		N	= north
B123 (B with a number, no hyphen)	= in Britain, a secondary road		N123 (N with a number, no hyphen)	= in Belgium, France and Spain, a national highway
blk	= block			
boul	= boulevard		N-IV (N with a Roman numeral, with hyphen	= in Spain, a special class of national highway
ch	= *chaussée* (road)			
ctr	= centre		R	= right
D123 (D with a number, no hyphen)	= in France, a secondary road		rd	= road
E	= east		RR	= railroad/railway
E123 (E with a number, no hyphen)	= a pan-European highway		Rt	= route, numbered highway (usually followed by a number)
jog	= as in 'jog R', a turn (in this case to the right) immediately followed by another opposite turn so that one continues in approximately the original direction of travel			
			S	= south
			sq	= square
			st, str	= street, *straße*, *straat*, etc.
			T	= T intersection
			W	= west
km	= kilometre		Y	= Y intersection
L	= left		yd	= yards

In addition to each listed building and most noted ones being located on a city map or by written directions, listed and noted buildings are also plotted on an outline map of the country. On the country maps:

▲	= ***	▲	= **	▲	= *
■	= no astericks	●	= a 'note'	⊡	= a town plan

(The *s are explained under 'Relative importance' below). Only the most important building in each location is indicated.

On local maps all listed buildings are shown by a ▲. Only those noted ones not immediately adjacent to their listed buildings are also shown by a ●.

For almost all of the rural entries, the instructions and a good road map should provide sufficient information. However, it is always desirable to have detailed maps of cities and towns. Except in Britain, these are normally available – if not always free – at local tourist offices. Even more useful, in most of the countries for which they are published, are the Michelin Guides. These guides provide small but excellent plans for most towns of any size. They are particularly useful because they give up-to-date information on one-way streets. (Curiously, the maps in the British Michelin are far less complete and thus much less useful.) The most consistent series of individual maps covering larger cities are the Falk Plans, most of which are based on a special projection system that magnifies the typically more dense central section of a city. Because the city maps in this book are generally based on this special Falk Plan projection, the shapes of certain street intersections and other details may differ from those of more conventional maps.

To avoid confusion when reading signs and maps, native place names and spellings have been used in the directions and are given along with the common English equivalent, if any, at the top of each entry. (The European, rather than the American method of designating the floors of a building is also consistently used, i.e. 'ground floor' = US first floor; 'first floor' = US second floor, etc.)

Finally, the names of some towns are given in the following form: Barcelona/Pedralbes. This indicates that the building is located in a contiguous suburb, Pedralbes, of a major city, Barcelona.

THE LISTINGS

In addition to the directions and the photographs – generally quite straightforward exterior views intended both to give some overall impression of the building and to make it easier to find – the listing for each building provides the following information:

Name, if any, and use There is an index of building types which groups all buildings intended to serve a similar purpose.

Architect There is also an index of architects which gives their other listed or noted works.

Dates Usually given as a range of years, these represent the dates found in the literature. Ideally they should indicate the span of time from the beginning of design to the end of construction. More often they just represent the period of construction.

Style The classification of buildings by 'style', more common in US than European architectural guides, is primarily intended to help those without a background in architectural history better to understand the philosophical and aesthetic context for a building's design. If no such label seems helpful, it is omitted. This tends especially to be true of recent buildings. To aid readers who may be less familiar with these terms, many of them are discussed briefly in the introduction where they are shown in bold face.

Relative importance An * or ** or *** next to the reference number represents an attempt to indicate the relative value (in ascending order) of experiencing first hand that building or place as it exists today. In assigning these ratings many factors were taken into account, including (in varying proportions): historical importance, present condition, accessibility, context and also – and this is something much harder to define or defend – any quality or qualities which make that personal encounter a pleasurable, or memorable, or evocative experience. Like the indication of style, these evaluations are intended to be of use primarily to the lay reader.

Comments The comments on the buildings are not meant to be objective or exclusively descriptive. They vary as much as the buildings themselves. Some may call attention to a little-known architect or discuss an unusual building type. Some describe a building's role in the history of modern architecture. Others may discuss more generally an aspect of design or the interaction of buildings with their settings. These are impressions of buildings not as two-dimensional abstractions on a printed page but as tangible artifacts that may be encountered on a city's streets or in open country; newly minted, or gracefully carrying their years or sadly aged; representatives of a specific type or unique creations; little-known or world famous; successes or failures.

A SUGGESTION

Although the Introduction which follows attempts to summarize in a few brief pages the origins and development of modern architecture, it is in the nature of this book that the comments on each building must stand on their own. But, taken together, the hundreds of individual entries and notes also form a kind of fragmented, kaleidoscopic history and critique of two centuries of modern architecture. To get the most from the individual listings – from the unavoidable references to movements, events, innovations, styles, personalities – the book should first be read as a whole. To counteract, in some small way, its necessarily non-chronological organization we suggest that, after the Introduction, the national sections should be read in the following order: Britain (**GB**) and France (**F**), where the Industrial Revolution and the quest for new means of architectural expression began in the eighteenth and nineteenth centuries; Austria (**A**), Belgium (**B**) and Spain (**E**), where the first modern-seeming style, the turn-of-the-century Art Nouveau, found its fullest expression; Germany (**D**) and Holland (**NL**), where between the World Wars the irrational and the rational, in rapid succession, reached brief, brilliant apogees; and finally Scandinavia (**DK, S, SF,** and **N**), Italy (**I**), Switzerland (**CH**), Portugal (**P**) and Ireland (**IRL**).

TWO FINAL REQUESTS

Be considerate At all times the utmost respect should be shown to the occupants of any building. The fact that a building is listed here does not imply that it may be entered or that it may be photographed from within the property. In the case of most public, non-residential buildings, obtaining permission when necessary is usually not difficult.

Because of considerations of privacy, occupied single-family houses have generally been excluded, except those which are visible from the street. However, it is unfair to the residents of any dwelling to ask to see the inside of such a building, particularly as you may be only one of many visitors on a given day.

For future editions Sir Nikolaus Pevsner wrote that a guidebook should not be judged until its second edition. For future editions we would be pleased to hear from readers, care of Weidenfeld & Nicolson, 91 Clapham High Street, London SW4 7TA, if:

You would like to see a building or place added to this guide.

We have made a factual error. We have done our best, but the odds against us are long.

A building has been renumbered or a street name changed – a surprisingly common occurrence.

Something has happened to render the directions useless, such as a changed traffic pattern.

A building has been altered or destroyed. Increased recognition and publicity should help save important buildings from demolition, but undoubtedly some will be lost.

D. J. De W. & E. R. De W.

INTRODUCTION
An Historical Overview

By the beginning of the eighteenth century, the mature Baroque, a form of Classicism born of the Counter Reformation, had become in varying forms the universal language of architecture throughout Catholic and Protestant Europe. The Classical system of architecture represented the ancient world of Greece and Rome, then still a semi-mythical, golden age. However, the system was understood primarily from only a few examples of Imperial Roman architecture and from the famous ten books on architecture, *De architectura*, by the Roman architect Vitruvius, which, significantly, had survived without illustrations. Baroque Classicism was hierarchical, symmetrical and proportioned according to the prescribed ratios of the five Classical orders, because it, and the Classical orders, were believed to be made in the image of man. And man, in turn, was made in the image of God. The most common and conspicuous architecture, as distinguished from merely utilitarian buildings, was religious; and the cruciform plans of most churches even more explicitly reinforced the identity of architecture, man and God.

Perhaps the building which best reflected the role of architecture as a model of the cosmic and social order was the palace of the Sun King, Louis XIV, at Versailles. (For two centuries Versailles was emulated in various ways from one end of Europe to the other.) With its outbuildings it was an idealized miniature city of ten thousand, while its gardens were a model of the proper subjugation of nature. The roads on one side of the palace and the grand *allées* of clipped trees on the other radiated toward the horizon. At the centre of these lines of authority was the bed of the king – God's anointed on earth. Versailles, like the churches of the Counter Reformation, reaffirmed that God was in heaven, and mankind was put on earth to multiply and to subdue it.

But by the beginning of the eighteenth century there were already the first signs of a radically different way of idealizing the relationship of mankind, architecture and nature. Painters like Nicolas Poussin (1593/4–1665) and Claude Lorraine (1600–82) had come to depict in their landscapes a version of 'untamed' nature wherein architecture, or architectural ruins, existed in nature without dominating it, and were even subject to its laws of decay. In England as the eighteenth century progressed this new sensibility would give rise to theoretical writings on the nature of beauty, and would lead to the picturesque 'natural' landscapes of Capability Brown (1715–83) and Humphry Repton (1752–1818) – the *jardins anglais* of the Continent – in which architecture was no longer part of a system of formal gardens that architecturalized the landscape. Rather a much simpler architecture, often incorporating emblematic temple forms, would come to occupy these landscapes as if it were a creation not of man or God, but of nature itself.

By the beginning of the eighteenth century there were also the first suggestions of a new attitude towards the idea of style. For the first time since the Renaissance, Gothic architecture (the name 'Goth-ic' originally implied 'barbarian') could be seen as having some value in its own right. Sir Christopher Wren completed the Tom Tower, 1681–2, in Oxford in a Gothick manner that he felt harmonized with

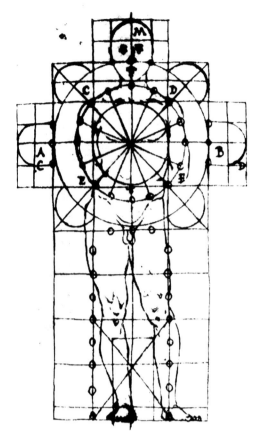

In the Classical system man was the measure of all things. This drawing by the Renaissance architect Francesco di Giorgio demonstrates the direct relationship between the human form and the plan of a church.

its existing late Gothic base, and Sir John Vanbrugh built for himself a Gothick castle, 1717–26.

These were among the first small signs of change, the first indications that an age of reason, inquiry and doubt – whose eighteenth-century beginnings are now called the Enlightenment – would gradually succeed an age of belief and received knowledge. But while the Gothic might seem an acceptable alternative under certain circumstances, 'architecture' in the eighteenth century meant Classical architecture. There could be no question of abandoning Classical architecture, only of re-examining its origins and meaning. If it was possible to speculate on the role of God in heaven, kings on earth, and mankind in nature, then the meaning of architecture, of Classical architecture, also had to be considered anew.

Vitruvius had written that architecture – that is the Classical temple – was derived from a 'primitive hut'. The need for a renewal of the Classical system led to a kind of deification of the primitive hut, which reached a peak in the middle of the century with the publication in France (and almost immediately in English in Britain), of the Abbé Laugier's influential *Essai sur l'architecture*, 1753. It also gave rise to **Neo-Classicism**, a reborn Classicism purified of theatrical Baroque distortions and eventually represented at its most extreme by the pure temple form (F-10b, D-67). It was an architecture that turned inwards upon itself and no longer assumed that it represented an accepted social order. Rather, it increasingly became architecture about architecture. Later, as the Revolution overtook France, it gave rise to proposals of unrealizable scale and scope, such as Etienne-Louis Boullée's Newton Cenotaph or Claude-Nicolas Ledoux's Ideal City of Chaux (F-53), whose forms and details often symbolically 'spoke' of function or, sometimes very explicitly, of cosmic meaning – or meaninglessness. The term **Architecture Parlante** was coined by mid-nineteenth-century French architects in reference to these projects, and to their own works (F-11), which were meant to 'speak' in this way to the observer as the Gothic cathedrals had once done.

Of almost exactly the same date as Laugier's *Essai* were the publication of the first encyclopedia, the discovery near Naples of the buried Roman city of Pompeii (I-54b), and the almost equally important 'discovery' not much farther from Naples – if one can discover structures that have been standing in plain sight – of the tough, primitive 'Greek Doric' temples at Paestum (I-54a). Europe began systematically to make an inventory of its world. As it did so, it gained a clearer sense of time and place. It found high civilizations, past and present, not all of whose architectural accomplishments were part of the Classical tradition (GB-44). It learned that Rousseau's Noble Savage lived in a variety of

Top *One of several versions of a gigantic monument to Newton – the eighteenth century's ideal of the rational, inquiring intellect – proposed by E.-L. Boullée, c.1784.*

Above *'House for the Directors of the Loue', c.1773–9, from C.-N. Ledoux's series of projects for his Ideal City of Chaux – an extreme example of Architecture Parlante.*

'primitive huts'. The Classical past, now better understood, ceased to be a single golden age. It became at once both more distant and far richer, and no longer governed by simple immutable rules. For the first time there were accessible publications of measured drawings, not just of Roman architecture, but also that of Athens as well as the primitive Doric of Paestum and the almost Baroque elaboration of Hellenistic Asia Minor. As the complexity of the Classical past came to be better understood, so too, if more slowly at first, did that of the Gothic. Nor were only the external appearances of ancient buildings – the proportions and ornamentation – subjected to scrutiny. Construction details and methods were identified, or at least speculated upon, and plan variations related to building use were noted. Parallel to this cataloguing of the past was the need to design buildings for a variety of new uses, or uses previously incorporated in houses and palaces, or traditionally housed in buildings not designed by architects. These included shopping arcades (F-3), museums, offices and factories (F-53).

By the mid-eighteenth century, the Industrial Revolution was beginning radically to transform Britain and to a lesser extent France. The initial importance of the Industrial Revolution lay not so much in the new technologies that came with it (GB-59) (they would only affect architecture later), but rather in the way it catalysed a change in the nature and perception of society, cities and the landscape. It also accelerated the shift of power from the old landowning class to a new more urban, mercantile and professional class. Although most of the intellectual changes necessary for the eventual development of 'modernist' sensibilities were felt throughout Europe during the eighteenth century, the Industrial Revolution took an additional century or more to spread across the Continent. That is why this book is subtitled 'Buildings since the Industrial Revolution', rather than 'Buildings since the Enlightenment'. And that is why there is such a great range in the dates of the earliest buildings listed for each country.

In France these changes led to the development of **Rationalism**, an attempt to devise a systematically designed, scientifically constructed architecture. Rationalism in architecture, as in other aspects of life, assumes that there are universal laws that can be applied without exception, and generally without concern for any specific physical, historical or architectural context. Although there was considerable overlap between Rationalism and Neo-Classicism in the decades around the turn of the nineteenth century, one figure, Jean-Nicolas-Louis Durand, epitomized Rationalist thought. A teacher of civil engineering, he published a volume of graph-paper-based, standardized designs for buildings of all types. Durand's book continued to be used well into the nineteenth century, especially by foreign students seeking to enter the École des Beaux-Arts who sought to understand the French way of thinking about design. Durand's Rationalism, which was concerned primarily with the logic of the building's plan and only in a very general sense with that of its use, might perhaps more correctly be called **Classical Rationalism**. (The term Rationalism was also later misleadingly adopted in Italy to describe the International Style of the 1920s and 30s throughout Europe. But more on that below.)

Structural (or **Gothic**) **Rationalism**, on the other hand, is concerned primarily with the logic of structure and construction. Its greatest exponent was the mid-nineteenth-century theorist Eugène-Emmanuel Viollet-le-Duc, although it had permeated Jacques Germain Soufflot's Panthéon (F-10) a century earlier. Significantly, both men were involved in the structural restoration of Gothic churches.

Design for a concert hall by Viollet-le-Duc, c.1864: in effect a 'corrected' Gothic design using iron as Viollet-le-Duc believed Gothic architects might have done, had it been available to them.

The changes in French architectural theory during the eighteenth century coincided with the refinement of the academic Beaux-Arts system of education and with the academicization of French architectural practice. Through most of the nineteenth century the leading French architects were thus forced to become *de facto* public servants. This role often allowed them time to study the design of their buildings in greater detail than could their colleagues in other countries, but it also tended drastically to limit the number of buildings they could produce. On the other hand, in Britain and to some extent elsewhere on the Continent the eighteenth century had seen a gradual shift from the master-mason-architect and the amateur or gentleman-architect (Wren had been a professor of astronomy) towards such true professional architects as Sir John Soane (GB-8). Compared to that of most of their antecedents, the output of this new breed could be prodigious.

In France the revival of the Gothic was never fully accepted. Rather it was England, where there was no entrenched academy, which saw the greatest development of the **Gothic Revival**. Beginning with the papery sham **Gothick** of innumerable eighteenth-century garden follies (D-23) and of the urban Commissioners' Churches of early-nineteenth-century Britain, there gradually evolved sound built work and a body of theory, especially in the writings of the A. W. N. Pugin (GB-3) and John Ruskin (GB-49). The Gothic Revival reached its peak during the third quarter of the nineteenth century in the muscular, self-assured, polychrome **High Victorian Gothic** (GB-14a). Three major interrelated currents can be felt in the Gothic Revival: romanticism, nationalism and functionalism.

The Gothic Revival, which was in part an emotional response to the Industrial Revolution, was an architecture of mood and evocation. Its romanticism was an escape to an ideal pre-industrial, pre-Reformation past. (Pugin was Catholic and many other British Gothic Revival enthusiasts were High Church Anglican quasi-Catholics.) In Germany, this escapist aspect of the Gothic Revival re-emerged in Expressionism.

Protagonists of the Gothic saw it, not Classicism, as the natural national style of Northern Europe. In England it was even argued by the over-zealous or ill-informed that the Gothic was specifically English. In Germany identical arguments held it was German. Ultimately this idea that an architectural style could be specific to a particular country would give rise to National Romanticism.

Understandably, the Gothic is first and foremost associated with churches. The architecture of churches, especially Gothic ones, reflects functional patterns of use that are thoroughly codified, predictable and presumably immutable. To paraphrase Le Corbusier, a church – or at least a Victorian Gothic church – is 'a machine for praying in'. Clearly once such an attitude had been developed in connection with churches it was easy to extend it to other buildings as well. The Gothic Revivalists could also see about them (and grudgingly admire) all sorts of industrial products and machinery that exhibited the moral fitness for purpose they were seeking in their own work (GB-7). There can be no doubt that the Victorian Gothic owed much of its toughness to the influence of Victorian industrial design (see also GB-31). In our century, this aspect of the Gothic Revival was taken up, along with the term Functionalism, by the protagionists of the International Style.

Because there was no Gothic Vitruvius, no codified orders with set proportions, and because in any case the Anglo-Saxon tradition looks to precedent rather than codified rules, British Gothic Revival architects had to become acutely aware of incident and variation in old buildings. Once architects developed this skill of seeking and sketching the pleasing detail or lucky accident, it was almost inevitable that they would begin seeing, appreciating and replicating the anonymous or vernacular architecture that was usually far better suited than the Gothic to their secular commissions.

Initially, this British **Neo-Vernacular** architecture tended to be rather Elizabethan (GB-33). But following the pattern of most revivals, its own evolution paralleled that of the architecture upon which it was based – first in the synthesized early-eighteenth-century **Queen Anne** of the 1880s (GB-15) and then in the sometimes cottagey (GB-73), sometimes more urban **Free Style** of the turn of the century. However, in the Edwardian era some carefully studied and extremely romantic country houses, based on very specific local vernaculars, were produced by architects associated with the Arts and Crafts Movement.

Some of the most important developments in British design during the nineteenth century were only tangentially concerned with architecture. A large part of the Industrial Revolution was based on an international trade in luxury goods – fine cloth, china, etc. By the middle of the century there was great concern in Britain about the quality of British design. The most spectacular result of this desire to improve

British design standards was the Great Exhibition of 1851, the first world's fair, which was housed in the gigantic prefabricated iron and glass Crystal Palace. The assumption behind the Exhibition was that art could successfully be married to industrial production. But there were also those who reacted against the very nature of industrial employment and industrially produced goods.

During the second half of the century, William Morris (GB-26) and the **Arts and Crafts** Movement centred on him pursued a medieval utopian dream of spiritual renewal through artistic craftsmanship. Morris was a dedicated socialist who also worked prodigiously in a dozen different artistic and literary fields. He held that art could only be valid in the absence of machinery. Although the Arts and Crafts Movement included architects closely associated with the Queen Anne style and later the Free Style, its most important designs were for fine goods: wallpapers, silver, furniture, fabrics, finely printed books. These, together with the newly emergent architecture and interior design magazines such as *The Studio*, proved a most effective means of transmitting the movement's ideals and style. Thus the new sensibility easily crossed the Channel to France (F-12) and Belgium (B-3) where it soon evolved into **Art Nouveau** and then rapidly spread to the rest of the Continent. In Italy it was even called **Stile Liberty** after London's great Arts and Crafts emporium (GB-6a). In Germany, where its characteristic sinuous curves gained a certain angularity, it was known as **Jugendstil** (D-53, 57). In Austria, where it took on a Classical Rationalist character, it was called **Secession** (A-2). In Spain, as part of the nationalist, Rationalist language of Gaudí and his contemporaries, it became **Modernisme** (E-2).

In Scandinavia, and particularly in Finland, this new art for the new century yielded much of its role to a **National Romanticism** which shared the same British Arts and Crafts roots. Although National Romanticism has been well understood specifically in terms of Finland's history (SF-1), examples are to be found in most other countries. Hungary, which speaks a language related to Finnish, produced a quite similar National Romantic architecture. Elsewhere in Scandinavia the National Romantic Stockholm Town Hall (S-3) and the **Baltic Style** Gruntvig Church (DK-13) stand out among a handful of similar buildings in each county. In Czechoslovakia a rather peculiar style called **Cubism** was strongly identified with nationalist aspirations. So too was the archaic Neo-Classicism in which the Slavic architect Jože Plečnik built after the First World War in Czechoslovakia and Yugoslavia. Le Corbusier's earliest chalet-like houses in his native Switzerland are clearly National Romantic. And in America Frank Lloyd Wright's **Prairie School** (NL-46a) and its concurrent mass-produced counterpart, the Mission Style, were explicitly National Romantic. National Romanticism also clearly underlay some aspects of German Expressionism (D-28) and the Amsterdam School (NL-21), about which more later.

Typically, National Romanticism flourished in countries or regions which felt politically, culturally or economically threatened. Like National Romanticism in literature, and especially in music – as in the work of Jean Sibelius or Bedrich Smetana – it tended to search out folkloric models. But local, often transitional variations of more conventional historical styles were also drawn upon. Although in most instances it was directly associated with the Arts and Crafts Movement of the decades around the turn of this century, an interesting argument could be made that Portugal's Late Gothic Manueline architecture,

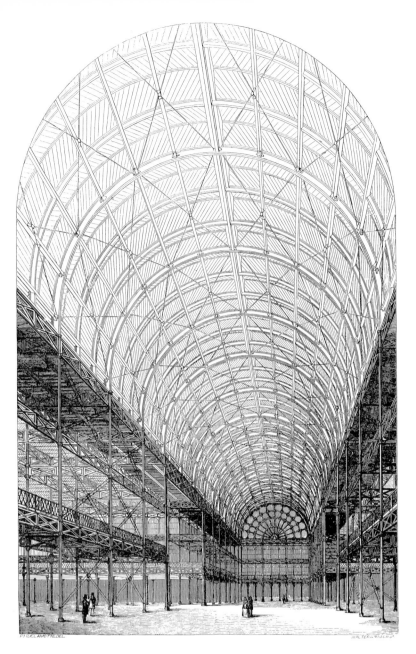

The iron and glass Crystal Palace built by Sir Joseph Paxton for the Great Exhibition of 1851.

which exhibits certain British connections, was nationalist and romantic in character. Clearly some sort of Nationalist Romantic impulses also underlay eighteenth-century arguments for specific national origins of the Gothic and for various nationalist invented Classical orders. (Such orders were used in the older part of the US Capitol.) In nineteenth-century France a complex theory evolved linking the Gothic and the Greek (F-28), which resulted in a nationalist style called **Néo-Grec**. Since the Second World War National Romanticism has occasionally reappeared in non-Western countries.

The eclipse of Art Nouveau in about 1910 was almost as rapid as its spread in the mid 1890s. In the shadow of impending disaster, there was a strong turning back toward Neo-Classicism, especially in Germany (D-16b). But there were also signs of movement in other, very different directions. In 1904 Tony Garnier exhibited his revolutionary Cité Industrielle project (F-54), which he had first designed in lieu of the usual

Prix de Rome winner's archaeological reconstruction of an ancient ruin. In 1907 a number of German industrialists, architects and industrial designers formed the Deutscher Werkbund (D-1), which in the ill-fated summer of 1914 held an important industrial and architectural exhibition in Cologne. In 1910–11 the exhibition and publication in Berlin of Frank Lloyd Wright's work had an immediate and profound effect on progressive architects throughout Europe. In addition to the well-documented impact of Wright's work in Holland (NL-1), its influence is also visible in Gropius and Meyer's Model Factory at the 1914 Werkbund Exhibition and, more subtly, in Le Corbusier's Villa Schwob (CH-17). In the same year that Wright was discovered by European architects, Gropius and Meyer began their epochal Fagus-Werke (D-35). (Once, when such questions seemed much simpler and more important, the Fagus-Werke could be proffered as the 'first modern building'!) And in 1914 a group of Italian architects, soon to be known as the Futurists, held the first exhibition of their radical architectural and urban designs (I-29b).

Despite these harbingers of the new century, August 1914 marked the true end of the previous one, much as the conclusion of the Napoleonic Wars had marked the nineteenth century's true beginning. Four years later the old order lay in ruins in the blasted, stinking mud of Europe's collective madness. Britain, France and Italy were drained. Russia's new dawn was the hope of many, the horror of others. Austria's ancient empire had quietly crumbled into a handful of small states. And Germany, then still only fifty years old as a unified country, knew defeat, a deflected revolution, loss of territories, partial occupation and, eventually, hyper-inflation.

From Germany's turmoil **Expressionism** emerged – a fantasy architecture which dreamed simultaneously of futuristic, crystalline 'city crowns' and of a handcrafted, medieval Gothic golden age. Like a deceptively vigorous young tree rising from the roots of a newly cut giant, it flourished briefly and spectacularly, mostly on paper, during those first few years of the Weimar Republic, before inflation was brought under control and real building could begin again. (In Holland these same few postwar years were also the heyday of the 'soft', smoothly contoured brick Expressionism of the **Amsterdam School** (NL-5), which was able to build far more than its German counterpart.) With the return of financial, if not social stability much of German Expressionism's futuristic aspect disappeared, as its more progressive proponents returned to the rational, functional technology they had just begun to explore before the war. Only the conservative, Arts-and-

The office block of Gropius and Meyer's Model Factory at the 1914 Werkbund Exhibition in Cologne reflects clearly the influence of Frank Lloyd Wright.

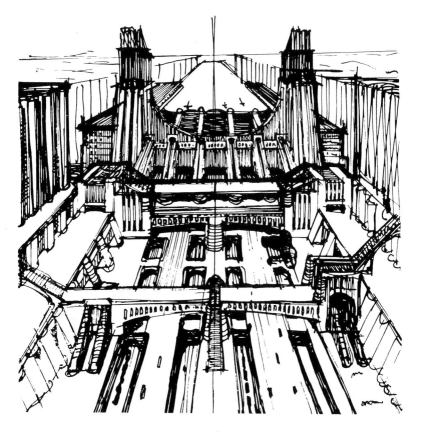

Antonio Sant'Elia's Futurist project for a combined airport and railway station, 1912.

Crafts-oriented Gothic Expressionism flourished through the rest of the 20s, especially in northern Germany (D-5).

In the early 1920s the major figures in German architecture, Gropius, Mies van der Rohe, Mendelsohn, etc., all temporarily suppressed their own varying stylistic inclinations and, like the most modern-minded younger architects elsewhere on the Continent, rapidly turned toward a radically new, white, orthogonal architecture devoid of ornamentation or overt historical references, an architecture that, not by accident, looked like the superstructures of ships. In Germany, where it was centred, this machine-like architecture (in a sense it was a rational metamorphosis of Expressionism's futuristic utopia) came to be called **Neue Sachlichkeit** (New Objectivity) or **Functionalism**. (In Italy, where it frequently had identifiable Classicist overtones, it unfortunately came to be called **Rationalism** – to the continuing

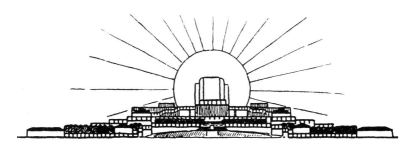

Bruno Taut's Stadtkrone *– part civic centre, part cathedral, part magic mountain.*

confusion of architectural discussion!) By 1932 a pair of Americans, Philip Johnson (D-37) and Henry-Russell Hitchcock, had rechristened it the **International Style**, despite those who wanted to believe that the new architecuture had gone beyond style.

In practice there was no clear line of separation between the theoretical implications of the terms Neue Sachlichkeit and Functionalism. Neue Sachlichkiet, as characterized, for instance, by the social housing of Ernst May in Frankfurt (D-52a), suggested a radically technocratic, orthogonal architecture whose outward appearance theoretically expressed little but the logic of its construction. The term Functionalism, on the other hand, implied that the building's programme, i.e. the uses for which it was intended, assumed a more assertive role determining the plan, massing and details. Such Functionalist considerations underlay the articulation of the new Bauhaus building, 1926, which Gropius and Meyer built at Dessau (East Germany). However, the careful asymmetrical balancing of its main masses and smaller elements also has much in common with the compositional devices of the Dutch **De Stijl** movement, whose architect adherents (NL-46) had by then already been absorbed into the International Style. Headed by Gropius during the peak of its influence in the 1920s, and until its closure in 1933 by Mies van der Rohe, the Bauhaus was essentially an industrial design school which only belatedly began to teach architecture. In fact, few architects of importance seem to have been trained at the Bauhaus, although several major figures did teach there.

In 1928 a group of the leaders of the new architecture, the Modern Movement as it would come to be called, representing a number of countries, met in Switzerland to form Les Congrès Internationaux d'Architecture Moderne, or CIAM. It was to be the first of ten such meetings held during the following twenty-eight years. CIAM codified, and eventually helped to ossify, the general theoretical foundations of the Modern Movement, especially concerning urban design. Through CIAM, architects came to present themselves explicitly as urban designers and social reformers. (The self-evident failure of CIAM-based urbanism in the 1950s and 60s would be a primary contributor to the rise of the more reactionary aspects of Post-Modernism in the 70s.)

Although the International Style would live on at least until the late 1950s, the peak of its influence as a representation of an international consensus – albeit one dominated by Germans – was probably reached at the 1927 Weißenhof housing exhibition at Stuttgart (D-60). (There is a tradition of such housing exhibitions in Germany, where modern architecture has long been closely identified with large social housing areas.) Only three years after Weißenhof the Nazis forced the Bauhaus out of Dessau and the great migration of European architects to America began.

Germany may have been the epicentre of the International Style, but the style's one figure of mythical proportions was a French–Swiss architect/painter living in Paris (who was blind in one eye). Le Corbusier, *né* Charles-Edouard Jeanneret, took the raw facts of the International Style and made epic, often tragic, poetry of it (F-22).

Le Corbusier, however, was virtually alone in France, aside from some relatively minor figures, and of course the Classical Rationalist master of concrete, Auguste Perret. For the most part modern architecture in France meant the superficialities of **Art Deco** – named after the 1925 Exposition des Arts Décoratifs, and also known by half a dozen other names, including **Moderne, Jazz Modern**, etc. (GB-9, I-48). It was an often quite conventional architecture, typically overlaid with modernistic motifs which owed much to the Viennese architect Josef Hoffmann and his Wiener Werkstätte arts and crafts guild (A-2a). Perhaps because it required enthusiasm and money, but no rigorous ideological engagement, the greatest surviving Art Deco monuments are to be found in America.

Le Corbusier's Villa Savoye of 1929–31 (F-45) may have been the aesthetic high point, the single unsustainable moment of equilibrium, of the International Style. After that there was a loss of rigour and, as the 30s wore on with continuing economic depression and the consolidation of Fascism, a widespread retreat toward monumentality or the vernacular.

After the Second World War there was no outburst of revolutionary architecture comparable to that which had followed the First World War. The destruction was far too widespread and too intense, the need to provide shelter too great. For the first time war had been waged systematically against cities themselves. The Modern Movement put itself forward as being ready not just to build the desperately needed housing but also to reconstruct the shattered cities. In fact there were those who viewed the devastation of the old urban fabric not as a loss but as an opportunity. Beginning with Le Corbusier's project for a city of three million of 1922 and his Plan Voisin for Paris of 1925, the Modern Movement had advocated as a 'necessity' the wholesale demolition of existing cities, save perhaps for the occasional monument, and their reconstruction as arrays of tall buildings standing in park-like settings (GB-28).

Because of postwar shortages of materials and, one must presume, an ambivalent attitude towards the fruits of technology, the prewar interest in integrating vernacular forms and attitudes into modern architecture – of humanizing it – became for a time even more intense. Exposed brick walls and pitched roofs were the order of the day. In Italy, where the exploration of vernacular architecture had proved attractive to certain modernists during the war years, this vernacular modernism was identified with the **Neo-Realism** of the cinema (I-11). Elsewhere it was called **Empiricism**, or **Scandinavian Empiricism**. Bright sun-filled photographs of Swedish housing projects, where it always seemed to be summer, were regular fare for European architectural magazines in the first grim postwar years.

In Le Corbusier's hands these needs led to a different solution: not comfortable materials and forms delicately assembled, but raw, board-marked concrete (F-63) and rough peasant masonry (F-26) which were to prove seminal to the development of Brutalism. During these years Le Corbusier developed his Modulor system of proportional measurement, which attempted to base the dimensioning of all building elements upon units drawn from a graduated scale of harmonically linked dimensions and to re-establish a connection, through those units, to the dimensions (and proportions) of an 'ideal' human body.

Gradually the self-assurance of the International Style reasserted itself. However, the old enthusiasm for tough machine-age technology had been moderated – except, perhaps, for the I-beam Neo-Classicism of Mies van der Rohe in America (D-13). In its place came the delicate, non-tectonic, almost mannerist abstraction of the **Late International Style** (DK-18). By the late 50s, the myth of a unified, scientific and effective modern architecture began to seem rather threadbare. But, to paraphrase George Bernard Shaw, perhaps the problem with the Modern Movement was that it was never properly tried. Certainly in most parts of Europe the great postwar modernist experiment, now so

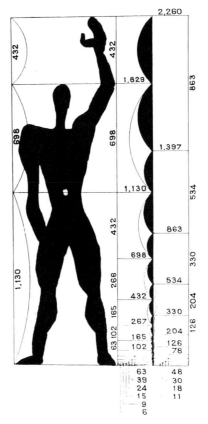

Le Corbusier's Modulor Man became the measure of all things in his Modulor proportional dimensioning system. Its graduated series of units of measure was derived from the Classical proportional numerical ratio known as the 'Golden Section'.

freely criticized, was always severely compromised by political, technical and economic circumstances. And Scandinavia's generally more positive experience with the Modern Movement suggests that it cannot be dismissed so easily as a total failure. Some day we may even come to feel that the true failure of twentieth-century planning and urbanism – in which modernist dogma merely reflected the adamant demands of the culture – was in its total capitulation to the car.

In 1956 there was an open split between the older, generally more German, Neue Sachlichkeit-oriented founding generation within CIAM, whose technocratic urbanism was effectively a product of group introspection, and a younger generation that looked to Le Corbusier for aesthetic guidance and to the social sciences for its urbanistic values. CIAM, the personification of the Modern Movement, went quietly to its grave, while the younger architects, the generation of Aldo van Eyck and Alison and Peter Smithson, who had been charged with setting up CIAM's abortive tenth and last congress, formed a new group called Team X. For a brief time Team X attempted to maintain that international dialogue which was the only hope for achieving a unified theoretical basis for modern architecture and urbanism. However, Team X had no formal organization or mechanism for renewal. Within a decade this last group having any claim to represent architecture as a discipline based on a coherent body of knowledge had been left behind by changing events, and no one seemed to care.

When the final reaction against the delicately abstract last phase of the International Style began a decade after the end of the war, it took

Robert Venturi's house for his mother, 1963. Venturi's 'gentle manifesto', Complexity and Contradiction in Architecture, 1966, opened the floodgates of Post-Modernism.

a number of extreme and sometimes contradictory forms, including **Neo-Expressionism** (D-14), a revival or continuation of the Expressionism of the 20s. There was also a general tendency to over-emphasize, overexpose, or overrationalize the structural system (B-8) and, occasionally, the mechanical system (F-6); to build monumentally (NL-24) or picturesquely (GB-55); and to treat each building as if it was so important and new that everything about it had to be specially designed and custom-built. Much of this coexisted, perhaps a little uneasily, under the name of **Brutalism**, and its ultimate expression was the megastructure, that building-as-machine which, like the mis-understood monster in a B-movie, might grow to unpredictable pro-portions or even threaten to consume an entire city (GB-86).

Soon that too evoked a reaction. The book *Complexity and Con-tradiction in Architecture*, 1966, by the American architect Robert Venturi, touched off a revolution or perhaps, to be more correct, a counter-revolution, the effects of which have still not sorted themselves out. Venturi's own ironic blend of historic allusion and banal modern technology was at first sometimes called **Pop-Architecture**, in rec-ognition of its links with the Pop Art of the 1960s. Now, together with a once more revived and generally rather abstract, pitched-roofed **Neo-Vernacular** (GB-34), as well as various resuscitated Neo-Classicisms – including escapist Neo-Palladianism in England and a nightmarish **Neo-Rationalism** in Italy (I-32, 33) – and all sorts of **Formalism** (A-2), it is part of that very unsatisfactory agglomeration known as **Post-Modernism**.

AUSTRIA

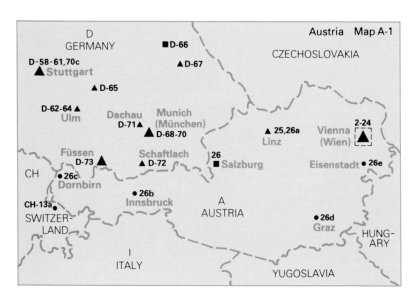

Austria Map A-1

D
GERMANY
CZECHOSLOVAKIA
■ D-66
D-58-61,70c
▲ Stuttgart
▲ D-67
▲ D-65
D-62-64 ▲
Ulm
Dachau
D-71▲
Munich
(München)
▲ D-68-70
2-24
▲ 25,26a
Linz
Vienna
(Wien)
▲
Füssen
D-73 ▲
Schaftlach
▲ D-72
26
■ Salzburg
Eisenstadt ● 26e
CH
● 26c
Dornbirn
● 26b
Innsbruck
A
AUSTRIA
CH-13a ●
SWITZER-
LAND
● 26d
Graz
HUNG-
ARY
I
ITALY
YUGOSLAVIA

Austria (Österreich)　　　　A-1

Just as post-Habsburg Austria seems almost an appendage to the city that once dominated Continental Europe's last heterogeneous empire, so too Austria's modern architecture is essentially that of Vienna. Even the few noteworthy buildings erected outside the capital are often the work of Viennese practitioners.

Language note Austrian German is like German German, but used more conservatively. Expect to encounter ß in lieu of ss more often and also considerably more Fraktur, that Gothic Germanic lettering which, for the untutored, can prove something of a trial.

Vienna (Wien)　　　　A-2

In Vienna, more than in Europe's other capitals, one can still sometimes strongly, suddenly sense the presence of empire. It is not just because of the broad belt of late-nineteenth-century public buildings and open spaces that collectively constitute the Ringstraße. There is also something else here, something more ephemeral – that can make even London or Paris seem to have been little more than imperial parvenus. None the less, Vienna seems to know that those cities remain alive to the world in a way that she is unlikely ever to be again.

Once Vienna was the cosmopolitan capital of central Europe. (Shopfronts here still sometimes wistfully announce long-vanished provincial outlets in Prague or Baden-Baden or Budapest.) From Vienna an Adolf Loos could once as readily have obtained commissions in Brno or Venice as in Linz or Salzburg. Once architects with names such as Fabiani (A-14), Plečnik (A-9) and Basset (A-13) came to Vienna to build.

During her last uncertain century of glory, Vienna even took up, in her own stiff-necked way, Venice's former role as the perpetual masked ball of Europe. Yet Vienna had an inferiority complex *vis-à-vis* 'the West' – so much so that Loos, admittedly an extreme Anglophile, felt called upon to publish a magazine entitled *The Other: A Periodical for the Introduction of Western Civilization into Austria*.

Imperial Vienna was equally the world of Strauss as of Freud, a world into which the fifty-year-old academician Otto Wagner almost surreptitiously introduced modern architecture. Admittedly Wagner's rhetoric was more radical than his buildings. But they, despite their Neo-Classical garb, were radical enough. It can also be argued that it was Wagner's two brilliant young pupils, Josef Hoffmann, founder of the Wiener Werkstätte (see A-2a) and Josef Olbrich, the leading architect of the Secession – Vienna's variant of the Jugendstil or Art Nouveau, who together stimulated this transformation in their old master. Perhaps so. But despite their facile talents and no lack of enviable commissions (B-12, D-53), none of their work ever approached in modernity the magnificent central hall of Wagner's Postal Savings Bank (A-10).

Equally intriguing to today's eyes and minds is the realization that Imperial Vienna was also the city of Adolf Loos, a man whose theories and designs have yet to be properly set in a fully satisfactory frame of reference. Loos stood partly in Otto Wagner's camp, or, perhaps more accurately, both he and Wagner stood in that of Rational Neo-Classicism (see A-10 and -22). Certainly Loos cared little for the work of Hoffmann and Olbrich, or for most other manifestations of the Viennese Secession. More than them, Loos identified himself with the modern industrialized world: with the West. As a young man he had visited the United States and, during his three-year stay from 1893 to 1896, he encountered the works of H. H. Richardson and Louis Sullivan. As an old man, he was to be part of the Paris of Le Corbusier, *l'Esprit Nouveau* and Dadaism (F-30).

But between came the First World War. For Vienna, the music suddenly stopped and all the guests departed, each with his own bit of empire. The Viennese were left alone with the past still ringing in their ears. Even now, after another world war – with the political, economic and physical cleavage having been made as absolute as if Vienna were at the tip of a peninsula – a sense of unreality persists. Vienna's suicide rate is among the highest in Europe. And her most creative architects produce some of the most abstractly Formalistic, unbuildable designs in Europe. Much of this Formalist architecture is derivative, inspired originally it would seem by the American Louis Kahn. There have also been a number of highly original if even less practical projects, such as Hans Hollein's now famous Surrealist photomontages: aircraft carriers set, like medieval cities, amidst verdant hills; and supersized railway wagons similarly sited, like twenty-first-century Par-

thenons, or at least like latter-day Walhallas (D-67). Some of these projects have tended to be highly geometricized, often abstract, again almost Surrealist, including studies for such things as 'urban transportation' nodes of a scale and scope rarely encountered in New York or London, much less Vienna – in a real sense, the modern counterparts to the late-eighteenth-century fantasies of Ledoux (F-53) and Boullée.

A-2a In 1900, enthusiastic art students triumphantly drew the Scots architect C. R. Mackintosh and his designer wife Margaret through the streets of Vienna in a flower-covered carriage. Such was the impact of a Secession-sponsored exhibition of their work (GB-85). And such was the importance of the decorative arts in *fin-de-siècle* Vienna, for the exhibition had consisted primarily of furnishings. (Paradoxically, despite Vienna's own exotic-erotic tendencies – one needs but mention the paintings of Gustav Klimt – Vienna seems not to have adopted the Mackintoshes' 'spooky' style of decorative illustration.) The Mackintoshes' work not only strongly affected the development of the Secession (A-24), but also – in philosophy as much as style – that of Josef Hoffmann's profoundly inventive and productive workshop, the Wiener Werkstätte. (It is no coincidence that the Werkstätte was initially financed by the

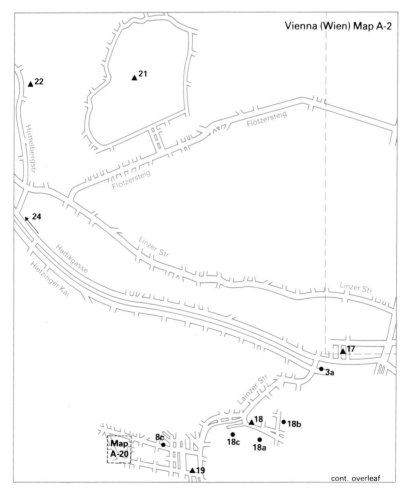

Vienna (Wien) Map A-2

cont. overleaf

cont. from previous page

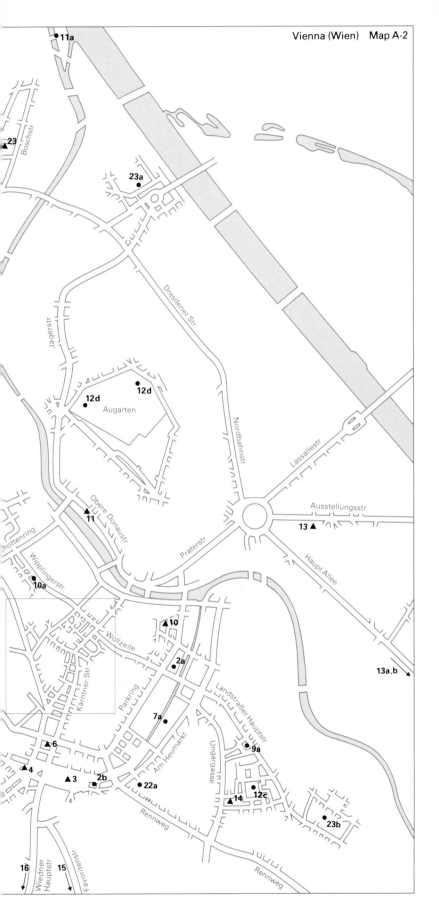

Vienna (Wien)   Map A-2

Mackintoshes' only Viennese client.)

The **Museum für angewandte Kunst**, at Stubenring 5, has a major collection of items produced by that Arts and Crafts Guild, which supplied the artistic decorations for most of Hoffmann's major commissions. *U-Bahn: Wien-Mitte*

Vienna (Wien)　　　　　　　　　**A-3**
* **Wiener Stadtbahn** (stations and architectural embellishments of the 'S-Bahn', the municipal railway system) 1894–1901
Karlsplatz, Hofpavillon (A-3a), and along the following lines: from Heiligenstadt to Penzing; and from Hütteldorf to Meidling-Haupstraße, to Landstraße, to Heiligenstadt, and back to Meidling-Haupstraße
Otto Wagner; Karlsplatz with Josef Olbrich
Neo-Classicism/Secession (Art Nouveau)
Map A-2 / U-Bahn: Karlsplatz

[From the end of the Empire in 1918 until recently, little was done to change the extensive Stadtbahn system, to which Wagner's contributed thirty-six stations along some twenty-five miles of four separate lines. One of these lines (Heiligenstadt to Penzing) is only now being brought back into service after having been all but abandoned in the 1920s. Most of the others have been converted to U-Bahns (undergrounds) and many of the stations have been modernized. Of the two Karlsplatz pavilions only one remains, now restored and used as a coffee-house. The Hofpavillon has also been restored.]

On the whole, too much has been made of Wagner's designs for the municipal railways – a situation the municipality seems to be trying to 'rectify' through its modernization programme. Aside from the stations themselves, his contribution to the system was essentially limited to the 'clothing' of its British-designed engineering work. To a generation that has learned

A-2b The **Historisches Museum der Stadt Wien**, at the Karlsplatz, has on display the living room of Adolf Loos's own apartment as well as some of Otto Wagner's beautifully rendered presentation drawings. It also has paintings by Klimt and other Secessionists. *U-Bahn: Karlsplatz*

to appreciate Victorian engineering in all its raw vigour they seem, for the most part, irrelevant. Only the latest stations – Karlsplatz and the Hofpavillon – stand apart from their over monumental peers.

The Karlsplatz is the most Secessionist, the most modern and the most often illustrated – and this may be partly responsible for the exaggerated reputation of Wagner's Stadtbahn work. It is, in fact, as industrialized and prefabricated as Giumard's Paris Métro pavilions (F-17). Just as Guimard's Métro entrances reinforced his obsession with prefabrication and standardization, so too this pavilion marks the beginning of a sequence of experiments with new materials and techniques that eventually led to Wagner's most radical later works (A-10, 21).

A-3a The **Hofpavillon** at Schönbrunner Schloßstraße is a light-hearted Belle Epoque parody of the official 'Maria Theresa' style. *U-Bahn: Hietzing*

Vienna (Wien)　　　　　　　　　**A-4**
** **Ausstellungshaus der Wiener Sezession** or **Sezessionhaus**
(exhibition gallery) 1898
Friedstrichraße 12
Josef Olbrich
Secession (Art Nouveau)

Map A-2 / U-Bahn: Karlsplatz
[The interior has been completely modernized and some rear windows filled in. Old photos and drawings suggest that the ornament and lettering once had some colour – or, more likely, were gilded, as the laurel leaves of the dome once were.]

For *fin-de-siècle* Vienna, the erection of the Sezessionshaus on so prominent a site symbolized both the position within the art world that the Secession had already established for itself and the, at least limited, acceptance of the new kind of architecture that it represented. (It also marked the beginning of Olbrich's brilliant but brief career.) Such a symbol, intended to have a strong, immediate impact, might be forgiven a certain amount of tinsel and falsefrontery.

After three-quarters of a century, the 'dome' is still an original, amusing idea. The main façade, with its sarcophagus-like entrance portico entablature (note the snake 'handles') spanning between two super-scaled pedestals, interestingly evokes the spirit of the eighteenth century's revolutionary romantic Neo-Classicists (F-53), even as it also anticipates Frank Lloyd Wright's then developing formal language.

Vienna (Wien)   **A-5**
* **Wohnhäuser** (apartment buildings)
Majolikahaus 1898–9
Linke Wienzeile 40
Linke Wienzeile 38 1898–9
Köstlergasse 3 1910
Otto Wagner
Secession (Art Nouveau)
Map A-2 / U-Bahn: Kettenbrückengasse

Even if Wagner's fame now rests elsewhere (A-3, 10. 11), the bulk of his earlier practice consisted of just such typically Viennese apartment buildings, most of whose existence Wagner came to deny.

Despite differences between them almost as great as their similarities, the earlier two of these buildings were constructed simultaneously. But they were intended to serve differing social classes, a fact reflected in their budgets and hence in their façades. The tile-covered Majolikahaus, the most unusual of the three and something of a *succès de scandale*, was built by Wagner as a personal investment and thus afforded him the rare opportunity to build solely to suit his own aesthetic and technical ideals. The product of this freedom is a satisfying, disciplined building whose wild Art Nouveau polychromy is tensely balanced by its sober modularity.

The once-gilded plaques high on the façade of No. 38 are by Kolo Moser, who later was to become one of the Wiener Werkstätte's finest decorative artists.

Linke Wienzeile 38

A-5a Less than a mile away, at **Neustiftgasse 40** and **Döblergasse 4**, are two later, 1909–12, Wagner apartment buildings. These, like the Villa Wagner II (A-22), reflect his last, almost Perret-like – or is it Garnier-like (F-54)? – mode. *U-Bahn: Lerchenfelder Straße*

Vienna (Wien)   **A-6**
**Österreichisches Verkehrsbüro
Zentrale** (Austrian Travel Agency)
1976–8
Opernring 3–5
Hans Hollein
Post-Modernism
Map A-2

Hollein is one of those rare architects – Peter Behrens (D-52) was a more extreme example – who is a facile, talented designer and yet so responsive to the ever-changing currents of architectural fashion that his own personality and beliefs tend to become the background to a constantly evolving overlay of *au courant* issues and imagery. Here, in the manner of Robert Venturi, or even more that of Charles Moore, he created a Post-Modernist game of allusions and icons suggestive of exotic places appropriate to a travel agency, which are also references to the work of fashionable architects, past and present. Thus the palm tree columns come not from a tropical isle but quote directly from John Nash at Brighton (GB-44), while the Indian pavilion owes much to Lutyens. More subtle is the frag-

mentary column base, recalling not just ancient Greece but also (perversely, in miniature at the size of a true column) the design of a widely published eighteenth-century French folly house shaped like a broken column. So too the cashiers' cages. They have been likened to Rolls-Royce radiators, but their proportions suggest equally caricatures of Phillip Johnson's A.T. & T. building in New York. Less witty is the theatre ticket desk with its Michael Graves-inspired bevelled cornice and already dated petrified drape. *Und so weiter.*

A-6a Because Hollein is probably the best-known Austrian architect since Hoffmann, even the smallest or most ephemeral of his few built works have been widely published. Among these is a series of diminutive, intensely designed shops – of which the **Retti candle shop,** 1965, at Kohlmarkt 10, is perhaps the most intense. A carefully 'machined out' block of space, it is too thoughtful and permanent to be mere interior decoration; too utilitarian, if barely so, to be sculpture. *U-Bahn: Stephansplatz*

A-6b Just across the street from the Retti

shop, at Kohlmarkt 9, is Max Fabiani's **Artariahaus,** 1901–2.

A-6c Another Hollein-designed boutique, more conventionally architectonic but less intriguing, is **CM,** 1966–7 on Tegetthoff-straße. *U-Bahn: Stephansplatz*

A-6d The façade of Hollein's **Schullin jewellery shop,** 1974, at Graben 26, reflects a fascination with grids and with the 'erosion' of built forms – both of which were to become avant-garde clichés in the later 70s. *U-Bahn: Stephansplatz*

Vienna (Wien)   A-7
Glashaus der Bundesgärten
(greenhouse) 1902
Burggarten
Friedrich Ohmann
Neo-Classicism/Secession (Art Nouveau)
Map A-2 / U-Bahn: Karlsplatz

Imperial Vienna had two architectural schools, one headed by Wagner, the other by Ohmann. Like Wagner, Ohmann was something of a conservative radical who, even when embellishing these 'Imperial-Royal' gardens, felt free to continue his decorative and tectonic explorations. Here, probing the possibilities of iron and glass, he gave the main pavilion generously bevelled edges which seem always able to catch the sun. In large part through his shaping of these glass surfaces, he was able to endow with an almost greater sense of substance than the rigorously Classical masonry with which they are enframed. Tellingly perhaps, when one considers the approaching end of the 'old order', the form language of the masonry calls to mind images from reactionary/revolutionary late eighteenth-century France.

A-7a Ohmann's fresh assurance – in a more openly Secessionist manner – is also to be found in the statues, columns, walls

and pavilions with which, in 1903–6, he embellished the banks of the canalized river Wien where it passes through the **Stadt-park.** The south end neatly ties in with one of Wagner's S-Bahn (now U-Bahn) stations (A-3). *U-Bahn: Stadtpark*

Vienna (Wien)   A-8
* **Looshaus** (originally Goldmann & Salatsch store and flats) 1910–11
Michaelerplatz 3
Adolf Loos
Rational Neo-Classicism
Map A-2 / U-Bahn: Stephansplatz

[Originally GOLDMANN & SALATSCH was spelled out in simple gilt letters across the centre of the upper façade, providing some sense of focus. Loos's fittings for the store, have also been removed. The only remaining Loos interior, a stairwell, is accessible from the side street.]

The architecture produced by architectural theoreticians and critics is often at best an acquired taste. Adolf Loos was such a critic-theoretician who was equally at home in the editorial office and the architect's atelier. The influence of his polemics should not be underestimated. Nor should that of his architecture – even if his drawings can be thought childish, and even if his buildings seem peculiarly cerebral, ascetic and, in a sense, diagrammatic compared to those of his Secessionist contemporaries.

In the Vienna of 1910 Loos seemed a radical and the Looshaus was the object of considerable public outrage. Yet, perversely, he was in fact a man very much of his time and place – acutely conscious of living in the industrialized twentieth century but essentially conservative and strongly conscious of continuity. Like Wagner's at 'am Steinhof' (A-21), his work was, at least in part, a kind of knowing, mannered restructuring of the past to suit the needs of a vastly different present.

Later, in the 20s, his buildings (as opposed to his writings or some of his rather innovative unbuilt projects), were, not surprisingly, deemed more important for their clear simplicity than for any specific stylistic modernity. After his death, the Fascist penchant for somewhat similar Neo-Classical forms may have even further obscured his avant-garde credentials. Today our understanding of Loos's more 'difficult' designs is becoming clearer as we gain distance from past polemical struggles.

A-8a Loos's **Kniže shop,** 1913, survives at Graben 13. *U-Bahn: Stephansplatz*

A-8b Perhaps the most often illustrated Loos interior is that of the diminutive **Kärntnerbar** (Loos Bar), 1907, in the Kärntner Durchgang. Unfortunately, over the years it has lost both its Secessionist

Vienna (Wien)   **A-9**
* Zacherlhaus (offices and shops) 1903–5
Bauernmarkt and Brandstätte 6
Jože Plečnik
Secession (Art Nouveau)
Map A-2 / U-Bahn: Stephansplatz
Chroniclers of particular periods or 'schools' of architecture tend to concentrate exclusively on their leaders – on the Wrights and Le Corbusiers – or, as here in *fin-de-siècle* Vienna, on a group of leaders: Hoffmann, Olbrich, Loos and Wagner. In doing so it is easy to overestimate those carried along by more famous colleagues, or underestimate those held back by the success of others. Vienna's *Belle Epoque* knew several such figures, among whom Fabiani (A-14), Lichtblau (A-18b), Ohmann (A-7), and especially Plečnik come immediately to mind.

Plečnik may not always have been consistent, but at his best, as here, he was disciplined, original, self-assured and comfortably urbane. His sense of scale was humane, not monumental; his choice of materials appropriate to the city, but also appropriate to its citizens; his forms and details lively and interesting, but not disruptively romantic.

In short, this is a building that honours equally the city in which it stands, the client who commissioned it and the architect who designed it. That is the way things ought to be, but rarely are.

Vienna (Wien)   **A-10**
*** Postsparkasse (postal savings bank) 1904–6 (front), 1910–12 (rear)
Georg-Coch-Platz 2
Otto Wagner
Rational Neo-Classicism/Secession (Art Nouveau)
Map A-2 / U-Bahn: Schwedenplatz
With its bolted-on façade of granite, marble, and – at the top – dark glass; with its aluminium, almost mechanistic, victory angel-like acroteria; and with its repetitious, modular, non-hierarchical massing, this is

painting, by Gustav Jagerspacher, of a wizened old waiter perpetually on duty, and Loos's remarkably Pop Art-like leaded-glass American flag canopy. Yet in all other respects this small room still appears as it does in old photos (only a little dog-eared). So completely unchanged is it that like other places in Vienna, time here seems slightly out of joint. *U-Bahn: Stephansplatz*

A-8c The greater part of Loos's practice consisted of houses and apartments. Unfortunately, most of the better-known examples have been lost or altered over the years. **One surviving Loos house,** 1913, is at the corner of Sauraugasse and Nothartgasse. Like his well-known Haus Steiner, now altered beyond recognition, it has a building-regulation inspired round roof.

A-8d The **Haus Moller,** 1928, one of Loos's later, partly International Stylized houses, is at Starkfriedgasse 19.

A-9a Much smaller, but no less intense, is Plečnik's **Karl Borromäus Brunnen,** 1909, a delightful little fountain and park-square, in the Karl Borromäus-Platz. *U-Bahn: Landstraße*

A-9b Two blocks down Bauernmarkt from Zacherlhaus is one of Vienna's more felicitous modern structures: Franz von Matsch's **clock-bridge,** 1914, spanning the Bauernmarkt at Hoher Markt. *U-Bahn: Stephansplatz*

a radical vision of a revitalized Neo-Classicism. It is also as close as Wagner's work ever got, geographically or metaphorically, to receiving the imprimatur of a location on Vienna's Ringstraße. But behind this still 'acceptable' façade the last overt stylistic references have almost disappeared. In their stead is the most convincingly modern, non-industrial architecture of its time – excepting only perhaps the best of Tony Garnier's notably similar but unbuilt and not entirely datable projects (F-54).

Behind this façade is an architecture of simple forms and little ornament; of dark wood panelling and specially designed Thonet furniture for ceremonial rooms (where the Kaiser's portrait still hangs!); of mechanically-cut stone employed as today we might use pre-cast concrete or some

Vienna (Wien) A-11
* Schützenhaus Wehranlage 'Kaiserbad' (dam control and equipment storage building) 1904–8
Donaukanal (Danube Canal) near Obere Donaustraße 26
Otto Wagner
Secession (Art Nouveau)
Map A-2 / U-Bahn: Schottenring
[The dam itself is no longer used. The control building was partially restored *c.* 1971.]

Compared with his Postal Savings Bank (A-10), this might not seem to be one of Wagner's major innovative works. Yet it is of interest both for its freedom from Neo-Classical references and for its frank expression of its unusual purpose: the annual assembly and disassembly of a seasonal dam whose hinged iron framework was collapsed on to the canal bed when not in use. When raised, this framework provided a track on to which a mobile crane could be rolled from the control building. The crane was then used to insert sluice gates into the framework to maintain a navigable depth of water in the canal. Power for both operations – raising the framework and inserting the gates – was

Vienna (Wien) A-12
* Flacktürme (anti-aircraft towers)
1940
See A-12a-d below
Friedrich Tamms
Map A-2
[The original 88 mm finials have been removed.]

Civil engineering is so named to differentiate it from the earlier, military sort that determined the forms of most European cities. Only in our own century has the military involvement with urban architecture been almost entirely destructive, and even then there have been exceptions. Here Hitler and his minions seem to have emulated Sixtus V, the sixteenth-century pope who placed obelisks at spatially significant points throughout Rome – monuments which, through the centuries, came to be the city's organizing foci. But Hitler erected as his spatial nodes a half-dozen megalithic fifteen-storey concrete towers

plastics; of aluminium, then still new, exotic and rather expensive, used perhaps for the first time to make 'architecture' of heating ducts; of glass, tautly curved in a membrane-like ceiling, or massively thick in translucent structural floors; of reinforced concrete, often expressed if not exposed. And it is in the symbolic, central banking room that most of these elements coalesce into a singular, white, light-filled space – one wherein ultimately resides much of Wagner's reputation, and even, to a degree, that of the whole Secession.

A-10a Among Wagner's earlier works, the only anticipation of this space is the former banking hall, now a surreal storage room, of the **Wiener Länderbank**, 1882–4, at Hohenstaufengasse 3. *U-Bahn: Schottentor*

provided via a windlass which, when in use, projected from the building's upper stories.

One would be hard pressed to cite a more invitingly precocious example of architecture as machinery, or vice versa.

A-11a Earlier, in 1894–8, Wagner had designed the architectural accoutrements for a larger **seasonal dam at Nußdorf**, which is assembled from a permanent bridge-like structure.

Esterházy Park

whose bleak bluff walls, several feet thick, are topped by even thicker cantilevered platform roofs. These were deployed in a rough triangle around the city's heart.

Despite their size, these towers have not become urban foci. However, they have been the subject of several daring urbanistic proposals which would begin to make them so. One scheme envisioned doubling or tripling their height by building what would have been Vienna's only skyscrapers on top of them. Another foresaw huge cantilevered platforms constructed on them, creating a 'park in the sky' on the Augarten pair and a city centre heliport on the Stiftskaserne tower.

Urbanistically, the Stiftskaserne tower will always be the most important. It exactly, startlingly, and no doubt deliberately terminates the Hofburg's central axis. At present, however, it is too low to be effectively seen from the Ring. Only as one backs away from it, towards the Michaelerplatz, does it begin to play an impressive role in the total composition.

To some Viennese these structures are undoubtedly an embarrassment. To others they are an important reminder of one of Europe's least civilized moments. Not surprisingly, most of the cities once graced with them have spent fortunes on their demolition.

A-12a Esterházy Park.
U-Bahn: Kettenbrückengasse

A-12b Stiftskaserne (on axis with Hofburg). *U-Bahn: Kettenbrückengasse*

A-12c Arenberg Park.
U-Bahn: Landstraße

A-12d Augarten (a pair).
U-Bahn: Friedensbrücke

Vienna (Wien)   **A-13**
** Riesenrad (Ferris wheel) 1896–7
Kratky-Baschik-Weg, Prater
Walter Basset
Map A-2 / U-Bahn: Praterstern
[In deference to the lady's age, her load of cabins has been reduced by half.]

This is not the world's first Ferris wheel (that was created by George Washington Gale Ferris for Chicago's 1893 Columbian Exposition), but, thanks in part to Harry Lime, it must be the best-known one.

Built, like the Eiffel Tower (F-16), as the centrepiece of a world's fair, its original justification was not just the ride but the view. Eiffel's tower was an unspecialized support structure into which a vertical transportation system had to be fitted. The Ferris wheel, on the other hand, was an organic synthesis of transportation and structure – but one so specialized that, unlike the tower, it has remained a toy ever since.

A-13a There are two other interesting structures in the park-like Prater area: Otto Schönthal's **Trabrennbahn** (trotting track grandstand), *1912 SW on Haupt Allee (Map A-2→) / L on Trabrennstr / on R;*

A-13b And Otto Erich Schweizer's concrete **Stadion** (stadium) at Prater-Krieau, 1931. *Abt ½ mi (1 km) further on Haupt Allee (Map A-2→) / L on Meiereistr / on R*

Vienna (Wien)   **A-14**
Portois und Fix (shop fitters)
1898–1900
Ungargasse 59–63
Max Fabiani
Rationalism/Secession (Art Nouveau)
Map A-2
[Some simple but distinctive lettering and lamp standards have been removed from the ground-floor façade. The mezzanine-level spandrels, which originally were only above the doorways, now also span the large shop windows.]

Although many pre-First World War buildings in Vienna reflect or suggest an identifiable sort of 'Viennese Rationalism', nowhere else, except perhaps in aspects of Wagner's later efforts (A-5a, 10) is there so clear an example of such an astylar classical Rationality.

Vienna (Wien)/Favoriten   **A-15**
* **Zentralsparkasse** (branch savings
bank, with community culture centre)
1975–9
Favoritenstraße 118
Günther Domenig
Neo-Expressionism
*S on Favoritenstr (Map A-2→) abt $1\frac{1}{4}$ mi
(2 km)*

One does not quite know where to begin.
Is it Expressionist? Post-Modern? Surrealist?
High-Tech? Organic? Yes, all those and half
a dozen more. It's insistent! Exciting!
Creepy! It is among the most truly original
works of architecture realized in the past
twenty years. Looking at each aspect one
could say, 'Hasn't this or that been done
before?' Perhaps so, but never in such a
synthesis of contradictions, nor with such
integrity. 'Soft-sculpture' stairrails are not
stucco but concrete. 'Organic' ductwork is
High-Tech stainless steel. The well-detailed,
orthogonal façade and trusswork appear to
be melting. Prosaic fluorescent light fixtures
form organic chains and patterns that
weave around ductwork and trusses. A
gigantic grasping hand and blue concrete
'water' deny that the only messages are
about tectonics. The relative Rationality of
the working spaces – away from the staircase – similarly denies that all is organic,
or symbolic. So many chances taken! Bravo
for a truly original mind in this age of dull,
book-thumbing 'radicalism'!

Vienna (Wien)   **A-16**
Rehabilitationszentrum Meidling
(hospital) 1966–8
Unter-Meidlinger Straße 26–28
Gustav Peichl
Formalism
*SW on Wiedner Hauptstr (Map A-2→) /
L on Reinprechtsdorfer Str / R at Y on
Triester Str abt 1 mi (1.3 km) / R on Unter-
Meidlinger Str / third blk on R /
S-Bahn: Meidling*

For reasons which are not clear – perhaps
the re-emergence of some sense of cultural
inferiority or an attempt to recapture the
spirit of a grandiose architectural heritage –
post-Second World War Austria has produced a remarkable amount of idealized
(i.e. unbuildable) architecture and urbanism. When, as here, such thinking is applied
to a real architectural problem, the result-
ant building can never achieve the total
geometric rigour of its paper counterparts.
None the less, one looks in wonder at the
unyielding completeness of this hospital
whose triaxial symmetry demands that all
its components must be in threes, sixes,
nines, etc.

How extraordinary to have the self-
assurance to build a hospital, of all things,
as if the science, technology and social
theory that are its primary *raison d'être* will
remain as immutable as this fantasy.

A-16a Across Unter-Meidlinger Straße is
Karl Kirst and Robert Oerley's slightly
Expressionistic and considerably more
humane **George-Washington-Hof**
housing, 1927–30.

Vienna (Wien)   A-17
Wohnhaus (social housing) 1924–5
Penzinger Straße 35–37
Theiß & Jaksch
Expressionism
Map A-2 / U-Bahn: Hietzing

Most of Vienna's interwar municipal housing is tinged with some sort of German Expressionism, ranging from the Gothicky (A-23b) to the Mendelsohn-esque (A-23). In this particular small development the Expressionism is more classically biased – albeit not in the mode of the usual uninspired nineteenth-century Viennese apartment building vernacular, nor in that of Hoffmann's abstract mannerism. Rather the quoining, the projecting heads and, not least, the sensibilities underlying the stuccowork pattern of the central façade, seem to be freely, if loosely, drawn from Central European Renaissance usages.

Ultimately the impetus here may be as much nationalistic as Expressionistic. But its appeal lies in the economy of means.

Vienna (Wien)   A-18
* **Haus Primavesi** (house) 1913–15
Gloriettegasse 14–16
Josef Hoffmann
Neo-Classicism
Map A-2 / U-Bahn: Hietzing

Two of Hoffmann's buildings stand well above the rest: the simple, elegant Purkersdorf Sanitorium, 1903–11 (A-24), and the opulent Palais Stoclet, 1904–15 (B-12). Before them, he had built Anglo-Art Nouveau houses. Following them, he turned increasingly toward a stark, cryptic Neo-Classicism which at its best, as here, had a certain stage-set-like grandeur. Thanks mainly to Hoffmann and/or the uncertainty of the times, this mode gained a substantial if short-lived popularity. For many it represented a necessary purgative after the excesses of Art Nouveau – and before those of Expressionism. For others, including Hoffmann, it was to become a dead end.

A-18a Just down the street, at Gloriette-

gasse 21, is an **Art Nouveau house,** which, with its Baroque overtones, is strangely reminiscent of a house type then also popular with some of Frank Lloyd Wright's lesser-known suburban contemporaries. Not that Chicago has anything quite like the malevolent eye that keeps watch here.

A-18b A little further in the same direction, at Wattmanngasse 29, is a small **National Romantic apartment building,** 1914, by Ernst Lichtblau. Its façade is an Arts and Crafts adaptation of Germanic vernacular architecture. That at the same time it seems to anticipate the later International Style strip window may or may not be a coincidence.

A-18c In the opposite direction – physically, spiritually, and temporally – is the neat **group of International Style houses,** 1932, at Franz Schalk-Platz 3–7, by C. S. Drach.

Vienna (Wien)   **A-19**
Konzilsgedächtniskirche (church)
1966–8
Lainzer Straße 138–140
Josef Lackner
Formalism
Map A-2

The almost biaxial symmetry, the central altar, the careful attention to details, the air of calm self-assurance, these all typify many contemporary Austrian churches. If, within that context, this church has a fault, it is that an overly massive organ loft dominates its interior. Conversely, of most interest here is the inventive handling of the exterior walls. They are constructed of gigantic concrete blocks whose unusual surface texture appears to be the result of having filled semi-porous forms with many small batches of a high-aggregate-content concrete. Furthermore, these 'blocks' have been imaginatively, and quite appropriately, conjoined with crisp, smooth, pre-cast-like, poured-in-place concrete work around the doors (and elsewhere) to achieve a paraphrase of traditional quoining – but with the conventional roles of the modular and the more homogeneous materials reversed.

Vienna (Wien)   **A-20**
* **Werkbundsiedlung** (housing exhibition) 1930–2
Various architects, see A-20a-o below
International Style
Map A-2

[Although its maintenance may not always have been the best and a few of its houses were lost in the war, the area remains almost as built.]

There are obvious and potentially misleading parallels between this Werkbundsiedlung and its famous namesake in Stuttgart (D-60). Both share a common impetus, ideology and aesthetic, as well as similar, low-density suburban locations – albeit Stuttgart's free-standing middle-class villas were far more costly than Vienna's working-class row houses.

Yet Stuttgart's Weißenhof Siedlung truly reflects the position of the best, and most orthodox, modernists during those pre-Hitler days when the amount of modern architecture being built in many German cities exceeded that of some entire European countries. The Weißenhof Siedlung was a high-water mark, the definitive and remarkably consistent standard of comparison for the whole International Style. The same cannot be said of Vienna's exhibition. Although it involved twice as many architects, much of the local talent (not identified here) justifiably never escaped obscurity – even if Hoffmann, and especially Loos, are not names to be ignored.

In Germany the best housing, the standard against which the Weißenhof Siedlung must be judged, included the likes of Siemensstadt (D-18). In Austria the analogous standard of comparison was the more conservatively monumental Karl Marx-Hof (A-23).

The more interesting surviving houses and their architects are:

A-20a **Woinovichgasse 13–19,**
Adolf Loos
A-20b **Woinovichgasse 14–20,**
Gerrit Th. Rietveld

Werkbundsiedlung
Map A-20

A-20c **Woinovichgasse 9,**
Richard Neutra
A-20d **Woinovichgasse 11,**
H. A. Vetter
A-20e **Woinovichgasse 10–12,**
G. Guevrekian
A-20f **Woinovichgasse 32,**
Josef Frank
A-20g **Woinovichgasse 34, Engelbrechtweg 4–6 and Veitingergasse 71–73,** Hugo Häring
A-20h **Veitingergasse 79–85,**
Josef Hoffmann
A-20i **Veitingergasse 87–93,**
André Lurçat
A-20j **Veitingergasse 107–109,**
Ernst Plischke
A-20k **Jagdschloßgasse 68–70,**
Helmut Wagner-Freynsheim
A-20m **Jagdschloßgasse 76–78,**
J. F. Dex
A-20n **Jagicgasse 8–10,**
Clemens Holzmeister
A-20o **Engelbrechtweg 5–7,**
Oskar Strnad

Vienna (Wien) A-21
** Anstaltskirche Heilig Leopold or Kirche 'Am Steinhof' (chapel of state
mental hospital) 1903–13
Baumgartner Höhe 1
Otto Wagner
Rational Neo-Classicism
Map A-2

[The church was faithfully restored *c.* 1971, except that the external copperwork was not regilded. Permission to visit must be obtained in advance.]

Vienna is a city of anomalies, but it is surprising how easily one comes to accept them. This marble and gilt edifice, set high on its commanding hilltop, is far more magnificent than any parish church in the city – yet it is only a hospital chapel. Although Neo-Classical in form, it is radically modern in detail: a traditional monument whose materials, expression and method of construction, and even to some extent its function, have been thought out afresh. For instance it is a marble church, but not one built of solid stone, nor does it pretend to be. Rather the marble is a veneer, bolted on in the most direct and obvious manner. Similarly, because site, circumstances and culture demanded a dome, Wagner built one. He even gilded it so that it could be seen for miles. But he neither built it of masonry nor, unlike so many of its sheet-metal Baroque forbears, did he make it appear to be masonry. Instead, like some tensely inflated sheet-copper balloon (invisibly supported by internal iron trusswork) it is unmistakably light – more so even than

the lacily transparent foliage of Olbrich's Sezessionshaus dome (A-4).

Viewed from within, however, the height of such a city-scaled dome might have been overwhelming, especially to the ill. Wagner therefore halved the interior volume with a hung 'vault' whose grid of gilded T-iron supports gives the space texture and scale, even as it, along with some strip skylights, serves to deny the structural implications of the vaulted form. The interior is further enriched with stained glass, wrought metalwork and Kolo Moser mosaics. Although these represent the most Arts and Crafts side of Wiener Werkstätte, they are comfortably in tension with the predominant pragmatic Rationalism – perhaps best personified by the hygenic, continuously running holy water fonts.

Vienna (Wien) A-22
* Villas Wagner I and II (own houses)
1886–8 and 1905–13
Hüttelbergstraße 36 and 38
Otto Wagner
Neo-Classicism and Rational Neo-Classicism respectively
Map A-2

[The right pergola of Villa I was enclosed in 1895, the left in 1900.]

What a contrast between these two adjacent houses built by and for the same man! The earlier is a traditionally grand summer pavilion, a suburban counterpart to Wagner's palatial townhouse/studio, and, not surprisingly, the subject of persistent rumours that it was originally intended for a prince. It is the peacock's plumage of a man whose prior success had been more that of the entrepreneur than that of the architect – a man whose success had been as much financial as artistic.

The later house reflects an older man who had forsaken material achievements in favour of more difficult artistic ones.

Villa Wagner II

It is a simple, unpretentious, dwelling – save perhaps for the Kolo Moser glass above the door. Yet it was as radical as any European house of its day.

The builder of the first Villa Wagner would have been all but forgotten were it not for the builder of the second.

A-22a **Wagner's town house,** 1889–91, is at Rennweg 3. *U-Bahn: Karlsplatz*

Vienna (Wien)   **A-23**
* Karl Marx-Hof (social housing) 1927
Heiligenstädter Straße 32–92
Karl Ehn
Expressionism
Map A-2 / U-Bahn: Heiligenstadt

Between the wars Vienna's staunchly
socialist government undertook a vast programme of high-quality public housing
construction. At the time it was an effort
almost without parallel. Some 60,000
dwellings were built, many in huge hollow-
centred complexes that surrounded large
park-like courtyards.

Karl Marx-Hof may not have been the
biggest, the best or even the most monumental of these, but its marvellous
centrepiece line of flagpole-tower-topped
archways has come to be a popular, if
unflattering, ideogram for a social ideal
which was genuinely humane. Ironically,
these arches lead to nothing more important than an S-Bahn (now U-Bahn) station.

Once, in more troubled times, Karl Marx-
Hof did, however, know another sort of
symbolic glory. In 1934 it became famous
as a fortress – on the socialist side, naturally – during a brief, bloody, civil war.

A-23a Marx's co-author has the dubious
honour of having lent his name to Vienna's
most monumentalized housing: the **Friedrich Engels-Hof,** 1930–3, by Rudolf
Perco, on the Friedrich-Engels-Platz.

A-23b One of the most pleasant, if less
aggressively modern, of these superblocks
is Schmid & Aichinger's vaguely Gothicky-
Expressionist **Rabenhof,** 1927–9, at
Baumgasse 29–41.

Purkersdorf [near Vienna]   **A-24**
*** Evangelische Anstalten
Krankenhaus** or **Purkersdorf
Sanitorium** 1903–7
Wiener Straße 72–80
Josef Hoffmann
Secession (Art Nouveau)
W from Vienna on Rt 1 (Map A-2→)
*→ WEST AUTOBAHN-LINZ (E-5) / bear R on
Wientalstr (Rt 1) just before beginning of
autobahn / on L just beyond Purkersdorf
town limit sign*

[The mansarded top floor is a later
addition, the original roof having been flat.
At the time of writing the building was said
to be vacant and deteriorating.]

Despite obvious debts to Wagner, the
Purkersdorf Sanatorium, more than any
other Secessionist building, reflects the
Mackintoshes' influence. Their example
can be seen in the plain unornamented
white plaster walls and white-painted
woodwork; in the lack of overt Neo-Classical references, a strict symmetry notwithstanding; and, most obviously, in all
the tiny square windowpanes.

Purkersdorf was Hoffmann's first major
building. More important, it was the first
decorative commission for Hoffmann's
newly-founded Wiener Werkstätte. Unquestionably this building was the basis
for much of Hoffmann's reputation as a

pioneer modernist. In the context of his
total output, however, its apparent pre-
dictive modernity is something of an exception. Still, despite the mature Hoffmann's
opulent Classicist tendencies, and despite
some rather more convincing and only
slightly later houses by Loos, Purkersdorf
may well be the earliest Germanic anticipation of the International Style – an anticipation which, as it happens, owes much
to its international ancestry.

Linz   **A-25**
* St Theresia-Kirche (church)
1958–62
Losensteinerstraße
Rudolf Schwarz
Romantic Rationalism
W from Linz ctr on Rt 139 (Unionstr) past autobahn / L at CAMPING *on Landwiedstr / second L on Losensteinerstr / on R*

The architecture of our era has, temporarily at least, achieved a heterogeneity without historic parallel. Undoubtedly the time must come when scarcity of energy and resources, more than aesthetic or cultural considerations, will force the establishment of a new homogeneity – that is, a new vernacular tradition. Until then, however, almost *any* group of theoretically consistent variations on a particular building design will remain significant. Wright's Prairie and Usonian houses, Le Corbusier's Maisons Citrohan (F-59) and Unités (F-63), and Aillaud's 'snakey' housing (F-40) are examples of such groups that come to mind.

St Theresia Kirche is representative of another interesting if less well known group. Each of these Schwarz-designed churches is a tall, flat-roofed elliptical space, with all the acoustical advantages and disadvantages inherent in such a form. They also share, to varying degrees, a frankly exposed concrete structure and other reflections of a Rationalist/Brutalist attitude towards materials and details. Aside from the number and location of the generically similar, 'tacked-on', semi-oval side chapels, the greatest differences between them are in the nature of the infill walling (stone, stucco, brick) and in the treatment of the fenestration, which can be crucial to the success of this particular design, and which Schwarz never handled more simply and convincingly than here. His strict adherence to a regular window grid both disciplines and modulates the single, con-

tinuous, flowing wall surface. When combined with the expressed regular structural system and the semi-apparent curving grid of lights, it transforms a potentially amorphous, even dull space, derived from an essentially weak and 'pretty' form, into a space charged with dynamic tension.

One reason for the consistency of these churches – including the less obviously related Heilig-Kreuz-Kirche in Bottrop, West Germany (D-41) – may be that Schwarz is the author of the only theoretical treatise on church design to have been written by an important twentieth-century architect.

Other Schwarz oval churches, all in Germany, are:

A-25a St Michael-Kirche, 1954
Gellert-Straße 39, Frankfurt;
A-25b St Maria Königin-Kirche, 1956–9, Kohlweg 48, Saarbrücken;
A-25c St Bonifatius-Kirche, 1960–4, Volpertshäuser Straße 1, Wetzlar.
A-25d Also in Linz is the **'Austria Tabak' tobacco factory,** 1930–4, by Peter Behrens & Alexander Popp. It is the last work of an aging pioneer (D-16, 56). *E from Linz ctr along river abt ½ mi (1 km) / on R at junction of Untere Donaulände and Rechte Brückenstr*

Salzburg   **A-26**
ORF-Studio (radio and television studios) 1968–73
Nonntaler Hauptstraße 49d
Gustav Peichl
High-Tech Rationalism
E along S bank of river to Rudolfsplatz (sq) at end of Nonntaler Brücke (bridge) / S (away from river) around E side of bldg facing br / R at Y on to Nonntaler Hauptstr

Here is a true architectural machine: rationally assembled from slick industrial components; functionally, almost diagrammatically organized to suit its complex and highly technical programme; responding primarily to its own internal requirements (like all machines) – and not to its site or surroundings (Salzburg's fortress hovers overhead). How appropriate then, that this self-absorbed building is only one of a series of virtually identical regional studios Peichl built for the ORF.

The others include:

A-26a ORF-Studio Linz, 1968–73.
S from Linz ctr on Landstr abt ½ mi (1 km) / L on Blumauerstr / at Franckstr 2a
A-26b ORF-Studio Innsbruck,

1968–72. N from Innsbruck ctr (at Hofburg) on Rennweg
A-26c ORF-Studio Dornbirn, 1968–72. *On Höchsterstr*
A-26d ORF-Studio Graz, 1968–81. With stuccoed walls. *At Buchgraben 51*
A-26e ORF-Studio Eisenstadt, 1968–82. This one (again stuccoed) also sports some diminutive Aldo Rossi-esque, pennant-topped, turret-ventilators, along with some other ventilators of a perhaps more Freudian character, all rendered in stainless steel. Peichl, it should be noted, is a well-known satirical cartoonist publishing his work under the name 'Ironismus'. *At Marbergerstr 20*

BELGIUM

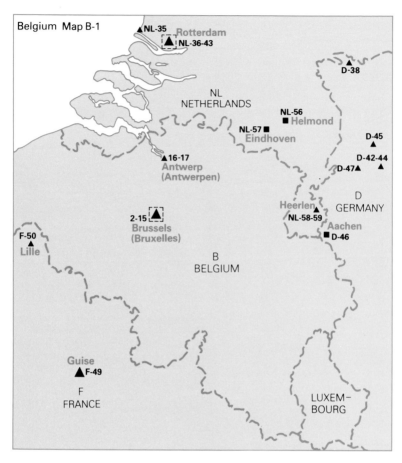

Belgium Map B-1

NL-35
Rotterdam
NL-36-43

D-38

NL
NETHERLANDS

NL-56
Helmond

NL-57
Eindhoven

D-45

D-42-44

D-47

16-17
Antwerp
(Antwerpen)

D
GERMANY

Heerlen
NL-58-59

Aachen

2-15
Brussels
(Bruxelles)

F-50
Lille

B
BELGIUM

D-46

Guise
F-49

F
FRANCE

LUXEM-
BOURG

Antwerp (Antwerpen)	B-16-17
Brussels (Bruxelles)	2-15

Belgium (Belgie/Belgique)　　B-1

Established in 1830 for the convenience and security of Europe's great powers, Belgium for long served as their battleground. Today its location, *laissez-faire* economics, and cultural bifurcation – being half Germanic (Flemish) and half Latin (Walloon) – have made it a Eurocrat's haven: Nato, the EEC, and dozens of multinational corporations are all established in and around Brussels.

Certainly as a people the Belgians have little sense of a national or cultural identity that they can call their own. Traditionally the French-speaking minority has ruled, maintaining and to an extent transmitting to the rest of the population the peculiarly French point of view that any place other than Paris is by definition provincial. Naturally the Dutch-speaking Flemish populace receives some cultural stimulus from Holland. But as Belgium is conservative and Catholic while Holland is liberal and more Protestant, those links are not particularly close.

This cultural tension and lack of national identity has allowed most investment and development to remain in the hands of private individuals rather than public institutions. By European standards there is relatively little public transport. Similarly there are relatively few housing projects, but many private houses – including most of postwar Europe's larger and more tasteless examples. (This even though, or perhaps because, Belgium has a disproportionately high number of architectural schools and architects.)

Perhaps these circumstances suggest why Art Nouveau, originally a shallow-rooted hybrid limited to the two dimensional 'applied arts', was able suddenly to blossom into a three-dimensional architectural language in the liberal *nouveau-riche* Brussels of the early 1890s. (Although it was then momentarily a political and artistic hotbed, Brussels has never been Europe's most cosmopolitan capital.) They may also explain why later Belgian architecture was never able to fulfil the promise of that first flowering.

Language note Belgium is uncomfortably bilingual – uncomfortable to the extent that even well-educated Walloons (French speakers) often know little Flemish (Dutch) while many Flemings prefer not to speak French. It is also frequently hard to know where the linguistic boundaries lie. Generally, Antwerp and the north, including Brussels's suburbs, are Flemish. Brussels is officially bilingual, but leaning towards French. The south is Walloon.

Most Belgian towns and many streets have names in both languages. These can sometimes look quite different although they usually mean the same thing, e.g. Haanstraat and rue du Coq. We have tried throughout to give names in the appropriate local language, but be prepared for frustrating inconsistencies on the part of the Belgians. To add one final bit of confusion, French speakers will frequently substitute 'y' for 'ij' in the spelling of Flemish proper names, e.g., Stynen for Stijnen. (For other confusions involving 'ij', see NL-1: *Language note*.)

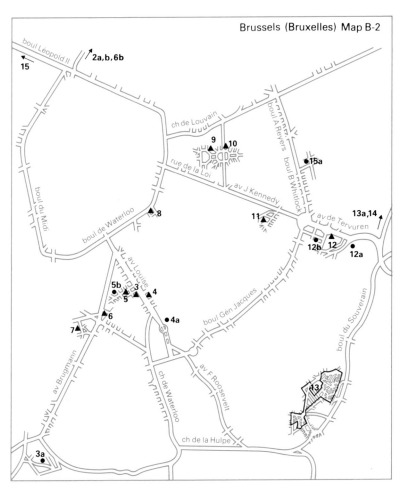

Brussels (Bruxelles) Map B-2

Brussels (Bruxelles)　　　　B-2

The core of Brussels is centred upon the Grand Place with its famous gilded guild houses, the elegant Galeries Saint-Hubert (a group of three arcades, the Galeries du Roi, de la Reine, and des Princes) 1846, and some unfortunate postwar pseudo-medieval 'restorations'. Surrounding this are miles of three- and four-storey row houses – a low-density version of the once widely imitated nineteenth-century Parisian urbanization pattern that is still being extended here, long after its demise in other Northern European cities. Ironically, in many of Brussels's most urbane and appealing older inner-city quarters examples of this sort of development are now being sacrificed to speculators, who are rapidly rebuilding the city at the actual densities of nineteenth-century Paris, but with all the 'charm' and 'urbanity' of suburban twentieth-century Paris.

Of some interest is Brussels's system of selective traffic improvements. For the most part a by-product of the 1958 World's Fair,

these consist primarily of a number of short tunnels which carry smoothly, and often also merge or divide, traffic that otherwise would be fighting its way through many of the city's most heavily used intersections. Although this must be a costly solution, it is a far better one – physically, visually, and acoustically – than the monstrous viaducts that are coming to dominate important urban spaces in other European cities.

B-2a In the centre of the fair site, and of the boulevard du Centenaire, is an additional legacy of that otherwise forgotten world's fair. The **Atomium**, now three decades old, still sits – alone, graceless, decrepit, and remarkably dated – amid the debris of a party that no one ever remembered to clean up properly. *N from inner ring road on quai de Willebroeck (Map B-2→) ⇨ allée Verte / L on av de la Reine past B-6b / L just before junction with autoroute on av de Madrid / L on av de l'Atomium*

B-2b Near by is the **Grand Palais du**

Heysel, a large exhibition hall by Joseph van Neck, 1935. A somewhat more useful relic than the Atomium, its pyloned main entrance and ziggurat sides appear innocently Art Deco to some, and suspiciously Fascistic to others.

Brussels (Bruxelles)   **B-3**
* Hôtel Tassel (house, now Mexican Embassy) 1892–3
6 rue Paul-Emile Janson
Victor Horta
Art Nouveau
Map B-2

[Carefully restored in the mid 80's. Interior may be viewed by advance appointment only.]

Rarely can one say that a particular building was the first of its style or genre. There are at least a half-dozen claimants to the title of *'first skyscraper'*, even though an enterprising Minneapolis architect did try to patent the idea and collect royalties on it. And there are even more entrants in the *'first* modern building' sweepstakes (e.g. D-16, 36).

But Horta's Hôtel Tassel was clearly the first true Art Nouveau building. Before it, there was only a vague something in the air: only hints within the regional architecture of Catalonia (E-3), which seem in any case to have gone unnoticed outside Spain; or suggestions in motifs emanating from England via Arts and Crafts magazine illustrations; or premonitions in goods sold by shops such as Liberty's (GB-6a) and in the discovery of non-European two-dimensional graphic art – both by poster designers and by such differing sorts of painters as James McNeill Whistler and Jan Toroop; or anticipations in the discovery of the aesthetic possibilities of such 'new' materials as terracotta, malleable iron, and stained glass.

The Hôtel Tassel was a seed crystal in this supersaturated ambience. Suddenly,

although the very name was not to be coined for several years, Art Nouveau architecture was to be found everywhere.

B-3a One other oft-mentioned claimant to the title of 'first Art Nouveau building', despite its overwhelmingly English Arts and Crafts derivation and a date of 1895–6, is Henri van de Velde's house, **Bloemen-werf,** at 102 avenue Vanderaey in suburban Uccle.

Brussels (Bruxelles)   **B-4**
* Hôtel Solvay (now a couturier house) 1894–8
224 avenue Louise
Victor Horta
Art Nouveau
Map B-2

[The large, stained-glass winter garden on the second floor was destroyed by a bomb during the Second World War.]

Almost as if he were suffering from a kind of *horror vacui,* Horta applied his decorative genius uniformly throughout this incredibly expensive yet somehow dull house. Only the chandeliers – like frozen showers of stars – have a real vitality. Everywhere else there is a feeling that, even this early in his career, success was coming too easily. Or was it that where there is an almost unlimited budget, restraint, and discipline are apt to be overwhelmed by the simple need to spend?

B-4a **Hôtel Hallait** (house) at 344 avenue Louise, 1902–5, is also by Horta.

Brussels (Bruxelles)   **B-5**
Maison Ciamberlani (house, now
Bulgarian Embassy) 1897
48 rue Defacqz
Paul Hankar
Art Nouveau
Map B-2

[The now mostly obliterated murals are
examples of sgraffito, a technique wherein
many thin layers of pigmented plaster are
uniformly applied to a surface and then
selectively removed to produce a fresco-like
effect. Here, weathering has continued that
erosion, reducing large areas of both murals
to a single colour.]

During the mid-1890s Belgium saw the
parallel emergence of two sorts of Art
Nouveau architecture. The first and more
important (B-3), based on the work of Horta
and Van de Velde, and characterized by
more fluid linear ornamentation, was epitomized by, among other things, Hector
Guimard's Paris Métro entrances (F-17). It
was that 'Franco-Belgian' version of the
Art Nouveau which quickly came to be
replicated, with varying degrees of faith-
fulness, from Madrid (E-29) to Moscow.

This house is an example of Belgium's
'other' Art Nouveau, a variant developed
by Hankar and others that never spread
beyond the Low Countries. It was less a
new, ahistoric style than an extension of
nineteenth-century Gothic Rationalism,
combined with certain National Romantic
features – here the 'Flemish' windows and

the Northern Renaissance mural beneath
the cornice. (The other mural is more conventionally Art Nouveau.)

B-5a The **adjacent house**, 50 rue
Defacqz, 1898, is also by Paul Hankar –
part of the top floor is a later addition.

B-5b **Hankar's own house**, 1893, is
at 71 rue Defacqz.

Brussels (Bruxelles)   **B-6**
** **Musée Horta** (Horta's house, now a
museum) 1898–1901
25 rue Américaine
Victor Horta
Art Nouveau
Map B-2

Few modern architects deserve, much
less have, a museum dedicated to their
work – only four other European examples
come to mind: Le Corbusier (CH-3 and F-
22), Gaudí (E-12a), and Aalto (SF-35d).
The well-restored interiors of Horta's own
home typify his best work. (He apparently
had no 'early' or 'tentative' period and
produced virtually all of his important
buildings in the space of ten years.)
Although modest when compared to many
of the houses he created for his clients, this
house-turned-museum is, quite fittingly, its
own primary permanent exhibit.

The museum also contains a library, a
study centre, offices for an architects'
association, and space for changing exhibitions, while in the large rear yard, gaunt
fragments rescued from now destroyed
Horta buildings bear witness to the fact that
architecture is both the most durable and
the most transient of art forms.

Horta's lost works include the Maison du
Peuple, 1895, a political party headquarters whose complex yet rational structure and programme made it the most
important single building of the Franco-
Belgian Art Nouveau.

B-6a The building next door, 23 rue
Américaine, was originally **Horta's**

studio. Now a private house, its upper and
ground-floor windows have been somewhat modified.

B-6b A partial explanation for Horta's
apparent invention-at-a-stroke of a new
architecture, utilizing glass and iron extensively, may be found in the remarkable but
little-known **Serres Royales du
Château de Laeken** (royal conservatories), 1874–93, at 61 avenue du

Parc Royal, built by his mentor, Alphonse Balat. Horta certainly would have intimately known, and might even have worked on, this extensive complex. [Only open to the public for about one week a year, usually in May: inquire at the Government tourist office.] N *from inner ring road* (*Map B-2→*) *on quai de Willebroeck* ⇨ *allée Verte* / L *on av de la Reine* ⇨ *av du Parc Royal abt* 2½ *mi (4 km)* / *in palace grounds on R*

Brussels (*Bruxelles*)   **B-7**
* **Clinique du Docteur Van Neck**
(orthopaedic clinic, now offices) 1910
53 rue Henri Wafelaerts
Antoine Pompe
Rationalism
Map B-2

[Originally the pilasters extended about three feet above the roof line. The first (gymnasium) floor windows on either side of the balcony were bricked up to the height of the lintel over the doors and all three first-floor windows were filled with hollow hexagonal glass blocks – like those in the Castel Béranger staircases (F-19) – thereby forming an almost continuous band of faceted glass. The two windows to the right of the entry have been similarly enlarged and then, ironically, painted white, greatly damaging the composition's delicate balance. The metalwork originally accented the façade in a distinctive blue. It has been painted to match, and becomes confused with, the cream-coloured woodwork.]

The decade between the waning of Art Nouveau and beginning of the interwar era produced some interesting theories and projects, but little notable architecture. It was a period of change, uncertainty, and reaction.

This building, Pompe's first, reflects that time at its best: shedding the old reliance

upon ornament, with only the metalwork here showing traces of Art Nouveau; and searching for a newer, simplified grammar suitable to a new age. Yet there are echoes of older vocabularies, the arch, the Rationalists' exposed beams, the bay windows. In spite of its misadventures in remodelling, one can still see what an exciting hybrid composition it was.

Brussels (*Bruxelles*)   **B-8**
Banque Lambert (bank) 1958–64
24 avenue Marnix
SOM (Skidmore, Owings & Merrill)
Miesian
Map B-2

By the end of the 1950s postwar America was settled and secure. It had gone to college on the GI Bill, got a good job, and now wanted to be reassured of its recently acquired sophistication. So, afraid of making mistakes and believing that it had no modern tradition to draw upon, America turned once more to Classicism, to the low-risk, abstract, conservative architecture of Mies van der Rohe and his followers. As a result, SOM became the biggest architectural firm in America, if not the world. Huge sums of money were devoted to demonstrations of the many, frequently outlandish ways in which it is possible to support structurally, or pretend to support, a modularized, compartmentalized, sterilized, more-or-less Miesian box.

In a generic sense, then, this particular building will be thoroughly familiar to any American: the empty plaza concealing the large volumes of space that would not fit within the box, and also the set-back ground floor, hidden behind curtains as if it is not there, because the Miesian formulae say it should not be there.

The only new twist here is that the pre-

cast façade elements are load-bearing. (Structural pre-casting seemed new and exciting then.) Each of these little column units, rigidly fixed to the edge of the floor slab, is hinged, mid-column, to identical units above and below. (Note how this imagery – but not the actual, expensive and absurdly articulated, structural system – was soon mimicked in the curtain walls of a neighbouring speculative office building.)

Brussels (Bruxelles)   **B-9**
* Hôtel van Eetvelde I (house, now offices) 1895–7
4 avenue Palmerston
Victor Horta
Art Nouveau
Map B-2

[Interior accessible by appointment.]

Horta had bigger, more sumptuous commissions (B-4) and he built more elaborate, but now lost, sequences of spaces. But of his surviving works none combines the richness and the inventiveness to be found in this, one of his earliest houses. Its metal façade is perhaps Horta's most modern. It employs iron rationally to create an entire frame – as distinct from his frequent simple substitution of iron lintels or posts for stone ones. The interior is even more remarkable, especially when viewed from the distance of almost a century. There is banded marble in the *conciergerie*, an onyx dado in the front parlour, gilt bronze everywhere, and – the

pièce de résistance – a two-level glass-domed winter garden spatially uniting all.

B-9a The **Van Eetvelde House II**, 1898–1900, at 2 avenue Palmerston, was built by Horta as an adjunct to the first.

B-9b No. 3 avenue Palmerston is yet another Horta house, the **Hôtel Deprez – Van de Velde**, 1895–7.

Brussels (Bruxelles)   **B-10**
* Maison Saint-Cyr (private house) 1900–3
11 square Ambiorix
Gustave Strauven
Art Nouveau
Map B-2

Possible first impressions notwithstanding, the twenty-four-year old designer of this delightful ornamental orgy possessed problem-solving skills that were quite the equal of his decorative abilities. Because light can be a critical problem on so narrow a site, Strauven built an almost all-glass façade. But he set this 'curtain wall' just far enough behind the apparent façade-line to provide shade in summer without excluding the low winter sun. He also thereby gave each of the principal floors a full-width balcony, which on the ground floor he extended forward to make an extra-deep projecting porch. Even the curious curve of the front steps, the only exception to the façade's otherwise rigid symmetry, is doubly logical as it both eases access to the basement entrance and keeps the circulation path to one side of the porch.

Finally there is the large, round, top-floor

window, part of an epidemic of similarly shaped openings on Brussels's Art Nouveau houses (B-5, 11). It is, to be sure, a perfectly reasonable masonry form. Moreover, it is a dormer. (Note the patches of shingles between it and the party wall.) Technically this house is only three floors high and so may have been less heavily taxed.

Brussels (Bruxelles)/Etterbeek   **B-11**
* Maison Cauchie (Cauchie's own house and studio) 1905
5 rue des Francs
Paul Cauchie
Art Nouveau
Map B-2

Paul Cauchie was not an architect but a muralist, who so composed the façade of his own house that it would demonstrate his craft to its best advantage. And, as he was not otherwise aligned with one of the local 'schools' of Art Nouveau architecture, only the circular window and the technique of his sgraffitto murals are particularly Belgian. In most other respects this clever pastiche of Secessionist and Mackintoshian elements is yet another testimonial to the then-rapidly increasing influence of the period's new architectural and 'artistic' magazines.

Brussels (Bruxelles)/Woluwe-St-Pierre **B-12**
** **Palais Stoclet** (house) 1905–11
279 avenue de Tervuren
Josef Hoffmann
Viennese Secession (Art Nouveau)
Map B-2
[Not open to visitors.]
Formidable! Overwhelming! Adjectives seem inadequate when describing Hoffmann's, the Secession's, and Brussels's most important house – if indeed, a fifty-room bronze-trimmed marble mansion occupying acres of urban land can even be considered a 'house'. Do the dining-rooms of 'houses' contain twinned mirror-image Gustav Klimt mosaic murals? – handmade, like all the decorative elements here, by Hoffmann's Secessionist Wiener Werkstätte Arts and Crafts guild.

Not surprisingly, the Palais Stoclet is full of contradictions – hence, in part, its appeal. It appears so classically impassive. (The tower, although Romantic in conception, has all the lyrical warmth of a bowling trophy.) Yet, for the period, its plan is relatively free and open, its overall street elevation is not unduly symmetrical and its detailing is generally free of explicit classical language. The flat white marble walls even seem, like much here, to foreshadow the International Style – except that behind their parapeted tops there is not the flat roof which would become so dear to the next

generation. Rather, above the walls there appears just enough of the traditional, almost vernacular, sloping roof, so that one cannot help being particularly aware both of it and of the semi-dormered top floor windows which, perversely, make the walls appear as if they had been left unfinished.

In a sense, that roof sums up the whole building. Unlike much of Art Nouveau, the Palais Stoclet wants to be modern – not just escapist and, coincidentally, novel. It wants to be coldly, calculatingly part of a new man-made world. Yet, not just in name, but in the labour and wealth lavished upon it, it *is* a palace.

B-12a Just to the east, at 333 avenue de Tervuren, is an **International Style house** by Huibrecht Hoste, 1933, which demonstrates a curious form of architectural preservation. A large apartment building has been grafted on to it.

B-12b Near by, at 6 rue du Collège Saint-Michel, but worlds away from the Palais Stoclet socially and economically, is the **Fabbri studio** by Emile Lambot, 1900. In its unassuming modesty this small building – a happy blend of Rationalist tectonics and Arts and Crafts decoration – could hardly differ more from the Palais. Yet, in their conservative modernity, they do share a kind of kinship.

Brussels (Bruxelles)/   **B–13**
Watermael-Boitsfort
Cité-Jardin Floréal
(garden suburb) 1920–9
avenue des Archiducs (both sides)
Louis van der Swaelmen, *et al.*
English Arts and Crafts
Map B-2
By all rights this should be somewhere in the home counties around London. It belongs with Letchworth Garden City (GB-37) and the rest of the semi-utopian experiments in semi-suburban living inspired by Ebenezer Howard. Its planning, its cottagey architecture, its green cosy ordinariness are English, not Belgian.

B-13a **Kappellenveld**, 1924–7, in Bruxelles/Woluwe–St-Lambert, is another Van der Swaelmen garden suburb, for which Huibrecht Hoste and Antoine Pompe, among others, designed houses.

Like several similar contemporaneous projects, it represents a kind of architectural advance over Floréal. But its planning and landscaping are so determinedly uninteresting that the complex as a whole seems dull in comparison. *E on av de Tervuren (Map B-2→) / L on boul de la Woluwe, abt 1¼ mi (2 km) / R on av E. Vandervelde / on both sides of rd for three blks beginning just past church at top of hill*

Brussels (Bruxelles)/   B-14
Woluwe–St-Lambert
** **Maison de la Médecine** (student
housing) 1969–75
avenue Chapelle-aux-champs
Alma Métro Station 1969–82
avenue de l'Assomption
Lucien Kroll
*E on av de Tervuren (Map B-2→) / L on boul
de la Woluwe, abt 1¼ mi (2 km) / E on av E
Vandervelde / abt 500 yds (m) on L
(immediately opposite B-13a)*

Maison de la Médecine

There are interesting and substantial
differences between these two related projects. Kroll's housing is virtually the sole
major European example of what might be
called the architecture of 1968 – the *ad hoc*
construction with 'available' materials that
became emblematic of the US 'drop-out'
generation. However, unlike its typical
American counterpart, the builders, clients,
and designers here were not one group but
three. While this housing may look like an
urban Drop City, its participatory design
process was closer to that advocated by
certain Dutch theorists, or practised by
Ralph Erskine (GB-76). Today flaws in the
ad hoc detailing are becoming evident. Or,
as some would have it, they are being mag-
nified by lack of maintenance. None the less
these innocently idealistic buildings so

accurately mirror the spirit of their times
that they transcend such shortcomings.
Indeed they are more than mere architecture. They are social documents and
works of art – almost a kind of folk art.

The Alma métro station is also art-like
but, compared to the housing, more obviously and conventionally so. Clearly there
were still improvisational embellishments
(the foliage-painted glass) and details that
demanded on-site judgements, not to
mention on-site cutting and fitting (the
pleasingly irregular glass canopy). But
something is missing. Perhaps because the
moment of the late 60s had passed, or
because there was no participating client,
there could not be the same spontaneity.

Brussels (Bruxelles)/   B-15
Berchem-Ste-Agathe
La Cité Moderne (planned suburb)
1922–5
place des Coopérateurs
Victor Bourgeois, with Louis van der
Swaelmen, city planner
International Style
*W on boul Léopold II (Map B-2→) ⇨ av
Charles Quint / L on rue Laurent Heirbout
(fourth st past basilica, just before light)/just
past jog in road and along second st on R*
[Poorly maintained.]

Despite its name, la Cité Moderne makes
no real pretence at being a city – garden
or otherwise. But of the half-dozen experimental housing areas built near Brussels
between the wars, it is architecturally the
most interesting. In particular it marks both
the beginning and a high point of Victor
Bourgeois's career. The quadruple corner
house, for instance, strikingly parallels

Erich Mendelsohn's better-known Berlin
double villa (D-11a). As might be expected
from its date, la Cité Moderne is also somewhat naive. The distinctive long zigzag
blocks – an attempt to provide windows on
two walls of most rooms – have particularly
strange, if spacious, floor plans and must be
expensive to heat. Experience, and carefully
developed minimum standards, would soon
enough put an end to such experimen-
tation, and with it to the architectural
vigour of most social housing.

B-15a Bourgeois was one of the two best-
known Belgian International Style architects. (The other was L. H. de Koninck who
for the most part built houses, the best of
which – and some were very interesting
– have not survived.) Of Bourgeois's later
International Style efforts, the slickest is
the **Maison Jespers** (house and studio),
1928, at 149 avenue du Prince Héritier.

Antwerp (Antwerpen)   **B-16**
* Art Nouveau Wijk (Art Nouveau
area) *c.* 1900
Cogels Osylei, Generaal Van Merlenstraat,
Waterloostraat and Transvaalstraat
J. Bascourt, E. Dieltiens, J. De Weerd, *et al.*
Art Nouveau
S from Centraal Station on Pelikaanstr (on
W side of tracks) / L at fourth underpass
on to Gen Van Merlenstr (middle street of
three) / area consists of four blks around
intersection of Gen Van Merlenstr and
Waterloostr

Because all extreme styles become diluted
through diffusion, these modest, semi-
vernacular Art Nouveau houses seem
almost more mid-nineteenth-century
Rationalist in spirit. None the less this district, with its exuberant if not sophisticated
ornamental ironwork and ceramics, must
constitute the largest, most homogeneous
collection of Art Nouveau buildings
anywhere. Of special interest are:

B-16a The set of matching houses decorated with **mosaics of the four
seasons,** at the intersection of Waterloostraat and Generaal Van Merlenstraat.

B-16b The remarkable **mosaic depic-
tion of the Battle of Waterloo** at
Waterloostraat 11.

B-16c The area's **best individual
house,** at Cogels Osylei 80.

Antwerp (Antwerpen)   **B-17**
* Liberaal Volkshuis 'Help U Zelve'
(political hall, now offices) 1898
Volksstraat 40
Emile Van Averbeke, with Van Asperen
Art Nouveau
SE from Antwerp ctr on Frankrijklei ⇨
Amerikalei / R on Schildersstr (see B-17a
below) / R after Museum, on to
Volkstr / on L
   [Interior destroyed.]
   All that remains is a fantastic façade
including what must be the all-time cham-
pion split or broken pediment.

B-17a On Schildersstraat, just across from
the north-east corner of the Koninklijk
Museum, is a **house,** *c.* 1900, by F. Smet-
Verhas. Perhaps built for some retired sea
captain, it uses what appears to be the bow
of a real sailing boat as part of a remarkable
corner balcony. *See directions above*

SWITZERLAND

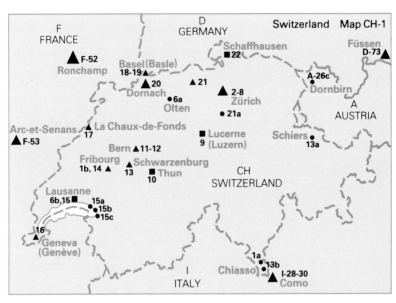

Switzerland   Map CH-1

F FRANCE
D GERMANY
Füssen
Schaffhausen ■ 22
▲ D-73
▲ F-52 Ronchamp
Basel (Basle) 18-19▲
A-26c ●
▲ 20
▲ 21
Dornach
● 6a
▲ 2-8 Zürich
Dornbirn ●
Olten
● 21a
A AUSTRIA
Arc-et-Senans ▲ 17 La Chaux-de-Fonds
▲ F-53
Bern ▲11-12
■ Lucerne 9 (Luzern)
Schiers ● 13a
Fribourg 1b, 14 ▲
Schwarzenburg ▲ 13
■ Thun 10
CH SWITZERLAND
Lausanne 6b,15 ■
● 15a
● 15b
● 15c
■ 16
Geneva (Genève)
1a ●
13b ●
Chiasso ●
I-28-30 ▲ Como
I ITALY

Switzerland (Confederatio Helvetica/Schweiz/Suisse/Svizzera)   CH-1

In architecture as in most other things, Switzerland lives up to its popular reputation. It is conservative, conscientious and not unduly innovative. There were only three pre-Second World War Swiss architects of lasting international significance, Le Corbusier, Hannes Meyer and Robert Maillart. But Le Corbusier, in his formative years, had access to the most progressive architectural minds in Germany, while his later epochal career was wholly identifiable with France. Meyer, the far too little-known successor to Walter Gropius as head of the Bauhaus, was also an expatriate. And Maillart, whose reputation probably peaked with the postwar enthusiasm for structural aesthetics, was in fact an engineer.

Since the war, the French-speaking and, to a lesser extent, the Italian- and German-speaking Swiss architectural communities have tended to reflect in their work the prejudices and enthusiasms, strengths and weaknesses of their respective counterparts in France, Italy and Germany. In the case of French Switzerland this has tended, at best, to mean rather stale Corbusiana and, at worst, sterile French Formalism. Therefore, until the 70s, 'modern Swiss architecture', as the world knew it, was essentially German-Swiss architecture. It differed from that of Germany in its generally more romantic expressiveness – as seen both in its tendency towards a rectilinear fragmentation of mass and detail and in the often refined Brutalism of its impeccable concrete construction. And it is this Swiss architecture, as exemplified by the work of Förderer & Zwimpfer (CH-22, 22c) among others, which, for the first time, began to have some influence outside Switzerland. More recently the architecture of the Italian-speaking Ticino, and particularly that of Mario Botta, has begun to achieve unprecedented international recognition. Botta's reputation is based largely upon a series of exquisitely crafted, abstractly geometric houses – which must demand a great deal of their occupants. Typically they suggest the work of Louis Kahn in conception and detailing, with just a touch of Carlo Scarpa's ornamentalism. Botta worked for both Scarpa and Kahn. They also tend to be inaccessibly located. There are, however, two non-residential Botta buildings that can be visited:

CH-1a The **secondary school** at Morbio Inferiore, 1970–7, is almost a pure example of Kahnian Brutalism with interior spaces reminiscent of his Bryn Mawr College dormitory. Unfortunately, its main building, like a line of eight identical symmetrical pavilions, leaves one with the uneasy sense that Botta put one of his little pavilion houses into a Xerox machine and ran off eight enlarged copies.

CH-1b The more recent **Banque de l'Etat de Fribourg/Freiburger Staatsbank,** 1977–82, does even less for his reputation. A hulking, sullen geometric building placed between two acutely intersecting streets, it is composed of two severe cubic masses – one facing each street – joined together by a huge cylindrical 'bay window' apparently made from an old-fashioned, unlovely 1950s curtain-wall system. *At junction of av de Pérolles (Rt 11) and route des Arsenaux, near RR station*

Language note Four languages are spoken in Switzerland: German, French, Italian, and Romansh – an almost extinct Latin-based tongue. Because, with a few exceptions, one language dominates any given area, all building and street names are given in the appropriate regional language. Although 'ö' and 'ü' seem to be the common usage in German here, they are sometimes also written as 'oe' and 'ue'. As in Germany, 'ß' and 'ss' are interchangeable in certain circumstances, but because 'ß' predominates it has been used here.

Zürich   **CH-2**
Mehrfamilienhäuser Doldertal
(flats) 1935–6
Doldertal 17 and 19
Alfred & Emil Roth, with Marcel Breuer
International Style
E from Quaibrücke (bridge) on Rämistr / R opposite University on Gloriastr, abt $\frac{1}{2}$ mi (1 km) / R on Bergstr / third L on Doldertal / on L

These two buildings, originally to have been three, are Breuer's only significant prewar, pre-American works. Designed with an enjoyable spatial complexity that is frequently missing from Germanic architecture of the period, they clearly show Breuer to have had, even then, almost Baroque inclinations.

Zürich   **CH-3**
** Centre Le Corbusier (museum)
1962–7
Bellerive Straße and Höschgasse
Le Corbusier
Neo-Expressionism/Rationalism
S from E end of Quaibrücke (bridge) on Uto Quai ⇨ Bellerivestr, abt $\frac{3}{4}$ mi (1.2 km) / in park on R

[Le Corbusier's last architectural statement, designed to house an exhibition on mankind, later used to exhibit Le Corbusier's own work.]

In its way the Centre Le Corbusier created almost as startling a first impression as had Notre-Dame-du-Haut at Ronchamp (F-52) a decade earlier. But there is a basic difference between these two buildings. Ronchamp was a manifesto to the world at large. It was an exaggerated statement of Le Corbusier's evolving attitude towards form, materials, and space. This pavilion seems to be more a private gesture whose importance derives from the uniqueness of its steel construction within the body of Le Corbusier's work. Like Harvard University's Carpenter Center, which he designed at about the same time, it is autobiographical and retrospective, if more subtly so.

The Centre Le Corbusier consists of two independent structures of steel, a material which he otherwise almost never employed for major structural elements. The larger, a pair of huge open-sided umbrellas, symbolically relates the smaller enclosed exhibition pavilion resting beneath it to the scale of the park and the city, and also, it would seem, to the whole history of monumental Classicism. These great canopies further serve, almost incidentally, to shelter the open terrace atop the lower structure.

It is, however, the lower structure that seems so unexpected in relation to Le Corbusier's previous buildings and projects. Yet it is perfectly plausible when seen as the fruition of several long-standing theoretical concerns which, in different ways, had been reflected in his earlier work. The pavilion is assembled of steel-flanged modular, load-bearing panels dimensioned, like the rest of the building, according to Le Corbusier's 'modulor' proportional measuring system, and infilled with various combinations of neoprene (rubber) gasketed glass and/or brightly enamelled sheet metal. These panels are bolted together in such a way that their flanges, bolts, and other precise but chunky exposed structural details contrast satisfyingly with the slick non-structural infilling, just as the irregular pattern of the infill elements also contrasts with the regularity of the structural connective grid.

He may not have meant it as such but Le Corbusier could not have built himself a more epigrammatic epitaph.

Zürich   **CH-4**
* Hochhaus Zur Palme (shops and offices) 1959–64
Bleicherweg und Genferstraße
M. E. Haefeli, W. M. Moser, R. Steiger & A. M. Studer
Late-International Style/Structural Neo-Expressionism
W from Quaibrücke (bridge) / R on Talstr / L on Bleicherweg / ahead on L

Zur Palme was something all too rare: an office building conceived not as a box on stilts in the middle of a windswept plaza, but rather with careful thought as to what was needed and possible in order to get the most benefit from this particular site for both the owner and the public. As a result, Zur Palme's tower stands above a two-storey base, covering most of the site, which contains shopping arcades and a large mezzanine level for the professional and other offices to which greater public access is needed. The roof of this base serves as a car park and is edged by an ingenious precast folded-plate snow shelter which shields the cars from view, while helping, by its scale and mansard shape, visually to link the base with the office tower above.

The tower does stand on eight large columns, clearly aligned with the structural grid of the base, but only two stand free for their total height beneath the tower, and one is neatly encircled by the parking deck's double helix access ramp. These large columns collect the weight of the tower from some one hundred smaller ones lining the corridors and façade – where the multitude of columns appears unfortunately busy. That aside, this is a lively argument for articulate and meaningful complexity: a building which avoids most of the problems associated with urban office towers and enriches its surroundings.

CH-4a There are some pleasant and, for-Switzerland, rare **Art Nouveau buildings** just to the west on Bleicherweg.

Zürich   **CH-5**
* Kantonsschule Freudenberg
(secondary school) 1956–60
Bederstraße and Steinentischstraße
Jacques Schader
Late-International Style
SW on Bleicherweg from Zur Palme (CH-4) / angle R at Y on to Bederstr / at first R past RR tracks

There is a common misconception, particularly in the New World, that architectural sensitivity to a site with strong natural characteristics can only be expressed through the organic integration of the building into its surroundings, in the manner of Frank Lloyd Wright (S-30, SF-37). There is, however, another more traditional way of relating a building to a designed or manipulated 'natural' setting, even if that setting amounts to no more than the simple meadow in which Le Corbusier placed the Villa Savoye (F-45) – an object both as appropriate and as alien there as a spacecraft on the surface of the moon. It is based on the principle that building and site must each remain true to its own reality and that by so doing each can best serve as a foil to the other.

Perhaps there is no more artificially natural a site than a well-matured 'English' landscape, such as surrounds this austere, slightly abstract, white school – almost as if the building were some strangely displaced ocean liner (to invoke a surreal technological analogy with considerable precedent in modern architectural theory). Yet despite the long tradition of verdant campuses, it seems at first impossible that the needs of a secondary school could be made compatible with so 'natural' a setting – even allowing for such necessities as an experimental garden and playing fields.

It was presumably in response to this problem that Schader built a two-storey-high platform, containing among other things three gymnasia, around the highest point on the site. On the platform he placed two classroom buildings. The assembly hall is situated on a lower adjoining platform of its own. This two-level, three-building, platform-campus has sufficient, but carefully delineated, hard open space to serve the students' outdoor social and circulation needs. Students are not barred from using the grounds, but access to and from the platform-campus is only possible by three well-defined routes – one being via the lower platform level while the other two follow stairs and ramps that climb up to the

campus through the trees. (In a small echo of that other, Wrightian attitude towards the *genius loci*, two trees actually pass through holes in one of the ramps.) This separation of most activities from the grounds, for most of the time, assures that the landscaping will continue to function as a foil to the school's hard elegance.

Zürich   CH-6
* Freibad Allenmoos (public swimming park) 1938–9
Ringstraße
M. E. Haefeli & W. M. Moser
International Style
N from Zürich ctr → FLUGHAFEN on Stampfenbachstr, abt 1 mi (1.5 km) / L at Y on to Hofwiesenstr, abt 1 m. (1.5 km) / R on Ringstr / on R

Allenmoos is representative of urban Switzerland's tradition of creating very urbane yet 'natural' open-air public swimming parks. The landscaping, which has had forty years to mature, is lush and inviting. Nor are the concrete buildings that border the park without technical interest, although collectively they are somewhat disjointed. The public dressing-rooms, for instance, incorporate thin-shell roofs spanning forty feet, while the roofs of the private cabins and the refreshment pavilions are, for the period, daringly cantilevered.

CH-6a There are several other early examples of this pleasant Swiss institution. One such is Frey & Schindler's **Strand-**

bad, 1937–9, on the banks of the river Aare in Olten. *On W bank of river, S of Alte-Brücke (wooden bridge)*

CH-6b Another, on Lausanne's lake front, is the **Plage Bellerive,** 1936, by Marc Piccard at avenue de Rhodanie 23. Unfortunately an enlargement of the site in 1964–6, destroyed the relationship that once existed between the building and the lake. *On lake front, just W of city ctr*

Zürich/Oerlikon   CH-7
* Hallenstadion (indoor stadium)
1938–9
Wallisellenstraße 45
Karl Egender
Rationalism
N from Zürich ctr → FLUGHAFEN on Stampfenbachstr, abt 2½ mi (4 km) / R on Wallisellenstr / on L

Here is an 'ancestor' the Brutalists overlooked. And like the best of the buildings they did rediscover (GB-57), it is not the accidental result of some vernacular or engineering genesis. No, this is the sort of work many may talk of but few produce:

tall hard walls patterned by raw concrete framework; brick infill and industrial glazing tensely curved at front and rear; sharply broken sides exposing aggressive outward-thrusting ribs; a strong cornice whose pattern of beams, purlins and rafters, set in deep shadow, contrasts with the tautness of the light-coloured walls below. Inside the same tensions again: a far from insubstantial two-and-a-half acre roof, linked to the stands only by glass, floats over everything – its entire four-million-pound load accommodated, almost too matter of factly, on four steel columns.

Zürich/Altstetten   CH-8
* Reformierte Kirche (church)
1938–41
Pfarrhausstraße
Werner M. Moser
Scandinavian Empiricism
W from Zürich → BASEL and BERN on
Badenerstr, abt 3 mi (5 km) / L on
Affolternstr → LUZERN & ST GOTTHARD /
first R on Pfarrhausstr / on L

The manner in which the nice but ordinary old parish church was retained as a chapel, almost enshrined within the new parish centre, says much about the mood of the late 30s: the need for reassurance and for symbols of the stability and humanity that infuse this church. More than most non-Scandinavian buildings of its day, it reflects that mood while still retaining the integrity of its own vision of modernity.

There is no reversion to folksy motifs here, no cowering before those who were then calling modern design 'cultural Bolshevism'. Indeed, the attitude towards materials and form is at times disconcertingly inventive.

Lucerne (Luzern)/Schönbühl   CH-9
Wohnhochhaus Schönbühl
(apartment tower) 1965–8
Langensandstraße
Alvar Aalto
Late-International Style
Einkaufszentrum (shopping centre)
1966–7
Langensandstraße
Alfred Roth
S from Lucerne ctr along lake shore →
RICHARD WAGNER MUSEUM */ on L at edge*
of city

For those who cannot get to Finland, or even Wolfsburg (D-32), here is an opportunity to experience Aalto first hand. It may not be Aalto at his best, but his touch is to be found throughout this block of flats – from his 'signature' door handles to a particularly complex, distorted version of his recurrent 'fan-emerging-from-a-rectangle' plan motif (D-30, SF-14, 38, 39).

If Aalto does not quite live up to his own standards here, Roth probably exceeds his. It is as if a certain romantic Scandinavian 'looseness' had rubbed off on him, so that, despite the limitations imposed by a rooftop car park, his shopping centre is a little lighter and less rigid than one might otherwise have expected.

CH-9a Facing directly on to the river Reuß, which flows out of the lake through Lucerne, is the **St Karlikirche**, 1930–5, a large, unpretentiously elegant, well-proportioned church designed by Fritz

Wohnhochhaus Schönbühl

Metzger. Unfortunately it stands behind an unimaginative colonnaded porch that is, at best, an awkward response to its dramatic riverside site. *W from Lucerne ctr → BASEL and BERN / R at KANTONSPITAL-FRIE-DENTHAL / across river on R*

CH-9b Of both the same vintage, 1935, and the same conservative elegance is Armin Meili's **landing stage** for the lake's excursion steamers. However, it is the sharp-prowed turn-of-the-century boats themselves, with their gleaming engines and great articulated paddles, that really should not be missed. *In Lucerne ctr, opposite the RR station, on S side of beginning of river*

Thun   CH-10
Boilerfabrik (boiler factory) 1958–9
Bernstraße 19
Atelier 5
Corbusian Brutalism
N from Thun ctr on Rt 70 (→ BERN) / on
L at junction with Rt 6 (→ SPIEZ and
INTERLAKEN)

It might seem like too much 'architecture' in too small a package. But it also contains offices, a showroom and, on its roof, the owner's apartment and garden. This arrangement has some distinct advantages, including privacy, a view, the convenience of 'living over the store' and, potentially, a less costly house, if not a less

costly garden, since everything up to and including the ground floor of the house is a necessary part of the factory below.

Bern   **CH-11**
Universitäts-Institut (lecture halls
and laboratories) 1931–6
Sahlistraße
O. R. Salvisberg & O. Brechbühl
Rationalism
*NW from Bern ctr → BIEL on Länggasstr /
L at Bühlstr (where Biel rd turns R) /
two blks on R*
    Compared to the tough-minded, prewar
work of O. R. Salvisberg, the postwar Swiss

Brutalists seem wilfully picturesque. Salvisberg's Universitäts-Institut is a carefully
proportioned, three-storey building with
raw concrete load-bearing walls. Its most
powerful elevation is banded by endless
ranks of closely spaced identical windows,
whose relentless progress is measured only
by a series of uniformly spaced lecture halls
which project, almost menacingly, from
and above the uppermost floor.

Bern   **CH-12**
* Siedlung Halen (row housing)
1959–61
Stuckishaus
Atelier 5
Corbusian Brutalism
*NW from Bern ctr (→ BIEL) on Länggasstr
⇨ Halenstr (in park) / first L after
Halenbrücke (bridge over river Aare) /
→ SIEDLUNG HALEN*
    Halen is a slightly precious, seventy-nine-
family, mini-hill town of clustered row
housing. At the time of its construction
much was made of the fact that it provided
its occupants with more communal and
individual amenities, and with a more
urban sense of place, than might have been
expected given its modest budget. All of
this was presumably made possible because
structural elements frequently serve two
dwellings instead of just one; because the
utilities system includes a single central
heating plant, instead of seventy-nine separate units; because the ratio of expensive
exterior surfaces to building volume is not
as high as it would be with free-standing
houses; and because there is a single
common parking garage, another shared
structure, under one of the buildings –
which has the added advantage of keeping
cars out of the community.
    That an aggregation of some 350 people
can support a small village shop and a
swimming pool is not to the credit of the
architects. What the architects *are* responsible for here is the sense of place. Unfor-

tunately most of Halen's external spaces are
unimaginative and physically cramped –
so much so that, when coupled with the
insular nature of the houses themselves,
they would seem likely to discourage,
rather than encourage, the sorts of spontaneous social contacts that transform
'housing' into a community. It may be,
then, that Halen's reputation should stand
simply on the fact that it was built at a time
when the prevailing CIAM 'tower in a park'
ethic strongly discouraged such human-
scale housing. And perhaps its greatest
failing is its small size: had it been a community of several thousand people, its
potential economic and social advantages
might well have been better realized.

Roßgrabenbrücke

Schwarzenburg [*near Fribourg*]   CH-13
* **Roßgrabenbrücke** and
Schwandbachbrücke (bridges)
1932 & 1933 respectively
Schönentannen-Hinterfultigen road
Robert Maillart
*E from Schwarzenburg on Rt 74 / L at
Schönentannen →* FULTIGEN & HINTER-
FULTIGEN

Maillart's bridges can be found throughout Switzerland. Many, like this pair, are
on minor roads. Although these two
examples do not include the earliest, the
longest, or the most dramatic (CH-13a),
they are in a location that will not give the
average flatlander acute vertigo and they
afford the opportunity of comparing two
types of Maillart design in one place.

The Roßgraben bridge, the first
encountered, is a 269-foot three-hinged
arch of the type used in his more spectacularly sited efforts. Although it may look
massive, the arch itself is but eight inches
thick. The remaining visible structure is
only thin vertical stiffening ribs.

The shorter Schwandbach bridge is a
daring curved example of a more innovative and difficult design. Here the upturned
edges of the roadway itself are stiffened to
redistribute the concentrated vehicular

loads on to the arch which, being so thin,
must carry its burdens only by simple compression and could not otherwise accommodate such unevenly distributed forces.

That Maillart's work is important to the
history of concrete design is widely recognized. Here, however, the beauty and
simple elegance of these structures transcend such considerations.

CH-13a Above the little mountain town
of Schiers, near Davos, is Maillart's **Sal-
ginatobelbrücke,** 1929–30, one of the
longest and surely the most dramatically
sited of his bridges. *N from Davos on Rt 28
abt $18\frac{1}{2}$ mi (30 km) / in Schiers follow uphill
rd behind church, keeping to R at Ys / several
miles on narrow, unpaved, precipitous rd*

CH-13b Maillart's only interesting building, *per se,* is the **Punto Franco bonded
warehouse,** 1924–5, in Chiasso. A
simple, wide-span shed with a marvellously delicate concrete truss roof, it is now,
unfortunately, sandwiched between a pair
of larger, more prosaic neighbours. *S →*
CHIASSO *from motorway E9 abt 900 yds
(m) / R between* GULF *and* SHELL
stations / inside fenced area at end of rd

Fribourg   CH-14
***Université Miséricorde** (university)
1938–41
Route du Jura
Fernand Dumas and Denis Honegger
Perret-esque Rationalism
W from Fribourg ctr → LAUSANNE *on Route
des Alpes / R →* UNIVERSITÉ *on Route du
Jura / on L just past RR tracks*

For most French-speaking architects of
the 20s and 30s the work of Auguste
Perret, not the International Style, epitomized progressive architecture at its best.
Curiously this little-known, multi-function
academic building represents that ideal
more elegantly than almost any work of
the time to be found in France. If one can
overlook the occasional bits of Classicist
formalism and period ornament, not to
mention the parody of Le Corbusier's Swiss
Pavilion (F-34) at the main entrance, it *is*
a respectably modern effort.

Lausanne   **CH-15**
Vallée des Jeunes (exhibition
building, now children's park) 1964
Vallée du Flon
Michel Magnin
Neo-Expressionism
S then W from Lausanne RR station →
GENÈVE ⇨ *av des Figuiers / exit from
roundabout at Lausanne Sud (where autoroute
NI-E4 → Geneva begins) →* CAMPING */ first
R into car park / ahead on R*
[Originally an entranceway to the 1964
Swiss National Exposition.]

Even more than their German- and Italian-speaking counterparts, most French-Swiss architects seem in their work to be 'French' first and 'Swiss' second – if at all. Perhaps no other modern culture can equal the French as creators of 'poetic' architecture. While almost all of these rebellions against Cartesian logic and classicist moderation seem disastrous to everyone but the French, once in a while one of them achieves some success.

Here the programme could hardly have been more appropriate: a pair of pavilions, connected by an elevated walkway, intended to serve initially as the entrance and introduction to a fair. Yet a propitious programme is, by itself, no guarantee of success. When setting out to build a fantasy one must maintain just as much self-discipline, albeit applying different standards, as under more conventional circumstances. One must invent rules based

not on the usual standards of rationality and efficiency, but rather on the need to delight, surprise, charm, or amuse, without seeming to overstrain either one's own talent or the observer's temporarily suspended standards of reasonableness. All of this M. Magnin has done.

CH-15a Behind a wall on the busy shoreline road in Vevey, toward the east end of Lac Léman, is the **house Le Corbusier built for his parents** in 1923. [*Closed to public.*]

CH-15b Further along the same side of the shore road in Clarens-Montreux is the similarly secretive, now somewhat modified **Villa Karma** which Adolf Loos remodelled, 1904–6, by adding a ten-foot thick swath of new construction around an existing house. [*Closed to public.*]

CH-15c The exacting standards of Swiss construction are particularly evident in what must surely be Europe's best-designed and landscaped motorway system. Consider, for instance, the **prefabricated pre-stressed concrete viaduct,** 1966–9, by A. Piguet, that carries route E2 for several miles along the eastern end of Lac Léman. An elegant but expensive solution, it seems to have been dictated primarily by a desire to avoid the massive visual impact of conventional cut and fill construction.

Geneva (Genève)   **CH-16**
* Maison Clarté (studio apartments)
1930–2
rue St-Laurent and rue Adrien-Lachenal
Le Corbusier
International Style
*S from pont du Mont-Blanc / first L on quai
Gén Guisan ⇨ rue Versonnex / R at place
des Eaux-Vives on to rue des Eaux-Vives / L
at top of hill on to route de Malagnou /
immediate hard L on to rue Adrien-Lachenal
/ on R*

One might expect this beautifully controlled, machine-like, steel-framed block of two-storey flats to be better known and more widely respected. Despite an uncertain junction with the ground, it is far more convincing than most apartment blocks of its time – not to mention its being one of Le Corbusier's few large prewar buildings and one of his few realized antecedents of the epochal postwar *unités* (F-63). Unfor-

tunately it coincided in time, scale, and residential function with two other precursors of the *unité*: the Pavillon Suisse (F-34) and the Armée du Salut (F-35). These not only employ much of Clarté's detailing, its most successful aspect, but also incor-

porate a number of more advanced planning concepts, innovations in the use of materials, and new details of their own.

Few buildings of the period could stand comparison with those two, and even Clarté is not one of them.

La Chaux-de-Fonds   **CH-17**
* **Villa Schwob** (house) 1916
rue du Doubs 167
Le Corbusier
Rational Neo-Classicism
NW from av Léopold Robert (main st) on to rue de la Fusion
[Not open to the public.]

Here, in this city of watchmakers, Le Corbusier was born – as Charles-Edouard Jeanneret – in 1887. At the local school of applied arts he received his only formal artistic training. And here he built his first half-dozen houses, as well as one now lost cinema. The earliest of these houses, two National Romantic chalets built in 1906 and 1909, exhibit far more self-assurance than might be expected in the first designs of a provincially trained teenager.

Le Corbusier's last work in La Chaux-de-Fonds was the Villa Schwob. By the time he came to build it, a decade later, he had travelled through Italy and the Near East and had experienced, first hand, the work

of the most progressive architectural minds in Europe (D-40, 40a, F-18, 54). As a result, the Villa Schwob is a kaleidoscopic mirror – reflecting but also distorting and fragmenting many of the architectural concerns of the moment. It reflects the 'discovery' of traditional Islamic architecture and the revival of interest in Rationalism and in the irrational mythos of geometry. In it are to be seen the formal symmetries of Neo-Classicism (and of Wright); the flat roofs and broad cornices of Asia Minor; and, subtly in evidence for the first time in Le Corbusier's work, an enthusiasm for regulating lines and mathematical proportions.

In 1923, an illustration of the Villa Schwob with superimposed '*traces régulators*' was published by Le Corbusier in the pamphlet *Vers une architecture* – the single most influential piece of propaganda in the history of modern architecture. The Villa Schwob was for long the only one of his earlier works that he acknowledged.

Basel (Basle)   **CH-18**
* **Antoniuskirche** (church) 1926–31
Kannenfeldstraße 51
Karl Moser
Perret-esque Rationalism
NW from SBB Bahnhof (RR station) S of river → FRANCE / abt 1½ mi (2.5 km) on L

For its time the Antoniuskirche was a bold excursion into the then still largely unexplored realm of raw, unadorned concrete. Admittedly Moser must have been aware of the concrete church which Auguste Perret, then unchallenged master of the material, had built only a few years earlier at Raincy (F-36). But Moser chose a quiet, restrained approach to the material, rather than Perret's more inventive ornamentality. He also diverged from Perret's basic plan the better to meet both his own artistic needs and the demands of his more difficult, urban site. In particular he added

a remarkable old-new element – the *porte cochère*. This gateway, neatly fitted beneath the organ loft, connects the street with a courtyard formed by the church and its attendant secular buildings. It also serves as the symbolic city-scaled doorway of the church: a colossal false opening eighty feet high, which is the first of a series of six successively smaller portals. The final and smallest of these, only some fifteen feet high, frames the actual *porte cochère* within which are the modest doors leading into the nave. Rarely in modern architecture has there been so graphic an example of scale manipulation to accommodate functional, urbanistic and symbolic requirements. Yet throughout history such devices have been commonplace enough. Gothic cathedrals, for instance, often have huge door surrounds, sometimes covering half the façade, even though the actual doors

may be only a dozen feet square and may in their turn contain other quite small openings for everyday use.

Unfortunately the imaginative boldness of the entrance was not matched by the tower. A 'skyscraper style' affair, it might have looked *au courant* as late as 1940, but it is decidedly dated today. Ironically, underneath its stylization, the tower's main structure is a giant up-ended Vierendeel truss, which, if left exposed, would have made it a far stronger and less datable companion to the entrance, as well as to the exposed steel tower of the neighbouring Johanneskirche (CH-19).

CH-18a Also by Moser is Basel's **Badischer Bahnhof** (railway station), 1912–13, in which Saarinen's Helsinki station (SF-3) seems to have acquired the garb of Schinkel's Neo-Classicism.

Basel (Basle)   **CH-19**
*Johanneskirche (church) 1936
Metzer Straße and Mülhauser Straße
K. Egender & E. F. Burckhardt
International Style
N from Antoniuskirche (CH-18) on Kannenfeldstr → FRANCE / R on Mülhauser Str / on R

Here is the first modern Swiss church with neither explicit ornamental and historical reminiscences nor spatial and structural ones. Its school and parsonage wing is almost as straightforward an example of International Style as one could hope to find. Yet the church proper is not. It has the hardness of an earlier, more rigorous modernism – of the Maison de verre (F-13), the radically Rationalist projects of Hannes Meyer, and some of Le Corbusier's work (CH-16) – blended with premonitions of the romantic reaction that emerged during the late 30s.

Possibly it represents an attempt, in the face of rising Fascism and uncertainty about the future, to overcome the self-assured abstractness of the International Style. The detailing and interior of the

church, particularly its metalwork, feel almost Brutalist – which is one alternative to abstraction and simplification. At the same time the exterior, with its traditionally focal tower, enclosing churchyard and, perhaps most significant, not quite flat non-parapeted roof, hints at the then emerging vernacular sensibility of the following fifteen years. Certainly that roof, with its comfortable sheltering eaves, illustrates the qualities that many found so lacking in the orthodox International Style.

Goetheanum

Dornach [near Basel]   **CH-20**
** Goetheanum (religious/philosophical society HQ) 1925–8
Heizhaus (central heating plant) 1913
Rüttiweg 45
Glashaus (glass-carving studio) 1913–14

Hügelweg 59
Rudolf Steiner, *et al.*
Expressionism
S from Basel on Rt 18 → DELEMONT / E at Reinach → DORNACH / → GOETHEANUM
   [Work on the interior of Goetheanum still continues.]

Rudolf Steiner was by profession a pedagogue, philosopher and student of the works of Goethe. Shortly before the First World War he founded Anthroposophy, a philosophy-cum-religion derived from Theosophy (NL-1) but incorporating many of Goethe's as well as Steiner's own theories of education, medicine, drama, dance, art and architecture.

The first Goetheanum was begun in 1913, in part to provide a suitable setting for the annual production of Steiner's Anthroposophist mystery-drama cycle. It was a strange structure, built up of massive wooden sections that were carved in place as if they were stone. Aesthetically, as well as chronologically, it stood somewhere between Art Nouveau and Expressionism. Yet it was less clearly related to the architectural thought of its time than the present building, to which there were some interesting contemporary parallels, including Czech 'Cubist' architecture.

In 1922 an arsonist destroyed the first, highly personal Goetheanum, so that we now know it only through photographs, through fragments of wood ornament, and,

most directly, through Steiner's glass-carving studio, the Glashaus, which although much smaller and simpler generally reflects the style and spirit of that original Goetheanum. From this earlier period there also remains a heating plant, the Heizhaus, which more clearly anticipates the second Goetheanum.

The present building, built 'on the foundations' of the first, is a massive, raw, reinforced concrete construction reminiscent of some Second World War fortifications. This mode of construction was both fireproof and particularly suitable to the execution of Steiner's design, which consisted solely of a clay model he made shortly before his death. Steiner also left behind a number of trained associates, as well as a body of both theoretical writings and practical precedents, including those embodied in the houses surrounding the Goetheanum. In later years these teachings and buildings have provided the design criteria for the interior of the Goetheanum as well as for the many 'Steiner-style' schools and clinics that are still being built by Anthroposophists throughout the world (NL-30).

Brugg/Umiken   **CH-21**
* Terrassensiedlung Mühlehalde
(stepped housing and studios) 1962–71
Am Bruggerberg
Scherer, Strickler & Weber (Team 2000)
Brûtalism
W from Brugg ctr across river Aare →
BASEL / *1 mi (1.5 km) on R*

Stepped or terraced housing such as this is a seductive idea that attracts most architects at least once in their careers. Typically, such stepped buildings must overcome added expenses imposed by both the more difficult construction conditions and the need for costly inclined elevators – or must accept severe limitations imposed by not having these (CH-21a). Only in Switzerland have advanced construction techniques, the price of scarce flat land, and high living standards combined to make stepped housing not only feasible but even common.

CH-21a Near Zug is a smaller **stepped housing development**, 1958–61, by Stucky & Meuli. From most angles all one can see of these twenty-five houses is a fragmented series of outward leaning planters, their potentially overwhelming angularity broken by all sorts and sizes of vegetation, including even some small trees. (When confronted with a few square feet of bare ground, the Swiss householder can be relied upon to plant *something*.) That these buildings read as only a series of disassociated planes is, of course, not due to the vegetation but to the steepness of the site and the extent to which the planters have been cantilevered so as to both enlarge the terraces and ensure privacy. Even for Switzerland this is a steep site. *N from Zug ctr →* ZURICH / *second R past RR bridge on Metallstr / first R on to Industriestr / up hill on L*

Schaffhausen   **CH-22**
Kantonsschule (secondary school)
1963–6
Munotstraße
Förderer & Zwimpfer
Brutalism
From Schaffhausen ctr → MUNOT up
Emmersburgstr to Munotstr / on R 200 yds
(m) before fort (Ch-22b)

The works of Förderer & Zwimpfer all bear a strong family resemblance. Here the main differences from the norm are the emphatic aluminium detailing and, more important, the bolder, more vigorous sculpting of such necessary large-scale elements as the canopied link with the existing school and the high retaining walls. These features lent themselves well to the sort of treatment that this firm previously gave to planters, benches and other smaller elements (CH-22c).

One would like to think that the increased scale of these sculptural manipulations reflected a recognition of the school's prominent position on the Munot. However, some of Förderer & Zwimpfer's later work in Schaffhausen continued to evolve further in the same direction, so that it was no longer bold – just clumsy. The appropriateness of scale found here seems, then, to have been a happy accident of timing and location.

CH-22a Further down the street towards the fortress is the **Kindergarten Munot,** 1932, by Wolfgang Müller. This diminutive school lays claim to the hard-to-prove distinction of being the first modern stepped (or, as they are generally known outside the UK, 'terraced') hillside building.

CH-22b The **Munot fortress** itself, said to be constructed after a design by Dürer, has been converted to provide a number of modern recreational facilities without diminishing its medieval character.

CH-22c Below the Rhine falls in nearby Neuhausen is the **'Park' café-restaurant,** 1961–3, another particularly sculptural example of Förderer & Zwimpfer's ability to integrate architecture and landscape. → RHEINFALL / *on W side of falls / → signs*

WEST GERMANY

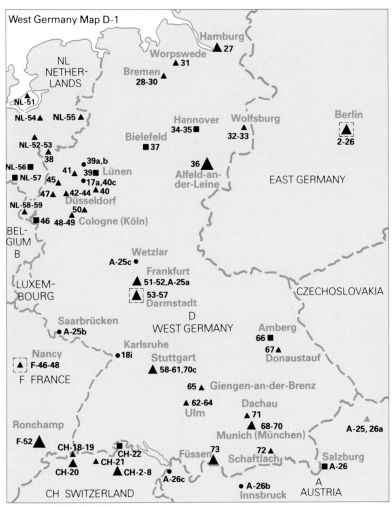

West Germany Map D-1

NL NETHER-LANDS

NL-51

NL-54▲   NL-55 ▲

NL-52-53
38 ▲

NL-56■   41▲ 39■ ●39a,b
■ NL-57 45▲   Lünen
        47▲ 42-44 ▲40 ●17a,40c
NL-58-59   Düsseldorf
        ■46 48-49 50▲ Cologne (Köln)

BEL-GIUM
B

Hamburg ▲ 27
Worpswede ▲ 31
Bremen 28-30 ▲

Hannover Wolfsburg
34-35■   32-33 ▲

Bielefeld
■ 37

36 ▲
Alfeld-an-der-Leine

Berlin
▲ 2-26

EAST GERMANY

Wetzlar
A-25c ●

Frankfurt
▲ 51-52,A-25a
▢▲ 53-57
Darmstadt

D
WEST GERMANY

LUXEM-BOURG

Saarbrücken
● A-25b

Nancy
▢▲ F-46-48
F FRANCE

Karlsruhe
● 18i

Amberg
66 ■
67▲
Donaustauf

Stuttgart
▲ 58-61,70c

65 ▲ Giengen-an-der-Brenz

▲ 62-64
Ulm

Dachau
▲ 71

CZECHOSLOVAKIA

Ronchamp
F-52 ▲

CH-18-19 ▲ ■ CH-22
        ▲ CH-21
CH-20 ▲ ▲ CH-2-8

Füssen
▲ 73

Munich (München)
68-70 ▲

72▲
Schaftlach

A-25, 26a

Salzburg
■ A-26

● A-26b

A
AUSTRIA

● A-26c

CH SWITZERLAND

Innsbruck

West Germany (Deutschland) D-1
The collapse of Germany's old High Baroque, her indigenous Classical architecture, coincided with the final dissolution of her old polycentric political order, and of the Holy Roman Empire, during the Napoleonic era. For Germany the nineteenth century was a time of national political consolidation, not one of architectural innovation – with the exception of Schinkel's brilliant Neo-Classicism. By the beginning of the twentieth century Germany was a single state and had 'proved' herself militarily. Now, ready to compete with Britain for the world's

markets, Germany wanted her products to be as well designed as those of her competitors. Good design would have to become not just national policy but a patriotic duty.

In 1907, an alliance of manufacturers and architects established the Deutscher Werkbund. This still-extant organization was meant to formulate both aesthetic and technological standards for all German manufactured goods. The national government also sent cultural attachés abroad to report on foreign advances in architectural and industrial design (D-22). Even local ducal governments such as Hesse (D-53) and Saxe-Weimar founded schools for the encouragement of design through 'artistic handicrafts' (*Kunstgewerbe*): Saxe-Weimar's school in time evolved into the Bauhaus. Then, just as all these efforts were beginning to bear fruit, they were overwhelmed by the First World War.

Germany's defeat was followed by five years of revolution, readjustment and hyperinflation. It was a time of studied architectural irrationality, during which few designs ever left the drawing board. It was also a time of catharsis and, perhaps, the necessary prelude to a complete break with historicism.

The return of financial stability brought a return to the ideology of a rationalized design aesthetic derived from the rationality of industrial production – a sensibility for which there had been little time since 1914. Now, at least for some, there was to be no stylistic confusion and no remembrance of the past. For a decade, from 1923 to 1933, the Bauhaus flourished, the great white *Siedlungen* (housing areas) embodying new social values rose (D-7, 8, 18, 52a) and Germany was the undisputed focus of modern architecture's first full flowering. Later, after the Nazi-impelled diaspora of modernist architects – first to Russia and then to Scandinavia, England and America – the perception of her pivotal role during these crucial years, and even more so that of the Bauhaus, would come to be curiously reinforced and to take on almost mythic qualities.

The Second World War brought another defeat – and division. Germany is again fragmented, not just between East and West but, within the West, into a federation of relatively autonomous states (*Länder*). Geographically, and to some extent socially and architecturally, these states mirror their pre-1870 namesakes. Although, predictably, West Germany has maintained high standards of building design and construction, if not always of planning, it has also developed distinct regional styles – in Berlin, for instance, or in the Stuttgart region to the south or around Hamburg to the north. West Germany is perhaps Europe's most

polycentric country. It has no great capital to draw wealth and talent from culturally impoverished provinces. Berlin, Munich, Düsseldorf, Cologne, Hamburg, all compete on approximately equal terms. If Germany does not know the excitement of a London, neither has it the desolation of a Liverpool.

None of Germany's cities remains, more than forty years after the war, as heavily damaged as do their British counterparts. The first-time visitor could even find it easy to believe that German cities suffered far less from Allied bombs than America's cities have from her own bulldozers and automobiles. For anyone who experienced Cologne, or even Munich, shortly after the war, the lack of visible damage is almost disturbing. Even pockmarks in stone buildings have often been cut out and repaired. Not to dwell upon past mistakes may be healthy. To obliterate all traces of them so totally seems less so.

Finally we should note that because of the post-Second World War realignment of Eastern European political boundaries many of the more important pre-First World War German buildings now lie in Poland. Most of Karl Friedrich Schinkel's works are in East Berlin (D-26). Others are at Potsdam in East Germany, where Erich Mendelsohn's Einstein Tower is also located. Walter Gropius's once badly damaged, but now impeccably restored, Dessau Bauhaus is also in the East. The majority of Germany's early modern architecture was built in the more industrialized West, however, and it did survive the war. There were losses, to be sure: both August Endell's spooky Jugendstil photographer's studio in Munich and Mies van der Rohe's early Expressionist Liebknecht-Luxemburg Monument in Berlin were demolished by the Nazis. The war itself claimed Otto Bartning's famed steel church in Essen, some of Mendelsohn's urban commercial buildings and many other lesser works. But towns grow outward, and it was the old dense historic urban cores of German cities that suffered the most. Often the modern buildings in the suburbs seem to have escaped almost unscathed. Ironically, one of Germany's greatest individual losses of modern architecture occurred only after the war, when Mendelsohn's finest department store, the Schocken in central Stuttgart, fell victim to over-zealous traffic engineers.

Language note Fraktur, the difficult archaic German Gothic alphabet, has all but dropped out of use in West Germany. All that remains of it is the letter 'ß', which is still often substituted for 'ss'. Occasionally one will also encounter 'ae', 'oe' and 'ue' substituted for 'ä', 'ö' and 'ü'.

West Berlin   D-2

West Berlin is an island, as surely as if surrounded by water. And, like any true island, it is a self-contained, self-concerned little world with a time scale of its own. Here there are only a few echoes of the other, dull if no longer shabby, adjacent Berlin, where the destruction of war is more in evidence.

Culturally and economically West Berlin is a part of that prosperous, materialistic Germany 90 miles away, where the catastrophes of the war are rapidly fading if unpleasant memories. But psychologically, West Berlin reflects its artificial insularity, even to the extent of having developed its own distinctive modern architecture – a

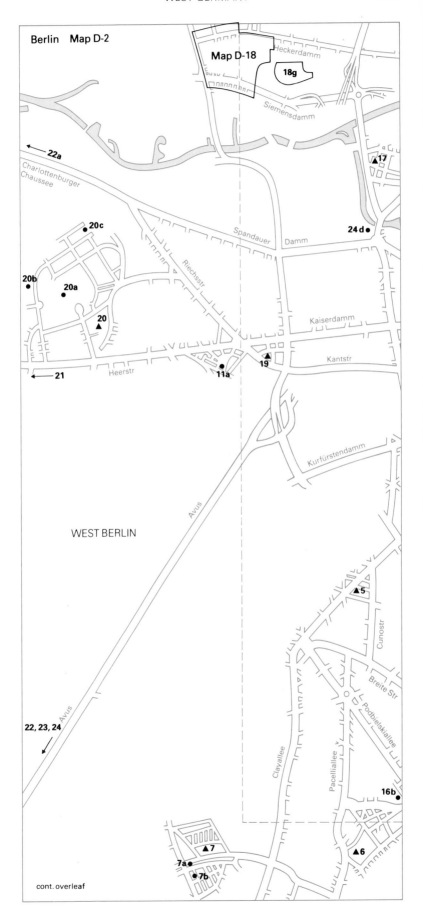

Berlin Map D-2

Map D-18

18g

Heckerdamm

Siemensdamm

22a

Charlottenburger Chaussee

▲17

20c

Spandauer Damm

24 d●

Riechsstr

20b

20a

Kaiserdamm

20
▲

Kantstr

21

Heerstr

19
▲

11a

Kurfürstendamm

Avus

WEST BERLIN

▲5

Cunostr

Breite Str

Avus

Podbielskiallee

22, 23, 24

16b
●

Clayallee

Pacelliallee

▲7

▲6

7a ●

● 7b

cont. overleaf

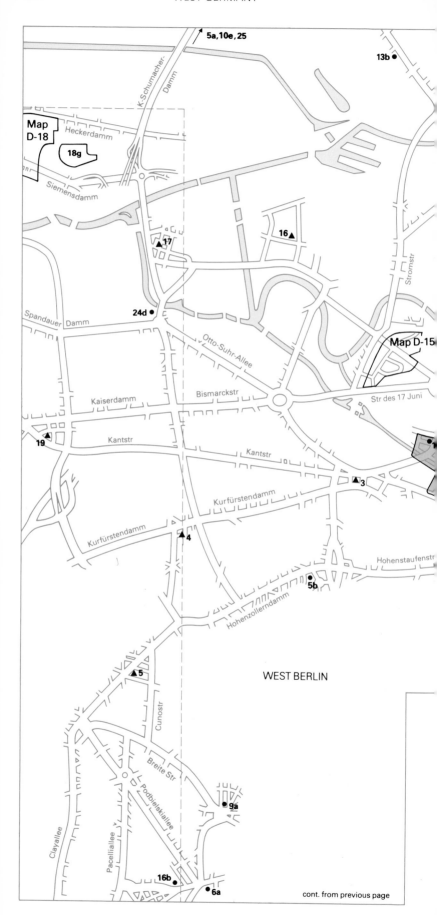

5a,10e,25

13b ●

Map
D-18

Heckerdamm

18g

Siemensdamm

K-Schumacher-Damm

17

16 ▲

Stromstr

Spandauer Damm

24d ●

Otto-Suhr-Allee

Map D-15

Kaiserdamm

Bismarckstr

Str des 17 Juni

19

Kantstr

Kantstr

▲3

Kurfürstendamm

Hohenstaufenstr

Kurfürstendamm

▲4

5b

Hohenzollerndamm

▲5

WEST BERLIN

Cunostr

Clayallee

Pacelliallee

Breite Str

Podbielskiallee

9a ●

16b ●

● 6a

cont. from previous page

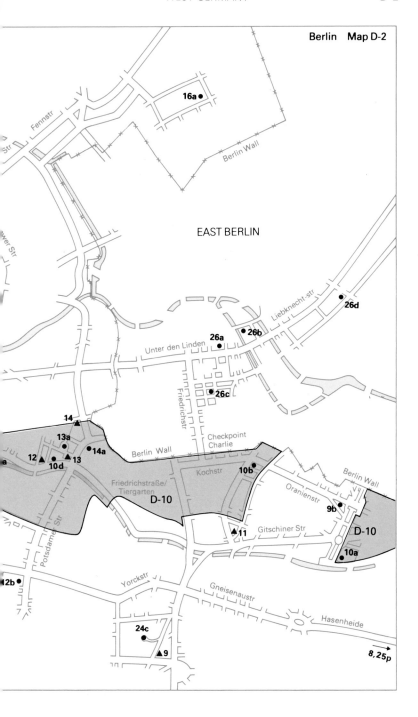

Berlin   Map D-2

somewhat coarse-textured, over-expressive recollection of the International Style that is rather too fond of bright paint.

There are, of course, the lingering echoes of the Cold War 50s. Most conspicuous is the Berlin Wall, which has a way of intruding unexpectedly, of suddenly blocking a street or cutting across a vista. Yet the old Berlin's centre, as well as much of its industry, is in the East: so that, apart from the Wall and the uninteresting postwar new commercial core along the Kurfürstendamm, much of West Berlin seems imbued with an almost *déjà-vu* sort of timelessness. It is a city of quiet, leafy suburbs

where one can still sense – better perhaps than anywhere else – the environments created by Central Europe's pre-First World War evolutionary bourgeois reformers (D-22) and also, later, by their more technocratic, but equally optimistic, Republican successors (D-8, 18).

The survival of this ambience may, of course, be only a by-product of West Berlin's disproportionately small number of cars and of the chronic emigration of the younger, more aggressive elements of its population: none of which makes suburban West Berlin any the less unique, tangible or appealing.

West Berlin/Charlottenburg **D-3**
* **Kaiser-Wilhelm-Gedächtnis-Kirche** (church) 1955–63
Breitscheidplatz
Egon Eiermann
Abstract Neo-Expressionism
Map D-2 / U-Bahn: Kurfürstendamm;
U-Bahn and S-Bahn: Zoologischer Garten

The 'Kaiser Wilhelm Memorial Church' is now more a memorial to prewar Berlin than to the Kaiser. Perhaps Berlin's best-known postwar building, it is not its most successful. The understated details and prismatic massing of Eiermann's church – soberly precise by day, glowing electric blue at night – do seem appropriate foils to the gaunt, war-shattered spire of the original, 1895, Gedächtnis-Kirche (an exception to the German tendency to sweep away unpleasant reminders of the war). But the functions of the church are divided among too many separate buildings of differing plan forms: octagon, hexagon, rectangle.

However, all that matters little because the siting, and therefore the existence, of the church is open to question. The old spire determined both the programme and site of the new church, which is surrounded by streaming traffic in the midst of West Berlin's 'Times Square'. Location alone dictated that this would be Berlin's best-known postwar building and also that Eiermann, who won the commission through a competition, could only make the best of difficult circumstances.

Berlin/Halensee **D-4**
WOGA Bauten (cinema, now theatre, offices, hotel and flats) 1926–8
Kurfürstendamm (Lehniner Platz), between Cicerostraße and Albrecht-Achilles-Straße
Erich Mendelsohn
Expressionism/International Style
Map D-2 / U-Bahn: Adenauerplatz

[The cinema has been externally restored, but internally totally transformed into an experimental theatre, 1976–81, by Jürgen Sawade.]

Always the best-known part of this complex, the rounded 'dynamic' cinema with its jutting pylon is now only the shell of Mendelsohn's design. But today Expressionist dynamism matters less than it once would have. Now these buildings seem more interesting as a group, both for the variety of their responses to differing programmatic requirements and for their adaptation of the then new architecture's design criteria to traditional urban land-use patterns.

West Berlin/Schmargendorf **D-5**
* **Kreuzkirche** (church) 1930
Hohenzollerndamm and Forckenbeckstraße
Ernst & Günther Paulus
Gothic Expressionism
Map D-2

One consequence of our century's sometimes too self-serving and polemical 'editing' of architectural history is that a building such as this church can remain virtually unknown, even though it represents both an ingenious attempt to solve an old and difficult type of site problem within a traditional vocabulary, and a skilful use of comfortable, natural materials.

D-5a Berlin's other interesting, if less convincing, major example of this sort of Expressionism is Eugen G. Schmohl's **Borsig office tower,** 1927, which lies partly hidden within a semi-suburban industrial enclave. *NE on Kurt-Schumacher-Damm (Map D-2 →) / NW on Scharn-weberstr ⇨ Seidelstr ⇨ Berliner Str / on L opposite U-Bahn: Borsigwerke*

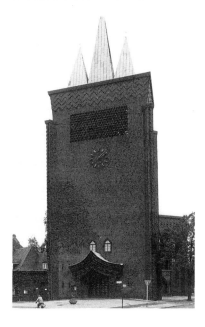

D-5b Fritz Höger's **Kirche am Hohen-zollerndamm** (church), 1931–3, at Hohenzollernplatz, is Expressionism reduced to the role of a new Neo-Gothic: built large and well, but neither inspired nor inspiring. *U-Bahn: Hohenzollernplatz*

West Berlin/Dahlem   **D-6**
** **Freie Universität** (Free University) 1962–73
Habelschwerdter Allee and Schwendener Straße
Candilis, Josic & Woods, with Jean Prouvé (curtain wall)
Brutalism/Rationalism
Map D-2 / U-Bahn: Dahlem-Dorf
  Low and elegantly curtain-walled, with brown-patinaed Cor-ten steel panels (see GB-74), it is a non-gridded but orthogonal two-storied system of pathways enclosing – as necessity dictates – auditoria, offices, classrooms and atrium-like bits of 'campus'.
  It is *not*, as has often been suggested, a megastructure. Megastructures are by definition exceedingly large, or large-scaled, as for instance, Cumbernauld Town Centre in Scotland (GB-86), Moshie Safdie's Habitat in Montreal, or Paolo Soleri's desert daydreams in the American south-west. Above all, like most more conventional buildings, they present readily identifiable images. The Free University does not – and to that extent is not so much a building as a built system. But, without a doubt, it *is* Architecture.

D-6a This is not Dahlem's only example of technologically uncompromising construction. One of Germany's biggest **'Victorian' greenhouses** – even if built just barely in our own century, 1905–7 (restored 1963–8) – was designed by A. Koerner for the nearby Dahlem Botanischer Garten (Botanical Gardens).
S-Bahn: Botanischer Garten

West Berlin/Zehlendorf   **D-7**
Groß-Siedlung Onkel-Toms-Hütte (social housing) 1926–31
Riemeisterstraße
Bruno Taut, Hugo Häring, O. R. Salvisberg, *et al.*
International Style
Map D-2 / U-Bahn: Onkel-Toms-Hütte / Taut's work is on Am Hegewinkel, Argentinische Allee and Wilskistr / Haring's work is on Eisvogelweg and Auerhahnbalz
  [The original colour scheme has been restored.]
  The site planning of this 'forest *siedlung*' (housing area), especially to the south of the U-Bahn, does not equal prewar British standards. In all other respects, however, this was and remains the perfect mature model of a technocratic, socially responsible, suburban housing scheme – especially when compared with the better-known Siedlung Britz (D-8).

D-7a Whatever its other advantages, Onkel-Toms-Hütte would make no sense without O. R. Salvisberg's combination **U-Bahn station** and **shopping area**, 1930, at its centre.

D-7b Just on the western edge of the *siedlung*, at Onkel-Tom Straße 85–91, are **four houses**, 1923, by Richard Neutra and Erich Mendelsohn.

West Berlin/Britz   **D-8**
** **Groß-Siedlung Britz**(social
housing) 1925–7
Fritz-Reuter-Allee
Bruno Taut & Martin Wagner
International Style
E on Hasenheide (Map D-2→) ⇨ *Buschkrug-*
allee / R on Blaschkoallee / L on Fritz-Reuter-
Allee / on R / U-Bahn: Parchimer Allee
[The original part is west of Fritz-Reuter-
Allee and between Parchimer Allee and
Stavenhagener Str. Extensions to the south
of Parchimer Allee date from 1930–1. The
famous 'horseshoe' is seen from Fritz-
Reuter-Allee.]

Britz, the first of Berlin's large-scale
housing areas, symbolized the promise of
both a new, more salubrious social housing
and a new technocratic, ahistorical architecture. It was presented as form linked
indissolubly with reform. But was it?

In many ways Britz was less than radi-

cal. There are, for instance, undeniable
Expressionist overtones in the alignment of
some of its streets and buildings so that
many of the still tile-roofed buildings are
neither oriented nor spaced in accordance
with climatic or other technical considerations. On the contrary, they often
adhere to the street lines in a conventional
manner, even as they attempt to deny that
fact through minor staggered setbacks and
other similarly picturesque devices.

However, the Britz which the world at
large knew was identified with the one
great, bright, park-centred horseshoe-
shaped apartment block that lies at its
heart. It presented an image of nature surrounded, but not overpowered, by pure
architecture seen through a theatrically
framed opening. This, not the lingering pic-
turesqueness or Expressionism, was Britz's
vision of a new scientific happiness.

West Berlin/Kreuzberg   **D-9**
**Verbandshaus der Deutschen
Buchdrucker** (bookprinters' union hall,
apartments and printing plant) 1924–5
Dudenstraße 10
Max Taut, with Franz Hoffmann
Map D-2 / U-Bahn: Platz der Luftbrücke

At one time Max Taut had drawn, but
not built, the most beguiling and escapist
of Expressionist fantasies. Here, just four
years later, all that remained of those
schemes was a certain dynamism of the
street façade. It was advanced work for its
day, but not radical – not like the factory/
administration wing to the rear. That is
a truly minimal Rationalist statement of
support and enclosure: a simple unadorned
concrete grid whose columns and girders
are proportioned to carry their loads most
effectively and whose interstices are filled
with conventional industrial glazing.

Nor is this just another 'Queen Anne
front' and 'Mary Ann behind'. Aside from
possible municipal dictates, the differences
between the front and rear blocks seemingly reflect the interaction of programme,
budget and site. Obviously the apartment
block belonged on the street and, as concrete was then still rather expensive, its
upper stories were, quite reasonably, built
with conventional loadbearing walls. The
rear block, on the other hand, had to
accommodate heavy vibrating equipment

as well as large ceremonial spaces. It *had* to
be of concrete. And, unlike conventional
masonry, concrete did not need applied
'dynamism' to demonstrate its modernity:
it *was* modern.

D-9a Five years later, 1929–39, Taut and
Hoffmann built the **Prussian Mines
Administration building** on Breitenbachplatz in the Wilmersdorf district. A
hard, logical, unfashionable building, its
steel frame is made manifest by a grid of
earthy terracotta fireproofing, large areas
of glass, and panels of obviously non-structural but still quite tactile, clinker brickwork. *U-Bahn: Breitenbachplatz*

D-9b At Oranienplatz 4–10 is an **office**

building designed by Taut in 1931–2. A logically technological building, it employs more advanced industrial materials to utilize effectively a tight, expensive urban site. This may not be quite so timeless a building. But only the traditional, monumental surface material of its street façade – as opposed to the glistening 'self-cleaning' white ceramic tiles that sheathe its light-well – distinguishes it from certain more recent, if not famous, Rationalist works. *U-Bahn: Moritzplatz*

West Berlin   **D-10**
* Internationale Bauausstellung or **IBA 87** (Formerly IBA 84, exhibition of urban reconstruction) Begun 1977 Hardt-Waltherr Hämer (planner, Kreuzberg), Josef Paul Kleiheus (planner, all other new construction)
Friederichstraße/Tiergarten and part of Südlicher Kreuzberg are shown on Map D-2

IBA 87 is a continuation of the German (and Berlin) tradition of housing exhibitions (D-15, 60). It is also a reaction against the 'brave new world' town planning, with its loss of traditional urban design values, represented by such exhibitions, and indeed against the Modern Movement as a whole. The IBA corporation itself built nothing. Working within existing building regulations, it developed planning guidelines and organized architectural/urban design competitions for those parts of the city in which it intervened.

There were three primary areas: Kreuzberg, Südlicher (south) Friedrichstraße/Tiergarten, and Tegel Harbour. Kreuzberg, traditionally working class, now mostly populated by hippies and Turkish 'guest workers', is half encircled by the Wall. Here the major emphasis was on self-help community involvement, the renovation of existing buildings, and the filling of gaps in a relatively intact urban structure. To the west of Kreuzberg, in Südlicher Friedrichstraße/Tiergarten, wartime bombing and postwar replanning had left far less of the original urban fabric. It is here that IBA 87 most closely resembles the traditional German housing exhibition. There are dozens of new buildings by almost as many architects, all presumably working to produce unified demonstrations of rediscovered traditional urban design values. Typically, runners-up in the competitions were asked to design buildings to fit winning master plans. Lastly, in the northwestern corner of the city is Tegel Harbour, one of Berlin's several pleasant lakeside recreation areas. Here the emphasis was on non-residential buildings.

Although the Friedrichstraße/Tiergarten planning competitions produced some remarkable projects, most remain unbuilt at the time of writing, while much of the completed work is not particularly memorable. In some instances the ideal of a meaningful whole is lost amidst the incoherence of too many small fragments by too many different hands (no matter how well designed the individual pieces might be). Much of the architecture is also technically prosaic and intellectually unconvincing. Even fewer projects have been completed at Tegel, but the generally less arcane Tegel designs may lose less when made into real buildings. Among the IBA projects completed at time of writing are:

D-10a The **Fraenkelufer block** by Heinrich & Inken Baller is the most successful of Kreuzberg's infill housing. The Ballers' work blends great technical skill and ingenuity with a romantic sensibility that strongly recalls the Gothicky German Expressionism of the 20s. In the best Kreuzberg tradition, much of the building (and its landscaped courtyard) lies within the block. It can be seen through the driveway entrance.

D-10b Much of the impetus for the reconstruction of Südlicher Friedrichstraße/Tiergarten came from an earlier polemical proposal by Rob Krier for Südlicher Tiergarten. Krier's 'White House', 1979–80, at 63–64 Ritterstraße, is part of his **Ritterstraße superblock plan,** which extends north to Oranienstraße. It was not built as part of IBA 87, but has been incorporated into it. Krier also designed the white Neo-Classical building (said to be based on a Schinkel design) on Feilnerstraße on the centre of the block. The rest of the buildings were designed by other architects within Krier's master plan.

D-10c The **Rauchstraße block,** also by Krier, may be one of the more successful because each building is free-standing. Krier designed the curved frontispiece at its east end – with the off-putting bust over the archway. Other buildings (from east to west) along the north side of the block are by Brenner/Tonon, Giorgio Grassi, Henry Nielebock and Aldo Rossi. On the south side they are by Valentiny & Hermann, Hans Hollein and Krier. (The end building is a prewar survivor.) Rossi's building is an agreeable surprise. It benefits enormously from its nineteenth-century Rationalist-inspired detailing and brickwork. Krier's plan required the end buildings be of brick and the six middle 'pavilions' of plaster.

D-10d Public buildings were also projected for Südlicher Friedrichstraße/Tiergarten in conjunction with IBA 87. Among them is the **Wissenschaftszentrum** (science centre), 1979–86, an addition by James Stirling to a grandiose nineteenth-century office building on the Reichpietschufer. Stirling's plan, a desperate, rather humourless joke, is composed from several abstract representations of iconic plan forms – a church, a castle keep, etc. – seemingly thrown haphazardly together. (The axial relationships between them is too subtle to be recognized *in situ* by most visitors.) Its elevations, which hardly acknowledge the plan, consist of an unremitting grid of square windows, set into the same storey-high stripes of alternating colours that Stirling first used to such ill effect on the Fogg Museum addition at Harvard University.

D-10e Gustav Peichl's **water treat-ment plant**, 1980–3, on Buddestraße, Tegel, was an ideal commission for an architect who thrives on mechanistic, symmetrical designs (A-16). Its control building looks like the superstructure of a giant ship. *NE on Kurt-Schumacher-Damm (Map D-2 →) / NW on Scharn-weberstr ⇨ Seidelstr ⇨ Berliner Str / R, in Tegel, on Waidmannsluster Damm / R on Buddestr / on L*

West Berlin/Kreuzberg   **D-11**
Haus des Deutschen Metallarbeiter-Verbandes (metal workers' union headquarters) 1929–30
Alte Jakobstraße 148–155
Erich Mendelsohn & Rudolf W. Reichel
International Style
Map D-2 / U-Bahn: Hallesches Tor
   Erich Mendelsohn was a convert from Expressionism to the International Style. Exhibitions of his matchbook-sized draw-ings of Expressionist fantasies had made him famous. But fantasies are hard to build and Mendelsohn was to be no mere paper architect. For him the International Style was not an ideology but a buildable lan-guage in which he could continue devel-oping his dynamic expressive vision; and so he co-opted it for his own formalistic ends.
   Here, thrusting its pavilion-like corner toward the intersection, is one 'Function-alist' office building that positively rejoices in the traditional formal restraints and possibilities of its wedge-shaped site. And thus it also anticipated and contributed to that more formalistic postwar modernism which rapidly destroyed the illusion of a single styleless and totally pragmatic new architecture. (The rear elevation is actually more dramatic than the front.)

West Berlin/Tiergarten   **D-12**
Shell-Haus (office block) 1931
Hitzigallee and Reichpietschufer
Emil Fahrenkamp
International Style
Map D-2 / U-Bahn: Kurfürstenstr
[Extension to rear, 1965–7, by Paul Baumgarten.]
   This is the International Style of the Establishment, not ideological but solid, suave, cosmopolitan – and, in this case, the most 'liberal' work of a basically con-servative architect. Dominated by the fretted rhythmic line of round-cornered bays, which in both plan and elevation build toward the taller entrance block, Shell-Haus ultimately seems more self-assured than exciting.

D-12a Near by is the new permanent home for the **Bauhaus-Archiv**, 1964–79, designed by TAC, the firm founded by Walter Gropius. *Three blocks W on Reich-pietschufer / on L*

D-12b Similar to Shell-Haus in scale, pro-gramme, date and general effect, is Bruno Paul's **Kathreiner-Hochhaus** (offices),

D-11a At Karolingerplatz 5a in the Char-lottenburg district there is a **double house**, 1922, by Mendelsohn. The 'dyna-mics' it reflects are not all architectonic. They are also those of the real world: of a young architect attempting, with mixed results, to reconcile his unbuildable revo-lutionary-industrial fantasies with the technical and economic realities of post-First World War Germany. *Map D-2 / U-Bahn: Theo-Heuss-Platz*

1929–30, on Potsdamer Straße at Kleistpark. However, its heavy spandrels and contrasting, expressively vertical corners, more closely prefigure the post-war Berlin style. *U-Bahn: Kleistpark*

West Berlin/Tiergarten   **D-13**
** **Neue Nationalgalerie** (art
gallery) 1962–8
Potsdamer Straße and Reichpietschufer
Ludwig Mies van der Rohe
Neo-Classicism
Map D-2 / U-Bahn: Kurfürstenstr

Mies's ultimate abstraction, nominally an
art gallery, in fact a monument to the pur-
suit of an ideal. It is the ultimate technical
transformation of the Neo-Classical temple
and, equally, the ultimate exquisite bore.
Only large sculptures and monumental
canvases can survive the crushing embrace
of this temple's crystal cella. The 'real'
museum – a beige and white nonentity
containing the main exhibition spaces – lies
below, buried within the granite podium.

The one intense architectural experience
which can be found here has nothing to
do with Mies, at least not directly. The
museum's collection contains a series
of minutely detailed romantic vignettes

of Karl Friedrich Schinkel's Berlin. When
juxtaposed in the mind's eye with the
ravaged yet still recognizable settings they
so lovingly depict (D-26a–c), these paintings evoke – in a way undreamt of by their
creators – precisely that romantic sense of
the 'sublime' transience of glory that so
preoccupied the early nineteenth century.

D-13a The adjacent Italianate church,
the **Matthias-Kirche**, 1846, which
seems to appear in every photograph of
the gallery, is the work of August Stüler.
While Mies studied the works of Schinkel
and was inspired by certain of his formulae,
Stüler studied with Schinkel the man, and
evidently partook of his humanistic spirit.

D-13b At **Afrikanische Straße 14–41**
is some housing designed by Mies in 1926–
7, a time when he was under the influence
of, if not inspired by, the International Style.
U-Bahn: Rehberge

West Berlin/Tiergarten   **D-14**
** **Philharmonie** (concert hall)
1956–63
Kemperplatz
Hans Scharoun
Expressionism
Map D-2 / U-Bahn: Kurfürstenstr

A difficult building to assess: is it the
last, but one of the most important, of the
authentic Expressionist works? Or is it an
impressive 'ghost' of a now forty-years-dead
movement conjured up by one of its last
surviving practitioners? To be correct, it
is both and neither. Although Scharoun's
magnum opus is explicable only in terms of
his unrepentant Expressionism, it is also
an eccentric, highly personal building that
demands, and to an extent deserves, judge-
ment by standards of its own.

The Philharmonie is well known as one
of the first and only concert halls wherein
the audience surrounds the orchestra,
rather than facing it as in a traditional
auditorium. But for Scharoun it was, above
all else, a 'landscape'. He likened its fragmented sloping seating areas to hillside
vineyards above which lights and acoustical clouds form a 'skyscape'. Nor would
it be unreasonable to extend the analogy:
to see cascades in the staircases; mountains

in the roofscape; a multi-imaged sunrise (a
recurrent Expressionist motif) in the circular stained-glass windows. The very richness of nature is expressed in the variety of
materials and details – although some of
these, their symbolic roles notwithstanding, have weathered badly. And at the
very centre of this metaphoric universe is
the orchestra, embodying mankind and
bringing life to the concert hall, the space
which is the building's *raison d'être* and the
sole symmetrical element to which all else
haphazardly adheres.

D-14a Scharoun also designed the nearby
Preußische Staatsbibliothek (Prussian State Library), 1964–78.

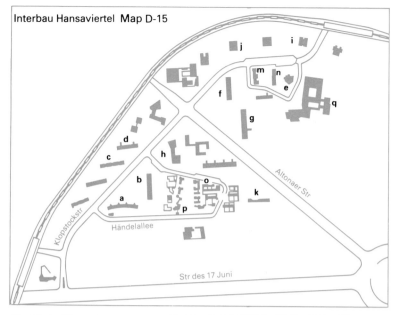

Interbau Hansaviertel Map D-15

West Berlin/Tiergarten   **D-15**
* Interbau Hansaviertel (permanent
international building exhibition)
1957–61
*Klopstockstraße, Händelallee and
Bartningallee*
Various architects, see below
Map D-2 / S-Bahn: Tiergarten or Bellevue
   If the Weißenhof Siedlung (D-60) marked
the apogee of the International Style then
this, Weißenhof's spiritual heir, clearly signalled the style's final eclipse. Here the
cream of the modernist Establishment (see
also D-20), working within accepted ideology, could only produce a tired, second-rate
environment.
   Fifteen individual *'objekte'*, all housing
unless identified otherwise, and/or their
architects, at least merit identification:

D-15a (*Objekt 7*) Walter Gropius. Not to
be compared with his prewar work at
Siemensstadt (D-18).
   D-15b (*Objekt 8*) Pierre Vago, Archetypical formalistic French façade manipulation.
   D-15c (*Objekt 9*) Wassili Luckhardt, a survivor of the 'heroic generation' of the
1920s, and Hubert Hoffmann.

D-15d (*Objekt 10*) Paul Schneider-
Esleben.
   D-15e (*Objekt 12*) Otto H. Senn. Typically
Swiss: intelligent, conservative, slightly
sculptural.
   D-15f (*Objekt 13*) Egon Eiermann.
   D-15g (*Objekt 14*) Oscar Niemeyer, Bra-
silia's designer, *sans esprit*.
   D-15h (*Objekt 16*) Alvar Aalto. Only
slightly better than the average here.
   D-15i (*Objekt 20*) Eugène Beaudouin &
Raymond Lopez.
   D-15j (*Objekt 21*) Van den Broek & J. B.
Bakema.
   D-15k (*Objekt 25*) Paul Baumgarten. The
best of the lot.
   D-15m (*Objekt 26*) Max Taut – another
survivor from the 1920s.
   D-15n (*Objekt 27*) Kay Fisker.
   D-15o (*Objekt 40*) Arne Jacobsen. Typ-
ically insubstantial.
   D-15p (*Objekt 45*) Sergius Ruegenberg &
Wolf von Möllendorff. A classic example of
the Scharoun-esque private house type that
flourished in Berlin in the 1930s and again
in the 50s.
   D-15q Also within the Hansaviertel area
is Werner Düttmann's **Akademie der
Künste** (academy of art) of 1959–60.

West Berlin/Moabit   **D-16**
**** Montagehalle der AEG-
Turbinenfabrik** (steam turbine
assembly hall) 1908–9
Huttenstraße and Berlichingenstraße
Peter Behrens
Neo-Classicism
Map D-2 / U-Bahn: Turmstr
   Once, when technology seemed to be
modernity, critics looked at this temple of
production and saw nothing but an unornamented, architect-designed factory built
entirely of honest exposed concrete, riveted
steel and industrial glazing. Some even
called it the first truly modern building.
   Perhaps they really did not see that the
concrete – always primarily a structural
material – was here merely filling gaps

within the steel frame; nor that the sloping
striated corners combined allusions to both
Renaissance quoining and archaic battered
masonry within their mannered non-sup-

portive solidity; nor that the polygonal pediments as well as the exposed steel 'columns' and 'cornice' were in fact also conscious Classical allusions that denied the reality of the building's structural triple-hinged arches. Today, the Turbinenfabrik seems less a statement of radical Functionalism than one of nationalist mercantilism – not that that makes it any less elegant, merely less 'important'.

D-16a Behrens was AEG's staff architect and industrial designer. The same classicist tendencies are to be found in all his AEG work – from typography to teapots. In fact, his slightly later AEG complex of 1910–12, on Voltastraße, the **Hochspannungsfabrik, Montagehalle** and **Kleinmotorenfabrik,** is not less but more Classical than the turbine factory. *U-Bahn: Voltastr*

D-16b Behrens's specific debt to the Classicism of Karl Friedrich Schinkel (D-26) can be seen in his contemporary, 1911–12, **Haus Wiegand** at Peter-Lenné-Straße 28–30. Appropriately it now houses the German Archaeological Society. *U-Bahn: Podbielskiallee*

West Berlin/Charlottenburg   **D-17**
Gustav-Adolf-Kirche (church) 1934
Brahestraße and Herschelstraße
Otto Bartning
Prematurely Late International Style
Map D-2 / U-Bahn: Jungfernheide

Otto Bartning may be best remembered for his many postwar *Notkirchen* (temporary wooden churches). With their prefabricated timber beams, often set between their predecessors' ruined walls, they seemed to exemplify the empirical, almost vernacular quality so typical of that period; a quality usually explained in terms of wartime or postwar shortages, but in fact also reflecting a reaction against the International Style's abstract technical imagery.

It has often been suggested that this romantic empiricism of the 1940s, or at least the discontinuity it seemed to represent in the development of modern architecture, gave rise to the flaccid Late-International Style of the next decade. But here already are those same romantic tendencies: the shattering of previously simple forms, both large and small; the renewed interest in symmetry; the use of contrasting rude or natural materials as accents; the expression and articulation of structure. Patently it had begun to develop much earlier.

D-17a Even earlier, 1929–30, is Bartning's round **Auferstehungskirche** (church) in Essen. It also seems so much like a cliché 1950s church that, despite old photographs, one wants to doubt the accuracy of its postwar restoration. *SE from Essen ctr on Steeler Str →* ESSEN-STEELE */ R beyond expressway on Kurfürstenstr / second L on Studenstr / on R*

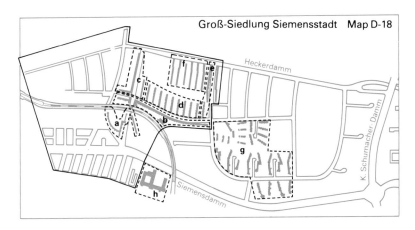

Groß-Siedlung Siemensstadt   Map D-18

West Berlin/Charlottenburg   **D-18**
* Groß-Siedlung Siemensstadt
(social housing area) 1929–31
Jungfernheideweg, at Goebelstraße,
Heilmannring and Heckerdamm
Hans Scharoun (site plan and **a**), Otto Bartning (**b**), Walter Gropius (**c**), Hugo Häring (**d**), Fred Forbat (**e**), Hans Henning (**f**), *et al.*
International Style
Map D-2 / U-Bahn: Siemensdamm

Siemensstadt is the most famous and influential of all those great German *siedlungen* that set the standard for housing in interwar Europe. Yet it does not truly represent the type (D-52a). It is not sufficiently earnest or scientific: its buildings are not all parallel, all identical, all pure white. It is, in fact, not sufficiently boring. Gropius is too elegant here. Häring is too folksy. As for Scharoun – his wilful manipulation of balconies and other elements must once have seemed scandalous!

D-18g There are some **postwar Scharoun buildings,** 1957–60, at Goebelplatz.

West Berlin/Charlottenburg   **D-19**
Haus des Rundfunks (radio station, now Radio Free Berlin) 1930–1
Masurenallee 8–14
Hans Poelzig
Rationalism/Expressionism
Map D-2 / U-Bahn: Theo-Heuss-Platz or S-Bahn: Witzleben

Hans Poelzig is one of modern architecture's shadowy figures: an influential teacher, but one who did not attempt to propagate a personal style, whose unbuilt projects have always been better known than his buildings. (Most of his buildings, in any case, either did not survive the Second World War or were isolated in its aftermath.) Born in 1869 and a contemporary of Frank Lloyd Wright, Poelzig was of that generation whose earlier works the chroniclers of the 'Modern Movement' could not let pass unrecognized. However, his later role as *éminence grise* to the younger Expressionists of the 1920s seems to have caused some embarrassment.

In this dark, hard relic of his later years one can only just sense, in its forms and in the choice and use of materials, some of the tension between Rationalism and Expressionism, between logic and emotion, which permeated his earlier work.

West Berlin/Charlottenburg   **D-20**
* **Unité d'Habitation** (apartment block) 1957–8
Heilsberger Dreieck
Le Corbusier
Brutalism
Map D-2 / U-Bahn: Olympia-Stadion

Despite its singular suburban setting, Le Corbusier's Berlin *unité* was part of the 1957 Hansaviertel housing exhibition (D-15). Its splendid isolation is variously attributed to Le Corbusier's intransigent aloofness and/or German inflexibility. In any case, if this is a more dramatic site than any the Hansaviertel could offer, it is also one which saves the other exhibits from invidious comparisons. Yet, like them, the *unité*, too, is flawed – at least compared to its prototype (F-63).

Perhaps with some justification, the Berlin authorities persuaded Le Corbusier to increase his ceiling heights. But without his permission further modifications were made: details were changed; the already minuscule seventh-floor shopping street was completed as apartments; the roofscape virtually disappeared; various bulky service functions were fitted in amongst the *piloti.* Not surprisingly, Le Corbusier sued.

D-18h Siemensstadt, being basically a factory town, also included **industrial buildings** such as that by Hans Hertlein, 1929–30, on Siemensdamm at Ohmstraße.

D-18i Another influential housing area with which Gropius was associated is **Siedlung Dammerstock,** 1928–9, in Karlsruhe. *S from RR station on Ettlinger Str ⇨ Ettlinger Allee → Dammerstock*

D-20a The nearby **Olympia Stadion** (Olympic stadium), 1934–6, by Werner March is one of the largest surviving Nazi communal structures.

D-20b To the west, across a former parade ground, is March's **Dietrich Eckardt Thingplatz** (now the Waldbühne) a 20,000-seat amphitheatre of the same date. Its combined Grecian form and Teutonic name – meant to evoke mingled 'racial memories' – demonstrates, if nothing else, the durability of Teutonic logic (see also D-67).

West Berlin/Spandau **D-21**
* Lebensrettungsstation (lifeboat station) 1969–70
Am Pichelsee
Ludwig Leo
Archigram-esque
W on Heerstr (Map D-2→) / L (past second bridge) on Am Pichelsee / 500 yds (m) on R
During the Pop Art movement of the 60s a group of young British architects calling themselves Archigram published a kaleidoscopically collaged sci-fi architecture comic book whose method was its message and vice-versa. Although the largely British-designed Centre Pompidou (F-6) owes much to Archigram, the group itself built nothing of importance. Peter Cook, the leader of the group, says this building is terrific. Admittedly it is Archigram-esque, on one side only. The others are representative of the contemporary 'Berlin School' (D-2). That minor inconsistency notwithstanding, Leo's effort – like Archigram's own futuristic fantasies – is (by turns) exciting, puzzling and ultimately unsatisfying. And why not? It shares the

D-20c Just to prove that those two structures are more '*Völkisch*' (i.e. Germanic) than specifically Nazi, March's similar nearby **Deutsches Sportforum** dates from as early as 1926–8.

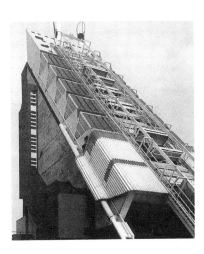

same caricature-like sense of unreality, with certain apparent 'working parts' that are really no more than ornaments. (And one must not even consider what practical justifications there might be for such a suburban skyscraper boathouse!)

West Berlin/Nikolassee **D-22**
Haus Freudenberg (house, now private hospital) 1907–8
Potsdamer Chaussee 48
Hermann Muthesius
English Arts and Crafts
SW on Avus → Wannsee (Map D-2→) / E on Potsdamer Chaussee / on L / S-Bahn: Nikolassee
This remarkably English house – derived mostly from M. H. Baillie-Scott – symbolizes a key link in the story of orthodox 'Functional' modern architecture. Its designer was a sometime civil servant, who for seven years, had been attached to the Germany embassy in London solely for the purpose of gathering information on British architecture. The results of his aesthetic espionage were then published as *Das englische Haus*, 1904–5, a large three-volume work through whose illustrations the houses of Baillie-Scott, Voysey, Mackintosh and other progressive British architects

came to be widely known to, and emulated by, their Continental counterparts.

Meanwhile, Muthesius's desire for a more lasting and potent vehicle with which to improve the quality and competitiveness of German design led him to found the Deutscher Werkbund (D-1, 60).

It might be noted in passing that an architectural attaché also served at the German embassy in Washington, DC. But as he failed to discover even Frank Lloyd Wright, both *Das amerikanische Haus* and its author soon slipped into obscurity.

D-22a One of Berlin's most rural landscapes – such as it is – surrounds the garden suburb of **Staaken,** 1914–17, designed by Paul Schmitthenner. Although Hanseatic in style and vaguely medieval in plan, it is essentially Anglo-Saxon in spirit. *W on Charlottenburger Chaussee (Map D-2→) ⇨ Brunsbütteler Damm / R along the Wall / R on Torweg / on L*

West Berlin/Zehlendorf   **D-23**
** **Pfaueninsel** (Peacock Island, now a
public park)
Schloß (sham ruined castle) and
Meierei (dairy barn in sham ruined
church) 1794–7
Johann G. D. Brendell
Kavalierhaus (guesthouse) 1824–5
Karl Friedrich Schinkel
Gothick
*SW on Avus → Wannsee (Map D-2→) W
on Potsdamer Chaussee ⇨ Königstr, abt 3 m
(5 km) / R on Nikolskoer Weg abt 1 mi
(1.5 km) / ferry to island abt 50 yds (m) /
Or, in summer, waterbus line 1 from
Wannsee (S-Bahn: Wannsee) abt 4½ mi
(7 km) or line 3 from Spandau (S-Bahn:
Spandau) abt 8 mi (13 km) to Pfaueninsel /
ferry to island*

Schloß, Pfaueninsel

[The Schloß originally had wooden
exterior walls. The island's stone temple
is the original front of the Charlottenburg
Palace Mausoleum.]

When humanist Classicism held sway
and man was the measure of all things
(from a column to the universe) architectural artifice desired artificial settings.
Later, when the Romantic Revolution
placed mankind and its works within
nature, not above it, it was no longer desirable to mould architecture and nature to
man's image. Rather one strove to discover
and express the unique essential meanings
of each. Thus the eighteenth century's
quest for archaic and arcadian prototypes;
for the Rousseauesque primitive hut; for
Neo-Palladian purity; for the Gothic's
natural organic logic. And thus too, the
quest for picturesque 'natural' settings.
This ideal, first formulated in and propa-
gated through seventeenth-century landscape paintings, had been finally realized in
eighteenth-century England. Upon reach-
ing the Germany of Goethe and Beethoven,
however, it came to a new and fuller – not
to say eventually overripe (D-73) – fruition.

Pfaueninsel's mock ruined church-cum-
cow barn and its sham castle, equipped
with a perversely high-technology iron
bridge, 1807, are remarkable for their
romantic innocence of archaeological accuracy. If nothing else, Schinkel's later Kavalierhaus, with its genuine Flamboyant
Gothic façade from a Danzig town house,
demonstrates the distance Gothic archaeology had come in just thirty years – and
also the distance it still had to go.

Pfaueninsel *is* unreal. It is as unreal, to
over-stretch perhaps a relevant analogy, as
Beethoven's *Sixth*. But it is also magical –
an enchanted isle – and never more so than
now when it lies within this other artificial
'island' that is Berlin.

West Berlin/Zehlendorf   **D-24**
* **Klein-Glienicke** (country estate,
with summerhouse and garden pavilions)
1824–6
Königstraße
Karl Friedrich Schinkel
Neo-Classicism
*W on Königstr from Nikolskoer Weg (D-23)
abt 1 mi (1.5 km) / on R just before
border / or continue W from Pfaueninsel
(D-23) via waterbus to Glienicker Brücke*

Owing to various accidents of war and
geography, Schinkel's better-known surviving monumental works are in East
Berlin (D-26), while only some of his 'smaller' efforts, such as Klein-Glienicke, remain
in the West. And even this, like the Pfaueninsel (D-23), is but a peripheral fragment
of the strangely suburban Prussian court
that grew up around the characteristically
named palace of Sans Souci.

There is little evidence here of that
Rationalism and technical inventiveness
with which recent generations have
perhaps too closely identified Schinkel.
Instead one finds another, equally authentic Schinkel: the royal favourite who
could combine Italian vernacular and
Renaissance forms with Greek details in
an attempt to produce a modern Prussian
architecture! Seen in these typically sandy,
Prussian woods, his quest seems, inex-
plicably, to have met with some success.

D-24a Although the product of a later
generation, *c.* 1850, the little half-round
pergola, with its diminutive primitive
Doric columns and caryatid centrepost,
seems also to belong here – especially when
compared with the more 'correct' but less
appealing nearby circular temple, the
Grosse Neugierde, which a maturing
Schinkel had copied in 1835 from the
Choragic Monument in Athens.

D-24b Coeval with the pergola is the
exquisite little Byzantine-Romanesque
Klosterhof, a decorative 'mausoleum' –

complete with a real tomb of a real 'philosopher', c. 1300 – assembled from fragments of an Italian monastery.

D-24c His dedication to Neo-Classicism notwithstanding, Schinkel was a man of his time. He could, when necessary, work in a variety of picturesque manners. Atop the Kreuzberg – a hill surrounded by typical late nineteenth-century inner-city Berlin tenements – stands a Schinkel-designed **cast-iron Gothic monument,** 1819–20. Commissioned to commemorate Germany's liberation in the Napoleonic Wars,

it is, at best, a stylistic and technical footnote to Schinkel's career. The site, however, affords an excellent view of the city. *U-Bahn: Platz der Luftbrücke*

D-24d Just to the east of the Charlottenburg Palace is a small, almost ascetically simple, Schinkel-designed **summer house,** 1824. It contains a number of his own Romantic paintings, (as well as those of Caspar David Friedrich and others), which lovingly and minutely depict the ever-blue-skyed Berlin of his times. *U-Bahn: Richard-Wagner-Platz.*

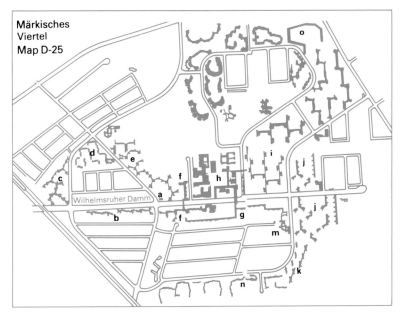

Märkisches Viertel
Map D-25

West Berlin/Wittenau   **D-25**
Märkisches Viertel (experimental housing area) 1965–70
Wilhelmsruher Damm
Werner Düttmann, Hans Müller & Georg Heinrichs (site plan), *et al.* (see especially D-25c, f, j, h, m and o below)
NE on Kurt-Schumacher-Damm (Map D-2→) ⇨ Oranienburger Str / R on Wilhelmsruher Damm / on both sides of rd / S-Bahn: Wittenau (Nordbahn)

As an exhibition of advanced architecture, and a model of social reform through built form – and a weapon against West Berlin's chronic emigration – the Märkisches Viertel was heir to the tradition of the large, often polemical, prewar Berlin *Siedlungen* (D-7, -8, -18). Indeed, a comparison with them can be enlightening. The individual apartments here are larger, but so too are the buildings. If more open space is given over to greenery here, that green space is also less identifiable with the individual dwellings; and a far higher proportion of the total open space is given over to cars.

Remarkably, despite the inevitable disharmonies that arise when thirty different architects 'express' themselves cheek by jowl – and here most did so in the nervous postwar Berlin Style (D-2) – this high-rise garden suburb still manages to suggest a physically coherent community. The area's

more notable buildings, all housing unless otherwise indicated, include:

D-25a Information pavilion, 1966, Wilhelmsruher Damm and Eichhorster Weg, Fridtjof F. Schliephacke.
D-25b Wilhelmsruher Damm 315–329, 1965–7, Karl Fleig.
D-25c Wilhelmsruher Damm and Finsterwalder Straße, 1966–7, Herbert Stranz.
D-25d Eichhorster Weg and Finsterwalder Straße, 1965–8, Hansrudolf Plarre.
D-25e Eichhorster Weg, 1967–8, Oswald Mathias Ungers.
D-25f Wilhelmsruher Damm, 1966–7, Ludwig Leo.
D-25g Wilhelmsruher Damm 107–157, 1966–8, René Gagès, with Volker Theissen and Werner Weber.
D-25h Communal and shopping centre, 1966–7, Wilhelmsruher Damm and Senftenberger Ring, by Hans Bandel & Waldemar Poreike.
D-25i Wilhelmsruher Damm, 1967, Hans Müller & Georg Heinrichs.
D-25j Wilhelmsruher Damm and Treuenbrietzener Straße, 1967, Ernst Gisel.
D-25k Dannenwalder Weg, 1967, Werner Düttmann.
D-25m School, 1967, Dannenwalder Weg, Günter & Ursel Plessow.
D-25n Kindergarten, 1966–7, Dan-

nenwalder Weg and Tramper Weg, by Fin Bartels & Cristoph Schmidt-Ott.

D-25o Senftenberger Ring, 1967, Shadrach Woods.

D-25p By way of comparison, on the opposite side of Berlin is the **Gropius-Stadt**, a contemporaneous and similarly

East Berlin (Ost-Berlin)   **D-26**

Although technically not within the scope of this book, East Berlin is so easily accessible that at least some of its more significant buildings must be noted. (*Map D-2 / non-Germans must enter East Berlin through Checkpoint Charlie*)

D-26a Karl Friedrich Schinkel's **Neue Wache** (guardhouse, now 'Monument to the Victims of Militarism and Fascism'), 1816–18, interior 1930, by Heinrich Tessenow, on Unter den Linden. Restored after

Hamburg   **D-27**
** **Chilehaus** (office block) 1923–4
Burchardstraße and Pumpen
Fritz Höger
Expressionism
S from Hauptbahnhof (central station) on Steintorwall / R just past four-towered building on R / straight ahead

Nominally Chilehaus honours the land where its builder had found his fortune. In fact it is intended to personify the spirit of twentieth-century Hanseatic Hamburg – then, as now, a proud shipbuilding, ship-owning city-province and a world port.

The knife-edged ship's-prow where Burchardstraße and Pumpen intersect – Expressionism's best-known image – is no accident. Parcels of land were rearranged to allow the Pumpen façade to curve so sinuously towards a more acute meeting with its neighbour. The final sharp wall juncture itself was made possible only through a similarly clever manipulation of the building's tiered upper-storey set-backs, and the insertion, at street level, of twinned, deliberately non-architectonic pavilions skilfully masking the reality of the site's blunted corner.

Those terracotta pavilions, set so inorganically into the flanking re-entrant corners, at first seem little more than anomalous echoes of Vienna's Arts and Crafts, Wiener Werkstätte. (Indeed they may be.) But, are they not also – in some other, metaphoric realm – the great salt sea breaking against the ship's racing bow?

D-27a Just across Burchardstraße is the **Sprinkenhof office block,** 1925–8, also by Höger, with Hans and Oskar Gerson.

large housing area named in honour of Walter Gropius. On the whole, it is a depressing amalgam of stale theories and timid forms. *SE on Hasenheide (Map D-2→) ⇨ Buschkrugallee ⇨ Rudower Str / R on Lipschitzallee / on both sides of rd / U-Bahn: Lipschitzallee*

war damage.

D-26b The **Altes Museum,** 1828–30, by Schinkel, facing the Lustgarten. Restored after war damage.

D-26c The **Schauspielhaus** (theatre), 1818–21, by Schinkel, on the Platz der Akademie. Restored after war damage.

D26d In front of the Alexanderplatz S-Bahn station, are **two office buildings,** 1930–1, by Peter Behrens.

Although similar in scale and rich brickwork, it lacks its predecessor's poetry.

D-27b In Hamburg's Botanischer Garten (botanical garden) is a modern version, 1961–3, of that quintessentially Victorian building type, the **greenhouse,** by Bernhard Hermkes & Gerhard Becker. While the Victorians were always working right up against the limits of the available technology, today's greenhouses can be more freely and picturesquely planned, and their structural support achieved by an almost limitless variety of means. Perhaps that is why the Victorians' efforts always seem more satisfying. *NW from Hauptbahnhof (central station) on GlockengieBerwall ⇨ Gorch-Fock-Wall, abt $\frac{1}{2}$ mi (1 km) / in Botanischer Garten on R*

Bremen   D-28
* Paula Modersohn-Becker Haus
(art gallery and shops) 1926–7
Haus Atlantis (multi-use centre,
cinema, etc.) 1929–30
Böttcherstraße 2
Bernhard Hoetger
Expressionism
*SE from Rathaus (town hall), on foot, across
Marktplatz and around Schütting (sixteenth-
century guildhall), behind which is entrance
to Böttcherstr*

[Both buildings were severely damaged
in the war. The new façade of Haus Atlantis
by Ewald Matare, 1956, reflects the spirit
of the Modersohn-Becker Haus rather than
that of the more nationalistic Haus Atlantis.
The Modersohn-Becker Haus, as rebuilt by
Max Säume and Günter Hafemann, is
much closer in fact and in spirit to Hoetger's
original. Few of the damaged elements seem
to have been reproduced exactly, however,
and some, such as the entrance hall ceiling,
have been drastically simplified.]

Paula Modersohn-Becker Haus

Böttcherstraße, or something like what
one now sees here, was the creation of
Ludwig Roselius, a successful import-
export   merchant   whose   taste   for
Expressionist art became entangled with a
number of pan-Germanic racist ideas. To
further their propagation, Roselius bought
and transformed this late medieval street.
By the time he had finished, only one of its
original houses remained, No. 6, Roselius
Haus, which is now a museum. All but
two of the rest were rebuilt by Runge &
Scotland, 1923–31, in a dry version of the
Low German nationalistic Baltic Style.

Roselius commissioned Hoetger, an
Expressionist sculptor-turned-architect, to
create Paula Modershohn-Becker Haus and
Haus Atlantis, the Böttcherstraße's two
most   important   monuments.   Haus
Atlantis, the later of these, was a curious
blend of mysticism and advanced technology. Its façade, gridded by a copper-clad
steel frame, might almost have seemed

a paradigm of rationality – despite the
strangely carved wooden spandrel panels
and the mansard roof-like parabolic vault,
studded with cylindrical coloured glass
blocks, that spanned the top-floor 'Hall of
Heaven'. However, a large part of its façade
was also overlaid by a mammoth crucifix-
like Nordic 'tree of life' set within a ring of
runes. The figure on it was said to represent
the ideal of individual sacrifice for the good
of the many. There was more in a similar
vein, which may help to explain why only
the remarkable staircase and a few other
elements devoid of overt nationalist/racist
messages survive of Hoetger's original Haus
Atlantis.

The Paula Modersohn-Becker Haus was
primarily to be a museum of her paintings.
Perhaps because of that, and because it was
conceived earlier, it seems always to have
carried a less strident message.

Bremen   D-29
Stadthalle (municipal sports and
conventional hall) 1955–64
Gustav-Deetjen-Allee and Hollerallee
Roland Rainer, Max Säume & Günter
Hafemann
Neo-Expressionism
→ STADTHALLE *(from almost anywhere in
city)*

The great buttresses bristle nervously
toward the town, visually and actually
resisting the tremendous pull of the hall's
taut tensile roof. Between them grandstand
stairways hang in cantilevered cascades.
Here is one of postwar architecture's more
deceptively dramatic moments – at least as
it can be abstracted by wide-angle black
and white photography.

In reality, the main elevation incorporates large areas of a too-insubstantial,
badly weather-stained blue cladding that
fails to provide the buttresses with any convincing tectonic frame of reference. Indeed,
taken together with the conspicuous corrugated sheathing of the end elevations, it
gives the building an air of impermanence,

or at least of a very tight budget. Even
the buttresses themselves, when closely
studied, become less satisfying. They
apparently strive to combine a Nervi-like
lyrical expression of stress (I–5) with a
Morandian Brutalist articulation of function (I-43), but in the end achieve neither.

Bremen/Neue Vahr   **D-30**
* **Wohnhochhaus** (apartment tower)
1958–62
Otto-Suhr-Straße
Alvar Aalto
Neo-Expressionism
*SE from Hauptbahnhof (central station) on
elevated rd / L at circle / third R past RR
on to Kurfürstenallee / → NEUE VAHR*

Here is architecture as disciplined yet
lyrical poetry: a white splayed sunflower-
head of dwellings, as if seen not at one
moment but through time, ever turning
sunward yet fixed to the necessary orthogonal ordinariness of its supporting stem of
sustenance.

Worpswede [near Bremen]   **D-31**
* **Haus Hoetger II** (Hoetger's own
house, now Hoetger Hotel) 1921–2
Weyerberg
Worpswede Café and Hotel (café and
hotel) 1925–7
Bergstraße and Lindenallee
Große Kunstschau (large exhibition
gallery) 1927
Bergstraße and Lindenallee
Bernhard Hoetger
Expressionism/National Romanticism
*NE from Bremen on Rt 74 / →
Worpswede / L at Y past second
WORPSWEDE sign (with town map) /
Worpswede Hotel and gallery on L /
for house → HOETGER HOTEL*

Haus Hoetger II

Hoetger's sequence of buildings in this
sometime artists' colony makes an interesting study in the development of one
man's very personal style: from the great,
heaped-up, sheltering roof of his studio
house with its primitive, almost neolithic
interior; through the café's more regular,
quietly assured trio of linked medieval barn
forms; to the exhibition hall – remarkably
modern inside and totally ahistorical, if still
Expressionistic, outside. It seems like the
record of a successful psychotherapy – with
the primitive fantasies and fears being exor-
cised one by one. Or, given Hoetger's
contemporaneous work in Bremen's
Böttcherstraße (D-28), were they only
being sublimated?

Wolfsburg   **D-32**
* **Kulturzentrum** (culture centre –
auditoria, shops, library, clubrooms, etc.)
1958–62
Rathausplatz on Porschestraße
Alvar Aalto
*→ STADTMITTE / next to Rathaus (town
hall) on E side of main st (Porschestr)*

Here are all those romantic, mannered
personal details and plan motifs, in spite
(or because) of which Aalto's most poetic
works usually stop just short of wilfulness.
Even the centre's dry, somewhat mechanical qualities – its papery, plaid Carrara
marble cladding and colourless interiors –
reflect that certain coldness which from
about this time crept increasingly into his
later works.

D-32a   The Hans Scharoun-designed

Wolfsburg Municipal Theatre, based
on a competition-winning scheme of 1965,
is more solidly built but less inspired than
his earlier similar efforts (D-14). *S from
D-32 on Porschestr / first R after Heinrich-
Heine-Str / on R*

Wolfsburg   D-33
Heilig-Geist-Kirche (church)
1958–62
Röntgenstraße 81
Alvar Aalto
Neo-Expressionism
S from Wolfsburg ctr (D-32) on Porschestr
abt ½ mi (1 km) / R on Röntgenstr (just past
pedestrian bridge) / 500 yds (m) on L

What much of the High German Baroque
is in respect to its Italian antecedents, this
church is to Aalto's masterpiece at Imatra
(SF-27), i.e. too much 'architecture' for the
available amount of building – while its
tower seems an ill-considered afterthought.

Hannover   D-34
Anzeiger-Hochhaus (newspaper
offices with penthouse cinema) 1927–8
Goseriede 9
Fritz Höger
Expressionism
W from Hauptbahnhof (central station) on
Kurt-Schumacher-Str / at end of st

As a *Hochhaus* (skyscraper) its nine
stories are not very convincing, nor has it
as dramatic a site as Höger's better-known
Chilehaus (D-27). None the less, in texture,
massing and ornamental detail it remains
a most satisfying example of a stylistic language whose vigorous youth was too often
given over to an 'Arts and Crafts' mysticism
and whose later maturity saw too many
shallow repetitions of stock motifs.

Hannover   D-35
**Historisches Museum am Hohen
Ufer** (historical museum) 1960–6
Pferdestraße and Burgstraße
Dieter Oesterlen
S from (D-34) on Goseriede / angle R
(following tram) on Goethestr / first L past
bridge on Leibnizufer / first L (across bridge)
/ first L / on L

Hannover lost most of its past to the war.
This museum interprets surviving artifacts of that past. It displays flags and
carriages, and crocks in glass cases – and,
indirectly, some of Hannover's remaining
architectural heritage. Visible through its
glass walls, a row of half-timbered houses
serves as a backdrop for displays of small
precious objects. In turn the rhythm of the
museum's own adjacent façade and cornice
line is sympathetically modulated to suit
that of the smaller, livelier houses.

The museum also incorporates the
remains of an old arsenal and a watch-
tower – two simple, substantial constructions, of greater historical than aesthetic value. Happily these have not been
allowed to become either untouchable
relics or undetectable restorations. The
museum has copied their rough limestone
for its own (non-loadbearing) walls, while
the museum's strong continuous cornice
hovers above old work and new alike.

D-35a The river Leine flows behind the
museum. Along its edge is a pathway
whose **mosaic paving** was created from
stone fragments of prewar Hannover.

D-35b Sheltering behind a delightful,
delicate nineteenth-century cast-iron pergola is a little glass **pavilion**, 1964–6,
by Arne Jacobsen, which serves as a nearly
invisible foyer for a seventeenth-century
orangery-turned-recital hall. It is so self-
effacing that it almost isn't there. Even
its columns are of glass. Not Jacobsen's
grandest or best-known work, but maybe
his most appropriate. *NW from Hannover ctr*
on Rt 6 (→ BREMEN) abt 2½ mi (4 km) / hard
R on Herrenhäuserstr (tram-line) / in
GROSSER GARTEN *abt ½ mi (1 km) on R*

D-35c Immediately adjacent to the
Grosser Garten's Baroque vision of nature
as artifice – note the splendid diminutive
outdoor theatre, 1685–1714 – is H.L.
Wendland's artificially natural, 'English'
Georgengarten 1835–42.

Alfeld-an-der-Leine [near Hildesheim]   **D-36**
*** Fagus-Werke (shoe-last factory)
1910–14
Rt 3
Walter Gropius & Adolf Meyer (elevations)
Edouard Werner (plan)
Classicized Industrial Vernacular
N from Alfeld ctr → HANNOVER / on R abt 500 yds (m) past RR station

[The Fagus-Werke has remained essentially unchanged since its completion three-quarters of a century ago.]

This familiar image of the best-known 'first modern building' is a fraud of sorts. Most of the buildings that lie behind Gropius's famous glass-walled frontispiece block are less than remarkable – a typically disjointed ensemble of sometimes only slightly architecturalized German industrial vernacular buildings: progressive perhaps, but hardly radical.

How, then, did this single element come to differ so from most of its neighbours, along with which it purportedly was designed? (And what was the role of the Fagus-Werke's financing and machinery – much of which came from Massachusetts, apparently accompanied by some sort of architectural advice!) More to the point, how did three generations of historians and critics of the 'Modern Movement' not only fail to explain satisfactorily, but often even to notice or at least mention, architectural inconsistencies between the parts of this factory which, experienced first hand, should have been troubling?

Bielefeld   **D-37**
Richard-Kaselowsky-Haus
(municipal art gallery) 1962–8
Artur-Ladebeck-Straße
Philip Johnson
On inner (E) side of ring rd, just N of junction with Rt 61 → Köln

So insensitive and ineffective, indeed impotent, a building would normally best be soon forgotten. But this particular monumental pomposity is a representative product of a man who helped define and propagate the International Style in America; and who, beginning as Mies van der Rohe's best-known disciple, became one of the most famous, long-lived and prolific postwar American architects.

In Houston or New Haven such archi-

tecture might once have looked interesting. Unfortunately, here, within the European context, even in this unpretentious provincial town, one can fully understand its meaninglessness.

Emmerich [near Arnhem, NL]   **D-38**
* Heilig-Geist-Kirche (church)
1962–6
Wassenbergstraße and Hansastraße
Dieter G. Baumerwerd
S from autobahn E36 → EMMERICH abt ½ mi (1 km) / L on Gerhard-Storm-Str / first L on to Hansastr / at end of rd on R

A picturesque suburban church composed of hexagonal concrete shell umbrellas: potentially the ultimate trite bore, but not here. The interior is predictable enough, yet skilfully handled, with the umbrellas being so substantial in proportion and material as to preclude any sense of preciousness. Externally it is virtually another building – almost Japanese. The umbrellas are visible only in section. And, seen thus, they seem to be giant, double-stemmed Y's or paired shed roofs, cantilevering from paired supporting columns. Similarly, the dominating sheer, brutally form-marked screen walls shel-

tering beneath these roofs are dematerialized into vast abstract Expressionistic canvases when seen from within. Even the difficult points of juncture between the external corners of the umbrellas are cleverly hidden behind large columnar buttresses, which from within again seem little more than wide mullions. In this case the poetic formalism is really rather clever – a genuine success in territory where so many others have found only failure.

Lünen, Ruhr **D-39**
Geschwister-Scholl-Gymnasium
(school) 1955–62
Holtgrevenstraße 6
Hans Scharoun
Neo-Expressionism
From Rt 54 in Lünen ctr → LÜNEN-SUD *on Parkstr / first L at Sporneckerplatz / on R*

Only Hans Scharoun could have produced such a lyrical, *ad hoc* architectural landscape – a fugue of pleasantly romantic, if escapist, forms and spaces created from a mad variety of sometimes incompatible or unsubstantial, and occasionally downright tacky materials. It is not for every taste and it does not always work. But beneath these idiosyncratic forms and details lies an organizational sense – a true functionalism – both richer and more convincing than that of most more 'logical' buildings. Children ought to love it!

Hagen, Ruhr **D-40**
* **Wohnhäuser Hohenhagen** (artists' colony houses) 1910–14
Stirnband 38–54
J. L. Mathiew Lauweriks
Expressionism
E from Hagen ctr on Rt 7 → ISERLOHN & AUTOBAHN */ R→*HAGEN-EMST *on Haßleyer Str / second L on Stirnband / on L / Prikker house is at far end*

In 1948 Le Corbusier wrote a book called *Le Modulor*, an explanation of his personal system of proportional dimensioning. In it he somewhat gratuitously mentions that, '... once, on a voyage of discovery, as he [Le Corbusier] was looking over a modern villa at Bremen, the gardener there had said to him: "this stuff, you see, that's complicated, all these twiddly bits, curves, angles, calculations, it's all very learned".' To this Le Corbusier only adds, 'The villa had belonged to someone called Thorn Brick (?), a Dutchman (about 1909)' – his parentheses.

There can be no doubt that in fact the city was Hagen, not Bremen, and that it was the last of this group of houses – built for the well-known Dutch painter Thorn Prikker – that Le Corbusier had seen. As for the 'voyage of discovery', it had been more philosophical than geographical, and had probably occurred in 1910 or 1911, when Peter Behrens, for whom Le Corbusier was then working, was building a house on the same street (D-40a), and when the Prikker house would also have been under construction. It is likely, then, that Le Corbu-

D-39a The similar, later, 1964–8, Scharoun-designed **school** at Marl-Drewer-Süd is even more romantic and often more fragile. It seems one of those buildings that survives only through the respect of its users. *E from Rathaus (see D-39b below) on Bergstr, abt $\frac{1}{2}$ mi (1 km) / R on Heisterkampstr ⇨ Breddenkampstr / R on Westfalenstr / on L at Y*

D-39b At the centre of Marl, such as it is, is a Van den Broek & Bakema-designed **Rathaus** (town hall), 1958–67. It is an orthodox 1950s CIAM-inspired complex whose programmatic elements are all neatly but simplistically segregated into discrete little packages. Better constructed than conceived, it is 'styled' in a weakened version of Marcel Breuer's sculpturesque Brutalism (F-14), in turn an imitation of Le Corbusier's postwar manner.

sier's 'gardener' was Lauweriks himself.

Forty years *is* a long time. The memory does play tricks. And, while Le Corbusier was never given to overstating the role of others in the formulation of his precepts, this statement reads almost like a deliberate, if none too explicit, clue for posterity.

In fact, a remarkable number of interesting and important figures were connected with and presumably affected by the Hagen art colony, which until the last decade has been remembered only in a surprising number of footnotes, passing references and unpublished theses. Aside from Lauweriks, Prikker, van de Velde and Behrens (see D-40a-d below) those involved included Bruno Taut, Walter Gropius, August Endell and Josef Hoffmann.

Equally remarkable, considering that these houses were Lauweriks's only built work, is the influence that his mystical Theosophical designs (see NL-1) and teachings appear to have had upon a wide spectrum of the next generation. In addition to Le Corbusier, those whom he affected included members of the Amsterdam School, as one might expect, and, less predictably, Gropius's early partner Adolf Meyer, a student of Lauweriks whose own present obscurity is almost as intriguing as that of his former teacher.

D-40a Behrens's **Haus Cuno,** 1908–11, now somewhat modified and used as a school, stands at the corner of Stirnband and Haßleyer Straße.

D-40b The key catalytic figure at Hagen was the millionaire art collector Karl Ernst Osthaus, whose own house, **Hohenhof,** 1906–8, at Stirnband 10, was designed by Henri van de Velde. It is now a guesthouse for the city of Hagen. *From Hagen (see directions above) L on second Stirnband (Stirnband is actually two parallel streets which were once connected at their far ends) / at end on R*

Bottrop, Ruhr **D-41**
* Heilig-Kreuz-Kirche (church)
1952–7
Scharnhölzstraße 31
Rudolf Schwarz
Rationalism/Neo-Expressionism
N from Bottrop ctr on Osterfelderstr ➪ Pierde Markt ➪ Horsterstr / L AUTOBAHN-MÜNSTER *on Friederich-Ebert-str / first R on Scharnhölzstr / one blk on R*

As with the religions they house, successful churches often intermingle the practical with the inexplicable. Most architects seem not to understand this, perhaps because they do not understand religion. Schwarz understood. Building churches was his vocation.

Here all is rational: the exposed concrete framing with its brick infill; the main façade's expression of trussed, wind-resisting window tracery; the simple free-standing square bell tower; the attached but separately articulated chapel and sacristy. Yet there is also something beyond pure reason. This is not meant to be just a building, but rather, metaphysically, the knowable fraction of a universal order:

Düsseldorf **D-42**
Warenhaus Tietz (now Kaufhof department store) 1906–9
between Heinrich-Heine-Allee and Königsallee
Joseph Maria Olbrich
Jugendstil
At the N end of Königsallee (N-S st paralleling canal in town ctr)
[Interior totally transformed.]

After Darmstadt, this comes as a disappointment. Here is neither the eloquence of the earlier Ernst-Ludwig-Haus (D-54) nor the invention of the contemporaneous Hochzeitsturm (D-57). Granted this is a department store, but is it not too obviously so? Is its Byzantine/Baroque roofscape not too pat and easy? As with some of Olbrich's larger private houses of this period, there is a feeling here of self-conscious, restrained high fashion – and of the *enfant terrible* who, no longer building for artists and aristocrats, finds himself 'leashed in' by the great bourgeoisie.

D-40c Van de Velde also remodelled the then **Folkwang Museum,** now Karl-Ernst-Osthaus-Museum, 1901–2, at Hochstraße 73 in Hagen. There, in accordance with his personal theories of art history, Osthaus displayed his collection of modern paintings and primitive art grouped together according to specific thematic categories. (Today the Folkwang Collection, now more or less conventionally hung, is in Essen.) *Hochstr, in Hagen ctr, parallels Frankfurter Str (Rt 54) just to SW*

D-40d Peter Behrens's other work near here, a quite 'cardboardy' **crematorium** of 1906–8, markedly reflects the Schinkelesque, Greek-vase-painting-like graphic style he adopted during the brief German post-Art Nouveau revival of interest in Neo-Classicism. *SE from Hagen → HAGEN-DELSTERN on Rt 54 / in cemetery past river*

a fragment, like the very space of the nave – with its 'west' end so insubstantially bounded by a translucent galactic swirl entitled 'Infinity'; a fragment, like the parabolic plan of the nave – with some vast extension implied in its projecting walls.

Metaphorically then this church may be not unlike the brilliant perigee of a comet: that brief moment of reflected glory which permits us to surmise the vast extensions of the comet's realm – but without which that realm is none the less real.

D-42a Diagonally across Heinrich-Heine-Allee, at No. 53, is the **Wilhelm-Marx-Haus,** 1921–4, by Wilhelm Kreis. It is a conservatively Gothic Expressionist 'skyscraper' – with a leopard in its lobby.

D-42b Kreis also built Düsseldorf's **Rheinhalle,** 1925–6, an Expressionist culture centre, planetarium, etc. *On bank of Rhine just N of Oberkasseler Brücke (bridge)*

Düsseldorf   **D-43**
* Thyssenhaus (office block) 1956–60
Jan Wellemplatz
Hentrich & Petschnigg
Neo-Expressionism
*On the N side of Düsseldorf ctr where Berliner
Allee-Kaiserstr crosses the Hofgarten*

Unlike their American counterparts,
European office skyscrapers, when built at
all, are rarely allowed to cluster. More typically their location is at least partially
determined by urban considerations, so
that, rising above the roofscape, they will
become the sort of urban landmarks that
church steeples, domes, and *campanili* once
were.

Thyssenhaus is a reasonably conventional twenty-five-storey office building – 'short' enough to disappear in New
York or Chicago – with a greenish-silvery
curtain wall that looks dated and a plan
that is perhaps over-elongated to be
efficient. Admittedly it is an elegant,
dynamic form: a remarkably effective and
photogenic corporate symbol. But that is
of secondary importance compared to the
implications of its assigned role as an urban
place-marker. Such close civic identification with symbols of big business is somewhat disquieting. It seems not a little unlike
the sense of identity and mutual self-inter-
est that once existed between city authorities and those of the church.

D-43a The adjacent **Schauspielhaus**
(municipal theatre), 1960–9, is by
Bernhard Pfau.

D-43b Düsseldorf's first large postwar
office tower, **Mannesmann Haus**,
1952–5, by Paul Schneider-Esleben, is

more conventionally designed and has a
less significant location on the Rhine
embankment in the old quarter of the city.
*At Mannesmannufer 1b, 1 mi (1.3 km) S of
Oberkasseler Brücke (bridge)*

D-43c The Mannesmann Haus's location
was undoubtedly determined by the presence of Peter Behrens's adjacent **Mannesmann office building**, 1908–12.

Düsseldorf   **D-44**
* Haniel-Hochgarage (garage)
1949–51
Grafenberger Allee 276
Paul Schneider-Esleben
*NE from Düsseldorf ctr (D-43) on Schadowstr
⇨ Am Wehrhahn ⇨ Grafenberger Allee /
abt ½ mi (1 km) on L*

Surely the most elegant parking garage
ever: a four-storey hard glass box of dark
crystal beneath projecting eaves. Those
eaves, part of a subtly folded roof, also
shelter and carry a cable-borne access
ramp – a slightly jagged, taut, light diagonal ascending in front of the dark, reflecting surfaces.

D-44a Conversely, and almost simultaneously in 1950–4, Schneider-Esleben
also built **St Rochus-Kirche**, which
looks like nothing so much as an outsize
hat. *N from Am Wehrhahn (see directions
above) on to Adlerstr / R on to Prinz-Georg-
Str / one blk on R*

Krefeld [near Düsseldorf]   **D-45**
* **Haus Lange** (house, now branch of
Kaiser Wilhelm Museum) 1928
Wilhelmshofallee 91
Ludwig Mies van der Rohe
International Style
*N from Krefeld ctr on Ostwall / R on Moerser
Str (→ MOERS) / R on Wilhelmshofallee /
500 yds (m) on R*

Ever present in Mies's work is a dichotomy between the tangible and the abstract.
The anonymous non-specificity – not to say
unusability – of his later grand, uncompromisingly steel-caged spaces (D-13)
needs no reiteration here, nor do their Neo-
Classical origins (D-26b).

This not quite doctrinaire International
Style house demonstrates both the extent
to which Mies, like so many others at the
time (D-60), tried to suppress his own architectural instincts, and the power with
which his basic inclinations asserted themselves none the less. His external materials,
for instance, are too real to be true to the
International Style. The brickwork of both
house and garden – substituted for the
style's almost mandatory white stucco – is

carefully dimensioned and laid in a rich-
textured English bond. The refined railings
are also at odds with the style's preferred,
often clumsy, pseudo-nautical pipework.
Even the plate glass, so precisely proportioned and deep set within its reveals,
seems too substantial.

Mies's own sensibilities also show
through in the interior. This is no 'dwelling
machine' without inhabitants. It is just a
set of well-proportioned spaces, neither
more nor less, and seemingly as suited to
its new role as it must have been to its
former.

D-45a Next door at 93 Wilhelmshofallee
is Mies's **Haus Esters** of the same date.
[Still a private residence.]

D-45b The **Kaiser Wilhelm Museum**
is typical of many similar progressive small
German museums. In addition to some Mies
drawings and the temporary exhibits displayed in the Lange house, its main collection includes graphic and decorative arts
representative of the Jugendstil and Bauhaus. *Westwall and Marktstr in Krefeld ctr*

Aachen   **D-46**
St Fronleichnam-Kirche (church)
1928–31
Düppelstraße
Rudolf Schwarz
International Style
*E from town ctr → KÖLN (AUTOBAHN) abt
1 mi (1.5 km) / R at circle (Europlatz) on to
Joseph-von-Görres-Str / L at Y (see also
D-46a below) / in second blk on L*

[Featureless as the interior seems today,
it was originally even more abstract, with
nothing on the walls; nor were there the
larger lighting units at the bottom of the
long chain-fixtures; nor, and this is more
important than it might seem, was the concrete frame's shadowy outline apparent on
the now no longer quite so white plaster.]

Other International Style churches do
not come easily to mind. In a sense this
simple means, these plain white surfaces,
could almost belong to an idealized Mediterranean peasant church; so too might the
basic symmetry, the deliberately pitched
vestigial roof, and the square windows set
traditionally within a massive apparently
loadbearing wall, which in fact is not. One
is also reminded of Le Corbusier, the self-
proclaimed archetypical modern man, who

alluded to a time 'when the cathedrals were
white', while knowing they had blazed with
barbaric colour – even as here Schwarz, the
proponent of a renewed archaic Chris-
tianity, sought his ancient faith in white,
twentieth-century asceticism.

D-46a By way of comparison, near by on Zeppelin Straße is **St Bonifatius-Kirche** 1959–64, one of Schwarz's many postwar churches. *R at Y from Joseph-von-Görres-Str (see directions above) on to Sedan Str / angle L onto Adalbertsteinweg / L on Zeppelin Str*

D-46b Near Aachen, and almost contemporary with St Fronleichnam, is the **Höhere Fachschule für Sozialarbeit** (social-work school), 1931, which Schwarz designed with Hans Schwippert. *SE → Burtsheid / L, past RR, on to Park Str ⇨ Friedrich-Ebert-Allee / L on Kappelen Str ⇨ Robert-Schumann-Str / at No. 25*

D-46c In a little park in the centre of Aachen is the **Elisenbrunnen,** a small fountain pavilion by Karl Friedrich Schinkel, 1823. *Just E of cathedral*

Mönchengladbach **D-47**
* **Stadtisches Museum Abteiberg** (art museum) 1972–82
Abteistraße 27
Hans Hollein
One blk E of Rathaus (town hall) in town ctr

What a fascinating, troublesome building. For twenty years Hollein seemed the perennial 'promising', if no longer exactly 'young' architect. He did a small shop here (A-6a, c and d) and an interior there (A-6), yet never the big project that would really be 'architecture'. But for ten of those years he was, in fact, working on this one commission – not huge but substantial, and a real building. Unfortunately, ten years may have been too long. He may have had too much time to worry out all the separate bits and pieces of a detailed programme for a strong client. (There may also have been some Post-Modernist notions of the building as a collaged metaphoric cityscape.) Thus it is difficult even to speak of this museum as 'a building'. It seems a collection of fragments: an eroded tower – too small to make any sense, with each floor plan preciously, precisely specific; an extendable grid of apparently identical square gallery spaces, each, it is said, tailored to house permanently a specific part of the museum's collection; a terraced hillside landscape curiously reminiscent of mountainside rice paddies. The museum is also rife with inconsistencies: the systematic *and* the random; the air of cold, detached sophistication *and* the gestures tying it into the surrounding urban fabric; the tactile, undulating brick retaining walls of the terraces *and* the hard, awkward metal and glass detailing – which looks in places as if it wants either to be slicker or more industrial than it is. Compared to all this, Stirling's Stuttgart museum (D-58) seems positively jovial and healthily straightforward, and even the simplistic, naïve self-assurance of Mies's Berlin museum (D-13) becomes a breath of fresh air.

Cologne (Köln) **D-48**
Gürzenich (municipal meeting halls) 1949–55
Quatermarkt and Gürzenichstraße
Rudolf Schwarz & Karl Band
Empiricism
S from cathedral on Unter Goldschmied ⇨ Quatermarkt / five blks on L

At the end of the war Cologne lay devastated. Standing almost alone amidst the broken walls and rubble was its cathedral (D-48a), a tragic witness to the coldly calculated ferocity of man's destructive urge. A few blocks away had also once stood the Gürzenich, a fifteenth-century Late Gothic communal hall, and, next to it, the almost equally venerable St Alban's church. Both had been reduced to shells.

Almost immediately, Rudolf Schwarz began to guide Cologne's rebirth. Schwarz was a man of moderation. For him there had been enough destruction. He saved whatever was left of the old – while taking advantage of new opportunities.

One such possibility, permitted by the relocation of St Alban's parish, was an expansion of the Gürzenich into the space between it and St Alban's. The raw interior walls and arches of the church itself were left to frame a space commemorating Cologne's 50,000 war dead – a space occupied only by Käthe Kollwitz's figures of two grieving parents. But this reconsecration of an already sacred place did not prevent Schwarz from using part of its exterior walls to enclose the Gürzenich's new lobby. Although the rooms he created between the buildings may now seem over-lyrical, or escapist, it is a tribute to his sensitivity and skill that the proximity of such secular uses does not violate the memorial.

D-48a Only the apse and part of the west front of **Cologne Cathedral** were built during the Middle Ages. All else is nineteenth-century work, 1824–80, that is too archaeological to be of interest here. However the fact of its completion, in part through a revival of medieval methods, is important. This enormous undertaking, Prussia's counterpart to the Walhalla (D-67), was controlled by an appropriately

Cologne (Köln)/Riehl   **D-49**
* **St Engelbert-Kirche** (church)
1930–2
Am Riehler Gürtel 50
Dominikus Böhm
Expressionism
N from Cologne ctr along river / first L past ZOO BRÜCKE (*see D-49a below*) → ZOO / → AMSTERDAMER STR / *R on Am Riehler Gürtel (first R past first light past underpass) / several blks on L*

Its conspicuous early concrete shell roof drew attention to St Engelbert's during the 'thin-shell' fad of the 1950s. Even today it remains among the few reasonably coherent attempts to use these efficient, if uncompromising, structural forms. The design succeeds, both visually and volumetrically. Little more than eight identical shells, all focused upon a single point and all contained in, and delineated by, a sheer circular brick wall, the structure does its work simply, without overpowering the church.

This circular plan-form strongly suggests, almost demands, post Second World War Catholicism's revived archaic 'religion in the round'. In 1930, however, such church plans were still essentially a Protestant innovation. Hence the arched, dramatically side-lighted sanctuary which grows somewhat unexpectedly from the formally 'complete' circular nave – a graft that appears more successful from within

than from without.

Of course the contradiction here between form and use may not just reflect a premature anticipation of ecclesiastical reform. Like its more truly concentric Protestant contemporaries (D-17a), St Engelbert's may unexpectedly, but not inappropriately, be an echo of Weimar Germany's utopian mystical dreams of crystalline 'city crowns' (*Stadtkronen*) and of 'cathedrals' of light – or of socialism!

D-49a At Krefelder Straße 45 is **St Gertrud-Kirche**, 1962–5, by Böhm's son Gottfried. *W from Zoo Brücke on Innere Kanalstr abt $1\frac{1}{4}$ mi (2 km) / L (by turning R)* → STADTMITTE, *on to Krefelder Str / abt 250 yds (m) on R*

Bensberg [near Cologne (Köln)]   **D-50**
* **Rathaus** (town hall) 1963–9
Engelbertstraße, Schloßberg
Gottfried Böhm
Neo-Expressionism
E from Cologne ctr on Rt 55 abt $9\frac{1}{2}$ mi (15 km) → (*Bensberg*) STADTMITTE / → RATHAUS

Here is a civil place maker of many, sometimes contradictory, aspects. In size and location it is less dominating than the neighbouring old Baroque 'New' Palace. But in image, if not function, it is an echo of prewar Expressionism's infatuation with the *Stadtkrone* (city crown), that glorious dream castle – part cathedral, part civic centre – which was to have been the urban utopia made manifest.

Unquestionably this is a building of its own time, yet it recollects, in mass and plan as well as in the relics it incorporates, the fortress that once occupied its site. It is essentially a modern office block – a fact clearly expressed in its strip windows – yet it is also a traditional Rathaus, complete with the traditional communal dining facilities and some equally traditional romantic cave-like interiors.

True, in a few places these varying realities do not quite all comfortably coalesce. The old and the new sometimes affect each other strangely. Thus the tapering central stair tower seems contrived when seen next to its medieval neighbours. But these are small quibbles, at least given the many, often conflicting, values – perpetually in tension, yet not unresolved – that are fused within this municipal magic mountain.

medieval, guild-like organization called the Bauhütte (literally: builder's hut) which also was to become the philosophical and etymological ancestor of the Bauhaus.

Frankfurt am Main   D-51
Museum für Kunsthandwerk
(museum of decorative arts) 1983–5
Schaumainkai 15
Richard Meier & Partners
Neo-Corbusian
On S bank of river directly opposite city ctr

Richard Meier's career has been distinguished by both the elegance and the consistency of his work. Unlike so many contemporary masters – such as James Stirling (GB-58, D-58), or Michael Graves – one can trace a continuous evolution in Meier's work from his early Corbusian pastiches to this elegant geometric fugue. Here he has given up Le Corbusier's more obvious idiosyncratic *forms* while creating a new synthesis based on Corbusier's design *principles* (F-22).

The geometric logic of this museum is keyed to the geometry Meier found in the plan and façade of the nineteenth-century Villa Metzler, which formerly housed the collection and is now part of the new museum. Meier's analysis of the villa's façade yielded a plaid-like grid which determined the rhythm and dimensions of Meier's own more explicitly gridded façade, while the villa's square plan became the basic unit of the museum's four-module by four-module grid plan. But the villa's impact on Meier's building does not end there. He treats it as one of four corner 'pavilions' which makes a complete square of his otherwise L-shaped plan. These pavilions may be thought of as a sequence, beginning with the villa and continuing clockwise in plan, although Meier's three pavilions progressively disintegrate into the fabric of his building. If all this seems an exercise in mannerism, Meier's most mannerist conceit is the second identical plan grid which he superimposed on the first at a skewed angle of $3\frac{1}{2}°$ (a device he first used elsewhere). While the first grid, aligned with the villa, shapes the exhibition spaces, the second, aligned with the gardens and riverside quay to the east, orients the internal circulation routes. Even though $3\frac{1}{2}°$ sounds like a small angle, the tension between these grids is strikingly evident in plan. But experienced inside the building, it seems little more than an excuse for some agreeably picturesque distortions.

D-51a The Villa Metzler is one of several grand bourgeois villas belonging to specialized museums that stand on the south bank of the river opposite the centre of Frankfurt. Another of these, radically transformed by O. M. Ungers in 1984, now houses the **German Architecture Museum**. In contrast to Meier's very deferential attitude towards the Villa Metzler, Ungers gutted his villa, inserted a symbolic 'house' within its shell, and submerged its base in a new one-storey, top-lit gallery structure. *W on Schaumainkai*

D-51b At Wilhelm-Leuschner-Straße 69 is a coolly **Rational office building**, 1930–1, by Max Taut & Franz Hoffmann. *S from Hauptbahnhof (central station) on Baseler Str / first R on to Gutleutstr / immediate L and across Baseler Str on to Wilhelm-Leuschner-Str / in first blk on R*

D-51c Frankfurt's Expressionist **Groß-markthalle** (wholesale market), 1927–8, by Martin Elsässer demonstrates that sometimes it is sufficient to believe in one's form language. Then anything can be done – even a 'futuristic' market hall. *E from Frankfurt ctr on Zeil to Alfred-Brehm-Platz / → tramline out SE corner / continue S to Sonnemannstr / directly opposite*

D-51d Near by and similarly scaled, stylish yet prosaically functional, is Egon Eiermann's **Neckermann Warehouse**, 1958–61. Unfortunately its most interesting façade lies partly hidden behind later additions. It can now best be seen from the rear. *E from D-51c under RR on to Hanauer Landstr ⇨ Rt 40 / abt 2½ mi (4 km) / on R*

D-51e In addition to his Berlin Rundfunks (radio station, D-21), Hans Poelzig's other surviving major work in West Germany is the **I.G. Farben building**, 1928–31, now US Army Headquarters. It is also his least appealing work. Curiously, despite both the tasteless vulgarity of its lavish use of marble and other unsubtle costly materials, and its innate conservatism, it is better known than the Rundfunks – probably because it appears to reflect more closely conventional modernist precepts. *N from An der Hauptwache on Groß Eschenheimer Str ⇨ Eschersheimer Landstr, abt 1 mi (1.5 km) / L on Furstenberger Str / three blks on R at Bremer Str*

Höchst am Main [near Frankfurt]   **D-52**
** Altes Verwaltungsgebäude
Farbwerke Höchst (administration
building, Höchst Dye Works) 1920–4
Werkgelände
Peter Behrens
Expressionism
W from Frankfurt am Main → HÖCHST *on
Mainzer Landstr / →* FARBWERKE
HÖCHST AG / → OST TOR / *ahead on R*

[Written permission is required for interior photography.]

Peter Behrens was something of an architectural weathercock. For thirty years his work accurately reflected each shift of the German avant-garde. First there was Art Nouveau (D-56), then various sorts of Neo-Classicism (D-16, 40a, 40d), here Expressionism, and later still, a reasonably progressive modernism (A-25d). Yet if Behrens was inconsistent, he was also remarkably adroit, both artistically and professionally. He not only built Höchst when others could only dream on paper, but he built it expensively and well.

Höchst may be a pastiche – marrying Germanic nationalistic motifs to Gaudí-esque forms, Wrightian spatial attitudes, and perhaps a soupçon of commercial symbolism – but it is a convincing pastiche. And its cave-like, almost mystical foyer, bounded by subtly coloured stalagmite columns, is as dramatic as any space achieved by any of the Expressionists.

D-52a Later in the 20s, under the leadership of its municipal architect, Ernst May, Frankfurt built large amounts of ascetic Rational social housing. Increasingly this architecture was attacked as 'cultural Bolshevism'. Finally May and many of his staff emigrated to Russia – vindicating their opponents. One of their last projects, and because it was largely designed by Mart Stam perhaps the most interesting, is the **Hellerhof** area, 1929–31. *N of Mainzer Landstr (see directions above) near edge of Frankfurt*

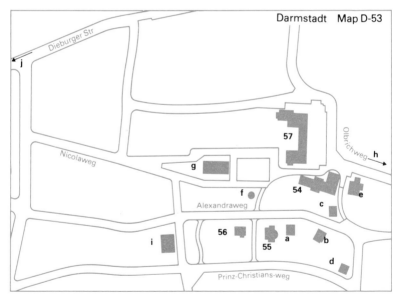

Darmstadt   **D-53**
** Mathildenhöhe (artists' colony)
1899–1914
Josef Maria Olbrich, *et al.*
Jugendstil

[Because the houses are all stuccoed, it may not always be readily apparent that most have been modified, some drastically so, as a result of war damage.]

If there were an acropolis of the Jugendstil – Germany's Art Nouveau – it would be the Mathildenhöhe. On this hill at the turn of the century, the Grand Duke Ernst Ludwig von Hessen established an art colony to which he attracted many of the best younger Germanic artists and which held a series of exhibitions in 1901, 1904, 1908 and 1914. Among these artists was the Viennese architect Josef Maria Olbrich, who, although he was to work for only ten years, would prove himself to be one of the most versatile and prolific designers of his generation. Almost every building on the Mathildenhöhe (unless indicated otherwise below) is, or before the war was, his work.

D-53a   **Haus Glückert II** (house), 1899–1901, Alexandraweg 25.

D-53b Haus Habich (house), 1900–1, Alexandraweg 27.

D-53c Olbrich's own house, 1900–1, Alexandraweg 28. Its entire upper half has been rebuilt in a most prosaic form, and is quite unlike the original.

D-53d Haus Deiters (house), 1900–1, Mathildenhöheweg 2.

D-53e Oberhessisches Haus (house), 1907–8, Olbrichweg 15. Now somewhat changed, it shows that in his last works Olbrich, too, was beginning to respond to the German post-Jugendstil revival of Schinkel's Neo-Classicism.

D-53f The round **pavilion** behind the chapel, 1914, is by Albin Müller. In both motifs and methods it more than any other structure here shows the impact of Josef Hoffmann's Viennese Arts and Crafts

organization, the Wiener Werkstätte.

D-53g Müller also built the **Neo-Classical pool,** 1914, in front of the chapel.

D-53h At the end of the pool once stood a set of **gateposts** by Müller, with lions by Bernhard Hoetger, 1914. The gateposts are now in the nearby park. E (Map D-53 →) abt two blks / across RR

D-53i The house at **Eugene Brachtweg 6,** 1908, now used for various sorts of temporary exhibitions, is by Alfred Messel. Messel's once not insignificant reputation rests on a now lost Berlin department store.

D-53j Hessisches-Landesmuseum, 1896–1906, at the Friedensplatz, is also by Messel. Not surprisingly, one of the greatest strengths of this excellent small museum is its Jugendstil collection. W (Map D-53 →) abt four blks / on R

Darmstadt **D-54**
* **Ernst-Ludwig-Haus** (artists' studios) 1899–1901, rear added 1904 for the second exhibition
Alexandraweg 26
Josef Maria Olbrich
Jugendstil
Map D-53
[Badly war-damaged. Exterior faithfully restored.]
The Mathildenhöhe was more than just artists' houses and studios. It was a semi-utopian community and, over the span of a decade, the scene of several exhibitions. The first of these, combining a summer-long inaugural fête with an arts, crafts and architectural display, was held in 1901. For the occasion a temporary restaurant pavilion was erected amid the trees on top of the hill and a temporary art gallery was built at its foot. On the brow of the hill and on axis with the gallery rose the Ernst-Ludwig-Haus – a kind of collective temple of creativity and the exhibition's spiritual focus. Flanking the axis between these two stood the artists' houses.
    The Ernst-Ludwig-Haus had to be both mundane and symbolic. On its north side, out of sight and shielded from direct sunlight, conventional glass clerestories illuminated simple, lofty work spaces. To the south, it presented a blank wall – a

backdrop against which Olbrich could, without actually misrepresenting the nature of the building, assemble a suitable hymn in praise of artistic labour.
    In front of the building he placed a pair of idealized figures – male and female. (It is not Olbrich's fault that thirty years on their type would become a totalitarian cliché.) The bronze angels behind them were 'borrowed' from Olbrich's old mentor in Vienna, Otto Wagner. The arched entrance canopy is at once the most clearly Art Nouveau and the most original part of the composition. Finally, there is the projecting roof, a device that suggests framing end pavilions where none exist and is also an allusion to another collective artists' studio built by an admired contemporary, Charles Rennie Mackintosh (GB-79).

Darmstadt **D-55**
* **Haus Glückert I** (now offices) 1899–1901
Alexandraweg 23
Josef Maria Olbrich
Jugendstil
Map D-53
[Restored essentially as built.]
Compared to Olbrich's other houses, at least as they were before the war, the exterior of this Baroque-gabled box hardly seems striking. Only its gilt patterned circular entranceway suggests that more lies within. It is a two-storey cube of space – a studio living room – cut into on one side by a balcony, while on the other it expands outwards through a great arch into an

ingle-nook. Its simple plastered surfaces are enlivened by extensive and, at least when taken individually, coherent systems of stencilled ornament: typically Viennese Secession chequered borders; some light-reflecting gilt; two tree-like 'candelabra'

that incorporate expanding rows of bare electric bulbs; and even symbolic 'smoke' rising above the fireplace. Curiously, this 'smoke' issues from a rather Victorian-Gothic mantelpiece – seemingly forty years out of place.

Darmstadt   **D-56**
Haus Behrens (Behrens's own house)
1900–1
Alexandraweg 17
Peter Behrens
Art Nouveau
Map D-53

[Not open to the public.]

When Peter Behrens came to Darmstadt in 1899, he was a promising young graphic artist with no architectural training and a taste for the more florid Franco-Belgian Art Nouveau. As his contribution to the 1901 exhibition, he designed and furnished this house. It was his first building and as such is notable primarily for its restraint. Two years later, still without any architectural training, Behrens left Darmstadt as an architect and industrial designer.

If this seems improbable, consider that by 1910 Walter Gropius, Le Corbusier and

Mies van der Rohe had all sought and found employment with him!

Darmstadt   **D-57**
* Hochzeitsturm (wedding tower, 1906, and exhibition hall for 1908 exhibition)
Mathildenhöhe
Josef Maria Olbrich
Jugendstil
Map D-53

[Interior of exhibition building drastically altered.]

One can sense here that as the Art Nouveau ebbed older ideals began to reassert themselves. The earlier theatrical ingenuity of the Ernst-Ludwig-Haus (D-54) gave way to an almost archaic serenity and a concern for craftsmanship. There is still drama, but of a more difficult sort. Even the tower, a wedding present from the Grand Duke to his new Duchess, is more intellectual, less visceral, which may be why its historical role remains somewhat ill-defined. Depending upon their own par-

ticular biases, critics have seen the beginnings of Expressionism in the up-raised hand-like roof – that *is* what it is meant to be – or an anticipation of the International Style in its 'wrap-around' strip windows. It might be of greater interest, however, to know more about the genesis of the modular grid of concrete trellises with which Olbrich surrounded the complex.

Stuttgart   **D-58**
* Neue Staatsgalerie (art museum, theatre and music academy) 1977–84
Konrad-Adenauer-Straße
James Stirling, Michael Wilford & Associates
Post-Modernism
K.-Adenauer-Str is NE portion of inner ring rd / on E side of rd

There is a curious parallel between the careers of James Stirling (Britain's most important postwar architect), Sir Edwin Lutyens (Britain's greatest twentieth-century architect), and Richard Norman Shaw (Lutyens's closest nineteenth-century counterpart). Each began working in a kind of vernacular style: rural and domestic for Shaw and Lutyens; industrial and technical for Stirling. Later, when that no longer sufficed, each turned to what Lutyens called the 'High Game' of mannered Classicism. While Shaw's mannerism

always remained subdued, Lutyens's at times almost overwhelmed his architecture (GB-36). However, it also gave his buildings vitality and a kind of meaning, even if they flew in the face of the twentieth century. One cannot help having similar thoughts about Stirling's recent work. Clearly, his Leicester and Cambridge University buildings (GB-58, 51) are *the* masterworks of postwar British architecture. At Oxford, in the last of his 60s triad of university buildings (GB-50), the mannerism evident in the first two begins to seem a symptom of a deep underlying malaise – the 'crisis' of confidence that has affected architecture since the early 70s.

Much has changed in Stirling's work since then. Many of the mannerisms and allusions are now explicitly historicist: the circular courtyard here that directly refers to Schinkel's Altes Museum in Berlin (D-26b); the stones 'fallen' from the walls (to ventilate the parking garage) that are almost a cliché of sixteenth-century Italian mannerism; the 'Egyptian' cornice; the U-shaped plan of the two gallery wings with

their traditional rooms arranged in enfilade; and the pitched roofed 'aedicule' at the street line announcing the axiality of the building – in lieu, Stirling says, of the traditional 'man on a horse' in front of the adjacent old portion of the museum. Many other allusions, however, are still references to Stirling's old repertory of modern precedents: the Corbusian curves and ramps; and the iron and glass canopies, suggestive of nineteenth-century industrial vernacular and Russian Constructivism. Much else also remains that is pure, High-Tech Stirling. But where does it all lead? Is he finding a way through modern architecture's crisis? Or is he merely learning to live with it?

D-58a Stuttgart's monumental **Hauptbahnhof** (railway station and hotel), 1911, 1917–19, 1922–8, by Paul Bonatz with Friedrich Scholer, is also on the inner ring road, at Arnulf-Klett-Platz. *Stuttgart ctr at NW corner of the inner ring rd (at Rt 27)*

Stuttgart   **D-59**
* **Hymnus-Chorheim** (choir school, kindergarten, community rooms and post office) 1968–70
Birkenwaldstraße 98
Behnisch & Partner
High-Tech Neo-Vernacular
N from Stuttgart ctr on Heilbronner Str / L on to Türlenstr / follow tram lines on to Birkenwaldstr / abt ½ mi (1 km) on R

The precise sources may be obscured, but they seem to be mostly Anglo-American, the picturesque array of shed roofs being derived from the San Francisco Bay Region Revival; the interior paintwork suggesting Pop Art-inspired super-graphics; and the choice of materials seeming somewhat Brutalist – British in the case of the patent glazing, American in that of the concrete block. Even the mannered use of large cement asbestos tiles as a paraphrase of

the region's delicate slate-hung vernacular, has 'Pop' overtones. Needless to say, all these sources have sources of their own. (Ultimately, most architecture *is* about architecture.) But that does not matter – at least not when the architecture works as well as this, is as coherent, and belongs so undeniably to its site.

Stuttgart   **D-60**
** **Weißenhof Siedlung** (Deutscher Werkbund housing exhibition) 1926–7
Am Weißenhof
Ludwig Mies van der Rohe (site plan), *et al.*
International Style
N (up) Birkenwaldstr from D-59 → signs / between Am Weißenhof and Rathenaustr

[After severe war damage and insensitive reconstruction, only about half of the original structures, most of which were single family houses, retained any semblance of their original appearance. These, however, are now being restored.]

The Deutscher Werkbund was founded as a somewhat mercantilist association of industrialists and designers. Even before the First World War it had already begun forging links between German architecture and German industrial design (D-1). In 1914, it sponsored a large and influential exhibition which included, among other things, Walter Gropius's somewhat Wrightian ideal factory (see page 20) and Bruno Taut's remarkable Glass Pavilion – one of

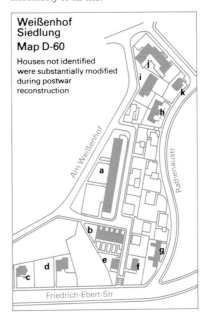

Weißenhof
Siedlung
Map D-60

Houses not identified
were substantially modified
during postwar
reconstruction

the most mystical Expressionist works ever realized, and certainly the most uncompromisingly technological.

After the war, these reform-minded propagandistic exhibitions continued. Yet of all the Werkbund's remarkable architectural efforts only the Weißenhof Siedlung survives, and even it has been transformed, both physically and as a symbol. Once, for its creators, it exemplified the mature homogeneity of the new 'objective' architecture (*Neue Sachlichkeit*). To its detractors, Nazi and otherwise, it was an 'Arab village' or an example of 'cultural Bolshevism' – either being a threat to both Family and Fatherland.

Now all that is past, and this exemplar of the new, anonymous functionalism is primarily a pantheon of the 'heroic era'.

The now lost or unrecognizable buildings were designed by Walter Gropius, Ludwig Hilberseimer, Bruno Taut, Max Taut, Hans Poelzig, Richard Döcker and Adolf Rading. The surviving buildings, containing about two-thirds of the original dwellings, are the work of the following:

D-60a Mies van der Rohe. The symbolically collective, but unrepresentative, **centrepiece apartment block**.

D-60b J. J. P. Oud. Radically Rationalist, but also slightly mannered, **row housing**.

D-60c Victor Bourgeois. A privately funded **'villa'** by a French-speaking Belgian. Technically it lies outside the bounds of this consciously all-Germanic response to the French 1925 Exposition des Arts Décoratifs.

D-60d and e Adolf G. Schneck

D-60f and g Le Corbusier. He, significantly, was considered Swiss, not French.

D-60h Josef Frank
D-60i Mart Stam
D-60j Peter Behrens
D-60k Hans Scharoun

Stuttgart/Zuffenhausen　　　　**D-61**
* **Wohnhochhäuser Romeo and Julia** (two apartment buildings) 1954–9
Schozacher Straße 40
Hans Scharoun & Wilhelm Frank
Neo-Expressionism
N from Stuttgart ctr on Rt 27 (Heilbronner Str) abt 3 mi (5 km) / R on Haldenrainstr (at ROT) sign / abt 70 yds (m) on L

One could be tempted to make a tortured analogy about the attempts of aging Shakespearean thespians to recapture sprightly youth – attempts that might be credible enough when seen across the footlights. But, as with this Romeo and Juliet – usually known only from flattering, dramatic, sunfilled photographs – the illusion is lost, amidst garish paint and arch gestures, when encountered close up. As here, art and craft may be assuredly in evidence, but the projected youthful spontaneity no longer quite convinces. (Fortunately, we are not given to making such analogies.)

Ulm/Neu-Ulm　　　　**D-62**
* **St Johann-Baptist-Kirche**
(church) 1921–6
Augsburger Straße 11
Dominikus Böhm
Expressionism
E from cathedral on Neue Str / → NEU-ULM across river / L on to Augsburger Str → AUGSBURG / in first blk on R

One's initial impression is of an extensively war-damaged, crudely repaired façade. Closer inspection suggests that, although the brick infill is of a rough texture, it is carefully laid and detailed. Perhaps, then, this is an ancient fabric which has been strengthened? In fact, no. Although the stones are old – having come from Ulm's former fortress – the church was built all of a piece. Once understood, this exercise in pseudo-primitivism seems to reflect an almost eighteenth-century sensibility. Certainly it does not prepare one for the space within.

The interior is still 'Gothic', perhaps even

D-61a A little further out on Route 27 in Kornwestheim is a curious, tapered-sided **water tower-cum-municipal office building**, 1933–5, designed by Paul Bonatz with Friedrich Scholer. *N from D-61 on Rt 27 (Heilbronner Str) abt $1\frac{1}{4}$ mi (2 km) / → KORNWESTHEIM / abt $\frac{1}{2}$ mi (1 km) on L*

more so than the façade, but of a more original sort: an abstract composition rendered in a crisply immaterial white stucco. It has neither mouldings nor ornament – only form. Columns melt into vaults and vaults into window walls. The space seems not so much constructed as envisioned. It is a tectonic N. C. Wyeth cloudscape. Unlike the insistent archaic reality of the exterior, one sees and can accept it for the theatrical illusion it is – suspended ferroconcrete magic and nothing more.

Ulm D-63

* Garnisonskirche, now
Pauluskirche (church, originally for the
military) 1908–11
Frauenstraße
Theodor Fischer
Jugendstil (interior)/
Eclectic National Romantic (exterior)
*E from cathedral on Neue Str / L on
Frauenstr / abt six blks on R*

[The interior was sympathetically renovated in 1970, when the original fixed pews
were replaced by chairs, thereby necessi-
tating the new terrazzo floor, and the fresco
was painted on the proscenium above the
altar. The crucifixion behind it is original.]

One should, perhaps, mention the undisguised use of industrial glazing and the
early exposed and expressed concrete
frame – even if part of it is carefully formed
into Ionic columns. There was a time when
architectural historians would have doted
on such facts, while ignoring Fischer's
eclectic nationalism. But the Garnisonskirche is appealing precisely because
of the freedom with which it draws upon
a whole range of stylistic and historical
resources, as well as technological ones. It
requires skill – not just lack of inhibition – to
successfully blend Romanesque, Baroque,
Classical and Jugend elements in a church
which, presumably for nationalistic
reasons, ignores the Gothic, and thereby
in a sense a French tradition of church
planning, in favour of older, if less common,
Germanic-Romanesque precedents. If the
effects of all this manipulation do not
always seem handsome, or even on
occasion resolved, they are never dull.

Ulm D-64

* Hochschule für Gestaltung or
Neues Bauhaus (school of design)
1950–5
Grimmelfingerweg
Max Bill
Rationalism
*W from cathedral on Neue Str, through tunnel
→ FRIEDRICHSHAFEN/JUGEND-
HERBERGE / continue past same / R on
Grimmelfingerweg / L at Y / at top of hill*

[The 'New Bauhaus' closed in 1968. At
the time of writing the building was being
used by another school.]

This would-be reincarnation of the
Bauhaus clearly demonstrates that Max
Bill's years at Dessau had not been spent
learning from Gropius, but rather from his
Rationalist, Marxist successor, Hannes
Meyer. There had been something almost
monastic about the first Bauhaus. It had
been so self-sufficient, so conscious of its
separateness from the community, so
imbued with a mysticism that had gradually become a mystique. One strongly
senses that heritage in this school's picturesque disposition on its hill-top site, in
its almost Cistercian asceticism, and in Max
Bill's cold, logical form language.

Giengen-an-der-Brenz [*near Ulm*] D-65
* Fabrik Steiff (teddy bear works)
1902–8
Margarete-Steiff-Straße at Schwibbogen Platz
Richard Steiff
Industrial Vernacular
*E from Rt 19 (15 mi – 24 km N of Ulm)→
GIENGEN / → STADTMITTE / at town ctr*

There is only the generous simple iron
frame, braced with diagonal tie rods and
set between the widely spaced layers of a
totally double-glazed curtain wall – only
that and no more.

Had an architect designed and publicized

this, his small place in history would have been assured. Were the Fabrik Steiff a generation older, histories of the 'Modern Movement' would, one assumes, have recognized and canonized it as an unprecedented radical vernacular precursor. Structurally, and 'machine-aesthetically', this American-influenced stuffed animal factory is well in advance of Gropius's famous Fagus-Werke (D-36), which in any case it antedates by several years. And its curtain-wall system is technically superior even to that of his Bauhaus, which was built more than twenty years later.

Could it be, then, that for buildings, as with people, ultimately it is not always a matter of what you are, but of who you know? Or, at least, who knows you?

Amberg   **D-66**
Thomas Glas Fabrik (glassware factory) 1967–70
TAC (The Architects' Collaborative)
Neo-Expressionism
E from Amberg ctr on Rt 85 (→ REGENS-BURG) 1 mi (1.6 km) past circle / R on Barbarastr / bear R across Leopoldstr on to Bergsteig / visible from end of rd on R

Even though TAC was founded by Walter Gropius, one senses here no real kinship with his epochal role in establishing the International Style. Despite arguments that its monumental hut-like form is designed to vent hot gases, this self-contained, 'temple-in-the-landscape' factory seems peculiarly American – or, at least, not particularly European. It is at once prettily abstract and arrogantly indifferent to site and circumstances. It is an ideogram that can too easily be understood from a single vantage point.

Donaustauf [near Regensburg]   **D-67**
* **Walhalla** (monument to the nation's heroes) 1814–42
Leo von Klenze
Neo-Classicism
E from Regensburg on autobahn E5 (7 mi – 11 km) → WALHALLA

Following the Napoleonic Wars, Germany was swept by a wave of nationalism. There were many calls for the erection of pantheons and national monuments to victory, or at least to liberation. Existing sentiment for the development of a 'Germanic' architecture was greatly reinforced. But what was to be its style?

Naturally there was a strong pro-Gothic camp. Beginning in the 1840s under Prussian sponsorship, it undertook the completion of Cologne Cathedral (D-48a) as a national shrine. Surprisingly, there was also an older (D-26a-c) and perhaps more numerous pro-Greek school. Their argument – not entirely unlike those of their American Greek Revivalist counterparts – suggested that, in addition to possible racial links, ancient Greece and modern Germany had each achieved something akin to cultural perfection. Therefore, it was held, the architectures of the two cultures ought to be as similar as the unavoidable differences in costume, climate and needs would allow. Walhalla – the Parthenon with an iron roof – perfectly embodies this ideal.

Despite the massiveness of its base, Walhalla seems to hang in the misty air above the Danube. Sited and seen as no true Greek

temple ever was, it is the Parthenon transformed. If not uniquely German, it is at least distinctly modern. And its name, superficially so inappropriate, somehow changes the way one sees this pure, most iconic of architectural paradigms. In this place it is no longer 'Greek', but rather the Walhalla of Nordic mythology.

D-67a Just outside Regensburg itself are some impressive, system-built structures housing the **Mathematics** and **Medical Faculties** of the University of Regensburg, 1967–71, by Heinle, Wischer & Partner. Although not friendly or cosy, they are a significant improvement on the huge, impersonal structures typical of the new universities built in Germany during the 60s. *S from Regensburg ctr or REGENS-BURG SUD exit of E5 → UNIVERSITÄT*

Munich (*München*)   **D-68**
* **Alte Pinakothek** (museum
reconstruction) 1945–57
Theresienstraße and Barerstraße
Hans Döllgast
Neo-Classicism
*N from inner (Altstadt) ring rd on Ludwigstr
/ L on Theresienstr / abt four blks on L*

Here is one of the relatively few postwar
German reconstructions that does not want
to deny the fact or effects of war – either
through total restoration or total modernization. Instead, the breached masonry of
Leo von Klenze's original elegant façade,

1826–36, has been repaired with simple
brickwork of a similar colour, thereby
lightly and poignantly suggesting, like an
artist's sepia cartoon of a long vanished
painting, the façade's now lost eloquence.

Equally interesting, if for different
reasons, is the more radical reconstruction
of von Klenze's bombed and gutted interior.
Its stark new lobby and vast, bifurcated
monumental stairway – built in place of
one originally located in an end pavilion –
have an abstract spatial grandeur that
Louis Kahn, and perhaps Mussolini, might
well have appreciated.

Munich (*München*)   **D-69**
Villa Stuck (house-studio, now
municipal museum) 1897–8
Prinzregentenstraße 60
Franz von Stuck
Neo-Classicism
*E from inner ring rd → MÜNCHEN-OST on
Prinzregentenstr / on S side of st beyond
river and angel monument*

The longer one studies the complex tapestry of *fin-de-siècle* architecture, the more
of its previously unnoticed but none the less
critical threads become apparent. One such
thread was a revival of interest in Greek –
as distinct from Roman or Renaissance –
Classicism. This interest had begun with
the birth of archaeology in the eighteenth
century (I-54a, b) and has periodically
reappeared during times of political and/or
artistic crisis. Occasionally it has provided
models that were directly copied (D-67).
More often it has been an indirect source of
inspiration (F-28) or just one among many.

In the 1890s, when the German academic Neo-Baroque had become a stale

formula, this enthusiasm for Greek art
again began to reassert itself. Franz von
Stuck's villa was only one product of that
renewed interest. Significantly perhaps,
Stuck was not an architect. He was a
painter whose involvement with the mystical Symbolist movement led, quite naturally, to an interest in things archaic. This
is not to say that he was concerned with
mere archaeological correctness, nor was
he attempting only to escape into the past.
Far from it. His rich polychromatic interiors
are as much Pompeian as Greek, while his
obvious concern for honesty and integrity
of materials reflects the most progressive
nineteenth-century attitudes.

Histories of modern architecture could,
and have, ignored the likes of this strange,
rather idiosyncratic house. But, just as the
medieval enthusiasms of William Morris's
generation helped lay the groundwork for
the familiar Arts and Crafts side of the Art
Nouveau (GB-39), so this sort of archaism
ushered in its equally important radical
Classicist variant (A-4).

Munich (München)   **D-70**
** Olympische Sportstätten
(Olympic park) 1968–72
Lerchenauer Straße and Petuelring
Günter Behnisch, Jürgen Joedicke, *et al.*,
with Frei Otto
NW from Munich ctr on Dachauer Str →
OLYMPIA-TURM / *in Oberwiesenfeld park
just W of tower*

Behnisch and Joedicke's competition-winning design is based almost entirely on Frei Otto's dramatic and all but proprietary tension structures. Otto, an engineer, must therefore take most of the credit, or criticism, for this enormous, expensive symbol of Germany's postwar economic and social rehabilitation.

It is tempting to suggest that this, the ultimate steel and plastic big top, is also symbolic of our century. Certainly no other period could have computer-calculated and hand-crafted so permanent an incarnation of so impermanent a structural type: a tent created for a few days' use, yet meant to last indefinitely.

D-70a To the north, across Petuelring, is the **Olympisches Dorf** (Olympic village), 1968–72, by Heinle, Wischer & Partner.

D-70b Directly to the east across Lerchenauer Straße from the Olympisches Dorf is Karl Schwanzer's distinctive **BMW corporate headquarters**, 1969–70.

Of course, it is mere coincidence that this isolated, distinctive, legless tower marks the location of BMW's motor-museum – which just happens to be adjacent to the Olympic park.

D-70c Frei Otto's office (**Institut für leichte Flächentragwerke**) at Stuttgart University is housed in a test section for his first large tent, the West German Pavilion at Montreal's Expo 67. Its original fabric covering has since been replaced by wooden sheathing and slates – an absurd-seeming substitution that actually looks quite reasonable, thereby saying much about the true nature of these structures. *SW from Stuttgart ctr →* VAIHINGEN / → ELTINGEN / *L at roundabout (Schattenring)* / → UNIVERSITÄT / *R at Universitäts Str / first R / on L*

Dachau [near Munich]   **D-71**
* Versöhnungskirche (church of
atonement) 1964–7
Konzentrationslager
Helmut Striffler
*NW from Munich ctr on Dachauer Str abt
13½ mi (22 km)* / → KZ-GEDENKSTÄTTE *to
camp / near crematorium*

Here one sees the terror beneath civi-

lization's mantle: it is logically efficient.

Ultimately, as words fail, so too must architecture. One cannot commemorate the victims of inhumanity. These cascading steps and curving walls are meant to be a relief from the surrounding deathly orthogonal order, even as the earth into which they lead gave final relief to tens of thousands who found themselves here.

Schaftlach [near Munich]   **D-72**
* Heilig-Geist-Kirche (church)
1964–7
H. B. von Busse
Neo-Vernacular
*S from E11 (at Holzkirken) on Rt 318 / R
at* SCHAFTLACH, *through village and across
RR / third L on to Fockensteinstr / one blk
on L*

New wooden buildings are rare in
Europe, even in those areas where timber
abounds. But that is not the only reason
this shed-roofed pine box seems so very
American in the manner of San Francisco's
1960s revived Bay Region style. Consider
only the way in which it makes 'architecture' of such structural 'necessities' as
the spidery king-post roof trusses, and of
the great laminated girder/gutter that
carries both the trusses, and the row of
sliding barn-type doors that discreetly
allows holy day expansion.

Granted the props supporting the side
walls seem self-consciously expedient, as do
the braces which 'architecturalize' the large
free-standing exterior cross. Yet, somehow,
such over-indulgences are not out of place.

The most American quality, however, is
also the least tangible: a peculiarly rich,
resinous aroma that evokes all the summer
camps, mountain lodges, or weekend
cabins one has never known.

Füssen [near Garmisch-Partenkirchen] **D-73**
** Neuschwanstein (Bavarian royal
palace-cum-sham castle) 1868–92
Eduard Riedel with Christian Jank
(1868–74), Georg Dollmann (1874) and
Julius Hofmann (1884–92)
Neo-Gothic/National Romantic
S from Rt 17, 2½ mi (4 km) E of Füssen →
HOHENSCHWANGAU *(another palace) /
Neuschwanstein is at top of hill, abt ½ mi
(1 km) (rd closed to private cars)*
[Never completed.]

Mad King Ludwig's archetypal Dis-
neyland castle: the ultimate Gothick folly,
the ultimate descendant of Marie An-
toinette's escapist Petit-Hameau at Versailles. Beyond the magnificence of the setting or the ambition of the undertaking,
one is struck by the completeness of the
conception – and the self-deception. The
pervasive unreality of the place is clearly
dependent upon a 'total design' ethic, not
unlike that which was to flourish to excess
at the turn of the century and then to return
again, in various guises, during Weimar
Germany's descent into the abyss.

Neuschwanstein is essentially a monument to, and setting for, Richard Wagner's
Teutonic 'music dramas' – total designs of
another sort that assumed the complete

dedication of all who became involved with
them. Not surprisingly, Ludwig's Par-
sifalian retreat exudes a Nietzsche-like
'artist-as-cult-hero' mythos, wherein the
royal patron's persona becomes confused
with those of his artist client's creations.

DENMARK

Denmark   Map DK-1

Ålborg · 19a
DK DENMARK
19-20 Århus
Fåborg · 5a
D GERMANY
S SWEDEN
S-29
S-28
Klippan
Fredensborg · 15a
18 Humlebæk
2-17 Copenhagen (København)

Denmark (Danmark)   DK-1

Danish architecture tends to be conservative – not reactionary, but thoughtfully, cautiously conservative. Despite being the link between Europe and the rest of Scandinavia, and despite longstanding ties with the world at large, Denmark has shown a remarkable degree of architectural insularity over the years. During the whole of the nineteenth century and well into the twentieth, Classicism prevailed here. At the turn of the century the profession's reaction against Art Nouveau, Jugendstil and Finland's National Romanticism was so strong that Danish architectural students were forbidden to study, much less design, in these modes. This is not to imply that the Danes do not care about good design, architectural or otherwise: it was Denmark that gave us Steen Eiler Rasmussen, one of the century's most sensitive observers of the built environment. And postwar Den-

mark's decorative arts long set the standard for simple, humane modernism. But, unlike the turn-of-the-century Jugendstil silverwork of Georg Jensen, Danish furniture and interior design of the 50s have not retained their original fresh appeal.

Between the wars Danish architecture slipped almost directly from Neo-Classicism into that peculiarly Scandinavian vision of an unaggressive, unpolemical, almost vernacular modernity, without ever really having succumbed to the International Style. Since the war the chief influences here have been – for reasons which remain not completely clear – Mies van der Rohe and the Japanese vernacular, with the latter sometimes being startlingly paraphrased. Denmark is by no means devoid of interesting modern buildings, but do not look for a Danish Asplund or Erskine, much less an Aalto.

Language note In an effort to rationalize spelling, the Danes are converting from the use of Å and Ø to Aa and Ö. However, the older forms still persist under certain circumstances. Both versions have therefore been used as encountered. Also, in any Danish alphabetical listing, æ, Å or Aa, and Ø or Ö, follow Z.

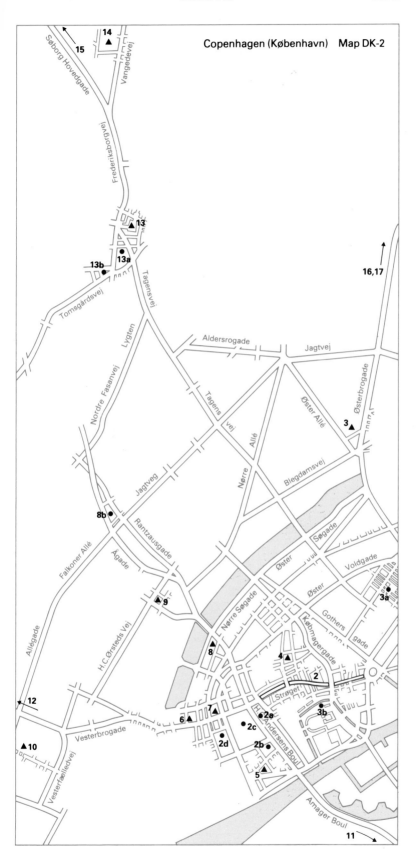

Copenhagen (København) Map DK-2

Copenhagen (København)   DK-2

Copenhagen was one of the first cities to ban cars from parts of its core, thereby making a pedestrian precinct out of the intimately scaled old shopping district. Collectively called Strøget, this sequence of narrow, shop-lined streets extends about half a mile from the Rådhuspladsen to the peacefully wooded Kongens Nytorv square. It also opens out unexpectedly at intervals into several other busy urban squares.

DK-2a Martin Nyrop's huge National Romantic **Rådhuset** (city hall), 1888–1905, at Rådhuspladsen, is one of the earliest Scandinavian examples of this genre.

DK-2b South-east from the Rådhuset on H. C. Andersens Boulevard is Jens Vilhelm Dahlerup's **Ny Carlsberg Glyptoteket** (art museum), 1892–7, whose façade is as assertively articulated as its name. And if

Art Nouveau never found favour in *fin-de-siècle* Copenhagen, that did not mean everything was just business as usual. The Glyptoteket's rear façade, 1901–6, by Hack Kampmann – architect of the police headquarters (DK-5) – has overtones both of Otto Wagner's radical Neo-Classicism and of the other fancies and follies erected by its beer baron patron (DK-10).

DK-2c Between these two turn-of-the-century monuments to earnest fantasy stands a triumph of nineteenth-century escapism: **Tivoli** (gardens), begun 1843, is one of Europe's unique experiences.

DK-2d Just south-west of Tivoli is the **Hovedbanegården** (central station), 1904–11, by H. Wenck. Its provincial Richardsonian façade hides an appealing, spacious grand concourse.

Copenhagen (København)   DK-3
Lægeforeningens Boliger (medical society housing) 1853–5
between Øster Allé and Østerbrogade
Gottlieb Bindesbøll
Rationalism
Map DK-2

This little 'village', an early attempt at the reformation of housing standards and a counterstroke to the high-density tenements being put up elsewhere in the city, was built on a then recently levelled section of Copenhagen's old fortifications. To modern eyes the spatial standards of the medical society's dwellings may seem impossibly minimal – although the typical Danish house is still diminutive by American standards. Perhaps more surprising, the toilets were not and still are not within the apartments. They, along with the

laundry, are shared. There are also communal meeting rooms, a kindergarten and shops.

DK-3a The immediate impetus for the medical society's housing reform efforts may have been partially English (there were some much publicized model workers' dwellings at the 1851 Crystal Palace Exhibition), but Copenhagen does have at least one remarkable precedent of its own for this sort of housing. The still extant **Nyboder area** was begun as a unified development as early as 1631. The original two-storey form can be seen at Skt Paulsgade 21–40.

DK-3b Quite another side of Bindesbøll is revealed in his romantically Neo-Classical **Thorvaldsens Museum**, 1839–48, at Porthusgade 2.

Copenhagen (København)   **DK-4**
* Universitets Biblioteket
(university library) 1857–61
Frue Plads and Fiolstræde
Johan Daniel Herholdt
Rationalism
Map DK-2

Of some significance in terms of local architectural history, this sturdy brick box is equally pleasing to mind and senses. Not surprisingly, its ancestry is primarily foreign, the cast-iron stacks probably having been inspired by Henri Labrouste's Bibliothèque Ste-Geneviève (F-11) and the rich but 'honest' brickwork deriving from Gothic Rationalist theory.

With its attenuated columns, old wood and older bindings, the stack room is indeed appealing, but there is true excitement in the monumental staircase. Although not really warranted by the entrance hall below, nor by the reading rooms above, this grand gesture none the less dominates the building, expansively filling the small space into which it is fitted. In fact, as if in self-justification, the structure of stair and building are so thoroughly integrated that they could not be separated without causing both to collapse. Thus a colonnade that grows out of the stairs first carries the upper-level floor, and then becomes an arcade-cum-railing around the top of the stairwell. The effect is reminiscent of the work of Herholdt's Philadelphian contemporary, Frank Furness – but gentler.

Copenhagen (København)   **DK-5**
Politigården (police headquarters)
1918–24
Hambrosgade and Niels Brocks Gade
Hack Kampmann, Åge Rafn, *et al.*
Mannered Neo-Classicism
Map DK-2

One wonders at the praise given this building by Steen Eiler Rasmussen, who usually had so deep a concern for the humanity of architecture and the built environment. This is so surreally unhospitable a place, full of mannerist proportions and details which, by their nature, must be at variance with the human scale. Had it been built as a pantheon or a war memorial, or as the police headquarters of a police state, one might argue that the architects had served the usual conventions admirably, and nowhere more so than in the two public courtyards: the open circular one, with its recollections of Charles V's palace in Granada, and beyond it the smaller impressively oppressive atrium.

The interior is more of the same – only different. Long corridors lined with identical doors of inhuman proportions end inevitably in round chambers from which lead other corridors. Occasionally, as one crosses an important axis, that fact will be marked over a door by some plaster embellishment, which, like other interior details, disconcertingly suggests the 30s decor of a Jean Harlow movie.

Some may find it witty. It *is* coldly elegant and it seems also to raise again the question of the compatibility of *Neo*-Classicism and democracy.

DK-5a The other well-known Danish contribution to Scandinavia's Neo-Classical revival is Carl Petersen's **Fåborg museum,** 1912–15, in Fåborg, a small town on the island of Fyn.

Copenhagen (København)   **DK-6**
Vesterport (offices and shops) 1930–2
Vesterbrogade 8
O. Falkentorp & P. Baumann
Map DK-2

Like Gunnar Asplund's Stockholm Public
Library (S-7), Vesterport exactly marks the
point of transition to 'modernism'. Unlike
Asplund's work, it is the sort of building
that could have been dressed up in any of
the inappropriate, borrowed clothes that
were common to the period. Instead, it is
sheathed in a handsomely extravagant
copper curtain wall which can be seen to
best advantage on the acutely angled rear
corner of the building.

DK-6a Den Permanente, the shop to
the left of the entrance, displays and sells
items of Danish design that have been selec-
ted for the store by a jury process.

DK-6b The **Astoria Hotel** across the
street was built by Falkentorp two years
later, 1933–5. By then the time of transition had definitely passed, but Falkentorp's concern for materials had not.
The Astoria is not stuccoed. It is entirely of
poured concrete, including the interesting
staircase at its opposite end.

Copenhagen (København)   **DK-7**
SAS Royal Hotel 1960
Vesterbrogade at Hammerischsgade 1
Arne Jacobsen
Late International Style
Map DK-2

More impressive when built than now,
and more so to Europeans than to Americans, its spirit and overall form strongly
evoke New York's once startling, now
almost forgotten, Lever House.

Time has not been kind to this sort of
architecture. No longer the new crystalline
prism glistening in an archaic world of
meaningless masonry, today it seems only
to have been the first harbinger of onrush-
ing tackiness. Nor, at least in this instance,
has it aged with grace. Years of dirt and
reality are far too apparent upon the
previous, flimsily immaterial interior surfaces. Because there is so little else to look
at, one is just that much more aware of
grimy streaks emanating from once hidden
air diffusers or of greasy stains on elegantly
sculptural, free-form leather chairs.

Copenhagen (København)   **DK-8**
Vestersøhus (apartments) 1935–9
Vester Søgade and Gyldenløvesgade
Kay Fisker & C. F. Møller
International Style/Scandinavian
Empiricism

Map DK-2

The power of this long uninterrupted
rhythmic façade demonstrates what can be
achieved through simple repetition – if the
basic elements are good enough. Not that
it is quite as simple as that. There are two

interlocking rhythms here, the basic balcony-bay module and a double module,
served by a single entrance at its base and
capped by a longer balcony at its top. At a
still larger scale, these upper balconies also
tend to read as a continuous cornice, unifying the building as a whole.

Copenhagen (København)　　　　　DK-9
H. C. Ørsteds Vej 54 (post office and
flats) 1939
Edvard Thomsen
International Style
Map DK-2

With its angled balcony bays and bright
yellow tiles – yellow and red are the Danish
Post Office colours – this is, for Copenhagen,
a lively, innovative little building. Above
the Post Office, two stories of apartments
employ an interesting variation of the balcony-bay system. Here, in contrast to the
large sheets of glass so highly prized at the
time, are external glass-block walls resting
on concrete spandrels that rise about thirty
inches above the floor line: an arrangement
which retains heat, allows greater flexibility
in the location of furniture, and yet admits
light generously.

The form of the balconies is also different,
if not unique. It offers openness and projection on its two outer sides, while retaining a sense of privacy, despite floor-to-
ceiling glass, on its two inner sides. Here,
then, is the 'destruction of the box' which
the International Style's corner windows,
roof terraces, *piloti*, and such were supposed to achieve. And it is imaginatively
accomplished in difficult circumstances,

Copenhagen (København)　　　　　DK-10
* **Elefanttaarnet** (elephant
tower/bridge) 1901
Dipylon (double-arched bridge) 1892
Ny Carlsbergvej
Hack Kampmann
Gothic Revival and Indian Revival
Map DK-2

From time to time a *nouveau-riche* merchant prince – or, as in Mr Carlsberg's case,
a beer baron – spends his money on some
fanciful caprice so devoid of 'taste' that no
one else would have built it, and so much
fun that it needs no further justification.

Around the corner, at Gyldenløvesgade 19, is the **Byggecentrum,**
a permanent display of Danish building
materials and techniques.

An earlier, 1922, Neo-Classical
housing scheme by Fisker is the
Hornbækhus flats at Ågade 126–134.

not just mindlessly suggested as was then
so frequently the case.

Unfortunately the upper floors lack the
same imagination, although the topmost at
least is surely a later addition.

Elefanttaarnet

Copenhagen (København)   **DK-11**
* **Skolen ved Sundet** (open-air school)
1934–8
Samosvej and Sumatravej
Kaj Gottlob
Scandinavian Empiricism
SE on Amager Boul (Map DK-2→) ⇨
*Amagerbrogade / L following tram-line
on to Holmbladsgade / R following tram on
to Østrigsgade / L on to Samosvej / in
second blk on R*

The Skolen ved Sundet (school by the
Sound) was but one of several such almost
diagrammatically functional schools (F-44,
NL-16) that grew out of an international
movement for the fresh-air treatment of
'delicate' or, more specifically, in this case
tubercular children. The south-facing glass
wall of the main classroom wing is organized into a series of bays, the module of
the ground-floor classrooms being carried

through the upper floor. The entire second
level of this wing is a solarium, equipped
with built-in cots and accessible by ramp.
In good weather all of the glazing of both
floors, essentially the entire south wall, can
be moved out of the way in sections. There
is also a courtyard between the classroom
wing and a service wing, which serves as a
sheltered play space in the frequently windy
weather here.

Now, with the virtual disappearance of
TB, the school is used for brain-damaged
children who are said to respond well to
the sentitivity of the original design.

DK-11a The more conventional **school**
across the street was built by Gottlob at the
same time. It is of the characteristically
Scandinavian hall type, in which the
classrooms are organized around a large,
balconied, two-storey interior court.

Copenhagen (København)/Vigerslev   **DK-12**
* **Hanssted Skole** (elementary school)
1954–8
Vigerslevvej and Rødbyvej 2
F. C. Lund & Hans Christian Hansen
Semi-Japanese
*W on Vesterbrogade (Map DK-2→) to Ålholm
Plads (oversize traffic-light in ctr of rd) / L
on Ålholmvej / second R, at circle on to
Vigerslevvej / three blks on L*

The Hanssted Skole reflects the best
postwar Danish architectural thought and
temperament. Fitted on to a tight suburban
site on a busy street, it makes the most of
its situation by spreading out in two wings:
one, containing those functions less likely
to be bothered by traffic, borders the street;

the other, containing the classrooms, faces
a quiet, landscaped buffer area between the
school and some neighbouring houses. The
acute angle formed by these wings shelters
a play area, perhaps the school's best space.

One senses that in spirit – not style – this
building seems to want to be Japanese, as
much as anything, but in a way quite
unlike so many other contemporary Danish
buildings. There is no mindless imitation
here. This is just what architecture should
be: materials, detailing, plans and elevations working together, not to project the
easy unity of simple forms that hides unresolved problems, but rather to create the
natural unity that comes from having
solved them.

Copenhagen (København)/Bispebjerg **DK-13**
* **Grundtvigs Kirken** (church and
housing) 1918–40
Tagensvej 256
P. V. Jensen-Klint and Kåre Klint
Baltic Style (National
Romantic)/Expressionism
Map DK-2

What else could possibly measure up to
that carefully calculated first view of this
upthrusting crystalline brick tower,
especially as seen in the low sun of a late
summer evening?

It is arguable whether this memorial
to Father Grundtvig, the founder of the
Danish Christian nationalist folk high-
school movement, is more nationalist
or Expressionist. Clearly it has a far greater
intensity than the surrounding houses or
even than its own nave. It would be
remarkable were it otherwise. The monu-
ment-tower could be shaped almost solely
by aesthetic considerations, whereas the
other parts had to fulfil functional needs,
and in the case of the housing had to do so
on a far tighter budget. Also with time
Jensen-Klint, and later during the 30s his
son Kåre, may well have become more concerned with, and inhibited by, a concern
for historical stylistic accuracy. But, then,
could anyone, except perhaps Gaudí –
creator of the greatest of all modern Chris-
tian-nationalist monuments (E-11) – have
maintained such a pitch of intensity over a
period of twenty-two years?

DK-13a Just down the street, on Fred-
eriksborgvej (paralleling the cemetery),
between Jacob Lindbergsvej and Tuborgvej,
is the **Bispeparken housing area,**
1940–2, by Kåre Klint, M. L. Stephensen,
K. Thorball, Knud Hansen, Vagn Kaastrup
and Friedrich Wasner. Here a rigorously
functional version of the balcony-bay
system has been incorporated organically
into buildings that rely on a palette of traditional forms and materials.

DK-13b Diagonally across Frederiks-
borgvej from Bispeparken, (just south of
the cemetery) is one of Denmark's earlier
modernist housing schemes, the **Stor-
gården flats,** 1935, by Povl Baumann
and Knud Hansen.

Copenhagen (København)/Søborg   **DK-14**
* **Munkegårdsskolen** (school)
1952–6
Vangedevej 178
Arne Jacobsen
Map DK-2

Possibly Jacobsen's best building. Unlike
most of his other postwar works, the detailing is reasoned and substantial. Nor has the
programme been forced into some abstract
package.

The classrooms are the essence and the
building blocks of the scheme. The school,
designed around the classrooms' special
programmatic requirements, is a grid of
major and minor corridors with pairs of
well-lit classrooms sharing large court-
yard-teaching spaces in the grid's interstices. It is these outdoor classrooms, each
individually landscaped yet consistent with
its fellows, to which the Munkegårdsskolen
owes its substantial reputation.

Copenhagen (København)/Bagsværd **DK-15**
Bagsværd Kirke (church) 1974–6
Bagsværd Hovedgade 189–91
Jørn Utzon
NW on Søborg Hovedgade (Map DK-2→) ⇨
Buddinge Hovedgade ⇨ *Bagsværd
Hovedgade* / *at Taxvej*

Jørn Utzon's name inevitably conjurs up
images of the great, heaped-up shell forms
of the Sydney Opera House. There are also
recollections of the false starts and compro-
mises that eventually led to his dis-
association from that national monument –
all stemming from the ill-conceived notion
that such a huge structural form (and functionally complex building) could be based
on a simple, scaleless competition sketch
from the opposite side of the globe.

How different, and how comfortably at
home, is this little suburban church. Its
blank, but ever so subtly Aalto-
ornamented, pre-cast concrete walls, and
the corrugated aluminium that covers its
tall nave, almost suggest an industrial or
agricultural building. But there are also
echoes of the nationalistic, stepped gable
walls of Utzon's earlier Fredensborg
housing (DK-15a) – thickened to become
glass-roofed corridors – and echoes, as well,
of the postwar Danish enthusiasm for
Japanese vernacular (DK-12). Between the
two corridor-walls, the nave is spanned by
exquisitely crafted, boardmarked, poured-
in-place concrete thin shells. Revived here
with great elegance and authority, they
recall the wooden ceilings in Aalto's Viipuri
Library (now in the USSR) and the Scandinavian tradition of wooden vaulting in
churches. Unfortunately, other aspects of
the interior are less convincing.

DK-15a Utzon's only notable earlier work
in Denmark is an area of **cluster housing
for the elderly**, 1962–3, at Fredensborg.
Its careful brickwork, fretted, tile-capped
gables, and familiar picturesque massing
strongly recall the Baltic Style – Denmark's
particular brand of National Romanticism
(DK-13). *S of Fredensborg on A6* / → SLOT
(palace) on Slotsgade / *on L*

Copenhagen (København)/Hellerup **DK-16**
Blidahpark (housing) 1932–4
*Strandvejen, between Phistersvej and
Maglemosevej*
Ivar Bentsen, *et al.*
International Style
N on Østerbrogade (Map DK-2→) ⇨
*Strandvejen (rd nearest water) abt 4½ mi
(7 km)* / *on W side of st*

Although its blocks of flats are all aligned
in rigid echelon formation, Blidahpark surprisingly makes quite an amiable
impression. This is mainly because of the
curving access street and the juxtaposition
of buildings that, although programmatically and stylistically similar, were
designed by different architects. Also,
because they were built well, avoiding
period clichés, the buildings have generally
aged with a certain grace, which is more
than one can say for most 'advanced'
housing schemes of the time.

Copenhagen (København)/ DK-17
Klampenborg
Søholm (row houses) 1950–5
Strandvejen 413
Arne Jacobsen
Scandinavian Empiricism
N on Østerbrogade (Map DK-2 →) ⇨ Strandvejen abt 7½ mi (12 km) / on L where rd runs along shore

It is difficult to believe that these houses, so different in feeling from the rest of his work, were really designed by Jacobsen. Possibly because he lived here himself, he forewent his usual slickness and simplicity of form to explore the picturesque possibilities of naturally textured materials and fragmented massing, as experienced in the fogs that frequently drift in off the sea.

DK-17a Søholm is part of a larger development begun by Jacobsen in the early 30s. Proceeding north along Strandvejen one encounters the **Ved Bellevue Bugt flats,** 1961, which are attached to the **Bellavista flats,** 1933, and beyond them what was originally a summer **theatre** and **restaurant,** 1937, now converted into a cinema and flats.

Humlebæk DK-18
** **Louisiana Museum** 1958, 1968–71, 1975, 1978–82
Gammel Strandvej 13
Jørgen Bo & Vilhelm Wohlert, with Niels Halby (1978–82)
Late International Style
E of coast rd (not A3) abt 6 mi (10 km) S of Helsingør / → signs

[The original museum and an auditorium addition, 1975, are to the rear of the site. The newer galleries are nearer the road: 1968–71 to the left of old house, 1978–82 to the right.]

It is the earliest galleries that shaped the unique spirit of this place. In them one meets that strangely self-contradictory final phase of the International Style which so strongly emphasizes plan and programme, yet treats overall form almost as a kind of sculptural exercise. At times it becomes definable as architecture only because plate glass completes the enclosure of the internal spaces. The origin of this approach probably lies in the Bauhaus 'basic design' teaching technique, which stresses, among other things, the concept of abstract design, in abstract surrogate materials, as a way of preparing the student for designing buildings – or doorknobs, or cities. Theoretically this allows the student to make the transition to organizing real buildings with real materials without the 'hindrance' of any architectural-historical preconceptions. Unfortunately, it also creates a tendency to treat buildings as if they were only cardboard models blown up to full size. Materials are painted or stained or plastered so as to obscure their true nature, while structure must fit in as best it can – one side of a roof being carried on solid masonry even as the other is propped up by minimal steel columns hidden in the framework of a glass wall.

These observations may sound like a condemnation of this particular building. Surprisingly, they are not. The lush surroundings, the sympathy of the programme to this approach, and the architects' undeniable skills, all combine to make this museum a delight. It never dominates its contents or its site, yet it retains a distinctive character of its own.

Praise is also due to the sculpture garden by landscape architect Ole Nørgård, despite its somewhat dissimilar character.

Århus   **DK-19**
* **Rådhus** (town hall) 1937–42
Rådhus Pladsen
Arne Jacobsen & Erik Møller
Scandinavian Empiricism
→ CENTRUM, *until tower is visible* /
→ TOURISTINFORM

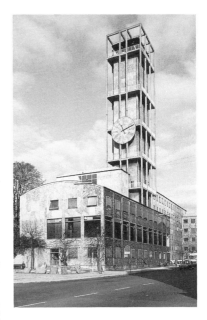

There is something uniquely Scandinavian about this sort of modern mannered Neo-Classicism – something beyond a foreshadowing of the cold sterility that was to vitiate most of Jacobsen's later works (DK-7). It is the sense of a disturbing surrealism: of Kafka's dark world, of the vistas and spaces of Piranesi's prison drawings, of the sets for the film *Metropolis*. As with other early Jacobsen works, the debt to Gunnar Asplund is particularly obvious in the detailing. But there is also a certain spiritual kinship between the romantic sensibility that gave rise to the stairs which disappear up and around the drum of Asplund's Stockholm library (S-7) and the almost penitentiary-like balconies and staircase within the light-well of the office block here – even if the direct prototype of this part can be found in Copenhagen's town hall (DK-2a). The most telling comparison, however, is with Asplund's law courts at Göteborg (S-27). When that building and this are considered together it is immediately apparent that Asplund is the master and Jacobsen the disciple.

Incidentally, the tower was not part of the original design. It was added by Jacobsen at the insistence of the Århus city fathers, who could not conceive of a town hall without a tower – no more than the orthodox modernists of the time could have imagined there ever again being a role for such explicit traditional symbolism in architecture.

DK-19a In Ålborg, about 60 miles (100 km) north of Århus, is one of Alvar Aalto's less well-known buildings, the **North Jutland Museum of Modern Art**, 1958–72, at 50 Kong Christians Allé. *W from A10–E3 (Hobrovej/Vesterbro) abt 500 yds (m) S of city ctr*

Århus   **DK-20**
Århus Universitet (university) 1931–69
Nordre Ringgade at Langelandsgade
C. F. Møller (1931–69) with Kay Fisker (1931–7) & Povl Stegmann (1931–42)
Scandinavian Empiricism
N of Århus ctr on S side of A15–E3–A10, just where A15 splits off

What other modern university can claim to be the product of one architect working over a period of almost forty years? As might be expected, Møller's buildings here are very consistent in design, some might say to the point of being dull and, following a common Danish practice of the 30s (DK-16), they are also all rigidly aligned on a slight bias to both conventional solar orientation and to the course of a several-times-dammed stream that bisects this bucolic campus. Because most of the buildings are located around the periphery of the campus (in order to create its idyllic sense of isolation) this uniform alignment does at least help relate them one to another.

Most of the 'architecture' here is concentrated in the main building, a delightful if slightly mannered example of a consciously folksy style. With its graceful arcade and an outdoor amphitheatre sheltered against its ivy-clad wall, it forms a dramatic upper end to the stream valley. Inside is a corridor treated like an arbour, with subtly snaking brick paving, and an auditorium which might be more believable if viewed as a chapel.

SPAIN

Spain Map E-1

F
FRANCE

•13a
Comillas

Lourdes
• I-37a

F-28e
•
Carcassonne

F-64
▲

26c
■

22
Girona ■

E
SPAIN

Barcelona
△
Reus   2-21, 26b
24
25a   23
Gandesa ●   Vistabella
▲ 32-33   ▲ 25
Segovia   El Pinell
de Bray

▲ 27-31
Madrid

26 ▲
Calpe

Spain (España)   E-1

Spain is an assemblage of diverse political, cultural and economic areas. Symbolically central and dominating all – part nerve-centre, part parasite – is Madrid (E-27). Surrounding it, and extending almost to the Atlantic and Mediterranean coasts, is the Spain of countless legends and Baedekers, a land still standing with one foot planted firmly in the nineteenth century (while the other, too often, is in the eighteenth). It is a relatively unpopulated, under-developed, unspoiled land. That it remains so is not due to any conscious design. Physical and land-use planning as they are known elsewhere in Europe seem all but non-existent in Spain – except where tourist money is involved. Rather, the preservation of rural Spain stems from a medi-

eval system of land tenure and a lack of local urban opportunities. Together these tend to drive people from the undeveloped regions towards Madrid or the coasts. Provincial Spain, which includes most of the country's land mass and ancient landmarks, is, not surprisingly, almost devoid of noteworthy modern architecture.

Spain is also a peninsula and its long coastlines are subject to great development pressures. On the north and west, facing the Atlantic, are the mushrooming industrial towns: Bilbao, La Coruña, Santander, Oviedo, El Ferrol. These can recall the worst of nineteenth-century Britain's Black Country – every bit as unplanned and as devoid of architectural interest. Simultaneously the Mediterranean coast, whose unspoiled beauty once equalled that of the French and Italian rivieras, has, with them, become the Florida of Europe, complete with the same sort of architectural and environmental insensitivity.

Then, still having to be considered apart from the rest of the country, there is Barcelona (E-2), the intellectual, cultural and economic heart of a restive Catalonia and also modern Spain's major centre of architectural creativity.

Travel note The heavily used Mediterranean coast road, as well as the main routes radiating from Madrid, are in a reasonable condition. Other roads, or at least their paving, can all but disappear for stretches.

Language note One will occasionally encounter extended versions of family names, which reflect both the paternal and maternal lineages. Thus, instead of Gaudí, one might find Gaudí y Cornet or Gaudí Cornet or, in Catalan, Gaudí i Cornet.

Barcelona   E-2

Often independent (in fact if not in name); once the capital of a far-flung, if short-lived, Mediterranean empire; the last stronghold of the Second Republic, under which it had virtual autonomy; for long Spain's only industrial city and still its richest and most cosmopolitan, Barcelona has also produced most of Spain's noteworthy modern architecture.

The city's most distinctive feature, aside from its mountain-ringed, seaside location, is its extensive grid of large, bevel-cornered, square city blocks. This grid is the product of an ambitious expansion plan, drawn up by Ildefonso Cerdà in 1859, but based upon Spanish Renaissance practices. Its generous tree-shaded streets and the 'plazas' created at each intersection deserve much of the credit for making Barcelona an enjoyable, urbane city.

Barcelona's grid is a product of the golden age of her bourgeoisie: a period when the city, grown rich on textiles, was known as the Manchester of Spain. In those years Barcelona patronized not just Gaudí but literally dozens of architects whose combined talents, and the means put at their disposal, equalled those to be found anywhere in Europe – or in the most comparable American city, Chicago.

The First World War put an end to most building in Barcelona. Then came depression, revolution and half a dozen years of promise followed by civil war. Good fortune, abetted by nationalism and a respect for her artistic and cultural heritage, spared much of the city's gloriously reckless, *nouveau-riche* self-aggrandizement – from the war and then, inadvertently aided by political and economic circumstances, from the peace as well.

The breadth and vitality of 'Modernisme', or Arquitectura Modernista, Barcelona's brilliant if still somewhat enigmatic turn-of-the-century architectural efflorescence, is by now well recognized. Understandably, Modernisme is often considered just another of the many names for – or at best a national variant of – Art Nouveau. But it is more than that. As can clearly be seen even in Gaudí's work, Modernisme is highly variable and unpredictable. At times it can be identified with the archetypal biomorphic Art Nouveau of Paris, Nancy and Brussels. But there are also strong and often dominant strains of a Viollet-le-Duc-inspired Rationalism, of National Romanticism, and of a surprisingly persistent Victorian eclecticism – all bound together, perhaps misleadingly so, by a great concern for artistic handcraftsmanship.

Modernisme's, or at least Gaudí's, exact role in the development of twentieth-century architecture has long been a matter of some debate. Was the even faster-to-flower French Art Nouveau totally unaware of the dramatic earlier developments (E-3) south of the Pyrenees? And

what was the relationship of the later works of Gaudí and Jujol (E-11, 23) to German Expressionism?

Modernisme's strongest early foreign connections seem to have been with the English Arts and Crafts Movement, but there is no clear evidence that Catalan innovations travelled back to that source. It is said, however, that, as a young man in the sway of Arts and Crafts ideals and also trying to 'find himself', Walter Gropius made his way to Barcelona. There, guru-like, was Gaudí. Gropius went back to Germany inspired by Gaudí's holistic workshop method of design and infused with the strong sense of purpose that eventually led to the founding of the Bauhaus and, as some would have it, to architecture's 'new age' – possibly a somewhat chauvinistic Catalan version of events. But still, Gropius *did* come to Barcelona and he *did* know of Gaudí. Were there others? Barcelona's relationship with the rest of Europe (again like that of Chicago) remains little understood and, potentially, an enlightening area of future study.

After a long post-Civil War hiatus, in the 1960s Barcelona began to rediscover and reassert itself. At the same time, following the final collapse of the Functionalist hegemony, modern architecture began to rediscover the true richness of its own past – including Art Nouveau and Expressionism. The generation of Catalan architects who came of age in this ambience has for the most part tended to work within some sort of vaguely Mediterranean regionalist style, often more Italian in origin than Catalan.

E-2a Las Ramblas is a wide promenade, above a vaulted-over river, whose vitality makes it a quintessential urban experience. It is also punctuated by some delightful Art Nouveau shops of a sort which in other parts of the city are now finally beginning to fall victim to prosperity and the urge to modernize. *Metro: Fernando*

E-2b Facing the Plaza Nueva and the Cathedral is the **Col·legi d'Arquitectes** (Architects' Association), whose gallery mounts some of Europe's best temporary exhibitions of local contemporary and historical architecture. *Metro: Jaime I*

Language note The language of choice for Catalans on both sides of the Pyrenees is often Catalan – a blend of French and Spanish. Although the names of architects are given here in Catalan, the directions use Spanish because, at least until recently, only Spanish street names have been posted. One may expect, however, to encounter the names Diagonal and Granvía used in reference respectively to Barcelona's Avenida del Generalísimo Franco and Avenida José Antonio Primo de Rivera. (Under Franco every Spanish town with at least two streets had one of each.)

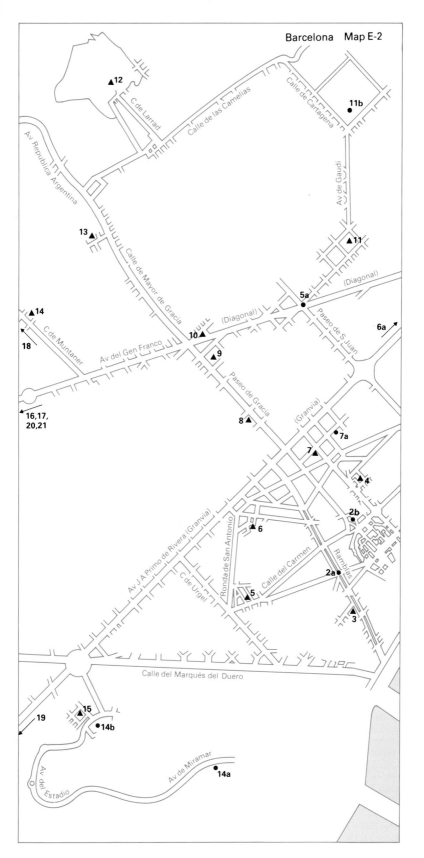

Barcelona   E-3
** Palau Güell (house, now theatre museum) 1885–9
Calle del Conde del Asalto 3–5
Antoni Gaudí
Neo-Mudéjar (National Romantic)
Map E-2 / Metro: Liceo

It is as if the ideas came to Gaudí as fast as he could get them built. Only then could he look at them and decide which to develop, which to drop, how to proceed.

The façade seems simple enough at first glance, with none of the Casa Vicens's (E-13) rash fragmentation and polychromy. For its day, it was remarkably coherent and regular. But then, in the centre, there is that pair of dramatic parabolic arches.

Gaudí was an excellent mathematician. He wanted to find those structural, i.e. masonry, forms which would most efficiently carry loads and would be seen to be doing so. (This was to become the major form-giving force in his work.) But these arches must be seen as more than just the theoretically optimal solution to what is, after all, a moderate stone span. Placed as they are, amongst tight neat rows of rectangular windows, and filled with vibrantly energetic iron grills, they are also tokens of the real innovations within.

Behind the façade, simplicity and regularity give way. The cellar, and especially its spiral horse ramp, is an orgy of exposed Catalan tilework, while above, in the house itself, a daringly attenuated parabolic dome covers a grand salon which also served as both chapel and concert hall. This dome, whose ultimate descendants were the towers of the Sagrada Família, incorporates Moorish elements, in particular the star-like perforations, within a structural form derived from African mud architecture. The smooth, sensual stone columns in this room – they too meld into tall parabolic arches – are another imaginative response to Moorish precedents. But they were to have no real place in Gaudí's later repertoire. On the rear façade an elaborate, starkly mechanistic-looking bay demonstrates the dramatic possibilities of an otherwise ordinary part of Barcelona's vernacular vocabulary (E-10). This minor triumph was also never developed further.

Finally, there is the first of Gaudí's many and ever more elaborate roofscapes – complete with his first tentative essays in sculptural forms and broken-tile mosaics.

Barcelona   E-4
** Palau de la Música Catalana
(concert hall) 1905–8
Alta de San Pedro 13
Lluís Domènech
Modernisme
Map E-2 / Metro: Urquinaona

Of all Gaudí's contemporaries – for whom patronage came, perforce, from the Establishment or not at all – Domènech was *the* Establishment architect. It was he who received the prestigious public commissions (E-1b), wherein a flamboyant display might be more highly valued than difficult-to-comprehend creativity.

And what a show he staged here: terracotta ornament in abstract patterns every bit as inventive as the best of Louis Sullivan's; acres of mosaic – sometimes combined with terracotta, sometimes cut into the brickwork; a great glittering viscous half-formed teardrop-shaped Tiffany-like skylight-chandelier suspended above the audience in the auditorium; half-arches tied back by some hidden restraint, defying gravity and common sense to support surprisingly conventional decorative lanterns; and the murals, some naive, some silly. Gilt, bronze and coloured glass are everywhere. So too are allusions to, and personifications of, music and Catalonia. There is so much ornament, so much decor, that it had to be

and looks like the work of many hands.

The site is tight and awkwardly shaped, particularly at the lobby end, and that, too, shows. This is, then, a building with many faults. But modesty, discretion and restraint are not among them. It is the sort of architecture that both made and killed Art Nouveau – and, now that it is safely dead, makes us delight in it again.

Barcelona   E-5
Església del Carme (church, parish
house, and school) 1910–14
Calle Antonio Abad and Calle Obispo Laguarda
Josep Maria Pericas
Rationalism
Map E-2
   [Locked except for Masses.]
   Despite certain appealing elements – the
honeycomb-topped school tower; the four
powerful exposed bays of the nave with
their undulating lower walls; and the hard,
moulded, engineering-type brickwork that
made both possible – despite all these and
more, in the end this building is a disappointment. Too many functions are
jammed into, and articulated on, this
almost medieval site. It cannot remain
coherent. And it seems a dead end, too,
a knowing, but powerless last stand of a
progressive regional style against external
forces – the architecture of which lost
causes are made, be they justified or no.

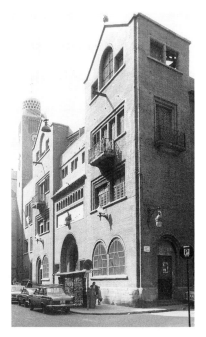

E-5a Pericas also designed the **Mossén
Jacinto Verdaguer monument,** 1913–
24, in the Plaza Verdaguer.

Barcelona   E-6
Dispensari Central Antituberculós
(tuberculosis clinic) 1934–8
Calle Torres Amat
Sert, Torres Clavé & Subirana
International Style
Map E-2 / Metro: Universidad
   Here, a few years after his Muntaner flats
(E-14) and no longer fresh from school and
his sojourn in Le Corbusier's office, Sert was
beginning to attempt to apply the Inter-
national Style's Functionalist tenets to
Catalonia's particular circumstances.

   The colour used here might once have
grated upon modernist sensibilities, and
even more so the grid of pollarded trees,
although they are most welcome in the
summer. This was only a first tentative
step towards the development of a modern
regional style. But for Spain's Civil War
there would have been others.

E-6a The credit for the TB clinic is sometimes given to a group known as
GATCPAC, of which Sert and Torres Clavé
were the prime movers. GATCPAC was

Catalonia's counterpart to CIAM, the Pan-
European Congrès Internationaux d'Architecture Moderne. Among other things,
GATCPAC operated the Republic's quasi-
official government planning and architectural agency. Its largest project, now
drastically altered and given over to military housing, was **Casa Bloc,** 1932–6, at
Paseo Torrás y Bages 105. *NE on Granvía
(Map E-2→) / N on Av de la Meridiana /
at* SAN ANDRÉS *exit straight on Calle de
Palomar two blks / R on Paseo Torrás y
Bages / on R*

Barcelona   E-7
* **Casa Sant Jordi** (offices and flats)
1929–31
Vía Layetana and Calle de Caspe
Francesc Folguera
Expressionism
Map E-2 / Metro: Urquinaona
   Casa Sant Jordi has not drawn much
attention over the years. But it is one of
interwar Europe's most quietly elegant
modern buildings.
   Basically, its design accords with Louis
Sullivan's Neo-Classical assumption that
the tall building is a metaphorical column.
It has a 'base' – the ground floor and, as
in Sullivan's work, a mezzanine. It has a
'shaft' – here six floors, evenly divided
between offices and flats but united by the
continuity of surface, by the projecting bays

(the 'fluting') and by the implication of a window grid. And it has a 'capital' – Sullivan's cornice-cum-attic, which here is the servants' hostel. To have used such a formula, under such potentially unsuitable circumstances, was a daring stroke. Yet, perhaps just because of the tension induced

Barcelona   **E-8**
** Casa Batlló (flats) 1904–6
Paseo de Gracía 43
Antoni Gaudí, with Josep Maria Jujol
Art Nouveau
Map E-2 / Metro: Aragón
[In that it is basically a remodelling of a building erected in 1874, Casa Batlló is not entirely Gaudí's work, but the transformation is so complete that it might as well have been.]
This is Gaudí's most conventionally Art Nouveau building and the building in which the hand of his chief collaborator Josep Jujol is most evident. The exterior ceramics, both front and rear, as well as the ironwork all seem to be Jujol's. But whether or just how Jujol's more apparent involvement with the Casa Batlló relates to its more overt Art Nouveau characteristics is still an open question.
Obviously this is one of modern architecture's most exciting demonstrations of colour as a means of architectural expression. Jujol's mosaics – like a glistening anticipation of a more impressionistic Joan Miró – are more coherent, if less spontaneous, than those on his better-known Park Güell benches (E-12). And within the public interior spaces there is another, very different use of ceramic colour. The combination light-and-stairwell is sheathed in simple blue tiles that subtly change in hue – from skylight to lobby – like a shaft of sunlight within a southern sea.

Barcelona   **E-9**
** Casa Milà or **'La Pedrera'**
(apartment building) 1905–10
Paseo de Gracía 92
Antoni Gaudí
Art Nouveau
Map E-2 / Metro: Diagonal
Here, once again, is Gaudí the disarming and unpredictable; Gaudí, who always disdained stucco, that mainstay of so many of his compatriots – and of most Art Nouveau architects. Seeking plasticity, he achieves effects in stone that they, with their easy stuccoed brickwork, could only suggest. But Gaudí has carved his façade as if from a single solid block! There is little he could have done with a cliffface that he has not achieved here by hollowing and undercutting this almost 'living' rock.
The two interior light courts reveal yet another Gaudí. Here the same loadbearing masonry is reduced to a minimum, and the inward-facing cylindrical façades read like curtain walls. Their function is not to shelter from the street's hot sun, but to give a maximum of light to kitchens and corridors. (There is also a rear façade opening on to the centre of the block.)
Sadly we are not accustomed to spirits who, so pragmatically yet with integrity,

by the differing window patterns between the stories of offices and those of flats, the more one studies Casa Sant Jordi the more one is convinced by it.

E-7a The **Casa Calvet**, 1898–1900, at Calle de Caspe 48, is by Gaudí.

E-8a Next door, at Paseo de Gracía 41, is Josep Puig's **Casa Amatller**, 1898-1900.

E-8b At Paseo de Gracía 35 is Lluís Domènech's **Casa Lleó Morera**, 1905.

can cultivate such varying attitudes within their work – much less within the same building. And if one stands back, across the intersection, it is possible to see in Casa Milà's roofscape a third, more familiar Gaudí.

Barcelona   **E-10**
* **Casa Comalat** (house) 1909–11
Calle de Corcega 316
Salvador Valeri
Art Nouveau
Map E-2 / Metro: Diagonal

Among the most successfully sensuous sculptural 'curtain walls' ever assembled, this façade is a party-wall-to-party-wall projecting bay created from a remarkably simple system of narrow roller-shuttered windows. Above it, the roof parapet is but extra frosting on the cake. Its sky-grabbing oculus accentuates the tension between the bifurcated upper parts of the bay. Only the provincial Art Nouveau ground floor, happily shaded by the bay, is something of a disappointment.

One might ask why this very effective curtain wall-bay device is not more widely used. In fact, Barcelona abounds with examples, but they almost all face the generally inaccessible interior courts of her large, hollow city blocks. This happens to be the rear and far more interesting façade of a building whose front is at Diagonal 442. (The rear façade of the Palau Güell, E-3, displays another equally inventive, if more machine-like, variation.)

Barcelona   **E-11**
*** **Temple Expiatori de la Sagrada Família** (church)
Plaza de la Sagrada Família
Antoni Gaudí
1883–93 (crypt and apse), 1891–1900 (nativity portals), 1903–26 (nativity towers), 1952–present (continuing work by others)
Gothic Rationalism
Map E-2 / Metro: Sagrada Família

[The construction site is open, for a fee, during working hours, and there is a public elevator in one of the towers. The present architects' atelier in the crypt may also be visited. It contains large plaster models of the church.]

Could anyone but Gaudí have built this incredible anachronism, in any city but the blend of the modern and the medieval that was his Barcelona? Gaudí was forced to accept an already constructed academic Gothic Revival crypt and ground plan. But upon these he envisioned an evolving series of design modifications, which were, he maintained, simply the result of his having developed the Gothic in accordance with modern advances both in mathematics and in the knowledge of materials and construction techniques. (Thus, for instance, in his later designs the nave pillars came increasingly to resemble multibranched trees.) This was consistent with both the Rationalist training that began his career and the Expressionist mood of his final version of the church. Gaudí also felt that, despite its almost medieval (now century-long) period of construction, the Sagrada Família was not to be the last of the old 'cathedrals' but the first of the new – which is how, in a secular age, he was able to build so convincing a religious work.

Following Gaudí's death in 1926, a group of younger architects finished the

three remaining, incomplete Nativity Towers in accordance with his detailed plans. Construction then ceased. Most of Gaudí's drawings, sketches and models for the church – which after several metamorphoses had taken on strongly Expressionist overtones – were destroyed in the Civil War.

Since 1952 work on the church has resumed, using modern equipment and new techniques. For the sake of economy, but with more than a little poetic justification, Gaudí's successors are also utilizing a continuous supply of stones from Barcelona's demolished older buildings. This renewed construction follows large-scale models carefully reconstructed from reproductions of the original drawings and models of Gaudí's final designs, as well as from extrapolations based on the previously constructed parts of the church. There is also, it would seem, a certain amount of improvisation. This has caused some resistance from those – mostly architects – who feel the new construction is lifeless, even if it does generally reflect Gaudí's intent. However, the citizens of Barcelona, acting perhaps more from Catalan nationalism than devotion, annually donate vast sums to the church's fund-raising drives.

E-11a Wedged behind a fence in a too

Barcelona   **E-12**
*** **Parc** or **'Park' Güell** (garden suburb, now municipal park) 1900–14
Calle de Larrad and Calle Olot
Antoni Gaudí
National Romantic/Rationalism
Map E-2

[The deterioration of the ceramics and rockwork is no worse than might reasonably be expected. Some careful restorations have been undertaken.]

Prominently displayed on its outer wall is the name Park Güell, with park spelt in the English way. As this might suggest, it is a direct outgrowth of British precedents. But, despite Gaudí's Arts and Crafts predilections, he was not the strongest link with England here. Rather it was his great patron – one of modern architecture's most important patrons (E-3, 17, 19, 20) Count Eusebi Güell. Güell's connections with the design-conscious British textile industry brought him into contact with the ideas then being advanced in progressive English design circles, including presumably Ebenezer Howard's visions of garden cities. It appears, however, that the Count anticipated a class of inhabitants for his community that would have made it more analogous to the fashionable London suburb of Bedford Park (GB-30), rather than the rural, cottagey suburbs (GB-37) which grew out of Howard's ideals. As for the Park Güell's curiously artificial ambience, that may have been an unavoidable by-product of grafting concepts quite specific to one culture on to another so radically different. Perhaps that is why only three of the sixty lots in Gaudí's plan were ever built on. But Güell's loss is our gain.

The architecture of the park divides itself into four distinct yet not discordant personalities – especially remarkable considering that all four were conceived at one time, by one man, as part of a single project.

The first is encountered in the surrounding walls, the gatehouses and the great axial cascade of stairs. All these elements share an underlying simple basic structure of rubble masonry bedecked with a confection of complexly surfaced, complexly patterned tile mosaic, whose surface contours often have a perversely indirect relationship to their polychromatic patterns. A wilder collection of forms and fancies would be hard to find – except elsewhere in Gaudí's *œuvre*. But as in all his work, these elements, both large-scale and small, are often symmetrical and subtly geometric. Save for the unexpectedly bold,

easily overlooked corner of the site, is the little 'temporary' **schoolhouse** Gaudí built in 1909 for the children of his workers. Its fluted, thin, shell-like roof is one of Gaudí's most dramatic demonstrations of the possibilities of Catalan tile masonry, and also of his own mastery of form and structure.

E-11b At the opposite (N) end of the Avenida de Gaudí is Lluís Domènech's extensive **Hospital de Sant Pau,** 1902–12. *Metro: Dos de Mayo*

Pop Art-like 'Park Güell' signs, however, none of these peripheral elements ever quite develops the vitality one expects of Gaudí.

The second and best-known of its architectural personalities is that of the projecting platform plaza (called the 'Greek theatre' by Gaudí). Or, to be more precise, it is that of the several-hundred-feet long serpentine bench-cum-parapet that forms the plaza's perimeter and also serves as the foreground to a magnificent panoramic view of Barcelona and of the Mediterranean beyond. Again, the plan of the plaza, and hence of this bench, is symmetrical. But not so its surface decoration – much of which is usually attributed to Gaudí's chief assistant, Josep Jujol. Covered by a polychrome mosaic of fragmented tiles and even bits of broken crockery, it surpasses mere architectural ornament. It is an important, vigorous contribution to the development of the twentieth-century eye.

But what a surprise, even in the context of Gaudí's work, lies beneath the forward part of the plaza. Here, where the community market was to have been, is a forest of freely adapted Doric columns. The subtly Moorish mood of this hypostyle hall springs from its not-quite-Greek, mosque-like column grid; while the pragmatic slight buttressing angle at which its outermost columns incline is also symbolic of the ethical and genetic bonds which Gaudí, as a disciple of Viollet-le-Duc, would have felt linked the Greeks to the 'Goths' (see F-28).

Finally, and least-known – perhaps

because they do not present as 'beautiful' or coherent a photographic image – are the park's super-rustic rockwork causeways and retaining walls. These linear constructions, so seemingly insubstantial, almost slapdash, are the organizers of the site. They define and separate the vehicular and the (often covered) pedestrian circulation systems. In spite of appearances, they were carefully conceived according to advanced principles and are solidly constructed, as their unfortunate continuing use by motor traffic demonstrates. Even the whimsical petrified trees and folk figures

standing before the raked buttress-columns of the long, overtopping, breaker-like retaining wall have a role to play as supports for the wall's outermost edge.

E-12a From 1906 until shortly before his death in 1926, Gaudí lived in one of the park's three houses. Built in 1904 by Francesc Berenguer, it is now operated by the Amics de Gaudí as a museum, the **Casa-Museo-Gaudí**. However, it contains more memorabilia than items of direct architectural interest. [Open irregular hours: check Col·legi d'Arquitectes, E-2b.]

Barcelona   **E-13**
** **Casa Vicens** (house) 1883–5
Calle de las Carolinas 22
Antoni Gaudí
Neo-Mudéjar (National Romantic)
Map E-2 / Metro: Fontana
[The elaborate garden and fountain have disappeared. Some of the original iron fence, identical to that still in place, has been installed at the Park Güell (E-12). A sympathetic addition was made in 1925 with Gaudí's cooperation. This is a private house, not open to the public.]

The careers of famous architects usually have modest, tentative beginnings. Often it is only after many years and marked philosophical and stylistic metamorphoses that the individual genius emerges. Not so in the case of Gaudí. At the age of twenty-six, in the very year he finished his architectural studies, be began to design this then suburban mansion – his first building.

At the time, even the better work being done by Barcelona architects reflected a sort of gawky, brick, Viollet-le-Duc-inspired Graeco-Romanesque-Gothic Rationalism (F-28). In this context the Casa Vicens must have been a minor bombshell. There was nothing tentative about Gaudí's presentation of his 'new' Iberian architecture. Although still Rationalist, it looked less to the Gothic than to Mudéjar, an archaic Hispano-Moorish vernacular style in which rubble masonry walls are tectonically gridded with a reinforcement of brick quoining and banding – a technique the Arabs had originally adapted from Roman practice. However, the house also owes at least as much to the English Arts and Crafts Movement, and, to a lesser extent, to the Japanophilia of the Aesthetic Movement. This later Anglo-Orientalism is clearly evident both in the design of the wooden lattice sunscreens, even though the idea for them is again Hispano-Moorish, and in certain of the beautifully preserved interiors.

Most obvious, and at the time shocking, must have been Gaudí's remarkably convincing use of what are, by themselves, rather garish floral-patterned tiles. Eventually multi-coloured ceramic decorations would become one of the most characteristic and effective aspects of Gaudí's work. It might be assumed that this was a

natural extension of a pre-existing Spanish tile tradition, and of Gaudí's general interest in Spanish ceramic construction materials. In fact Spain, unlike Portugal, provided almost no precedent for the wholesale use of exterior tiles. The simple truth is that Gaudí's first client happened to be a tile manufacturer!

The Casa Vicens's final distinction lies in its sinuous whiplash ironwork, whose general appearance, date and descent from the Arts and Crafts Movement make it a prime contender for the somewhat dubious title of the 'first manifestation of Art Nouveau', a distinction now usually accorded to a contemporaneous, 1883, book illustration by the British architect Arthur H. Mackmurdo. However, neither this nor the subsequent, even more thoroughly Art Nouveau, ironwork of the Palau Güell (E-3) seems to have had any significant, immediate influence in Barcelona, much less in the rest of Europe.

E-13a The quiet little summer resort of Comillas, on Spain's cooler north coast, contains another of Gaudí's earliest and most mannered houses, the villa **'El Capricho'**, 1883–5. It is adjacent to an almost equally remarkable and equally National Romantic Bishop's Palace. [Said to be accessible through the palace grounds, when open.]

Barcelona   **E-14**
Casa Sert (apartment block) 1930–1
Calle de Muntaner 342–348
Josep Lluís Sert
International Style
Map E-2 / Metro: Muntaner

Given its corner site, the symmetrical 'front' façade may be questionable, while the corner balconies are just stylishly silly. Still, this is Sert's first work and, even if there are few competitors for the distinction, it is also Spain's least provincial International Style building.

E-14a Sert's best prewar work, the long-lost Spanish Republican Pavilion at the 1937 Paris Exhibition, was the setting for the first display of Picasso's *Guernica*. It is fitting, then, that at the end of his career Sert was able to build a museum in Barcelona dedicated to his close friend and to Catalonia's other great expatriate artist, Joan Miró. However the **Fundació Miró**, 1975, is little more than a tougher restatement of the Fondation Maeght (F-61). *On Av de Miramar in Parc de Montjuich*

E-14b Another long-lost exhibition pavilion, Mies van der Rohe's famous **'Barcelona Pavilion'** – one of the German pavilions from the 1929 Barcelona Exhibition – has been rebuilt near its original site in the exhibition grounds.

Barcelona   **E-15**
Fábrica Casaramona (yarn factory, now police barracks) 1911
Calle de Méjico 11
Josep Puig
Rationalism/National Romantic
Map E-2 / Metro: Plaza España

The Catalan enthusiasm for virtuoso displays of brick and tile construction sometimes led, almost inadvertently it seems, towards an architecture that others, elsewhere, were struggling to evolve. Consider, for instance – without reading too much into it – this late work of a basically conservative architect. Admittedly it is a factory and not one of his more typical National Romantic-Gothic apartment buildings (E-8a). None the less, in it

he has combined explicit expressions, both real and symbolic, of the nature of the building's structure; of its special functions (as in the water-tank bulging from its tower); and of its 'free' plan which does not rigidly follow the site lines.

Barcelona   **E-16**
* Col·legi Teresia (school) 1888–94
Calle de Ganduxer 105
Antoni Gaudí
National Romantic
W on Diagonal (Map E-2→) / second R past Plaza de Calvo Sotelo ⇨ Calle de Ganduxer / ½ mi (1 km) on L (across Ronda del General Mitre) / Metro: Bonanova

A remarkable aspect of Gaudí's work is its vitality. Despite certain persistent motifs and tendencies no two of his buildings have more common elements than dissimilar ones. One cannot find such consistently striking differences in the work of any other modern master.

This convent school is a prime case in point. Built to a strict budget and lacking any of Gaudí's customary sculptural embellishments, it is, in plan and elevation, a repetitively modular rectangle organized around a central light-well corridor. Only its almost separate porch-cum-bay and main staircase recognize its axis of symmetry.

Barcelona/Pedralbes   **E-17**
* Pavellons Güell (stables, lodge and
dragon-gate) 1884–7
*Avenida de la Victoria and Paseo de Manuel
Girona*
Antoni Gaudí
Neo-Mudéjar (National Romantic)
*W on Diagonal (Map E-2 →) / R on Av
de la Victoria (at Plaza Papa Pío XII) →*
SARRIA-PEDRALBES / *on L at first
intersection*
[The entrance to the now vanished Finca
Güell – an estate, not built by Gaudí, which
was once, 1919–24, a royal palace.]

Barcelona/Bonanova   **E-18**
* Casa Bellesguard (house, now a
clinic) 1900–2
Calle de Bellesguard
Antoni Gaudí
National Romantic
*W on Diagonal, ½ mi (1 km) past Plaza de la
Victoria / R on Calle de Muntaner (Map
E-2 →) to end at Plaza Bonanova / continue
on Calle San Juan de la Salle (rd nearest
church) ⇨ Calle Bellesguard / on R*
    Gaudí was the greatest modern master
of fantasy. Yet, unlike his Classicist counterparts (GB-36, I-15), he did not use mannerism as his chief fantastical device. Only
in this fairy-tale castle – not to be confused
with his gingerbread (gate)houses (E-12) –
does one encounter a strong *double entendre*,
tongue-in-cheek mannerism.
    In certain respects, Bellesguard is a
reasonably conventional turn-of-the-
century villa, or at least it incorporates
many of the right conventional motifs. But
there is an attenuation to it – especially
about the windows. And most particularly
there is that almost maniacally ubiquitous,
precisely assembled, at times even mosaic-
like rubble rockwork. It is used everywhere:
for tracery, for mouldings, for the ironic
'smooth' rustications around the front
doors. Even the mansard roof and the tall
steeple, with its super-scaled cross-cum-
finial, are seemingly of rubble, although
their crispness of form – not to mention
logic – denies that.
    If for no other reason, Bellesguard is

    These modest (by Gaudí's standards) and
monochromatic buildings are interesting –
but not remarkable when compared to the
rest of his work.
    Not so the gate. With rippling iron-mesh
wings, sinuously coiled spring neck, fiercely
fanged mouth, raking red wrought-iron
talons and spiky spiralling tail, it is a fantasy
incarnate for the true dragon *aficionado*.

E-17a At **57 Paseo de Manuel
Girona** is another Gaudí gate, 1900,
which once lead to the Finca Miralles.

intriguing as an example of Gaudí's will-
ingness to try almost anything once. Generally, however, his efforts were more
profitably spent on more original and
logical creations – such as the structural
tile armature that supports this confection.

Garraf [near Barcelona]   **E-19**
** Bodegas Güell (wine cellars, porter's lodge and chapel) 1888–1900
Francesc Berenguer
National Romantic
S on C240 (Map E-2→) → CASTELLDEFELS *abt 7½ mi (12 km) / S of Garraf on L, abt 3¾ mi (6 km) S of Castelldefels (Caution: gatehouse appears suddenly after a bend – pass it by and turn around at a safe place)*
[Residence, not open to the public.]

There are few more overworked modern mythical figures than that of the 'promising young architect'. A few such, however, have been known to exist. Here, in his first building, Berenguer produced a functional, fantastical masterpiece which, in its freedom from ornamentation or historical references, equals Gaudí's own most extreme works of the time.

A *bodega* is an above-ground wine cellar. The sloping roof-cum-walls of the Bodegas Güell respond to the progressively diminishing spatial requirements of first the *bodega* itself, then a superimposed dwelling, and finally an attic chapel. They also reflect an attempt to counter the outward thrust of the vaulted ceilings of these spaces without having recourse to tie-rods or massive buttresses. The clearest expression of this – delineated in miniature and demonstrating that the forces do in fact resolve themselves – is the dramatically propped chapel porch, where the hewn angular columns and polygonal stonework strongly suggest Gaudí's later Crypt Güell (E-20).

This little eye-catching stone tent epitomizes the tensions that exist throughout the entire building: between the smooth, simple surfaces and the rustic rubble masonry with its semi-ashlar, cyclopean quoins and lintels; between the aggressively thrusting and that which is in repose; between the particularity of certain details and the coalescing unity of colour and material; between asymmetry and symmetry; between the rectilinear and the curvilinear; between the incomplete and the complete. It is not an easy building, but it grows on one.

Then there is the remarkable, tensile chain-net entrance gate, suspended from its graceful catenary support. The gatehouse itself, perhaps somewhat later than the *bodegas*, is not quite as convincing – in part because it lacks a single unifying material. Already it seems to suggest that, for whatever reason, Berenguer, the 'promising young architect', would not surpass his first brilliant originality.

Santa Coloma de Cervelló   **E-20**
[near Barcelona]
*** Cripta de l'Església de la Colònia Güell (Colònia Güell chapel/crypt) 1908–14
Antoni Gaudí
Expressionism/National Romantic
W on Diagonal (Map E-2→) ⇨ *N-II (→* MADRID*) to Molins de Rey, abt 8½ mi (14 km) / L across bridge / L →* SAN BAUDILLO, *abt 2 mi (3 km) / R just after RR crossing / → signs*

[Although the project was first proposed in 1898, design work apparently did not begin until at least 1908. As its name suggests, the present structure was to have been the crypt of a church, which would have been twice as high again. Although otherwise well-preserved and maintained, the exterior is coated with a thick layer of dust which obscures the small bright areas of broken-tile mosaic as well as the more subdued hues of the Miró-like windows. (They are post-Civil War replacements of the originals.) Of the church's three altars only the centre one is by Gaudí. His associate Josep Jujol designed the altar on the left as well as the calligraphy behind it. The other, set on a Gaudí column base, is by Josep Puig. The pews are by Gaudí (some are recent copies). Lying among the surrounding pines are the great monolithic columns that were to have stood within the church.]

The first impression of this, Gaudí's most original work, is of a crude, disorganized vigour: of a chaotic, almost random assemblage of leaning rubble walls, megalithic stone columns, crazily tilted brick piers, unorthodox arches, and irregular vaults. In fact, the crypt is a partial realization of an orderly, symmetrical, 'pure' compression structure. Gaudí even developed its design using a flexible, 'pure' tension model made of wires and weights (a photo is in the sanctuary), which accurately simulated the loads imposed on and by each part of the buildings, as well as the angles of the columns and shapes of the arches required to carry them. The model, being completely flexible, had to hang upside down. The one major exception to this careful structural analysis was the asymmetrical flight of steps leading to the unbuilt nave. Unlike the crypt these steps, which now serve as

the entrance porch, were never intended to support the great weight of the church or its 300-foot tower. And so they alone did not have to be constructed in such a way that the distribution of future loads could be precisely predicted and accommodated. Gaudí was able to build them even more imaginatively, if that is possible, of hyperbolic paraboloids – those light thin-shell structures whose subsequent incarnations in reinforced concrete (E-31) would be hailed two generations later as a tectonic breakthrough.

But it would be easy to overemphasize these structural considerations. Although they are interesting and necessary to a complete understanding of architecture such as this, it is far more important to see that, in part because of them, the Crypt Güell is one of the truly great modern examples of finely disciplined improvised art. And that, despite some current wisdom, is not a contradiction in terms.

E-20a Gaudí has sometimes been credited with planning and building the entire village. However, its other interesting buildings are all by Francesc Berenguer. Particularly noteworthy is the nearby linked **school and teacher's house**, 1911.

Tarrasa [near Barcelona] **E-21**
* **Masía Freixa** (house, now municipal music school) 1907
Parque San Jorge
Lluís Moncunill
National Romantic
W on Diagonal (Map E-2→) ⇨ N-II, →
MADRID, *abt 18½ mi (30 km) / R on C243*
→ TARRASA, *abt 9½ mi (15 km) / L in Tarrasa, before RR, on to Av del Caudillo (Rambla)* → CENTRO URBANO *(see E-21a) / L at Calle de Padre Llauradó / second L on to Calle de Galileo / first R on to Plaza de José Freixa y Argemí / in park*

No other Catalan architect, not even Gaudí, based his work so exclusively upon the direct expression of Catalan thin-tile masonry. Attenuated though they are, these arches and vaults are stuccoed masonry, not reinforced concrete. (In 1907, concrete used in such a manner

would have been even more unlikely.)

Aside from the nature of its structural forms, however, the most remarkable aspect of this building is simply that it is an unornamented, unelaborated architecture of structure, whose underlying philosophy is not unlike that more commonly associated with the works of Mies van der Rohe and his followers half a century later had been. Would that most of their efforts were as lively, original, and honest.

E-21a On the Avenida del Caudillo is Moncunill's **Aymerich i Amat factory** (now Sepauto S.A.). It has curved, thin-shell, north-light roofs which look like contemporary pre-cast concrete structures – and not at all as if they were made of inch-thick tiles in 1907. *On Av del Caudillo (Rambla) past Calle de P. Llauradó (see directions above) on R*

Girona (Gerona)   **E-22**
Farinera Teixidor (house and offices)
1910–11
Carretera de Santa Eugenia 42
Rafael Masó
Jugendstil (Art Nouveau)
W from Girona ctr on N141 → Anglés / abt $\frac{1}{2}$ mi (1 km) on N side of rd

This is one of Masó's earliest commissions, built when he had yet to visit Vienna, Munich or Darmstadt. (By 1912 he had.) It is therefore a pastiche of elements borrowed from sources he could have known only indirectly, in combination with a few 'Catalan' motifs – such as the great parabolic arch. Whatever these two buildings lack in sophistication is more than offset by the verve with which they were conceived. They pack in more 'architecture' than half a dozen typical buildings of their size.

E-22a Just down the street, at No. 19, is the **Casa Teixidor**, a block of flats by Masó, 1918–22, which could just as well have been built in Germany or Austria.

Vistabella [near Tarragona]   **E-23**
* Iglesia (church) 1918–23
Josep Maria Jujol
Expressionism/National Romantic
N from Tarragona on N240 (see E-23a) → LÉRIDA (LLEIDA), *abt 5 mi (8 km) / R →* PERAFORT, *before RR / →* SECUITA */ →* VISTABELLA */ on R in ctr of village*

[The church was badly damaged in the Civil War. Though it has been carefully rebuilt, only a little of Jujol's original painted interior decoration remains – near one of the side altars.]

The Bodegas Güell (E-19) and this tiny village church were the first and last flowers of Barcelona's architectural glory, and were also among the most original. Jujol lived in Gaudí's shadow more than any of his contemporaries and is deservedly most renowned for his decorative efforts, especially the inventive mosaics and ironwork he did for Gaudí (E-8, 12) – work of more originality than that with which he embellished his own buildings.

Only here, encouraged perhaps by the Expressionism then at its peak in Germany, did Jujol turn his surreal eye – with which he had so successfully transformed Spain's folk-Baroque – towards the Gothic and the acrobatic Catalan tile masonry he knew so well from the work of his master (E-20).

The result is a spectacularly picturesque building, especially considering that it is based on a very simple square ground-plan and a quite regular system of ribbed vaulting. Like many another great work of architecture, it always photographs larger than life; and it is all the more surprising for

being in so out of the way and unprepossessing a little village – not that such circumstances are unusual in Iberia (E-25). It also, again like the Bodegas Güell, has suffered from obscurity for far too long.

E-23a To the the left of the N240 (see directions above), at the Plaza Imperial Tarraco in Tarragona, is the **Administrativo Gobierno Civil** (government office building), 1961, by Alejandro de la Sota – an interesting derivative of the Italian mannered modernism of the 50s.

Reus [near Tarragona]   **E-24**
* **Barrio Gaudí** (social housing)
1964–9 (phase 1)
Avenida Barcelona
Taller de Arquitectura Bofill
Neo-Expressionism
W from Tarragona on N420 → REUS /
→ FALSET *and* MORA / → BARRIO GAUDÍ

Quantitatively, government-subsidized housing must be the most important category of construction in Europe – even though, when looked at in terms of imaginativeness, it must also be one of the least important. Beginning here, then, it has

been particularly interesting to watch the Bofill team use its fertile, if occasionally hyperactive imagination (F-38) within this technocrats' haven.

In this megastructure of a village they employed a deliberately simple palette of standard techniques and materials. These include a complex but orderly 90°/45° planning matrix and a sufficient number of differing arrangements of dwellings and shops to generate an almost endless variety of walkways, roof terraces and other public spaces – albeit always within the context of an overall symmetry.

El Pinell de Bray   **E-25**
* **Bodega Cooperativa** (wine co-operative) 1919–21
Cèsar Martinell
National Romantic
Between Gandesa and Tortosa on C221 (in some places also called N230) / →
PINELL / *just off of rd into Pinell*

[The *bodega* shows signs of war damage and *ad hoc* repairs. As with all good Spanish vernacular architecture, such tribulations only help it fit better with the surroundings.]

It *almost* blends into this remote Tarragonan village – which itself seems an organic extension of the rugged landscape. Only its size, a *gemütlich* frieze of happy imbibers across its front, and a thin canopy of flat tiled arches at its rear, distinguish Pinell de Bray's largest secular building. Nowhere does its exterior betray the thread-thin elliptical brick arches and struts which carry its roof over an enormous room containing forty-six huge wine vats (which do not occupy one quarter of its volume).

Few cathedrals have spans the equal of this, none the economy of means. Had Maillart (CH-13) built it of concrete it would be famous, but not more elegant.

E-25a Martinell built many such structures in this area. Most, although technically interesting, are less tectonically elegant. Another typical example is the **Co-op Agrícola** in Gandesa, 1919. *On N420*

Calpe [near Alicante] **E-26**
* **Xanadu** (resort apartments) 1966
La Manzanera (resort village)
Taller de Arquitectura Bofill
Expressionistic Neo-Vernacular
E from coast rds (E26 or N332) →
CALPE / → LA MANZANERA

The Taller (studio) Bofill have been notable as the most flamboyant and creative, if not always the most responsible, among postwar Catalan architects. Xanadu exemplifies their earlier work and attitudes. An architecture which would be hard to justify in most contexts at most times, its wilful romantic self-assertion may well have been necessary at that particular moment in this particular place. (Its actual location just outside Catalonia matters little.) Patently it could not, and should not, be justified in terms of any Functionalist ethic. It is what it was meant to be – an original, witty declaration of independence, which, like it or loathe it, cannot be ignored.

E-26a La Muralla Roja, the nearby indescribably red apartment building, 1969, is also by Bofill.

E-26b In the Barcelona suburb of Sant Justo Desvern is Bofill's **Walden 7,** a massive apartment complex, 1970–5, whose name, and presumably its programme, were inspired by B. F. Skinner's book *Walden Two.* Its intensively utilized dwelling units are meant to have, both individually and collectively, a psychological fitness of purpose as ideal urban dwelling-machines – or so suggest the architects. Unfortunately one is reminded that Skinner did much of his psychological research with rats in mazes.

E-26c Just over the French border, at Le Boùlou, on the Autoroute La Catalana (E4), is the Bofill-designed **Le Perthus monument,** 1974–7, a statement of Catalonia's past glories and present national aspirations. (It was commissioned, somewhat surprisingly, by the French regional highway authority.) Set on an artificial pyramidal hill, it is a roofless 'ruined' temple portico with an uncompleted set of Gaudí-like twisted, square red-brick columns seen against a false-front cella wall of orangey brick. All this symbolizes, it is said, both Catalonia's own incompleteness and the four fingers of the upraised battle-bloodied hand of the first Count of Barcelona – according to tradition the source of the Catalan flag: four red stripes against a golden background.

The impact of the monument is distorted and diluted, however, by the intrusion of extraneous symbolism which seems to relate solely to two trendy, 'high style' international architectural fashions, both cynically mannered and not at all appropriate to the issue of Catalan nationalism. Of these the witty, cardboardy, Venturi-esque brick 'shrubs' flanking the central axial stairs are, at worst, irrelevant. But so is the Classical form language of the monument itself. It, unfortunately, is far too easily identifiable with the severely, almost surreally, stripped-down Neo-Classicism that we tend now to associate with Mussolini's Italy, but which also flourished, especially on paper, under Franco. While the revival of interest in this occasionally inventive authoritarian architecture may have been inevitable, if not easily accepted, its use in this context seems nothing short of grotesque.

Madrid **E-27**
For the most part Madrid's governmental, institutional and business architecture is unexceptionally unadventurous. Yet, as is true of progressive areas throughout the country, residential architecture here is another story.

Upper-middle-class houses and apartment buildings, as well as occasional areas of workers' housing, can be quite pleasing. They are reasonably well constructed of masonry with – surprisingly in an economy such as Spain's – steel frames. They also evince a remarkably harmonious, if unexpected, blend of influences, including Spanish vernacular, Wright, and even Japanese vernacular – the more exotic among these apparently having been in part proselytized by Italian and perhaps German publications. Although this comfortable mode of design has hardly affected the country's vast, mass-produced lower- and middle-class housing projects, Spain none the less remains the only Southern European country to have developed anything even approaching a respectable modern urban vernacular.

E-27a As in the rest of the country, indications of planning are few and far between here. But Madrid was once the site of an unusual private attempt to build a linear city. In 1882 Arturo Soria, an engineer, proposed and eventually began developing his **Ciudad Lineal,** a horseshoe-shaped city, one kilometre wide and fifty-eight long, which was to wrap itself around Madrid. The key element of the Ciudad Lineal was an electric street railway running along a wide, tree-shaded boulevard.

Lacking the eminent domain powers needed to assemble the land, and having no enforceable covenants with which to control its development, Soria's partially completed Ciudad was eventually engulfed by Madrid's rapidly growing suburbs and today little remains. *E from Madrid ctr on Calle Alcalá abt 3¾ mi (6 km) / L on Calle Arturo Soria which is the spine of the Ciudad Lineal / Metro: Ciudad Lineal*

Madrid   E-28
Edificio Capitol (office building) 1931
Avenida de José Antonio 41
Luis Martinez-Feduchi & Vicente Eced
Expressionistic International Style
José Antonio (Granvía) is the city's
main shopping st / at W end on axis /
Metro: Sto Domingo

Had Erich Mendelsohn (GB-43) designed
a focal point for New York's Times Square,
it might well have been this theatrically
modern, blatantly commercial urban landmark.

Madrid   E-29
Palacio de Longoria, (now Sociedad
General de Autores España) 1900–2
Calle de Fernando VI 4
José Grases Riera
Art Nouveau
W from Calle de Alcalá on Av de José Antonio
(Granvia) / R on Calle de Hortaleza /
R on Calle de Fernando VI / on R /
Metro: Alonso Martínez

Hardly a seminal example of Art
Nouveau, this house reflects more money
than talent. Yet it may be of interest –
especially the palm-tree columns of the
orangery or the white and gold grand staircase with its stained-glass flowers. To
anyone familiar with Barcelona's prodigious architectural output during the
same period, however, it must primarily
reaffirm the conservative insularity of
Madrid – a city in which this is the only
significant representative of the first pan-
European modern style.

Madrid   E-30
** Torres Blancas (apartment tower)
1962–7
Autopista de Barajas (Avenida de América)
Francisco Javier Sáenz de Oiza
Brutalist Wrightian
E from Madrid ctr on NII (E4) / R at Calle
de Cartagena, just before beginning of
expressway (tower is to L but not directly
accessible) owing to no left turn and one-way
streets) / turn around and cross NII / first
R / on R

If, after the two masterpieces of his later
years, Falling Water and the Johnson's
Wax headquarters, Frank Lloyd Wright
had grown old with the grace to acquire
and keep important clients and with a more
abiding faith in his own earlier organic
principles, then his last works might have
been as convincing as this. Like the best of
Wright's efforts – from which Sáenz de Oiza
has so freely but intelligently borrowed

(directly and via Italy) – the Torres Blancas embodies just that blend of great honesty and abstract romanticism which is almost never to be found in the work of Wright's more fervent and obvious devotees.

This is a difficult but understandable building because its often fragmented forms are still individually and collectively comprehensible, even if not always strictly functional. The tower feels right in its details, in its use of materials, and especially in the gesture of the lobby that extends up through its full height. Most of all, and unlike most romantic modern architecture, it is not embarrassed about its real nature or role. It has not been disguised as sham machine or sham sculpture.

Sited at the boundary between urban city and suburbs, next to the main road from Barcelona and hence from Europe, Torres Blancas is a fanfare to Madrid. If not hedged in by other, lesser towers, it is and will remain an urban gesture *par excellence*. And in that, it is more right than Wright.

Madrid   **E-31**
* Hipódromo de la Zarzuela
(racecourse grandstand) 1935
Carretera de la Coruña (NVI)
Carlos Arniches, Martin Domínguez &
Eduardo Torroja
NW from Madrid on NVI → VILLALBA or LA CORUÑA (past Río Manzanares) / → HIPÓDROMO
[May be locked and hard to see off-season.]

Architects, driven one assumes by a mixture of admiration and envy, have been wont to include a certain class of engineers and technicians amongst their own ranks, including the likes of Buckminster Fuller, Robert Maillart (CH-13), P. L. Nervi (I-5, 36), the Mexican engineer-entrepreneur Félix Candela, and Candela's mentor, Eduardo Torroja.

It was Torroja's prewar work – his daring, graceful concrete shells – that most inspired the immediately post-International Style generation. They were searching for a new, more tectonic and often more romantic non-Functionalist rationale. They found it, in part at least, in Torroja's seemingly impossible semi-cylindrical vaults for the now lost Frontón Recoletos Jai Alai hall and, even more, in the delicate cantilevered canopies of this grandstand.

As Torroja was not an architect, our perception of his talents ultimately depends upon the calibre of his various architectural collaborators. And that is what makes La Zarzuela so satisfying. It is a successful association – perhaps a fortuitous one – of almost independent architectural and engineering elements, each so straightforwardly performing its assigned task that together they form a surprisingly harmonious whole.

Segovia   **E-32**
* Cooperativa Pío XII (social housing) 1967–9
José Joaquin Aracil, Luis Miguel &
Antonio Viloria
Neo-Vernacular
→ ACUEDUCTO ROMANO / up into old city on first rd E of aqueduct (Calle de San Juan) / R past second park / at end of st
How refreshing to find on this quite difficult site, which could have provoked tectonic overkill from most designers, such remarkably unaffected, guileless architecture. No part of these buildings needs to be explained away. They are comfortably in accord with the simple, functional Spanish vernacular tradition of earlier centuries. They could not have been more sym-

pathetic to their site without seeming over-sensitive – the recycled roof tiles having presumably been required by its historic setting. Yet they could not be more ahistorical.

Admittedly the site, directly beneath the old town, was a foil to the Cooperativa's simplicity and a prerequisite for its all-

important multi-level circulation system. Without it, the buildings might not have attracted any critical notice, nor would they work. That the architects took full advantage of the opportunities offered by the site is to their credit.

Segovia　　　　　　　　　　**E-33**
* Fábrica 'Acueducto Felvi'
(sausage factory) 1967–8
Carretera de San Rafael (N603)
Francisco de Inza
Neo-Expressionism
On N603, 2 mi (3 km) S of Segovia

Neither a masterpiece nor revolutionary, it is simply appealing, the way all architecture could and ought to be. It is functionally laid out, well detailed, comfortable in the landscape – thanks particularly to its earthy brick sheathing and the assured

presence of its six-storey, 150-foot long air-drying building. Only the perhaps over-expressive, tile-covered roofs seem questionable, and even their forms are not so flagrant as to be out of keeping with the factory's subtly pervasive romanticism. The architect insists that in this climate a completely flat roof is inappropriate – presumably because of thermal expansion and contraction. Hardly a plausible excuse, but it reminds us that an architect's most important acquired skill can be the ability to justify essentially aesthetic decisions.

FRANCE

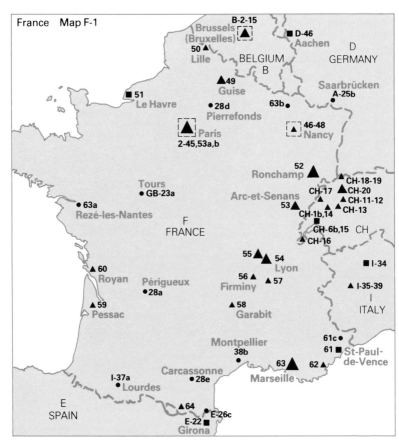

France   Map F-1

B-2-15
Brussels (Bruxelles)
50 ▲ Lille
BELGIUM
B
■ D-46 Aachen
D
GERMANY
■ 51 Le Havre
▲ 49 Guise
Saarbrücken
A-25b
● 28d Pierrefonds
63b ●
▲ Paris
2-45,53a,b
□ 46-48 ▲ Nancy
52
Ronchamp ▲
Tours
● GB-23a
Arc-et-Senans
53 ▲
CH-18-19
▲ CH-20
CH-17 ▲
▲ CH-11-12
▲ CH-13
CH-1b,14
CH-6b,15
CH-16
CH
● 63a
Rezé-les-Nantes
F
FRANCE
55 ▲ 54 ● Lyon
56 ▲ ▲ 57
Firminy
■ I-34
▲ 60 Royan
Périgueux
● 28a
▲ I-35-39
I
ITALY
▲ 59 Pessac
▲ 58 Garabit
Montpellier
38b
61c ●
61 ■ St-Paul-de-Vence
I-37a
● Lourdes
Carcassonne
● 28e
63 ▲ 62 ●
Marseille
E
SPAIN
▲ 64
E-26c
E-22 ■
Girona

Many of modern architecture's theoretical and technical roots can be traced, directly or indirectly, to eighteenth-century France – the France which fostered Europe's first social-political revolution and which, more than almost any other Continental country, participated in the early stages of the Industrial Revolution. Throughout the last two centuries, however, France's architecture, like her revolution, has been subverted by a society which, when not actively supporting such conservative institutions as the Ecole des Beaux-Arts, the school whose academic style and teaching method dominated French architecture and civic design for two centuries – under kings, emperors, and republicans alike, has been transforming some of its most progressive architectural impulses into divertissements for dilettantes. It is no accident that France invented the superficially ornamental, non-ideological Art Deco style, nor, conversely, that Le Corbusier, one of the greatest architects of the century, who was Swiss born and trained (in the crafts-school tradition), did his 'apprentice' work in Vienna and Berlin and did not finally settle in Paris until he was thirty.

From the idealized, unbuildable, romantic Revolutionary Neo-Classicism of Boullée and Ledoux (F-53), through the mastery of new materials and structural techniques of Hennebique, Eiffel, and Perret (F-41, 16, 18), and the pioneering restorations and voluminous theoretical writings of Viollet-le-Duc (F-28b–f) and other nineteenth-century French Rationalists, to Le Corbusier's utopian polemics (F-63) – whose global ramifications we are still experiencing – France's impressive architectural heritage has too often been ignored, re-

pressed or bowdlerized. France, like the United States, is becoming a land of isolated monuments; a land whose postwar growth has created an unplanned visual morass, a land of curious, contextless minor works which elsewhere would have led to something; a land of deflected talent working out often ingenious but ultimately unimportant exercises in formalistic pattern-making. Aside from the occasional villa or fashionable apartment, architectural innovations can have little effect in a highly centralized, bureaucratic country like France, unless and until they have filtered down through the governmental, corporate and cultural establishments. By then, such ideals have frequently become distorted parodies of themselves and can do more harm than good, as witness La Défense (F-27a) and the endless mechanistic, CIAM-inspired wastelands of postwar housing that now encircle every French city.

Paris   F-2

Cities by nature are artificial organisms. Until relatively recent times they have not even been capable of reproducing their own populations. And in many ways Paris seems, for better and worse, Europe's most artificial city. For centuries its physical growth was constrained by encircling walls which separated the Parisian from the rest of France – physically, spiritually, culturally, even economically. Ledoux's gatehouses, for instance (F-53a–b) – part of Paris's sixth, but not last, wall – were built as customs offices where goods entering and leaving the city were taxed. The final wall, marked by the present boulevard Périphérique, was not demolished until the late nineteenth century.

Continuous pressure for living space within its walls meant that Paris achieved population densities unequalled elsewhere in Europe. Although today these densities are much lower, modern Paris still remains, almost as if from habit, Europe's most densely populated city. Undoubtedly this contributes to its amazing sense of vitality. It must also be a cause of the tensions that periodically explode into riot, revolution and other forms of communal catharsis.

It was partly in an attempt to ameliorate just these conditions (not only by improving the water supply and sewerage, but also by providing mobility and clear fields of fire for Louis Napoleon's Imperial Guard) that Baron Haussmann's grand boulevards (F-5)

were cut through the most congested sections of old Paris. Yet, in spite of the bold precedents set by Haussmann, whose reforms were as much administrative as physical, Paris has not coped successfully with the realities of twentieth-century transportation technology and urban growth. Unlike London, where the Underground has always extended for miles out into the countryside, most of the impressively dense, heavily used Métro network is contained within the Périphérique – almost as if blocked by a physical barrier. Furthermore, Paris has never been as well endowed with a commuter rail service as London, a deficiency that is only now being corrected.

Trips which begin or end outside the Périphérique, including most suburban commuter journeys, are generally best made by car. Usually this means tens of thousands of single occupant cars working their way along the boulevards, around the Périphérique, or along the new expressways that have been shoehorned onto the banks of the Seine. Once they near their destinations it becomes a case of each motorized man for himself. At best he parks in the gigantic underground garages – as many as eight stories deep – built beneath every park, *place* and *rondpoint* in the city. At worst, and often, he parks among such of the trees as have been left on the promenades of the once civilized boulevards, including those of the Champs-Elysées.

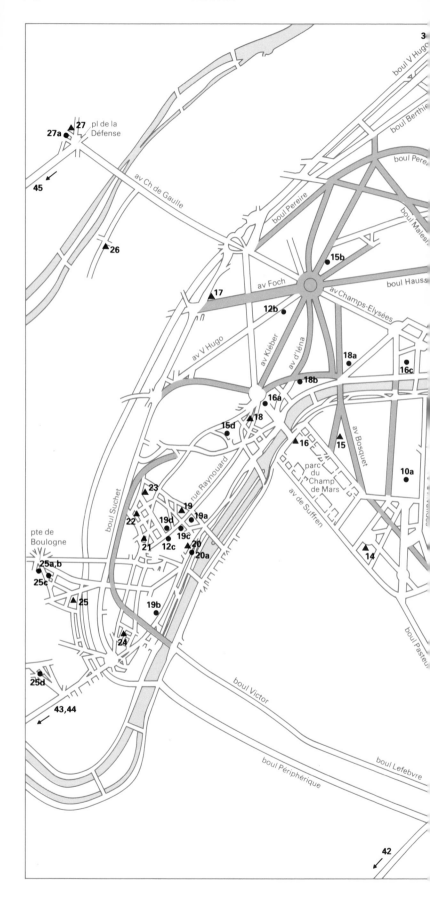

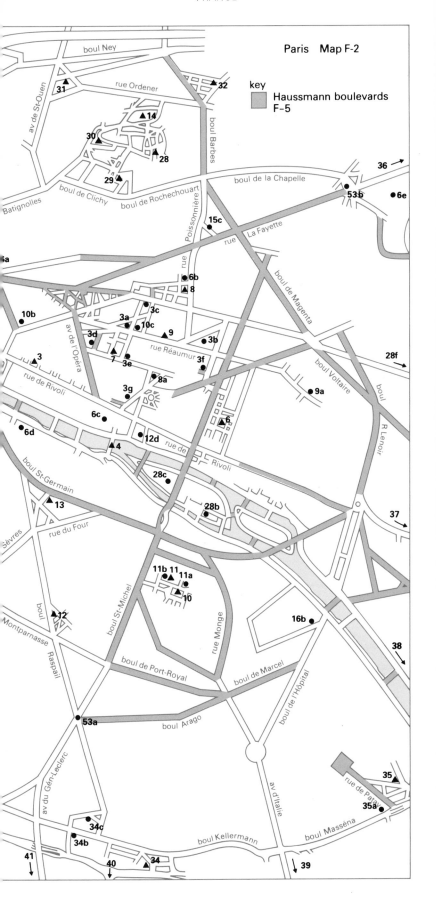

Paris   Map F-2

key

Haussmann boulevards
F-5

boul Ney
rue Ordener
av de St-Ouen
31
32
boul Barbes
14
30
28
29
Batignolles
boul de Clichy
boul de Rochechouart
boul de la Chapelle
36
53b
6e
15c
rue La Fayette
boul de Magenta
Poissonnière
6b
8
10b
3c
av de l'Opéra
3a
10c
9
3d
3b
3
rue Réaumur
28f
7
3e
3f
3g
8a
boul Voltaire
9a
R Lenoir
boul
6c
6
6d
12d
rue de
4
Rivoli
rue de Rivoli
boul St-Germain
28c
37
13
28b
Sèvres
rue du Four
rue du Four
11b 11
11a
boul St-Michel
10
12
16b
38
Montparnasse
Raspail
boul
rue Monge
boul de Port-Royal
boul de Marcel
boul de l'Hôpital
53a
boul Arago
35
av d'Italie
rue de Patay
35a
av du Gén-Leclerc
34c
boul Masséna
34b
41
40
34
boul Kellermann
39

Paris 1 and 4   **F-3**
** Rue de Rivoli
1801–11 (place de la Concorde to rue de l'Echelle); 1851–5 (eastward extension and full mansard roofs)
Percier & Fontaine
Neo-Classical Rationalism
Map F-2 / Métro: Palais Royal or Concorde

Anyone could have built it – block after identical block, the lines of its arcades and cornices barely interrupted by the intervening streets. The idea of the arcades was not new, nor by then technically very advanced. It required only a boldness of vision and a degree of organization.

Anyone could have built it. Yet who would have if not the French: the progenitors of the metric system and the Code Napoléon, of Haussmann and Perret; the nation that, more than any other, has set conceptual elegance above sentiment or chance.

Such bold, simple logic has undeniable appeal, especially in the earliest section of the rue de Rivoli, where the Tuileries lie before it and the old city is at its back. It would only be later, elsewhere, with other technologies and sensibilities, that such logic would lead to a thousand desperate and dull urban landscapes.

F-3a The rue de Rivoli's immediate Parisian ancestor – in quality if not quantity – is the **rue des Colonnes,** 1797–8, variously attributed to Bernard Poyet or N.-A.-J. Vestier. Although only a few years earlier, it distinctly reflects the style of the more revolutionary period in which it was cast. *Métro: Bourse*

F-3b ·Street arcades were not the only covered walkways in nineteenth-century Paris. There were also many glazed shopping passages – especially in the area north and east of the nearby Palais Royal. Among the earliest of these to survive more or less intact is the **passage du Caire,** 1799, connecting the place du Caire and the rue St-Denis. *Métro: Réaumur-Sébastopol*

Other arcades in the area include:

F-3c The **passage des Panoramas,** 1800, between the rue St-Marc and the boulevard Montmartre, and its continuation, the **passage Jouffroy,** 1845–57, across the boulevard Montmartre. *Métro: Montmartre*

F-3d The **passage de Choiseul,** 1825–7, between the rue des Petits-Champs and the rue St-Augustin. *Métro: Pyramides*

F-3e The **galerie Colbert,** 1825–6, and the adjacent **galerie Vivienne,** 1828, between rue Vivienne and the rue de la Banque. *Métro: Bourse*

F-3f The **passage du Grand-Cerf,** 1824–6, between the rue Dussoubs and the rue St-Denis. *Métro: Etienne Marcel*

F-3g The **galerie Véro-Dodat,** 1822–6, between the rue Croix-des-Petits-Champs and the rue Jean-Jacques-Rousseau. *Métro: Palais Royal*

The pont des Arts before reconstruction

Paris 1 and 6   **F-4**
* pont des Arts (footbridge) 1800–3; rebuilt 1978
quai de Conti to quai du Louvre
L.-A. de Cessart and J. Lacroix-Dillon
Map F-2 / Métro: Pont Neuf
[Various arches had to be replaced over the years because of collisions with barges. After several were knocked out at once in the early 70s, the bridge was 'accurately' rebuilt in 1978 with fewer, longer spans.]

The pont des Arts was built somewhat later than the Iron Bridge at Coalbrookdale (GB-59), and was not especially daring in its spans – hence its recurring difficulties. Still, it was the first iron bridge in France, and its prominent site, logical design, and lack of ornamentation are noteworthy.

Nineteenth-century view of the avenue de l'Opéra looking from the Opéra towards the Louvre, before the central section of the avenue had been cut through

Paris   F-5

*** Les Grands Travaux de Napoléon III

(the rebuilding of Paris including: boulevards de la Tour-Maubourg, Haussmann, St-Michel, du Palais, de Strasbourg, de Sébastopol, St-Germain, Voltaire, Diderot, Richard-Lenoir, Malesherbes, de Magenta, Beauséjour, Ornano, Barbes; avenues George v, Foch, de Wagram, de l'Opéra, Kléber, Henri-Martin, Georges-Mandel, d'Iéna, Marceau, Hoche, Mac-Mahon, Niel, Daumesnil, Bosquet, de Friedland, Duquesne; rues La Fayette, Rivoli (extended), etc.) 1853–69
Baron Georges-Eugène Haussmann, Préfet de Paris
Map F-2 (shaded streets)

From l'Opéra to her tourist-trodden sewers, much of the Paris we know today is Haussmann's. The almost entirely rebuilt or restored Ile de la Cité is his. So, too, are the boulevards that slice through pre-revolutionary Paris and give order to her nineteenth-century suburbs.

It was Haussmann's Paris rather than that of the Bourbons that Le Corbusier's radical-utopian planning proposals of the 1920s (so remarkably influential despite consistently disastrous results when emulated) would have swept away. But it was also Haussmann – the *'artiste démolisseur'* – who had set Le Corbusier the example. Haussmann was godfather to the Paris street scenes of a thousand Impressionist canvases. But a later generation would also canonize him as the patron saint of urban renewal.

Paris 4   F-6

*** Centre Georges Pompidou or Beaubourg

(cultural centre)
1970–7
rue St-Martin and rue Rambuteau
Piano & Rogers
Archigram-esque
Map F-2 / Métro: Rambuteau

This machine for the propagation of the arts must be the best-known postwar building in Europe. Like the Eiffel Tower (F-16), it has come to be identified with Paris in the popular consciousness. Indeed, because no two other modern European buildings have so caught the general public's attention, it might be useful to look at some telling parallels, as well as contrasts, between Europe's most famous modern architectural monuments.

The Eiffel Tower now seems to epitomize the more fondly remembered aspects of a then youthful era of industrial self-confidence. But in its own time its height, shape and naked structure caused it to be greeted

with almost universal contempt by writers, artists and aesthetes. On the other hand, Beaubourg, the perhaps unintentional (pre-oil crisis) epitaph to that same era – and to our confidence in modernity for its own sake – can hardly, despite itself, be seen as a serious intrusion on the ravished post-De Gaulle Paris skyline. And it has been received with nearly universal enthusiasm.

Like the Eiffel Tower after the Franco-Prussian War, Beaubourg seems a calculated attempt to reassert France's cultural (and technical) eminence – in this case after the post-Second World War emergence of New York and London as major art centres. But Beaubourg is not truly French. It is the product of a London-based Anglo-Italian design team. And it is a megastructure, one of the rare built examples of an idea strongly advocated by Le Corbusier, but which evoked only shallow formalistic responses in France itself. Beaubourg is also the almost sole full-scale realization of the mega-tech imagery of the English Archigram Group (D-21). The most French aspect of Beaubourg is its very existence. Along with the Louvre, Versailles, the Arc de Triomphe, Haussmann's boulevards (F-5), and the Eiffel Tower, here the French have once again translated into reality a grandiose social/architectural vision at a time when other nations lacked the means or the will. To be somewhat cynical, France, through the acquisition of Beaubourg, significantly strengthened one of the world's greatest 'collections' of architectural monuments in the area of its greatest weakness (despite Le Corbusier). In the process, eyes were diverted from the almost concurrent destruction of Les Halles, a comparably important, modern urban monument.

Technologically, the Eiffel Tower was a paradigm of Rational structural efficiency at the expense of virtually all usable space, not to mention spatial flexibility. In contrast, Beaubourg is a model of Expressionistic structural (and mechanical) excess, elegantly diagrammed, in the name of spatial flexibility. Highly articulated technology once more serves here as a new order of ornament. But there is one difference from most such exercises. Here everything really is what it seems to be and really does what it seems to do – regardless of how great the cost. (Consider only the weather-proofing problems when most of the bones and guts of a building lie outside its skin.)

Returning to our comparison one last time, the Eiffel Tower became an icon of Paris. Beaubourg, on the other hand, is in many respects just a building, a big and very expensive one which to a great extent must be judged by standards applicable to any other building. It is not unique in the functions it houses, nor in its style (broadly speaking), nor in its disregard for those codes and traditions that gave such a strong organic coherence to the Paris that Eiffel's tower so long stood above, and for. If Beaubourg presents the most radical possible contrast to the fabric of the adjacent Marais district, one of Paris's most ancient quarters, it is also Beaubourg, not necessarily Paris, which benefits more from that juxtaposition. Two adjacent Beaubourgs would have had a far less, not more, favourable impact. And had it risen instead at La Défense (F-27a), how much would the world have thought of it then?

F-6a Only a few blocks away stood another famous monument of nineteenth-century Paris and an antecedent of Beaubourg, Victor Baltard's famous Halles Centrales (central markets), 1854–66: ten elegant, Rational, iron and glass pavilions bound together in two groups by road-spanning arcades. For a century these market halls housed the richly vital commerce of cuisine. Ironically, in the 1970s they were destroyed by the same dispassionate 'rational' bureaucratic thinking that had permitted Haussmann to reshape Paris (F-5) – and to build them.

A far less elegant but still surviving iron structure by Baltard is the **église St-Augustin**, 1860–71, in place St-Augustin. It is an eclectic stone-walled pastiche of a church whose iron piers and vaults are carefully concealed from the outside. *Métro: St-Augustin*

F-6b There is one earlier, 1851–5, iron church in Paris, **St-Eugène**, 4–6 rue Ste-Cécile, by Louis-Auguste Boileau and Adrien-Louis Lusson. It demonstrates that there were some in Paris willing to use bare iron, albeit still in Gothic form – and willing even to express externally the curvature of iron vaulting. *Métro: Bonne Nouvelle*

F-6c At the time of writing, yet another modern monument is being added to France's national collection. I. M. Pei is building a vast **underground museum extension** beneath the large courtyard of the Louvre – similar, presumably, to his underground extension to the National Gallery in Washington. But this time, in lieu of Washington's modest fountain-skylight, a tasteless giant glass pyramid is to fill the centre of the space. A fitting counterpoint to La Défense (F-27a) at the other end of the Champs-Elysées.

F-6d Across the Seine from the Louvre is the **Musée d'Orsay**, or Museum of the Nineteenth Century – yet another of the string of new Parisian cultural monuments. It is housed, appropriately, in Victor Laloux's Gare d'Orsay, 1898–1900. If only Gae Aulenti, the Italian architect entrusted with the conversion, 1980–6, had known what to make of Laloux's supremely confident Beaux-Arts fusion of overwrought ornament and radically Rational iron-and-glass construction. Aulenti's infill is cold and sterile, and, despite massive, battered masonry walls, strangely temporary in feeling. Would that it actually were temporary.

F-6e Some sense of the opportunity lost at Les Halles can be seen at the **Grande Halle at la Villette**, 1867, by Jules de Mérindol. After the international scandal surrounding the destruction of Baltard's masterpiece, the Villette Halle – in fact an abattoir – was converted into a cultural and activities centre, 1982–4, by Reichen & Robert.

Paris 2   **F-7**
** **Bibliothèque Nationale** (library
reading room and bookstacks) 1853–69
58 rue de Richelieu
Henri Labrouste
Néo-Grec/Rationalism
Map F-2 / Métro: Bourse

[The stacks are closed to the public.
Entrance to the reading room requires a
reader's ticket, but the space can be seen
from the lobby.]

Unlike his earlier Bibliothèque Ste-Geneviève (F-11), with its subdued but powerful
façade, neither the street elevation here nor
that facing the entry courtyard gives any
hint of what lies hidden within. None the
less, technically and spatially this is the
more remarkable building. It contains the
first cast-iron library stack system – complete with structural glass floors designed
to transmit light down to the lowest level.
Furthermore, in the ceiling of the reading
room Labrouste turned the uncertain
tensile strength of this new structural
material to further advantage by forming it
into nine iron and faience domes supported
on a grid of semicircular iron arches
perched on tall thin iron columns. Spatially
this is far more dynamic than the twin
barrel vaults of his previous library. And,
at no cost to the structural or visual logic,
it allows an even distribution of ocular sky-

lights, one in the centre of each dome,
throughout the room. Altogether an
elegant solution – even if its underlying
logic was soon negated by the introduction
of steel and electricity.

Paris 9   **F-8**
* **Central téléphonique** (telephone
exchange) 1911–12
15 rue Bergère
François Le Coeur
Rationalism
Map F-2 / Métro: Poissonnière

There were other early attempts (F-12),
in addition to Art Nouveau, to develop a
new ahistorical style. As is true here, these
also frequently involved responses to new
social requirements as well as to the new
functional and technical ones. In this case
the entire top floor was given over to service
and recreational facilities for the employees.

F-8a There is another interesting, and
earlier, 1890–1, Rationalist **Central
téléphonique** by Jean-Marie Boussard at
46 rue du Louvre. It is entirely covered
in white-glazed brick, except for the north
façade which is almost an all-glass curtain
wall. *Métro: Les Halles*

Paris 2   F-9
* Le Parisien Libéré (newspaper
offices) 1903–5
124 rue Réaumur
Attributed to Georges Chédanne
Art Nouveau/Rationalism
Map F-2 / Métro: Sentier

More than any comparable European
structure of its kind and time, this is the
definitive urban office building stripped to
the bare necessities of light and support,
with a minimum of wasted space or
inflexibility. Except for the curvature of
some minor structural elements, which
might have been only marginally more
efficient had they been straight, there is
hardly a suggestion of ornament in the
entire building.

F-9a An interesting comparison might be
made with Hector Guimard's only **office
building,** at 10 rue de Bretagne, which
may have been designed as early as 1913
but was not completed until 1919. It is also
a Rationalist, steel-framed, bay-windowed
structure, but the projection of its two
remarkable bays increases progressively
with each succeeding storey.
Métro: Filles du Calvaire

Paris 5   F-10
** Panthéon (formerly church of Ste-
Geneviève, now secular shrine to France's
national heroes) 1755–90
place du Panthéon
Jacques-Germain Soufflot
Neo-Classicism
Map F-2 / Métro: Maubert-Mutualité

[After the Revolution two short bell
towers, which had not been part of
Soufflot's original design, were removed
from above the corners of the pediment –
this in honour of the first change of status
from religious to secular. At the same time,
1792, all the windows were filled in and
some of the ornament recut by Quatremère
de Quincy – this in the name of a purportedly greater archaeological precision.]

In 1753, Marc-Antoine Laugier, a Jesuit
priest, published his influential *Essay on
Architecture*, a seminal Neo-Classicist tract
which, in the best theological tradition,
called for a return to first causes and, in
particular, to the Rousseauesque primitive
hut – it then being the assumed basis of
all Classical architecture. In effect he, like
other theorists in that 'Age of Reason',
wanted to revive the Greek temple in its
pure, rational simplicity: just columns,
lintels and a roof. Hardly a reasonable response to the climate or the needs of eighteenth-century France, but one whose
general acceptance as an ideal clearly demonstrated that the old Renaissance-
Baroque continuum had lost both meaning
and vitality. Neo-Classicism was, then, not
a prolongation of the old system but the
first of those stylistic revivals commonly
associated with the nineteenth century.

The Panthéon was not a direct result of
Laugier's book. The two arose separately in
response to the temper of the times and
reflect important differences of attitude.
Soufflot's church, for instance, was meant

to be Byzantine in plan – albeit that was
held tantamount to being Greek at a time
when, through suitably Byzantine exercises
in Gallic logic (see also F-28), Greek culture,
and thus all things Greek, were held to be
spiritually and genetically French! Contemporary critics even found it consistent
with this line of reasoning to hold that
Sainte Geneviève (as it was then known)
was Gothic! Not that they were completely
without justification. Soufflot was one of
the first architects to understand that the
Gothic was not simply an ornamental style,
nor just another order like the Doric or
Ionic, but rather a system of structural
logic. He understood that logic and daringly
used it to produce the lightest, most structurally efficient building post-Renaissance
Europe had yet known. It was so light, in
fact, that a popular fear for the stability
of its dome forced Soufflot to replace the

supporting column clusters beneath it with the present more substantial piers.

In a sense, popular opinion was right. Both philosophically and technologically Soufflot had stretched the Classical system beyond its natural limits of scale and proportion. It was not possible for him to span the distances between his columns with single stone lintels. Instead, he had to employ flat arches laced together with an elaborate system of wrought-iron ties. And so, ironically, Neo-Classicism's first major monument also marks the first serious revival of Gothic structural technology, and even points toward the eventual development of reinforced concrete.

F-10a An enlightening comparison can be made between the Panthéon and Paris's other major domed monument, Jules Hardouin-Mansart's Baroque church of **St-Louis des Invalides,** 1680–1708, at 2 avenue de Tourville. *Métro: Varenne*

F-10b Another Paris church, the **Madeleine,** 1806–28, by Alexandre-Pierre Vignon (interior, 1828–45, by Jean-Jacques Marie Huvé), on the place de la Madeleine is, externally at least, one of modern Europe's few temple-form buildings (but see also D-67). *Métro: Madeleine*

F-10c A more modern programme fitted into a less pure temple form is the **Bourse** (stock exchange) by Alexandre-Théodore Brongniart, 1808–15, in the place de la Bourse. [Iron roof added 1823–6, wings 1895–1903.] *Métro: Bourse*

Paris 5   **F-11**
** Bibliothèque Ste-Geneviève
(library) 1839–50
place du Panthéon
Henri Labrouste
Néo-Grec/Rationalism/Architecture Parlante
Map F-2 / Métro: Cardinal Lemoine
[Although the main reading room may be entered and photographed only with permission, it can be viewed from the corridor.]

Most histories of modern architecture at least mention the Bibliothèque Ste-Geneviève, if only to note the slender iron columns and lacy iron arches within its main reading room. Indeed, it must be both one of the better-known nineteenth-century buildings and one of the least understood. Its exposed structural iron is early, to be sure, but hardly the earliest (GB-59, 64). Far more to the point, that ironwork does not reflect a single-minded interest in technical innovation for its own sake – no more so than does the seldom noted fact that this was the first artificially lit library. It merely suggests the breadth of Labrouste's intense questioning spirit and his desire to interweave many kinds of reality and meaning. His was an attempt to unite necessity with allusion; to bring the past, through art, archaeology and of course the written word, into the present.

Appropriately Ste-Geneviève was also an attempt to confront the reality of Gutenberg and of Luther: the reality of the printing press and of the universal vernacular literacy which had deprived architecture of its traditional communicative role. For Labrouste, architecture could no longer illustrate social structure and myth in the manner that the cathedrals had done when they were the 'bibles of the poor'. In a sense he felt post-Renaissance architecture could only be about architecture, past, present and future. Ste-Geneviève's exquisitely precise façade clearly, one might say organically, describes its internal organization. It even lists the writers, from Moses through to the latest mid-nineteenth-century scientist, whose recorded thoughts lie on the shelves immediately behind their incised, and once coloured, names. Yet this is no easy building to 'read', much less one to be quickly 'scanned'. Nor is there space enough here even to paraphrase its multiple meanings and allusions. As with a rich but difficult epic, successive rereadings are their own reward. For each new generation, Ste-Geneviève has always struck some responsive chord – even for those who thought they could see nothing more in it than technical innovation.

F-11a Just across the rue Valette, facing the place du Panthéon, is the **librarian's house,** 1847, also by Labrouste.

F-11b The similarly subordinated façade to the left of the library is a **former entrance to the Collège Ste-Barbe,** 1840–52, designed by Labrouste's older brother Théodore.

Paris 6   **F-12**
** **Maison à Gradins** (social
housing) 1911–12
26 rue Vavin
Henri Sauvage
Rationalism
Map F-2 / Métro: Notre Dame des Champs

There is a striking resemblance between
the Maison à Gradins and Tony Garnier's
Cité Industrielle (F-54), first exhibited in
Paris in 1904. Just as Garnier had done
with various aspects of his utopian project,
Sauvage derived the detailing and basic
design of this unique, radical, ziggurat-like
apartment block not from aesthetic considerations but from a desire to reform the
living conditions of urban workers. (Ironically, as with some other famous proto-
typical social housing schemes (F-63), the
occupants here were not to be workers.)
But this building led to little else. After the
First World War, Sauvage built only one
additional, more refined version (F-32).
This building may also have contributed to
an influential project by the Italian Futurist
Antonio Sant'Elia (I-29a-b).

F-12a As early as 1903–5 Sauvage,
together with Charles Sarazin, had built
the **Logements Hygiéniques à Bon
Marché** at 7 rue de Trétaigne. An almost
styleless concrete-framed housing block, it
originally had a communal roof terrace.
Métro: Jules Joffrin

F-12b Sauvage's   steel-framed   **Cité
l'Argentine,** an apartment block and
arcade at 111 avenue Victor-Hugo, shows
that even as late as 1906 he had not quite
left Art Nouveau behind. *Métro: Etoile*

F-12c The most extreme example of Sauvage's ability to abandon style completely –
when the need arose – is the block of
studio apartments of 1926 at 65 rue la
Fontaine. Even a knowledgeable observer
could be forgiven for assuming that it had
been put up in the 50s by some unre-
markable modernist – or, ironically, in the
80s by an *au courant* Post-Modernist.
Métro: Michel-Ange-Auteuil

Paris 7   **F-13**
** **Maison de verre** or **Maison
Dalsace** (house and doctor's
office) 1929–31
31 rue St-Guillaume
Pierre Chareau, with Bernard Bijvoet
International Style High-Tech
Map F-2 / Métro: Sèvres-Babylone

[Both the house and the courtyard in
which it is situated are closed to the public.
At present one can only catch a glimpse
through an archway.]

What appears to be a remodelling of an
existing building is, in fact, an entirely new
house slipped beneath the upper stories of
an old building whose top-floor tenant
refused to be budged from her apartment.

Behind the sheer, glass-block façade –
whose construction progress Le Corbusier
is said to have followed daily – is a timeless
vision of an aesthetic appropriate to an
industrial era: a careful collage of industrial

F-12d Sauvage collaborated with Franz
Jourdain on the Art Deco extension and
unfortunate renovation (1926–30) of
Jourdain's **Samaritaine department
store,** 1901–10, between the rues de la
Monnaie, Baillet and de l'Arbre-Sec on the
Right Bank of the Seine. Until then la Samaritaine's original façades had been one of
the chief glories of the French Art Nouveau.
Marvellously wrought riveted iron ornament rioted – in a subdued way – over
carefully delimited areas of its exposed
structure, while enamelled metal panels,
reminiscent of Alphonse Mucha at his best,
filled any other surface that was not glass.
At the time of the renovation, when Art
Nouveau was in extreme disfavour, most of
the embellishments of the façades, including a beautiful entrance canopy, were
removed, and all the enamelwork, save for
a large panel bearing the stone's name, was
painted over. (Some of Jourdain's original
ornamental intent remains visible on the
short rue Baillet façade.) It is surprising
that, despite the extent of the vandalism
they suffered – in part at their own creator's
hands, the older façades still look whole.
Métro: Pont Neuf

components intended to allow the inhabitants continuously to reshape their living
spaces. To a degree, the assurance and
flexibility of the Maison de verre is reminiscent of the similarly intense Schröderhuis (NL-46). Yet by comparison this
house makes Rietveld's earlier masterwork
seem like a fragile, precious piece of period
furniture.

Paris 7   F-14
* **Unesco** 1953–8
place de Fontenoy
Marcel Breuer & Bernard Zehrfuss, with
Pier Luigi Nervi (engineer)
Neo-Expressionism/Brutalism
Map F-2 / Métro: Ségur
[The glass sunshades were a later
addition, as is the large underground
western extension with its six sunken
courtyards. The lobby is open to visitors
and tours of the rest of the building are
available. There is also a Japanese garden
by Noguchi, a large Alexander Calder
mobile, Miró murals, etc.]
Over the years critics have consistently
found this building to be disappointing, disorganized and tainted by political compromise. The political charge was inevitable.
The UN is the ultimate political body, and
it had acted lamentably with regard to the
usurpation and emasculation of Le Corbusier's design for its New York Headquarters – much as twenty years before Le
Corbusier had been unjustly deprived of
the right to build his competition-winning
League of Nations design.
Here, if anything, the opposite was true.
The Unesco commission was taken from an
architect who was not producing results

and given to a man who had been both a
renowned teacher at the Bauhaus and a
sometime partner of Walter Gropius. But
Breuer's prior experience had been primarily as a furniture and house designer.
At the time he had no major building to his
credit, nor were his training or philosophical background appropriate to this
traditional urban site on a critical location
in one of the most complex and important
axial sequences in Europe's most formal
city – as is especially evident from the Eiffel
Tower (F-16) which stands astride the same
axis. No matter how dogmatically modern
Breuer wanted to be, he was obliged to
respect the symmetry and outline of the
place de Fontenoy. Hence Unesco's unusual
(if not brand-new for Breuer) and here quite
successful three-winged plan.
All this having been said, Unesco
remains, sadly, one of the better large
postwar buildings in Paris – if only because
when Breuer designed it, he was still essentially breaking new ground and he gave the
building some thought. However, much of
the credit must also be due to Nervi, who
was responsible for shaping the *pilotis* and
the entrance canopy, and, most significant,
for making possible the huge folded-plate
structure that houses the auditorium.

Paris 7   F-15
Immeuble d'appartements
(apartment building) 1901
29 avenue Rapp
Jules Lavirotte
Art Nouveau
Map F-2 / Métro: Ecole Militaire
The nineteenth century's interest in construction technology led to the development of architectural terracotta, a ceramic
material whose plastic and polychromatic
possibilities made it exceedingly popular
among all but those with the strictest historicist sensibilities. For some reason French
Art Nouveau – in contrast to that of some
other countries (A-5, E-8) – rarely exploited
the full aesthetic possibilities of this
material, even though ceramics were as
much a part of the nineteenth-century
French technical heritage as were the glass
and metal that Art Nouveau regularly
employed with such assurance.
This particular ceramic façade, although
Lavirotte's and Paris's most successful,
reflects little understanding of the material's potentials and limitations as an architectural medium. True, it does incorporate
some unusual conceits and does not lack
inventiveness, and even has what one
takes to be a sense of humour. Yet if ever
there was a hotchpotch, this is it.

F-15a Around the corner at **3 square
Rapp** is another more typical Lavirotte
ceramic façade of 1899 with vaguely
Baroque overtones.

F-15b Lavirotte's well-known **Céramic Hôtel** of 1904, at 34 avenue de Wagram, is even more coherent, and even less interesting. *Métro: Ternes*

F-15c At 14–16 rue d'Abbeville are **two Lavirotte buildings** of about 1900. The façade of one is being devoured by writhing ceramic weeds, while that of the other is graced by a pair of large, amply endowed female figures. *Métro: Poissonnière*

F-15d The dullness of a more technically competent French terracotta **Art Nouveau façade,** by Charles Klein, 1903, can be seen at 2 rue Eugène-Manuel. *Métro: Passy*

Paris 7   **F-16**
*** Tour Eiffel (Eiffel Tower) 1884–9
champ de Mars
Gustave Eiffel
Map F-2 / Métro: Trocadéro

[Eiffel's personal apartment, above the top observation deck, has been converted into a TV transmitting station. The restaurants have also been rebuilt, with the loss of most of the tower's original paper-doily ornament. The only surviving ornament is within the great base arches. More recently, 1981–3, the original spiral stairs – down which Alec Guinness's Lavender Hill Mob descended so dazzlingly – have been replaced with lighter, more conventional zigzag ones. At the same time the original upper elevators were lost. But surely the greatest loss the tower has suffered was the elimination of the ever more elaborate interwar decorative lighting schemes that began as part of the 1925 Exposition des Arts Décoratifs. Financed as advertising by the automobile tycoon Citroën, they made the tower an even more dominant part of the Parisian skyline by night than it was, and still is, during the day.]

Eiffel, a pragmatic, pioneering bridge designer (F-58), built this 984-foot (300-metre) tower as a temporary centrepiece for the 1889 World's Fair. Since then, it has become the symbol of the tourists' Paris. At the time of construction it was consciously another kind of symbol, an assertion of France's recovery from the devastations of the Franco-Prussian War and the Commune. It marked Paris's readiness to resume its place as the *haute bourgeois* cultural capital of nineteenth-century Europe. The Eiffel Tower was virtually a unique object when built, all but devoid of prosaic useful functions. It was France's '300-metre flagpole'. Yet, because it stood in complete contrast to both its park-like setting and the roofscape above which it was seen, and because it was visible from throughout the city while at the same time rendering the entire city comprehensible from a single, central vantage point, it quite justifiably became the icon of Paris.

But what of the future? Already the cluster of office towers at La Défense (F-27a) looms menacingly on the horizon, while other infiltrators, closer to hand, further disrupt the traditionally uniform Parisian skyline.

F-16a The 'Mussolini Modern' group directly across the Seine on axis with the tower is the **Palais de Chaillot,** 1934–7, by Carlu, Boileau & Azéma. It is a souvenir of the 1937 World's Fair. *Métro: Trocadéro*

F-16b The 1889 Fair was also responsible for a second equally bold masterpiece of engineering, C.-L.-F. Dutert and Victor Contamin's **Palais des Machines** (machinery hall), whose massive three-hinged arches spanned 380 feet. This huge structure was destroyed during the 20s – a time when the Eiffel Tower was also threatened. The best remaining example of Dutert's work is the **Galerie de Paléontologie** (palaeontology gallery) 1895–5, at the Museum of Natural History on the rue Buffon in the Jardin des Plantes (botanical gardens). In addition to an iron structure, it incorporates some remarkable ornamental ironwork. *Métro: Gare d'Orléans-Austerlitz*

F-16c Also originally a single huge glass and iron exhibition space was H.-A.-A. Deglane, L-A. Louvet and A.-F.-T. Thomas's **Grand Palais,** 1897–1900, built for the 1900 Exhibition, on the avenue Winston Churchill. Its interior has suffered numerous remodellings over the years, however, while its Beaux-Arts façades always were stickily sweet fluff. *Métro: Champs-Elysées-Clemenceau*

Paris 16   **F-17**
** Accès des stations de Métro
(Métro station entrances) 1899–1903
(design in production until 1913)
Porte Dauphine
Hector Guimard
Art Nouveau
*Map F-2 / Métro: Porte Dauphine (between
av Foch and its northern lateral)*

[Of the 140 entrances originally erected,
about 90 of the simpler sort remain in place.
Part of one is at the Museum of Modern Art
in New York. Most of the more elaborate
examples were located in places of particular importance and vulnerability and,
except for Porte Dauphine, they are now all
lost. Another glassed pavilion will, it is said,
eventually be re-erected.]

These delightfully ornamented holes in
the ground have personified Art Nouveau
to generations of Parisians and tourists
alike. When first erected they also helped
to popularize the style, giving it yet another
of its aliases – Style Métro. Through the
intervening years, when the very name Art
Nouveau was anathema, they kept it and
Guimard from complete eclipse.

They are not, however, just style without
substance. The Métro entrances also represent one of the first attempts by an architect to design a systematized modular 'kit
of parts' – one suitable, within limits, to
the solution of a range of similar problems.
Depending upon how these parts were
assembled, an entrance could be made to
fit the requirements of almost any given site
or circumstance. Even today, when kept
free of the extraneous encrustations they
seem so readily to acquire, they remain
one of the liveliest, most successful street
furniture designs ever.

Paris 16   **F-18**
** Immeuble d'habitation
(apartment building) 1902–4
25bis rue Franklin
Auguste Perret
Rationalism
Map F-2 / Métro: Trocadéro

Despite a popular misconception, this is
not the first reinforced concrete-framed
building. That distinction probably rests
with de Baudot's church in Montmartre (F-
29) or with a now lost mill by François
Hennebique, although both are only a few
years earlier. Nor is this the first expression
of a structural frame on the façade of a
building. For years Rationalists had been
espousing that idea, and occasionally building it (F-37). In fact, perhaps because he
was still unsure of his concrete, Perret
covered it with terracotta. The more strictly
Neo-Classical and eminently Rational
Perret of later years (F-18b) might well
have dismissed the use of such cladding –
especially the mosaic flowers on the non-
structural infill panels – as no more than
a youthful aberration. (These ceramic
daisies, apparently the work of ceramicist
Alexandre Bigot, also appear, sometimes
along with Guimard-designed components,
on contemporaneous Art Nouveau buildings.)

Even though he tried to avoid it in his
later works, Perret's real innovation here
was the development of an irregular, albeit
symmetrical, columnar grid which wholly
responds to the building's interior spatial
requirements. Although not impossible in
the previous iron technology, this fore-
runner of Le Corbusier's 'free plan' structures was certainly better suited to the rigid
joints and inherently greater homogeneity
of concrete. Furthermore, Perret's façade
not only recognizes the fact that the build-

ing has a skeletal structure; it expresses
volumetrically the incipient free plan made
possible by that structure.

Regardless of how it was read by later
generations, however, this development
may partly have been the fortuitous result
of a shallow building lot, which made the
mandatory light-well unnecessary. Perret
was thus able to include its volume within
the façade, giving each of the principal
rooms even more light and air, and a better
view across the adjacent park to the Seine.
And so with this singular response to this
singular site, he extended his undeniable
reputation as a pioneer of new materials
and techniques into the areas of planning
and design – despite the evidence of much
of his previous and subsequent work.

F-18a '25bis' is one of Perret's three important prewar buildings. The next, in chronological order, was the Garage Ponthieu of 1905 (destroyed c. 1969), whose concrete frame Perret left unclad. The last was the **Théâtre des Champs-Elysées,** 1909–13, at 13 avenue Montaigne. Henri van de Velde was originally to have been its architect with Perret serving as engineer and structural contractor. Eventually Perret received the architectural commission as well. Although the hand of Van de Velde is perhaps still discernible, the theatre as built is primarily the work of Perret. It is best and most justly known for its complex concrete frame, which can be seen and appreciated only in drawings.
Métro: Alma-Marceau

F-18b A nearby Perret building that exemplifies both his unexcelled ability to use concrete and the basic conservatism of his mature designs is the **Musée des Travaux Publics** (museum of public works) of 1937, at the place d'Iéna.
Métro: Iéna

Paris 16   **F-19**
* Castel Béranger (apartment building) 1894–8
14–16 rue La Fontaine
Hector Guimard
Art Nouveau
Map F–2 / Métro: Jasmin

   In the summer of 1895 while working on designs for the Castel Béranger, Hector Guimard visited Brussels where he met Victor Horta and saw some of Horta's houses (B-3). Previously, Guimard's work had been well within the Gothic Rationalist orthodoxy of Viollet-le-Duc (F-24). His later work would employ a purely Art Nouveau vocabulary, one which was to become increasingly abstract with the passage of time. Only here and, to varying degrees, in a few smaller country houses – the best of which is now lost – is the vigour and inventiveness of Guimard's better Art-Nouveau ornament equalled in his handling of the building's materials and forms.

   The Castel Béranger is, then, an uneven, but not incoherent, mixture of two romanticisms. It has the Gothic Rationalist's honest concern for unadorned materials and expressed structure, frequently inspired by vernacular or industrial usage – as is to be seen, for instance, in the rubble masonry of the courtyard façades and in the use of several types of the then still very novel glass block. Juxtaposed with these are the sophisticated Art Nouveau concern for continuity, an interest in the implication of 'organic' relationships between parts, and a preference for highly plastic cast materials such as terracotta and iron.

   When Castel Béranger is compared to Guimard's later urban Art Nouveau work (F-21) one must see that the exciting freshness here represents a kind of hybrid vigour. The more mature Guimard would approach the design of large urban buildings within a more consistent, but also more limiting, theoretical framework – inevitable, perhaps, but the loss is ours as well as his. And how in that case did he continue for several more years to produce his little fantasy country houses?

F-19a As time passed, Guimard became increasingly involved with a semi-industrialized standardization of building elements: gutters, downpipes, ventilators, etc. Either because he continued to believe in what he modestly called '*le Style Guimard*', at least in small doses, or because it was too expensive to make new moulds, these elements retained their original Art Nouveau forms long after the style had disappeared from other aspects of his work. In fact, they almost became his trademark.

   They may be seen nearby on such late Art Nouveau **Guimard buildings** as 8–10 rue Agar (also known as 17–21 rue La Fontaine or 43 rue Gros), 1908–11, in which Guimard had a financial stake, as well as:

F-19b **142 avenue de Versailles,** one of Guimard's better apartment buildings, 1903–5, in his mature Art Nouveau style;

F-19c **11 rue François-Millet,** 1910; and

F-19d **60 rue La Fontaine,** 1910–11.

Paris 16   F-20
Immeuble d'appartements
(apartment building) 1934
42 avenue de Versailles
Jean Ginsberg, with François Heep
International Style
Map F-2 / Métro: Chardon-Lagache
   This apartment building was designed just at the moment of transition when the over-specific if still ascetic forms that first appeared in the villas of artists and dilettanti were beginning to find their way into the realm of speculative bourgeois flats.

F-20a Two years earlier Ginsberg, with Berthold Lubetkin, had built a smaller, more restrained **apartment building** at 25 avenue de Versailles.

Paris 16   F-21
Hôtel Guimard (Guimard's own house and studio) 1909–10
122 avenue Mozart
Hector Guimard
Art Nouveau
Map F-2 / Métro: Michel-Ange-Auteuil
[After Guimard's death, Mme Guimard, who was an American, wanted to assure the preservation of this house together with its interiors, which were then still intact. But, as the French government would do nothing to assist, she was forced to convert the building into flats. She gave most of the interiors and furnishings to museums – including New York's Cooper Union and Museum of Modern Art. The dining-room, however, remains in Paris at the Musée d'Art Moderne, while the bedroom is in Lyon's Musée des Beaux-Arts (F-54a).]
   As might be expected, Guimard lavished special attention on his own house. It was to be a harmonious total work of art reflecting the refinement of *'le Style Guimard'*. By 1909, however, it must have been painfully apparent that Art Nouveau was fading fast. Even Guimard's own ornament, once so violently alive, was becoming something like – but more tense and refined than – that of eighteenth-century French Rococo

furniture. Not so the organization of his façades. They still respond primarily to internal requirements and are just too lumpy, too circumstantial, to be called refined – if also too tasteful to be called vigorous!

Paris 16   F-22
** Maisons La Roche et Jeanneret
(double house, now Fondation Le Corbusier) 1922–4
10 square du Docteur-Blanche
Le Corbusier
International Style
Map F-2 / Métro: Jasmin
[Restored c. 1970. Open to the public.]
   The Maison Jeanneret, built for Le Corbusier's brother, is a modest dwelling, devoid of spatial gymnastics or even a separate exterior identity. Indeed, it is little more than an appendage or foil to the Maison La Roche, Le Corbusier's first uncompromising masterwork. Now, happily filled with Le Corbusier's paintings, furniture and models of his buildings, the Maison La Roche serves as the Fondation's exhibition space.
   Fittingly, it was in the Maison La Roche that Le Corbusier brought together for the first time the famous 'five points', which were to be the theoretical basis for most of

his later architecture, especially between the wars, and which also, therefore, underlay the entire International Style. These five points were:
1. Free-standing supports (*pilotis*): essentially the exposed ground-floor columns of a skeletal structure. They dramatize the greater distinction between building and site inherent in non-loadbearing-wall con-

struction. As used here by Le Corbusier for the first time, they are of simple form and uncertain necessity.

2. Free façades: another by-product of the skeletal frame. This means that windows, doors, etc., may be positioned and sized solely in response to the dictates of functional necessity, or at least in response to such aesthetic considerations as Le Corbusier's proportion-governing *tracés régulateurs*, an overlay of imaginary vertical, horizontal and diagonal regulating lines which could determine the relationships, sizes and proportions of all the façade elements, and of the façade itself. (Later in his career the role of the *tracés régulateurs* would be taken over by his Modulor system of proportional units of measurements.)

3. Strip windows: really an aspect of the free façade. They, like the *pilotis*, are said to appear here first, although something similar can be found in the contemporaneous Ozenfant Studio (F-34c).

4. A roof terrace: the natural corollary to the watertight flat roof, particularly in cities, where ground-level outdoor space is at a premium and frequently shaded. The terrace here is still rather rudimentary compared to such later examples as the Villa Savoye (F-45) or Marseilles Block (F-63).

5. A free plan: the truest expression of Le Corbusier's fresh architectural vision, it derives in part from his constant compositional experiments as a painter. Le Corbusier carefully positioned balconies, partitions, stairs, ramps and cut through walls (some two or three stories high) to compose 'pure' spaces of a sort only appropriate or possible within a structural system that is not being internally 'expressed'. Through all this he transformed the form-world of his purist canvases into the kinetic three-dimensional experience which he called an 'architectural promenade'.

Over the next forty years he was to develop this last point much further. He would choreograph columns and walls, employ a broad palette of textures and materials, and eventually attempt, in essence, to unify painting, sculpture and architecture. But this is the real beginning.

Paris 16   **F-23**
Cité Mallet-Stevens (houses)
1926–7
rue Mallet-Stevens
Robert Mallet-Stevens
International Style
Map F-2 / Métro: Jasmin

From our present perspective Le Corbusier's work seems to stand almost alone in that strange mélange of modernity and timelessness that was post-First World War Paris. (And noone did more than Le Corbusier himself to encourage such a perception.) At the time, however, two French architects were frequently equated with Le Corbusier. One was André Lurçat – now chiefly memorable for a single school (F-39). The other was Mallet-Stevens, whose works partook of the more slick sophistication then in vogue, even as they also tried to meet the International Style ideal of angular, white asymmetry.

Almost alone in a generation that had little love for Art Nouveau, Mallet-Stevens admired Hoffmann and Mackintosh, two members of that prewar movement who had had a strong, inflexible sense of style. Shortly after he had finished these five

fashionable houses, political and economic crises caught up with Mallet-Stevens and his era, and he, like Mackintosh and Hoffmann before him, lost touch with the temper of his radically changing times.

Paris 16   **F-24**
* Ecole du Sacré-Cœur (school, now
apartments) 1895
9 avenue de la Frillière
Hector Guimard
Rationalism
Map F-2 / Métro: Exelmans

[The ground level, originally open, has been filled in.]

If today those V-shaped pairs of tapered columns still demand attention, imagine their effect in an age of masonry construction. Admittedly their unorthodox arrangement does lend the structure considerable stability in one direction, although it is doubtful whether the average person at the time would have recognized that. More to the point, it lessens the spans of the heavily

laden girder that the columns support. The girder, in its turn, carries dozens of closely spaced I-beams between whose flanges nestle brick vaults which both serve as the first floor's sub-structure and also, at their outer ends, carry the slightly cantilevered exterior loadbearing walls. With each element so carefully articulated and delineated from its neighbour, and with similar, if sometimes symbolic, constructional articulation around the windows and elsewhere, this complex structure is eminently Rationalist. Indeed, it was directly derived from a widely disseminated, forty-year-old project by the great Rationalist theoretician Viollet-le-Duc.

However, even as he built this school Guimard was designing the Castel Béranger (F-19) and, turning away from this tectonic architecture, would soon be setting out on his Art Nouveau adventure. Is this, then, the end of a lineage? In a sense, yes. But add some concrete, retaining much of the iron in a more complex form, and what is the result? Le Corbusier's indispensable *pilotis* (F-63) which, in their turn, devolved into one of the major clichés of post-Second World War architecture.

Paris 16   **F-25**
Immeuble d'habitation (apartment building) 1933
24 rue Nungesser-et-Coli
Le Corbusier
International Style
Map F-2 / Métro: Michel-Ange-Molitor
[The penthouse was Le Corbusier's own home until his death in 1965. It now belongs to the Fondation Le Corbusier and, it is to be hoped, will eventually be made accessible to the public.]

Neatly turned out in its all-glass curtain walls, this is rather advanced work for its time – although hardly in a class with either Le Corbusier's Clarté block (CH-16), or the Armée du Salut (F-35), both of which are of about the same date. But such is the nature of speculative urban apartment buildings: they are so constrained by economic limitations and municipal regulations that their designers' and owners' options are almost nil – as witness the nearly identical front and rear façades here, as well as the more or less conventional position and massing of the bays.

Yet equally appropriate to its urban location, and to the urban mythos, is the single penthouse apartment. Designed especially for its artist-owner, and not bowing to any constraints save those he imposed upon himself, it is a very private place in which it is possible, if one desires, to expose a party wall's comforting rubble masonry or sculpt a set of stairs like those remembered from some timeless Mediterranean village.

F-25a Not too far away, near the south end of the Bois de Boulogne, at 6 rue Denfert-Rochereau in the suburb of Boulogne-Billancourt, is the **Maison Cook**, Le Corbusier's 1926 reinterpretation of the traditional row house. Unfortunately, its

once open ground floor, which made the conjoined front and rear yards seem luxuriously large, has since been enclosed.

F-25b **8 rue Denfert-Rochereau** is by Robert Mallet-Stevens, 1926.

F-25c Near by, at 9 allée les Pins, are Le Corbusier's **Maisons Lipschitz** and **Miestschaninoff** of 1924.

F-25d The **Hôtel de Ville** of Boulogne-Billancourt, 1931–4, at 20 avenue André-Morizet, is the only Parisian work of Tony Garnier. Do not be fooled by the fusty façade: Garnier saved himself here for the large internal circulation hall.
Métro: Marcel-Sembat

Paris/Neuilly   **F-26**
* **Maisons Jaoul** (double house)
1952–7
81 rue de Longchamp
Le Corbusier
Brutalism
Map F-2 / Métro: Pont de Neuilly
Here is Le Corbusier's most influential restatement of his hybridized, folkloric 'Catalan thin-tile vault' (with modern concrete edge beams) structural system – an idea which first appears in his work as early as 1916 and which, beyond that, has even earlier Rationalist antecedents (F-24). In

addition to the Maisons Jaoul, Le Corbusier also built two other houses incorporating similar versions of this system: the frequently published and now all but lost Maison du Weekend, 1934–5, and the Sarabhai House, 1955–6, in Ahmadabad, India. But both were low, sod-roofed buildings that presented little in the way of an externally photographable image, and one was built at an inauspicious time while the other is in an out of the way place.

The Maisons Jaoul on the other hand, are multi-storied, therefore presenting a more identifiable image and are in an accessible location. They, and the interest they generated in their less accessible counterparts, provided an impetus for a whole generation of architects – among whom those on the Continent stuck more or less closely to the original Corbusian prototype (CH-12), while their English and American counterparts almost immediately took the picturesque tectonics of these houses as the starting point for a wider range of variants and modifications (GB-29). Rarely has so modest a commission had so great an impact – excepting always some of Le Corbusier's earlier works (F-45).

Paris/Puteaux   **F-27**
CNIT, Palais des Expositions
(exhibition hall) 1957–8
place de la Défense
R. Camelot, J. de Mailly & B. Zehrfuss, with J. Prouvé (curtain walls), N. Esquillan & P. L. Nervi (engineers)
Map F-2 / Métro: La Défense
Overall, it is the structure that dominates. How could it not? The fluted concrete thin shell – some six feet thick but light and hollow – spans over seven hundred feet and covers more than twenty acres from only three points of support. It is, or was at the time of construction, twice the size of any other concrete clear span.

Jean Prouvé's curtain walls – like some Brobdingnagian reincarnation of traditional greenhouse glazing – are remarkably appropriate to, and in scale with, this huge anonymous building. But any addition to such a simple strongly geometrical shape is difficult at best, and the box-like projections from its sides are no exception.

F-27a Until recently the Champs-Elysées's axis had always seemed, from the vantage point of the Arc de Triomphe, to go on to infinity. Not any more. Now **La Défense,** the planning of which began in 1958, terminates the vista in a mini-Manhattan whose huddle of toy skyscrapers almost seems aware of its own absurdity.

Paris 18   **F-28**
* Sacré-Cœur (church) 1872–1912
Butte Montmartre
Paul Abadie
Néo-Grec/National Romantic
Map F-2 / Métro: Abbesses
Every tourist knows Sacré-Cœur, perhaps fortuitously glimpsed down some narrow street, or seen from the Eiffel Tower (F-16), gleaming hazily white on its distant hilltop. How could anything so appealing at the distance of half a city be so seemingly wrong close at hand? For that matter, why should a national expiatory church (a kind of penance for having lost the Franco-Prussian War) be so overtly oriental?

The model for Sacré-Cœur was St-Front at Périgueux, an unusual Romanesque church whose Greek-cross plan and distinctive turreted domes betray its kinship with St Mark's in Venice and, ultimately, with Byzantium. Its choice as the model for Sacré-Cœur reflects a theory, much favoured by Viollet-le-Duc, that there had been only two true forms of architecture. One was the Greek, no longer practicable but still the universal ideal, the other was the Gothic, descended from the Greek through a complex racial lineage, still adaptable to modern usages, and manifestly French.

Thus Rome's architecture, as well as all the derivatives from it, were but the borrowings of a lesser race. The fall of Rome had merely freed the 'Byzantine-Greeks' to develop their (implicitly superior) Byzantine style – which was to become the Romanesque. Later, according to this theory, these same Byzantine-Greeks passed the light of their artistic reason to those vigorous 'Aryans' who were to become the French nation and also the progenitors of the Gothic! Greek and Gothic were thereby linked, not only through the common rationality with which they responded to their respective circumstances, but also, as it were, 'genetically'.

If any building could demonstrate such a link, and thus France's moral superiority, it was the Byzantine-Romanesque church of St-Front. What could have been more natural at that time of national self-doubt than to bring St-Front to Paris?

F-28a St-Front *c.* 1120, is everything Sacré-Cœur wants to be – perhaps because Abadie himself extensively restored St-Front at the same time as he was building Sacré-Cœur. *In ctr of Périgueux*

F-28b By the nineteenth century, after hundreds of years of neglect culminating in the Revolution, many French churches were in dire need of such restoration. One of the most active and respected restorers was Eugène-Emmanuel Viollet-le-Duc, whose influential theoretical writings owed much to his restoration work – and vice versa. Chief among his restorations, in importance if not extent, was that of **Notre-Dame-de-Paris,** 1163–1270 (restored with J.-B.-A. Lassus, 1842–68). Without Viollet-le-Duc it would now have few of its famous gargoyles and statues, nor its sacristy, nor the tall spire above its crossing. Without him Notre-Dame as we

know it would hardly exist. *Métro: Cité*

Viollet-le-Duc, as much as any single individual, is responsible for our idea of what the Gothic ought to look like. Among his other restorations are:

F-28c Ste-Chapelle, also on the Ile de la Cité, built by Pierre de Montreuil, 1245–8. (Restored with J.-F. Duban and J.-B.-A. Lassus, 1837–83). With its original glass and repainted interior, it presents a particularly authentic if precious picture of the Gothic. *Métro: Cité*

F-28d The large **Château de Pierre-fonds,** 1390–1429, which he imaginatively (too imaginatively, some say) reconstructed, 1856–79, almost from a pile of rubble, so that it might serve as a country home for Napoleon III. *S from N31 between Compiègne and Soissons on D335, abt 4½ mi (7 km) / in ctr of town*

F-28e The ancient city of **Carcassonne,** fifth to thirteenth centuries, whose many-towered walls Viollet-le-Duc restored, 1852–79. Also then in an advanced state of ruin, they are now considerably more convincing than some of the 'medieval' houses they encircle. *From N113, E of Carcassonne ctr → LA CITÉ*

F-28f Among Viollet-le-Duc's wholly new works, only one, the **Mausoleum of the Duc de Mornay,** 1858, in Père-Lachaise cemetery, reflects the radical use of history that his writings might have led one to expect. *E on av de la République (Map F-2→) / R on boul de Ménilmontant to entrance / on chemin du Montlous in cemetery / Métro: Père-Lachaise*

Paris 18   **F-29**
* Eglise de St-Jean-de-Montmartre (church) 1894–1904
2 place des Abbesses
Anatole de Baudot
Gothic Rationalism
Map F-2 / Métro: Abbesses
De Baudot was a follower of Viollet-le-Duc and thus, despite the vaguely Islamic overtones of the ornamented structure of this church, a confirmed Gothicist. Here, because he was designing the world's first public building with a reinforced concrete frame, and because that building also was a church, it was even more natural that he turned to an essentially Gothic form of construction. This allowed him to express the nature of his material without relying too much on its then still uncertain tensile characteristics – a cautious approach but, in the face of municipal authorities who tried to demolish the church even before it was finished, a necessary one.

By the time St-Jean was completed, so was Perret's 25bis rue Franklin (F-18). Two years after that, in America, came the raw concrete cube of F. L. Wright's magnificent Unity Temple. *Sic transit gloria mundi.*

F-29a Simultaneously, 1899–1903, J. G.

Astruc was erecting the last of Paris's iron churches (F-6a,b), **Notre-Dame-du-Travail** at 59 rue Vercingétorix. Within its masonry walls is a light and delicate if decidedly unadventurous structure, fabricated entirely from stock rolled iron sections. *Métro: Pernety*

Paris 18   **F-30**
Maison Tzara (house and apartment)
1925–7
15 avenue Junot
Adolf Loos
Map F-2 / Métro: Lamarck-Caulaincourt

[The rear of the house faces the hameau des Artistes, and is reached via the staircase at 11 avenue Junot. Except for some new window casements it is externally unchanged. It is not open to visitors.]

Adolf Loos – radical Classicist, Anglophile and devoted Viennese, critic, theoretician and practical architect – built this house for the Dada artist Tristan Tzara. It was one of his last buildings and the only one to materialize from his five-year Parisian sojourn (1923–8). During the 20s, Loos's polemical writings, which unlike his architecture were not bound by particular programmatic constraints, technological requirements or considerations of style, retained much of their relevance – as they do today. By then, however, the time for his Neo-Classical gravity, symmetry, allusions and proportions had just about passed. Solidity and unrelieved symmetry had become all but unacceptable in the era of Le Corbusier's light white villas (F-22).

Like the work of other critic-architects, indeed like most of Loos's own earlier buildings and projects, the Tzara house seems at once radical and conservative.

Paris 18   **F-31**
Maison (house) 1913
185 rue Belliard
Henri Deneux
Arts and Crafts/Rationalism
Map F-2 / Métro: Port de St-Ouen

How tyical to find such a building in Paris. It is truly remarkable for its date: hard, clear, concise, with its concrete structure expressed, if not exposed, and its ornament essentially limited to the lively, ingenious patterning of its ceramic façades. But who was Henri Deneux? Apparently this is all that he built. Shortly after the First World War he abandoned the twentieth century for the thirteenth and began working on the restoration of Reims Cathedral, leaving to us only this of himself.

Paris 18   **F-32**
** Immeuble d'appartements et piscine (social housing and swimming pool) 1924–6
26 rue des Amiraux
Henri Sauvage
Rationalism
Map F-2 / Métro: Marcadet Poissonniers

The flats Sauvage had built in the rue Vavin (F-12) a dozen years earlier are, justly perhaps, more famous than these. However this building, which is less a fragment, and unlike its predecessor was actually intended for urban workers, somewhat better exemplifies the reformed housing type that Sauvage was attempting to develop. The set-back floors and white-tile façades, designed to bring light to both street and dwellings, are essentially unchanged from the earlier building. Only a greater overlapping of individual apart-

them, and a simpler, less ornamented – almost Constructivist or Futurist – exterior detailing suggest the passage of time, not to mention a world war. The main addition

Paris/Clichy   **F-33**
* **Marché couvert et Maison du Peuple** (market and assembly hall) 1937–9
39–41 boulevard du Général Leclerc
Marcel Lods & Eugène Beaudouin, with Jean Prouvé (curtain wall)
Rationalism
Map F-2
[Some minor damage (new doors, etc.) in the name of maintenance.]
Here is the medieval market/town hall updated and totally timeless. Below, largely open to the street, is a market hall with sheltering canopies all around, supported by bent steel beams which overhang the pavement and blur the distinction between the inside and out. Above is an unadorned, symmetrical, Miesian premonition: a truly flexible meeting hall with three glazed walls

Paris 14   **F-34**
** **Pavillon Suisse** (Swiss student hostel) 1930–2
7 boulevard Jourdan, Cité Universitaire
Le Corbusier
International Style
Map F-2 / Métro: Cité Universitaire
[Restored, with minor modifications, by Le Corbusier in 1957]
A complex yet simple building, it is even its own entrance canopy. At the peak of the International Style, it broke many of the then still new rules and began to suggest another, newer set – perhaps one reason it still looks so fresh. Gone is the white plaster. In its place is a cast-stone sheathing whose joints give a sense of scale by delineating storey heights, albeit not from floor to floor but from one windowsill or table height to the next. Gone too is that pure functionality of line and form. Previously, sculptural exceptions to the prevailing rational rectangularity were limited, if present at all, to the shaping of less permanent, non-structural elements. Here, the *pilotis*, the common room, the entire stair tower, are sculptured. They all play against the pure rectangular, mechanistic curtain-walled, steel-framed prism of the dormitory block, wherein only the slight variations of width and placement of the rectangular parapet openings suggest the freer plan of the director's top-floor flat.
Paradoxically, the most important 'innovation' in the Pavillon Suisse is the load-bearing rubble masonry of the curving common-room wall. For the first time in Le Corbusier's work no site condition, no primitive rural construction necessities can be called upon to justify this returning rustic romanticism, which, by its very pres-

here is the public swimming bath. It is neatly fitted into the leftover interior space created by the stepped configuration.

and a taller, skylit central section whose peripheral areas can be partitioned off for separate use. Enclosing all, with a minimum of fuss, is Jean Prouvé's spare sheet-metal craftsmanship – to call it a 'curtain wall' would be demeaning.

ence, admits to the end of the optimism of the first machine age.

F-34a The second building to the east is the **Brazilian students' hostel,** 1952–9. Le Corbusier, along with the Brazilian architect Lúcio Costa, is credited with designing this parody which mocks both the Pavillon Suisse and much of Le Corbusier's later work as well.

F-34b Some little distance west, at 61–63 boulevard Jourdan, is the **Dutch hostel,** 1931, by W. M. Dudok.
Métro: Cité Universitaire

F-34c Just north of the university at 53 avenue Reille, on the square Montsouris, is the early, 1922–3, and influential **Ozenfant Studio** which Le Corbusier designed for his then partner in purist painting and polemics, Amédée Ozenfant. Although well maintained, it has been extensively if subtly modified.
Métro: Cité Universitaire

Paris 19   F-35
** Cité de Refuge de l'Armée du Salut (Salvation Army hostel) 1929–33
12 rue Cantagrel
Le Corbusier
International Style
Map F-2 / Métro: Porte d'Ivry

[The Cité-Refuge was restored, after a fashion, in 1975. However, many details, from paint colours to glass blocks, are not correct.]

The main façade was once an absolutely flat and for some reason slightly canted curtain wall of both clear and obscure glass panels – these having been distributed in accordance with the needs of the spaces behind them. As the building was to be air-conditioned, Le Corbusier gave this southerly wall its remarkable flatness by simply not allowing any windows in it. His flaunting of faith in the ideal of brute-force environmental technology became totally irrational, however, when he refused to modify the curtain wall even though budget cuts had eliminated the building's air-conditioned equipment. Shortly after the war, Le Corbusier remodelled the unworkable façade – substituting a more regular pattern of rather unattractive opaque panels with opening windows for the obscure glass, and adding the *brise-soleil* system which now gives the wall its busy cluttered look.

Many of the sources of conventional architectural wisdom are strangely quiet about this building. It usually gets just the obligatory passing reference with perhaps a comment on its ocean liner-like superstructure, or on the neo-Platonic geometric purity of the foreground elements, or on the tension that once existed between both these and the original façade. And usually there is the same Le Corbusier photograph featuring prominently his favourite Voisin motorcar, an elegant geometric-mechanical analogy to his architecture which Le Corbusier wanted no one to miss. The same car appears in Le Corbusier's photographs of his other early buildings, but never more ironically and fittingly than here. Both motorcar and building epitomize Le Corbusier's infatuation with the promise of a once youthful technology. For him time and this experience quickly began to temper that ardour. Too many others, however, were captivated for far too long by the arguments – built, written and drawn by Le Corbusier – made by him during that first burst of enthusiasm.

F-35a Near by, at 24bis boulevard Masséna, is Le Corbusier's **Maison Plainex** of 1927. *Métro: Porte d'Ivry*

Le Raincy [near Paris]   F-36
** Notre Dame du Raincy (church) 1922–3
avenue de la Résistance
Auguste Perret
Rationalism
E on N3 (Map F-2→) / S → Le Raincy on D117 abt 1¼ mi (2 km) / R on av de la Résistance (D163) / abt 500 yds (m) on R
[Locked weekdays.]

In a sense this church is two semi-independent structures which, save for their proximity, have little organic relationship with each other. Most of what one sees from the street, the entrances, vestibules and tower, is the typical unlovely wedding cake that so often results when a Classicist strives for verticality. However, the main body of the building, a great shallow-vaulted nave, has frequently and justifiably been compared to High Gothic. It is Perret's masterpiece: not a parody but a restatement in concrete and glass of the Gothic quest for height, light, colour and weightlessness.

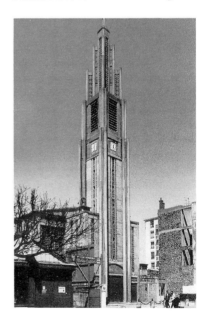

Noisiel-sur-Marne [near Paris]   **F-37**
* Usine Menier (chocolate factory)
1869–74
Jules Saulnier
Gothic Rationalism
*E on N34 (Map F-2→) / S in Neuilly-sur-
Marne on D194 / E on D75 ⇨ D217bis /
N→*NOISIEL */ L at main entrance to Menier
factory (follow outside of wall) →* QUAI */
factory bridges river abt 250 yds (m)
upstream*

Chicago's partisans – than which there
are none more partisan – trace the development of iron skeletal construction, of non-
loadbearing or 'curtain' walls, and ultimately therefore of the skyscraper, to
William Lebaron Jenney and the others
who rebuilt Chicago's Loop after the Great
Fire of 1871. Yet even as Chicago burned
this factory was under construction.

Spanning the river, supported by four
piers, the iron frame of the Menier factory
takes the form of a lattice bridge girder with

Marne-la-Vallée [near Paris]   **F-38**
* Les Espaces d'Abraxas (social
housing) 1978–83
Noisy-le-Grand
Taller de Arquitectura Bofill
Pre-cast Neo-Classicism
*E from Paris on autoroute A4 (Map F-2→)
abt 7½ m (12 km) / exit →* NOISY-LE-GRAND
on rue du Centre / on R

In a heartfelt competition project of
1974–5, the Taller (studio) Bofill attempted
to re-weave the tattered edges of the gaping
wound rent in the fabric of Paris by the
brutal destruction of Les Halles. Then,
developing the traditional site-planning
and architectural vocabularies they
adopted there, Bofill produced a series of
elegant, Classically inspired designs for
other urban parks and a parallel series of
housing designs. While Les Espaces d'Abraxas is part of that sequence, its grandiose
intensity sets it apart. It is in fact three
housing blocks: the curved 'Theatre', the
massive 'Palace' (also the theatre's stage
set), and, between them, the smaller 'Tri-
umphal Arch', which is, along with its
occupants, the sole actor on the stage. If
Bofill's initial reversion to Classicism was an
understandable response to the modernist
insensitivity to traditional urban fabrics,
then this may be a more desperately radical
reaction to the high-rise desolation of
postwar modernist suburbia.

Certainly Les Espaces is a statement. (The

diagonal and vertical structural elements
that are visible on the façade. (The elaborately patterned brickwork between them
serves merely as infill.) Even the window
surrounds and dormers are edged in an iron
framework which ties directly into the main
structure, while iron purlins carry the roof
tiles, and iron rods projecting from the iron
ridgepole support an elaborate ceramic roof
crest.

Chicago never knew that a technical
advance could be so exotically clothed.
From a reasonable distance the building –
mirrored as it is in the murky Marne –
looks, as its architect proudly proclaimed,
like 'an oriental tapestry'. Meanwhile the
chocolatey aroma of the factory is almost
overpowering.

F-37a Across from, and slightly to the
east, of the factory gate is a contemporaneous **model industrial village**
which Saulnier also built for Menier.

local authorities are said to view it proudly
as a civic monument.) But it is also a *Classical* statement, or at least a mannerist Classical statement. As such, it demands to be
evaluated by Classical standards. Mannerist
jokes require rules to make sense. The theatre's black glass columns are, one hopes,

such a joke. So too the doorways set into their bases, and the cluster of 'negative' or concave, pilasters used as lamp standards (with the lamps in their 'positive' capitals). This device reappears in the central portions of the smooth, ten-storey-high pilasters which line the 'Palace's' façade – not to be confused with the paired twelve-storey fluted pilasters containing the elevators.

But elsewhere, as in the awkward placing of the elevator columns on the end elevations, the Classical syntax has been so distorted and rearranged that parts of the building seem to be mumbling a kind of tectonic gibberish. And the observer, wondering which jokes were intended and which not, is left with the disquieting sense that, teetering on the brink of high kitsch, this could be a Liberace stage set designed by Albert Speer.

Having said all this, one must look past Bofill's 'statement' to the technical accomplishment which made it possible. Beyond the cardboardy Classicism, the quality and imaginative use of prosaic precast concrete technology is truly impressive. Never again can bad architecture hide behind the presumed limitations of pre-cast panel construction.

F-38a Bofill's first realized projects of this sort were **Les Arcades du Lac**, 1972–8, and **Le Viaduc**, 1974–81, at Montigny-le-Bretonneux, near St-Quentin-en-Yvelines – in reality two parts of one project. Les Arcades is a set of hollow square blocks, forming 'streets' between them, which has at its core a small circular urban piazza with a diminutive temple at its centre. Le

Viaduc is, as its name implies, a 'viaduct' of housing leading into the middle of an artificial lake. The uniform five-storey buildings here are far more prosaic than those of Les Espaces, although their Classical language seemed radical enough when they were first built.

F-38b Bofill's more recent **Antigonne housing** area, 1970–83, in Montpellier, returns to a slightly more Baroque version of the planning principals employed at Les Arcades. Its exquisitely crafted, uniformly seven-storey-high buildings, are garbed in a more conservatively correct Classicism. They shape streets and spaces that truly begin to suggest a 'palace of the people'.

F-38c Also in Marne-la-Vallée/Noisiel is the **Château d'eau des Quatre-Pavés** (water tower), 1971–4, by Christian de Portzamparc & Georgia Benamo. Encased in a polygonal, sloping-sided spiral of chain-link fence partially overgrown with vines, it invokes traditional images of the Tower of Babel – an association which somehow magnifies its presence.

F-38d The gigantic parody of Boullée – or whatever it is meant to be – just to the west of the Palacio d'Abraxas in Marne-la-Vallée is called the **Arènes de Picasso**, 1980–4. It was built by Manola Nunez, one of the founding members of the Bofill firm. *N on rue du Centre from F-38 / bear R on main rd around superblock containing F-38 and then L on to av du Pavé-Neuf / abt 500 yds (m) W of F-38.*

Villejuif [near Paris]   **F-39**
Ecole Karl Marx (school) 1930–3
avenue Karl Marx and rue Auguste Delaune
André Lurçat
International Style
S (via Porte d'Italie) on N7 (Map F-2 →) ⇨ boul M. Gorki, abt 2 mi (3 km) / R on av de Virty ⇨ av de la République / L on rue Auguste Delaune / on R

Here, amidst the unique anarchy of a working-class Parisian suburb, is one of the purest, most timeless prewar French buildings. Surprisingly it was designed by

a man who otherwise, in his work for the *beau monde* and the bourgeoisie, is notable for having never quite overcome the clichés of his day. Only here, somehow, was a Marxist municipality able to inspire Lurçat to give that little bit more.

F-39a Judging by the adjacent **Yuri Gagarin swimming pool**, by P. Chemetov and J. Deroche, 1969, Villejuif has retained intact, over the past forty years, both its political faith and its patronage of good architecture.

Grigny [*near Paris*]   **F-40**
** **La Grande Borne** (housing area)
1961–71
Emile Aillaud
Rationalism
S (Map F-2 →) on autoroute A6 abt 12½ mi
(20 km) / exit → GRIGNY */ continue S*
paralleling expressway / abt 500 yds(m)

In Aillaud's earlier housing areas scattered 'star' and (exclamation) 'point' blocks – both bad parodies of good ideas (S·16a) – stand in the middle of seemingly desolate flat plains, while around them other long, sinuous blocks of flats entwine like snakes coupling in a pinball machine. However, when one experiences first hand those earlier schemes, as well his later work such as this, against the background of France's more typical senile-CIAM slab housing, it must be admitted that there is method to the madness of his muse.

With the years trees tend to mellow his projects' more abstract qualities. But more important here, Aillaud gave up his silly 'point' blocks, which, with their unreasonable shape and chequerboard of windows, always seemed the most arbitrary, least convincing aspect of his earlier work. He has also remarkably, if surreally, landscaped La Grande Borne – again a fairly exceptional occurrence in French housing. Finally, and very significant for their overall impact, La Grande Borne's pre-cast wall panels (despite its curvilinearity, this *is* a highly industrialized architecture) have been sheathed with ceramic tiles in a wide range of strong, sensitively chosen colours which make the whole ensemble a delight to the eye – even before one discovers the two-storey Magritte-like ceramic mosaic murals or the ten-foot-high pigeons.

Bourg-la-Reine [*near Paris*]   **F-41**
* **Maison Hennebique** (Hennebique's own house, now a telephone exchange)
1900–4
1 avenue du Lycée-Lakanal
François Hennebique
S (Map F-2 →) abt 3 mi (4.5 km) on N20
⇨ *boul M. Joffre / R, in Bourg-la-Reine, on*
D60 (av Victor Hugo) / R on av du Lycée-
Lakanal / immediately on L

[Inevitably some modification has been made to suit the house to its new role. Most notable is the less than sensitive addition just below the large glass bay.]

Hennebique was a pioneering engineer and contractor of reinforced concrete. In a sense his home was his laboratory and sample kit. Here, with little apparent concern for overall effect, he demonstrated concrete's suitability for supporting a water tower or a wall-length all-glass projecting bay window; for cantilevering a massive oriel or making a watertight roof terrace; and even for creating dragons with reinforcing-rod tongues.

F-41a By way of contrast, around the corner to the rear, at 2 rue du Lycée and 1 rue Lakanal, is Hector Guimard's Art Nouveau **Chalet Blanc**, *c*. 1907–10.

F-41b Across and a little further up avenue Victor Hugo is the **Lycée**

Lakanal, 1882–96, by Anatole de Baudot. It is a quintessential example of nineteenth-century French Rationalist institutional architecture.

Orsay [near Paris]   F-42
* Piscine (indoor swimming pool)
1968–9
*avenue Delattre-de-Tassigny and avenue du
Parc de la Pacaterie*
Maillard & Ducamp
Brutalism
*S on N306 (Map F-2→) abt 15½ mi (25 km)
/ SE on N446 → Orsay / W from Orsay
ctr on N188 / R at first light past*

Meudon-Bellevue [near Paris]   F-43
* Maison Bloc (house) 1953–6
Sculpture tower 1962–6
6 rue des Capucines
André Bloc
Neo-Expressionism (tower)
*W (Map F-2→) across Pont de Sèvres →
SEVRES CENTRE / L at first light on to
N187 / L on to N306-A → MEUDON
/ R at light on to D181→CHAVILLE
/ first L on to rue des Capucines /
500 yds (m) on R / tower can be seen
from drive of adjacent housing*
[Not open to the public.]

From the founding of *L'architecture d'au-
jourd'hui* in the 30s until his death in the
60s, André Bloc was the editor of France's,
and one of the world's, most prestigious
architectural journals. Primarily through
this medium he exercised a significant, if
sometimes questionable, influence over
postwar French architecture.

The little he built also made itself felt,
even if not in a direct way. Constructions
such as this tower, or an earlier sculptural
'house', are not immediately translatable
into real architecture. But somehow they
seem to epitomize that ephemeral quality –
perhaps a serious attempt to integrate art
and architecture, or perhaps only an escape

*intersection with N446 / → GARE /
→ PISCINE / abt 500 yds (m) past bridge*
French architects tend to juxtapose borrowed elements in unexpected ways. Here,
decidedly unromantic concrete (raw but
not tactile), 'industrial'-looking brickwork,
and sixty-six-foot pre-cast thin-shell factory
roofing vaults are all combined in a building
that is light, airy and playful – and yet in
no way stickily pretty.

Sculpture tower

from dreary over-Rational reality – which
has made French architecture so dis-
tinctively and often so unsubtly French.

Suresnes [near Paris]   F-44
* Ecole Nationale de Plein Air (open-
air school) 1932–6
*rue de la Procession and rue de Pas Saint-
Maurice*
Marcel Lods & Eugène Beaudouin
Rationalism
*W (Map F-2→) across Pont du Suresnes
(N185) / L at Y→VILLE DE SURESNES /
R after second RR bridge on boul Washington
⇨ boul L. Loucheur ⇨ rue de la Poterie ⇨
rue de la Procession / at top of hill on R*
[Large parts of the school are sheathed in
an early form of pre-cast concrete panelling,
which in places has had to be shored up.]

During the 1920s the International Style

feigned an image of industrial modernity
in advance of the available construction

technology. It was meant to be a self-fulfilling promise of the future.

During the 30s, when many leaders of the International Style had begun to turn towards romanticism and rusticity, a new group – perhaps partly fired by all the technological rhetoric – began seriously to develop an architecture actually based on new materials, applied technology and scientific knowledge. And when, as here, they also had to respond to complex and detailed programmatic requirements, their work was capable of achieving an exciting mechanistic logic, both because so many of the elements became multi-functional and because every form seemed to have some particular *raison d'être.*

The special built-in potential for modifying this school on an hour-by-hour basis also lent it an extra sense of mechanistic fitness to purpose. Or, as one commentator wryly noted, everything was so new, so complexly specific and so fragile, that none of it ever did work quite right.

Poissy-sur-Seine [near Paris]　　　F-45
*** Villa Savoye or **'Les Heures Claires'** (country house) 1929–31
82 chemin de Villiers
Le Corbusier
International Style
W on N13 (Map F-2→) abt 2 mi (3 km) / W on N190 → Poissy / W from Poissy ctr on D30 ⇨ rue de la Maladrerie / R just past water tower (at Y with 'island' in intersection) on rue de Villiers / behind wall at end of rd
[The house was completely restored *c.*1968. Unfortunately a large school complex has been allowed to encroach insensitively upon the site, thereby greatly diminishing the intended juxtaposition between pristine nature and an equally pristine artifact. The building is open to visitors.]

There is no more important, fascinating or enigmatic building in the entire history of modern architecture. Looking back over the preceding decade, or over the last few centuries, it seems to come from nowhere and from everywhere. It is out of place but not disturbing. In it living would be a challenge and a pleasure; yet it seems natural, almost preferable, without furniture or the cluttering realities of day-to-day existence.

Nor is it merely polemical. It is a philosophical abstraction, one whose unworldliness even Le Corbusier was never again to recapture. On many occasions he did restate the basic physical concept: the pristine cubic volume from which the forces of internal necessity have thrust certain elements. But the Villa Savoye's moment was fleeting. Born in the post-First World War collapse of the old order, its self-assured concern with universal truths, an obvious prerequisite for such a classic point of equilibrium, could not long survive in the face of insistent reality. The political-economic crisis of the late 20s and early 30s that introduced the new era of reactionary nationalism also saw the arbitrarily confident, prismatic architecture – as suitably rendered on paper as in plaster – give way to the psychic security of romantic forms, rustic masonry (F-34) and, eventually, *béton brut* (F-63).

Nancy Map F-46

* Nancy   F-46

Despite its French name, Art Nouveau was not an exclusively French invention. Many of its constituent aspects were essentially British in origin and, as regards architecture at least, Belgian in development – which perhaps is why Paris enjoyed less than its accustomed advantage over other French cities as a centre of Art Nouveau design and production. Thus it was possible for Nancy, a traditional handicraft metal-working town, to become a focus of Art Nouveau creativity quite the equal of Paris, with its own especially overripe, over-wrought version of the style. But her moment of glory was short-lived and now all that remains of the 'School of Nancy' is a handful of buildings and a museum:

F-46a The **Musée de l'Ecole de Nancy,** at 38 rue du Sergent-Blandan, is housed in a mansion of the period, if not of the style. It undoubtedly contains not just the best collection of objects of the School of Nancy but one of the best collections of Art Nouveau anywhere. In its yard is an aquarium pavilion, 1906, attributed to Eugène Vallin.

F-46b In addition to the two houses listed separately below (F-47, 48), other Art Nouveau buildings of some interest in Nancy include a house by Lucien Weiss-enburger, 1904, at **1 boulevard Char-les-V**, and:

F-46c Another Weissenburger house, 1905, at **52 cours Léopold**.

F-46d The former **Hôtel Excelsior,** by Weissenburger and Alexander Mienville, 1910, at 1 rue Mazagran, whose café interior was, until its closing in 1975, a particularly well-preserved period piece.

F-46e **Two large houses** by Emile André, 1902 and 1904, at 69 and 71 avenue Foch.

F-46f The **Maison Huot,** 1902–3, also by André, at 92 quai Claude le Lorrain.

F-46g The **Banque Nationale de Paris,** 1910, by André & Charbonnier, on the rue St-Jean, at the rue Chanzy.

F-46h A house by Biet & Vallin at **22 rue de la Commanderie,** 1901–2, which is especially notable for its ironwork.

F-46i The **Graineterie Job** (seed shop) by H. B. Gutton, 1900–1, restored c. 1975, at 52 rue St-Jean. A marvellous little building – the nineteenth century's idea of half-timber rather literal-mindedly meta-morphosed into a kind of 'half-iron'.

Nancy   **F-47**
* Villa Majorelle (house, now
government offices) 1901
1 rue Louis-Majorelle
Henri Sauvage
Art Nouveau
Map F-46

[The ground-floor front porch has been
filled in and various changes made at the
rear.]

Nancy's best Art Nouveau building is
the youthful work of a Parisian architect,
whose reputation rests almost entirely on
two, seemingly styleless blocks of flats
(F-12, 32). It has been argued, therefore,
that the design of this house should be
ascribed not to Sauvage, its architect, but
to Majorelle, its owner. Majorelle was a
furniture designer, a decorator of some note
and indeed a leading figure in the School of
Nancy. Certainly the building's more sculptural accoutrements – downpipes, terracotta ornament, carved wood furnishings
and fitments – do seem to betray Majorelle's
facile, if non-tectonic, hand.

The house itself, however, has a hard aggressiveness and a Rationalist handling
of certain elements, particularly the struc-
tural woodwork around the roof, reminiscent of the young Guimard. It cannot be
the work of Majorelle or any other Nancy
designer. It is architect's architecture.

Nancy   **F-48**
Maison Bergeret (house, now offices)
1903–4
24 rue Lionnois
Lucien Weissenburger
Art Nouveau
Map F-46

All that is missing are the ubiquitous
thistle and pine motifs symbolic of the then-
lost nearby provinces of Alsace and
Lorraine. Otherwise, this is quintessential
School of Nancy architecture: traditional in
form; conservatively stylish in its furniture-
like ornament; and beautifully embellished
inside with gilt, rich woods, wrought iron
and vibrantly hued glass.

Guise, Aisne   **F-49**
** Familistère (communal housing)
1859–70
Jean-Baptiste Godin
Industrial Vernacular
N from Guise ctr on N360 ⇨ rue André
Godin, abt 400 yds (m) / on R just before
small river
[The somewhat less ascetic right-hand
wing was built last.]

Throughout the nineteenth century
there was a powerful, persistent impetus to
establish ideal agricultural and industrial
communities. Many of these, especially in
America, were religious in origin. Others
were socialist. Some were both.

Charles Fourier was not a pragmatic man
of action. But, being French, he was able
to describe with great exactitude both his
idealized agrarian commune, which he

called a *phalange* (phalanx), and the 'phalanstery' that was to house it. Although there were a number of independent attempts to establish Fourier-esque communes, none of these, including several in America, ever enjoyed the resources and/or the longevity required to build a true phalanstery as envisaged by Fourier. Ideally such a structure was to accommodate an entire 1600-person *phalange* – 'coincidentally' the population Le Corbusier was to choose for the Marseille Unité (F-63) – in three hollow blocks joined at the corners. Within, cantilevered 'street-galleries', one for each storey, were to circumscribe the perimeter of each block's courtyard.

As its name implies, the Familistère is

not quite a phalanstery. For one thing its courtyards were glazed so that they might better serve as the foci of all sorts of large-scale communal activities. Also the Familistère accommodates only 1200 persons; it is industrial, not agrarian – having been established by an altruistic industrialist next to his factory; and, although it incorporates a crèche and other communal facilities, it was based, as its name suggests, upon the nuclear family.

After the Second World War, the last of the more advanced aspects of the commune including cooperative ownership of dwellings and factories, were finally lost. Only the Familistère itself remains, a testament to a remarkable social experiment.

Lille   **F-50**

* Maison Coilliot (house and ceramic shop) 1898–1900
14 rue de Fleurus
Hector Guimard
Art Nouveau
W from Hôtel de Ville (see F-50a below) in Lille ctr around Porte de Paris (roundabout) / R on boul Papin / R at light / immediate L on rue Jean Bart / fifth R at roundabout (place P. le Bon) on to rue de Fleurus / half blk on R

During the critical five-year period around the turn of the century when Art Nouveau was at its zenith, Guimard constructed only one major building, a long-lost, little-known auditorium which may well have been his masterpiece.

This shop, his only other urban building of that period, illustrates the large scale, the less refined forms and the interaction between building and context that typify Guimard's work during those years. It is a building dominated by tensions, and not just those endemic to Art Nouveau as a whole. There are tensions between the implication of a solid façade and the penetration of that façade by the street's space; between the urban industrialized terracotta masonry which forms the façade at street level, before thrusting upwards alongside the adjacent buildings, and the almost medieval 'house'-shaped timber two-storey porch; and, because of the angle at which the party walls meet the street, between the orientation of the outer façade as mandated

by law and custom, and that of the inner façade as it responds to internal necessities.

F-50a Lille's **Hôtel de Ville** is a classic example of how thoroughly out of step the French can be when they put their minds to it. This magnificently 'Victorian' pile was built in the 1920s.

Le Havre   **F-51**

Quartier Moderne (postwar reconstruction of the town's centre) 1944–54
Auguste Perret
Rationalism
Along both sides and to S of av Foch

As the twentieth-century incarnation of nineteenth-century Classical Rationalism, Perret served in the later decades of his long career as official France's 'acceptable' modern architect, when and if it felt the need for one. Thus, in 1944, when Perret was already seventy, he was commissioned to reconstruct the entire heart of this town, even while Le Corbusier was fighting to build his single Marseille Unité (F-63).

In the long run Le Corbusier's effort got most of the glory, and from his supposedly very technological building came Brutal-

ism, a rustically romantic rationalization of compromise. At Le Havre this inconsistency was reversed. Concrete was Perret's material, and his arcaded, corniced, pilastered city was built utilizing the then most advanced modular concrete prefabrication technology.

F-51a Nothing demonstrates Perret's mastery of concrete more than l'église St-Joseph, 1952–9, the church he built for Le Havre. The height of a thirty-storey

Ronchamp, Haute-Saône [near Belfort] F-52
*** Chapelle de Notre-Dame-du-Haut (pilgrimage church) 1950–5
Le Corbusier
Neo-Expressionism
From N19 in Ronchamp → N.D.-DU-HAUT *(under viaduct and up hill to car park)*

[In keeping with the traditional character of pilgrimage churches, Ronchamp is an all-the-year-round tourist attraction. If possible, avoid visiting it on weekends, holidays and holy days.]

It must have been difficult for Le Corbusier's disciples to keep up with some of his seeming changes of course. Even when he first gave life to this little nun's coif-cum-seashell of a hilltop church, only the faintest gasp was heard in the short stunned silence. Then came the tumultuous applause that has yet to die down completely. Some declared it the greatest building of all time. Others were even less restrained in their praise. Eventually a few voices could be heard saying, 'Of course, it can all be traced back to his early work.'

Today, after a third of a century, there is still no denying the impact of that fantastic

office building, it also serves as a landmark far out to sea.

Seen from within, the fussiness of certain details, the uneasy fumbling for precedent all disappear. Then there is only the presence of the tower. Rising to incredible heights above massive piers, it thrusts open the space overhead – dominating the light-filled chamber below but never oppressing it. *W* → *sea, from Le Havre ctr (Hôtel de Ville) on av Foch / L on boul François Ier / abt four blks on L*

prow with its oversailing roof, all so solidly anchored by the towers' smooth solidity. Undeniably, this is one of the strongest single images in all of modern architecture. And Le Corbusier develops that one image slowly before your eyes as you climb towards it. But like any building, Ronchamp is not perfect. It has its 'better' side. And while the exterior as a whole is masterful, the interior, though still remarkable, does not have quite the same power.

Arc-et-Senans, Doubs   F-53
** Les Salines Royales de Chaux
(royal saltworks) 1775–9
Claude-Nicolas Ledoux
Neo-Classicism
N from D472 at Mouchard (junction N83) → ARC ET SENANS

[A partial restoration in the 1920s left the interesting, if not historical, concrete

work inside the processing sheds. In the 1970s more extensive renovations were undertaken, especially in the central administration block. The philosophical differences between these two restoration campaigns, separated by half a century, are interesting and apparent. One of the peripheral pavilions houses an exhibition describing the life, times and work of

Ledoux, including his famous project for an ideal city which he conjured up around the real Chaux during the years of the Revolution. Les Salines, now a centre for speculation about the future, is open to visitors.]

Ledoux, along with Friedrich Gilly, Etienne-Louis Boullée and some others, symbolizes a turning point in architectural history. His is the generation of radicals which stands as a delineator between the Renaissance-Baroque epoch and our own. In their idealized and mostly unrealizable projects, they anticipated or paralleled the political and social revolutions of their time. Directly and indirectly, their projects have affected successive generations of 'revolutionary' architects.

The first generation, whose lives sometimes overlapped those of the revolutionary romantics, included Sir John Soane (GB-8) and Karl Friedrich Schinkel (D-26a-c). Without abandoning their freshness of vision, these successful practising architects toned down their predecessors' sense of radical unreality. Subsequent revivals of interest in Ledoux and his contemporaries have also coincided with periods of social revolution: 1830, 1848, 1870, the early 1920s, and the late 1960s. One of the first histories of modern architecture, published in 1933, was even titled *Von Ledoux bis Le Corbusier* (From Ledoux to Le Corbusier). More recently, in the 1960s, Louis Kahn and others, in semi-conscious emulation of Ledoux's generation, designed projects

Lyon   **F-54**
** **Cité Industrielle** (unbuilt project for an ideal industrial city) 1899–1917
Musée des Beaux-Arts (art museum),
place des Terreaux
Tony Garnier
Rationalism
Place des Terreaux is at N edge of Lyon ctr midway between the two rivers, just in line (E-W) with place where the Saône (coming from W) begins to flow parallel to the Rhône
The inclusion of this project, which is a series of drawings not a built work, is unique in this volume – just as the extent and specificity of Garnier's masterwork is almost unique in the history of modern architectural projects.

Having left Lyon in 1889, Garnier spent the next ten years in Paris studying at the Ecole des Beaux-Arts. He proved himself a master of the elegant irrelevances that had become the Ecole's stock in trade. Eventually, with a much admired scheme, he won the Prix de Rome, an honour intended to allow its recipients several years in Rome absorbing the glories of the ancients.

Garnier spent most of his four-year Roman sojourn devising an ideal industrial city for a population of about 35,000 inhabitants on an imaginary site, but one typical of the Lyon region. This scheme, first exhibited in Paris in 1904, was the most explicit visualization to date of an idealized industrial urban environment. It must have had a stunning impact. As the exact contents of the original exhibition are uncertain, however, its specific influence is now difficult to trace. To complicate

which often far overreached the limits of technical or economic feasibility.

For someone casually encountering Les Salines, or 'Chaux', for the first time, they may seem simply to represent a Classicism little different from other, better known eighteenth-century buildings, despite the semicircular site plan and the monumental mannerism of the cave-like entrance. Compared with his later unbuilt projects for symbolic geometric houses and huge monuments, many of which were envisaged as part of his utopian aggrandizement of Chaux, this may seem tame stuff. But, unlike his ideal projects, this was a real problem involving a real industrial process, the production of salt from local brine springs. (Salt was a royal monopoly and an important source of government revenue.) Here he had to use real materials and, most particularly, he had a real budget. In fact Les Salines must be one of the first factories designed by a professional architect.

F-53a Two of Ledoux's monumental, and once numerous, Parisian toll houses, 1785–9, have also survived more or less intact. One, the **Barrière d'Enfer,** at the place Denfert Rochereau, Paris 14, is now an entrance to Paris's Catacombs. *Map F-2 / Métro: Denfert-Rochereau*

F-53b The other is the circular **Barrière de la Villette,** at the place de Stalingrad, Paris 19. *Map F-2 / Métro: Stalingrad*

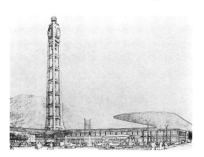

matters further, Le Corbusier, who could not have seen the 1904 exhibition, sought out Garnier in Lyon as early as 1908. What additional material might he have been able to see then? And if he visited Garnier, who else did as well?

The Cité Industrielle as we now know it is the greatly revised and expanded version which was published in 1917. It included work done in Lyon during the preceding thirteen years. Although at the end of the First World War this project would still have seemed radical, less than a decade later its imagery, if not its programme and scope, would have ceased to be so. Yet it remains fascinating even today as one of the last, and by far the most graspable, of a long line (F-49, 53) of modern utopian and/or socialist architectural visions.

F-54a The museum also has a **Hector Guimard room** (see F-21).

F-54b For a multitude of reasons, not the least of which is that the times changed and Garnier did not, his buildings, even where closely identifiable with the Cité Industrielle, never share its sense of excitement. The best-known of these is the municipal **abattoir** (slaughterhouse), 1906–24, in the quartier de la Mouche. *S from Lyon ctr along quai on E bank of Rhône ⇨ av Leclerc ⇨ av T. Garnier / on L just after st separates from river*

F-54c Near the abattoir is the **Stade Olympique** (stadium) of 1913–19. *Continue past F-54b to av Jean-Jaurès / across st to L*

F-54d The largest of Garnier's municipal projects is the residential quarter **Etats-Unis** of 1928–35. Built to house 12,000 persons in six-storey walk-ups, it is a far cry from the idealism of three decades earlier. *E from Lyon ctr on av Berthelot abt $1\frac{1}{2}$ mi (2.5 km) / angle R on boul des Etats-Unis / on both sides of st*

F-54e More dramatic than any of Garnier's built projects is the **Avenue de l'Hôtel de Ville**, 1931–4, by Maurice Leroux, in suburban Villeurbanne. Flanking this two-block boulevard, which leads to the city hall, are two dozen closely spaced, identical white apartment towers. Rising from a continuous two-storey base at the pavement line, they break near their tops into six stories of ziggurat-like setbacks. These two rows of buildings are in turn terminated – at the far end of the boulevard from the city hall – by a taller pair of pylon-like apartment towers. There is nothing else quite like it anywhere. Unfortunately, a small nagging voice in the back of one's head keeps saying, 'Cecil B. DeMille proudly presents . . .' *E from F-54 across river Rhône on Pont Morand (bridge) ⇨ cours Vitton ⇨ cours Zola abt 2 mi (3.5 km) / on R*

Eveux-sur-l'Arbresle [near Lyon]   **F-55**
** **Couvent de Ste-Marie-de-la-Tourette** (built as monastery, now retreat centre) 1953–60
Le Corbusier
Brutalism/Neo-Expressionism
W from Lyon on N7 → MOULINS and VICHY / L at L'ARBRESLE / L on D19 (→ EVEUX) / → LA TOURETTE $\frac{1}{2}$ mi (1 km)
[La Tourette now functions as a retreat or study centre. The church is open daily. The rest of the monastery can only be visited on certain days: check locally.]

The best of Le Corbusier's postwar work is rife with semi-resolved relationships. Eliminate the quirky rules, the necessary exceptions, and there would remain at most a technocratic fantasy – a film set for *Metropolis* or *2001*. Leave only the artistic aspects and there is merely a one-man sculpture show that is its own gallery. Le Corbusier's brute mechanistic, industrial – if not necessarily industrialized – architecture seems at times to be seeking some sort of justification in the apparently extraneous gestures that do not quite fit his own systems.

This is, perhaps, a little like Le Corbusier's view of himself. He might have championed rigour, rationality and conformity for the masses, but he assumed exceptions would always be made for their leaders. Occasionally, if not often, the exception became the entire building (F-52). More characteristically, as here, Le Corbusier worked at the edge of a precipice. Behind him lay the safe, necessarily grey world of order and technocracy, before him an enticing wilderness of the will into which he continuously made forays. Maintaining his equilibrium in this way was exhilarating and risky; it produced troubled, or occasionally flawed, masterworks.

La Tourette is one of Le Corbusier's most influential late buildings and it offers an impressive photogenic dynamism. It is, for instance, an immediate antecedent of Boston's City Hall of 1962–5, a building which, in turn, has had many equally unanticipated progeny.

La Tourette is a dramatic building not quite attuned to its site: hard and square, its geometric strength is almost overpowered by surface-breaking detail. There is almost too much exception, not enough system. It is a cloistered monastery whose outward orientation leaves the cloister as little more than a light-well. It is a building of occasionally uncomfortable personal gestures: of unstable-looking angled arches cut from exposed foundations; of a pyramidal dunce-cap roof that overwhelms a tiny private oratory chapel.

Yet, protruding from the north wall of its great bare box of a church is the lower-level chapel, whose divergent, upward-thrusting light-catchers mark the hours as they modulate the ever-changing sunlight and transmit it to seven small altars ranged below. This sequestered place, with its red, yellow and blue colour-saturated walls and ceiling, is one of the most intensely moving, persuasive and personal spaces in all of modern architecture.

Maison des Jeunes et de la Culture

Firminy, Loire   F-56
*** Maison des Jeunes et de la
Culture** (youth centre) 1957–65
Stade (stadium) 1960
Unité d'habitation 1960–8
Le Corbusier
Brutalism
*E from N88 (rue V Hugo) in Firminy on to
boul St-Charles →* MAISON DE LA CULTURE
/ *youth centre and stadium are abt 500 yds
(m) on L / to reach unité, R from roundabout
at supermarket / at top of hill on R*

Because this group of buildings was a 'monument' to a municipal administration which held power during better times, it has now become a political scapegoat. At the time of writing the *unité* had been internally partitioned from top to bottom and only one half was heated and occupied. Behind the stadium a half-completed church by Le Corbusier stood derelict.

None of Corbusier's three completed buildings here can be considered a major success. Overall, the *unité* is probably the best of the lot. Yet it is only one of several more or less equally emasculated descendants of the original, 1946–52, Marseilles Block (F-63).

Near by, but not physically or spiritually related to the *unité*, is the youth centre. The obvious, unnecessary, but once faddish structural Neo-Expressionism of its drooping catenary roof and thrust-resisting façades is almost an embarrassment, particularly coming from the atelier that created Ronchamp (F-52). Also missing here is that typical Corbusian aloofness of architecture from site, which, in its extreme form, elevated his buildings on their famous *piloti*. Instead, the long rear side of the centre develops an unusual, for Corbusier, almost organic site relationship.

Decidedly least important among this trio is the stadium. It has none of the mannerisms or even the general sense of unpredictability normally associated with Le Corbusier's work. That it serves well as a foil to the youth centre's more appealing elevation is all to its credit. By establishing a tension in the space between the structures, both are enhanced. But, given the site and circumstances, that is no more than any good designer should have achieved.

Hauterives, Drôme   F-57
* Palais Idéal du Facteur Cheval
(Postman Cheval's dream palace)
1879–1912
Ferdinand Cheval
*E from A7, at Chanas, on D519 / S at
Beaurepaire on D538 →* ROMANS *to
Hauterives (abt 6 mi–10 km) / →* PALAIS
IDÉAL DU FACTEUR CHEVAL

Ferdinand Cheval was a postman in a rural part of France which to this day remains poor, bleak and rather wild. For thirty-three years while making his rounds he collected rocks and cobbles – the region's normal building material – that caught his fancy. From these he fashioned not so much a dream palace as a palace of miscellaneous visions, encompassing philosophy, giants, temples, trees, humour, furniture, people, nature: a whole life's experiences, real and vicarious.

This huge mass, whose creation was equally a physical and a spiritual feat, con-

tains passageways, grottoes, staircases, terraces on several levels and other elements more or less nominally associated with conventional architectonic construction. But this is not a building for use, not in any normal sense of the word. It is the summation of one simple, sensitive man's transfigured-petrified image of the world.

Garabit, Cantal   **F-58**
* **Viaduc de Garabit** (railway viaduct)
1880–4
Gustave Eiffel
*Crosses over N9 abt 7 mi (11 km) S of
St-Flour*
   [The lake is a later addition.]
   The graceful, powerful self-assurance of that parabolic arch! It springs from a wide, flat, hinged base, and as it rises it narrows and deepens, both to align with the deck truss overhead and to resist the localized bending stresses caused by heavy trains. Then, reversing the transformation, it continues its nimble leap through space to land on the opposite shore.

Pessac [near Bordeaux]   **F-59**
* **Cité Frugès** (workers' housing area)
1922–6
avenue Henri-Frugès and rue Le Corbusier
Le Corbusier
International Style
*W from Bordeaux (→ ARCACHON) on
N350 / L on to av Henri-Frugès, abt 1 mi
(1.5 km) past Pessac ctr / at end of rd*
   [Greatly modified: see below.]
   These houses (there are only a few basic designs, variously combined) were built for the employees of a wealthy Bordeaux industrialist. They represent an early partial realization of Le Corbusier's Domino and Citrohan house-type projects and, indeed, are Le Corbusier's only sizeable prewar group of any sort. They were also the object of his boldest early excursion into the realm of exterior colour – four typically impure 'purist' hues having been employed to the almost total exclusion of white.
   Today the predominant colour of the Cité is the muddied ochre typical of all French villages, while individual houses that have suffered no more than repainting during the past half century are rare indeed. So many were modified, for reasons often as much socio-psychological as functional, that their transformation even led to the publication of an influential book which attempts to document and explain the process. Thus the Cité's occupant-inspired metamorphosis may have become historically more important than the very fact of its having been built by Le Corbusier in the first place.

Royan, Charente-Maritime   **F-60**
* **Eglise de Notre-Dame** (church)
1954–8
rue du Château-d'Eau and rue de Foncillon
Guillaume Gillet
Neo-Expressionism
From N150–730 → CENTRE VILLE / *bear
R around post office /* → EGLISE NOTRE-
DAME

A most singular church: traditional,
axial and symmetrical; raw, expressive, full
of technical daring. Thrusting an oval of
thin, curved concrete blades towards the
sky, it is seemingly the fulfilment of one of
those escapist Expressionist fantasies that
arose from the chaos of post First World
War Germany: a Teutonic apparition translated into reality by a semi-Rationalist
Frenchman; a man-made magic mesa,
unaccountably set down in this seaside
resort town, with no understanding of the
cars and other, more prosaic buildings that
approach its concrete talus-slope base.

Like the Gothic cathedrals – its spiritual
forbears – this church wants to rise, unen-
cumbered, above a world which would not
need signs banning the half-naked, and

whose air would never be perfumed with
suntan oil.

St-Paul-de-Vence [near Nice]   **F-61**
Fondation Maeght (art museum)
1962–4
Josép Lluís Sert
*N from N7, 6 mi (10 km) W of Nice, on N85
and then D36 →* VENCE / → FONDATION
MAEGHT

Sert's talents are better represented by
his work in his adopted Boston than by his
extant European buildings (E-6, 14). Not
that there is anything particularly wrong
with this gallery. Sitting half-hidden on a
pine-covered hillside, the Fondation
Maeght even appears refreshingly modest.
Unlike other European museums designed
by American-based architects of the period
(D-13, 37), it is genuinely at ease with the
art it houses, and gives the impression of
not being excessively concerned about its
own 'importance' as a work of art. Or is
that only the result of an unfocused sense
of direction?

Le Corbusier's influence – via his Brazilian disciples, it would almost seem – is
clear enough, while the 'cute' delicacy of
the 'nun's coif' roofs is peculiarly
American. This is a confused architecture,
perhaps symptomatic, in part, of Sert's own
ambiguous nationality. Born a Catalan, a
disciple of the French-Swiss Le Corbusier
for whom he had worked in Paris, Sert
succeeded Walter Gropius as head of Harvard's Graduate School of Design.

F-61a Next to the gallery is a maze-like
sculpture garden designed in collaboration with Sert's fellow Catalan
expatriate Joan Miró. Based on even such
fragmentary evidence it is interesting to
consider the sort of museum Miró might
have created.

F-61b Nearby, in Vence, is the famous
Chapelle du Rosaire (chapel of the

rosary) decorated by Matisse, 1951. *From
Vence ctr →* ST-GENNET *on N210 / on R
(check locally for opening times)*

F-61c A little more distant, at La Gaude,
is another American-designed building of
the same period and aesthetic persuasion,
the **Centre d'Etudes et de Rech-
erches IBM** (research centre), 1960–2,
by Marcel Breuer. Here is more of the
precise, powerful, sculptured concrete work
so typical of the period. It is a paraphrase
of Breuer's Unesco building (F-14) in Paris –
where the design made considerably more
sense. The similarity of the *piloti* to concrete
cacti in this semi-desert setting is, one
assumes, unintentional. *N from N7 on
D118 (just W of river Var and Nice airport)
→ La Gaude / abt 6 mi (10 km) on R*

Port Grimaud [near St Tropez]   **F-62**
* Port Grimaud (resort town) 1965–9
Rt N98
François Spoerry
Neo-Vernacular
2½ mi (4 km) W of St Tropez

It has been almost twenty years since the designs for this pull-your-yacht-up-to-your-door, fake fishing village first startled the architectural world. Whatever the public's opinion may have been, the modernist establishment responded with incredulity, derision and hostility. And in retrospect one is inclined to think with fear as well. Vernacular materials and forms might have been acceptable, if the total effect was still undeniably modern. But here there was no interest in appearing modern.

The explicit stylish borrowings of a Robert Venturi might have caused scandal, but at least they still somehow appeared to be of this century, and they were as likely to look to neon Las Vegas as to Baroque Rome. Port Grimaud was not like that. It was unabashedly sham 'French Provincial'. And it was very appealing: a successful townscape thrown in the face of so many postwar modernist failures. (Admittedly, it was also built for the rich on the Riviera, not in some grey working-class Northern European suburb). Today, when one looks at Port Grimaud – with the mind's eye a jumble of Post-Modern columns, arches and pitched roofs – it is easy to forget that this fantasy village once raised such strong emotions.

Marseille   **F-63**
*** Unité d'habitation or **Marseilles Block** (apartment building) 1944–52
boulevard Michelet
Le Corbusier
Brutalism
S from Marseille ctr on rue de Rome (N559) ⇨ boul Michelet / beyond second roundabout on R / → signs

[Although the 'street' of shops on the seventh and eighth floors has never flourished financially, the hotel on the same level continues to function, and serves medium-priced meals in its restaurant.]

With this apartment block Le Corbusier aroused much of French public opinion and the modern architectural establishment. Architects, politicians and the man in the street either loved it or loathed it – and said so publicly. It was described as inhuman. What, then, would they have thought of today's French high-rise slab suburbs?

The interlocking sets of two-storey apartments – they extend the full depth of the building and wrap around elevator corridors that occur on every third floor – were said to be impossibly narrow. And so they were. But the proportions might easily have been corrected in later *unités*. (Originally there were to have been five on this site.)

The raw concrete, bursting upon a world of painted plaster and brick, was called brutal (*béton brut*) and ugly. But within a few years everyone would be using it.

The *unité* was a *succès de scandale* for a man who had already had more than his share. Le Corbusier had wanted to improve the lot of the millions who were caught in a desperate housing squeeze – a legacy of two world wars, the Depression and much bureaucratic ineptitude. Instead the Marseilles Block became almost a cultural monument, or freak show. Hundreds of curious visitors queued to see the apartments with the double-height living rooms, the shopping 'street in the sky', the rooftop kindergarten and the other communal facilities. Nevertheless, there has always been a long waiting list of prospective tenants.

Meanwhile, from its slightly surreal roof one can see its glass and chrome descendants gradually filling up a view which must once have been magnificent.

F-63a Of the four *unités* that were to follow elsewhere, none is as complete or as visually exciting as the Marseilles Block. In a sense this simply reflects the real world overtaking the ideal, or smaller visions overwhelming a grander one. At Marseille Le Corbusier may well have placed the shopping street where he did not because that location was practical, but because it made the *unité* more self-contained and, just perhaps, because it undeniably looks more dramatically 'functional' there than

Font-Romeu, Pyrénées-Orientales   **F-64**
*** Four Soleil** (solar furnace) 1966
N618 and D10–29
Henri Vicariot
W from Font-Romeu abt 2 mi (3 km) on D618 / at junction with D10–29
High in the Pyrenees the air is clear, the clouds few, the views magnificent. Set dramatically in the midst of it all is this almost equally spectacular and somewhat other-worldly complex. It is a fairly simple device. A field of giant steerable mirrors, arrayed over a south-facing slope, directs sunlight into a huge, shimmeringly multi-faceted, concave mirror which forms the entire north side of an eight-storey building. This mirror in turn focuses all its received energy into a single point of intense heat within a smaller, hammer-headed laboratory tower that stands before it. The sight of such a remarkable and starkly functional construction – made to harness the primal source of life and rising from an untouched landscape – should be a moving

it would on the ground. With its special *brise-soleils* (sunshades) and extra set of exterior fire stairs, it also helps scale down the Marseilles Block's oppressive massiveness. None of the later *unités* has such an extensive shopping street. Similarly none has as elaborate a system of *brise-soleil* built into its façade, nor as sculpturally effective a set of roof accoutrements and *piloti*. Some do not even have double-storey living rooms. It might be argued that stripped-down *unités* are better than none at all. But considering the hundreds of suburban pseudo-*unités* hulking about the outskirts of Europe's industrial cities, even that proposition seems doubtful.

Two of Le Corbusier's later *unités* are listed elsewhere (D-20, F-56). The others are the **Rezé-les-Nantes unité** (near Nantes), 1952–7, and:

F-63b **Briey-en-Forêt unité** (near Metz), 1957–9.

experience. But the mood of the place is broken by the ghastly blue curtain-walling of the main structure.

Then again, without that one mundane detail the laboratory, taken as a whole, would look even more like sixty-three Martians at an outdoor movie.

GREAT BRITAIN

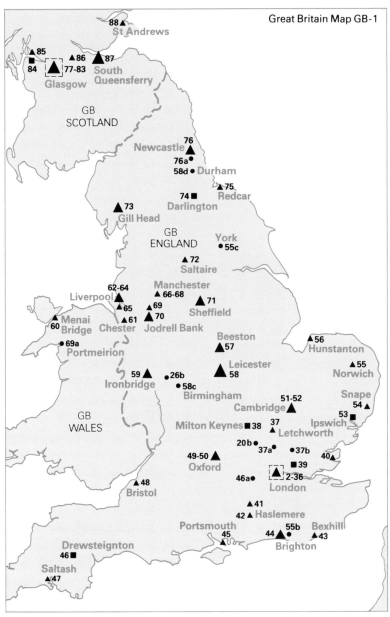

Great Britain Map GB-1

88 ▲
St Andrews

▲ 85
■ 84
77-83 ▲ 86 ▲ 87
Glasgow South
Queensferry

GB
SCOTLAND

Newcastle ▲ 76
76a ●
58d ● Durham
▲ 75
74 ■ Redcar
Darlington

▲ 73
Gill Head

GB
ENGLAND
York
● 55c

▲ 72
Saltaire

62-64
Liverpool ▲
▲ 65
▲ 61
Chester
Manchester
▲ 66-68
▲ 69
▲ 70
Jodrell Bank
▲ 71
Sheffield

60
Menai
Bridge
● 69a
Portmeirion

Beeston
▲ 57

▲ 56
Hunstanton

59 ▲
Ironbridge
● 26b
● 58c
Birmingham
Leicester
▲ 58

▲ 55
Norwich

Snape
54 ▲

51-52
Cambridge ▲

53 ■
Ipswich

GB
WALES

Milton Keynes ■ 38
37 ▲
Letchworth

20b ●
37a ▲
● 37b
40 ▲

49-50 ▲
Oxford
■ 39
46a ● 2-36
London

▲ 48
Bristol

▲ 41
42 ▲ Haslemere

Portsmouth
45 ▲
44 ▲ 55b ●
Brighton
43 ▲ Bexhill

Drewsteignton
46 ■

Saltash
▲ 47

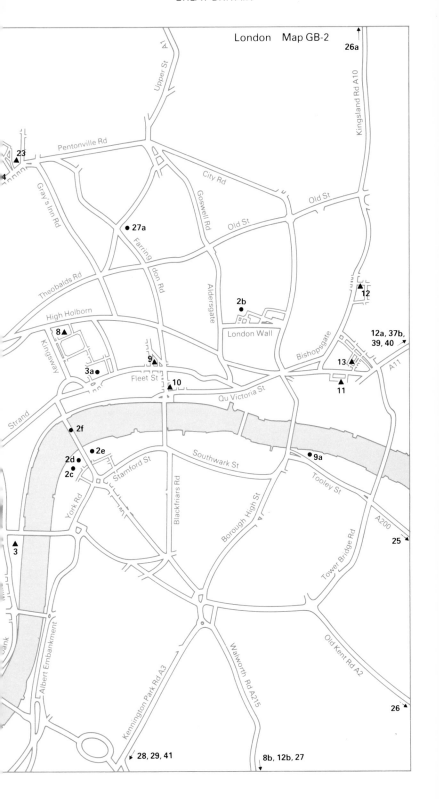

London   Map GB-2

Great Britain   GB-1

Technologically, if not always ideologically, modern architecture sprang from Britain's eighteenth-century Industrial Revolution. Industrialization created new building requirements (heavily laden multi-storey factories, 'fireproof' warehouses, vast railway stations), while also developing a whole range of 'new' materials (iron, glass, ceramics) and new means of distributing nationally older materials (brick, slate, stucco) whose use had hitherto been regional. It also led to what soon became standard solutions to these new problems (GB-24, 31, 63), as well as to new aesthetic formulas for older building types (GB-7, 73) – although pioneering examples of the former are often inaccessible, and the latter sometimes remain unrecognized for what they are. Unfortunately, modern rapacity, short-sightedness and ignorance have exacted on Britain's architectural heritage a toll even greater than that taken by the bombings and the scrap-metal drives of two world wars.

Britain's greatest single contribution to the idea of a modern architecture was the enormous, totally industrialized and prefabricated, iron and glass Crystal Palace, which was built to house the first true world's fair, Prince Albert's Great Exhibition of 1851. Today, even the great Vic-

torian train sheds – massively arched and only partially or smokily glazed (GB-19, 23, 24) – cannot truly recapture the translucent vastness of that ethereal enclosure. Only in the Palm House at Kew (GB-31) and a few other similar conservatories is it possible to sense, in miniature as it were, the full extent of the nineteenth-century's iron and glass audacity.

Clearly Victoria's reign saw the peak of British architectural inventiveness, even if much of that architecture did not come from architects but from engineers such as Isambard Kingdom Brunel (GB-47) and, in the case of the Crystal Palace, from Sir Joseph Paxton, a 'gardener' (and chief factotum to the Duke of Devonshire). And although Britain's tectonic pre-eminence did not carry over uniformly into the realm of more conventional architectural problems, William Morris's Arts and Crafts Movement and the partially overlapping Aesthetic Movement were among the most important foundations of Art Nouveau. Because of them, late-nineteenth-century British domestic architecture was widely acclaimed and emulated on the Continent (B-3a, D-22). But Edwardian Britain reacted strongly against the excesses of Art Nouveau. By 1914 Britain's pioneering progressive designers and architects had either been forced into eclipse or were seeking refuge in historicism.

During the first half of the twentieth century Britain increasingly became an architectural backwater, a trend that since the Second World War has been no more than partially reversed. Only the then little appreciated industrial work of Sir Owen Williams (GB-9, 57, 67) and the madly brilliant, mannerist exercises of Sir Edward Lutyens (GB-36) relieved the interwar tedium of upper-class and institutional Neo-Georgian or middle-class Neo-Voysey. Unfortunately, Lutyens's best works are country houses – of the sort familiar to readers of British detective fiction – and none of the better examples has yet been opened to the public.

London   GB-2

Once the world's largest city, London is still, by a substantial margin, Europe's largest. But deceptively so. London spreads out at such a comparatively low density that it rarely approaches the tight urbanity of Paris, much less that of Manhattan.

The existence of so large a city on so small an island guarantees its pre-eminence in all things, including architecture. With the Underground extending well into the country and commuter rail services available to places as distant as Brighton – far beyond the now inadequate green belt – the greater part of Britain's modern architecture is accessible from a single central location. Bearing this in mind, directions to buildings within a broadly defined Greater London metropolitan area are referenced from the London map.

GB-2a Many items displayed at the Great Exhibition of 1851 are now in the **Victoria and Albert Museum**. That

museum also owns a room that was decorated by William Morris at an early stage in his career, 1867, and the monumentally lush Art Deco former lobby of the Strand Palace Hotel, 1929, by O. P. Bernard. *Underground: South Kensington*

GB-2b The 'opportunities' presented by the reconstruction of London's war damage have not led to great architectural or urbanistic triumphs. Even the once much heralded **Barbican enclave,** 1959–81, by Chamberlin, Powell & Bon, is now freely criticized for being anti-urban in its isolation of the pedestrian from the hurly-burly of the city, while its clumsily picturesque, Brutalist architecture seems tired and dated. *Underground: Barbican*

GB-2c Another such lost opportunity, on an even more prominent site, is the South Bank Arts Centre. Its first building, the **Royal Festival Hall,** 1951, was designed by the LCC (London County

Council) Architect's Department as part of the Festival of Britain – of which it is the only survivor. Before its 1962 renovation this was a remarkably evocative souvenir both of the Festival and of that brief postwar movement of optimism when Britain still thought that she had 'won' the war and that all would be well once more. Now, except for some interior recollections of its former innocence, the Festival Hall is just dully respectable. *Underground: Waterloo*

GB-2d Even dull respectability is preferable to the elephantine enthusiasm which permeated the mid-60s additions to the centre: the **Purcell Room,** the **Queen Elizabeth Hall** and the

London/Westminster, SW1   GB-3
** Houses of Parliament 1835–60
Parliament Square
Sir Charles Barry, with A. W. N. Pugin
Neo-Gothic
Map GB-2 / Underground: Westminster
  [Pugin's Commons Chamber, a less spectacular effort than his decoration of the House of Lords, was burnt out by bombs in 1940 and flaccidly rebuilt by Sir Giles Gilbert Scott in 1950.]
  Many foreigners assume the Palace of Westminster to be medieval, while those who are a little more knowledgeable, including many Britons, too easily dismiss it as 'fake' Gothic. As a result, it is one of the best-known but least appreciated of modern buildings. And it *is* modern. Its iron and masonry 'fireproof' construction is modern. So is its built-in ventilation system the flues of which – concealed in turrets and pinnacles – picturesquely embellish its roofscape. Its scope, its complexity, its functional specificity are also modern. Even Pugin's scholarly, nationalistic, Gothic ornament reflects modern sensibilities (even though it clothes an almost perfectly symmetrical body, which Pugin disdainfully but with some justification called 'Grecian', meaning Neo-Classical).
  It is self-confident, larger than life and, despite its historical garb, a wholly appropriate symbol of that first industrial age.

GB-3a Barry and Pugin's Palace of Westminster replaced a rambling, medieval aggregation largely destroyed by fire in 1834. In addition to the Houses of Parliament, the Old Palace contained law courts. These were eventually rehoused in the **Royal Courts of Justice,** 1874–82, a mammoth Gothic ensemble on the Strand, which G. E. Street erected a gen-

Hayward Gallery, 1963–8, by the GLC (Greater London Council) Architect's Department. *Underground: Waterloo*

GB-2e On the opposite (east) side of Waterloo Road from the rest of the centre is the **National Theatre,** 1967–77, by Denys Lasdun & Partners. Although not as inelegant as its immediate predecessors, it is almost more convincing as city-scaled sculpture than as architecture. *Underground: Waterloo*

GB-2f The South Bank Arts Centre is linked to the north bank by Sir Giles Gilbert Scott's conservatively graceful **Waterloo Bridge,** 1939–45. *Underground: Waterloo*

eration later. By then the Gothic ideal held sway in Britain and it was possible to build a more correct, more organically coherent re-creation of Gothic architecture, but one which in this case – aside from a single grand circulation space – now seems far less interesting. *Underground: Chancery Lane*

GB-3b If Sir Giles Gilbert Scott was not at his best in the House of Commons, he is certainly seen in a better light in the elegant, but now sadly disappearing, prewar British **telephone booths** he designed. With its Greek fluting and domed top, the first version, Model No. 2 of 1926, has more than a whiff of Sir John Soane about it. Its successor, Model No. 6 of 1936, is a slightly smaller, slightly more Moderne restatement of the earlier design.

London/Westminster, SW1   **GB-4**
* **New Zealand House** (chancery offices) 1960
Haymarket and Pall Mall
Robert Matthew, Johnson-Marshall & Partners
Late International Style
Map GB-2 / Underground: Charing Cross

There is a school of thought which suggests that most buildings should be as efficiently unobtrusive as possible, leaving the occasional grand or monumental gestures to those few functions, places or occasions which truly justify them. Such was the nature of Baroque Rome and Georgian London. It is one reason why they worked, why their gestures – their squares, churches and palaces – are so effective.

At first glance New Zealand House seems to suggest that such a system could still work: that high-quality, self-effacing, truly functional buildings might again provide a neutral backdrop for important urban *foci*. But the sensitive incorporation within New Zealand House of John Nash and G. S. Repton's Royal Opera Arcade, 1816–18, (entered from Pall Mall), serves as a reminder that, at least for the present, here

the relationship is in fact reversed. New Zealand House is an ascetic, crystalline intrusion into a reasonably homogeneous Classical context. It is the exception and, as such, becomes unjustifiably more special than it would be as a part of the 'context'.

London/Westminster, SW1   **GB-5**
* **Economist Group** (offices, bank, and flats) 1964
25 St James's Street
Alison & Peter Smithson
Rationalism
Map GB-2 / Underground: Green Park

Although at the time they had but one large building to their credit (GB-56), the Smithsons' writings and projects dominated radical British – and to an extent international – architectural thought during the 50s. It was, then, somewhat ironic that their second major client was an establishment publishing house whose co-tenants were to include a bank and an addition to one of the most prestigious St James's clubs. To some of their followers this might have seemed a rare chance to plant an architectural bomb in the enemy's heartland, but the Smithsons could not have been more well-mannered nor, for the time, more respectful of traditional urban values. They maintained all three of the site's street lines as well as the St James's Street cornice line. They employed a travertine-like variety of London's traditional Portland stone. And they even made a gesture towards integrating the adjacent Boodles club building with their own.

In the mid-60s, any decision not to set a tombstone-like slab within an anti-urban plaza did, of course, represent a kind of radicalism. Yet, if the Smithsons had not totally sold out to the establishment,

neither had they lived up to their previous reputation as the *enfants terribles* of British architecture. If the Economist Group had come from almost any other office, it would probably have been accepted as a creditable if colourless contribution to the city's fabric. But, as the creation of two such outspoken theoreticians, who had so loudly proclaimed their desire to redirect radically architecture and urbanism, merely having avoided pitfalls hardly seems sufficient.

London/Westminster, W1   **GB-6**
National Radiator Building or **Ideal House** (office building) 1928
Great Marlborough Street and Argyll Street
Raymond Hood, with J. Gordon Williams
Art Deco
Map GB-2 / Underground: Oxford Circus

[The ground-floor display room has been gutted to make way for a succession of shops, but the damage could have been much greater.]

Although, as the name suggests, Art Deco is an essentially decorative style of Continental origin, its greatest architectural efflorescence came in America. Aside from the long-vanished pavilions of the 1925 Paris Exposition des Arts Décoratifs, from which it took its name, the best European examples of this mode were once to be found in Britain. Now, however, little of that remains: some superficially stylized and now fading factory façades and cinemas, the lobbies of the Strand Palace Hotel (GB-2a) and of Sir Owen Williams's Daily Express building (GB-9); and, the National Radiator Building, which, as it happens, was designed by and for Americans.

GB-6a Across Great Marlborough Street is the half-timbered **Liberty & Co.** annex, 1924, by E. T. & E. S. Hall, which was authentically constructed from the timbers of old wooden warships. During the waning years of the British Arts and Crafts Movement it must have made a most suitable setting for that store which, for nearly half a century, had been *the* merchandiser of high-class Arts and Crafts paraphernalia. Curiously, Liberty's façade on Regent Street was put up at about the same time by the same architects.

GB-6b Another London example of marginal modernity – perhaps in this case better called Moderne or Pacquebot Style – is the **Rainbow Room** of the former Derry & Toms Department Store, (now Marks & Spencer), 1933, by Bernard

George with C. A. Wheeler (another American) at 99 Kensington High Street, W8. It was originally designed for *thé dansants* and came complete with some of the snazziest 'conveniences' ever. As if to demonstrate that this sort of modernism was just a style, not a commitment, the store's roof was given over to an elaborate mock-Spanish garden. *W on Kensington Rd (Map GB-2→) / on L abt three blks past Kensington Gardens / Underground: High St Kensington*

GB-6c London's best-known American building, Eero Saarinen's **US Embassy,** 1958–61, on Grosvenor Square, is every bit as nervously, conservatively modern as Hood's – and far more forgettable.
Underground: Marble Arch

GB-6d Somewhat more distant is yet another Art Deco building with American connections, the perhaps over-publicized **Hoover Factory,** 1932–5, by Wallis Gilbert & Partners. *W on A40 (Map GB-2→) abt 6 mi (10 km)*

London/Westminster, W1   **GB-7**
* All Saints' Church 1849–59
7–9 Margaret Street
William Butterfield
Ecclesiological Neo-Gothic
Map GB-2 / Underground: Oxford Circus

Butterfield and his fellow-ecclesiologists – the leaders of Victorian Gothicism – were men of principle. Honesty was the one indispensable constituent of their work. Butterfield built in the Gothic style because he felt it was the best way in which to build, both morally and tectonically. But that did not mean he believed All Saints, Margaret Street, should seem to have been built in the agrarian Middle Ages. No, it had to be recognizable as a product of urban, nineteenth-century, industrialized Britain. Not to have made use of terracotta, stock brick or sash windows would have been 'dishonest' and abhorrent – particularly in a church.

London/Camden, WC2   **GB-8**
** Sir John Soane's Museum (his
own home) 1792–1834
12, 13 and 14 Lincoln's Inn Fields
Sir John Soane
Romantic Neo-Classicism
Map GB-2 / Underground: Holborn

Sir John Soane, the eminently respectable architect of the old Bank of England,
1792–1823 (now demolished), was very
much a man of his time. Yet he might also
almost have been of our own century. The
façade of his house brings to mind the more
Classicist side of *fin-de-siècle* Vienna's
Secession, while its interiors reflect a spatial
inventiveness that many of today's Neo-
Classicists could not hope to equal. Soane
used simple linear ornaments to punctuate
space; plaster to mould it – especially in
ceilings; mirrors to reflect, transform or
extend it; glass – often carried by iron – to
illuminate or dramatize it; and objects to
modulate it. He strove modestly for effects
which his Revolutionary Romantic French
contemporaries could only suggest in grandiose paper schemes. In his bijou breakfast
room, surreal monks' cave, and kinetic
picture gallery (hung with Hogarth oils),
he anticipated another century's
Hoffmanns (B-12) and Kahns – while
reducing its Philip Johnsons (D-37) to footnote status.

GB-8a **No. 19 Lincoln's Inn Fields,**
1868, is by Philip Webb.

GB-8b Soane's largest extant public
building is the **Dulwich Picture
Gallery,** 1811–14, in College Road. *S via*

*Elephant & Castle on A215 (Map GB-2→)
abt 3½ m (5.6 km) / L at Herne Hill on to
A2214 (Half Moon Lane) / R on Village
Way / R on Dulwich Village ⇨ College
Rd / gallery is about ½ mi (1 km) on R*

GB-8c Among the most radically primi-
tive of Soane's works are the **Royal
Hospital Stables,** 1814–17, in Royal
Hospital Road, Chelsea.
Underground: Sloane Square

London/The City, EC4   **GB-9**
* Daily Express Building (editorial
offices and printing plant) 1930–2
Fleet Street and Shoe Lane
Sir Owen Williams, with Ellis, Clarke &
Gallannaugh; lobby by Ronald Atkinson
Moderne (exterior)/Art Deco (lobby)
Map GB-2 / Underground: Blackfriars

Looking back to the years between the
two world wars, the eyes of most observers
were long-dazzled by the ascetic white
architecture of Le Corbusier and his few
fellow International Style 'heroes'. But
during those two decades there were as
many varieties of modernity as there were
names to describe them: Art Deco, Pacquebot Style, Jazz Modern, Moderne, etc.
Generally, time has not served these modes
well, and most surviving examples now
seem pretty thin.

Not so the Daily Express Building.
Thanks to excellent materials and work-
manship, this slick, streamlined black ziggurat still gleams with a sense of exciting
newness, while within, its Art Deco lobby
vibrates like the dawn of a new age.
However, as others have noted before, sun-
rises and sunsets can look confusingly alike.

GB-9a Most consistent in its Art Deco language, if never as spectacular as the Daily
Express lobby, is **St Olave House,** 1927–
32, the head offices of the Hay's Wharf Co.
on the south bank of the Thames. Designed

by H. S. Goodhart-Rendel, a gentleman-
architect who is now principally remembered for his perceptive critical writing, its
'front' façade, on Tooley Street, is pre-
sentable enough, but its 'important' façade
clearly is that seen from the river and from
both London and Tower Bridges.
Underground: London Bridge

GB-9b Another side of Sir Owen Williams – the engineer – is to be seen in his **BOAC Hangars**, 1950–2, at Heathrow Airport. The 336-foot concrete span was once the world's longest. *W on A4 (Map GB-2 →) / SW on A30 / just N of rd on S side of airport*

London/The City, EC4   **GB-10**
The Black Friar (pub)
New Bridge Street and Queen Victoria Street
H. Fuller Clark, with Henry Poole (sculptor)
*c.*1890 (extended 1919–24)
Arts and Crafts
Map GB-2 / Underground: Blackfriars

Although rather seedy now, more so within than without, the Black Friar pub still fascinates. It is a quaffer's Watts Chapel (GB-41) built of rich, durable materials and swarming with little fat friars.

How peculiarly British – such effort seemingly in aid of so prosaic a function. The ultimate purpose here, however, was not the glorification of ale, but rather the revival of 'artistic' craftsmanship.

London/The City, EC3   **GB-11**
** Lloyd's (insurance exchange)
1978–86
107 Leadenhall Street
Richard Rogers & Partners
High-Tech
Map GB-2 / Underground: Bank

Inevitably comparisons with two other major High-Tech buildings come to mind: Rogers's own earlier, more monumental Centre Pompidou (F-6), and Foster Associates contemporaneous, much larger Hongkong Bank tower in Hong Kong. Both Lloyd's and the Hongkong Bank are High-Tech office buildings for large financial institutions, with floor plans free from the mass of fire stairs, lifts, etc. that lies at the core of most conventional office buildings, but Lloyd's shares more of Beaubourg's picturesque toughness. Lloyd's open plan is required by a huge, exchange floor, known as 'The Room', which fills the base of the tower. The service functions are then left to fit themselves, as best they can, on to the remaining bits of site around the building's simple rectangular body – virtually the largest rectangle that could be squeezed on to the lot. Because the size of 'The Room' effectively determines the perimeter of the office floors above, those floors almost demand the atrium (topped with a Crystal Palace-like barrel vault) which rises the

entire height of the building in place of the usual internal service core.

London/The City, EC2 **GB-12**
Bishopsgate Institute and Library
1894
230 Bishopsgate
C. Harrison Townsend
Free Style/Art Nouveau
Map GB-2 / Underground: Liverpool Street

If Victor Horta had not invented the Franco-Belgian form of Art Nouveau architecture in 1892–3 (B-3), Harrison Townsend's early works might now be considerably better known, albeit not necessarily famous. Townsend's free but uneven blend of a vaguely Richardsonian English Neo-Baroque, with some Arts and Crafts motifs, is not comparable to Horta's richer, more original work, yet for its time and place Townsend's break with the past is notable. From it one can trace a path, circuitous though it might be, to that other, ultimately more significant, branch of the Art Nouveau, the Viennese Secession.

GB-12a Near by, in Whitechapel Road, is Townsend's **Whitechapel Art Gallery** of 1897–9 (upper storey now somewhat modified). It shows how little he, like Horta, was able to build upon his own first achievement. *E on Whitechapel High St (Map GB-2→) / abt three blks on L / Underground: Aldgate East*

GB-12b Further afield and later still is Townsend's **Horniman Museum,** 1900–2 – rather more sure-handed and

expressive but of the same mode, at 100 London Road, Forest Hill. *S on A215 (Map GB-2→), then on A2216 → Dulwich / on L 700 yds (m) before Forest Hill Station*

London/The City, EC3 **GB-13**
Holland House (office building) 1914
1–4 and 32 Bury Street
H. P. Berlage
Rationalism
Map GB-2 / Underground: Aldgate

[There was once a third façade in an alley off Creechurch Lane. Both façade and alley have given way to a large new building, of which Holland House has become an appendage. Many of the original surfaces and details of the interior public spaces were lost as recently as 1983.]

Externally, Holland House's terracotta cladding and regular modularity reflect Berlage's discovery of Louis Sullivan (on a journey to America in 1911). Internally, Berlage, the very Dutch and not surprisingly somewhat mystical follower of Viollet-le-Duc's Rationalism, was once far more in evidence.

The Kröller-Mullers, who commissioned this building, were among modern architecture's grandest private patrons (NL-52, 53). As can be seen at the corner of Bury Street and Creechurch Lane, their largesse was, in part at least, supported by shipping.

London/Westminster, SW1   **GB-14**
* Lillington Gardens Estate (social
housing) 1968–72
Vauxhall Bridge Road and Charlwood Street
Darbourne & Darke
Map GB-2 / Underground: Pimlico

Pragmatic Britain, with its terraced row
house tradition and its love of nature, was
among the first to reject the CIAM-inspired
housing ideal. One can sense the beginning
of that rejection at Park Hill (GB-71),
Thamesmead (GB-25) and elsewhere. Yet
rarely before Lillington Gardens was the
entire nature and quality of social housing
so thoroughly and reasonably restudied in
relation to a large, high-density urban site.
Lillington Gardens is not a compromised
fragment of a social or technical utopia.
Lillington Gardens *is*, in scale, texture and
function, a truly organic part of the city. It
contains a mixture of dwelling types, not
just sizes. Its dwellings are all near to the
ground. Many have direct street access
through small gardens. None has to rely on

elevators. Above all, Lillington Gardens is
not idealized nor 'proto-typical' – which
may be why it is not better known.

GB-14a Surviving in the midst of all this
radical reasonableness is G. E. Street's **St
James the Less**, 1860, a hard, polychromatic church, which in its own youth
seemed more radical than reasonable.

London/Chelsea, SW3   **GB-15**
* Old Swan House 1875–7
17 Chelsea Embankment
Richard Norman Shaw
Queen Anne 'Revival'
Map GB-2 / Underground: Sloane Square

Along with others of the immediate post-
William Morris generation, Shaw (who
was actually older than Morris) tried to re-
establish the vernacular Classical lineage
that had been lost during the Industrial
Revolution. Their goal was to graft a viable
new architecture, appropriate to nineteenth-century England, on to old post-
Renaissance English 'root-stock' – on to the
architecture of that period after the Classical vocabulary had already become well-
established but before the regional vernacular traditions had lost their vitality. For
them the Georgian, with its rigidly established formulas, was unacceptably restrictive. They chose instead to return to an
even earlier tradition, more or less that of
Queen Anne's reign (1702–14), in which
they believed they could find formal solutions to all sorts of functional difficulties.

In theory, it may have seemed to make
some sense. Yet such a projection of the
past, no matter how freely developed, into
a more demanding present could hardly
have been expected to prove satisfying for
long. The nineteenth century had programmatic requirements and offered technical opportunities for which there could
be no precedent. To fit within even such
an adaptable historical mode as the Queen
Anne Revival, architect and client alike
had to deny all the fruits of the Industrial
Revolution – which most were not willing
to do – or they had to use the 'Queen
Anne' simply as a convenient fiction through
which to escape from other, more strictly
codified, styles. Shaw, establishment
architect that he was, took the latter course.

Old Swan House is an elegant evocation
of something that never was. And, in one

very visible respect, it epitomizes all the
issues of precedent and historic fidelity that
both underlay and undermined the Queen
Anne Revival, because the romantic, ver-
nacular-seeming cantilevering of the upper
stories of Old Swan House (a half-timber
usage translated here into brick) is, not
surprisingly, only made possible by a
hidden iron framework.

GB-15a Next to Old Swan House, at 18
Chelsea Embankment, is Shaw's **Cheyne
House,** 1875.

GB-15b **Nos 9–11 Chelsea Embankment,** 1878–80, and No. 8, **Clock
House,** 1879, are also Shaw's work.

GB-15c Further to the west, just past
Oakley Street, at **38–39 Cheyne Walk,**
are the two surviving houses of a group,
1899–1901, designed by C. R. Ashbee, a
key figure in the Arts and Crafts Movement.

London/Chelsea, SW1   **GB-16**
* **Peter Jones** (department store) 1936
(extension on King's Road, 1964)
Sloane Square
Slater, Crabtree & Moberly, with
Sir C. H. Reilly
International Style
Map GB-2 / Underground: Sloane Square

Today the curtain wall is a thing of ill-
repute – often little more than exterior
'wallpaper' with which bad designers
clothe boring buildings. Such was not
always the case. Once, it was a custom-
designed component of expensive and prestigious, or at least stylish, architecture.

This curtain wall is a case in point. Utilized only where appropriate, easily turning
a difficult corner without recourse to any
quasi-Classical or quasi-Victorian tricks,
it is a rational response to particular problems, not merely the application of an
accepted formula. Such thoughtful design
characterizes the entire building. And see
how well it all has worn.

GB-16a Another London department
store, **Selfridges,** 1907–9, was designed
by the Chicago architectural and city planning firm, Daniel H. Burnham & Co, with
street elevation by Francis Swales.
Underground: Marble Arch

London/Kensington, SW3   **GB-17**
Michelin House (garage, now offices),
1908–9
91 Fulham Road
François Espinasse
*Map GB-2 / Underground: South
Kensington*

[Originally the larger windows contained
backlit stained-glass views of the Michelin
Man, who was also represented by statues
mounted atop the corners of the cornice.]

If Michelin House doesn't quite seem to
belong in London that may be because its
façades were prefabricated in France –
which is not to say that it would 'fit' in
Paris. Like the motor cars depicted in its
vitreous murals (joyously racing under
eternally sunny skies), or like its present-
day counterparts, the faience façades of
franchise-America, it owes no allegiance to
any particular place.

GB-17a Similar, but locally produced,
ceramic material encases **Debenham**
House, a contemporaneous, 1905–7,
Neo-Classical house, at 8 Addison Road,
Kensington, by Halsey Ricardo. Now occu-
pied by the Richmond Fellowship, its unex-
pected interiors reflect a fascination with
Byzantium that permeated the Edwardian
Arts and Crafts Movement. *W on A40
(Bayswater Rd) (Map GB-2→) abt
1½ mi (2.5 km) past Notting Hill Gate / L
on Addison Rd / on L*

London/Kensington, SW3   **GB-18**
Twin House 1891
14–16 Hans Road
C. F. A. Voysey
Neo-Vernacular
Map GB-2 / Underground: Knightsbridge

Not one of Voysey's better-known works
(GB-73), but a telling one – especially in the
context of its more classically proportioned
neighbours. It has the slightly medieval air
one might expect in an urban building
designed by this champion of rural vernacular sensibilities.

GB-18a **No. 12 Hans Road** is the
work of A. H. Mackmurdo, 1893–4. His
interiors and graphic designs of the 1880s
are often cited as a major source of Art
Nouveau. It is typical of progressive British architecture of the period that such a
sensibility is not more evident in the
façade of this house, elegant though it is.

GB-18b The **food halls of Harrods**
department store, just across the street,
are a remarkable example of Free Style (Art

Nouveau) ceramic work, 1902, designed
by G. W. J. Neatby.

London/Westminster, W2 GB-19
* Paddington Station 1850–4
Praed Street, Bayswater
Isambard Kingdom Brunel (engineer), with
Sir Matthew Digby Wyatt and Owen Jones
Map GB-2 / Underground: Paddington

Paddington has been likened to an English cathedral. The comparison is inevitable, and, as far as it suggests an attitude towards skin and structure, it is apt. Most obviously, the truss-supported arches recall the effortlessly 'floating' quality of Gothic timber hammerbeam roofs. At a more abstract level, one can also sense a certain paperiness of the volumetric surfaces and a delicate modularity which seems particularly characteristic of British architecture, be it that of the Late Middle Ages (such as the Henry VII Chapel at Westminster Abbey) or of James Stirling (GB-51).

Spatially the shed's three equal 'naves' and its double 'transepts' are more reminiscent of Spanish cathedrals: multi-aisled, polydirectional and slightly 'Moorish'. In fact others have also noted a certain 'Saracenic' flavour here. While these exotic sources might not be obvious to the casual viewer, they were very much in the minds of progressive nineteenth-century architects. They were obsessed by the idea of evolving, or synthesizing, a new style: one appropriate to a time in which materials,

methods of construction, scale, spatial possibilities and programmatic requirements were all being totally revolutionized. Not surprisingly, that century of colonialism took its search for new solutions and old precedents to every age and culture. Owen Jones was one of the foremost mid-Victorian advocates of such systematic renewal of architecture and design. (His *Grammar of Ornament* would, after half a century, still profoundly affect the young Frank Lloyd Wright.) In his own youth Jones had made the first serious modern study of the Alhambra – and so it is that this Anglo-Hispano-Moorish railway cathedral came into being.

London/Westminster, NW1 GB-20
* Penguin Pool 1934
London Zoo, Regent's Park
Tecton (Berthold Lubetkin)
International Style
Map GB-2 / Underground: Camden Town

It is telling and ironic that this delightful toy is Britain's best-known International Style monument.

GB-20a The corduroy concrete **Elephant House,** 1965, is by Casson, Conder & Partners.

GB-20b Tecton was also responsible for an International Style **Elephant House,** 1934–5, at Whipsnade Zoo in Bedfordshire. *N on A400 (Map GB-2→), then A1, then M1 / NW near Harpenden on A5 / L on B4540 →* WHIPSNADE *and* ZOO

London/Westminster, NW1 GB-21
* Aviary 1963
London Zoo, Regent's Park
Lord Snowdon, with Cedric Price and
Frank Newby
Structural Neo-Expressionism
Map GB-2 / Underground: Camden Town

Questions as to its true authorship notwithstanding, this is a most remarkable birdcage. Even if one is not interested in birds (or birdcages) there is still a good ten minutes' diversion to be had here, just making sure that it really does obey the laws of mechanics and gravity.

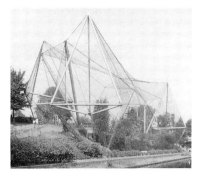

London/Camden, NW1 **GB-22**
* **TV-am** (television studios and offices
in a converted garage) 1982–3
Hawley Crescent
Terry Farrell Partnership
Post-Modernism
Map GB-2 / Underground: Kentish Town

Unlike its often more glitzy and jokey
American counterpart, European Post-
Modernism tends either towards the Neo-
Vernacular or the Neo-Classical. Glitzy,
jokey TV-am must be, then, Europe's most
American Post-Modern building. As befits
a breakfast-time TV service, its windowless,
silver sheet-metal street façade is a sunrise
'horizon' – one streaked with red, orange
and yellow streamlines which, above its
central entrance, become the ghost image
of a huge arch containing a neon-lit 'electronic' keystone. In the somewhat more
conventional rear façade, facing the Grand
Union Canal, the saw-toothed north-light
roofline and brickwork of the former garage
are still partially visible through the geometric paint and other accretions.
However, topping each rooflight gable is a
very domestic (and very British) blue-and-
white egg cup, complete with a sunrise-
golden egg (where Classical tradition has
taught us to expect a sphere or pineapple).
Within the centre of the building and paralleling these two façades is a long, atrium-
like circulation and reception space containing a number of strange elements
meant to be evocative of exotic settings – a
'temple', a 'ziggurat' and a 'desert' – all
derived from a quixotic iconographic programme. If nothing else, TV-am has an
appropriately stage-set-like air of unreality.

London/Camden, N1 **GB-23**
* **King's Cross Station** 1850–2
King's Cross
Lewis Cubitt
Italianate/Functionalism
Map GB-2 / Underground: King's Cross
[The original laminated wooden roof
beams were replaced with steel in the late
nineteenth century.]

No age could be more 'functional' than
the nineteenth century when it put its mind
to it. Here is a structure just as logically
organized and as devoid of ornament as
the locomotives it was built to serve. The
volumes of its two parallel sheds, one for
departures, the other for arrivals, announce
themselves on the façade. Indeed, with the
addition of a clock and a *porte-cochère*, they
are the façade. For once form decidedly does
follow function.

GB-23a The same scheme – in late Néo-
Grec trimmings – is to be found in Victor
Laloux's **Gare d'Orléans**, 1895–8, in
Tours, France.

London/Camden, NW1 **GB-24**
* **St Pancras Station and Hotel**
(now British Rail offices) 1868–74
Euston Road
W. H. Barlow (shed)
Sir George Gilbert Scott (hotel)
High Victorian Gothic (hotel)
Map GB-2 / Underground: King's Cross

Everyone knows that the nineteenth
century developed the now-ubiquitous skyscraper. But we tend to forget its more
daring large-scale spatial achievements. If
this 250-foot by 700-foot space can still
excite one (as fifty-storey office towers no
longer can), think of the effect it must have
had a century ago. There are other large
sheds on the Continent – as there also once
were in America. None. however, was so
large so early.

Happily the inherent merits of Scott's
hotel – dismissable so recently as a 'Victorian horror' masking the 'honest' train
shed – are again coming to be recognized.

London/Bexley, SE2   **GB-25**
* Thamesmead New Town
Begun 1968
Hartslock Drive
GLC (Greater London Council) Architect's
Department
Late International Style
E on A200 (Map GB-2→), then A206
abt 8 mi (13 km) → GREENWICH /
→ WOOLWICH */ →* PLUMSTEAD /
→ THAMESMEAD

The unwelcome, hostile future depicted
by the film *The Clockwork Orange* was por-
trayed in part by the early architecture
of Thamesmead. The choice was understandable. Yet Thamesmead was no more
than a partly Brutalist, partly picturesque
assemblage of fairly standard GLC concrete
panelwork. In addition to its size, the unreality of this place derived from its inten-

sively developed infrastructure, and
particularly its elevated walkway system,
which in turn reflected a desire to separate
the residents from both traffic and, one suspects, Thamesmead's eminently floodable
marshland site. Ironically, later phases of
development here reverted to a much more
'comfortable' Neo-Vernacular manner of
building.

GB-25a One of the last of the big, 'Futuristic', system-built housing projects in
London is the **Alexandra Road
Development,** 1969–79, by the
Borough of Camden Architect's Department. Its almost thousand-foot-long 'spine'
is a terraced, eight-storey high, virtually
one-sided block which effectively shields the
rest of the site from a railway cutting.
Underground: Swiss Cottage

London/Bexleyheath   **GB-26**
** The Red House 1859–60
Red House Lane
Philip Webb, with William Morris
Neo-Vernacular
*SE on A2 (Map GB-2→) abt 9½ mi (14 km)
/ E on A207 (Shooters Hill Rd ⇨ Crook
Log) abt 4½ mi (7 km) / R on Upton Road
/ third R on to Red House Lane / on L*
[The house is privately owned, and at the
time of writing was open to the public only
one afternoon a month. Check with
National Tourist Board for specific times
and dates.]

Webb may have been its architect, but
The Red House was William Morris's own
home, his youthful manifesto of a new life-
style intertwined with a new aesthetic. Its
immediate architectural roots lie in the
buildings and writings of such mid-
Victorians as William Butterfield (GB-7)
and G. E. Street (GB-14a): architects whose
deep moralistic convictions transformed
their work into a quest for the principles
that underlay the only building methods
which they felt were suitable to Britain,
and which also therefore had to underline
her rightful indigenous style – i.e. the
Gothic.

Following in this tradition, The Red
House was not an attempt to create Gothic
architecture at an inappropriately small
scale, nor was it meant to be a deceptive,
archaeologically correct, traditional vernacular cottage. Rather it was built in
accordance with those principles which, it

was assumed, local craftsmen would have
developed by 1859 had the evolution of
their vernacular tradition not been corrup-
ted by foreign influences, i.e., Classicism.

GB-26a Morris's boyhood home, **Water-
house,** in Walthamstow, (London/
Waltham Forest), is now the William
Morris Gallery. It contains a large sampling
of his firm's work along with other Pre-
Raphaelite objects. *N on A10 (Map GB-2→),
abt 4½ mi (7 km) / E on A503 ⇨ Forest
Rd / abt 2 mi (3.5 km) on L, in Lloyd Park*

GB-26b Further afield, in Wolver-
hampton, Staffordshire, is **Wightwick
Manor,** 1887 and 1893, a rather archaeological half-timbered house by Edward
Ould who was completely decorated and
furnished by Morris's firm. *W from Wol-
verhampton on A454 / R at* THE MERMAID
pub on to Wightwick Bank / up hill on L
[Open to the public.]

London/Southwark, SE15   **GB-27**
Peckham Health Centre (community
health centre) 1933–5
St Mary's Road
Sir Owen Williams
Rationalism
S on A215 (Map GB-2→) / E on A202
⇨ *Queen's Rd / R on St Mary's Rd (second
after RR viaduct) / on L /*
Underground: New Cross Gate

[Now a large conventional group practice and clinic.]

An understandable preoccupation with
the unhealthy effects of the smoky atmosphere of prewar London may help explain
the marked resemblance between this pioneering 'total health centre', which was just
as much concerned with the maintenance
of good health as with its restoration, and
some of the more characteristic products of
the contemporary open-air school movement (DK-11, F-39). Otherwise this is a
typical Owen Williams work – datable but
not dated. Its strict symmetry, emphasized
end pavilions and lack of stylistic motifs,

must once have made it appear old-
fashioned and boring. But at least it still
retains its sense of integrity.

GB-27a One near contemporary is the
Finsbury Health Centre, 1938, by
Tecton, in Pine Street, EC1. Its slick, out-
wardly bowing, symmetrical, glass-block
and tile façade seems abstractly formalist,
compromised, and unconvincing –
especially having come from a firm like
Tecton (GB-20, 35). *Underground: Angel*

London/Wandsworth, SW15   **GB-28**
* **Alton West Estate** (social housing)
1955–60
Danebury Avenue, Roehampton
LCC (London County Council) Architect's
Department
Corbusian Brutalism
*SW on A3 (Map GB-2→) → GUILDFORD
abt 4½ mi (7 km) / R on to Roehampton
Lane (→ ROEHAMPTON) / L on Danebury
Av / on both sides of rd*

The Alton West Estate, commonly called
Roehampton, was long a favourite example
of aesthetically pleasing, and thus one was
meant to presume well-designed, social
housing. It is also one of the more faithful
approximations to Le Corbusier's postwar
social housing schemes. The five *unité*-like
(F-63) slabs marching along the site's
northern boundary especially reflect
Corbusier idolatry of a very high order.

Since the late 50s much has been learned
of the social problems associated with this
sort of idealistic planning panacea. (One
needs but cite America's public housing.)
Yet Roehampton remains, and perhaps
always has been, seductive not for the
undoubted refinement of its architecture,
but because it is skilfully set in a well-

matured landscaped estate: a full-blooded
archetype of those abstract, two-dimensional and essentially symbolic *jardins
anglais* with which, in so many of his large-
scale housing proposals, Le Corbusier
attempted to breathe some meaning into
the voids between his buildings.

GB-28a Perversely, just south of Alton
West, on the Portsmouth Road, is the
earlier, 1952–5, **Alton East** (also by the
LCC Architect's Department). Its Scandinavian-inspired 'People's Detailing' represents an attempt at a kind of architectural
Socialist Realism.

London/Richmond upon Thames   **GB-29**
Langham House Close (flats) 1958
Ham Street
Stirling & Gowan
Brutalism
*SW on A3 (Map GB-2→) abt 5 mi (8 km)
/ bear R on A308 → KINGSTON / R in
Kingston→HAM on A307 (Richmond Rd)
/ L on Ham St / L on to Langham House
Close / on R*

The Corbusian Brutalist/vernacular
ancestry of Langham House Close can
never be in doubt. But already here Le Corbusier's rough, pseudo-Catalan peasant
vernacular (F-26) has begun to be transformed: it has become more precise and
regular; the loadbearing masonry more
carefully calculated and constructed. It

was still an attempt to re-create a vernacular – but beginning with buildings like this,
the source of inspiration increasingly was
the vernacular of the Industrial Revolution.

London/Hounslow, W4   G B - 30
* **Bedford Park** (garden suburb)
1874–90
Chiswick
Richard Norman Shaw, *et al.*
Queen Anne 'Revival'
*W on A4 (Map GB-2→) past Hammersmith
Flyover / R at Hogarth Roundabout →
CHISWICK / on to Devonshire Rd (see GB-
30a below) / across Chiswick High Rd on to
Turnham Green Terrace ⇨ The Avenue
/ along both sides of st several blocks deep /
Underground: Turnham Green*

Bedford Park was an early, middle-class translation of the artistic retreat (conveniently situated on a then newly-opened branch of London's far-reaching underground railway). Today, we think of it as the first garden suburb and hence as an ancestor of modern anti-urban town-planning – which it is. In its own time many considered it as much an aesthetic innovation as a social one – which it was.

14 South Parade, Bedford Park

G B - 30a The modest house illustrated is **14 South Parade**, 1889-94, by C.F.A. Voysey, perhaps the single most important building in the area. Although derived from ideals similar to those which animated Shaw's red-brick villas, it marks the beginning of the new, more logically considered, somewhat less picturesque, Arts and Crafts house (see GB-73). *South Parade is SW boundary of Bedford Park*

G B - 30b Nearby is Voysey's **Sanderson & Sons Wallpaper Factory**, 1902–3 (now Alliance Assurance). Although Voysey's approach to a commercial commission is interesting, it is evident that domestic architecture was his true forte. *W on Chiswick High Rd from Devonshire Rd (see directions above) / L at Heathfield Terrace / immediate L into Barley Mow Passage / on L*

London/Richmond upon Thames   G B - 31
** **Palm House** (greenhouse)
1845–7 (restored *c.* 1985)
Kew Gardens
Richard Turner, with Decimus Burton
Functionalism
*W on A4 (Map GB-2→) abt 7 mi (11 km)
/ SW at roundabout (at beginning of M4)
on A205 / on R just after river /
map of gardens at entrance gate /
Underground: Kew Gardens*

The schizophrenic nineteenth-century attitude towards sex, morality and art is proverbial. Less well understood is the similar attitude towards design. Victorian Functionalists could argue that buildings should be as pragmatic as clipper ships, and yet accept the idea that classical or allegorical allusions were a necessary aspect of painting and sculpture.

Only a few specialized building types permitted the creation of truly functional architectural 'clipper ships': building types such as train sheds (GB-23), exhibition structures (F-16, A-13) and, of course, greenhouses. Here, as with all Victorian conservatories, the pre-eminent needs to maximize sunlight, minimize heat loss and control the run-off of internal condensation dictated the Palm House's forms, detailing and materials. Architecturally, the critical decision came only after all those needs had been satisfied. And then, happily, it was decided to leave well alone.

G B - 31a The gardens also contain an assortment of **eighteenth-century follies**, 1760–3, including three little Greek temples, a 'ruined' arch and a pagoda, all by Sir William Chambers.

GB-31b Still standing in Kew Gardens is Kew Palace, 1631. It originally introduced into Britain those Dutch Baroque elements which, somewhat remarkably, two-and-a-half centuries later became major components of the nationalistic and rather syn- thetic Queen Anne 'Revival' (GB-15). Fittingly, also to be found here is **The Lodge,** 1866–7, a diminutive creation by Richard Norman Shaw's early partner, Eden Nesfield. It is often cited as the first Queen Anne-style building.

London/Hounslow   **GB-32**
* Great Conservatory, Syon House
1820–7
London Road, Brentford
Charles Fowler
Neo-Classicism
W on A4 (Map GB-2→) / SW at roundabout (at beginning of M4) on A205 / SW on A315 → BRENTFORD */ →* SYON HOUSE

In a British film comedy some years back there was a sequence in which the main protagonist dreamt he had died. The heaven at which he eventually arrived was Syon House Conservatory (with its stone- work whitewashed to match the iron). The image seemed wholly appropriate.

There is a semi-immaterial quality about this diminutive plant palace. Its classical pedigree is asserted in pediments, arches, quadrants and pavilions whose stony, solid self-assurance seems perpetually in the process of dissolving into the sketchy insubstantiality of wrought-iron tracery – and nowhere more so than in the traditionally dominant, here translucent, central dome.

The conservatory is, incidentally, a quite early example of iron and glass architecture: its earliest predecessors date only from the late eighteenth century.

London/Harrow   **GB-33**
* Grims Dyke (country house, now a hotel) 1870–2
Old Redding, Harrow Weald
Richard Norman Shaw
'Jacobethan' or 'Old English'
N on A5 (Map GB-2→) abt 8½ mi (14 km) / L on A410, abt 2 mi (3 km) / R on Clamp Hill ⇨ Old Redding (across A409) / R opposite THE CASE IS ALTERED *pub →* GRIMSDYKE HOTEL

As one of the most successful society architects of his day – W. S. Gilbert once lived here – Shaw, through his country houses, greatly influenced the development of English domestic architecture. Admittedly Grims Dyke still bears traces of an older, more naive narrative historicism, its substantial half-timbering being most certainly a sham. Yet it also reflects a greater concern for the appropriateness of its vernacular vocabulary than would typically be found in comparable establishment architecture of a generation earlier. Houses such as this became a critical link between the earlier, less accessible medieval enthusiasms of a William Butterfield (GB-7) or a

William Morris (GB-26) and both C. F. A. Voysey's new national vernacular (GB-73) and Sir Edwin Lutyens's elegantly mannered, cynical scholarship (GB-36).

Unexpectedly, thanks to the then newly emergent illustrated architectural journals, Shaw's houses also had a direct impact across the Atlantic. There, the resemblance between his use of tile hanging and the New England tradition of shingle siding struck a responsive chord, both originally having been derived from the vernacular of south-east England. And so, in a sense, Grims Dyke and its kind were also among the progenitors of the American Shingle Style.

London/Hillingdon   **GB-34**
Hillingdon Civic Centre 1974–8
High Street, Uxbridge
Robert Matthew, Johnson-Marshall &
Partners
Neo-Vernacular
*W on Bayswater Rd (Map GB-2→) / angle
R at Shepherd's Bush on Uxbridge Rd
(A4020) / abt 12 mi (20 km)*
Underground: Uxbridge

Brick string courses, dentil courses,
soldier courses and pilasters; brick-bearing
arches and sloping-faced walls; bull-nosed
bricks, moulded brick transitions from
round corners to square; 'cast-stone' lintels
with bead mouldings; tile roofs: a generation ago such masonry work seemed
dead and gone for ever. Yet here it is, all
heaped up into a picturesque, russet mountain of a building. The faceted floor-plan
geometry – echoed in the roofs – is derived
from the interplay between two struc-
tural/planning grids set at 45° to each

other. If the roofs evoke the homely, tile-
hung Kentish vernacular so beloved by
British Arts and Crafts architects in the
early decades of the century (GB-36), then
the brickwork calls forth images of more
sophisticated Continental designs of the
same period: the elegant, geometric Rationalism of H. P. Berlage (NL-52) and the
romantic civil monuments of the German
Expressionists (D-42b). Yet the building
seems to lack any philosophical under-
pinnings. Beyond the beautifully crafted
brickwork and romantically piled
roofscape, one searches in vain for some
sense of a driving spirit, some larger idea.
Perhaps that is why the re-used, trite Neo-
Georgian cupola from a previous municipal
building sits too comfortably atop the
council chamber roof. And perhaps it also
explains the often amorphous, charac-
terless quality of the interior spaces –
despite some volumetric gymnastics
beneath those big roofs.

London/Camden, N6   **GB-35**
* **Highpoint I and II** 1933–5 and
1938
North Hill, Highgate
Tecton (Berthold Lubetkin)
International Style
*N on A400 (Map GB-2→) → HIGHGATE
/ L just after Kentish Town Underground
station on Highgate Rd abt 1 mi (1.5 km) ⇨
West Hill across Highgate High St on to North
Rd ⇨ North Hill / 400 yds (m) on
L / Underground: Highgate*

The International Style came late to
Britain, and, in those last few prewar
years, it came primarily as a political
refugee. Although limited in its impact, it
was soon assimilated, becoming less dogmatic and less sure of itself.

Highpoint I, one of the earlier examples
of this refugee architecture, is well handled
but conventional Corbusiana. Mech-
anically Mediterranean in elevation, it has
a ground-floor plan almost' more reminiscent of Le Corbusier's purist paintings
than of his buildings – so much so that
there is a flight of external stairs leading
down to the rear garden, whose mannerist
impracticality, not to mention danger-
ousness, equals anything Le Corbusier's
latter-day New York disciples could devise.

And Highpoint II? There, just three years
later, absolutely all the steam has gone out

Highpoint I

of the argument, leaving little more than a
sense of compromise – and a remarkable
foretaste of the flaccid 50s. Consider only
those *porte-cochère* caryatids. At the time
they must have been deliciously naughty.
Now they just seem like echoes of Las Vegas.

Meadway Gate, Hampstead Garden Suburb

London/Camden NW11   **GB-36**
* Hampstead Garden Suburb
Begun 1906
Richard Barry Parker, Sir Raymond
Unwin, *et al.*
Central Square churches 1909–14
Institute 1909–20s
Sir Edwin Lutyens
Neo-Georgian (Central Sq); Arts and Crafts
Neo-Vernacular (shops and cottages)
*N on A400 (Map GB-2 →) ⇨ A1, abt 3½ mi
(6 km) / L on Northway / suburb is on
both sides of rd / Central Sq is straight ahead
four blks / commercial bldgs are NW from
Central Sq on Erskine Hill / L on Temple
Fortune Hill / R on Hampstead Way / R
at Finchley Rd /*
Underground: Golders Green

Not a new town in the sense that
Letchworth (GB-37) or Cumbernauld
(GB-86) try to be, Hampstead unambigu-
ously proclaims itself a garden *suburb*. But
unlike Bedford Park (GB-30), its denser,
village-like antecedent, Hampstead Garden
Suburb succeeded all too well in achieving the amorphousness that often accom-
panies mass-produced suburbia. It is not
that Hampstead does not reflect high
architectural and planning standards,

but, as Gertrude Stein once said of another
place, 'There's no there there.'

The suburb's only focal point is Lutyens's
Central Square. As might be expected, his
tense, somewhat cynical self-assurance is
markedly in contrast to the surrounding
sea of complaisant, subdued sentimentality.
The architectural nuclei of this square are
two almost matched churches: more or less
Gothic in form, country Georgian in detail,
and quite mannered throughout – from
the blank 'windows' surmounted by real
dormers to the timber roof-trusses interlaced with masonry.

Of Unwin's work the best by far are the
larger Neo-Vernacular commercial buildings on the Finchley Road, the garden
suburb's western boundary.

GB-36a One of the other Arts and Crafts
architects represented in Hampstead
Garden Suburb was M. H. Baillie-Scott. His
most interesting contribution is **Water-
low Court,** 1908–9, a stark, almost Mediterranean, cloistered apartment building.
*SE from Central Sq on Heathgate / R on
Meadway / L on Hampstead Way / L on
Hampstead Way / R on Heath Close /
through 'medieval' gatehouse at end of st*

Letchworth, Hertfordshire   **GB-37**
* Letchworth Garden City 1903–12
Richard Barry Parker & Sir Raymond
Unwin
Arts and Crafts Neo-Vernacular
*N from London on A400 (Map GB-2 →)
then on A1 about 31 mi (50 km) /
→ LETCHWORTH / → TOWN CENTRE*
[Although physically unchanged, Letch-
worth the socially utopianistic garden
city long since evolved into Letchworth
the lower-middle-class garden suburb.]
It almost seems sometimes as if there

were an inverse correlation between architectural over-inventiveness and the success
of new town developments – as witness the
apparent social difficulties of Cumbernauld
(GB-86) or the initial financial failure of
Reston, Virginia.

In addition to its importance as the first
garden city, Letchworth's basic architectural soundness and consistency must
also be acknowledged, undramatic though
these qualities may be. After all, its designers' chief concern was, rightfully, not
so much the buildings themselves but

the quality of their total setting.

GB-37a Letchworth's post-First World War successor, **Welwyn Garden City,** was begun in 1919 with Louis de Soissons as chief architect. From the start its designers recognized that it would not be a grand social experiment, but merely a significant improvement upon the normal pattern of uncontrolled suburban sprawl – all of which may or may not excuse its unimaginative Neo-Georgian architecture. *Just off A1 halfway between Letchworth and London* / → WELWYN / → TOWN CENTRE

GB-37b **Harlow,** Essex, begun 1947, was long cited as the best post-Second World War British new town. If nothing else, it is at least typical of the time, having been designed by Frederick Gibberd in that watered-down British variant of Scandinavian Empiricism, which was then sometimes referred to as 'People's Detailing'. In certain parts of Harlow, such as the shopping centre, this embalmed vision of naive postwar optimism now seems remarkably depressing. *E, then N on A11 from London* ⇨ *M11, or E on A414 from Welwyn* / → HARLOW / → TOWN CENTRE

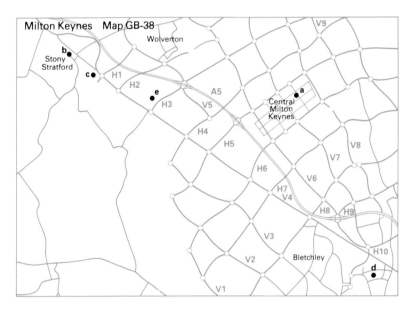

Milton Keynes Map GB-38

Milton Keynes **GB-38**
Milton Keynes (new city) Begun 1969
Rt A5
Derek Walker and Milton Keynes Development Corporation Architects, with Lord Richard Llewelyn-Davies (plan)
N on A5 (Map GB-2→) / *on A5 midway between Luton and Northampton*

Britain's current premier new town, or 'new city' as it wants to be called, has a car-oriented, low-density plan based on an irregular, non-hierarchical grid of arterial streets. Eventually there are to be 250,000 inhabitants spread over Milton Keynes's forty-nine square miles. If it lacks the architectural consistency of some of its earliest precursors, its general architectural quality is well above average. The buildings produced by the Development Corporation's own design team, including most of the commercial and industrial structures, are generally Miesian – some rather literal-mindedly so, others elegantly detailed and High-Tech. The housing, most of which is in rows or clusters, is the work of many firms and generally reflects the comfortable Neo-Vernacular common to contemporary British housing. Considerable attention has also been given to the landscaping. Indeed, the architects confidently predict that in a few decades the city and its inhabitants will have virtually disappeared amidst the

newly planted trees.

GB-38a In addition to the intensively developed **Central Shopping Building,** 1973–80, by the Corporation Architects on Midwinter Boulevard, a few other individual buildings worth noting are:

GB-38b The **Cofferidge Close Infill Development,** 1972–6, by the Corporation Architects. This small shopping precinct is carefully fitted into the middle of a block in the centre of Stony Stratford, an old village now absorbed into the fabric of Milton Keynes.

GB-38c The **Calverton End Adventure Playground,** 1974–5, by Archigram – a sad, tiny, fragment from one of the most widely published and influential avant-garde architecture groups of the 60s.

GB-38d The **Bletchley Leisure Centre Pool,** 1970–4, by Faulkner Brown–Hendy–Watkinson. Under a glass dome large enough to accommodate palm trees, it captures something of the spirit of Japan's elaborate, enclosed, High-Tech tropical swimming 'beaches'.

GB-38e The **Kiln Farm 7 'High Tech' Special Employment Units,** 1984–5, by the Corporation Architects.

Great Warley, Essex   **GB-39**
Church of St Mary the Virgin
1902–4
Rt B186
C. Harrison Townsend, with Sir William
Reynolds-Stephens (interior decoration)
Neo-Vernacular (exterior)
Free Style (interior)
*E from London on A11 (Map GB-2→), then
A12, then A127 →* SOUTHEND-ON-SEA *abt
18½ mi (30 km) total / L on B186 →*
WARLEY / *abt 1 mi (1.5 km) on L in a wood*
[Most of the original glass was lost during
the Second World War.]

A delightful little place, reminiscent of
some happier, mythical past – and ideal
future – when mankind could find pleasure
in work: a dream which, even today, shapes
our ideals of art and life.

Yet no two people ever dream of quite the
same golden age. Great Warley's architect
seems to have envisaged a simple, guileless
world in which indigenous skills and
materials could be used pragmatically to
satisfy communally-felt needs. On the other
hand, Great Warley's decorator – and here
one must invoke an older, less pejorative,
sense of that term – saw not a world of
sturdy yeomanry, but rather one fit for their
traditional overlords. His dream was of the
illuminated world of a Book of Hours or of
a bright tapestry of courtly love. Although

by the standards of the time his may have
been a restrained vision, today it seems
almost uncomfortably sweet.

Even though the effect could not have
been intended, in a sense Great Warley
recaptures the experience of a whole generation. After the delights within have
begun to jade, it is refreshing to step back
into an apparently more real world.

Burnham on Crouch, Essex   **GB-40**
* Royal Corinthian Yacht Club
1931
Belvedere Road
Joseph Emberton
International Style
*E from London on A11 (Map GB-2→), then
A12, then A127 →* SOUTHEND-ON-SEA *abt
19 mi (30 km) / N on A130, abt 3½ mi
(6 km) / E on B1012 ⇨ B1010 ⇨ B1021
→ Burnham on Crouch / R at far side of
town ctr on Belvedere Rd / at end of rd*
[The lower 'deck' has been further cantilevered on some awkward beams. The
self-consciously ship-like portholed basement is also an unfortunate addition.]

In 1932 Henry Russell Hitchcock and
Philip Johnson published their definitive

little book *The International Style* – they
coined the term. Only one British building
was listed (compared to five for Czechoslovakia) and this it.

Compton, Surrey   **GB-41**
* Watts Memorial Chapel 1896–7
Mary Watts
Arts and Crafts Eclectic
*S from London on A3 (Map GB-2→) past
Guildford / L on to B3000 ½ mi (700 m)
past A31 exit) →* COMPTON / *first L past*
WATTS GALLERY / *abt 350 yds (m) on R
in cemetery*

Mary Watts was the wife of G. F. Watts,
a then-renowned painter, and a serious
artist in her own right. But unquestionably she was an architectural amateur. Note
the lack of continuity between the chapel
and its attendant ambulatory, her only
other architectural effort. Or consider the
even more marked difference between
the chapel's 'Italianate - cum - Byzantine -
cum-Tudor-timber-translated-into-brick'
exterior and its strange, and equally eclectic, waxy-surfaced gesso interior, whose
horror vacui and other-worldliness are remi-

niscent of the spookier Dutch Symbolist
painters. However, Watts's primary sources
of ornamental inspiration are clearly – and
if anything too archaeologically – Celtic.
(All of this evinces a complete familiarity

with the popular exoticisms of the day.)

The story of the chapel's painstaking, hand-crafted construction reflects a dogged devotion to the precepts of William Morris. And, although Watts would have been shocked to hear it so called, in a sense it is a folly, just because it is so literal-minded, so terribly earnest. It lacks that crucial imaginative spark with which a Mackintosh, a Sullivan or a Wright would have metamorphosed these same elements. Yet because of that essential naivety, the Watts Chapel perhaps all the more readily exposes some of the tangled and otherwise less easily discernible roots of the turn of the century's flight from reality.

Haslemere, Surrey **GB-42**
* Teaching and Social Wing, Olivetti Training Centre 1968–73
Hindhead Road
James Stirling & Partner
On rd W from Haslemere → HINDHEAD

This is not a large building, nor a whole building. (It is an addition to a radically remodelled, tile-hung country house, *c.* 1900, by E. J. May.) Yet, despite its lack of age and size, it is encumbered with a fair amount of 'historical' significance. Most obviously it was in effect the diminutive coda to Stirling's picturesque/heroic work of the 60s (GB-51, 58). It also must stand – almost alone – as a surrogate for an entire generation of younger British designers of the late 60s and early 70s whose High-Tech and/or appropriate-tech projects filled the pages of the then very irreverent and anti-establishment *Architectural Design* magazine. If a design could be inflated, recycled, assembled from 'kits of parts', or made of GRP (fibre glass) panels, *AD* would publish it – and no one would build it. Lastly, this building must represent the high point of the 'good design is good advertising' strategy that Olivetti pursued so successfully for decades.

The wing itself consists of only three elements: a pair of long straight classroom blocks sheathed in identical modular GRP wall/roof panels (they sit rather unexpectedly on brick foundations); a square, GRP-clad, multi-purpose space which can be subdivided by drop-down partitions into four smaller square rooms (so small that one wonders if they were worth the effort);

and an all-glass connecting space which both ties the GRP sections together and links them to the old house. The angled disposition of the two classroom blocks was intended, it is said, to save some old trees. Their alternating stripes were originally to have been of the much stronger colours that Stirling typically prefers, but the local planning authority intervened.

GB-42a The **transformation of the existing house**, 1968–73, was carried out by Edward Cullinan, who was suggested for the job by Stirling. It suffers from a kind of High-Tech detailing whose forced 'festive' qualities seem less comfortable with the old work than does Stirling's more straightforward industrial-type detailing. The external changes are less apparent, but a thicket of chimneys which once crowned the house has been reduced to just two.

Bexhill, East Sussex **GB-43**
* De La Warr Pavilion 1933–5
Seafront
Erich Mendelsohn & Serge Chermayeff
International Style
S from A259 → Bexhill ctr / → DE LA WARR PAVILION

On its own merits the De La Warr Pavilion would be worthy of some note, there being few good International-Style buildings in Britain. But it is perhaps more significant as a 'documentation' of Mendelsohn's famous German department stores, particularly the Schocken store in Stuttgart which survived the war only to fall victim to a street widening project.

Inevitably there are some differences from its antecedents in Germany. There, the dynamic stair tower, with its linear chandelier, would not have projected arbitrarily from the middle of a seaside façade. Rather, commanding a busy street intersection, it would have been a place-marker in the urban fabric, the means through which the building turned the corner, and, of course, an advertisement. Thus if the

flanking blank-sided, box-like auditorium to the pavilion seems a 'tacked-on' afterthought, that is because, in relation to the stair tower – and to Mendelsohn's earlier work – it is.

Brighton, East Sussex   **GB-44**
**** **Royal Pavilion** (seaside villa)
Old Steine
John Nash
1815–22
'Indian' (pseudo-Mogul)
In Brighton ctr on E side of A23, one blk from sea front

Yes, it is modern: in that the acceptance of the exotic was a prerequisite for the devaluation of all historical styles, and in its exploitation of iron, both as structure (the kitchen's palm-tree columns) and as a means of prefabrication (the bamboo staircases).

But never mind all that. Just take it on its own terms. Suspend disbelief and be bemused.

GB-44a Adjacent to the Royal Pavilion is **The Dome,** a glass-domed former royal riding school (now concert hall), 1804–8, designed by William Porden. This building's almost accidental adoption of an 'Indian' mode inspired that of the pavilion itself.

GB-44b Although too late to be of any technical interest, the nearby iron **Palace Pier,** 1898–9, demonstrates nicely how, in less than a century, a royal idiosyncrasy had become the commoners' fancy.

Portsmouth, Hampshire   **GB-45**
***** **Tricorn Centre** 1967
Marketway and Charlotte Street
Owen Luder Partnership
Brutalism
S on M27 ⇨ M275 → GOSPORT and DOCKS / on L just beyond traffic roundabout

There is a dichotomy between Brutalism the ethic and Brutalism the aesthetic. The Rationalism of the former is often at odds with the Expressionism of the latter.

Tricorn's large-scale elements – market, parking garage, access ramp, department store, housing – are all logically, if doggedly, endowed with such differing and functionally specific overall forms that they relate to each other in an almost diagram-like fashion. There is also a logic of sorts underlying the stylistically mandatory use of exposed unretouched concrete. Yet what sort of logic stands behind so many of the smaller-scale design decisions: the spherical light scoops, the curved spandrel panels, the redundant columns? Nor is there any obvious reason for the apparent absence of overall unifying formal devices: of modularity, respect for the street line, etc. Admittedly, Tricorn is an extreme example. Its architects purportedly wanted to dominate and control the inevitable clutter of its individually designed shop fronts. But was it necessary to fight clutter with chaos?

Drewsteignton, Dartmoor, Devon **GB-46**
Castle Drogo (country house)
1910–30
off A382
Sir Edwin Lutyens
Neo-Gothic
4 mi (6.5 km) NE of Chagford on A382
[Less than half the original design was completed. Owned by the National Trust and open to the public.]

Lutyens is the epic figure in twentieth-century British architecture. Although he never broke with the styles of the past, the brilliance of his designs must rank him at least with Wagner, Berlage, Perret, Asplund or Aalto. One has to go as far back as Soane to find a British architect of comparable productivity and power. Lutyens was a builder of country houses – of houses which early in his career spoke with shire accents and hinted of long, rich evolutions, and that, as his career progressed, became increasingly formal without losing vitality. Typically his houses were cleverly planned, richly detailed and wickedly witty. Often too they melded seamlessly with one of Gertrude Jekyll's dream-like country gardens. Lutyens's *magnum opus* was not a house but a palace, the Viceroy's House in Delhi – that incomparable stage set for the last act of Empire.

He also built office blocks for his country-house clients, but somehow his sensibilities did not hold up as well amid the commercial realities of the City.

Unfortunately Castle Drogo is not representative of Lutyens's country houses. It is built, too literally like a castle, of solid stone. Sited on a rocky outcrop overlooking Dartmoor, it also lacks the usual garden setting. Lutyens's best houses resonate like a bright, bittersweet passage from Elgar. As its unlovely name suggests, Castle Drogo is dark and stiff. It is, however, the only major Lutyens house open to the public.

GB-46a One Lutyens palace open to the public is the extraordinary **Queen Mary's Dolls' House** at Windsor Castle.

Saltash, Cornwall [near Plymouth] **GB-47**
* Royal Albert Bridge (of the former Great Western Railway) 1859
Isambard Kingdom Brunel
Just W of Plymouth on A38 / RR bridge parallels road bridge

This is not architecture nor, in 1859, was it a pioneering use of iron. Even as a bridge it represents something of a dead end. Yet in its uncompromising gutsiness it epitomizes everything that nineteenth-century architects knew they lacked. The architects of that age never saw *their* work signed in four-foot-high block letters. They would have deemed it vulgar and brash – all the while subconsciously knowing that Brunel was the true, supremely confident man of their time.

Incidentally, Brunel also designed the rest of the gargantuan (seven-foot gauge) Great Western Railway, including its locomotives and even the steamships *Great Eastern* (for half a century the world's

largest) and *Great Britain* (GB-48a), which were to have continued the railway's service on to America.

Bristol, Avon **GB-48**
* Clifton Suspension Bridge
1829–54
Isambard Kingdom Brunel
Neo-Egyptian
W from Bristol ctr on A4 → Avonmouth / R just after (under) bridge → CLIFTON / → bridge signs

During its three and a half difficult decades of intermittent construction the towers were denied their intended Egyptian ornament. By the time of its completion Brunel was already five years in his grave, and the early suspension-bridge-building boom had passed. Historically Clifton is of no great significance. It is not even representative of Brunel's work. But seen from the gorge below, leaping 700 feet from one

cliff face to the other, it does much to redeem an age too easily remembered only for its industrial ugliness and squalor.

GB-48a Bristol is also the home of the **SS *Great Britain*,** 1845, Brunel's only surviving ship. → *signs*

GB-48b There are so few examples of extreme English Art Nouveau that the ceramic façade executed by G. W. J. Neatby for Henry Williams's **Edward Everard Building,** 1900–6, at Broad and John Streets, is notable simply because it exists – even embedded in an uninspired redevelopment project. Otherwise it is merely a competent piece of craftwork, animated only by a sense of 'duty', 'high purpose' and the 'nobility of artistic labour'. Would that it had also been enlivened by other more interesting qualities, such as elegance, wit or even simple unrestrained enthusiasm. *From E on A4 continue straight on to Victoria St ⇨ High St ⇨ Broad, St / on R*

GB-48c Bristol's only other early modern building of any real interest, Charles Holden's **Municipal Library,** 1905–7, never quite lives up to the promise of its curious resemblance to the contemporaneous work of Charles Rennie Mackintosh (GB-79, 83). *SW from end of 'floating' harbour on College Green ⇨ Deanery Rd / on L just past Cathedral*

Oxford   **GB-49**
** **University Museum** 1855–60
Parks Road
Deane & Woodward, with John Ruskin
Neo-Gothic
N from Oxford ctr on Banbury Rd (A4165) / R on Keble Rd / R on Parks Rd / on L

How typically Victorian. The face it presents to the world, except perhaps for its plain triangular dormers and mechanistic four-chimneyed 'chapter house', seems conventionally enough in the mould of that progenitor of High Victorian Gothic, John Ruskin. And Ruskin was, in fact, very much involved here, especially with the never completed programme of ornamental stone-carving (column capitals, window surrounds, etc.) which was to have been both a compendium of biological specimens and a demonstration of the possibility of reviving medieval craftsmanship.

Within, however, lies the real nineteenth century, ingeniously solving new problems with new materials in an old formal language. A great cloister garden – it can be called nothing else – has been roofed with iron and glass, just as the nineteenth century 'knew' Gothic builders would have done had they but had the materials. The forms are traditional, as is their (albeit exaggerated) articulation, and so too the method of laying the glass roof 'slates'. Only the

spatial effect is unprecedented.

Is it mere chance that this big, boney room is filled so happily with big boney dinosaurs?

GB-49a Just across the street is William Butterfield's **Keble College,** 1867–83.

Oxford   **GB-50**
** **Florey Building, Queen's College** (residence hall) 1968–71
St Clement's Street
James Stirling
High-Tech Brutalism

E from Oxford ctr on High St (A420) / bear L on St Clements (A420) at roundabout just past bridge / immediately on L

Most good artists experience crises, times when a particular line of development has been taken as far as, if not further than, is useful. Stirling here carried the mannerism and historicism of his Cambridge and Leicester work (GB-51, 58) past the point of diminishing returns. Florey *is* a brilliant, witty *tour de force*: a masterpiece of neurotic late-60s longing for more heroic times. But now it too has become part of the past, a moment no longer to be revived.

GB-50a Near by Sir Leslie Martin & Colin

St John Wilson's **St Cross Library**, 1964, on St Cross Road. *E from Oxford ctr on A420 / L before bridge on Longwall St / R on St Cross Rd / at bend in rd*

GB-50b More dated than precisely datable is Arne Jacobsen's **St Catherine's College** of 1960–7. *NE on Manor Rd from St Cross Library (GB-50a) / on R after stream*

Cambridge   **GB-51**
** History Faculty Library 1964–9
West Road
James Stirling
Brutalism
W from Trumpington St on Silver St / R on Queens Rd / L on West Rd / in ctr of blk on L

If Leicester (GB-58) launched Stirling's mannered, High-Tech new Brutalism, Cambridge saw its apogee. Although not as overtly mechanistic as his Leicester laboratories, this building is every bit as technological and eclectic. The huge quadrant of double-glazed tent roof over the reading room dominates everything. Even the library's single, focal, control desk is pinioned by its 'centre pole', while in the upper corridors one can read the roof in section and delight in its maze of tubular trusses and brightly painted mechanical equipment.

Inevitably there is a temptation to speculate upon Stirling's sources. Is he alluding here to the nineteenth-century cast-iron dome of the British Museum reading room, or perhaps to the *1984*-ish eighteenth-century utilitarianism of the Panopticon, Jeremy Bentham's 'idealized' asylum-cum-factory-cum-prison? Certainly the antiseptic glass-eyed corridor walls looking down upon the reading room reinforce the latter association.

On a more prosaic level, there are all the potential problems raised by Stirling's almost total reliance upon glass as a skin for the building. The reading room faces south-east, which may be an acceptable compromise. But what is it like to spend a sunny late spring afternoon in one of those westward facing greenhouse-offices?

GB-51a Probably the only modern architect better known than Stirling to have built in or around Cambridge was Walter Gropius. Gropius's later works are unfortunately always rather disappointing, and **Impington Village College**, 1936–9, with Maxwell Fry, a programmatically interesting utopianistic school and community centre, is no exception. *NW from Cambridge on A604 and then B1049 → Histon, abt 2 mi (3 km) / R on New Rd → IMPINGTON / 350 yds (m) on R*

GB-51b To the west of the library, on West Road, is **Harvey Court**, a graduate students' dormitory, 1960–2, by Sir Leslie Martin & Colin St John Wilson, with Patrick Hodgkinson. This once widely published building was apparently designed for another, more urban site: an explanation of, if not an excuse for, the minimal recognition of its Victorian garden setting. But no such circumstances can explain away a colonnaded front façade which, in its sterile, unacknowledged Neo-Classicism, is little more sophisticated than the shallowest cliché architecture of its time. Nor can one fully account for the presence of romantic-organic materials and details (misappropriated from Alvar Aalto) in a building that makes a rhetorical point of being hard-nosed. *Just to W of GB-51*

GB-51c A fragmentary but more blatant and consistent Brutalist polemic is Wilson's little addition to the **School of Architecture**, 1958–9, on Trumpington Street. *S from Cambridge ctr on A10 (Trumpington St) → London / on R at edge of city ctr*

Cambridge   GB-52
** **Clare Hall** 1966–9
Herschel Road
Ralph Erskine
Scandinavian Empiricism
*W from GB-51 on West Rd / R at T /
L on to Herschel Rd / on L*

This is not a building that can be comprehended quickly. One must take time to study it – detail by detail, element by element, vista by vista. Its architect Ralph Erskine is a hybrid creature, an Englishman who lives in Sweden (S-25, 30, 32, 32c). When seen in that over-centralized, over-homogenized·country, his work evokes the British picturesque tradition. In Britain, the homeland of Brutalism, it impresses one with its Scandinavian sensitivity to detail and material. (However, there is no denying that Erskine's delicate, often unconventional forms and details do take some getting used to, and that they might become tacky without careful maintenance.) Clare Hall embodies the ideals that an entire generation of Scandinavian-inspired postwar British architects – Erskine's generation – sought but were never able to find (GB-28a).

Ipswich   GB-53
Willis Faber & Dumas Offices 1975
Princes Street at Friars Street
Foster Associates
Minimalist High-Tech
*S from Ipswich ctr on Princes St, two blks /
on L at Friars St*

The undulating all-glass curtain wall, so evocative of Mies van der Rohe's earliest glass office tower projects, has been refined to the absolute minimum. By day there is nothing but dark, faceted reflectiveness from pavement to skyline. By night it becomes translucent and is seen to be suspended from the thinnest possible floor slabs, while those floor-slab edges cantilever in turn from abstractly round columns. The sinuousness of the wall adds further to the sense of abstraction. Only the awkward pipe railing breaks the skyline seems too tangible and out of character. After finding one's way inside one is confronted by a dramatic atrium extending through the two floors of offices into a bright rooftop penthouse. Surprisingly in an office building, the atrium is threaded together by a sequence of escalators rising through all three floors. The atrium, the expensive escalators and the totally open plan of the upper two office floors reflect a socially progressive attitude towards Willis Faber's employees. So too do the swimming pool at the rear of the lobby and the grassy roof terrace surrounding the penthouse. Here, it would seem, is that union of elegant efficiency and social reform which the Modern Movement for long promised but too rarely provided. However ...

The innovative social programme came from the client, not the architects. The abstract immateriality of the curtain wall would have been compromised had it been made of energy-efficient insulating glass, which of necessity has heavily outlined edges. The photogenic images of older neighbours reflected in the curtain wall are only possible because the older buildings are there to be reflected. (Two such curtain walls facing each other would tell a very different story.) The ground-floor space fronting the street, which could have been let out for shops or have contributed in some other way to the vitality of the street, remains black and dead by day, while by night it reveals, in artful High-Tech display, the building's plumbing – all of which says something about the architects' and their client's attitude towards *non*-employees.

Snape, Suffolk   **GB-54**
* The Maltings (concert hall) 1965–7
Rt B1069
Arup Associates
Neo-Industrial Vernacular
*E from A12 on to A1094 → ALDEBURGH /
S on B1069 → Snape / abt 1 mi (1.5 km)
on L, just past bridge over river Alde*

The Maltings is part of an old grain processing complex – otherwise still in use – whose malting house has been converted into a concert hall for a summer music festival in one of Britain's few remaining unspoiled regions. The hall is in reality a new space, created by the selective demolition of several major interior walls, and reroofed in a manner that somewhat resembles nineteenth-century industrial vernacular construction when seen from within and, more deceptively, mimics at a larger scale the roofscape of its demolished predecessor when seen from afar.

Norwich, Norfolk   **GB-55**
* University of East Anglia
1964–70
Denys Lasdun & Partners
Brutalism
*W 4 mi (6 km) from Norwich ctr on B1108
(Earlham Rd) / → UNIVERSITY OF EAST
ANGLIA or UNIVERSITY PLAIN*

Over two dozen universities have been established in Britain since the war. All have had the benefit of master plans and of far more extensive and effective overall architectural controls than have, for instance, their American counterparts. None the less, only at East Anglia did this orderly pre-planned growth process generate a vital coherent organism – as opposed to the more typical collection of individual buildings. (At least, up to a point, but see GB-55a.) Nor, unlike some of the new German universities, has East Anglia's unity been achieved through monotonous industrial modularity.

This is an articulate, romantic, picturesque architecture. And it is English to the core, in spite of, or perhaps all the more because of, its eclectic modernity. Indeed, the dramatic ziggurats of the futuristic parkside façades of the residence halls seem – once one has seen their *ad hoc* backsides – to be true descendants of all those peculiarly English eighteenth-century setpiece garden follies and shams.

GB-55a Just beyond the end of the residence halls is Foster Associates' **Sainsbury Centre for Visual Arts,** 1978, an elegantly detailed, mostly aluminium-panelled box, whose vast plate-glass end walls reveal a single huge interior volume spanned by an exposed space frame. It is so self-assertively High-Tech that it doesn't seem to give a damn about the organic unity of the rest of the campus, despite the gesture of an elevated walk-way leading back to Lasdun's buildings.

GB-55b Among Britain's other new universities only **Sussex University,** begun 1963, by Sir Basil Spence, Bonnington & Collins, has a strong, coherent self-image. If anything it is too coherent and too much an image – the highly tectonic vocabulary

of Le Corbusier's Maisons Jaoul (F-26) having been reduced here to a structurally dubious kind of wallpaper. *NE from Brighton on A27, abt $3\frac{1}{2}$ mi (5.6 km)* → FALMER / → UNIVERSITY

GB-55c The most tectonically, if not Teutonically (D-67a), systematized of the new English universities – utilizing the CLASP pre-cast concrete panel system – is the **University of York,** 1965–8, by Robert Matthew, Johnson-Marshall & Partners. *S from York ring rd* / → UNIVERSITY

Hunstanton, Norfolk **GB-56**
* Secondary Modern School
1949–54
King's Lynn Road and Downs Road
Alison & Peter Smithson
Brutalist Miesian
S from Huntstanton ctr on A149 / on L at edge of town

[There have been several later additions. The original portion of the school is nearest the water tower.]

The Smithsons, Brutalism's propagandist-parents, and Rayner Banham, its

official biographer, all regard the Hunstanton School as the first true Brutalist manifesto. Given the typically picturesque, often self-consciously crude architecture usually identified with that movement (GB-45), it may now be difficult to see much here that is 'Brutal'.

If today this once strident-seeming school is little more than an historical reference point, it can at least still remind us of how much the general critical eye has changed since 1950 and, conversely, of how little it had evolved before.

Beeston, Nottinghamshire **GB-57**
** Boots Pharmaceutical Factory
1930–2 (wet-process block), 1932–8 (dry-process block)
Thane Road
Sir Owen Williams
Rationalism
W from Nottingham ctr on A453 / S on ring rd (A6514) / R just before river on to Thane Rd / at end of rd

Because Sir Owen Williams was an engineer, his buildings embody a technical competence and complexity far beyond that achieved by most of his International Style contemporaries. And because his work was

too substantial for the abstract, idealistic 20s and 30s it remained relatively unrecognized until after the war, when the Brutalists rediscovered these factories. Now, when so many International Style buildings have come to look stale and shallow, Williams's tectonic self-assurance seems more convincing than ever.

GB-57a The **administrative headquarters** are by SOM (Skidmore, Owings & Merrill), 1966–8. *R of entrance gates*

GB-57b The adjacent John Player's **Horizon Factory** is the work of Arup Associates, 1968–71.

Leicester   GB-58
*** **Engineering Faculty,** Leicester
University 1959–64
Mayor's Walk
Stirling & Gowan
Brutalism
SE on A6 from Leicester ctr abt 1 mi
(1.5 km) / R on University Rd / L on
Mayor's Walk / at end of car park

Here Brutalism veers decisively away
from its early quasi-vernacular, almost pri-
mitivist emphasis upon the construction
process. Instead there is an enthusiasm for
the *ad hoc* adaptation of *contemporary* industrial materials – as distinct from those of
'yesterday' or 'tomorrow'. Also, almost for
the first time, there is a consciously archaeological use of motifs from the 20s, modern
architecture's 'heroic period', as it was then
coming to be called. Thus the two auditoria
are a direct reference to Russian Constructivism – albeit that the larger room's
mannered, sideways cantilever is distinctly
Stirling's own conceit. There is more one
could mention as well: the industrial
glazing system set at a 45° angle to form
'traditional' north lights; or the effect of
axonometric projections (a type of drawing
which creates a non-perspective bird's-eye
view) when used as a design tool.

GB-58a Just to the north is Arup Associates' **Attenborough Building** for
the Arts and Science faculties, 1968–70.
In addition to sympathetically and successfully responding to the laboratory's distinctive formal vocabulary, it is notable as
an attempt to design a naturally ventilated,
non-air-conditioned tower. Hence the
unusual 'no-draught' windows and cruciform plan.

GB-58b To the north of that is Denys
Lasdun's **Charles Wilson Social
Centre,** 1963–7.

GB-58c An interesting comparison can
be made with Arup Associates' coolly
rational **Mining, Minerals and Metal-
lurgy Department** at Birmingham University, 1966. Arup Associates are

basically – or at least were originally –
engineers. In a sense they continue an old,
curiously British lineage that leads through
Sir Owen Williams (GB-57) back to Brunel
(GB-47) and those other heroic figures of
early industrial Britain. It is hardly surprising then, given the architects and the
programme, that this is very much a tech-
nologist's architecture. It is pure, simple,
elegant and just a bit too idealized: too ready
to accommodate all the unpredictable
potential future needs of scientific study
within its prefabricated structural-
mechanical matrix of clustered columns
and paired girders. Its 'architecture'
lies not in the capacity to accommodate
the piping and duct-work of a modern
laboratory, but in the theoretical capacity
to accommodate their periodic rearrange-
ments. *SW from Birmingham ctr on A38,
abt 3 mi (5 km) / R on Edgbaston Park Rd
/ L on Pritchartts Rd / 300 yds (m) on R*

GB-58d Another elegant Arup structure
in an academic setting is the **Kingsgate
Footbridge** over the river Wear, 1962–
3, at the University of Durham. *E from
Palace Green on Duncow Lane and its continuation across North Bailey St*

Ironbridge, Shropshire   GB-59
** **The Iron Bridge** 1776–9
Abraham Darby III (iron founder)
*S from Wellington on B4169 →
Coalbrookdale / L beyond town on A4380 /
abt 1 mi (1.5 km) on R*

There are those for whom technology
is the essence of modern architecture. In

their aetiological myths this first all-metal
structure has – in part because of it symbol-
like elegant simplicity – long been presented
as an essentially ancestorless original
antecedent which simply willed itself into
existence, *machina ex deo* as it were, in this
appropriately primitive and picturesque
little valley.

Britannia Railway Bridge

Menai Bridge, Gwynedd   **GB-60**
* Menai Road Bridge 1818–26
Thomas Telford
W from Bangor on A5 → HOLYHEAD / at Menai Straits

Menai was not quite the earliest of the modern suspension bridges (i.e., those carrying stiff, flat roads) but, with a main span of some 550 feet, it was the first really big one. Here engineering and metallic construction technology finally and prominently came into their own. Although architecture, *per se* had some time since ceased to embody mankind's highest technological capabilities, achievements like this began to make that fact self-evident.

GB-60a Just to the south-west stands Robert Stevenson's tubular **Britannia Railway Bridge** of 1845–50. This more daring and more architectonic structure originally consisted of two continuous iron box beams, each over 1500 feet long and with two 460–foot central spans. The supporting arched trusses were added only in 1970–1, after the original structure had been weakened by a fire.

* Chester   GB-61
It may be just as well that there is no 'important' modern architecture to be found here. Chester must be experienced as a whole. It personifies a particular postwar British concern for the preservation and enhancement of 'townscapes' as living, organic – not to say romantically picturesque – assemblages.

Born as a Roman walled military camp, Chester became an important medieval seaport whose two main cross-axes, Eastgate/Watergate and Northgate/Bridge Street, developed into double-level arcaded shopping streets – the 'rows', as they are called. Eventually the river Dee silted up, leaving Chester to become a sleepy backwater. When the late nineteenth century rediscovered it, Chester was a bit of 'ye olde England' ripe for restoration. In the flush of their self-confident enthusiasm, the Victorians could not help adding a little something of their own. They developed a pedestrian way some two miles in circumference along the top of the old town walls and connected it to new shops, arcades and offices. (The best part is the delightfully elaborate Eastgate Bridge and the section of wall-footpath immediately to its south.)

Liverpool   **GB-62**
* Oriel Chambers 1864–5
14 Water Street and Covent Garden
Peter Ellis Jr
Rationalism
NW from St John's Centre on Crosshall St / L at T on to Dale St ⇨ Water St / several blks on R

[The rear half was destroyed in the war and replaced by a 'sympathetic' addition.]

Its projecting ranks of plate-glass oriel windows make Oriel Chambers appear to be one of the most technologically modern of nineteenth-century buildings. Anyone familiar with mid-nineteenth-century cast-iron façades (GB-78) might understandably assume this to be a highly developed example of that genre. Despite the extensive use of iron in the courtyard elevations, however, the street façades – what little there is to them – are in fact constructed primarily of stone. (Only as a result of war damage were they found to contain some iron as well.)

The use of stone, like the more elaborate cornice line, may have been an attempt to placate critics of so radical and apparently

insubstantial an architecture. If that was Ellis's motive he did not succeed. He completed only one other similar building before he and his architecture slipped into an obscurity from which the buildings alone have been rescued.

GB-62a Ellis's other building, **16 Cook Street,** 1864–8, is best known for its courtyard elevation – the façade being

Liverpool **GB-63**
** Albert Dock 1841–5
Jesse Hartley
Rationalism
S from E end of Water St on B5036 (along waterfront) / R just past pierhead at SALTHOUSE–ALBERT DOCK / *ahead to L*

[The dock, vacant and under threat of demolition when photographed, has since been reprieved.]

The Albert Dock can be seen simply as an early example of pure, unornamented functional design or, equally, as a pioneering example of 'fireproof' construction – even its roof being inverted iron-plate 'ships' hulls. But the spirit of this place transcends such technical considerations and depends upon other, less tangible, qualities. It lies rooted in memories – memories

more conventional. *Cook St is a continuation to the E (with a slight jog) of Brunswick St, which parallels Water St one blk to S*

of frail wooden hulls and forests of masts which once sheltered within this sombre space; memories of the world's wealth that once passed through here.

Liverpool **GB-64**
St Michael-in-the-Hamlet 1814–15
St Michael's Church Road
Thomas Rickman
Neo-Gothic
S from Liverpool ctr on A561 → St Michael's Hamlet / R (from Aigburth Rd) on to St Michael's Rd / L on St Michael's Church Rd / on L

Well before it was truly common, much less cheap, iron had come to have many architectural applications. Here, for instance, it provided a totally prefabricated internal structure – probably the second ever (GB-64a) – as well as a variety of elaborate but inexpensively reproduced ornamental components, including pinnacles, railings, tracery, etc. Previous architectural uses of iron had been dictated by structural necessity or a desire for novelty (D-23). Here the new technology was seen primarily as a means of replicating and therefore minimizing skilled hand labour.

Ironically, the reason for this labour-saving ecclesio-technical innovation was a wish to bring the established religion to the working classes. It all came to nought, however, when the presiding bishops decided not to consecrate further churches made from such an ungodly material – always excepting, of course, those pre-

fabricated iron edifices which continued to be shipped unassembled to missionary congregations throughout the Empire.

GB-64a Rickman's first prefabricated church was **St George's,** Everton, 1812–14. Generally quite similar to St Michael's if less thoroughgoing in its use of iron, it may not be long for this world. *N from Liverpool ctr on A59 →* PRESTON */ R at Y on to Everton Valley / first R on to St Domingo Rd / abt two blks on R*

Bebington [near Liverpool] **GB-65**
* Port Sunlight (industrial town)
1887–*c.* 1900
W. H. Lever (site plan), William Owen (architect)
Arts and Crafts Neo-Vernacular
S from Liverpool (through tunnel) on A41 abt 3 mi (5 km) / R at roundabout → PORT SUNLIGHT

With its almost too familiar cottagey architecture and its thoughtful separation of traffic – pedestrian from (horse-drawn) vehicular – Port Sunlight represents the ultimate refinement of the sophisticated nineteenth-century model industrial village. And in its cosy picturesque manner it really is appealing. Perhaps just because Port Sunlight was the product of an anach-

ronistic benevolent despotism, it reflects a verve not to be found in its larger, more famous successors (GB-37) – which were, in contrast, the progeny of reform societies or government bureaucracies.

Manchester   **GB-66**
* York House 1911
85 Major Street
Harry S. Fairhurst & Son
Functionalism (rear elevation)
SE from town hall on Princess St / L on Hart St / in first blk on L across a car park (rear elevation)

York House is an architectural *objet trouvé*. For some thirty years it must have seemed just another conventional Edwardian commercial building, if anyone noticed it at all. And so it might have remained, had not the Second World War blitz removed most of its neighbours. Only then was its remarkable all-glass sloping rear elevation fully exposed to view.

Although designed simply to facilitate the inspection of cotton cloth, and presumably innocent of any aesthetic intent, this façade soon became a pilgrimage site for a rising generation of Brutalist-inspired architects. And when, for a time, its existence was threatened, it also became a minor *cause célèbre*, stimulating some of the earliest 'preservation-through-reuse' schemes to have come from the modernist establishment.

GB-66a Speaking of crystals in the rough, Manchester's **Barton Arcade,** by Corbett, Raby & Sawyer, 1871, is one of the more complex examples of its genre. *On E side of Deansgate just S of St Mary's Gate*

Manchester   **GB-67**
* Daily Express Building 1939
Great Ancoats Street
Sir Owen Williams
Moderne
SE from town hall on Princess St / L on A62 (Mosley St ⇨ Oldham St) / R on Great Ancoats St / on L

Inevitably one must compare this Daily Express plant to Sir Owen's earlier building on Fleet Street (GB-9). Not surprisingly, by 1939 and in this more provincial setting some of the intensity, the easy dynamism, is gone. Although the vocabulary employed is much the same, its use here is more pragmatic. The stair tower does not generate the vertical accent it once might have, nor do the window-washing machine tracks turn the corner with the same elegant, but difficult, continuity. But the

truly important difference lies within. Here there is no longer any place for Art Deco tinsel: instead, behind a ceiling-to-pavement wall of glass, one faces the pure raw power of the press room – nothing more, nothing less.

Manchester/Victoria Park   **GB-68**
First Church of Christ Scientist
(now a community centre) 1903–8
Daisy Bank
Edgar Wood
Arts and Crafts/Free Style
S from Manchester ctr on A34 (Oxford Rd) abt 1¼ mi (2 km) / L at Rusholm Pl ⇨ Daisy Bank / one blk on R

True English Art Nouveau architecture, as opposed to interior or exterior decoration (GB-39, 48b), hardly exists. This cleverly arranged mélange, with its overtones of Edwardian Neo-Baroque and of Baillie Scott's Neo-Vernacular, is about as innovative as provincial English architecture of the period could be.

GB-68a In Hale, Cheshire, a more distant Manchester suburb, is Wood's **Halecroft,** 1890, a large and late 'Aesthetic' house which now contains local government

offices. *S from Manchester ctr on A56 / E on A560 → Stockport / R at T on to A538 / L at Y on to Ashley Rd / L on to Hale Rd / at no. 253, abt 1½ mi (2 km) on L*

GB-68b At 224 Hale Road is **Royd House,** Wood's own almost Art Deco flat-roofed concrete-framed house, 1914–16 – the same progressive but somewhat restricted talent in yet another style.

Knutsford, Cheshire   GB-69
* **Various buildings** 1895–1908
Richard Harding Watt, *et al.*
Arts and Crafts Eclectic
S from Manchester on A56, then A556, then A50 / E on A537 (→ Macclesfield) / L under RR on to King St / tower and coffee house ahead on L / Ruskin Rooms and some houses in Drury Lane further on R (just past post office) / for villas, continue on A537 past King St / R on Leigh Rd

If anything could be more English than one architectural folly, it would be a town full of them. And so we have Richard Harding Watt's embellishment of Knutsford: not the only such place in Britain, just the most interesting. It includes a memorial tower dedicated to the novelist and social critic Mary Gaskell; 'The King's Coffee House', and 'Ruskin Rooms' in honour of the godfather of High Victorian Gothic, John Ruskin; an assortment of curious nooks, alleys and vistas; and both modest dwellings and some substantial middle-class villas. There are suggestions here of Lutyens, Mackintosh and the more Germanic sort of Art Nouveau. But mostly there is a bemused sensitivity to form and detail, combined with a fine manneristic disregard for the niceties of scale.

Nowhere is there a more delightful modern example of the amateur architect at work, except perhaps in the almost contemporary concrete fantasies built by Dr Mercer in Doylestown, Pennsylvania.

Memorial tower and coffee house

GB-69a The closest British analogy to Knutsford is Clough Williams-Ellis's more recent 'seventeenth-century Italian village'-cum-resort at **Portmeirion**, Gwynedd, Wales. He, however, was a professional architect – which may be why his work seems less imaginative and exudes a saccharine self-importance. Some years ago Portmeirion also served, most suitably, as the setting for 'The Prisoner', a remarkable, surreal television series. *S from Bangor on A4087 ⇨ A487 / L abt 1 mi (1.5 km) after Porthmadog*

Jodrell Bank, Cheshire   GB-70
** **Radio Telescope** 1957 (enlarged 1970–1)
E from Knutsford (GB-69) on A537 abt 4½ mi (7 km) / S on A535 abt 3 mi (5 km) / → signs / W of rd

Some will object that although it is one of the world's larger structures the great 'dish' at Jodrell Bank can hardly be called architecture. Others might see in it the shape of things to come: a foretaste of an exciting, inevitable, Archigramesque, Buckminster-Fuller future.

Rising above a morning mist, it evokes a more elemental response, bringing to mind a much earlier monumental observatory. And, as with Stonehenge, the very presence of it sends tingles down one's spine.

Sheffield, South Yorkshire   **GB-71**
** **Park Hill** (social housing) 1961–6
South Street, Talbot Street and Duke Street
Sheffield Architect's Department
Brutalism
SE from Sheffield ctr on A616 →
NEWARK / *on hill on R*

It is not immediately obvious that this perfect paradigm of Brutalism, so enormous and stark, could house a successful, happy community – especially in Britain where there is no long-standing apartment-dwelling tradition. Yet Park Hill does work. Ask the residents. Notice the absence of litter and vandalism.

There are, of course, some mitigating factors. The individual 'maisonettes' – little two-storey 'houses' plugged into the megastructure – open on to exterior corridor balconies ('streets in the sky'), which, because of the sloping site, eventually lead back to the ground, and which also, with the assistance of goods lifts, allow milk and

other small delivery vans to come right to everyone's door.

Is Park Hill a justification of its style-cum-philosophy, an example of social reform via Brutalist built form? Probably not. Despite its psychological links with the earth, the physical reality of Park Hill differs little from some of America's now thoroughly discredited public housing. If here, somehow, it works, its success apparently derives less from the care taken by its designers than from the special efforts of the social workers who, when it was new, helped its occupants to transform Park Hill into a true community.

GB-71a By way of comparison, the adjacent and similar **Hyde Park** development, 1966, had the benefit of the same architects but not of nearly as much social assistance for its tenants. Reputedly it has yet to achieve the same coherent, stable sense of community.

Saltaire, South Yorkshire   **GB-72**
* **Saltaire** (industrial town) 1853–65
Victoria Road
Lockwood & Mawson
Italianate (the mill)
N from Bradford on A650 / R on A6038
→ SALTAIRE / *Victoria Rd is the main st*

There is one small, pleasant urban green, while down at the foot of the hill, next to the canal, a 'Greek' church and Italianate

mill confront one another tellingly. The mill is of some interest for its extensive, if largely inconspicuous, use of iron.

Only as a totality is Saltaire important. It is one of the earliest, best-preserved pioneering planned factory towns. As such, it is also an antecedent – by way of the likes of Port Sunlight (GB-65) – of such garden cities as Welwyn (GB-37a) and Letchworth (GB-37).

Gill Head [on Lake Windermere]   **GB-73**
** **Broadleys** (country house, now
Windermere Motor Boat Racing Club)
1898–9, stables 1900
Rt A592
C. F. A. Voysey
Arts and Crafts Neo-Vernacular
*On lake side of A592, just S of junction with
B5630*
[Interior shown by appointment only.]

Owing to a distorted historical perspective, Voysey was for too long simplistically
categorized as a 'pioneer of modern architecture', one whose restrained white peb-
bledash stuccoed houses were thus no more
than an imperfect anticipation of the International Style. This idea was first put
forward during Voysey's own lifetime: he
died only in 1941. It appalled him. He
loathed what he called that 'hatless' Mediterranean architecture. He wanted his
work to be, and he believed that it was, the
first truly *British* vernacular – as opposed,

for instance, to Kentish (GB-26), Cotswold
or Cornish. He saw it as an appropriate
response to Britain's climate and as an
appropriate use of those British materials
which for the first time, thanks to the railways, could be assembled from all parts of
the country: Welsh roofing slates, dressed
stone from the limestone belt, hardware
from the industrial Midlands, etc. Once
Voysey had developed this rationale and its
accompanying tectonic formula, he applied
it consistently throughout his career and in
all parts of the country.

Although Voysey may have had some
effect upon a later generation of Continental architects (e.g. A-2b), his influence
was most pervasive in Britain's rapidly
developing middle-class suburbs. During
the interwar years vast tracts were built in
a remarkably consistent, if diluted, sort of
Voysey vernacular. They could have been
inspired by far worse models.

Darlington, Co. Durham   **GB-74**
Cummins Engine Factory 1965
Rt B1273
Roche & Dinkeloo
Meisian
E from Darlington on B1273 / on R

Only Americans could have created such
a temple of industry – where even valve
handles protruding from the lawn seem like
votive offerings. Kevin Roche's elegantly
gutsy Meisian vocabulary and the raw Cor-
Ten steelwork are perfectly suited to each
other. Cor-Ten is a copper-bearing alloy
with a rich brown patina which has an
organic, timeless appearance, quite analogous to that of bronze. But it is also – you
should excuse the expression – more rustic,
and thus more appealing to modern,
romantic sensibilities which would much
prefer a well-weathered Greek temple to a
fresh, correctly painted one.

GB-74a The adjacent **Chrysler-
Cummins Factory,** 1964, is by Eero
Saarinen & Associates. As Roche and
Dinkeloo were those associates, obvious
comparisons can be made. It might also
be mentioned that the ultimate client for
both buildings was J. Erwin Miller – a man

who may have caused the construction of
more high-quality modern architecture
than any other individual, corporation or
institution. Most of these riches are in Columbus, Indiana, Mr Erwin's country
company town.

Redcar, Cleveland   **GB-75**
* **Public Library** 1966–71
Coatham Road and Ridley Road
Ahrends, Burton & Koralek
Brutalism
E from Middlesbrough on A1085 / →
REDCAR *on A1042 / past second*
roundabout on R

It is refreshing to find a building that employs industrial materials frankly and imaginatively without becoming involved with silly, or unjustifiable High-Tech imagery.

Constructed largely of corrugated semi-structural sheet metal and engineering brick, with an exposed, welded light-steel

framework, this library has a simple open plan. Its 'architecture' resides primarily in its detailing, especially that of its almost industrial-vernacular-like sawtoothed roof system, whose hexagonal north lights are in fact the interstices of Verendeel roof trusses. Curiously, although these north light monitors do face north, their presumptive *raison d'être* (glare-free indirect lighting) is contradicted by the skylights set within their flattened tops, not to mention those places where their angled southern sides are also glazed. Fortunately Redcar is a North Sea-side town whose skies must be overcast frequently, even by British standards.

Newcastle-upon-Tyne   **GB-76**
** **Byker Redevelopment** (social
housing) 1968–80
Ralph Erskine
Neo-Vernacular
E from Newcastle ctr on A695 ⇨ Shields Rd,
abt 1 mi (1.4 km) / on R

Byker is one of the most architecturally and socially successful examples of urban reconstruction to be found anywhere. In 1968 it was a windswept hillside community of thousands of tightly packed, smoke-blackened terraces, interspersed with the occasional church and pub. A decade later only the churches and pubs, *and the community*, remained. (The old Byker community was kept largely intact, and *in situ* throughout the reconstruction.) Byker, or more correctly the Byker Wall, may also be the best-known social housing since the Marseilles Block. Whether it will be equally, and one hopes more beneficially, influential remains to be seen.

The Byker Wall is just that: an almost uninterrupted wall of housing, five to eight stories high and four-and-a-half miles (seven kilometres) long, which sinuously encircles the northern and eastern perimeters of this south-facing sloped site. It protects Byker from the North Sea winds and traps the sun, creating its own micro-climate, as if Byker were a kind of walled garden. (Once the wall was also to have separated Byker from a proposed motor-way.) Its sheer, almost solid, northern side – all the dwelling rooms face south – is a bold, abstractly patterned tapestry of jumbo-sized

multi-coloured bricks. Its white, light-reflecting southern face is alive with windows and wooden-railed, shed-roofed balconies and brings to mind the ancient, balcony-encrusted Greek monasteries at Mount Athos. Most dwellings are two- or three-storey maisonettes and have both their own balconies and exterior balcony/corridors leading to lifts. The Byker Wall is a powerful, appealing, efficient building. But it is only twenty per cent of the Byker community. Equally important are the dozen little neighbourhoods that shelter beneath it – each with its own variations of a few standard house types, each planned in consultation with its residents.

GB-76a A characteristically 60s British Brutalist attempt at urban place-making is the **Trinity Square shopping complex,** 1964–7, by Luder & Worthington, in suburban Gateshead. Like Luder's more widely publicized Tricorn development at Portsmouth (GB-45), it is a big articulated concrete framework into which, for the most part, individual lessees

must insert their own shops. Here, however, the form vocabulary is less wilful, more consistent, and perhaps a shade more mechanistic.

Admittedly, Newcastle itself is an unlovely industrial town to which the importation of Brutalism, like that of coals, might seem unnecessary. Gateshead, however, is just an ill-defined tract of suburban sprawl, to which this may be a not inappropriate antidote. *S from Newcastle on A692 (High-level Bridge)* → GATESHEAD *on to West St / ahead on L*

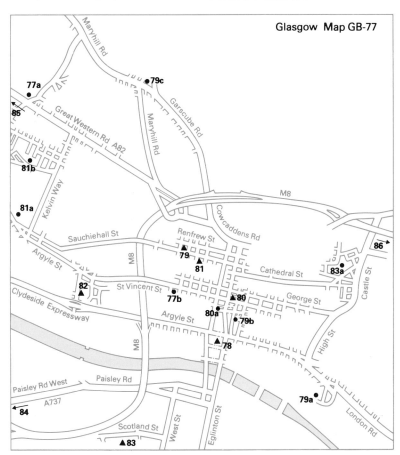

Glasgow Map GB-77

Glasgow
GB-77
Glasgow was once the Chicago of Scotland – 'The Second City of the Empire' – back in the steam age before the First World War. While the world has changed since then, for many years Glasgow just decayed, and then, more recently, suffered relentless urban renewal demolition. But still, some of Europe's more remarkable early modern buildings remain hidden among the ghosts of its prosperous past.

GB-77a One delightful survivor is **Kibble Palace,** James Kibble's gossamer greenhouse which was originally erected, *c.* 1860, at Coulport, and was re-erected in Glasgow's Botanical Gardens in 1872–3. It now gives the impression that only habit – and the stiffening influence of all those

panes of glass wedged between its thin twisted ribs – still hold aloft its great flat dome.

GB-77b The work of another remarkable Glaswegian Victorian, Alexander 'Greek' Thompson, must also be mentioned. His Greek Revival architecture – in fact more nearly Egyptian Revival in all but ornament – is uniquely suffused with a sensibility that elsewhere at the same time led to the creation of the muscular High Victorian Gothic. The façades of his office blocks include some curious anticipations of devices later used in Chicago by Louis Sullivan. The most dramatic surviving Thompson building is the **St Vincent Street Church,** 1859, at 265 St Vincent Street.

Glasgow   **GB-78**
* 'The Iron Building' (A. Gardner &
Son) 1855–6
36 Jamaica Street
John Baird I
Rationalism
Map GB-77

Although there are many mid-nineteenth-century American commercial
buildings with cast-iron façades, this is one
of just a few in Europe. With its repetitious
modularity and large amount of glass – so
reminiscent of the similarly Rational, if far
less interesting, corporate Miesian curtain-
walled idiom – it seems disconcertingly
more in the spirit of the 1950s than of the
1850s.

Glasgow   **GB-79**
*** Glasgow School of Art
1896–9 (centre and east wing)
1907–9 (west wing)
167 Renfrew Street
Charles Rennie Mackintosh, with Margaret
Macdonald Mackintosh
Free Style (Art Nouveau)
Map GB-77

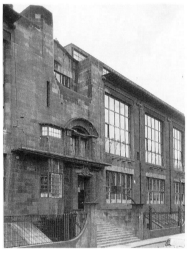

[There is a recent Post-Modern addition
by Gillespie, Kidd & Coia. An important
collection of architectural drawings and
watercolours from several of Mackintosh's
other commissions is displayed in the Mackintosh Room (the original boardroom) and
the newly opened Furniture Gallery. The
school has books for sale about its building
and about the Mackintoshes.]

Here, without a doubt, is one of the most
fascinating and important modern buildings. Aesthetically it speaks for itself. Historically one need but cite the publicity it
received in contemporary journals such as
The Studio, as well as the tremendous
immediate impact it had in Vienna (A-24)
and, perhaps less directly, the influence it
exerted upon the entire Germanic art
world.

By far Mackintosh's largest commission,
it evolved surprisingly little during the thirteen years from the competition-winning
initial conception to its completion. While
the design of the building is essentially
Mackintosh's alone, some of the interior
artwork may well be equally attributable to
his wife Margaret. The original boardroom
in the east end is typical of the Mackintoshes' early, more domestic, interiors –
being painted throughout in a creamy off-
white with pale lavender accents. The most
striking interior space, the library, is in the
later west wing. Although it is furnished
entirely in dark wood, a series of huge
bays – actually taller than the room – and
a more varied palette of accent colours
make the library visually and spatially more
exciting. Indeed, like the western exterior
door frame, it hints curiously at the coming
of Art Deco.

Leading up from both these major rooms
are two similar, but not quite identical,
staircases – with that to the east decidedly
the more satisfying. They epitomize Mackintosh's ability to find life in a deliberately
limited and potentially unpromising range

of forms, colours and materials. Here he
made 'Architecture' of a line of juncture
between the two types of wall surface; of
changes that occur to the stair treads as
the conditions at their edges change; of
small tiles that pick up odd glints of light
at unexpected moments; and of black iron
strapwork that cages the top landings. And
connecting those landings is an enclosed
loggia known as the 'hen run', the most
delightful place in this remarkable school.
On a sunny day it alone might induce one
to enrol as a student.

GB-79a Gillespie, Kidd & Coia, the architects of the school's Post-Modern addition,
were also responsible for one of Britain's
better small essays in hard-nosed, if still
romantic, Brutalism: **Our Lady and St
Francis Secondary School Annex,**
1964, on Charlotte Street near Glasgow
Green.

GB-79b Mackintosh's earliest major
work, the **Glasgow Herald Building,**
1893–5, at Mitchell Street and Mitchell
Lane, was designed while he was still an
employee of the firm of Honeyman &
Keppie. As it was built only three years
before his epochal School of Art, the
restraint shown here may reflect the influence of his employers, although presumably
the Art Nouveau details are his own.

GB-79c As with the Herald Building, it appears likely that Mackintosh had less than a free hand with his only church, **Queen's Cross,** 1896–9, at Garscube Road and Maryhill Road. This is particularly apparent in the exterior. Other than the tower which Mackintosh cribbed from a church in Somerset and a few Art Nouveau touches, it is quite conventionally Gothic.

Glasgow **GB-80**
Office building (rear elevation)
1908–9
84 St Mary's Alley
John A. Campbell
Rationalism
Map GB-77

Is this 'architecture' or oversight? Was this what Campbell really believed in (as opposed to the progressive Neo-Baroque front façade at 84–94 St Vincent Street)? Or was this rear alley elevation just something to be turned over to some nameless draughtsman – who, presumably, was much impressed by Mackintosh? Unfortunately for the grey city of Glasgow, it is only in sites such as this that one finds large areas of glass and also glazed brickwork.

GB-80a Mackintosh's **Daily Record Building,** 1901, on Renfield Lane at Hope Street, has a similar grime-resistant façade. On its lower portion he even attempted to play with the juxtaposition of glazed brick and stone.

The interior, although also superficially Gothic, is consistently more progressive in spirit – especially the nave's wooden barrel-vaulted ceiling and exposed iron tie-beams. But only the king-post truss ceiling of the small parish hall really suggests what was so soon to come. The church is now leased by the C. R. Mackintosh Society. It is both the society's information centre and a meeting place for the Maryhill community.

Glasgow **GB-81**
Willow Tea Rooms (now Henderson's the Jewellers) 1903–4
199 Sauchiehall Street
Charles Rennie Mackintosh
Free Style (Art Nouveau)
Map GB-77
[Restored, 1979–80, by Keppie, Henderson & Partners.]

Of the various tea rooms Mackintosh produced for Miss Cranston this is the only one which still survives. Although before its restoration the interior was far from intact, the former main tea room can now be visualized much as it once must have looked. The magnificent doors of the Room

de Luxe should also be seen: they are up the stairway, at the first-floor front.

GB-81a The Glasgow Museums and Art Galleries have **furniture and paintings by Mackintosh** on display at the Art Gallery and Museum, Kelvingrove. A section of the Chinese Room, a part of the former Ingram Street Tea Rooms, has been reconstructed in the museum.

GB-81b Glasgow University has recreated the principal interiors from the **Mackintoshes' own home,** 1906–14, using the original furniture and fittings, in its new Hunterian Art Gallery.

Glasgow   **GB-82**

*** Industrial redevelopment,
Anderston Cross Renewal Area**
1966–9
Finnieston Street at Clydeside Expressway
Jack Holmes & Partners
Industrial Vernacular
Map GB-77

Cumbernauld Town Centre (GB-86) may project the image of a megastructure, but this multi-factory building comes closer to the reality. The ground level is completely taken up by off-street vehicular circulation and loading docks. Above it a single manufacturing floor covers almost the entire site, following exactly the long curving street frontage of the property. The roof of this second level, in turn, is mostly a parking area that projects, cornice-like, over the pavement line – both to the building's visual and, presumably, functional advantage. On this parking level is a north-lighted factory as well as several large loft towers supported on *piloti*, which here for once really do make sense.

The only false note is someone's idea of a Kahn-esque stair tower attached to one of the loft blocks. This gratuitous bit of 'architecture' detracts from an otherwise honest and impressive ensemble.

Glasgow   **GB-83**

Scotland Street School (now a
museum of education) 1904–6
225 Scotland Street
Charles Rennie Mackintosh
Free Style (Art Nouveau)
Map GB-77

Because of its size, programme and date, this is necessarily a less exciting building than Mackintosh's School of Art (GB-79). The treatment of the fence and porter's lodge is more overtly mannered than anything in his previous work, while the stepped-back elements at either side of the stairs, as well as the stairs themselves, are prophetic of things then yet to come (F-12). Inside, only the stair towers are of any real importance.

GB-83a Glasgow's other Mackintosh school is the **Martyrs' Public School,** 1895, at Parson Street and Glebe Street.

Kilmacolm [*near Glasgow*]   **GB-84**
Windy Hill (house) 1899–1901
Rowantreehill Road
Charles Rennie Mackintosh
Scottish Baronial/Free Style
W from Glasgow (Map GB-77→) on A737
abt 7 mi (11 km) / R on A761 ⇨ Bridge of
Weir Rd (in Kilmacolm), abt 6 mi (10 km)
/ L on Rowantreehill Rd / on R at top of hill
[Not open to the public.]

The exterior of Windy Hill still looks much as it did when Mackintosh finished it. His even is the spiritual dichotomy between the main body of the house, so typical of the best British romantic work of the time, and the flat-roofed, slot-windowed, tower-like right-hand wing, which seems to anticipate some of the more *avant-garde* Continental work of the immediate post-Art Nouveau period a decade hence.

Helensburgh [*near Glasgow*]   **GB-85**
* Hill House 1902–4
8 Upper Colquhoun Street
Charles Rennie Mackintosh
Scottish Baronial/Free Style
NW from Glasgow on A82 (Map GB-77→),
abt 11 mi (18 km) then on A814→
Helensburgh, abt 8½ mi (14 km) / R on
Sinclair St / cross RR tracks / L on
Kennedy Dr / R on first st / on R

[Owned by the National Trust for Scotland. Open to the public.]

Larger than Windy Hill (GB-84), and on a more generous if less dramatic site, the exterior of Hill House does not quite have the spark of its predecessor. It seems a little too stolidly nationalistic and too cottagey-picturesque for its size. But sheltered within those solid walls is a world of exquisite

delicacy and inconceivable innocence. Nothing quite like it has survived from those brief, bright Edwardian days.

Cumbernauld [*near Glasgow*]   **GB-86**
* Cumbernauld Centre 1965–7
H. Hugh Wilson & D. R. Leaker
E from Glasgow on M8 (Map GB-
77→) / NE on A80, abt 12 mi (19 km) /
→ CUMBERNAULD TOWN CENTRE

Rarely has a building – or as the fashion of the day had it 'megastructure' – received so much publicity and been such a failure.

In an effort to accommodate this 60s mega-cliché to the realities of the Scottish climate, extensive areas of glass panelling have been added. But if retro-fitted glass might make Cumbernauld Centre useable,

nothing can save the town as a whole from the effects of the planning decision that placed its already indifferent housing a quarter of a mile away from the Centre, across bleak open fields. Nor can one help wondering how much better the residential areas might have been had the Centre been built with more conventional, and presumably less costly, techniques. If only the all too apparent sacrifices had produced some quality somewhere. The inhabitants seem to feel this way as well. Otherwise why else the intense vandalism the Centre has suffered?

South Queensferry [near Edinburgh] **GB-87**
*** Forth Railway Bridge 1881–90
Sir John Fowler & Sir Benjamin Baker
*NW from Edinburgh on A90 / best seen from
South Queensferry or car park at S end of
Forth Road Bridge*

It must be seen to be believed. For sheer
guts there is nothing else quite like it. Even
saying that its spans are almost 1200 feet
long does not really mean much. Its vastness only becomes apparent when, high
above and barely discernible, an insect-like
train slowly crawls through those tangled
steel girders. Compared to this, Eiffel's
Tower (F-16) is only a World's Fair souvenir.

St Andrews, Fife **GB-88**
** Andrew Melville Hall (residence
hall) 1964–9
St Andrews University
James Stirling
Brutalism
*N from St Andrews ctr on A91 / on L past
RR tracks*

As is true of all Stirling's buildings, one
is confronted here with a powerful, rich
conception. But, unlike his other collegiate
efforts (GB-50, 51, 58), Melville Hall lacks
the colours, incidents and materials that
can mitigate the inhuman, mechanical
nature of his aesthetic. The smoothness,
precision and crispness of the pre-cast concrete is undeniably spectacular. And it,
along with the hard white plaster, large
areas of glass, extruded aluminium and
pure, hard, blue flooring, makes this a
strong architectural 'statement' – but one
that might be seriously questioned as a
living environment.

Conversely it could be argued that here,
in Scotland, Stirling felt the need to trap
and intensify all the available light. The
stairways, for instance, extend to the roof,
where each ends in a glasshouse – a miniature translucent catalogue version of the
archetypal primitive hut – which serves
both as a skylight and as a pseudo-outdoors
place to which the students can escape from
their not so spacious rooms.

ITALY

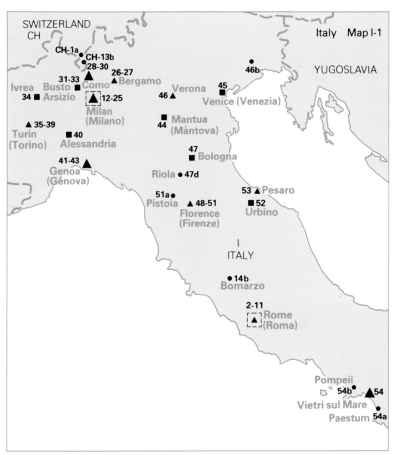

Italy Map I-1

Italy (Italia)   I-1

Despite the darkly imagined prisons of the eighteenth-century Romantic architect and engraver Giovanni Battista Piranesi – whose greatest influence fell outside Italy – modern architecture developed no real Italian roots until the 1914 exhibition of Antonio Sant'Elia's Futurist fantasies (I-29b). In some respects these picked up where Piranesi had left off. Just as his engravings had a century earlier, Sant' Elia's drawings too served as a source of romantic imagery to fire architectural imaginations north of the Alps. This was particularly true in Germany, where Erich Mendelsohn and the Expressionists early came under the influence of Sant'Elia's visions of glorified speed, monumental machines, organizational complexity and impersonal experience. In these Sant'Elia closely reflected the ideals of the leading Italian Futurist poet-propagandist, F. T. Marinetti. When Sant'Elia, a fervent nationalist, was killed early in the First World War, Marinetti co-opted his work and influence, using them to help politicize modern Italian architecture and move it towards a nationalist and essentially pro-Fascist position.

Because of this link between Futurism and Fascism, Italy never experienced the sort of wholesale repression of modern architects or their work that was later to occur in Germany. But naturally such immunity had its price. The most progressive Italian architects of the period could not be as creative or productive as their pre-1933 German counterparts, although they did design a number of large and influential temporary exhibitions as well as some public buildings. The single most highly regarded prewar modern building in Italy, the Palazzo del Terragni in Como (I-28), was in fact built as a regional Fascist headquarters. But if Italian progressive architecture was compromised through 'coexistence', the Italian version of totalitarianism's favoured stripped Neo-Classicism (I-2b, 2h, 4) rarely sank to the depths of mediocrity achieved by the Nazis. Prewar government buildings in Italy are frequently as good as, or better than, the official architecture of liberal New Deal Washington. Indeed most of the postwar American buildings so glibly labelled

'Mussolini Modern' do not approach some of their namesakes in modernity, let alone integrity or inventiveness.

At least until the disturbing development of a stark, high-fashion neo-Fascist Neo-Classicism (I-24), virtually all postwar Italian architects have shared a love of inventive detail, even if they held almost nothing else in common. Using glass, steel, and, less frequently, concrete, Italy's architects can achieve effects unequalled in Europe – presumably, in part, because of cheaper labour and less restrictive building codes. The same formal inventiveness is also applied to stucco, brick and stone, but with a wilful disdain for the haphazard character of Italian building maintenance.

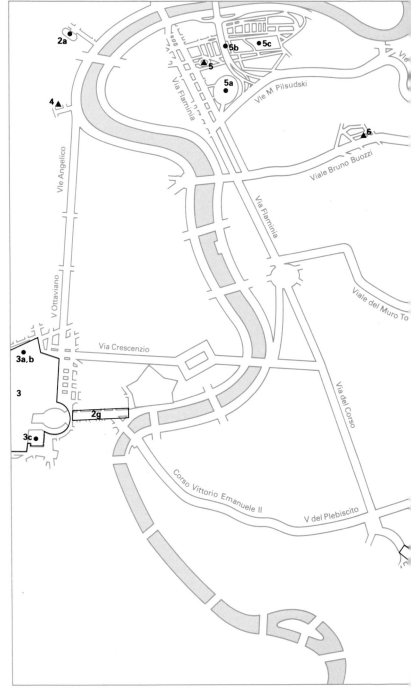

Thus within a few years plaster peels and stones shift, opening cracks from which the occasional plant may begin to sprout. All this might be suitably romantic in ancient buildings, or in ruins, but it does not accord well with the current Italian geometrical/industrial aesthetic, no matter how painstakingly handmade.

In view of their enthusiasm for inventive detailing, it is hardly surprising that Italian architects also devote considerable energies to the construction of elaborate and imaginative interiors. The design of shops, offices, apartments and exhibitions has become one of the most characteristic and convincing aspects of Italian architecture. Because of this it is difficult to list a fully representative sampling of the best current Italian work. Apartments and private homes are inaccessible to the average traveller, while shops, particularly the trendy, design-oriented sort, are notoriously transient. Anyone interested in experiencing Italian interior design, other than those examples listed (I-16b, 41a–c, 50b, 51b), should tour the fashionable shopping districts of Milan and, to an extent, of Rome.

Rome (Roma)   I-2

Rome, Italy's political capital and largest city, is very much a city of bureaucrats in a country where the private sector commissions most of the best architecture. As such, it has ceased to be Italy's architectural capital. But this was not always the case. Under Mussolini, the city assumed a perverse sort of architectural leadership. 'Il Duce' promoted many schemes for its improvement, expansion and embellishment – including several partially or wholly realized large-scale building projects.

I-2a The **Foro Mussolini**, now **Foro Italico**, by Marcello Piacentini, 1927–32, is reminiscent of Hitler's more infamous theatrical parade grounds at Nuremberg

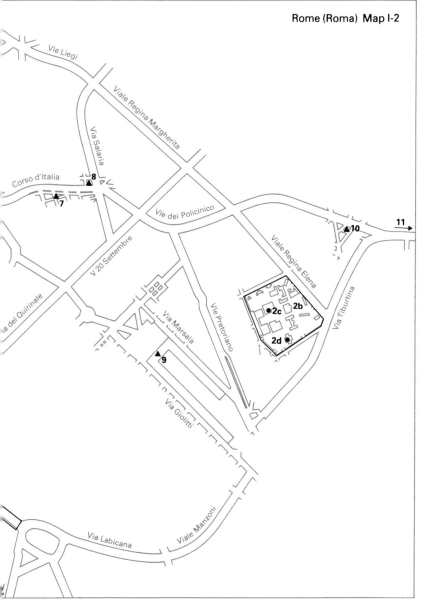

Rome (Roma) Map I-2

and Berlin (D-20a). Of all Mussolini's civic undertakings it bears most strongly the regime's stigma – as witness Piacentini's **Stadio dei Marmi,** whose gross statuary ominously embodies Fascism's essential inhumanity.

I-2b By comparison, the **Città Universitaria,** 1932–5, is not nearly so sinister, although its general layout and colonnaded entrance were also designed by Piacentini. Possibly it was not deemed to be as politically symbolic. Many of its buildings, despite their Neo-Classical overtones, are the work of architects committed to more progressive ideals – hence the pervasive air of compromise.

Among the most interesting of these are:

I-2c Istituto di Fisica (physics), 1934–5, by Giuseppe Pagano.

I-2d Facoltà di Matematica (mathematics), 1934–5, by Gio Ponti.

I-2e Istituto di Mineralogia (mineralogy), 1934–5, by Giovanni Michelucci.

I-2f Planning under Mussolini, unlike architecture, was consistently more conservative, or at least parochial. At best it produced functional traffic circulation schemes such as Rome's **Via dei Fori Imperiali.**

I-2g At worst, and most notably, it resulted in the **Via della Conciliazione,** which connects St Peter's with the Tiber, much to the detriment of Bernini's piazza.

I-2h The last of Mussolini's building schemes, and undoubtedly the one with the most curious history, was the Esposizione 42, or E42 district, now called **EUR** (Esposizione Universale di Roma), 1935–41 and 1948–58, again by Piacentini, *et al.* Intended to serve first as the site of a proposed 1942 World's Fair, it was then supposed to become a nucleus of Rome's suburban expansion. As had been the case at the Città Universitaria, Piacentini, the 'official' architect, was chosen to head a design team composed largely of progressives. E42, however, was not to be a secluded academic retreat: it was to be a showcase for the 'new Italian culture', a vision of the future under Fascism. Unlike the university, it could not be compromised.

In due course, an orthodox site plan emerged, appropriately modernized Neo-Classical buildings were designed, and construction began. In 1941, amidst growing suspicions that 1942 would not be a good year for World's Fairs, construction was halted. In 1948 the new democratic government decided to continue the project as a more or less conventional urban development. It changed the name to EUR and, strange as it may seem, finished the area in the prewar idiom – arches, columns, cornices, acres of marble and all. The momentum of Italy's bureaucracy may in part underlie this anomaly, but it does not completely explain some of EUR's later additions. *S from Rome (Map I-2→) on Via di San Gregorio / L on Via delle Terme di Caracalla ⇨ Via Cristoforo Colombo (Rt 148)* → EUR

I-2i The most remarkable of these later additions, architecturally and symbolically, must surely be the **Christian Democratic Party building,** by S. Muratori, 1955–8, which is almost more Neo-Classical than any of its Fascist predecessors. *On the Piazza L. Sturzo.*

Among those predecessors are:

I-2j The **Palazzo dei Congressi,** 1938–52, by Adalberto Libera. *On the Viale della Civiltà del Lavoro*

I-2k The arcaded **Palazzo della Civiltà Romana,** 1940–2, by La Padula and Guerrini. *Facing the Palazzo dei Congressi at the opposite end of the Viale della Civiltà del Lavoro*

Roma (Rome)   **I-3**
Città del Vaticano (Vatican City)
Map I-2
The Vatican is not normally associated with modern architecture. However, there are a few exceptions:

I-3a The first break with tradition came in 1932 with Giuseppe Momo's **spiral ramp** leading to the Vatican Museums and Galleries. This conical space does not compare unfavourably with Frank Lloyd Wright's similarly spiralling Guggenheim Museum (1943, 1956–9), which it antedates. Especially notable are the subtle but distinct lengthening and foreshortening effects achieved when the space is viewed from above and from below respectively.

I-3b Beyond the ramp lies the **Museo Gregoriano Profano Pio Cristiano e Missionario** (museum of non-religious art), 1967–70, by Fausto, Lucio & Vincenzo Passarelli. Unfortunately its display mounting system is so unnecessarily complex and obtrusive that, despite the basically good intentions, it overwhelms the objects presented.

I-3c If the new museum has its difficulties, Pier Luigi Nervi's **Papal Audience Hall,** 1971, is an unqualified disaster. It is a heavy-handed Las Vegas-Baroque box whose fumbling, indifferent deference to the presence of St Peter's Basilica succeeds only in accentuating an irreconcilable gulf. *Just S of St Peter's*

Rome (Roma)   I-4
Palestra per la Scherma (fencing
academy) 1934–6
*Viale delle Olimpiade and Via Roberto Morra
di Lavriano*
Luigi Moretti
Monumentalized International Style
Map I-2
[Derelict since 1960.]

Perhaps no other Italian architect of the
period could have designed this school, for
this purpose, in the heart of Mussolini's
personal showplace, the Foro Mussolini
(I-2a), without losing completely either his
wit or his dignity. Even the wretched
'official art' mosaic covering one of the academy's larger walls had to have clothing
added to its over-nude fencers, in order –
so the official explanation went – that their
indecency might not corrupt public morals.

Probably the Party officials who commissioned this building never realized how
good it is. It *is* dignified, but in an organic
way, so that while suggestive of stability,
it is neither conventionally massive nor
colonnaded.

Rome (Roma)   I-5
* Palazzetto dello Sport 1956–8
Piazza Apollodoro 10
Pier Luigi Nervi, with Annibale Vitellozzi
Formalism
Map I-2

The position which Pier Luigi Nervi, an
engineer, enjoyed as postwar Italy's most
famous 'architect' is at least partly due to
the factional, politicized nature of Italian
architecture. This was abetted, perhaps, by
his success in obtaining commissions
whose engineering content so predominated that their 'architecture' often
consisted of little more than the glazing
between structural elements. It may be just
as well that this was so. Among the buildings whose overall design Nervi presumably controlled, (I-3c, 36) only in the
Palazzo del Lavoro in Turin (I-38) do the
more architectural elements seem as competent as Nervi's primary structure.

The two enclosed sports arenas he
designed for the 1960 Olympics tend to
bear out this point. They represent two
versions of the same basic design, differing
primarily in size: a 200-foot span, 5,000-
seat capacity for the Palazzetto dello Sport,
versus a 300-foot span, 16,000 seat-
capacity for its larger, younger sibling, the
Palazzo dello Sport (see I-5d below). Yet in
some ways they are quite different. The
Palazzo, for instance, has nothing like the
ring of graceful, if unfortunately propped-
up, Y-shaped supports with which the
Palazzetto resists the great outward thrust
of its dome. These struts, part of the Palazzetto's primary structure, are the element
upon which its pleasing liveliness depends.
They seem to be tying an almost buoyant
dome to the ground – an illusion reinforced
by the dynamic shell-like fluting of the
dome's edge.

Internally both spaces are dominated by

the delicate ribs of their domes. But, again,
it is the Palazzetto, with its ribs interlacing,
like the centre of some gigantic sunflower,
that is the more pleasing. Like most of
Nervi's designs, both of these structures are
essentially diagrams of the path through
which they accommodate stress. As their
rib patterns plainly show, they direct all of
their lines of force, via a compression ring,
around a common point at the centre.
Thus, despite their efficient appearance
and utilization of advanced concrete technology, they are quite traditional in the
disproportionate concentration of carrying
capacity and weight at their centres. Compared, for instance, to a geodesic dome, they
are not in fact an especially efficient means
of spanning such spaces – which again
raises the question of whether Nervi the
engineer-turned-architect does not owe his
renown to Nervi the structural poet.

I-5a Adjacent to the Palazzetto are two
other Nervi designs, the **Stadio Flami-
nio,** 1957–60, designed with Antonio
Nervi, and:

I-5b The **Viadotto di Corso Francia**
(viaduct), 1959–60.

I-5c The **Villaggio Olimpico** (Olympic
Village), 1957–60, by Cafiero, Libera, Luc-

cichenti, Moretti & Monaco, is on the far side of the viaduct from the Palazzetto.

I-5d The structure supporting the dome of Nervi's **Palazzo dello Sport,** 1958–60, is subsumed within the substructure of its grandstand – leaving a rather stolid and untectonic circular glass wall to become the Palazzo's exterior. Within, the spoke-like ribs of the dome have had their potential elegance diminished by a band of cut-out lighting recesses, which confuses the dome's apparent structural logic by dividing its undersurface into three concentric rings of light and shade. *Through and past* EUR (*see I-2h*) / *rd splits around Palazzo*

Rome (Roma)   **I-6**
* Casa del Girasole ('Sunflower House' apartment building) 1947–50
Viale Bruno Buozzi 64 and Via G. Schiaparelli
Luigi Moretti
Mannerism/International Style
Map I-2

[Canopy over stair slot a later addition.]

At second glance certain aspects of this small, pleasant block of flats may seem a bit odd. What appears simple and straight-forward is not. The major street façade is a flat composition of abstractly alternating bands of stucco and shutters. But there is a deep light slot slashed up its centre and wedge-shaped balcony extensions that make the façade wider than the building – a little like two Wild West false-fronted buildings put bottom to bottom and laid sideways. Similarly, the side-street elevation is modern vernacular with 'punched out' windows and a series of saw-toothed bays, so angled that the rearmost rooms might catch some sun. (What could be more direct and functional?) The saw-toothed motif is repeated again in the cornices flanking the light slot, only this time arbitrarily at two different heights and angles, like a cock-eyed split pediment. (What could be more non-functional?) Then there is the paper-thin 'rusticated' stone 'basement', where joints which one would normally expect to be vertical run at sharp angles – echoing the saw-toothed motif; where surface textures vary from super-smooth to super-natural; and where,

emerging from the masonry next to one of the windows, is a fragmentary leg, a classically sculpted fragment seeming very much at home in these alien modern surroundings.

To the cognoscenti all this may sound familiar: false fronts, deep slots which expose a building's inner workings, gratuitously angled elements, a conscious juxtaposition of the vernacular with the arty, a general air of mannerism. During the late 60s these became hallmarks of certain avant-garde American architects, and in particular two who had an intimate knowledge of Rome – Aldo Giurgola and Robert Venturi. Not surprisingly, Casa Girasole is mentioned in Venturi's influential book, *Complexity and Contradiction in Architecture.*

Rome (Roma)   **I-7**
* Edificio per negozi, uffici e abitazioni (shops, offices and flats) 1963–5
Via Campania and Via Romagna
Vincenzo, Fausto & Lucio Passarelli
Picturesque Rationalism
Map I-2

It is unorthodox; it is contradictory: however, experienced *in situ* the Passarellis' creation proves not only pleasing but remarkably rational, at least within its own terms of reference. Immediately above street level the smooth dark-glass sheathing of its office floors carefully maintains the traditional urban building line, while it also politely mirrors older neighbours and bits of sky. Above that the highly articulated penthouse apartments fully, if romantically, make the most of their commanding site – also in the best urban tradition.

In a sense, one is presented here with two perfectly reasonable solutions to two different design problems. The only difficulty is that they happen to be piled one on top of the other – and, perhaps, that the seemingly less substantial is below. One's first instinct is to wish that the logical, distinctive structural system, which plays such a visually important role in organizing the dynamic apartment levels, were more in evidence in the office floors. But then, if fully exposing and expressing the structure might have made the building more comprehensible, might it not also have made it more boring? Much more interesting is the Passarellis' solution. They left out just enough glass panels from the curtain walls (but did not omit their glazing bars) to reveal one of the columns for its full length – thereby both creating a series of small, otherwise pointless balconies and saying to the concerned observer, 'It's all rather more logical than you might have supposed.'

Rome (Roma)   **I-8**
* La Rinascente (department store)
1957–61
Piazza Fiume
Albini & Helg
Rationalism
Map I-2

Ever since its initial conception, in a somewhat different form, much has been made of this building – in terms of the final product, perhaps too much. As might be expected of Albini & Helg, the detailing has an unusually articulate clarity. Indeed, the exposed steel frame is so aggressively articulated that it unavoidably brings to mind the timberwork of some ancient Japanese temples. One even suspects that much of the potential for structural continuity, an important advantage in welded steel construction, must have been sacrificed to this articulation.

Equally articulated in its own way, and perhaps indirectly responsible for the over-extended structure, is La Rinascente's exposed aggregate pre-cast wall system. The concrete, made with red marble aggregate, is ground to a smooth terrazzo finish, which gives an appropriate air of hard mechanistic authority to the projecting channel-shaped modular panels into which it is formed. The distribution and the variable widths of these panels are in turn governed by the size and location of the service elements they contain, and by the nature of the store's structural system. Ducts and pipes originating in the attic are fed downwards inside the panels, which terminate at various floors in accordance with their service requirements. The resulting patterns of crisply angled mechanical service chases alternating with flat panels – patterns that are more complex on the upper floors, less so on the lower – are further accentuated by the shadows of the projecting spandrel beams which play upon them, and by thin (perhaps eight-inch) horizontal white bands cast into the panels at about head height on each floor. All of this enlivens and subtly imprints a sense of scale onto a potentially dull, windowless, and otherwise almost scaleless, construction.

Rome (Roma)   **I-9**
* Stazione Termini (railway station)
1947–50
Piazza dei Cinquecento
Montuori, Vitellozzi, Calini, Castellazzi, Fatigati & Pintonello
Abstract Neo-Expressionism
Map I-2

Talking with Italian architects who were students in the early 1950s, or reading the literature of the period, one encounters the sense of excitement, of promise, that was personified by this building. Maybe it was just that relatively little else was actually being built. More likely it was a certain Oscar Niemeyeresque quality of unreality: the novel non-tectonic forms; the huge spaces; the five-storey office block designed to look like ten; the sense of scale so different that one did not quite know how to react to it; the vision of things to come that, perhaps, made one a little uneasy.

Much was said at the time about how, in their great modesty, the architects and planners had saved a bit of Rome's ancient city wall. And well they should have! Always featured prominently in photographs of the station, the wall at least was tangible and tectonic.

Today, like Niemeyer's Brasilia, this naive vision of the future is rapidly becoming an anachronistic image of the past.

Rome (Roma)   I-10
* Edificio per abitazione (apartment
building) *c.* 1930
Via della Lega Lombarda and Via G. della Bella
M. Marchi
Expressionism
Map I-2

Like certain kinds of plants, architects
sometimes cast their seed to the winds – via
the printed word and rotogravure. As a
result, their progeny may come to light
in rather unlikely places. It is not just
the mildly Expressionist details and
proportions but the startling terraced configurations that would make this building
seem exotic almost anywhere. Discounting
the unlikely possibility of fully independent
invention, the most plausible source for this
idea is Hans Poelzig's 1916 Expressionist
project for a House of Friendship in Con-
stantinople – a scheme which was little
less than a modern reincarnation of the
Hanging Gardens of Babylon. This obscure
block of flats is to the best of our knowledge
the only prewar building to explore the
potential of Poelzig's remarkable project.

Rome (Roma)   I-11
* Quartiere INA, Casa Tiburtino
(social housing) 1949–54
Via Tiburtina 1020
Mario Ridolfi, Ludovico Quaroni, *et al.*
Neo-Realism (Nationalist Neo-Vernacular)
E on Rt 5 (Map I-2→) → TIVOLI / *on R*
just inside city limits

During the late 1930s Northern Europe
began to develop a stylized folksy mode of
design – soon to be called Scandinavian
Empiricism – as a reaction to the de-
personalized architecture then emanating
from the avant-garde on the one hand and
from increasingly conservative governments on the other. In Italy an analogous,
if more determinedly folkloric, reaction –
known as Neo-Realism – developed at the
end of the war. For a time, certain Italian
architects went about the countryside col-
lecting and analysing examples of vernacular planning, use of materials and
construction details. They then incorporated these into their own work.

The movement, which was romantic,
unclassical and therefore, in a sense, un-
Italian, did not last long – about the length

of time required to complete Casa Tiburtino.
Its studied picturesque aesthetic was out of
keeping with the Italian formalist tradition,
and its equally studied identification with
vernacular building techniques made it
increasingly   uneconomical   with   the
passage of time. None the less, Casa Tiburtino, like its vernacular prototypes, argues
forcefully for the ideal of dwellings and
neighbourhoods which possess some sense
of familiarity, and with which the individual can identify.

Milan (Milano)   I-12
Milan's reputation as a design-conscious
city, although deserved, must be considered
within the Italian context. Milan is the
financial and industrial capital of the
country. Some of its apparent sophistication may simply represent wealth combined with a business-like approach to
problem-solving and an enthusiasm for the
appearance, if not always the realities, of
technological efficiency. Milan seems, for
instance, little more able than other Italian
cities to shape its own growth. Throughout
the postwar era (and long before the rise of
Rossi – I-24, 33) the attitudes controlling
development of its central area remained
consistent with those established during
the Fascist period. However, the results
thus far are no worse than Louis Napoleon's Paris (F-5), and far preferable to the
usual unimaginative application of CIAM's
pseudo-scientific urbanistic theories.

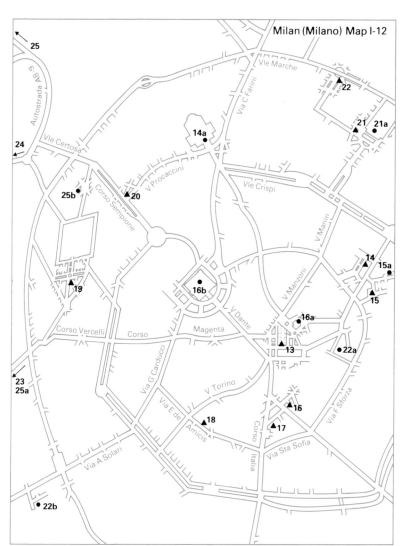

Milan (Milano) Map I-12

Milan (Milano)   I-13
** Galleria Vittorio Emanuele II
(arcade) 1865
Piazza del Duomo
Giuseppe Mengoni
Neo-Classicism
Map I-12

This arcade is one ancestor of the shopping mall. But the difference between these
two building types rests not simply in a
more advanced technology that can
exclude pigeons and climatic vagaries from
shopping expeditions, while potentially also
creating a setting of greater spatial complexity. If that were all there was to it, then
we might really be better off today, despite
the lost delights of walking under airy
glazed iron spider's webs, and despite the
loss of the sense of scale and stability derived
from ordered façades such as these.

There is, however, another difference –
in a sense one beyond the scope of the
assignment usually presented to the architect, but none the less germane to the
nature of these building types and to the
way in which we experience them. A shopping mall, with its vast windswept asphalt
parking prairie or its grim, grimy garage, is
a dead-end destination hermetically sealed
from other aspects of everyday life. Arcades,
on the other hand – if they are to succeed,
and some do not – must be an integral part

of the urban fabric. People must use them not just with some specific objective in mind but because they are a convenient, pleasant way to get from one place to another. Milan's Galleria is one of Europe's most successful spaces not because it is the biggest of its kind, but because it is an important, natural part of the everyday lives of the Milanese.

Milan (Milano)   **I-14**
Casa Castiglione (house, now offices of Unione del Commercio) 1900–3
47 *Corso di Porta Venezia* (rear elevation on Via Marina)
Giuseppe Sommaruga
Stile Liberty (Art Nouveau)
Map I-12

[Almost immediately after its construction, outraged public opinion forced Sommaruga to remove two large nude figures which had flanked the entrance. The interior was rebuilt, 1971, by Eugenio Gerli. The façade, entrance hall and some principal interior spaces remain intact.]

The 1902 Turin fair was a triumph for the fully ripened Art Nouveau. Yet in Italy that style never became absorbed into the vernacular to the extent that it did elsewhere, and even the few interesting Italian examples tend to be identifiable with foreign – primarily French – sources.

In this context Sommaruga's work stands apart. He was innovative, not just imitative. Although he certainly took inspiration from foreign sources, he looked more to the relatively restrained Viennese Secession than to the emotive Art Nouveau of France and Belgium. There is, however, an element of mannerism which particularly distinguishes his work within the context of the Italian, or for that matter of any other, Art Nouveau. Sommaruga reached back to the sixteenth century to resurrect conceits, colossi and, as is especially evident here, rock-like rustication of a sort rarely to be found since the days of the Orsini Gardens.

I-14a Almost the only other examples of *fin-de-siècle* mannerist Italian architecture are to be found among the hundreds of mausolea – ranging from something short of the sublime to the completely ridiculous – in Milan's **Cimitero Monumentale**.

I-14b Except perhaps for their mannerism, and a certain cult status they achieved during the 60s and 70s, the sixteenth-century **gardens of the Villa Orsini**, near Bomarzo, have nothing to do with modern architecture. But they are more fun – assuming a slightly warped sense of humour – than many better-known, or more elaborate, examples of their type. *E from Autostrada del Sole at Attigliano, abt 56 mi (90 km) NW of Rome / → signs.*

Milan (Milano)   **I-15**
* **Palazzo Fidia** (apartment block) 1924–30
Via Mozart and Via Melegari 2
Aldo Andreani
Neo-Mannerism (National Romantic)
Map I-12

Some will undoubtedly find this confection misplaced in a guide to modern architecture. We must admit to being fascinated by so talented an architect seemingly so out of step with his time – if not his place. However, the Palazzo Fidia may not be quite as retrogressive as its jokey stylistic preoccupations suggest. It may, in fact, be as much a product of its time as were the contemporaneous romantic skyscraper fantasies of the American architectural illustrator Hugh Ferriss or the Gothic utopias of the German Expressionists. If not convinced by the street façade, have a look at the rear.

I-15a Another interesting, albeit more historically minded Neo-Mannerist design of the period – an **apartment building** whose façade is dominated by frescoed colossi – is in the nearby Via Cappuccini.

Milan (Milano)   I-16
* Torre Velasca (office and apartment
tower) 1958
Via Velasca and Corso di Porta Romana
BBPR
Rationalism/Neo-Vernacular
Map I-12

Here is a curiously contradictory attitude
towards urbanism. On the one hand, there
is a serious attempt to ameliorate the
impact of a large skyline-breaking building,
including the unusually mellow quality of
its concrete cladding, the picturesque
'random' fenestration pattern of its interchangeable windows and infill panels (in
theory, a simple reflection of the functional
needs of individual tenants), and, of course,
the famous romantic silhouette. Evidently
this was intended as much to harmonize
with the nearby cathedral as to accommodate the apartments occupying those
upper floors. And on the other hand? An
unimaginative, sterile, formalistic entrance
pavilion plunked down in the middle of
what must be Italy's least inviting piazza.

I-16a A BBPR effort with more consistent
urban credentials is the **Chase Manhattan building**, 1968–70, at the Piazza
Meda.

I-16b BBPR were responsible for the renovation of and displays in the **Castello
Sforzesco museum**, 1954–63. Although these now strike one as being
subtle and effective, in the context of the
unassertive architecture of the 50s they
must have seemed *almost* revolutionary.

Milan (Milano)   I-17
* Uffici e abitazioni (offices and flats)
1949–57
Corso Italia 15
Luigi Moretti
Neo-Expressionism
Map I-12

Why does this building remain virtually
unknown? Its complicated programme is
skilfully and articulately fitted on to a tight
urban site. The glazing, which accounts for
so much of its surface, has a tense self-
assurance, ranging in scale from the slot-like access
balcony openings to the cantilevered end of
the block of flats, are convincing in their
controlled, abstract dynamism.

It is, in a sense, urban-scaled sculpture.
Yet it never overwhelms the passing pedestrian. Granted, in the hands of the wrong
person, or even in too great a quantity,
such architecture could become tiring.

Perhaps the reason for its obscurity lies
in the highly politicized nature of Italian
architectural criticism. This is sophisticated
arty architecture for the rich, constructed

at a time when there was an emphasis
on folksy Neo-Vernacular buildings for the
poor (I-11). Then there may also have been
many who found Moretti's past political
involvements (I-4) ideologically unacceptable, whatever the merits of his work.

Milan (Milano)   I-18
Autorimessa (garage) 1949
Via Edmondo de Amicis 20–22
Tito Varisco-Bassanesi
International Style
Map I-12

This building is a bit stylized, but in a
subtle and pleasantly period sort of way.
And the sculpted forms do not contribute
to the efficient working of a parking garage.
However, if non-symbolic functionality
were the sole criterion of architectural
excellence, the study of architectural
history would be very dull – not least for
students of the Renaissance and the

Baroque. Consider instead how this
example of a vexing and uniquely modern
building type is both recognizable for what
it is and still worth a second look.

Milan (Milano)   **I-19**
Clinica Colombo (house, now a private hospital) 1909
Via Buonarroti 48
Giuseppe Sommaruga
Art Nouveau
Map I-12

In spite of certain mannerist and Art Nouveau elements, this building will seem strikingly familiar to anyone who knows the 'Prairie School' houses built around Chicago at about the same time by Frank Lloyd Wright's early contemporaries. Although it is possible that Sommaruga could have seen some of that work, much of it has only been published since the 60s. One cannot help wondering, then, if there was not some other common source – aside from Wright's own designs, which were at the time little known in Europe – for certain aspects of what was almost a common transatlantic vocabulary. Possibly such a source could have been Vienna (see A-18a). At the time, there were demonstrable architectural links with Chicago and its large German-speaking Catholic population. One could imagine similar cultural connections with the former Habsburg imperial territories in nearby northern Italy.

Milan (Milano)   **I-20**
Casa Rustici (flats) 1934–5
Corso Sempione 36
Lingeri & Terragni
International Style
Map I-12

Although it fits comfortably within the bounds of the International Style, this large block of flats also shares with Terragni's other works (I-28, 29) certain attitudes and elements that were not common to progressive architecture of the period. In particular there is a strong sense of order imposed by the concrete frame, and a Futurist-inspired dynamic handling of the semi-exterior spaces. The frame almost everywhere is delineated upon the façades. And when the central court cuts deeply into the building's volume, the frame emerges to become a series of Constructivist, or Sant'Eliaesque (I-29b) bridge-like balconies. While maintaining the sense of a continuous flat façade plane, there develops a tension between the apparently prismatic structure and the more complex volumes described by the dwellings it contains.

Milan (Milano)   **I-21**
* Torre Pirelli (office tower) 1955–60
Piazza Duca d'Aosta 3
Gio Ponti, with Pier Luigi Nervi
Neo-Expressionism/International Style
Map I-12

This 400-foot tower is one of the earliest, best-known and most influential of Europe's once rare tall office buildings. But how much of its elegance is due to Ponti's undoubted skill as a form-giver and how much to Nervi's concrete poetics? Nervi's structure employs two paired sets of shear-stress-resistant hollow triangular shafts (the tower's pointed ends) as well as two additional sets of tapered supports (visible at the façade's inflection points). For all its ingenuity, however, this solution has had a much greater impact on novelty-conscious architects than on structural engineers.

As an urban gesture or as an advertisement for Pirelli's corporate design sophistication the Pirelli Tower's success is undeniable. As a functioning office building whose inefficient, inflexible plan forfeits the most valuable floor area to structural overstatement, it seems – at least to American eyes – somewhat naive.

I-21a Across the Piazza Duca d'Aosta is Milan's monumental railway terminus, the **Stazione Centrale,** 1912, 1925–31, by

Milan (Milano)   **I-22**
* Edificio per abitazione (apartment block) 1960–3
Piazza Carbonari 2
Luigi Caccia Dominiani
Catalogue Neo-Vernacular
Map I-12

Romanticism and Rationalism interact here to produce an exciting tension. This building is little more than a severely rectangular prism completely sheathed with plain glazed tiles – except for its simple, unpretentious aluminium window system. But those windows have been used in anything but a simple manner. Just about every conceivable size, shape and combination of the window system's elements – which include built-in shutters and, in some configurations, exposed blank panels to house them – is to be found somewhere on these otherwise flat, featureless façades.

Out of this apparent chaos there emerges a kind of order. It results from the limited palette of materials, from a consistent floor-to-floor dimension, and from a structural system that is able to accommodate differing apartment plans within the simple prismatic building form. Ultimately, therefore, the appeal of this building derives from Caccia Dominiani's strong sense of discipline – highly personal though that may be. Without that discipline the intriguing underlying tension, and all else, would have been lost.

I-22a An earlier, 1954–7, more conventional or perhaps more urban essay, in which Caccia Dominiani employed these

Milan (Milano/Baggio)   **I-23**
* Istituto Marchiondi (boarding school) 1953–9
Via Noale 1
Vittoriano Viganò
Brutalism
W from Piazza Gambara (Map I-12→) on Via Anguissola / immediately angle R on Via delle Forze Armate → BAGGIO / L at Y on to Via Cividale del Friuli ⇨ Via Bagarotti / R on to Via Gozzoli / L at T and first R on to Via Val d'Intelvi Isorno / L on to Via Mosca / R on Via Noale / on L

With its Le Corbusier concrete and Terragni tectonics, this boarding school for problem boys was one of postwar Italy's more influential buildings. Yet, some critics' expectations notwithstanding, its influence was mainly felt outside Italy. Rough, raw materials and hard-nosed Brutalism were never very appealing to Italian architects who, especially since the war,

E. Montuori. The original, competition-winning design for the Stazione dates from 1912. At that time the exhausted Art Nouveau (Stile Liberty in Italy) was rapidly giving way to a resurgent Neo-Classicism – although, interestingly, this competition also gave rise to some of the most dramatic Futurist projects (I-29b). Construction was delayed by the First World War and its aftermath until well into the Fascist period, with results that can be seen, unevenly intermingled, throughout the building.

same materials, is the pair of office buildings at **Corso Europa 10–12.**

I-22b Caccia Dominiani's witty, and in a sense improvisational, **Loro e Parisini** factory administration block, 1956–7, at Via Savona and Cavalcavia Don L. Milani, exemplifies his penchant for combinations and uses of vernacular materials. Perhaps the *ad hoc* detailing – like the building's unusual form – is in part a response to specific functional and aesthetic constraints imposed both by the severely limited site and by the nature of the existing factory building. *Map I-12*

have tended to favour more lyrical forms of expression. Nor, it seems, were those critics correct who found this school repressively harsh and prison-like. Despite the hard use

Milan (Milano/Gallaratese)   **I-24**
Gallaratese 2 (social housing) 1968–73
Via Falck 37
Aldo Rossi
Neo-Rationalism
S from Piazza Kennedy (Map I-12→) →
Quartiere Gallaratese on Via Vigorelli ⇨
Via Croce / continue across Piazza Bonola on
Via Falck

The relentless logic of this columbarium for the living exceeds that of anything built under Mussolini. Much of Rossi's architecture – happily for the most part confined to the printed page – seems to be a reaction against postwar Italy's materialistic, *laissez-faire* version of CIAM modernism. One must suspect, however, that the deathly chill of this building may also have been a response to the atmosphere of political violence then nearing its peak in Italy.

it must suffer at the hands of its occupants, it shows, by Italian standards, no serious signs of deliberate abuse.

I-24a The adjacent **Gallaratese flats**, at Via Cilea 34, 1968–74, by C. & M. Aymonino, *et al.*, are more typical of the Italian avant-garde of the period. *To S of Gallaratese 2*

Milan (Milano/Baranzate)   **I-25**
* Chiesa Mater Misericordiae
1956–8
Via San Paolo and Via Erba
Mangiarotti & Morassutti
Formalism
N from Piazza Kennedy on autostrada A8-9 (Map 1-12 →) / first exit (→VARESE) / L on to Via Boccioni ⇨ Via G. B. Grassi (→ BARANZATE) / R→ BARANZATE-NOVATE / first L / at end of st

Standing four-square on an artificial knoll in the middle of an enclosure, this rectangular glass-walled church is externally almost featureless, save for the protruding ends of its cruciform pre-stressed roof beams. One enters not via the large 'ceremonial' door but through a smaller, more inviting entrance which leads past a chapel and then up into the church. Inside one finds oneself in a remarkable prism of light. True the roof hovers overhead, supported on four slender free-standing columns, and a similarly free-standing choirloft is at one's back. But these only tend to focus attention on the altar, while perhaps also preventing the church from becoming too much an ethereal abstraction – as if it could, in the face of several plaster saints and the usual indifferent maintenance.

I-25a It would be difficult to imagine a more straightforward church than the **Chiesa della Madonna dei Poveri**, 1952–6, by Figini & Pollini, on the Via Osteno in Milano/Baggio. It is just low aisles, a high dark nave and a tall 'light-catcher' over the altar – all within a chunky brick and concrete box. From outside it does not even admit to its differing interior ceiling heights. Just because the

excess drama and symbolism of so many postwar churches is so unconvincing, this one seems more refreshing for its sound proportions, use of light and sense of focus. *W from Piazza Gambara (Map I-12→) on Via Anguissola / immediate angle R on Via delle Forze Armate, abt fifteen blks / R on Via Osteno / on L*

I-25b The **Chiesa di San Ildefonso**, 1954–5 by Carlo de Carli, on the Piazzale Damiano Chiesa, reflects a gratifyingly honest approach to structure and material. From its hexagonally based, trilobed plan, there evolves a space whose impact, under a less Spartan discipline, could have been destroyed by over-elaborate detailing and too many materials. *Map I-12*

Bergamo   I-26
* Società Cattolica di
Assicurazione (offices, flats, shops,
parking and cinema) 1967–71
Via Daniele Piccinini and Rotonda dei Mille
Gambirasio, Zenoni, Barbero & Ciagà
High-Tech Mannerism
NW from Bergamo ctr → CITTÀ ALTA on
Viale Papa Giovanni XXIII ⇨ Viale Vittorio
Emanuele II / L at Via Tasca–Via
Petrarca / one blk on L

In many differing ways this is an exciting,
provocative building. It is exciting in its
multiplicity of functions, in its rigorous
detailing and utilization of advanced
materials, in its profusion of dynamic forms,
and particularly in its urbane humanity. It
contains, in addition to two floors of offices
and several parking levels, a below-street-
level cinema, a row of large multi-level
penthouses and a semi-arcaded floor of
shops – originally intended to be part of a
pedestrian circulation system leading to the
city's main shopping street.

It is, however, provocative in its sometimes less than practical 'functional'
elements and in the curious insertion of a
parking level between the two office floors –
at the obvious extra expense of providing
both a space-consuming, two-storey ramp
and insulation and weather-proofing for
thousands of additional square feet of
exterior surfaces. And then, once one
realizes it is not an optical illusion, there is
the problem posed by that part of the building facing the circular piazza (the Rotonda
dei Mille). Each of the three curtain-walled
façades of its two floors of offices and its
ground-level shops creates a concave, one-
storey-high cylinder segment approximately equal in radius to the piazza, but
not quite concentric with it or with the
façades of either of the other two floors. The
architects say they did this to enliven what
would otherwise be just another pre-
tentious little Parisian-style circular

piazza – as if the very presence of their
building would not have precluded that. As
it is, the Società Cattolica looks not unlike
a stack of children's blocks that has been
knocked slightly askew.

I-26a Nearby is a **block of shops and**
offices, 1968, also by Gambirasio,
Zenoni, Barbero & Ciagà. Towards the side
street it presents an interesting fibreglass
façade, while its required 'old' façade
facing the Via XX Settembre is carefully
shown at the corner to be exactly one brick
thick. *Down st, past I-26 garage entrance*
/ first L / at end of blk on R

I-26b On the edge of Bergamo, on the Via
Borgo Palazzo, is a **large furniture**
store, 1969, by the same architects. Built
in the form of a stepped rectangular helix,
it too makes extensive use of fibreglass and
displays beautiful concrete work. *SE from*
Bergamo ctr → BRESCIA / on L

Bergamo   I-27
Convento dei frati Francescani
(Franciscan monastery and school) 1972
Via Baioni
Gambirasio, Zenoni, Barbero & Ciagà
Modular Formalism
N from Bergamo ctr → PELLEGRINO on Rt
470 / on L at edge of town

As it has for centuries, the development
of Italian architecture still tends to follow a
course independent from that of northern
Europe. Gothic never was really at home

in Italy, nor were Art Nouveau and the
International Style. But there have also
always been exceptions – the occasional
trans-Alpine seeds that have taken root in
the warm Italian soil. One of the latest is
this aggregation of church, school and
cloistered monastery – a 'northern' building quite on a par with its American, British
and Dutch counterparts.

In plan it is a rhythmic plaid of 'served'
areas, each three modules square, separated from one another by a 'servant' grid

of single-module-wide integrated structural-mechanical-circulation spaces. One suspects that some Italians might accuse this monastery of being too technocratic, of having no soul. Seen from the other side of the Alps, however, it seems quite spirited, especially when compared to many conceptually similar buildings (D-67a, GB-58c, NL-55). The freedom with which the possibilities of its modularity have been exploited could be a lesson to those architects for whom rigid modular geometry was once a tool, then became a crutch and finally a strait-jacket.

Como   **I-28**

** **Palazzo del Terragni** (originally Casa del Fascio, Fascist Party offices, now border patrol offices) 1932–6
Piazza Terragni
Giuseppe Terragni
International Style/Rationalism
Across st and RR from Piazza Verdi at rear of cathedral

The Palazzo del Terragni is Italy's most important prewar modern building. Indeed, it is as convincing as anything built here *since* the war. For years, however, it received little recognition outside Italy.

In addition to most critics' ideological qualms about finding any merit in a 'Fascist' building, it must also have seemed uncomfortably Classical in spirit. Although asymmetrical and free of specific stylistic references, its self-assured, elegant underlying Classicism would have been evident and unacceptable in the more socially concerned 1930s, 40s and early 50s. The times demanded at least an image of humanism and/or functionalism.

Only in the late 50s could the salient characteristics of this, Terragni's masterwork, finally begin to be appreciated: the spaces and details stripped to severe rectangularity; the Neo-Classical Rationalism of its reliance upon a regular post and beam structural system as the primary form determinant; the emphatic use of such monumental materials as bronze, marble and heavy glass. Together these make some of the postwar generation of architects (D-37) seem more Terragni's true contemporaries.

Como   **I-29**

* **Novocomum** (flats) 1927–9
Viale Senigallia and Viale Vittorio Veneto
Giuseppe Terragni
International Style
W from Piazza Cavour (on lakeside) on Lungo L. Trento / first R past park / one blk on L

Terragni's first major work betrays a youthful reliance on the stock International Style elements: white walls, corner windows, pipe railings. But he also had sufficient knowledge of other, more exotic sources to have intelligently borrowed the unusual round corner pavilions from Russia's Constructivists. This is one of the few built examples of early Constructivist influence in Western Europe. Not that the citizens of Como were impressed. They came to see the strange new building, decided it looked like an ocean liner, and promptly dubbed it 'The Transatlantic'.

I-29a The **War Memorial**, 1933, at the end of the Viale Vittorio Veneto, is Terragni's simplified version of one of Sant'Elia's

famous visionary drawings – the closest that any of them ever came to realization.

I-29b There is a permanent exhibition of reproductions of Sant'Elia's drawings on the top floor of the **Villa Olmo**. *W along lakeside* → VILLA OLMO

Como   I-30
Asilo Sant'Elia (kindergarten) 1936–7
Via A. Alciato and Via dei Mille
Giuseppe Terragni
International Style
*S from I-28 on Viale Lecco / →MILANO /
bear L at circle / bear L just past church on
L / bear R at circle / R on Via dei
Mille / two blks on R*

Just to prove that Terragni was not
always concerned only with questions of
form and style, this pleasant little kindergarten turns an anonymous face to the
street, while its rear, composed mostly of
industrial glazing, shelters the play area
from cool mountain winds.

Busto Arsizio/Castellanza   I-31
Istituto tecnico industriale
(technical college) 1968
Viale Borri and Via Azzimonti
Enrico Castiglioni
Neo-Expressionism
*S from Busto Arsizio → LEGNANO (on Viale
Duca d'Aosta) / on R 500 yds (m) past RR*

Castiglioni is primarily known for his
unbuilt – and sometimes unbuildable – projects, involving large, 'poetic' thin-shells.
Many problems face the dreamers of radical
forms who actually want to build them but
who do not have a large budget (such as
Eero Saarinen had for his TWA Terminal
in New York and his Dulles Airport in
Washington); or who do not have access

to the appropriate vernacular construction
techniques (such as were available to
Gaudí); or who perhaps simply do not have
the skill to transform an idealized formal
concept into a real building made of real
materials for real people.

This school is just that sort of over-
ambitious project. Presumably because of
the expense of the complex curved concrete
structure, most of the materials and detailing are disappointingly pedestrian, as is particularly evident in the major circulation
space – despite its skylight, three-storey
height, and what is meant to be a dynamic
free-flowing form. Perhaps, at best, this is
an object lesson in the risks of building
paper fantasies.

Busto Arsizio   I-32
Scuola (school) 1964
Enrico Castiglioni
Neo-Expressionism
*N from Busto Arsizio ctr on Viale Duca
d'Aosta / L opposite Mizar factory (abt
½ mi/1 km) past roundabout / one blk on L*

If this school seems more successful than
Castiglioni's technical college (I-31), that
may be partly because it is smaller and
in some ways more conservative. Here at
least the rough rubble masonry and concrete shapes look less as if they had been
designed in modelling clay with the inten-
tion of being executed in a plastic. The
concrete work provides an interesting and
original demonstration of the material's

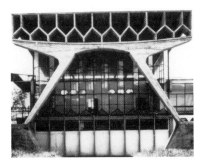

possibilities, even if the forms produced do
not seem totally suited to their functions.

Fagnano Olona [near Busto Arsizio]   **I-33**
Scuola elementare (school) 1972–6
Via Pasubio
Aldo Rossi
Neo-Rationalism

Here is the archetypal product of what is usually referred to by its proponents as Neo-Rationalism or 'Tendenza'. However one is hard pressed, despite the accompanying rhetoric, to see more in it than a deeply disquieting exhumation of the most dehumanizing manifestations of the 'efficient' Fascist state – not as epitomized by the architecture of Terragni (I-28), or even that of Piacentini (I-2a, b, f), but cynically and self-consciously it would seem, by that of the extermination camp.

Ivrea   **I-34**
Officine Olivetti (factory) 1934–57
Via Jervis
Figini & Pollini
Rationalism
From autostrada E21 → IVREA / abt 1¼mi (2 km) on R

Throughout the world Olivetti has come to be identified with sophisticated design – both in its products and in the architecture it commissions. (GB-42). In addition to being on occasion over-enthusiastically credited with having the first all-glass curtain wall, this particular building marks the beginning of Olivetti's sponsorship of advanced design.

Turin (Torino)   **I-35**
Turin has a remarkably 'American' grid-iron street plan. It is also, appropriately enough, the Detroit of Italy. As such, it has a decidedly no-nonsense technological bias.

I-35a One of the earliest expressions of this attitude – pre-dating Fiat, or Ford for that matter – is the 550-foot **Mole Antonelliana**, begun in 1863 by Alessandro Antonelli as a synagogue and completed, 1878–89, as a museum of the Risorgimento. Its present pinnacle is a faithful reproduction of the original which blew down. *E from central station on Corso V. Emanuele II, abt five blks / L on Via S. Massimo ⇨ Via Montebello / abt nine blks on R at Via Ferrari*

I-35b Turin's best-known example of

I-34a Olivetti has also commissioned many other buildings in Ivrea. Among these is a hexagonally planned employees' **dining and recreation centre**, 1953–9, by Ignazio Gardella. Although suffering from the usual Italian maintenance versus materials and detailing conflict, this elaborate facility is remarkably well integrated into its sloping wooded site immediately behind the factory.

I-34b In the centre of Ivrea is **La Serra**, a mini-megastructure, 1967–75, by Cappai & Mainardis, containing social and residential facilities for visiting Olivetti personnel.

technology as architecture is the **former Fiat factory**, 1919–26, by Giacomo Matté-Trucco, at present vacant and awaiting its proposed transformation into a university. It is a vast and competent but by American standards not exceptional concrete-framed structure whose primary claim to fame is that it has a high-speed automobile test track (banked curves and all) on its roof. This unique facility, which certainly influenced such later projects as Le Corbusier's Linear City, is best viewed from the Parco Europa, on a hill directly across the river from the factory. *To reach park, E on Corso V Emanuele II / R at T, past river, on to Corso Moncalieri / L just beyond Piazza Zara on to Via Sabaudia → PARCO EUROPA-CAVORETTO / factory itself is located at Via Nizza and Via Cortemilia*

*** Salone B e C, Palazzo delle
Esposizioni** (exhibition halls) 1948–50
Parco del Valentino
Pier Luigi Nervi
Empiricism
*E from Turin ctr on Corso V Emanuele II /
R on Corso Massimo d'Azeglio / at end of
park on L*

These two halls are the earliest, and for
many years were the best, of Nervi's extant
works – his much publicized aeroplane
hangars having been destroyed during the
Second World War. With their two distinct
patterns of ribbed vaults, each assembled
from hundreds of individual pre-cast
elements and bonded together by steel bars
and cement grout, they represent an

achievement in concrete whose lightness
and breadth of span was at the time unprecedented. One must, however, overlook the
decidedly unexceptional buildings of which
they are a part.

Because these halls lack the raw vigour
of most pioneering structures, they – and
especially the open-ended Salone B – have
now come to seem less exciting. Even
Nervi's staid Palazzo dello Sport (I-5d),
whose dome simply paraphrases the
vocabulary of the Salone B's vault, is a
more impressive space because of its greater
consistency and coherence. Today, one is
primarily attracted here to the smaller,
more self-contained Salone C, whose structure is closer in spirit to Nervi's now almost
mythical, long-lost aeroplane hangars.

Padiglione sotterraneo
(underground exhibition hall) 1958–9
Parco del Valentino
Riccardo Morandi
Brutalism
In park just N of I-36

In marked contrast to the somewhat
fussy vaults of Nervi's nearby exhibition
halls, Morandi's structure emphasizes vigorous, almost brutal forms and textures.
The greatest difference between them,
however, is that all 115,000 square feet of
Morandi's lie buried beneath a park.

I-37a **A similar structure by Pierre
Vago,** 1958, is to be found beneath the

lawn in front of the Basilica at Lourdes,
France. → BASILICA

* Palazzo del Lavoro (exhibition hall,
now trade school) 1960–1
Via Ventimiglia, Zona Esposizioni Italia 61
Pier Luigi Nervi & Antonio Nervi
Rationalism
*S from I-36 on Corso M. d'Azeglio ⇨
Corso Unità d'Italia / R on Corso Maroncelli
/ R on Via Ventimiglia / on R*

This is now what one expects of Nervi: a
forest of sixteen gigantic concrete columns,
each cruciform at its base and gradually
tapering to a cylindrical top. These support
sixteen huge multi-ribbed square steel
umbrellas – each separated from its neighbours by six-foot (two metre) wide strips of
glass. It is such an enormous building that
multi-storey mezzanines remain almost
unnoticed between the outermost rows of

columns and the elegant, wind-braced
curtain walls. And it is so assured a building that no element, large or small, disturbs
the sense of total coherence. It is Nervi's
most architecturally persuasive design.

Turin (Torino)   I-39
* Edificio per abitazione (apartment
building) 1964
Piazza Pitagora
P. de Rossi, S. Zaretti, E. Luzi
Rationalism
*W from RR station on Corso V Emanuele II
/ L on Corso Castelfidardo / angle R on
Corso Orbassano / abt 1¼ mi (2 km) on R*

At least since the Baroque, if not before,
Italian architecture has been so preoccupied with spatial and/or decorative
effects – often at the price of logical construction and a natural use of materials –
that one is left unprepared to respond
adequately to buildings such as these little-
known suburban apartment towers. Only
three humdrum materials are employed
here: tinted 'hammered' structural glass,
stock brick and poured-in-place concrete.
These materials could not have been
assembled in a more straightforward way.
Here 'architecture' is an integral part of
construction, not a system of embellishments.

The glass balcony railings that dominate
the façades represent an economical vernacular technology which, in Europe,
matured more than fifty years ago and has
been widely used ever since. Its use here
helps make possible such 'luxuries' as extra
balconies and roof decks. The brickwork is,
of course, only an infilling – and under
many circumstances still the lowest cost
curtain-wall material available. But it is
also substantial and honest. No hidden
angle irons support these walls at each
floor level or over the windows. Instead,
the floor slabs project and do the job themselves, while concrete lintels span the
window openings. Nor is the unusual
pattern of projecting bricks at the corners
just a way of providing 'ornament'. It also
eliminates the need for special corner bricks
or other tricky and expensive details.

Even the concrete frame is left just as it
came from the formwork: unglamourized,
unmonumentalized, unbrutalized. It is, in
spite of appearances, only a slightly more
imaginative than usual example of flat-
plate construction, that classic of efficient
contemporary vernacular structural systems which trades savings in the cost of
formwork and finishing against the use of
extra steel and concrete, and which, from
a floor-planning viewpoint, is one of the
most flexible ever devised. In a sense, the
only difference between the structure of
these buildings and that of a typical low-
cost American housing block is the imagination used to develop the system's potential.

I-39a By way of comparison there is a
somewhat more urban block of **flats,
shops and offices,** 1959, by BBPR at
the junction of Corso Francia and Via Cibra-
rio. Although admittedly conservative,
with a strange prewar Dutch flavour, this
building has languished in unjustified
obscurity – in part because it is a younger,
less flamboyant successor to BBPR's photogenic and once highly controversial Torre
Velasca (I-16). *W from RR station on Corso
Vittorio Emanuele II / R on Corso Inghil-
terra / abt ½ m (1 km) on L*

Alessandria   I-40
Dispensario antitubercolare
(tuberculosis clinic) 1935–8
Via Gasparolo 4
Ignazio Gardella
International Style
E from N10 at S edge of city on ring rd →
AEROPORTO, *abt 900 yds (m) / L on Via
Gasparolo / at end of blk on R*

With the passage of time, and ever more
distant diffusion from its Franco-German
epicentre, the International Style increasingly came to accommodate itself to local
conditions and sensibilities. In this instance
the accommodation was primarily to the
southern sun, involving the substitution of
pale colours for the usual pure white, and
the introduction of sun screens and cantilevered projections over the usual strip
windows – which here are divided into eye-
level and clerestory strips.

I-40a Gardella also built the **group of
apartment buildings,** 1951–2, at 11,
15 and 17 Corso Teresio Borsalino. *Corso
T. Borsalino is another segment of ring rd on
S side of city*

Genoa (*Génova*)   I-41
Uffici comunali (municipal office
building) 1952–61
Via Garibaldi 9 (rear)
Franco Albini
*Via Garibaldi is in the old (now pedestrian
only) part of town / on N side of st behind
Palazzo Doria-Tursi, 1574, now Municipio
(city hall)*

Genoa's city hall is an elegant, symmetrical, inward-looking Renaissance
palazzo wrapped around a large, double-
loggiaed courtyard. Entering on axis
through a dimly cool entrance hall, one
passes up a flight of steps leading into the
bright, colonnaded court. At the far end
a grand double staircase leads to the principal floor. Taking the right-hand set of
steps and turning left through a doorway
on the landing leads one to another courtyard, where again there is an axial alignment – but now it is with one of the terraced
wings of Albini's symmetrical office
addition.

The new building is cut into the hill on
three sides, but on the fourth it is open to
the sun with a view over the palazzo to the
old town and the sea beyond. Although it
is experienced as an independent design,
the addition responds to its immediate surroundings by continuing the sequence of
offset axes. They in turn visually link this
alliance of the sixteenth and twentieth centuries with a nineteenth-century lift tower
connecting lower and upper parts of the
city, which emerges further up the hill, but
is otherwise 'off axis' in relation to the old
palazzo below.

Here are Classical assurance and humanity spanning four centuries and all the
more delightful for being so unanticipated.

I-41a As could only have happened in
Italy, Albini made his reputation as an
architect largely through the design of
interiors and exhibitions. Just west of
the city hall is the eighteenth-century
Palazzo Bianco, whose art galleries
Albini designed in 1951.

I-41b Across the street is the seventeenth-
century **Palazzo Rosso,** also transformed
into an art gallery by Albini, 1952–61.

I-41c Also in the old quarter, within the
Cathedral of San Lorenzo, is a small **sub-
terranean treasury**, 1952–6, by Albini.
The entrance is difficult to find, but it is
worth the effort.

Genoa (*Génova*)   I-42
Edificio per abitazione (social
housing) 1958–62
Forte di Quezzi
Luigi Carlo Daneri
Corbusian Brutalism
N on Corso Torino (through tunnel) ⇨ *Corso
Sardegna / angle R at end of st on to Via
Fereggiano / first L on to Viale Virginia
Centurione Barcelli / at end of rd almost at
top of hill*

In the 1930s Le Corbusier published projects for linear city-cum-apartment buildings with highways on their roofs. Since

the war that idea, and/or its image, has had
a number of progeny (F-40, GB-71) – none
of which have included the roadway, its
basic form-giving *raison d'être*. However
this building, surely one of Europe's longest,
most closely resembles its parent both programmatically and formally. Like Le Corbusier's projects, it is well suited to its curving
hillside site. The linear continuity of the
structure as it follows the contours of the
hill should have facilitated construction on
a difficult site. It also permits the covered
access balconies to function more effectively as 'streets in the sky' – as opposed to

those of more conventionally fragmented developments whose individual buildings may serve only a tenth of the population.

As with most of the building types that Le Corbusier 'invented', this one was intended to conserve open space. The Forte di Quezzi housing once stood in dramatic isolation high on the green hills overlooking Genoa. But now the once verdant hillside is smothered with shoddy imitations – some so badly built and so thoughtlessly placed that sections of them have been known to break loose and slide down towards the city below.

Genoa (Génova)   I-43
** Viadotto sul Polcevera
(autostrada viaduct) 1960–7
Autostrada A10 over Polcevera river
Riccardo Morandi
Brutalism
Carries A10 abt 2½ mi (4 km) W of Genoa ctr / For more dramatic view from below: W from Stazione Principe (central station) on Via S. Benedetto ⇨ Via Buozzi ⇨ Via Milano / R on Via A. Cantore → AEROPORTO (under RR) / first R past river on Via Rolla ⇨ Via Greto di Cornigliano / abt ¾ mi (1.3 km) / To experience piers close up: continue and then R across river just after going under bridge / R at T on Via Walter Fillak, which passes through pier / (Note juncture of structure with roof on W side)

Like Nervi, Morandi is an engineer who designs buildings (I-37), but bridges are his forte – and the bigger the better. (This is but a fragment of the causeway he built across Venezuela's Lake Maracaibo.) It can be argued that such structures inevitably contribute to the confusion and blight they so frequently overshadow. Here, at least, the scale of the bridge – it is as much a question of its proportions as of its size – differs so radically from the buildings below that, in a sense, they can almost ignore each other.

Mantua (Mántova)   I-44
Cartiere Burgo (paper factory)
1960–2
Viale Poggio Reale and Strada Montata 13
Pier Luigi Nervi
Structural Neo-Expressionism
N from Mantua ctr on N62 → VERONA / R after lake → VERONA-MODENA-AUTOSTRADA A22 / on R

The twin towers dominating this 450-foot-long factory support a 'suspension bridge' that serves as its roof. Because this arrangement concentrates the loads being carried, rather than transmitting them through a multitude of small elements as was Nervi's usual practice, and perhaps because this was his first essay in tensile construction, the structure has a vigour more reminiscent of Morandi's work (I-43) than of Nervi's. Undeniably, this is a dramatic solution to the problem of housing a huge, continuous-process paper-making machine within a column-free space. But is it a necessary solution? (Spanning crosswise would have been more conventional and less costly.) Or – in design-conscious Italy – is this another example (I-21) of High-Tech corporate image-making?

Venice (Venezia)   **I-45**
Inevitably Venice is more museum than
city. It is, after all, Europe's most important intact historic urban environment.
Europe's other cities – those that survived
the two world wars – are primarily products
of nineteenth-century expansion and
reconstruction. Even the heart of Florence
suffered 80 per cent demolition, in the
name of urban renewal and street realignment, as late as the 1880s. Venice is also
the only European community of any size
to have escaped completely the tender
mercies of the car. It is this absence of motor
vehicles which, thus far, has saved Venice
and which also makes it – aside from its
historic and aesthetic importance – significant to urban designers.

Verona   **I-46**
* Museo di Castelvecchio (museum
installation in castle) 1957–64
Corso Cavour
Carlo Scarpa
*Three blks NW of Roman arena on Via Roma
at river*
   Carlo Scarpa was less an architect than
a sculptor of place and space. A lifelong
teacher who built little, he truly believed
that god was in the details. Scarpa
approached the installation of Verona's
Castelvecchio Museum as a Zen monk
might approach the organization of a landscape. Which is not to say that there is
anything overtly Japanese in Scarpa's
work, although he owed much to Frank
Lloyd Wright, who was profoundly influenced by Japanese art and architecture.
But everything here is poetry – the shaping
of space and light, dialogues between
artifacts, controlled views and paths, detailing that is neither reticent nor obtrusive.

I-46a Scarpa's last built work, completed
after his death by Arrigo Rudi, is the
Banco Popolare di Verona (bank head
offices), 1974–81, on the Piazza Nogara.
*NE from Roman arena on first st to R of
church / first L / first R / on R*

I-46b Like some other postwar European
architects (E-30), Scarpa may have been
truer to the implications of Wright's teachings than Wright was himself. The power

I-45a Since the Second World War Venice
has missed the opportunity to gain major
buildings by Le Corbusier, Frank Lloyd
Wright and Louis Kahn. However, the
pavilions of the Venice Biennale
form, at least in theory, a significant collection of mementos of many well-known
modern architects. Among them are:
Austria, 1934, by Hoffmann; Holland,
1954, by Rietveld; Finland, 1956, by Aalto;
Canada, 1958, by BBPR; 'Artbook', 1950,
and Venezuela, 1954 (now modified), both
by Scarpa. It is in fact generally just as
well, particularly in Aalto's case, that the
Biennale grounds are usually locked and
the pavilions out of sight – except for the
few months of the exhibition which is held
in even-numbered years.

and poetic imagery of Scarpa's **Brion-
Vega Cemetery,** 1970–81, in San Vito
di Altivole, would have been inconceivable
without Wright. But Wright would have
been incapable of creating a work of such
sustained intensity, craftsmanship and
attention to detail. *N from Padua on Rt 307
abt 14 mi (32 km) → Castelfranco Veneto / San Vito di Altivole is abt 6 mi(10 km)
N of Castelfranco / B-V cemetery is entered
through town cemetery*

Bologna   **I-47**
Edifici per esposizione (exhibition
building) 1964
Quartiere Fieristico
L. Benevolo, T. Giuralongo & C. Melograni
Neo-Expressionism/Neo-Liberty
*N from ring rd at Piazza di Porta Mascarella
on Via Stalingrado →* FERRARA */ →* FIERE
   As befits a setting for industrial fairs,
these buildings exude an aura of high technology. Big structural frames emerge from
one carefully detailed block, briefly touch
ground and pass on into the next. Each
element, from truss to downpipe, articu-
lates itself from its neighbours and
announces the fact of its existence in its
own distinctive colour. Moveable interior
partitions are formidably constructed of
corrugated steel. Even the coloured glass

windows enlivening the end walls look as if they were meant to serve some obscure technical function. Overdone? Perhaps, but these are exhibition buildings. They should have an air of exuberance, despite a necessarily warehouse-like programme.

I-47a The same architects designed the uninspired **administration building,** 1970–1, with its connecting pair of semi-circular exhibition spaces, which in contrast suffer from too much inspiration incoherently assembled.

I-47b Also in the exhibition area (next to the modern art museum) is a reincarnation of Le Corbusier's **Pavillon de l'Esprit Nouveau,** that counterblast to Art Deco with which he infiltrated the 1925 Paris Exposition des Arts Décoratifs – much to its organizers' dismay. Because it was known for sixty years only through published drawings and photographs, subsequent generations may have underestimated its influence. During its brief existence, this simple two-storey model apartment and diorama must have been seen by, and may

have converted to Le Corbusier's cause, more architects and members of the public than all his prewar buildings combined.

I-47c Bologna is a city of arcades – a traditional, now largely ignored, means of rendering urban environments more habitable. One modern building that continues this tradition, as well as bearing witness to the persistent Italian taste for mannerism, is Giovanni Michelucci's **Istituto Matematico** (University of Bologna mathematics building), 1964–5. *NE from Bologna ctr on Via Zamboni to ring rd / at Piazza di Porta S. Donato 5*

I-47d In Riola, a small town about 28 mi (45 km) south-west of Bologna (on Rt 64), is Alvar Aalto's only significant Italian work, the posthumously constructed **Church of Santa Maria Assunta,** first commissioned in 1966 but not begun until more than a decade later. A crisp building, perhaps to the point of stuffiness, and possibly not as sensitive to its site as might be hoped, it is neither the best nor the worst of Aalto's later designs.

Florence (Firenze)   **I-48**
Stazione ferroviaria di Santa Maria Novella (railway station) 1934–7
Piazza della Stazione
Giovanni Michelucci, *et al.*
Moderne
N from river on Viale Rosselli (at fourth bridge W of Ponte Vecchio) / R on Via Alamanni (just before underpass) / L at Piazza della Stazione

Along with the orthodoxies of the International Style, the 1920s and 30s produced a number of alternative images of modernity – from Art Deco (GB-6, -9) to the stripped Neo-Classicism of Auguste Perret (F-18b). This terminus reflects in part one such style or attitude, which owed as much to industrial design, then still in its brief vigorous youth, as it did to architecture. Applied with equal enthusiasm to everything from toasters to 'cities of tomorrow', the industrial design imagery of the period leaned heavily on the romanticism of speed and travel. It was 'streamlined', which in architecture usually meant having functionally unjustifiable rounded edges. It was ornamented with 'speed marks' – long thin parallel lines emblematic of blurring motion. Its motto was more likely to be 'form symbolizes movement' than 'form

follows function'. Most buildings designed in this idiom, particularly in Britain (GB-6d) and in America where it was especially prevalent, are more amusing than memorable.

Here, however, sophisticated designers employing functional planning concepts, made this stylized modernism into a serious architecture of bold symbolic gestures – such as the broad band of glazing that acts as a visible connection between the railway on one side of the building and the city on the other. This glazing, which is as symbolically important from without as it is from within, sweeps up over the station's *porte-cochère* and along the length of the waiting-room ceiling, before finally being absorbed by a cross-axis of canted glass. This lowers the ceiling and acts as a line of visual demarcation between the concourse (the city) and the platforms (the way to the hinterlands).

Symbolism of this sort always caused difficulty for the more orthodox International Style designers. Their ethics demanded extensive functional rationalizations. Only with the emergence of Post-Modernism and the revival of eclecticism could this sort of design – with all its possibilities and pitfalls – again come to the fore.

Florence (Firenze)   **I-49**
Villino Broggi-Caraceni
(house) 1910–11
Via Scipione Ammirato 99
Giovanni Michelazzi
Art Nouveau
*E from Ponte Vecchio on N embankment / L
on Viale Amendola (at second bridge) /
second R at circle on Via Scialoia / first R on
Via Scipione Ammirato / in first blk on R*

Never mind that this 'French' Art
Nouveau building is in Italy, or that it was
built as Art Nouveau was dying, unla-
mented, in Northern Europe. Michelazzi's
ornamental terracotta here is as good and
gristly as any that can be seen this side of
Paris.

I-49a More urban and Italian is Michelazzi's **Casa-galleria,** 1911–13, at Via
Borgognissanti 26.

Florence (Firenze)   **I-50**
* Edificio per abitazione (flats) 1965
Via Piacentina 129 and Via Don G. Bosco
Leonardo Savioli & Danilo Santi
Brutalism
*E from Ponte Vecchio on N embankment / L
at Via del Campofiore / three blks on L*

Were there a prize for the 'busiest building in Europe', this block of flats might well
win. It appears to be a reimportation from
Japan of a thoroughly metamorphosed
version of Le Corbusier's postwar concrete
architecture (F-63) – an architecture which
in Japan had sparked, or at least
coincided with, a frenzy of activity more
vigorous and creative than anything to be
seen in Europe or America during the same
period. Certainly that same vigour and
inventiveness is also much in evidence
here – almost to the exclusion of discipline.
Still this is a beautifully crafted building and
it would look considerably less improbable
in tighter, more urban surroundings.

I-50a The nearby Nervi-designed **municipal stadium,** 1930–2, is best known –
possibly more so than it deserves – for its 'fly-
ing' helical staircase. *NW from I-50 on Via
del Campofiore / L on Viale T. Mamiani
⇨ Viale E. Duse / R on Viale Manfredo
Fanti / on L*

I-50b Savioli's rehabilitation of the upper
floors of the **Church of Orsanmichele**
is quite disciplined, thoroughly Italian –
and worth the climb. *On W side of Via dei
Calzaiuoli, two blks N of Piazza della Sig-
noria / upper floors accessible via open bridge
from adjacent building*

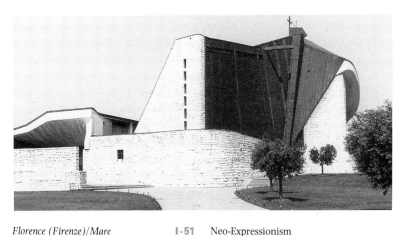

Florence (Firenze)/Mare   **I-51**
*** Chiesa di San Giovanni
sull'Autostrada del Sole** (Church of
the Autostrada) 1961–4
Autostrada del Sole
Giovanni Michelucci

Neo-Expressionism
Exit 20 from Autostrada (A1) → CHIESA
This is no mere roadside chapel. Built by
the autostrada company as a monument,
or expiatory offering, it is dedicated to the
men killed while constructing the highway.

But other than its memorial function, and the need to incorporate large quantities of art, its programme must have presented little challenge.

An unfettered commission for a monument such as this might seem all an architect could wish for. Yet an absence of constraints has undone many a designer, including in this case Michelucci, who compounded his troubles by imposing relatively few restrictions upon himself. Thus the floor plan, half of which is devoted – without particular purpose – to complex multilevel circulation arrangements, has no sense of an organizational rationale. Nor, save for the roof over the main entrance, has the building any regular structural geometry. While Michelucci does limit himself to only three materials – rubble masonry, rough form-marked concrete and rolled metal roofing – each, as he has treated it, represents the least discipline-imposing choice. His concrete, for instance, is sculpted, hung like cloth, and formed into props, beams, trusses, bents and cantilevers. While many

Urbino   **I-52**
Collegi Universitari (university residence hall) 1964
Giancarlo de Carlo
Brutalism
SW from Urbino on Rt 73a → AREZZO or
COLLEGI UNIVERSITARI *abt ½ mi (1 km) /*
up hill on R

Hanging in the Uffizi Gallery in Florence is a portrait of Federico da Montefeltro, Duke of Urbino, one of a pair of the duke and his duchess by Piero della Francesca. Every inch the aristocrat, and wearing a remarkable red hat, he sits in front of an apparently stylized landscape of delightfully bumpy little hills.

The duke is long gone. His magnificent palazzo has become a museum. But the 'unreal' backdrop of the Umbrian landscape remains as it was in the picture – a vista that this dormitory town overlooks, as once did the duke. De Carlo's buildings cascade down the slopes of a hill just outside the city walls with such an air of self-assur-

Pesaro   **I-53**
* **Villa** (house) 1902–7
Via Repubblica 1
Giuseppe Brega
Art Nouveau
Via Repubblica is Pesaro's main EW axis /
on N side at sea front

What could be more appropriate for such a genteel seaside town? Here is the architectural counterpart of those serving platters encrusted with ceramic seaweed and denizens of the deep that sometimes adorn the walls of 'atmospheric' seafood restaurants.

lesser architects have arrived at tectonic anarchy through incompetence, few have achieved it with such skill.

I-51a The **Casa di Risparmio e Borsa Merci** (bank and commodities exchange), 1950–2 and 1965, on the Piazzetta San Leone in Pistoia, is representative of Michelucci's typically far more restrained urban work. This restraint may reflect his strong sensitivity to existing urban environments, especially those of old homogeneous cities like Pistoia and Florence, where most of his buildings are located. It may also reflect his personal loyalty to the immediate postwar idealization of the vernacular. *S from Piazza del Duomo past Batistery on to Via Roma / an addition to 1909 'Renaissance palazzo' bank on L*

I-51b In the **Uffizi Gallery** Michelucci was responsible for the simple but elegant rebuilding of several rooms, the first ones encountered on the upper floors, containing the earliest paintings.

ance that they are commonly held to have few peers among the small group of modern pseudo 'hill towns' (CH-12, F-62). One is surprised, then, to find on closer inspection that, despite the college's overall liveliness of form and subtle siting, there are no places in its extensive system of exterior stairways and walkways that seem designed to reinforce communal life.

Vietri sul Mare [near Salerno]   **I-54**
** **Ceramica Solimene** (ceramics
factory) 1954
Piazza Vittorio Veneto
Paolo Soleri
Wrightian Neo-Expressionism
*From Autostrada del Sole at Vietri sul Mare
exit R on to Via Roma / 250 yds (m) on L*

[The right side of the building, as one
faces it, is Soleri's work. The left side, by
another architect, faithfully copies Soleri's
façade elements, but makes no attempt to
compete with his interior space.]

The interior of Soleri's first and only
European building betrays the year he
spent studying with Frank Lloyd Wright.
By that time – the late 1940s – Wright's
conception of an organic architecture had
finally and firmly shifted its emphasis from
the honesty of materials and structure to
the mythic/allegorical qualities of form,
pattern and space.

Spiritually, there are few closer parallels
to Wright's work than this tall skylighted
studio. With its untectonic structure and
spiral ramp, it almost demands comparison
with Wright's Guggenheim Museum – the
closest contemporaneous embodiment of
Wright's then-evolving attitudes. But even
this early in his career Soleri was too independent and inventive merely to copy the
'master'. His vigorous plant-like concrete
columns, whose suggestion of an arch-
itectural/biological analogy foreshadows
his later projects, are especially striking in
this respect.

If the Ceramica has a major fault it is the
decidedly weak relationship between the
interior work-space and the façade. A
curving line of inverted conic segments
covered by a tapestry-like mosaic of glazed
and unglazed pots, the façade even more
strongly prefigures Soleri's later bio-anal-
ogous mega-city projects. The residual triangular interstices between these segments
are filled by an almost refreshingly non-
poetic industrial glazing.

I-54a Not much further down the coast,
south of Salerno, stand the ruins of the
ancient Greek city of **Paestum**. The mid-
eighteenth-century's 'discovery' of its vigorous, early Doric temples, *c.* 450 BC, signalled a new perception of history –
architectural and otherwise. It also led to a
new awareness of how much had been
omitted from that one over-codified late
Roman treatise, Vitruvius's *De architectura*,
which had for so long served as the final,
irrefutable authority on a seemingly immutable Classicism. *25 mi (40 km) S on Rt
18 / → PAESTUM*

I-54b About halfway between Salerno
and Naples is **Pompeii.** The discovery of
this petrified Roman city at almost exactly
the same time as that of the temples at
Paestum (I-54a), did much to demytho-
logize the ancient world. And because
Pompeii made it more real, it eventually
became both more mundane and more
remote. *N from Salerno abt 18 mi (30 km)
on Rt 18 / → POMPEII*

IRELAND

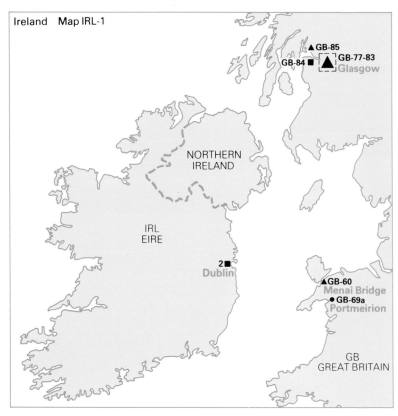

Ireland Map IRL-1

▲GB-85
GB-84 ■ ⌐¬GB-77-83
         ▲ Glasgow

NORTHERN
IRELAND

IRL
EIRE

2■
Dublin

▲GB-60
Menai Bridge
● GB-69a
Portmeirion

GB
GREAT BRITAIN

Ireland (Eire) IRL-1
Ireland is a relatively poor country which, during the last 150 years, has suffered revolution, civil war, famine and mass emigration. Today its population is about half that in 1835, and its most talented and ambitious young architects, such as Kevin Roche (GB-74), often feel that they must emigrate to succeed. All of this is by way of explanation for our solitary Irish building.

But before the great famine Ireland produced, and has preserved, an enviable wealth of Georgian architecture, both urban (Dublin's many fine squares and public buildings) and rural (e.g. Castletown House and Folly). This is the architecture one should experience in Ireland.

Dublin IRL-2
Trinity College New Library
1960–7
New Square
Ahrens, Burton & Koralek
Brutalism
Main (pedestrian) entrance to campus at College Green and Grafton St in Dublin
ctr / → BOOK OF KELLS / adjacent to Old Library

To build in the company of distinguished older buildings is among the most difficult and potentially rewarding tasks an architect can face. Here the challenge was compounded by the need to squeeze the New Library into a very tight slot. In part the solution to that problem lies beneath the paved forecourt, which conceals both two-thirds of the New Library's book stacks and a link to the Old Library, 1712–32, by Thomas Burgh. The remainder of the building sits to the rear of its site where, modestly but without self-effacement, it assumes the guise of abstract, scaleless sculpture.

This is not a new idea in such circumstances: Yale University's Beinecke rare books Library is merely a more celebrated and pompous version of the same thing. But rarely has it been done with so little sense of compromise. If only the same could be said of the elevator-cum-stair shaft inserted into the Old Library building. (It completes the underground connection between the two working libraries while isolating their joint circulation system from that of tourists visting the *Book of Kells*.) Somehow this small but important part of the scheme went awry.

IRL-2a The adjacent **Trinity College Museum,** 1853, is by Deane & Woodward.

NORWAY

Norway (Norge)   N-1

Scandinavia or no, Norway has not the architectural and design sophistication one might expect. But the scenery is magnificent and its vernacular structures, both old and new, are often appealing.

Language note Ø and Ö are interchangeable in the Norwegian alphabet, as are Å and Aa. While Ö and Aa are supposed to be the correct modern forms, Ø and Å seem to be employed more frequently, and are therefore used consistently here. But be prepared to see words spelled in either form. Æ, Ö, Ø, Å and Aa always occur after Z in alphabetical listings.

Norway   Map N-1

Oslo   N-2

For elegance of design, nothing can compare with the Viking ships at the **Vikingskiphuset** (on the Bygdøy peninsula, west of Oslo centre, at Huk Aveny 35).

N-2a Less mythic, and more mystic, is the **Vigelandsanlegget** (Vigeland sculpture garden) in Frognerparken. While Oslo's most unusual designed environment is not in the same class as Stockholm's Millesgården (S-21), it is at least a monument to the persuasiveness of Gustav Vigeland, who talked the city of Oslo into financing his entire life's work. This huge axial composition centres on an Art Nouveau fountain (originally intended for an altogether different setting) and incorporates a sculpture-encrusted bridge, a monumental stele, several sets of wrought-iron gates, acres of mosaic paving and various other freestanding sculptures.

Vigeland's adjacent studio building

Oslo   N-3
* Rådhuset (city hall) 1917–50
Fridtjof Nansens plass (entrance)
Arnstein Arneberg & Magnus Poulsson
Monumental Moderne
Near the inner harbour
[Check tourist office for times when interior is open to public.]

Here is a full-blown example of the Scandinavian enthusiasm for large and lavish town halls, one so long in construction that it clearly records the changes in theory and taste which occurred during its gestation. In spirit, and particularly in its carefully balanced asymmetrical details, it evokes the anomalous idea of an avant-garde Beaux-Arts (of about 1930). Its plan and massing are symmetrical but, unlike traditional Beaux-Arts compositions, they do not build up around the main axis. On the contrary, its otherwise entirely brick front façade is neatly, and rather manneristically, split down the middle by a vertical band of stone.

The interior, much of which is covered with murals and other decorative work, is later and slightly less formal in feeling.

shows traces of Perret influence. *W from Oslo ctr on Drammensveien / R on Halvdan Svartes Gate / park is on L, studio on R*

N-2b Of minor architectural historical interest is the work of Henrik Bull. His Richardsonian Romanesque buildings, completed thirty years after Richardson, carry some competent Jugendstil and National Romantic details. Most notable is the **Historisk museum,** 1897–1902, at Frederiks gate 2 (at Kristian IV's gate) and:

N-2c The **Regjeringsbygningen,** 1898–1906, the only built wing of a never-completed government office building at Akersgata 42 – at Apotekergata.

N-2d The **US Embassy,** 1958, at Drammensveien 18, is one of Eero Saarinen's less than successful diplomatic efforts (see also GB-6c). *On S side of Drammensveien opposite W end of Slottsparken*

Oslo   **N-4**
Sjøfartsbygningen (office building)
1916–18
Kirkegata 7 and Rådhusgata
Ingvar Olsen Hjørth
National Romantic
Eight blks E of Rådhuset (N-3) on L

Because its spare but sophisticated veneer of motifs drawn from Scandinavia's 'Folk Baroque' tradition reflects the prosperity Norway experienced as a neutral country during the First World War, Norwegians refer to this sort of architecture as 'War Baroque'. The lobbies, redecorated in the 30s, are low-key Art Deco.

N-4a At the east end of Rådhusgata is Bredo Berntsen's **Haven Lager**, 1916–20, a customs warehouse of the same period built entirely of concrete.

Oslo   **N-5**
Samfunnshuset (political social centre)
1940
Arbeidersamfunnets plass 1
Ove Bang
International Style
N from Domkirke (cathedral) on Torggata abt five blks / on R

A complicated building by one of Norway's best prewar modernists, it contains a large auditorium, a cinema and smaller meeting rooms, all hidden behind a unifying veneer of offices. Some interior finishes have recently been changed from those of a low-budget International Style aesthetic (e.g. linoleum) to others now apparently deemed more befitting the self-image of a prosperous workers' association (e.g. marble!).

Oslo   N-6
St Hallvard kirke (church and
monastery) 1958–66
Enerhauggata 4
Kjell Lund & Nils Slaatto
Brutalism
*NE from Domkirke on Storgata / angle R on
Brugata ⇨ Grønlandsleiret / L on
Tøyengata / R on Heimdalsgata / R on
Enerhauggata / on L*
  [Locked.]

Sitting atop a hill in a redevelopment
area, this deceptive square brick building
contains a round concrete church.
Although it owes much to the latter-day Le
Corbusier, this is no mere stylistic copy. By
local standards it is well thought out and
quite sophisticated.

While the monks might disagree, the
shape of the church itself – particularly its
downward swelling roof – seems almost
sensuous.

Oslo/Ullernasen   N-7
* Terrassehus (terraced flats) 1964
Anne-Tine & Mogens Friis
Øvre Ullern terrasse 45
Vernacularized International Style
*W from Oslo ctr on E18 ⇨
Drammensveien / exit at* BOGSTAD
CAMPING */ L on Vækerøveien R on
Ullernchausséen / L on Bærumsveien / R
on Hoffsjef Løvenskiolds vei (see N-7a
below) / R on Øvre Ullern terrasse / at end
of rd*
  Although they may not measure up to

similar groupings elsewhere (CH-21), these
six terraces containing fifty-four flats are
well sited in a beautifully wooded ravine
and present a positive image of a humane
yet highly technical modern architecture.
But there's a catch. The terraces, which are
as many as twelve levels high, provide no
direct horizontal access to most of the apartments. Some residents must climb as many
as six flights of stairs!

N-7a There is a **house by Ove Bang**,
1937 at Hoffsjef Løvenskiolds vei 32.

THE NETHERLANDS

Netherlands
Map NL-1

51c
▲ 21
Bergen
▲ 51
Dronten
Haarlem
22 ▲   51b
▲ 2-20
Amsterdam   Drienerloo
23 ▲   55 ▲
24 ▲   ▲ Hilversum   Apeldoorn
48-50   ▲ 54
25-34
▲ The Hague   ▲ 44-47
35 ▲ (Den Haag)   Utrecht
▲ 36-43   52-53
Rotterdam   ▲ De Hoge Veluwe

NL
THE NETHERLANDS   ▲
                        D-38   D
                               GERMANY

                                    D-39a,b
                               ●   D-39
Helmond   ■
■ 56   ▲ D-41
57 ■   ● D-17a,40c
Eindhoven   ▲   ▲
                        D-45   D-40
B-16-17 ▲ Antwerp   ▲ D-42-44
(Antwerpen)   ▲   ▲
B   D-47   Düsseldorf
BELGIUM
B-2-15   D-48-49 ▲   ▲ D-50
Brussels   58-59 ▲   Cologne
(Bruxelles)   Heerlen   (Köln)
                    ■ D-46

The Netherlands/Holland (Nederland)   NL-1

Holland is a small country, yet in the first third of this century it made major contributions to the development of modern architecture, while in general the quality of its ordinary architecture and town planning was, and still remains, the most consistent and humane in Europe.

This did not come about by chance. It is the result of Holland's particular history, geography, and demography. By the seventeenth century their natural resources had made the Netherlands rich and had fostered the development of Europe's first dominant middle class.

Nineteenth-century Holland saw little architectural innovation, although it did eventually produce some interesting examples of Gothic Rationalism (NL-3a), as well as a few, mostly unbuilt, designs that suggest that Henry Hobson Richardson's work had been seen and appreciated. In the 90s there were also some echoes of the Art Nouveau that was then sweeping neighbouring Belgium. But, curiously, it never really caught on with the Dutch.

Only with the turn of the century did a number of new attitudes begin to emerge. Most apparent among these was a different kind of Rationalism: hard, clean, sculptural, geometric and expressive of building construction (NL-3, 10). It made H. P. Berlage not only Holland's leading architect, but also her first modern architect of international repute. In part this Rationalist architecture also appeared strikingly new because it reflected the interest that most of the younger Dutch architects, and, less obviously, many Symbolist painters, such as Thorn Prikker and Jan Toorop, had in 'magic numbers' and in regulating lines and other systems of proportion. Many of these esoteric concerns stemmed from Theosophy, a late-nineteenth-century mystical religion-cum-philosophy which became remarkably influential in certain Dutch intellectual circles – with repercussions that were, and indeed still are, felt throughout Western architecture.

At this time Holland also experienced a somewhat belated flowering of the Arts and Crafts Movement. But rather than harking back to the Middle Ages, as had William Morris, there developed a strong interest in the architecture and textile designs of Holland's Indonesian colonies. This sense of identification with distant colonies eventually contributed to the fantastic, seemingly un-Dutch imagery of the Amsterdam School and perhaps, to an extent, to the development of German Expressionism as well. Perhaps its 'artistic', i.e. not wholly architectural, background caused the Amsterdam School to develop so unevenly. From start to finish it did not produce a single important interior space, nor a building plan or site plan of real significance. Although by European standards the Amsterdam School seems not to have been over-dependent on polemics, mottoes and manifestos, one of its more memorable, if less auspicious slogans was, 'Public, I despise you!'; this despite the remarkable circumstances of civil patronage under which it flourished (NL-11). It is not too surprising then that the school, at least in its most picturesque form, barely survived the death of its leader Michel de Klerk in 1923.

The last important external influence on the development of modern Dutch architecture was the work of Frank Lloyd Wright. The sheltering quality of his buildings, their diminutive sense of scale and the geometry with which they are suffused all seemed to strike particularly responsive chords in Holland. His work was apparently first seen by several prominent Dutch architects in a publication of 1900. Thus when William Gray Purcell, a Prairie School architect from Chicago was in Holland some six years later, he found Berlage already well acquainted with Wright's work. (Wright's later widespread exposure was due to the simultaneous exhibition and publication of his work in Berlin in 1910–11 by Wasmuth, the leading German architectural publisher.) Berlage finally visited America in 1911. Although personally more impressed by the works of Richardson and Louis Sullivan, he brought back and disseminated widely a favourable opinion of the Wrightian Prairie School architecture. By 1916 Robert van't Hoff, who worked briefly for Wright in America, was building a Prairie School house in Holland at Huis ter Heide (NL-46a).

During the First World War, neutral Holland remained isolated from the devastation and subsequent social upheaval of the war, but not from its horrors, which the Dutch may have seen more objectively than could the combatants. In this climate the influence of Wright's work combined in various ways with other current trends to help nurture both the hard abstract aesthetic of De Stijl (NL-46) and the soft romanticism of the fully ripened Amsterdam School.

It is worth noting that the only major pre-First World War example of direct Wrightian influence in Europe outside Holland was Walter Gropius and Adolf Meyer's model factory for the 1914 Werkbund Exhibition in Germany. Meyer was a student of J. L. M. Lauweriks (D-40), a particularly mystical Dutch architect who had visited the US in 1909.

During the first decades after the Second World War, Dutch architecture included few works of a power, poetry or significance comparable to that of prewar Dutch architecture. Competent architecture of the period is to be seen throughout the country, but gone or muted, with a few exceptions, are the fascinating outbursts of ego and polemic, or even the arty enthusiasms. And there is little satisfaction to be had from later developments: from the meaningless symmetry and geometry (NL-24), smirking pop coyness (NL-55b), frenetic romanticism (NL-56), structural overelaboration (NL-54), and, God help us, architectonic metaphysics (NL-34).

Language note The simple grammar of written Dutch – if not the pronunciation of the spoken language – make it perhaps the easiest Germanic language to puzzle one's way through. One difficulty that may be encountered is with the use of 'ij' or IJ, the Dutch equivalent of the English 'y', whose place it takes in alphabetical listings. Thus *style* in English is *stijl* in Dutch. However, on signs and other special typographical situations, 'ij' is often found looking like 'ij'. Occasionally in proper names, or when written by or for the benefit of foreigners, it will appear as 'y'.

Amsterdam   NL-2

Amsterdam is not just tree-shaded canals reflecting glistening rows of Northern Baroque gables. It personifies the Dutch sense of continuity and harmony: conservative, but never reactionary. Amsterdam is the embodiment of an attitude of mind that has developed through centuries of struggle to control the Dutch landscape and to keep it from the North Sea – a contest in which there has been little room for error or impulse.

Another constant threat is the car. As is true everywhere in Holland, Amsterdam tries to encourage the use of bicycles. It also has an excellent tram system and has even built a sub-sea-level subway. The campaign to limit cars has been effective, but parking within the old city probably ought to be banned altogether. Like Venice, old Amsterdam was designed for water transport. Wheeled vehicles which try to drive, make deliveries or park alongside the canals are, in effect, appropriating the pavements of Amsterdam's watery boulevards.

Amsterdam is also a city whose old core

developed concentrically and organically – pearl-like within successive layers of bulwarks. Outside De Singelgracht, the last old defence line, nineteenth-century Amsterdam grew in a regulated but unimaginative manner. However, because transport and building techniques had not radically changed, it kept much the same scale and density it had had before. With the new century that pattern was bound to change. The extension of tram lines, which transformed adjacent villages into commuter suburbs, simply added to the impetus of the Garden City Movement and other reform groups who were advocating new, lower-density living patterns. And in 1900, before things got seriously out of hand, the Dutch Parliament passed a law allowing Amsterdam and other cities to buy up all their surrounding buildable land. Since that time, following a series of masterplans and other more detailed schemes that are constantly being updated, Holland's cities have leased out development land in large plots to housing cooperatives, workers' associations and entrepreneurs. That is why the newer parts of Amsterdam exhibit neither the philistine indifference nor the rare strokes of brilliance that accompany less well-regulated speculative development. Nor, at least in the case of those areas built before the Second World War, do they sink to the depths of technocratic mediocrity – well-meaning or otherwise – typical of so much municipal housing.

NL-2a H. P. Berlage's **Amsterdam Zuid** (Amsterdam South), 1915, is one of the first and most famous of Amsterdam's suburban development areas – if only because of the

Amsterdam   **NL-3**
*** De Beurs (stock, grain and commodities exchanges) 1897–1903
Damrak and Beursplein
H. P. Berlage, tile murals by Jan Toorop, wood-carvings by Mendes da Costa
Rationalism
Map NL-2
[The former grain exchange now serves, with the addition of low-suspended lighting fixtures, as an exhibition space.]
   More than that of any other country, modern Dutch architecture can be said to have stemmed from the precepts of one man, Hendrik Petrus Berlage, as embodied in this one building. There had been the earlier work of P. J. H. Cuypers (NL-3a), and both Berlage and Cuypers owed much to Viollet-le-Duc's Gothic Rationalism. But Cuypers looked to the great French theorist's Gothicism, while Berlage emphasized his Rationalism. The Beurs in its turn gave rise to two separate Dutch schools, radically differing in philosophy and style.
   The Amsterdam School was the earlier of these to flower and the first to fade. It drew its inspiration from the almost mystical spirit that subtly pervades the Beurs, becoming explicit in only a few bits of ornament, and in the building's organic sensitivity to materials, especially to brick. It also gained from Berlage the notion that there could be an architectural language

Amsterdam School architecture to be found within it (NL-11, 12, 13, 14). However, Berlage built nothing there himself.

NL-2b Two much smaller developments from the 20s are **Betondorp** (literally, concrete village), a garden city, 1922, by D. Greiner, J. B. van Loghem *et al. E on Vrijheidslaan (Map NL-2→)* ⇨ *Gooiseweg, abt 1½ mi (2.5 km) / L on Rozenburglaan / first R / first R on Duivendrechtselaan* ⇨ *Onderlangs / on L, abt three blks deep, for entire length of st),* and:

NL-2c A **housing area,** 1921–5, at Purmerweg and Purmerplein in Nieuwendam, by B. T. Boeyinga, *et al. N through IJ-Tunnel (Map NL-2→) / exit E →* NIEUWENDAM *on Purmerweg / beginning about ½ mi (1 km) on both sides of st*

NL-2d Outstanding among postwar developments is Van den Broek & Bakema's **Amstelveen shopping centre,** 1961, which is far more successful than their famous Lijnbaan (NL-42). Amstelveen is, indeed, one of Holland's first acceptable postwar examples of ordered urban growth. *S on Amstelveenseweg (Map NL-2→) / abt 2½ mi (4 km) on L*

NL-2e Holland was the first non-Scandinavian country to establish an architecture museum, the **Stichting Architectuurmuseum,** and also – curiously as a separate institution – a national architectural archive, the **Nederlandse Documentatie Centrum voor de Bouwkunst,** both in Amsterdam at Droogbak 1A.

dependent solely upon the embellishment and articulation of volume and surface, rather than on the massive application of conventional ornament.
   On the other hand, the Dutch Functionalists, drew upon the integrity of the Beurs – its sense of wholeness and continuity – and upon Berlage's Rationalism: the honest, logical expression of structure, mechanical services and function. These are qualities most particularly to be found inside the building: in the structural expressiveness of its load-bearing brick masonry and of the iron trusses spanning its great exchange spaces; in the bevelled and quoined glazed surfaces of its brick walls (wherever they are in contact with people); and in the forthright handling of its mechanical services, be

they the exposed and delightfully decorated drainpipes or the electrical conduit trenches covered by removable iron plates, which are visibly, and in a sense ornamentally, incorporated into the corridor floors.

Amsterdam **NL-4**
* **Het Scheepvaarthuis** (shipping company offices) 1911–16
Prins Hendrikkade and Binnenkant
J. M. van der Meij, with Michel de Klerk & P. L. Kramer
Extended by Van der Meij 1926–8
Amsterdam School (Expressionism)
Map NL-2

Economically, the nineteenth century had not been good to the Dutch. With the new century the situation changed so markedly that Holland's shipowners were able to celebrate better times by building the Scheepvaarthuis – a judicious bit of conspicuous consumption. Their architect Van der Meij was a relatively young man with a passion for the expressive possibilities of brickwork. Among the other artists and architects also brought into the project were the even younger P. L. Kramer and Michel de Klerk, who were responsible respectively for the building's interiors and its incredibly tortuous ironwork.

Unlike the socialist Berlage, these men firmly believed in art for art's sake. They also believed in not letting the client have too much to say in the design. The shipowners obligingly gave their young architects a liberal budget, at least until the war began, and allowed them to indulge in some oriental fantasies, which, although possibly appropriate to the shipping business, had been developing for some time under the

NL-3a P. J. H. Cuypers's largest and most influential building – in effect the most clearly identifiable ancestor of the Beurs – is the **Rijksmuseum,** 1877–85, at Stadhouderskade 42.

influence of Symbolist artists such as the Indonesian-born Jan Toorop.

For their money and forebearance the shipowners got a remarkably original building. If the Scheepvaarthuis shows hints of Art Nouveau and, perversely, of Berlagian Rationality, its jutting angularity even more clearly foreshadows aspects of the Expressionism that was to develop in postwar Germany, where a major Dutch building can hardly have been unknown. Under the leadership of De Klerk and Kramer the Amsterdam School, Holland's unique form of Expressionism, would soon become more smugly sensuous, if also more comprehensible. But here is where its forms and images began to coalesce.

Amsterdam **NL-5**
** **Eigen Haard** (housing, post office and school) 1913–19
Zaanstraat, Oostzaanstraat, Hembrugstraat
Michel de Klerk
Amsterdam School (Expressionism)
NW on Zaanstraat (Map NL-2 →) abt three blks / on R

As the Scheepvaarthuis (NL-4) was the Amsterdam School's first creation, so Eigen Haard was one of the most extreme examples of the school's voluptuous

maturity. Perhaps being the first of its kind, and also De Klerk's personal 'manifesto', explains certain inconsistencies – such as between the lyric grace of its 'village' steeple and the almost demonic vigour of the little post office attached. Yet, despite its undoubted originality and De Klerk's general control of its design, ultimately Eigen Haard is but one more example of the school's façade architecture – brilliantly delightful, but perfectly willing to sacrifice all else for superficially picturesque ends.

Amsterdam   **NL-6**
* De Telegraaf (newspaper offices and printing plant) 1928–30
Nieuwezijds Voorburgwal 225
J. F. Staal
Late Amsterdam School (Expressionism)
Map NL-2

Early in his career Staal could best be identified with the Amsterdam School. But his later, mature work is more notable for its refined assurance than for its consistency, ranging as it does from a kind of cubist Amsterdam School style (NL-23) to a remarkable absence of 'style' (NL-14). Staal was, it seems, almost too responsive to both programmatic considerations and, more significantly, to the widely differing contexts in which he built.

Here, despite De Telegraaf's much larger size, its crisp restraint fits well among Amsterdam's elegant, urbane older buildings. Like the best of these, its façade is basically a simple brick grid with large multi-paned windows – although these are partly set before the wall in a rather Scandinavian manner. Also in the best Dutch tradition, Staal's few ornamental flourishes are limited in scope and size. One of these, the tower's elaborate illuminated pinnacle, was intended, like the entrance gate below, to serve both as an embellishment and as an advertising-identification symbol. It spells

out 'De Telegraaf', but at a scale too discreet to be legible.

This tower, whose form is another romantic echo of Scandinavia, also houses a large goods lift. Its oblique orientation, although self-consciously picturesque, is not wholly capricious, reflecting as it does the diagonal building-lot alignments that prevail in this part of Amsterdam.

Amsterdam   **NL-7**
* Cineac (newsreel cinema) 1934–6
Reguliersbreestraat 31
J. Duiker
Constructivist International Style
Map NL-2

[Since the photograph was taken, the dramatic original sign has been demolished and the glazed entrance covered over. The free-standing cylindrical box office is apropos, but not original.]

It is fitted to its awkward site with a skill that can only be appreciated from drawings, while its interior is nicely evocative of its times – in a clean-lined if not exciting way. But seen from the street (despite its size, one of Amsterdam's busiest), this now sadly mutilated little cinema was once was the most spectacular European anticipation of the American Post-Modern architecture of the late 60s. In the manner of Robert Venturi or Charles Moore, it was an aggressive, intriguingly ambiguous montage of witty architectural conceits blended with explicit and symbolic messages about the newsreels which were once to be seen within. It incorporated an assemblage of neon signs, a part of the original design, twice its own height. Projecting over its rounded entrance, the upper half of its carved-out cubic form remains an abstract, monumental street-scale 'cornice'. And beneath that, the public

street space is drawn into the theatre by an enticing, glistening, bright glass-enclosed projection booth which dramatically displays the 'technical wonder' of the cinema.

NL-7a By way of extreme contrast, across the street is one of Europe's best-preserved examples of the more atypical exotic school of movie palace design, H. L. de Jong's **Tuschinski Cinema**, 1918–20.

Amsterdam **NL-8**
Het Studentenhuis (shops, student
dormitories and apartments) 1958–66
Weesperstraat 7–57
Herman Hertzberger
Brutalism
Map NL-2

[The Dutch are remarkably tolerant of
disorder on the part of their offspring. Hertzberger is even said to be pleased with the
graffiti and posters beneath which parts of
his effort here have from time to time
entirely disappeared.]

If, by Dutch standards, this is a large
building, particularly given its location in
Amsterdam's old centre, it is also a sensitive
urban element that serves well as a bridge
between the scale of the old town and that
of the widened boulevard on to which it
principally faces. Even its Brutalist use of
materials is not accompanied by the sculp-

tural manipulations that are so commonly
a part of that genre. The seemingly omitted,
set-back fourth floor (the play area and
access balcony for the apartments above) is
also a response to the height of older,
smaller neighbours.

Amsterdam **NL-9**
* **Het Hubertushuis** (house for single
mothers) 1973–81
Plantage Middenlaan 33
Aldo van Eyck
Map NL-2

[Hubertushuis is not open to the public.
However, there is an excellent little book
on it, including a section by Addie van
Roijen-Wortmann, the client, published by
the Stichting Wonen in Amsterdam.]

Van Eyck is a curious figure. Although
British- and Swiss-educated, his sense of
detail has always seemed quintessentially
Dutch. As a leading member of Team X, the
group which sounded the death knell of
the old CIAM orthodoxy, he is typically
accounted a key personality in the history
of postwar architecture. Yet before the
Hubertushuis he could only be credited
with one major work, Amsterdam's
municipal orphanage (NL-19) – another
very child-centred, sheltering, private
building. Interestingly, like so many
important works of architecture, both
buildings had very strong clients. In most
respects, however, they are radically different. Where the orphanage is free-standing

on a large open site, solid, introverted,
subdued and systematically tectonic, the
Hubertushuis is deliberately urban, inter-
woven with two old adjacent buildings,
consciously transparent, brightly coloured,
and, at times, almost *ad hoc* in its detailing.
If the Van Eyck of the orphanage can be
thought of as an architect's architect, then
this Van Eyck is more an artist's architect.
Here, everything is more spontaneous, less
concerned with rules and principles than
with the joy of creation. Only one thing
remains the same – no visitors, please.

Amsterdam **NL-10**
** **American Hotel and Café**
1898–1901
Leidseplein 28 and Marnixstraat
Willem Kromhout
Rationalism/Jugendstil
Map NL-2

[The interiors of the hotel – but fortunately not that of the café – have been
redecorated beyond recognition. There is a
sympathetic Amsterdam School addition by
G. J. Rutgers, 1928, facing the canal.]

Amsterdam's two major *fin-de-siècle*
monuments both mark the pinnacles of
their creators' careers. But whereas
Berlage, the architect of the Beurs (NL-3),
is also remembered for his many other
buildings and writings, this is in effect
Kromhout's sole legacy. Although he continued to practice for some years, Kromhout built little else of significance and that,
having been in Rotterdam, is now mostly
lost. It is, then, not quite so surprising that

the American Hotel is far less well known
that it deserves to be.

The key to understanding this very tectonic building lies in its loadbearing-wall

structure, whose articulation in response to programmatic requirements combines an almost Richardsonian vigour with a Viol-let-le-Duc-inspired agility. However, its ornament and original decor, where not specifically Dutch, show more than a trace of Anglo-Viennese influence – as derived, perhaps, from the English Arts and Crafts magazine *The Studio*. This spirit is best

sampled in the café, which, despite its true provenance, seems to evoke the mood of a progressive pre-First World War Viennese coffee house. Lingering here over coffee and a newspaper, one almost believes that the arrival of a customer in full period regalia, either civil or military, would cause not the slightest stir – least of all among the staff.

Amsterdam   NL-11
Volkswoningbouw (social housing)
1921–2
Vrijheidslaan and Kromme-Mijdrechtstraat
Michel de Klerk
Amsterdam School (Expressionism)
Map NL-2
[Most of these façades have been subtly changed to increase interior light. Win-dowsills were lowered and balcony rails cut down. Only the windows of the little pepper-pot bays remain at their original height. But they too have lost the narrow horizontal 'ladder window' mullions so characteristic of the Amsterdam School.]

After the First World War, Amsterdam established a 'Committee for the Design and *Outward Appearance* of Buildings'. It was intended to assure the harmony and urbanity of Berlage's newly planned Amsterdam Zuid (NL-2a) by coordinating and guiding the work of the speculators, cooperatives and building societies then developing the area. It was a situation almost without parallel. The committee actually cared. And it attempted to fulfil the second half of its charge by distributing the responsibility for the 'outward appear-ance' of these buildings among the best of the Amsterdam School. Often, as is the case here, these architects merely put the proverbial 'Queen Anne front' on some decidedly 'Mary Ann' behinds. Even the fees for such work seem not to have been calculated in the usual manner, as a percentage of the construction cost, but rather per metre of façade length – pre-sumably in tacit recognition that the actual buildings and floor plans were designed by the contractor or developer.

It was an unusual arrangement, but not unprecedented – one need only remember Haussmann's Paris (F-5) – and it undoubt-edly benefited Amsterdam. That the lack of concern for the dwelling spaces behind their façades seems not to have over-strained the social consciences of Amster-

dam School architects may suggest why nothing the equal of Rotterdam's Spangen housing (NL-37) was built here.

NL-11a The housing just to the north and east on Holendrechtstraat, 1921, by M. Staal-Kropholler, demonstrates that, even before De Klerk's death, and even in the hands of one of its better practitioners, the Amsterdam School almost immediately began to lose its initial punch (NL-5).

NL-11b One of the last (1927) most sim-plified examples of the Amsterdam School's **linear-façade architecture** is the stretch of Hoofdweg north of the Mer-catorplein designed by H. T. Wijdeveld. Wijdeveld was the editor of *Wendingen*, a journal devoted to the school and also one of its greatest artistic triumphs. Ironically, *Wendingen*'s special 1925 issue on the work of Frank Lloyd Wright was instrumental in establishing and disseminating the Wrightian vocabulary that rapidly sup-planted that of the Amsterdam School.

Amsterdam   NL-12
* **De Dageraad** (housing) 1920–1
Henriëtte Ronnerplein and Thérèse Schwartzeplein

Michel de Klerk
Amsterdam School (Expressionism)
Map NL-2
[These two identical squares are sym-

metrically disposed about P. L. Takstraat (NL-13). The backs of the blocks can be seen from the yards of the pair of identical schools on that street.]

Despite their faint resemblance to rows

Amsterdam   **NL-13**
De Dageraad (housing) 1921–3
P. L. Takstraat and Burgemeester Tellegenstraat
P. L. Kramer, with Michel de Klerk
Amsterdam School (Expressionism)
Map NL-2

After De Klerk, Kramer was the Amsterdam School's other, perhaps more progressive, driving force. De Klerk was at his best in unorthodox, collage-like juxtapositions, patterns and uses of conventional materials, which were often incorporated into strangely traditional, almost archaic contexts (NL-5, 12). Kramer, on the other hand, typically used his equally prosaic materials in a much simpler, more straightforward manner to produce some remarkably unconventional sculpture-like architecture.

However, if Kramer's work was less impractical than De Klerk's, it was no more socially concerned. And that is a problem with the Amsterdam School – as compared, for instance, with Germany's more utopian-idealistic, if often unbuilt, brand of Expressionism. Most of the School's buildings might as well have been as solid and lifeless as the little blocks of plasticine in

Amsterdam   **NL-14**
Hoogbouwflat (apartment tower) 1929–32
Victorieplein 45–47
J. F. Staal
Map NL-2

When Berlage laid out Amsterdam Zuid (NL-2a) in 1915 he treated the district as an extension of the existing fabric, and not as either a garden suburb or the sort of intensely urban sub-centre which might dilute Amsterdam's characteristic monocentricity. Victorieplein was the closest to a traditional large-scale urban space that Berlage was willing to allow in the eastern, earlier part of this new district. As the focus of Victorieplein Staal's tower is, in effect, a consciously non-monumental, non-symbolic urban place-marker. And it is Amsterdam Zuid's only tall building.

Given its role, and the district's close identification with the Amsterdam School (NL-11, 12, 13), not to mention Staal's previous Amsterdam School connections (NL-19b–d), one might have expected something more Expressionist here. However, the area developed slowly. When Staal came to build his tower, De Klerk and the Amsterdam School were both some years dead, while the later Dutch romanticisms of the 30s and 40s (imported from Sweden or dredged up from the past) were

of outsize jam pots, these surrealistically scaled pseudo-suburban villas, and the squares they dominate, are De Klerk's most convincingly workable urban design.

which its adherents modelled their often brilliant façade designs.

NL-13a Shortly after finishing De Dageraad, Kramer became Amsterdam's semi-official 'bridge architect'. In that role he was responsible for designing the city's many Amsterdam School bridges, including that spanning the nearby Amstel canal where it joins the Amstel river.

yet to develop. So just this once Staal achieved a pure, classically restrained solution: a building so free of stylistic references that it could quite plausibly have been built a quarter of a century later. One suspects that Berlage, who had no great enthusiasm for the Amsterdam School, must have been pleased to have so unaffected a focus for his greatest urban scheme.

Amsterdam   **NL-15**
Atelierwoningen (studio
apartments) 1934
Zomerdijkstraat
P. Zandstra, J. H. L. Giesen & L. K. Sijmons
International Style
Map NL-2

The tight, slickly smooth, less articulated and decidedly more arty International Style of Le Corbusier or the Bauhaus remained essentially foreign to Holland, where a much tougher home-grown variant developed, especially in and around Rotterdam (NL-38, 39, 40). It is strangely reasonable, then, that one of the few Dutch buildings to resemble the more typical International Style is to be found in the home of the Amsterdam School, not in Rotterdam – even if, being in Amsterdam, it is characteristically clad in brick and not white stucco. What is most surprising, though, is its assurance and, after almost half a century, how fresh it remains.

Amsterdam   **NL-16**
* Openluchtschool (open-air school)
1929–30
Cliostraat 40
J. Duiker
International Style
Map NL-2

[The gatehouse was built a few years later. The mullions are thicker replacements of the originals.]

One of the most remarkable aspects of Duiker's work is the freshness of vision he brought to each new project, even though his form language is seemingly consistent. Here he took his cue from the emphasis that the open-air movement gave to fresh air and sunshine (DK-11, F-44). He minimized his building to an extent that had previously only been suggested by the most radical and theoretical of projects, such as Mies van der Rohe's 1922 proposal for a concrete office building.

Using the simplest sort of exposed concrete skeleton, which barely recognizes the existence of its encompassing glass curtain wall, Duiker built the school as a transparent tower pavilion. Then, taking advantage of the site's solar orientation, he set the pavilion at a forty-five-degree angle to

the gatehouse, thereby presenting it in the most transparent way possible – as compared to a normal orientation wherein the intervening full width of the ceilings would have left much less sky visible through the glass. In his quest for transparency, Duiker even turned the stair/hall core at a 45° angle within the tower, further decreasing the building's apparent solidity and incidentally improving the classroom layouts.

The result of all this careful, tidy manipulation is a construction of consummate elegance, marred only by the ground-floor wing which, as is often true of appendages to otherwise flawless pavilions, seems an awkward afterthought.

Amsterdam   **NL-17**
Montessorischool 1934
Anthonie van Dijckstraat
W. van Tijen, with Mart Stam and
Lotte Besse
International Style
Map NL-2

Both Van Tijen and Stam were masters of a highly technical, albeit still humane architecture, as this light, airy school clearly demonstrates. But rarely had they the need or the opportunity to design with such expediency as here on this tight urban site. This school has an almost romantic quality reminiscent of some of the better Scandinavian work of the time. Yet while the then emerging Scandinavian Empiricism, even at its best, is self-consciously arty and 'of its period', this matter-of-fact building is remarkably timeless.

NL-17a The adjacent **row of five houses**, 1935–6, at 4–12 Anthonie van Dijckstraat is by the same team of architects, although here it is Stam who is usually credited with the actual design.

Amsterdam   **NL-18**

* Nationaal
Luchtvaartlaboratorium
(aeronautical laboratories) 1937–46
Fokkerweg
Van Tijen & Maaskant
Scandinavian Empiricism
Map NL-2

Of all the countries that succumbed to the romantic reaction of the troubled years before and after the Second World War, few gave up as much and gained so little in return as did Holland.

Here is an exception: a rare example of interesting, original Dutch architecture of the period. But even it is suffused with the somewhat clumsy, vernacular-like forms and details of Scandinavian Empiricism, another romantic Nordic import. Curiously, the best such buildings here are often, as in this case, not the work of an Expressionistic native of Amsterdam, but rather of a formerly strict Functionalist like Van Tijen.

Amsterdam   **NL-19**

* Burgerweeshuis (municipal children's home) 1958–60
Amstelveenseweg and IJsbaanpad
Aldo van Eyck
Map NL-2

[The building is closed to the public.]

For someone who has seen Burgerweeshuis only from the outside, it may be difficult to understand the following that Van Eyck and this building – for a decade his only major independent work – once had among American architectural students. Nor did the influences all flow one way. Reminders of the work of Louis Kahn and of the then-current New Haven architectural establishment abound here. There are 'punched out' windows, industrial vernacular materials, and an exposed structure assembled from pre-cast concrete elements, including even perforated beams resembling Kahn's much-favoured Vierendeel roof trusses.

This modular constructional system, indeed the building's entire organization, reflects Van Eyck's attempt to create a technically updated, more open version of the

traditional Islamic cellular adobe construction. All of this gives Burgerweeshuis, with its hundreds of square concrete domes, a curiously picturesque ascetic rationality – at least as seen on paper or from above, and as experienced from within. But the choice of so exotic and introverted a prototype here may be quite appropriate. Islamic architecture is meant to give not just physical shelter from the heat and sun, but also social shelter within a culture which makes so marked a distinction between space that is aggressively public and space that is all but inviolably private. So too Van Eyck would argue that his primary concern was to offer psychological shelter to the children – mostly here as a result of various domestic difficulties – whose home this temporarily becomes.

NL-19a Diagonally across the intersection is Gerrit Rietveld's last major work, the **Rietveldacademie**, an art academy, 1965. Its neatly detailed glass walls exhibit a very different attitude towards the nature of architecture in a North-Sea climate.

Amsterdam **NL-20**
De Drie Hoven (housing and care centre
for the elderly) 1967–75
L. Bouwmeesterstraat and L. Chrispijnstraat
Herman Hertzberger
Rationalism
W on Schipluidenlaan (Map NL-2→) ⇨
Pieter Calandlaan / on L at L.
Bouwmeesterstr

Despite the common, but misleading, use
of the word 'Functionalist' to describe International Style modernism, one of the most
telling charges made against modern architecture is that it usually creates boring,
anonymous, interchangeable boxes which
do not in fact reflect the functions they
house. Dutch architects have been particularly sensitive to this problem (but see
also B-14, GB-76). Over the past two
decades some of them have developed
design techniques using interchangeable
modular elements, which allow a building's
initial group of occupants to help determine
the organization of its façades and plans.
Thus, presumably, the building truly
reflects the needs and desires of its first
occupants – if not necessarily of subsequent
ones. (It is also arguable that such methods
are no more than a 'scientific' way of producing picturesque variety.)

Hertzberger's work, and particularly Drie
Hoven, represents another way of attempting to deal with the same problem, while
maintaining a simple but rigorously systematic approach to materials and detailing. Here, despite his typically assertive
geometry and tough-minded prefabricated
components, he attempts to modulate
different parts of the building better to fit its
programmatic needs. He does this by using
variations of certain components –
especially three different lengths of pre-cast
beams and a modular wood and glass infill
wall panel system. In other smaller ways,
such as the addition of lower glass panels
to permit views from wheelchair height,
he also responds to the special physical
requirements of Drie Hoven's occupants.
Similarly he attempts to meet their psychological needs through the shaping of spaces
that permit both privacy and community,
and by providing opportunities to 'take pos-
session' of the building's spaces with mementos, plants, etc. But was it really
necessary to be quite so tough, and so
colourless?

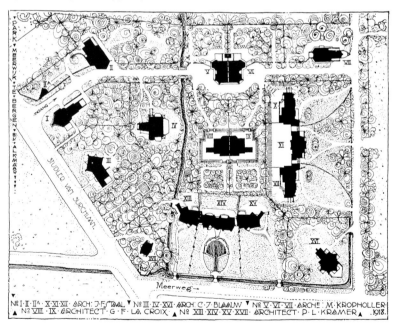

Nᴼ I·II·IIᴬ·X·XI·XII· ARCH: J·F/ TAAL ▼ Nᴼ III· IV·XVI· ARCH: C·7· BLAAUW ▼ Nᴼ V·VI·VII·ARCHᴱ· M·KROPHOLLER·
▲ Nᴼ VIII· IX· ARCHITECT· G·F· LA CROIX ▲ Nᴼ XIII·XIV·XV· XVII· ARCHITECT· P·L· KRAMER ▲ .1918.

Bergen [near Alkmaar] **NL-21**
** Park Meerwijk (houses)
Studler van Surchlaan
NL-21a Tuinhuisje (XVII),
P.L. Kramer, 1915–16
NL-21b Zofar, Elifaz, and **Boldad**
(X, XI, XII), J.F. Staal, 1916–18
NL-21c De Ark (II), J.F. Staal, 1916–
18. Perhaps the best individual house to
come from the Amsterdam School.

NL-21d De Bark (I), J.F. Staal,
1916–18
NL-21e Meerhoek (XVI), J.C. Blaauw,
1916–18
NL-21f Borschkant (III), J.C. Blaauw,
1916–18
NL-21g Beek en Bosch (IV),
J.C. Blaauw, 1916–18
NL-21h Beukenhoek (VII), M. Staal-
Kropholler, 1918. A remarkable boat-

shaped house by one of the too few important women architects.

NL-21i **Meezennest** and **Meerlhuis** (V, VI), M. Staal-Kropholler, 1918–19
NL-21j **Double house** (VIII, IX), G. F. La Croix, 1918
Amsterdam School
NW from Alkmaar → BERGEN / L in Bergen (at light) on to Oosterweg ⇨ Loudelsweg / angle L on Studler van Surchlaan / park on L
[Bergen's informally laid-out roads are at times hard to differentiate from bicycle paths. One additional triple house by Kramer at Park Meerwijk burned in 1921.]

Despite what its name might suggest, those elements of the Amsterdam School which were not drawn from Indonesia and other exotic sources derive largely from the rustic timber and thatch of the Dutch countryside. Could there, then, have been a better place than this suburban, even semi-rural setting for the still-coalescing Amsterdam School to have demonstrated its principles? And could they have built it at a more propitious time – when, even in a neutral country, modern materials were scarce and escapism was bound to be at its strongest?

Only Michel de Klerk, the Amsterdam School's universally acknowledged leader, is missing from this rustic Wießenhof Siedlung (D-60). Because, even as Park Meerwijk was rising, De Klerk was already hard at work on his own manifesto-'village', the eventually far more influential Eigen Haard complex (NL-5).

NL-21k Bergen's little **shopping centre**, 1962, is by Van den Broek & Bakema. *In Bergen ctr*

Haarlem **NL-22**
* **Tuinwijk Zuid** (housing area)
1920–2
Zonnelaan, Tuinwijklaan, Vijverlaan
J. B. van Loghem
S from Haarlem ctr on Kleine Houtstr ⇨ Kleine Hout Weg (see NL-22a below) / on Oosterhoutlaan / R on Middenlaan / L on Vijverlaan / second R on O. A. Zonnelaan / on R
Tuinwijk – literally 'garden village' – is most immediately impressive for its unflinching modernity and effective use of its site. Only later does one begin to realize that, unlike the other more advanced (non-Amsterdam School) Dutch architecture of the immediate post-First World War years,

Van Loghem's remarkably controlled vocabulary is not derived from the work of Frank Lloyd Wright. And, unlike that of the Amsterdam School itself, it is not adapted or contrived for some primarily visual effect. Rather it seems truly to reflect the functional needs and the possibilities of modern flat-roofed row housing, especially in its use of balconies and roof terraces.

NL-22a Much of Van Loghem's later work, mostly built around Haarlem, is a little too safely *au courant*. One interesting exception is his **Sportsfondsenbad**, an enclosed swimming hall, 1932–5, in the Frederikspark. *R from Kleine Hout Weg (see directions above) on Baan / in park on L*

Aalsmeer **NL-23**
* **Bloemenveiling** (flower auction hall)
1927–8
Van Cleefkade
J. F. Staal
Late Amsterdam School (Expressionism)
SE from E10, abt 10 mi (16 km) S of Amsterdam → AALSMEER / R → CENTRUM / ahead on R
[To see the flowers and the auction one must arrive quite early. For details, contact any VVV tourist office.]

A certain flamboyance underlies this restrained, basically conservative building. But, then, the process of auctioning off flowers by the bargeload (the barges actually pass through the building) is itself picturesque, even gaudy.

NL-23a Aalsmeer has an interesting, rather Constructivist school, the **ULO-School**, 1930–2, by J.G. Wiebenga. Unfortunately it has lost many of its more mechanistic details. *Continue along Van Cleefkade (see directions above) / third R on*

Zijdestr / second R on to Dorpsstr / first R on to Schoolstr / on R

NL-23b In the opposite direction, at 217 Van Cleefkade, is a **combination house and barn** by the Amsterdam School's leading figure, Michel de Klerk. Built in 1923, the year of his death, it seems to point towards the evolution of a more practical, yet still conservatively romantic language, much like Staal's. *NE on Van Cleefkade ⇨ Oosteinderweg / on L*

Ter Aar [near Leiden]   **NL-24**
* Raadhuis (town hall) 1970
J. van Stigt
Kahn-esque
N from Alphen a.d. Rijn (abt $7\frac{1}{2}$ mi–12 km E of Leiden) → TER AAR, abt $3\frac{3}{4}$ mi (6 km) / L across canal and through village / on L just past church in middle of rd

This diminutive village hall is an interesting, well-designed example of its genre – although soon its fashionable super-symmetry may seem a short-lived, quaint throw-back. A whole world of this architecture just would not work. It is too aggressively self-centred, too anti-urban. It is incapable of relating to other buildings except through a rigid, universally imposed formal geometry, or – as is the case here *vis-à-vis* the neighbouring church and the road – through a minutely studied, picturesque and ultimately precious, pseudo-archaic site plan. Both of these siting techniques typify, and in current usage frequently derive from, the powerfully monumental work of Louis Kahn, as does much else in this building. Needless to say, neither approach is especially practical or appropriate in most 'real world' situations.

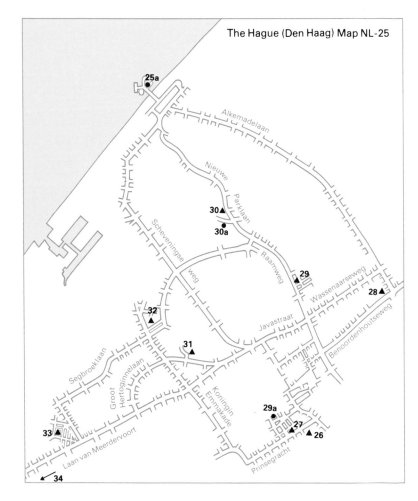

The Hague (Den Haag) Map NL-25

The Hague (Den Haag)   NL-25
Den Haag, also known as 's-Gravenhage, is the seat of government of Holland. (Amsterdam is the nominal capital.) It is also a seaside town composed of pleasant, often Wrightian suburbs.

The Hague (Den Haag)   **NL-26**
* **De Bijenkorf** (department store)
1924–8
Grote Marktstraat
P. L. Kramer
Amsterdam School (Expressionism)
Map NL-23
[The hexagonal great court, one of the few Amsterdam School public interior spaces of any sort, has been filled in, and the whole interior, except for the stairwells, is unrecognizably renovated.]

Here is one of the few non-residential Amsterdam School buildings, and also one of the best. Before most of the more famous International Style stores (GB-16) were built, Kramer had effectively overcome a major design problem inherent in the department store – one that the 'Functionalists' never tried to face: a department store with conventional windows on its upper floors either had to present a neat, orderly exterior image at the cost of functional efficiency within, or, as almost invariably happened, it had to make the most efficient use of its internal sales areas at the cost of windows that were messy, painted over or in other ways unappealing. Kramer fragmented his translucent but

NL-25a In the beach-front suburb of Scheveningen is **De Pier,** one of Europe's few interesting twentieth-century pleasure piers, 1960, by Maaskant, Dijk & Apon.

essentially non-transparent windows into glittering or glowing ornament (depending upon the time of day and weather) – thereby allowing De Bijenkorf effectively arranged sales areas, without making it look from the street like a dull, claustrophobic box.

The Hague (Den Haag)   **NL-27**
* **Coöperatie De Volharding** (co-op store, now office building) 1928
Prinsegracht 39
J. W. E. Buijs & J. B. Lürsen
De Stijl
Map NL-25
[The movie marquee-like spandrels originally carried advertisements.]

This building is not quite as unique in Holland as it would be elsewhere. From J. J. P. Oud's earliest post-First World War projects through the work of W. M. Dudok and others in the early 1930s, Dutch architects regularly designed otherwise straightforward, even sedate buildings – schools, factories, apartment blocks, stores – that went slightly cubistically berserk in just one place. For obvious reasons, these De Stijl-esque ornamental extravaganzas usually, as here, incorporated the building's main entrance, staircase and lifts. Yet De Volharding is different. It has a far greater unity than most such buildings because *all* of its exterior is fashioned from various sorts of glass. Of course at night, illuminated from within, this crystalline building

is transformed. It becomes a city-scale luminescent sculpture, advertising its presence as it once advertised its products.

The Hague (Den Haag)   **NL-28**
Flatgebouw Nirwana (apartments)
1927–30
Benoordenhoutseweg and Willem Witsenplein
J. Duiker and J. G. Wiebenga
International Style
Map NL-25

[At the time of writing the Nirwana stood half empty and in some disrepair.]

If Duiker is, unjustly, one of the less appreciated International Style architects, then this, even more unjustly, is one of his less appreciated works. Originally it was to have been part of a group of five similar buildings, all connected at their corners via access balconies – of which the present curious projecting corner balconies seem to be vestigial remainders. With only four three-bedroom apartments per floor, each with its own large corner living-room, the Nirwana represents an interesting departure from the usual modern Dutch slab block in which each apartment is the full width of the building. Yet, presumably because the distribution of winter sunlight among the apartments is far from equal, this otherwise interesting design never found favour in Holland.

The Hague (Den Haag)   **NL-29**
* **Nationale-Nederlanden** (insurance company, originally De Nederlanden van 1845) 1918–27, expanded 1953–4
Groenhovenstraat 2
H. P. Berlage
Rationalism
Map NL-25

[Only the half of the building abutting the car park (then a canal) was built in the 20s, at which time it was just two storeys high. The postwar expansion was carried out by W. M. Dudok, who followed Berlage's plans, and meticulously reproduced Berlage's cornice, corner and tower details.]

This could almost be a contemporaneous American urban factory – Berlage had been a fascinated pre-First World War visitor to America. It has the same generally unarticulated massing; the same exposed concrete frame filled with brick, glass block, and steel sash; and even the same, so typical, central tower – a feature that at once denotes entrance, accommodates stairs and elevators, and holds aloft the obligatory flag-pole.

But Berlage took this stock formula and made something more of it. He chose and used his materials carefully. He played the basic flatness of the façade against the intricately complex yet well-ordered pattern of the exposed concrete frame. And when he did cut into the building's prismatic volume, he did so just enough to enhance the tower's outward thrust and to achieve some enlivening articulation, but without sacrificing the basic simplicity of the form.

NL-29a In the centre of The Hague, at Kerkplein, is an earlier **office building**, 1895, with modifications of 1902 and 1909, which Berlage designed for the same client. As present it seems unused and may not be long for this world.

The Hague (Den Haag) **NL-30**
Rudolf Steiner Polikliniek (clinic)
1927–9
Nieuwe Parklaan 26
J. W. E. Buijs & J. B. Lürsen
Expressionism
Map NL-25

    Although this small hospital might seem to be the work of some particularly organic adherent of the Amsterdam School, its nominal architects were usually given to more rectangular fantasies (NL-27). In a sense Rudolf Steiner (CH-20) was the real designer here. Although he had died two years before the building was begun, his precepts were embodied in this unornamented, almost animistic, architecture – as indeed they still are in all the Anthroposophist schools and clinics that continue to be built by his followers.

    However, Steiner's ethic/aesthetic also owes much to Theosophy, a nineteenth-century mystical philosophy-cum-religion which flourished in Holland, and which strongly influenced the Amsterdam School. So there was, then, some connection here with Amsterdam – but via Switzerland!

NL-30a Near by, at Wagenaarweg 30, is a **house by Henri van de Velde**, 1902–3.

The Hague (Den Haag) **NL-31**
** First Church of Christ Scientist
1925
Andries Bickerweg 1 and Groot Hertoginnelaan
H. P. Berlage
Rationalism
Map NL-25

[Locked except for services.]

    Apart from his turn-of-the-century Amsterdam Bourse (NL-3), most of Berlage's more intriguing work post-dates his 1911 American visit. In these later buildings, he came increasingly to rely upon symmetry as an organizational tool. Often this was a traditional symmetry, but it could also involve the asymmetrical juxtaposition of symmetrical plan fragments in almost mannerist expositions of virtuosity, which sometimes seem to have been created as much for their own sake as out of any consideration of site or programme. Nor was this tendency merely some aberration unique to Berlage's later years. From Frank Lloyd Wright's early buildings on, modern architects have periodically rediscovered and been fascinated by the tensions that arise from creating an asymmetrical whole out of complex parallel and cross-axial symmetries.

    In this particular situation, the offset entrance axis and portico also serve to relate the more assertive form of the nave to the subdued, reflective one of the reading room. There are other tensions here, too, beyond those usually inherent in this sort of design. There is a tension between all the formal sensibilities associated with centuries of symmetrical monument-making on the one hand, and the sense of compromising expediency and, inevitably, of romanticism, implicit in asymmetrical design on the other. There is also a special tension between the image of the church proper as one of many free-standing buildings in a suburban park-like setting, and the sense of the reading room as an extension of a traditional canalside townscape.

The Hague (Den Haag)   **NL-32**
* Gemeentemuseum (municipal museum) 1919–35
Stadhouderslaan 41
H. P. Berlage
Rationalism
Map NL-25

[At the opposite end of the reflecting pool from Berlage's long entrance loggia is an unspectacular but respectful addition by Schammhart & Heijligers, 1965, intended to house temporary exhibitions. The museum's collections include works by Mondrian and other members of De Stijl, as well as a room of Art Nouveau most of which is Belgian and German in spirit.]

Berlage's last work, the culmination of various projects dating back to 1907, evokes in its masterly rhythms and rich structural-spatial sequences something grander even than its own substantial self.

From the street it is a complex play of shifting surfaces ordered by strong window patterns, while twin minaret-chimneys seem to deny the possibility of a simple, dominant, central element. (Indeed, lying at the museum's heart is a courtyard of no great symbolic or programmatic importance.) All this is reflected – further fragmented, yet enlarged – by sheets of water, and then drawn into difficult coherence by an interplay of imperfect symmetries. Berlage's sources here may be many and varied – from ancient Islam to Frank Lloyd Wright – but they are never blatant.

Close up, which is how one lives with a building, the museum is more impressive for its careful but inventive detailing; its functionality; its delight in materials; and its plain, workmanlike solidity.

The Hague (Den Haag)   **NL-33**
Papaverhof (housing area) 1920–2
Magnoliastraat
Jan Wils
Wrightian
Map NL-25

Composed of larger- and smaller-scale prismatic rectangular elements rendered in roughcast stucco, Papaverhof surrounds its own semi-private park. Ingeniously, it combines the efficiency of row housing with the light airiness of double houses. There is little else in Europe of such an early date and so large a scope that reflects as complete and sure a modernity.

Papaverhof is not a product of the De Stijl group. If it is reminiscent of that move-

ment, or vice versa, that is only because De Stijl owes much to Frank Lloyd Wright, while Papaverhof owes him *almost* everything.

The Hague (Den Haag)   **NL-34**
* Pastoor van Ars Kerk (church)
1969
Aaltje Noordewierstraat 4
Aldo van Eyck

Brutalism
SW from city ctr on Laan van Meerdervoort (Map NL-25→) abt 2½ mi (4 km) / L beyond park on Aaltje Noordewierstr / on L
Van Eyck's second major work confirmed

the suspicions generated by his first (NL-19): he can be too cerebral for his own good. This church, though interesting, typifies the architecture of that ever increasing group of theorist-architects for whom creativity is anything but a spontaneous act.

One almost feels there should be footnotes scattered about the building, such as:
1. *In the nave:* The church has no windows, receiving its light instead very indirectly via skylights, because Van Eyck is a devotee of Islamic architecture. The viewer must imagine the delight this cool space might afford if one had just stepped in from the hot, dusty, narrow streets of a casbah, rather than from the swirling damp grey mists of coastal suburban Holland.
2. *On the nave ceiling:* The beams run

inefficiently the 'wrong' way, so as not to disturb the spatial and metaphysical continuity between pastor and parishioners.
3. *At the main entrance:* The unusual door reflects Van Eyck's well-advertised aversion to conventional doorways.
4. *On the exterior walls:* Although this is obviously a modestly priced building, the decision to use porous concrete block in the damp Dutch climate was as much aesthetic as economic. It stems from a stark, hairshirt 60's asceticism – in this case of American origin.
5. Etc.

Like most treatises thick with footnotes, however informative they may be, a 'reading' of this church can prove rather heavy going.

Hook of Holland (Hoek van Holland) **NL-35**
* Woningbouw (workers' housing)
1924–7
2e Scheepvaartstraat 91a–113a
J. J. P. Oud
International Style
From E8-36 → CENTRUM *on to Prins Hendrikstr / L on Lichttorenstr / first R / on L*

The diminutive workers' flats within are well organized, with tight, almost symmetrical floor plans that typify Oud at his best. But the rounded shop-pavilions at the ends of both blocks – unexpected in the context of Oud's previous Neo-Classical and

De Stijl inspired work – are the most visible 'architecture' here. Photographs of the shops were once published as if they were of the whole building. Despite their early date, the shops are reminiscent of the over-expressive and often superficial, but widely transplanted, commercial International Style of the late 30s – 'Streamlined Moderne' as they might have been called in California. Beautiful though they are, there is something of the stage set here. Somehow it is not surprising to find that, out of sight in the rear, the gleaming twentieth-century surfaces revert, in part, to quite ordinary nineteenth-century brick.

Rotterdam NL-36
'Rotterdam will pursue the way of true construction with a deathly chill in its veins and Amsterdam will be destroyed by the fire of its own dynamism,' wrote Erich Mendelsohn in the early 20s. Although his imagery, like his famous early sketch projects, may have been immoderate, Mendelsohn accurately reflected a then-common perception of Rotterdam as a bulwark of 'Functional' architecture in a Holland gone slightly mad. One does not want to belittle the likes of Van der Vlugt, Van Tijen, Van den Broek and J. A. Brinkman but, compared to Amsterdam or even The Hague, Rotterdam is not exceptionally

well-endowed with first-class modern buildings. Nor can this situation be blamed entirely on the German bombing of 1940. That crime, which occurred after Holland had surrendered, destroyed some 30,000 buildings within the city's ancient core. Yet among them the only major works of modern architecture to be lost were an early housing area and the De Stijl Café de Unie by J. J. P. Oud, and W. M. Dudok's powerful De Bijenkorf department store.

Since the war, Rotterdam has become the world's largest port. If the reconstruction of its old centre no longer seems so inspiring (NL-42), the excitement of its harbour helps to make amends.

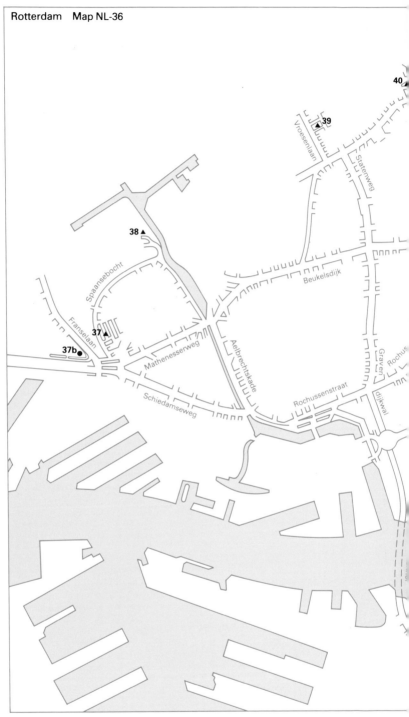

Rotterdam   Map NL-36

Rotterdam   **NL-37**
** Spangen (social housing) 1919–21
Spaansebocht, Justus van Effenstraat
M. Brinkman
Rationalism
Map NL-36

Given its post-First World War date, the conservative, unarticulated exterior of this large four-storey block hardly appears promising. But to pass through one of the archways leading into its cloistered interiors is to enter a humane vision of what 'housing' might become – a vision which only in the past few decades has

begun to be reproduced and then usually in a diluted form (NL-8, GB-71, 88).

Spangen is coherent yet not dull, a place where over 700 people can find a sense of community. Opening directly on to the ground level of its central sequence of spaces are two floors of flats, each having, in the traditional Dutch manner, its own private entrance. Above, a similar number of two-storey apartments are served by a system of wide corridor-balconies. These walkways provide not just access but also a public, social and play area immediately in front of each apartment's front door –

perhaps the first consciously conceived and built modern example of such a 'street in the sky'.

Today it seems incredible that this modern master-work went almost unrecognized for more than a quarter of a century. But, during the heyday of the International Style, Spangen's image of the future may not have appeared sufficiently radical – as compared, for instance, to Le Corbusier's visionary housing projects. Today Spangen's courtyards seem all the more convincing for their remarkable simplicity and frankness, their denials of easy or glossed-over solutions, and their exposed, articulate use of concrete. Most important, Spangen, unlike its better-known contemporaries, is not a vast dream project (F-54), nor the fancy of some philanthropist (F-49): it is municipally constructed housing.

Rotterdam   **NL-38**
* Fabriek van Nelle (coffee, tea and tobacco factory) 1926–30
Van Nelleweg
Brinkman & Van der Vlugt, with
Mart Stam
International Style
Map NL-36

Although well known in its own time, this factory has since become one of the less-appreciated major buildings of its period.

The International Style monuments whose reputations have always predominated are those which are at once simple and complex. Two of them come particularly close to Van Nelle in scope, time and spirit. The earlier, Gropius's Bauhaus of 1925–6 (now in East Germany), reflects in its fenestration and articulate massing the diverse administrative, residential and educational functions of a professional trade school. Yet its elemental forms and surfaces are simple, orderly and prismatic. Similarly, Le Corbusier's Armée du Salut, of 1929–33 (F-35), is, or at least was once, basically a sheer-sided mass rising up from behind several major free-standing geometric elements and topped by, as it were, a Cubist's reinterpretation of the Château de Chambord's fantasy roofscape. In part it is an unmistakable transformation of that primary architectural paradigm of the period, the transatlantic liner, whose clean sheer hull was topped by, and contrasted with, an extremely fragmented but equally functional superstructure.

Van Nelle, despite its size, elegant detailing and consistent functional honesty, has

Now, if only the cars could be kept out.

NL-37a Just by way of comparison, the immediately adjacent **Spaansebocht social housing,** of a similar scale and date, 1918–20, is by J. J. P. Oud, who was then Rotterdam's municipal architect.

NL-37b Just to the west (across the railway tracks) is **Oud Mathenesse,** a slightly later (1923) but more village-like 'semi-permanent' housing area designed by Oud for newly arrived rural immigrants. Also known as **Het Witte Dorp** (the white village), its modern houses shelter beneath traditional, steep red-tile roofs, so that it has more the feel of a comfortable country community than does its better-known International Style counterpart, De Kiefhoek (NL-43).

never been as influential as these two buildings, nor has it even been as influential as many smaller, simpler (often even simplistic) buildings and unbuilt projects. Architecture that is as generally pragmatic as this factory does not easily present a complex but still comprehensible overall image – one that invites in-depth analysis, yet can readily be retained and transmuted. Rather, its true functionality is apt to have been purchased at the cost of such easy aesthetics – as is even more likely to be true of a building's ability to adapt gracefully to evolving circumstances. Thus, despite ever changing production requirements, Van Nelle does apparently still work well. And unlike many of its better-known contemporaries – including the Armée du Salut – it has maintained the freshness of its First-Machine-Age youth.

NL-38a Holland's **'Telefoon' booths** are still made to a 1933 design by Brinkman & Van der Vlugt.

Rotterdam NL-39
De Eendracht (apartments) 1931–5
Vroesenlaan and Navanderstraat
J. H. van den Broek
International Style
Map NL-36

Admittedly this particular block of flats, Van den Broek's most important independent work, avoids the dogmatic, regimented site-planning that was to bedevil progressive Dutch architecture for the next forty years. And the apartment plans do, with the aid of sliding partitions and Murphy beds, squeeze accommodation for six into only 700 square feet, which is ingenious if nothing else. But something *is* missing here. Unlike the contemporaneous work of Van Tijen, who was also solving many of the same sorts of problems (NL-40), this architecture has no real guts. And, unlike the work of Van der Vlugt (NL-38), it also has no real soul – not even a technocratic one.

Rotterdam NL-40
* Flatgebouw, Bergpolder (social housing) 1933–4
Abraham Kuyperlaan and Dr de Visserstraat
W. van Tijen, with Brinkman &
Van der Vlugt
International Style
Map NL-36

Between the wars Rotterdam developed a particularly cold, calculating brand of Functionalism. Theoretically devoid of artistic preconceptions, it claimed to have no use for aesthetics, even for the machine imageries of Le Corbusier or the Bauhaus. Despite all that, in Rotterdam a low-cost social housing block such as this could still develop a spare sort of elegance, with not a form, space or element whose purpose or harmoniousness could be questioned.

There is a temptation here to say that form really can follow function and thereby produce great architecture. But would this block be so desirable were it, and its park-like site, not serving as a foil to all the surrounding low-brick cosiness? And would one really want a whole neighbourhood, much less a city, of such blocks? These are questions which, despite the evidence of a thousand over-orderly high-rise suburbs, too many European architects and planners took far too long to face.

what larger apartments (as opposed to two at Bergpolder). Finally, because of a hint of romantic fragmentation, this block relates a bit more comfortably to its setting – people, buildings and suburban greenery alike. Paradoxically it also seems a bit more Brutalistic, for much the same reason. It may not be as historically important a building as Bergpolder, but it is a slightly easier one to accept. [Many of the balconies have been enclosed.]

NL-40a Van Tijen & Maaskant's **Flatgebouw Kralingse Plaslaan**, 1937–8, at Kralingse Plaslaan and Ramlehstraat, is basically a reprise of the Bergpolder flats but built in concrete rather than in the more difficult-to-maintain wood and steel. It was also intended primarily for more affluent residents without children, there being only one bedroom in most of its some-

NL-40b Just down Kralingse Plaslaan, at No. 38, is a **house**, 1926–30, by Brinkman & Van der Vlugt. It was built, apparently at great expense, for the owner-director of the Van Nelle factory (NL-38). The technical imagery of some of its interior details and fittings are said to rival those of the Maison de verre (F-13). [Not open to the public.]

Rotterdam NL-41
Industriegebouw-oostzeedijk
(industrial 'flats') 1947
Oostzeedijk 208–224
Van Tijen & Maaskant
Scandinavian Empiricism/Neo-Industrial
Vernacular
Map NL-36

Van Tijen's struggle against the conservative historicizing influences that gave rise to the Delft School is almost triumphant here. Admittedly his prewar buildings may have been more uncompromising

(NL-40), but in those days he had been a part of what has since been dubbed modern architecture's 'heroic generation'. He had been one among many. In the 40s it must have seemed at times that he was struggling alone, as he tried and ultimately rejected several alternative ahistorical, if still romantic, design modes.

Rotterdam   **NL-42**
* **De Lijnbaan** (shopping centre) 1949–5
Van den Broek & Bakema
1949–54
Late International Style
Map NL-36
The Lijnbaan, once the most famous example of postwar Dutch architecture, or rather urban design, is also one of the most disappointing. This unimaginative, semi-covered pedestrian street is too wide to be intimate and too narrow to be grand. It might be exciting in a city of 70,000, but not in one of 700,000.

Ultimately, Rotterdam might be best served if the ageing Lijnbaan were treated like the temporary postwar expedient that increasingly it seems to resemble.

NL-42a The nearby **De Bijenkorf Department Store**, 1953–7, on Cool-

From his efforts came Holland's best link with Scandinavian Empiricism (NL-18), and also this building. with its strong but indirect allusions to the traditional, tall canalside warehouses that are as much a part of Holland's industrial vernacular tradition as are her windmills.

singel, was designed by Marcel Breuer. It and the Lijnbaan deserve each other. The sculpture by Naum Gabo in front of Breuer's store deserves somewhat better.

Rotterdam   **NL-43**
* **De Kiefhoek** (housing, shops, church and recreation area) 1925–9
Eemstein and Heer Arnoldstraat
J. J. P. Oud
International Style
Map NL-36
De Kiefhoek, Oud's and Holland's best-known International Style work, is one of two 'such 'villages' (NL-37b) of simple but elegantly efficient small row houses set amid the apartment blocks of working-class Rotterdam. Intended to house country people who were not used to city life, these dwellings, with their individual entrances

and backyards, could not be more in contrast to the CIAM-inspired ideal of high-rise 'social housing' (NL-40).

Utrecht   **NL-44**
As much as Haarlem or Amsterdam, Utrecht is one of Holland's most historic cities. However, its tight old core retains a medieval, provincial, inland character quite different from the well-ordered, worldly Renaissance or Northern Baroque ambience of the more low-lying Dutch sea-ports. Because the old town is on higher ground, some of Utrecht's canals, and especially Oude Gracht, are situated within such deep cuts that they and their quays take on the character of a multi-level circulation system – with the broad, lower canalside quays linked to the cellars of the adjacent buildings by spacious under-street vaults. In earlier eras heavy water-borne commerce was thus segregated from the city's normal pedestrian and vehicular traffic. Today, these quays and vaults are used for everything from outdoor dining to the building of small boats. Such a physical separation of circulation systems has been a long-standing but rarely realized urban ideal – from at least the time of Leonardo to (but not ending with) the skyways of downtown Minneapolis.

Unfortunately Utrecht also differs from most Dutch towns in another important respect. Some of her canals, as well as Sybold van Ravestyn's remarkable railway station, have been allowed to fall victim to the ill-conceived Hoog Catharijne renewal scheme, whose main beneficiaries seem to be the automobile and Utrecht's annual trade fair.

NL-44a The Modern Art Department of Utrecht's Centraal Museum is located at Maliebaan 42. in the Fentener van Vlissingenhuis, a typical nineteenth-century upper-middle-class dwelling. Devoted primarily to **artefacts of the Dutch Arts and Crafts Movement**, it contains whole rooms by Lion Cachet, executed in a style that might best be called East Indies Gothic, as well as work by Jan Toorop, Thorn Prikker, Theo van Doesburg and, appropriately enough in Utrecht, some of Gerrit Rietveld's De Stijl furniture and models of his architectural works. *E from Utrecht ctr →* AMERSFOORT *on to Biltstraat / R, just before RR, on Snellenlaan ⇨ Maliebaan / on R*

Utrecht **NL-45**
* Muziekcentrum Vredenburg
(concert hall and shops) 1975–9
Vredenburgplein
Herman Hertzberger
Rationalism
Next to Hoog Catharijne shopping centre

Hertzberger believes that because life is complex and ever changing, architecture must be able to accommodate – and reflect – that complexity. It is significant, then, that in this intriguing, difficult building one does feel something peculiarly resonant of the contradictions between constraining orderliness and almost anarchic vitality

that characterizes twentieth-century Dutch society. The structural system and detailing are carefully thought through and highly systematic. Yet the materials are prosaic, sometimes insubstantial, and, in the case of the concrete block, almost guaranteed to weather gracelessly. There is a relentless column grid and a vocabulary of metalwork and window details which suggest a very precise kind of rationality. But they add up to a picturesque impression – one of cubic details, angled wall planes and piled up volumes. There is not only justifiable self-assurance here, but perhaps also a bit of pleasure playing the *enfant terrible*.

Utrecht **NL-46**
*** Het Schröderhuis (house) 1924
Prins Hendriklaan 50
Gerrit Rietveld
De Stijl
E from Utrecht ctr → AMERSFOORT / on to Biltscheweg / first R past RR (at light) / first L (at light) on Prinsesselaan / straight across roundabout, bearing L along L side of park / L on Prins Hendriklaan / on L just before flyover
[The house was restored *c.* 1984. It is closed to the public.]

De Stijl was more a movement in art than in architecture. Its best-known protagonist was the painter Piet Mondrian. The Schröder House is the most important and virtually the only extant example of De Stijl architecture. It is also Rietveld's first building and by far his finest. It combines his cabinet-maker's feel for the assembly of small articulate components with an aesthetic sensibility that owes much to the theories of De Stijl's mercurial impresario, Theo van Doesburg.

A factor of fundamental significance in most major works of architecture – and one all too easily overlooked – is the influence of the client. By all accounts Rietveld's client here, Truus Schröder, was an extraordinary person. She, more than most architects of the time, seems to have understood and accepted the notion that a building might be more truly functional if it is in effect rearrangeable. Although the façades of Mrs Schröder's house have made it famous as an early icon of modernity, the greater innovation lies in the plan of its upper floor. This singular sun-filled space,

whose existence may be largely attributable to Mrs Schröder, is ingeniously divisible by folding and sliding partitions into as many as six separate rooms, including three bedrooms with washbasins. Such a spatial and programmatic innovation must be seen as at least semi-independent of the external sculptural creation which contains it. In combination they make this a unique work of art which, more than almost any modern house in Europe, must be preserved and made accessible to the public – not just as an artefact but as an embodiment of ideals.

NL-46a Because De Stijl clearly owes something to Frank Lloyd Wright, it might be noted that Robert Van't Hoff's **Villa Henny,** 1915–16, is in nearby Huis ter Heide. The Villa Henny is an absolutely convincing clone of a modest suburban 'Prairie' house of about 1905. Van't Hoff had worked briefly for Wright in America. *NE from Utrecht → Amersfoort on E8 / on N side of rd at Huis ter Heide (near Hotel Dijnselhoek), just E of crossroads → ZEIST*

Utrecht   **NL-47**
* **Woningblok I** (row houses) 1930–1
Erasmuslaan 5–11
Gerrit Rietveld
International Style
*Continue E on Prins Hendriklaan from NL-46
just past flyover / on L*

Few of Rietveld's later works are well
known. None better deserves greater recognition than these beautifully simple, but
not oversimplified, row houses. They must
rank among the best and most typical creations of Holland's distinctly technological
vision of the International Style. Yet they
remain in obscurity. Is this in spite of, or
because of, the nearby Schröderhuis?

NL-47a Rietveld also designed the adjacent **Woningblok II,** 1934, at Erasmuslaan 1–3.

NL-47b Rietveld's most technically interesting building of the period is a **chauf-
feur's home and garage,** 1927–8, on
Waldeck Pyrmontkade, which is constructed of one-by-three-metre pre-cast
concrete modules set within a steel frame.
Although this unusual construction has
since been stuccoed over, its steel framework is, strangely enough, faithfully delineated on the new surface. *W → Utrecht ctr
from NL-46 on Prins Hendriklaan / L on
Rembrandtkade / first R (across canal) /
first L on Waldeck Pyrmontkade / on R*

Hilversum   **NL-48**
* **Raadhuis** (town hall) 1924–31
Hoge Naarderweg and Koninginneweg
W. M. Dudok
Wrightian
*NW from Hilversum ctr on 's-Gravelandseweg
/ R on Koninginneweg / two blks on R*

Of all the architects practising in Holland
between the wars, none was more prolific
nor more generally respected than Dudok.
Because he never became deeply involved
in the struggles between the rival stylistic
schools, he could profit from their dis-
coveries while avoiding the difficulties of
trying to maintain some theoretically 'correct' position. Here, for instance, in his
greatest surviving work, Dudok has combined, and wholly assimilated, elements
taken from Frank Lloyd Wright, both
directly and via Berlage; from the Amsterdam School; from De Stijl; and, with
most subtlety, from the Stockholm City
Hall (S-3).

NL-48a For more than two decades,
beginning in 1915, Dudok was Hilversum's
municipal architect – a role which, while
allowing him to undertake a limited
amount of outside work, gave him an
almost unparalleled opportunity to direct
Hilversum's then rapid growth, to design
a wide variety of municipal buildings, and
to plan whole residential quarters. In addition to the Vondelschool (NL-50), the best of
his work includes the public baths, housing
and the **Dr H. Bavinckschool,** 1921–
30, on Bosdrift. *S from Hilversum ctr on
Havenstr ⇨ Bosdrift, abt 1 mi (1.5 km) on L*

Hilversum   **NL-49**
*** Grand Hotel and Theatre
Gooiland** (hotel, now housing for the
handicapped, and cinema) 1934–46
Emmastraat 2 (hotel), *Luitgardeweg* (cinema)
J. Duiker & B. Bijvoet
International Style
*At SW corner of ring rd circling city
core / cinema is around corner from hotel*

Most styles tend to evolve, if they last
long enough, in one or both of two not
always conflicting directions: mannerism
and Baroque elaboration. (Although these
terms were first applied to stages in the
development of post-Renaissance Classicism, they have since been seen to have an
almost generic applicability.) As is evident
here and elsewhere (D-11, 17), within
fifteen years of its first emergence, the idealistic white architecture of the 20s and 30s
began to develop an almost surreal insubstantiality and a Baroque plasticity, in
which once rectangular plan forms could
seemingly become curved as if made of
rubber. These traits would long survive in
resort hotels and cut-price suburban
schools, even after the orthodox International Style had all but disappeared.

The origins of such debased form languages are often to be found in innovations
by masters of an orthodox style, like Duiker

Hilversum   **NL-50**
* De Vondelschool (school) 1928–9
Schuttersweg 36
W. M. Dudok
Wrightian/International Style
*W from Hilversum ctr on Vaartweg abt
$\frac{1}{2}$ mi (1 km) / R on Schuttersweg / abt
800 yds (m) on R*

Like most of Dudok's efforts, this is a
thoroughly modern yet essentially conservative building. Consider only the thin
white cornice, which is good detailing and
visually effective, but disallowed by the
canons of the High International Style
orthodoxy; or the solidly Dutch, traditionally detailed masonry, against which
the cornice stands in contrast; or especially
the explicitly romantic and thus even more
'unacceptable' delicate little Wrightian
entrance executed in red and blue glazed
bricks. Altogether just the sort of building
that caused Dudok to be so well thought
generally of – except by the more extreme
partisans of both Rotterdam's technocratic
Functionalists and the Amsterdam School.

or Mendelsohn, who are seeking solutions
to specific formal problems. Duiker's
dilemma here stemmed from the need to fit
a programmatically complex building into
a tight urban site, which he did admirably,
while still providing a major external
space – a roof terrace surrounded by hotel
rooms above the restaurant and lobby.
Surely it would be unfair to fault Duiker for
subsequent misuses of his organic distortions of conventional forms, which were
for him only one aspect of a clever solution
to a difficult problem – just as unfair as it
would be to blame the seventeenth-century
Baroque architect Borromini for all the later
evolutions, perversions and dilutions of the
dramatic, didactic, Counter-Reformation
architecture that he had helped to create.

NL-49a Just outside Hilversum at Loos-
drechtsebosje 7, is Duiker & B. Bijvoet's
Zonnestraal Sanatorium, 1926–8.
Once one of their most mechanistically
elaborate, impressive works, it has had
numerous extensive alterations and
additions, some of which are deceptively
integrated into the original fabric. *S from
Hilversum ctr on Havenstraat ⇨ Bosdrift / → LOOSDRECHT, abt 2 mi (3 km) / L
at ZONNESTRAAL / → PORTIER / 100 yds
(m) on R*

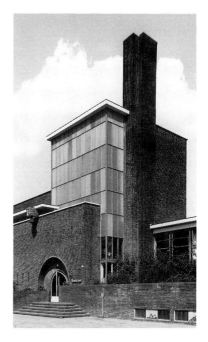

Dronten, Oostelijk Flevoland   **NL-51**
* De Meerpaal (community centre)
1967–8
F. van Klingeren
W from Rt 91 in Kampen → DRONTEN /
→ CENTRUM / *at ctr sq*
   De Meerpaal, once enthusiastically
described as an 'electronic agora', is an
enclosed space, but somehow not 'indoors',
where people, particularly teenagers, can
just 'hang out' or participate in those activities through which a sense of community
is maintained.
   Specifically it is a beautifully minimal,
but never precious, 165-by-230-foot glass
box. Situated wholly or partially within it
is an assortment of semi-independent and,
it must be admitted, somewhat graceless
stuccoed forms. These contain a theatre, a
café-restaurant, offices and other ancillary
facilities. But the almost apologetic manner
in which these elements have been inserted
confirms the true nature of De Meerpaal –
the major portion of whose space remains
free to house anything from films to art
exhibitions, dances and basketball games.
   De Meerpaal would be a welcome asset

De Hoge Veluwe [near Arnhem]   **NL-52**
* Jachtslot St Hubertus (hunting
lodge) 1915–17
Hoofdingang
H. P. Berlage
Rationalism/Architecture Parlante
→ HOGE VELUWE / *→* ST HUBERTUS /
100 yds (m) off rd at edge of small lake
   [The building is within the Hoge Veluwe
National Park for which an admission fee
must be paid. The interiors can only be seen
by groups of twenty to forty who have made
an appointment in advance. The landscaping is by Henri van de Velde.]
   The history of this former private
hunting park and its buildings is in part
the story of one of the twentieth century's
most unusual art collectors. Madame
H. E. L. J. Kröller-Müller was heir to a
fortune, which her husband greatly
expanded and she expended. Her art collection (NL-53a) included works by the
Dutch *fin-de-siècle* Symbolists Jan Toorop
and Thorn Prikker; by the De Stijl painters
Piet Mondrian and Bart van der Leck; and,
most especially, by Vincent van Gogh, who
was represented by no fewer than 270
works. With almost equal enthusiasm she
'collected' architecture, often in the form
of unbuilt projects. Or rather she collected
architects – and good ones at that.

in any small town. In a place as new and
raw as the Flevoland polders it seems a
necessity.

NL-51a The little unpretentious Dutch
modern-vernacular **shopping centre**
adjacent to De Meerpaal is more urbane
and appealing than anything to be seen in
the self-conscious, and once much-
discussed, architectural showcase town of
Nagele, on the Noordoost Polder (NL-51c).

NL-51b Even by Dutch standards, the
polders on the floor of the former Zuiderzee,
now IJsselmeer, present such an extensive,
flat, dull landscape that it is easy to forget
the magnificent technological feat which
makes their existence possible. An idea of
the scope of these undertakings can be had
from the even newer nearby **Zuidelijk
Flevoland** polder. *SW from Dronten abt
$12\frac{1}{2}$ mi (20 km)*

NL-51c The **Noordoost Polder,** another adjacent, partially prewar area, has
already begun to develop a softening sort
of patina. *N from Kampen on Rt 91*

   The first of these was Peter Behrens,
whom the Kröller-Müllers commissioned to
design a large house. Behrens erected a full-
scale wood and canvas model before his
scheme was rejected. The whole process
was then repeated – mock-up, rejection and
all – by Mies van der Rohe, who had until
then worked for Behrens.
   The Kröller-Müllers then hired H. P.
Berlage, who also unsuccessfully submitted
designs for the house and for a museum.
However, Berlage did construct a model
farm, the Holland House office building
(GB-13), and, of course, the St Hubertus
hunting lodge.
   Berlage had a penchant for improbable
schemes whose scope and symbolic content

seemed to require complex, unorthodox symmetries. Among such projects were his proposal for Lenin's mausoleum and his first, huge version of the Hague Gemeentemuseum (NL-32). This hunting lodge as mini-palace is the perfect embodiment of that propensity. It is meant to symbolize St Hubertus, patron saint of hunters, whose conversion is attributed to an encounter with a stag bearing a radiant cross between its antlers – an image now more familiar in Europe as the trademark of a German beer. Thus the spreading wings of Berlage's hunting lodge (encompassing the entrance court) are said to simulate the stag's antlers, while the tower stands surrogate for the cross – in addition to having once enabled observation of the game that was to be shot. The rationale for this exercise in symbolism is not more improbable than any of those given by other architects in justification of their more extreme designs; the history of architecture is filled with fascinating if not always memorable buildings whose curious symbolic functional intentions should not be allowed to obscure their other virtues.

The Hoge Veluwe park, like the Kröller-Müllers' art collection, was a gift to the state.

De Hoge Veluwe [near Arnhem]   **NL-53**
Rietveld Paviljoen (sculpture pavilion)
1955, re-erected 1965
Rijksmuseum Kröller-Müller
Gerrit Rietveld
→ HOGE VELUWE / → KRÖLLER-MÜLLER / *in sculpture garden, accessible only through museum (NL-53a)*
[The present pavilion is a reconstruction. The original was designed for one summer's use during an open-air festival in Arnhem.]

Despite the intended impermanence so well reflected in its simplicity of means and materials, Rietveld's little pavilion is now permanently and comfortably situated in one of Europe's finest outdoor collections of modern sculpture. It is itself as much sculpture as architecture. As a creation of his later years, and being free of any but the simplest programmatic considerations, it almost seems to be a non-dogmatic reappraisal, or restatement, of those spatial/compositional principles with which, more than three decades earlier, Rietveld had first designed his De Stijl furniture and then his epochal Schröderhuis (NL-46).

NL-53a During the 20s, the Kröller-Müllers hired Henri van de Velde as their architect (see NL-52). He built not only their long-delayed house near The Hague, 1928–30 (now the Canadian Consulate), but also two other country houses, two workers' houses, a warehouse, and another model farm. Van de Velde's major project, however, was the grandiose original Hoge Veluwe museum. (Construction was halted in 1922 and only the foundations and a scattering of unused building stones now remain.) The present **Kröller-Müller museum**, 1937–54, originally intended to be temporary, was Van de Velde's final work for them. It contains a substantial collection of De Stijl art. The newer wing, 1969–72, is by W. G. Quist. It does much to overcome Van de Velde's stiff, uninspired axial design, while capitalizing on the old building's best space – the sculpture hall – by re-orienting the museum's entrance towards it.

Apeldoorn   **NL-54**
* **Centraal Beheer** (corporate headquarters) 1969–73
Prins Willem Alexanderlaan 651
Herman Hertzberger
Kahn-esque
S from Apeldoorn ctr → ARNHEM / on L at edge of town

Hertzberger, one of Holland's most prominent architects, has always shown an awareness of what is new and interesting. Yet he has never been a mere stylemonger. Here, however, despite the promise and originality of his earlier works (NL-8), he came perilously close to the edge. The entire tectonic vocabulary here is drawn from the work of Louis Kahn. Hertzberger's salva-

tion is the vitality of the interiors, which reflect his concern that each user be able to 'shape' his or her own space, and the undeniable skill with which he assembled his over-articulated American borrowings.

Drienerloo [near Enschede]   **NL-55**
* Hallencomplex (machine laboratory)
1964
TH-Twente (technical university)
Van Embden, Choisy, Roorda van Eysinga,
Smelt & Wittermans
High-Tech Rationalism
Between Enschede and Hengelo on Rt 92 /
→ TH-TWENTE / first R inside gate /
100 yds (m) on L

Even on a campus where most of the architecture is interesting, or at least provocative, one must be struck by this elegantly detailed modular laboratory block. But is not its visual impact too much the result of unnecessary structural gymnastics? Is there any real justification for those free-standing exterior columns, whose offset burdens must be balanced by heavily counterweighted king-post tie-rods? Is this not structural extravagance?

Possibly it is not. In the first place, the roof panels were made slightly smaller than the structural grid, so that the residual spaces between them could function as skylit clerestories – hence the need to cantilever the four points of roof support away from each column. Secondly some, if not all, of these exterior columns may one day become interior columns. They would then have to bear the weight of additional roof panels where now these are counterbalanced by the tie-rods. But if the exterior columns were located in line with the exterior walls, and therefore in line with the corners of the roof panels they support, thereby avoiding the need for tie-rods, then any expansion would require the replacement of these columns with new ones like those actually used. And that would be more trouble than any caused by the present counterbalancing act.

NL-55a The university's student dining-hall, the **Mensa,** 1964, is by Piet Blom. In its youth it was said (more or less by way of an excuse), that this more-American-than-Dutch building was descended from an old barn – the source, presumably, of its pitched roofs, arched doorways and general air of rusticity. Such was the way in which one explained away the slightest historicism or allusion to the *genius loci* when Robert Venturi's first house and Charles Moore's Sea Ranch were still new. It is a thoughtful, well-executed work which deep in the woods of some summer camp would be a delight, but which is rather 'cute' for an academic setting.

NL-55b Just beyond the Mensa is Blom's student centre, **De Bastille,** 1970. It is both more ambitious and less successful, despite some interesting if theatrical interior spaces. Even more than the Mensa, it tries to incorporate too many incompatible foreign ideas (primarily American ones derived from pop culture and commercial symbolism), in this case at the expense of its strongest, most Dutch feature: its 'plaid' grid of structure and services. If only Blom had put more effort into developing the possibilities of this organizational system – and less into trying to assimilate transitory foreign enthusiasms.

NL-55c Just inside the campus gate, to the right and across the canal, is a small, highly refined if symmetrically precious, former **faculty dining-pavilion,** 1964, by J. van Stigt, which now serves as administrative offices.

NL-55d The **railway station in nearby Enschede,** 1949, is the work of H. G. J. Schelling, as is:

NL-55e The **station in Hengelo,** 1950. Both are interesting and not unpleasant examples of a very Perret-esque architecture which otherwise is almost unknown in Holland.

Helmond   **NL-56**
Paalwoningen ('pole' or 'tree' houses)
1973–8
Markt
Piet Blom
In Helmond ctr, on Markt (the central sq)

It is hard to know which is the more astonishing, the design of these cube houses, each balancing on one corner, or the fact that they were built. One is inclined to wonder if a certain kind of once fashionable mushroom, rather than any tree, led

to their creation. If the three upper sides of each cube function almost logically as roofs, the lower ones would make curious floors and are not much more reasonable

Eindhoven   NL-57

Although it has no buildings of particular architectural merit, at least by the more stringent criteria that must apply in Holland, Eindhoven's centre is one of the most comfortable and workable to be found among Europe's new, small industrial cities.

Heerlen [near Maastricht]   **NL-58**
* Het Warenhuis Schunck
(department store) 1934–6
Marktplein and Kerkplein
F. P. J. Peutz
International Style
From E39 → HEERLEN CENTRUM */ R on Geleenstr / L on Kruisstr (NL-59 is to L) / first L past church / L on Bongero / in first blk on L*

[At the time of writing the building stood empty, the Schunck store having moved to an anonymous box several blocks away.]

There is a curious silence in architectural literature about both this building and its architect. The all-glass curtain wall – admittedly an unpractical sheathing for a department store – and the general massing and detailing are reminiscent of, and no more dateable than the contemporaneous work of Sir Owen Williams (GB-57). This is,

Heerlen [near Maastricht]   **NL-59**
* Raadhuis (city hall) 1939–47
Raadhuisstraat
F. P. J. Peutz
Mannered Modern Neo-Classicism
From E39 → HEERLEN CENTRUM */ on central sq*

There are few better examples of the change a few years, and perhaps a different client, can make in an architect's work (NL-58). But do not be deceived by initial appearances. Peutz produced here a marvellously witty design. Its carefully casual fenestration, its consciously juxtaposed mouldings and orders of totally incompatible scale, its artfully undisguised

as walls. Yet, with their sloping walls and built-in cabinetry, the compact interiors of these wooden 'Alice in Wonderland' houses appear comfortably boat-like.

NL-57a Of some importance to the student of the De Stijl movement is Eindhoven's **Stedelijk van Abbe Museum** at Bilderdijklaan 10. Its collection contains a number of De Stijl artefacts, including a model of Theo van Doesburg's only important architectural work, the long-destroyed Café-Cinema L'Aubette, 1927.

in fact, one of the most technical-seeming products of a decade which by its midpoint was markedly turning away from such extreme expressions of faith in technology.

It deserves to be better known and more important, and it must be preserved.

almost-false front, and its most modern monumental interior staircase all seem more suggestive of the too-knowing 70s than of the often unduly-innocent 40s.

PORTUGAL

Portugal Map P-1

5-7 Oporto (Porto)

P PORTUGAL

E SPAIN

Sintra 1b

▲1a, 2-4 Lisbon (Lisboa)

Faro● 7a

Portugal   **P-1**
Architecturally Portugal is one of the most pleasing countries in Europe, but most of her architectural glories are of the past. The *azulejo* (ceramic tile) industry, which once produced an endless variety of imaginative tile patterns, and sheathed countless buildings – causing whole towns to glisten and shine – now dully, repetitiously, mimics tasteless French 'modernistic' designs. Still, the builder's vernacular architecture here is frequently better than its French counterpart, owing in part, perhaps, to innate conservatism and in part to influences from neighbouring Spain (E-27).

Such self-consciously modern architecture as there is in Portugal tends to follow the latest fashionable Spanish or Italian prototypes. However, in a country which once cheerfully merged Moorish, Baroque and even Oriental influences, and which also produced as vigorously ornamented a style as the Late Gothic Manueline (as seen at Tomar and Batalha), it should not be surprising to find a penchant for essentially decorative architecture.

P-1a There was a small, National Romantic revival of Manueline in the nineteenth century. The best examples of this are the **Estação do Rossio** (railway station) in Lisbon, 1887, by J. Limonteiro, *At S end of Av da Liberdade*, and:

P-1b The expansion and embellishment of the **Palácio da Pena** (palace) at Sintra, 1839–85, which was carried out by a German amateur architect, Count Eschewege – hence its northern romantic echoes of Neuschwanstein (D-73). *On Serra de Sintra / entrance off N247-3 S of Sintra*

Lisbon (Lisboa)   **P-2**
* Santa Justa Lift 1898–1901
Rua do Ouro and Rua de Santa Justa
Gustave Eiffel
Iron Gothic
S from Rossio (P-1a) one blk → river on Rua do Ouro / R on Rua de Santa Justa / at end of blk

Unlike Eiffel's bridge in Oporto (P-5a), this unusual example of vertical public transport is apparently a product of his office and not his own personal design. Although Lisbon is a hilly city with several picturesque funiculars, the Santa Justa Lift seems to tie the upper and lower towns together more effectively than they do. This is partly because, as a free-standing tower, it is a highly visible symbolic link. But more important, it helps its users to understand better Lisbon's complicated multi-level topography – in other words there is a spectacular view from the top.

P-2a In addition to the Santa Justa Lift,

Lisbon offers a couple of other spatial experiences. The more conventional of these, the lobby of the **Eden Cinema**, 1930–5, by Cassiano Branco, is a grand, almost man-

nerist, composition of staircases and bal-
ustrades that leaves one wishing its
architect had been able to finish the rest of
the building. *Adjacent to Estação do Rossio
(P-1a) on Praça dos Restauradores*

P-2b As much an environmental as
an architectural experience, the **Estufa
Fria** ('cold stove'), 1910–30, by Raul Cara-
pinha, occupies several acres of the Edward
VII Park. The entire land surface within the
Estufa, an old quarry, has been transformed
with rocks and boulders into a series of
planting areas and niches interlaced with
diminutive streams and ponds. It is like a

cross between the Moorish and Japanese
traditions of garden design – all set beneath
a lattice-work that reproduces the atmosphere of a rain forest (many of the plants
are from Brazil) by retaining moisture and
moderating the summer heat. The Estufa
Fria is a wholly original conception. Unfortunately its execution might have been
more imaginative. If only it had some of the
wit and sophistication of Gaudí's rockwork
(E-12), or the enthusiasm of Ferdinand
Cheval's (F-57). *N from Rossio (P-1a) on Av
da Liberdade / L around roundabout on Av J
A de Aguiar / R on Rua Castilho / at far end
of park on R*

Lisbon (Lisboa)   **P-3**
**Ingreja do Sagrado Coração de
Jesus** (church and community
centre) 1962–7
Rua Camillo Castelo Branco
Nuno Portas & Teotonio Pereira
Neo-Liberty
*N from Rossio (P-1a) on Av da Liberdade / R
just before roundabout on to Rua Alexandre
Herculano / second L on to Rua Castelo
Branco / on R*
Superficially this church, community
centre, cinema, cafe and pedestrian pass-
ageway owes too much to Spain and Italy.
But in pre-revolutionary Portugal it was
enough that such an ambitious yet disciplined complex could have been built at all,
considering the then staunchly conservative nature of both the government
and the client. Externally it is flawed only
by the finish of its pre-cast panels – the
first ever made in Portugal! – whose fuzzy,
exposed aggregate surfaces clearly seem
incompatible with the otherwise insistently
hard geometric detailing. Within the
church this same unaccommodating geometric aesthetic leads to the only other

serious problem, a violent clash with the
familiar furnishings and bric-à-brac
brought from the parish's old church.

P-3a There is an interesting **office
building** with a multi-level shopping
arcade, 1970, by Pereira, on the Rua
Braancamp. *W on Rua A. Herculano five blks
/ R on Rua Castilho / at end of first blk on R*

Lisbon (Lisboa)   **P-4**
Fundação Calouste Gulbenkian
(museum and offices) 1960–9
Avenida de Berna
Cid, Pessoa & Atouguia,
with Sir Leslie Martin
Late International Style
*N from Rossio (P-1a) on Av da Liberdade /
angle R at roundabout on to Av Fontes Pereira
de Melo / L on to Av A Augusto de Aguiar /
abt ½ mi (1 km) on R*
There is a strong similarity between this
deceptively large complex set in a lavishly
landscaped park and the art collection it

houses. Each exudes a conservative but
exceedingly knowledgeable good taste that
leaves no possible doubt as to the incredible
sums expended on the enterprise.
Do not expect to find anything startlingly
new here. At the same time, the building,
and even more the collection, are very fine.
There may be only a few examples of any
one artist or object type, but almost
invariably they are of the highest calibre,
be they the small, disquieting visions of pre-
Revolutionary France by Hubert Robert or
Sarah Bernhardt's incredible Lalique Art
Nouveau jewellery.

Oporto (Porto)   P-5

To the casual observer Oporto may seem somewhat less sophisticated than Lisbon. Yet because it is the country's business capital, it once benefited disproportionately from its greater foreign connections. Two notable architectural fruits of these contacts are:

Oporto (Porto)   P-6
Garagem Comercio (garage and offices) 1926–30
Rua do Almada and Rua Elisio de Melo
Rogerio Azevedo
International Style
E from Av dos Aliados (Oporto's central N-S open space) on Rua Elisio de Melo / on R at end of first blk.

For its date it would be worthy of some note in any country. Here it is remarkable, and not only for its period orthodoxies. Although, strangely, there are no shops at ground level, the combination of uses and the expression of the office floors disconcertingly anticipate postwar trends. And if the grand corner entrance seems to

P-5a Gustave Eiffel's **Ponte Maria Pia,** a railway bridge over the Douro, 1877, which is similar to his bridge at Garabit, France (F-58), and;

P-5b An **Art Nouveau shopfront** worthy of Paris. *Rua de Santa Catarina and Rua de Santo António, just off Praça da Batalha*

have been misappropriated from a bank, that may say something about the sort of people who could afford to own cars here.

Oporto (Porto)   P-7
Escola (school) 1970–2
Largo de Tomé Pires
Carmo Matos (Dept of Educational Construction), with A. Brandão
W from Oporto ctr on Av da Boavista / L abt 2 mi (3 km) past Praça de Mousinho de Albuquerque (roundabout) on to Rua de Sagres (opposite Av do Dr Antunes Guimarães) / bear R / on L

Compared to Spain, the standards of public construction in pre-revolutionary Portugal were relatively high – even though this meant fewer of the badly needed classrooms and dwellings were actually built. Certainly the quality of this school leaves little to be desired. More surprising, given the ultra-conservativism of most pre-revolutionary government architecture, is the integrity of the design. This

particular building represents an advanced stage of a programme to build standardized secondary schools throughout the country, which meant that its architects were able to put more effort into the design, knowing that the cost would be spread over a number of buildings. They were also able to make refinements in later schools based on experiences with early ones – as a comparison of this school with the first of its series at Faro will show.

It is all the more curious, then, that the gymnasia here and at Faro are both of an identical and considerably less satisfying design – which may be a comment on the nature of bureaucracies rather than on the inconsistencies of designers.

P-7a The **Faro School** is on the main road (N125) leading west out of town.

SWEDEN

Sweden   Map S-1

31-32▲
Kiruna   ● 32b
            Svappavaara

Luleå
32c

▲30
Borgafjäll

S
SWEDEN

SF
FINLAND

N
NORWAY

●1a

SF-28-30
Turku ▲

▲N-2-7
Oslo   ●SF-4d

Stockholm
▲ 22-24   2-21 ▲
Örebro   24a ●Södertälje

25 ■
Tibro

▲ 26-27
Göteborg

Klippan
DK-18 ▲   28 ▲ ▲29
        Hälsingborg
DK   ▲
DENMARK   DK-2-17

Map S-2   Stockholm

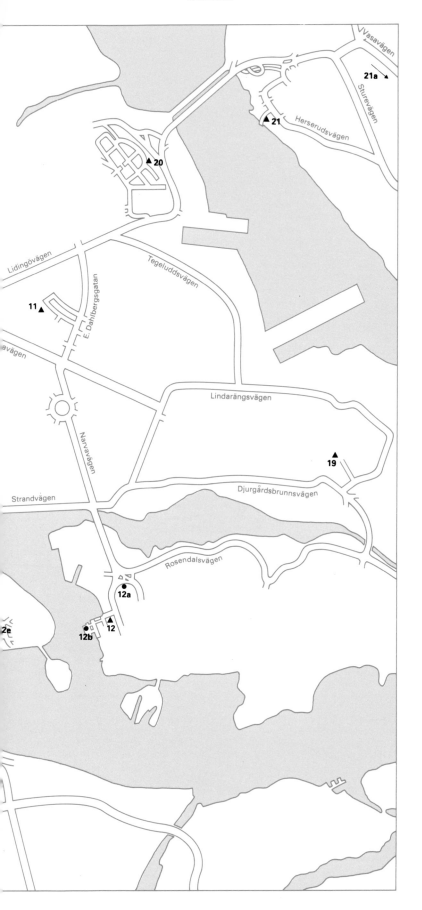

Sweden (Sverige)   S-1

When the Swedish Architecture Museum (S-2e) was founded some years ago, one of its basic premises was that modern Swedish architecture had begun in 1927 with the conversion of Gunnar Asplund from Neo-Classicism to the International Style (S-7), which in Scandinavia is still called Functionalism. Subsequently Asplund, who was as thorough as he was brilliant, chose to build the 1930 Stockholm Exhibition in a radical, almost Constructivist, version of the International Style. And with that, almost overnight, all Scandinavia adopted the new creed. It is a story one hears throughout the region. Although it sounds almost too much like the tale of some saintly bishop of the early church single-handedly converting an entire heathen nation, it is fairly accurate. However, the Swedes for a long time accepted it so literally that they badly neglected their own pre-1930 modern architecture.

In a way this is typical of Sweden's architectural establishment. It seems to place little emphasis on historical or aesthetic issues – which may be why, despite the number of creative Swedish architects since Asplund's time, none of them appears to have become the focus of a philosophical or stylistic school. Instead, a great deal of thought and attention is given to prosaic planning and design standards, if not always to their ultimate sociological impact. It is not surprising that outside Sweden, Swedish architecture has for so long been strongly identified with housing, community centres and the like. Unfortunately, since the time of the influential early projects so glowingly reported to the postwar world, there has been little improvement upon the then quite acceptable housing and satellite community design standards. Indeed, the direct user involvement which once played so important a part in the design process has almost disappeared, and with it much of the (admittedly at times over-optimistic) 'humanism' of Sweden's architecture.

Most Swedish housing is built and owned by a few large co-operative societies. And, as the economics of scale in the building industry have changed, these co-ops have increased the size of both their individual buildings and their total housing projects. The latest housing areas near Stockholm – if thirty miles can be called near – are huge aggregations of identical ten-storey slabs housing as many as 40,000 people. For better or worse, these still incorporate rote versions of those same planning criteria which once, when applied to communities of 5,000 housed in four to six-storey build-ings, earned so much praise both for Swedish planning and indirectly for Swedish architecture. Careful attention is still paid, for instance, to the complete separation of vehicular and pedestrian traffic. But because of the increased scale of the new shopping centres – needing to serve a population of 300,000 – most new housing areas are within walking distance of only the most minimal range of convenience shops. Consequently, the carefully arranged pedestrian circulation networks are largely useless, and apparently unused, save for persons going to or from the underground.

Stockholm's only planned suburban centre of any architectural interest is Vällingby (S-18). Significantly it is one of the earliest, and although not ideal, it still is one of the best.

Language note In alphabetical listings, Å, Ä and Ö always follow Z.

S-1a Mitigating the sterile reality of this over-organized urban utopia is the fact that most Swedish families (or so it seems) have some isolated rural retreat, in a sense their *real* home, where they spend every possible hour of the short, sun-filled Nordic summer. The romantic apotheosis of the Swedish summer house is **'Little Hyttnäs'**, 1884–1912, the studio-home of the painter Carl Larsson. Overlooking a small river at the edge of Sundborn, a village in Dalarna – Sweden's most 'Swedish' province – it is a rambling assemblage of buildings and parts of buildings, some old and some added, or moved to the site, by Larsson.

Little Hyttnäs remains today as Larsson recorded it in the innumerable illustrations of artistic bourgeois domesticity (peopled by his own family) that have endeared themselves to generations of Swedes. The house reflects – in many often subtle and original, but essentially conservative, ways – some of the most advanced design sensibilities of its time: sensibilities Larsson may well have encountered first-hand in Vienna, Brussels, Darmstadt, Glasgow or London; sensibilities that almost always lead back, if one traces them, to William Morris and the Arts and Crafts Movement. Yet Morris was a utopian socialist and a man with a dark, at times almost tragic, nature who can be seen as larger than life, while Larsson – as represented both by his paintings and by his diminutively scaled home – appears just the opposite. He seems to have been a deeply satisfied man, one who greatly enjoyed, amidst his bright rooms, all the little pleasures an ordinary person could reasonably expect.

Stockholm   S-2

Sweden is well on its way to becoming one of the most centralized countries in Europe – centralized, of course, in Stockholm, its capital. In response to this rapid expansion Stockholm has sponsored some of the most coherent, right-minded, and yet at times soulless suburbs to be seen anywhere in the postwar world. And it has also fostered some of postwar Europe's more needlessly destructive urban renewal. Through precise administrative controls and its actual ownership of most of the surrounding countryside Stockholm is able, to a remarkable degree, to dictate the nature and form of its expansion. Unfortunately, despite this municipal sponsorship of its development and despite a reliance upon large apartment blocks, the underlying design ethic seems doggedly anti-urban. Indeed, the retention of green space within the expanding city is nothing short of phenomenal, especially considering the large areas already occupied by water. When seen from the telecommunications tower (S-19), the new suburban Stockholm almost disappears amidst lakes and trees – and over the horizon.

S-2a Hötorgscity, Stockholm's first modern urban redevelopment venture, 1953–62, at one time had a significant reputation as an example of good urban design. That it did typifies the confusion of Swedish planning with Swedish architecture which has existed in the minds of many outsiders. Architecturally, with the possible exception of the Dux building by Backström & Reinius – and then one is speaking primarily of its lobby – Hörtorgscity is hardly worth a mention. Even its multi-level circulation system, the planning innovation for which it is best known, was evidently a fortuitous by-product of a prewar decision to cut Kungsgatan, one of the city's main shopping streets, through an inconvenient hill. *T-bana: Hötorget*

S-2b Only some twenty years after its inception did the project's first positive architectural dividends begin to appear, with the construction of the **Sergels Torg** traffic roundabout and its associated underground shopping areas, and of Peter Celsing's adjacent Temporary Parliament Building and Cultural Centre (S-5) – all of which are in part built over a motorway. *T-bana: Hötorget*

S-2c The cave-like **stations of Järva, Täby and Botkyrka T-bana** (underground) lines beneath central Stockholm, 1973–8, were designed by S. L. Arkitecktkontor, in conjunction with various artists whose work was made an integral part of the station designs.

S-2d Contemporary planning aside, much of central Stockholm remains romantically appealing, especially as seen from the water. One of the better such views of it is to be had from the deck of the sailing ship **Af Chapman,** now a student hostel with a café on the deck.

S-2e On Skeppsholmen Island, near the *Af Chapman*, is the **Swedish Architecture Museum.** It mounts interesting temporary exhibitions on a variety of architectural topics and maintains photographic files of recent Swedish buildings.

Stockholm   **S-3**
*** **Stadshuset** (city hall) 1902–23
Hantverkargatan 1
Ragnar Östberg
National Romantic
Map S-2¹ / T-bana: Centralen

It might be argued that this imaginative assemblage of historical allusions is not modern architecture. Yet spiritually, if not technologically, it could hardly have arisen in any previous period. Even though its imagery is borrowed from distant times and places – the Baroque seventeenth century, Gothic Venice, the Islamic Near East – it reflects a sincere attempt, typical of the period of its inception, to establish a traditional basis for a modern regional architectural style. In fact, a careful study of Asplund's work, not to mention that of Aalto and many other Scandinavian architects, shows a lasting debt to the Stadshuset.

Most of the Stadshuset's fabulously exotic, if disjointed interior can be seen only on a guided tour. It is also possible for the reasonably fit to visit the top of the tower. This involves a ride in a lift, several flights of steps traversing a large, dim, domed space – spookily filled with sculptors' trial pieces – through whose floor protrudes the oculused dome of a reception room below, and then about four turns around the uppermost part of the tower on an eerily lit ramp, until finally one emerges on to an open belfry. There are two additional platform levels above that, if one is in the mood and the weather permits.

And far below, set by the water's edge in the west end of the garden, an unexpected diminutive fountain provides delightful respite from all this knowing and extravagant fantasy.

Stockholm   S-4
* Läkarsällskapets Hus (Swedish
Medical Society) 1905–6
Klara Ö. Kyrkogata 10
Carl Westman
Eclectic Art Nouveau
Map S-2 / T-bana: Hötorget
 [Permission to enter must be secured in
advance.]

One is reminded of an issue of *The Studio*
from its turn-of-the-century heyday.
Passing from room to room is like thumbing
through articles illustrating various
examples of then avant-garde decor. And,
as in those illustrations, the relation of one
room to the next can be a bit vague at
times. Still there *is* an underlying consistency, even if it is only a uniform patina –
like that of the fragile yellowing pages of an
oft-opened journal.

Stockholm   S-5
* Kulturhuset and **Riksdaghus-
provisoriet** (Cultural Centre and former
temporary Parliament House) 1966–71
Sergels Torg
Peter Celsing
Map S-2 / T-bana: Hötorget
 These buildings close off the south end of
Sergels Torg/Hötorgscity.

 The Cultural Centre contains, or will
contain, a small theatre and cabaret, exhibition spaces, a library, shops, restaurants
and the headquarters of several cultural
organizations, including eventually the
Swedish Architecture Museum (S-2e).
Although the centre appears to be and in a
sense is two separate buildings, it is
designed to function as a single unit. The
theatrical and administrative elements are
placed in the large stainless steel-sheathed
block to the rear, while most of the other
functions occupy the glazed frontispiece on
Sergels Torg.

 The huge column-free space intended to
house the larger theatre, its stage, flyloft
and lobby, was first fitted out as an
assembly hall, with appropriate ancillary
spaces, for Sweden's new unicameral parliament. The remainder of this block was
then given over to parliamentarians' offices
and committee rooms.

Stockholm   S-6
Eden Hotell (hotel) 1927–9
Sturegatan 10–12
Björn Hedvall
International Style
Map S-2 / T-bana: Östermalmstorg
 Asplund deserves the credit he gets for
transforming Scandinavia's architectural
allegiance from Neo-Classicism to the International Style (S-7). But he was not entirely
alone in this effort, nor even necessarily the
first. Here is a building as uncompromisingly modern, albeit more German
than Scandinavian, and also earlier than
any of Asplund's modernist designs.

Stockholm   S-7
* Stadsbiblioteket (Stockholm city
library) 1921–8
Sveavägen and Odengatan 51–55
Gunnar Asplund
Neo-Classicism
Map S-2 / T-bana: Odenplan

With its discordant stylistic and/or philosophical discontinuities, this library records
the conversion to 'Functionalism' of *the*
leader of Scandinavia's Neo-Classical
revival. With the exception of the café built
into its podium which today, after violent
protests, is occupied by a MacDonalds ham-
burger restaurant, the transformation may
not at first seem so obvious. But the original
designs envisaged additional Classical ornament, heavy cornices and a central dome
rather than the present flat-topped drum.
Their deletions were a significant symbolic
act.

Spatially, however, the impact of this
building transcends all questions of style:
one need only cite the interior of the drum,
so strongly reminiscent of projects by late
eighteenth-century French revolutionary
romantic Neo-Classicists, or the unexpectedly disquieting stairs, echoing with
unseen footfalls, which curve darkly up out
of sight within its thick walls.

S-7a Another powerful proponent of
Scandinavia's Neo-Classical revival was
Ivar Tengbom, who built the sombre
Stockholms Enskilda Bank, 1915, at
Kungsträdgårdsgatan 8.
T-bana: Kungsträdgården

S-7b Tengbom's **Konserthuset** (concert hall), 1920–6, on the Hötorget, is
perhaps the single best-known example of
the style. *T-bana: Hötorget*

Stockholm   S-8
** Engelbrektskyrkan (church)
1906–14
Östermalmsgatan 20
Lars Israel Wahlman
National Romantic
Map S-2 / T-bana: Tekn. Högskol.

For a people reputedly so serious about
life, the Swedes can build remarkably
romantic fantasies – even though sometimes those fantasies (S-3) may carry
additional messages of nationalism. The
nationalistic allusions here primarily recall
Sweden's early, decidedly primitive Gothic
rather than the more sophisticated Northern Baroque which served as a point of
departure for some of Wahlman's contemporaries. This choice allowed him
greater latitude in his use of structure and
ornament than might have been possible
with the Classically-based Baroque, no
matter how freely adapted, because of its
more formal canons of design. Even Östberg
in his magnificently eclectic Stadshuset (S-
3) had to compartmentalize his borrowings,
so that the less unconventional and more
mutually congenial styles dominate the
exterior, while his extreme exoticisms are
carefully insulated from each other in separate interior spaces. Wahlman, on the
other hand, was able in this church to integrate the traditional and the exotic, the
adapted and the invented, into one reasonably coherent whole.

S-8a The various architects who built the
fashionable immediate **neighbourhood**
to the north and west of the church,
c. 1907–14, were quite sympathetic to it
without ever imitating its more extreme
external stylistic elements.

Stockholm　　　　　　　　　　　**S-9**
* Kungliga Tekniska Högskolan
(Institute of Technology) Begun 1917
Valhallavägen 79
Lars Erik Lallerstedt (1917–45)
Nils Ahrbom (1945–60)
Gunnar Henriksson (since 1960)
National Romantic
Map S-2 / T-bana: Tekn. Högskol.

To walk through first the older and then the newer parts of this campus can be rather depressing. In spite of the beautiful site and a remarkable consistency sustained over more than sixty years of construction, Lallerstedt's successors could not maintain his standards.

Clearly, Lallerstedt had no qualms about using the interplay of symmetry and asymmetry to help create the romantic dynamic uphill axis, which, through all its plazas, arcades and courtyards, never quite reaches a spatial climax. Regrettably his successors were unable to sustain this tension or fulfil the expectations his work arouses.

S-9a The **Kårhus** (student centre), 1930 and 1952, at Drottning Kristinas Väg 15, is by Sven Markelius.

Stockholm/Frescati　　　　　　　**S-10**
** Universitetsbiblioteket (library)
Allhus (student centre)
Activerum (sportshall) 1973–83
Stockholms Universitet, Fiskartorpsvägen
Ralph Erskine
Map S-2 / library and Allhus are in ctr of campus / sportshall is several hundred yds (m) N of Allhus

The student-owned and operated Activerum, the last of the three Erskine buildings to be completed, is a huge, subtly distorted, wooden Quanset (Nissen) hut. In a sense, it is Erskine's version of Robert Venturi's decorated shed. The Allhus and library were designed together as Erskine's response to a programme that had originally called for a single building. The Allhus, which incorporates a nineteenth-century exhibition building as a dining hall, is a loosely vernacular-like brick and timber structure whose most uninhibited forms and details always remain strongly tectonic. Of the three it is closest in character to Erskine's earlier work (S-30, GB-76). The library has the most demanding role to fill. It is the focal point of the university and a kind of frontispiece mediating between the coldly slick main academic building – Södra Huset – and the park-like campus, which was once a royal hunting preserve. It is also one of the masterpieces of Erskine's career.

Between Södra Huset and the library itself is a high vaulted concourse, intended to serve as a major interior public space. (Erskine's office explicitly thought of it as like a railway terminus.) It is a space filled with action and incident: steel trusses and props supporting arched timber roof beams,

Universitetsbibliothek

angling gangways connecting the upper levels of the library with Södra Huset, faceted thrusting bays, angled end walls penetrated by roof props. Yet it is not an escapist or sentimental space. It is as High-Tech rough and romantic as Stirling's mannered university buildings of the 60s (GB-51, 58). But unlike them, it is designed from the heart, not just the head. Perpendicular to the main concourse is a multi-level 'street' called Bokens Gata, the spine of the two-million volume library. The entire library, including Bokens Gata, rigorously follows a square-column grid. Not surprisingly, the grid is eroded (in a very Rationalist manner) near one entrance to accommodate a small grove of ancient oaks, and is cut off at a slight angle across the front to afford a better view – or so it is said. However, there may also have been a desire to break the technocratic parallel alignment of Södra Huset with the science building across the campus.

Stockholm   **S-11**
* Olaus Petri kyrka (church, parish
centre and apartments) 1955–9
Armfeltsgatan 2–12
Peter Celsing
Post-Modernism
Map S-2 / T-bana: Stadion

Here, arguably, is the first Post-Modern
building. Its concrete frame and stuccoed
walls, its unarticulated shapes and conventional components are all decidedly,
consciously prosaic. Within the church
itself there is a conspicuous absence of dramatic light scoops or other easy spatial (or
symbolic) clichés. Rather, this is an architecture of subtleties – as typified by Celsing's

use of slightly differing floor-tile textures to
define spaces within the church; or by his
application of an almost no-cost, unifying
and scale-modifying wide cornice-like band
of contrasting colour to the upper part of
the exterior walls; or by the ever so slight,
but enlivening and articulating (and again
almost cost-free) 'kink' that occurs at a
necessary but otherwise insignificant construction joint between the religious and
residential parts of the building.

Today this sort of self-conscious
amalgam of high art and low technology
no longer seems radical, even if it is still not
quite commonplace. In 1959 it would have
been almost without precedent.

Stockholm   **S-12**
* Liljevalchs konsthall (art gallery)
1914–16
Djurgårdsvägen 60
Carl Bergsten
Neo-Classicism
Map S-2

This century has become all too familiar
with buildings, especially commercial ones
(GB-66, 80, I-26a), which have some sort
of historical style at the front, where an
image is needed, even though they may
have the most rational sort of construction
in the rear. This art gallery is just that
sort but, perversely, reversed. Here the front
part, which would have been quite *au
courant* in 1914, is replete with references
to factory construction and to the then very
contemporary Rationalist work of Auguste
Perret (the prismatic concrete columns and
coffered ceiling of the front gallery), while
the rest of the building is more traditional.

Obviously this jokey inversion is not the
work of a dogmatic theoretician. But then
Bergsten was never that (S-26). Nor is it
the only such game being played here. At
one end of the first exhibition gallery is a
staircase, the focal point of that space. It
leads first to a landing which gives access to
a tea room, and then to a balcony running
beneath the clerestory windows that encircle the gallery. Close inspection reveals, however, that although the stair
treads are of a full width as far as the
landing, the second run and the balcony
itself are just wide enough to permit access
for washing the windows or adjusting spot-

lights. They are indeed a sort of functional
trompe-l'œil which, when seen from below,
is quite believable. Few progressive designers of the time could have taken
themselves so unseriously.

S-12a A short way towards the city and
on the other side of Djurgårdsvägen, is Agi
Lindegren's remarkable little **Biologiska
museet** (biology museum), 1893, which
looks and feels as one has always imagined
a nineteenth-century exhibition building
should – including the sign that unself-
consciously wraps itself around the
entrance portico.

The exterior form of the museum is that
of a freely-adapted *stavkyrka* (a medieval
Scandinavian wooden church), but its
interior is pure Victoriana: one huge 'natural' setting for stuffed animals surrounding a most remarkable double spiral staircase and viewing platform.

S-12b Of course one could not be this
close to the ship **Wasa** without visiting it.

Stockholm   **S-13**
Katarinahissen (lift and bridge-
restaurant) 1935–6
Slussen
Eskil Sundahl & Olof Thunström
Constructivism
Map S-2 / T-bana: Slussen

Like Eiffel's Santa Justa Lift in Lisbon
(P-2), this combination restaurant and vertical public transport could justify its existence solely by the view it affords. It has the
distinction of being one of the few extant
structures reflecting something of the spirit
of Russian Constructivism.

Stockholm   **S-14**
**** Skogskrematoriet, Skogs-
kyrkogården** (forest crematorium)
1935–40
Sockenvägen
Gunnar Asplund
Scandinavian Empiricism
S on Rt 73 (Map S-2→) to SKOGSKYRKO-
GÅRDEN *exit / L on Sockenvägen / R into
cemetery / T-bana: Skogskyrkogården*

After they won the design competition
for the Forest Cemetery in 1917, Asplund
and Sigurd Lewerentz collaborated on the
development of its general plan. Then
during the succeeding two decades, each
individually designed several of its buildings. The earliest, Asplund's Skogskapelle
(forest chapel) of 1920, is a simple wooden
structure with a shingled roof and whitewashed walls. The sculpture over its
entrance is by Carl Milles. The next,
the Uppståndelsekapellet (Resurrection
chapel), 1927, by Lewerentz, is a high point
of the Scandinavian Neo-Classical Revival.

There can be no comparison, however,
between either of these and Asplund's
Forest Crematorium. The power of the
building in its setting evades description.
As one climbs a gentle hill, the colonnaded
porch and great free-standing cross appear
quietly against the sky, whose changing
moods are also then found captured in a
small still pond at the crest of the slope. (At

the pond's edges, the sky merges imper-
ceptibly and surreally into the grassy
hilltop.) Inside the porch, beneath an asym-
metrically-placed oculus, a monumental
bronze sculpture by Joel Lundqvist reasserts
life, or afterlife, amidst tranquillity. The
floor of the porch slopes gently down
towards the chapel itself, subtly but com-
pellingly focusing the space. (The bronze
and glass wall between chapel and porch
can be lowered into the ground so that,
when possible, services can be held partly
or wholly in the open air.)

There is a reassurance in this unity of
architecture and site which derives not
from its dignity or its elegance of conception, but rather from its integrity of use and
meaning. Tragically, Asplund himself died
in the year of the chapel's completion. He
was cremated and his ashes interred here.

S-14a Another major Stockholm project
by Asplund, now somewhat modified and,
because of over-enthusiastic traffic engineering, difficult of access, is the **Statens
Bakteriologiska Laboratorium** (State
Bacteriological Laboratory), 1933–8, on
Storgatan in Solna. Its gatehouse interestingly anticipates, by about thirty years,
the Post-Modernists' enthusiasm for false
fronts. *NW on Solnavägen (Map S-2→) / L
on Sundbybergsvägen / L on Järnvägsgatan / L on Lundagatan / at end of rd on L*

Stockholm/Björkhagen   **S-15**
* Markuskyrkan (church) 1956–60
Malmövägen 51
Sigurd Lewerentz
Brutalism
*S on Rt 73 (Map S-2→) to first exit past
bridge (Skanstullsbrön) / →*BJÖRKHAGEN
(via Olaus Magnus Vägen ⇨ *Sparrmans-
vägen / L on Finn Malmgrens Vägen
/ R, under RR, at* BJÖRKHAGEN */ L on
Malmövägen / on L just before Björkhagen
Station / T-bana: Björkhagen*

If the Markuskyrkan is compared with the similar church Lewerentz designed at Klippan (S-29) six years later, the Klippan church is seen to be the more convincingly coherent, whereas this delights the visitor with its innovative vigour. Indeed, the relationship here between form and structure can be quite naive, not to say jarring, with curiously inappropriate combinations of materials mimicking the nave's brick vaulting. This church also suffers from a traditional linear hierarchical plan and an unfortunate, if typical, tacked-on space for Holy Day worshippers.

But if the Markuskyrkan has its limitations as a church there is true poetry in its exterior ambience – much enhanced by the often pale Scandinavian light. The paving, for instance, is made of various industrial ceramic units, including the huge pie-shaped bricks used in power plant chimneys. And they, like the beautiful little retaining wall that runs half-hidden through the trees on the far side of the site, are laid with a care and subtle sureness that one might expect in a Japanese garden.

Stockholm/Gröndal　　　　　　　S-16
Galjonsbilden (housing) 1947–52
Gröndalsvägen and Sjöbjörnsvägen
Sven Backström & Leif Reinius
Scandinavian Empiricism
SW (Map S-2→) on E4 / exit →
LILJEHOLMEN *on Liljeholmsinfarten*
/ angle L on Liljeholmsvägen / R on
Lövholmsvägen / angle R on
Gröndalsvägen / 400 yds (m) on R

Sweden's reputation for humane housing design rests primarily on early postwar projects such as this, and decidedly not on its more recent efforts (S-1). This pleasant but irregular site, which now might be passed over in favour of a location more amenable to mass production techniques, has been cleverly utilized to accommodate offices, shops, and housing in a combination of towers, row houses and stepped flats – among which these last, set into the side of a hill, are decidedly the most interesting. Indeed, their expansive terraces and generously glazed façades make them as seductive as any housing in Sweden. They project the image of a truly new housing type – like those proposed at different times by both the Expressionists and Frank Lloyd Wright, but never really achieved by either. They suggest the possibility of a new kind of human-centred, nature-oriented urbanism; one which would maintain the traditional densities and social amenities, but would also reflect the tectonic texture and the scale appropriate to its human builders and occupants,

rather than those imposed by industrialized construction components and over-large financial institutions.

S-16a The same architects also designed the earlier area of linked three-lobed 'star'-plan housing, 1943–7, just to the north, across Sjöbjörnsvägen. This peculiarly Swedish housing type was developed to maximize the efficiency and variety of the dwelling units while providing sheltered semi-enclosed courts between the wings of adjoining star-blocks.

Stockholm　　　　　　　S-17
Kollektivhus (co-op apartment)
1934–5
John Ericssongatan 6
Sven Markelius
International Style
Map S-2

A building can be rather like a seashell, shaping and shaped by the organism that created and lives within it. Often the original organism dies, or builds itself a new shell, leaving the old to be filled by a new life form which, hermit-crab-like, must adapt itself to fit its borrowed home.

Such was the case with this building. It was designed for a group of families: in theory, workers, artists and intellectuals; in fact, only artists and intellectuals. They were to live semi-communally with their own child-care centre and a central kitchen that supplied both a ground-floor restaurant and the deliberately kitchenless apartments (via dumb waiters). But with

the passing of the original communards the organism they had created withered away too, even though many of the present occupants are their children. Now the communal kitchen serves an ordinary res-

taurant, the child-care centre is a conventional nursery school, and the flats have had kitchens squeezed into them. Only the shell survives, but it is an interesting specimen despite all that.

Stockholm/Vällingby   **S-18**
Vällingby Centrum (suburban shopping and civic centre) 1952–6
Sven Markelius (plan), Sven Backström & Leif Reinius (shops)
Scandinavian Empiricism
W on Norr Mälarstrand (Map S-2→) / W at roundabout on Rt 275 (Drottningholms-vägen) / → VÄLLINGBY / T-bana: Vällingby

Vällingby Centre, one of the earliest and most widely respected of Stockholm's suburban centres, has all the subtlety and sophistication of a carnival. There is nothing wrong with such places of exotic amusement. But their throw-away architecture needs to do no more than provide a momentary diversion from everyday life.

To have to live with it, day by day, might prove less than satisfying.

All that said, however, Vällingby still has no real peers among Stockholm's later suburban centres. The simple truth is that they offer nothing new – except ever greater size. They have neither Vällingby's sense of fun, forced though it may be, nor the spatial interest of its open areas.

S-18a Vällingby's **St Thomas kyrka**, 1959, by Peter Celsing, is not quite up to his other work, although the nave might be an interesting space were it not for the obtrusive lighting fixtures and organ pipes. *Just NW of Vällingby ctr on Kirunagatan / T-bana: Vällingby*

Stockholm   **S-19**
* Kaknästornet (telecommunications tower) 1964–7
Djurgårdsbrunnsvägen
Hans Borgström & Bengt Lindroos
Map S-2

This sort of half-work, half-play civic electronic monument is almost exclusively a European phenomenon. (America's private communications companies, even those that could afford such conspicuous, specialized structures, feel no need to build them.) Typically these towers contain television and radio antennae for government-run broadcasting services, microwave relays for government-run telecommunications systems, and an observation platform and restaurant. Also typically the restaurant, and sometimes the observation deck, revolves, so that its necessarily circular form – which its designers usually treat with no great finesse – then dictates that the remainder of the structure will be circular as well.

Here, where nothing revolves, the architects have doggedly stuck to a scheme of various-sized square plan forms that overlap at 45° angles. Undoubtedly, there is in this a reaction to the round tower cliché. But it is not an over-reaction. It does work: this tower's forms and its materials –

primarily bronze glass and slip-formed concrete – are always under control. Unlike so many of its sort, the Kaknästornet is an elegant, vigorous and welcome addition to the city skyline.

Stockholm/Hjorthagen S-20
Hjorthagens kapell (chapel) 1907–9
Dianavägen
Carl Bergsten
Jugendstil
Map S-2 / T-bana: Ropsten
[The church was beautifully restored in the late 60s. Some changes were made at that time, but they are almost indistinguishable from the original work in both spirit and quality.]

The contrast between interior and exterior is striking. The outside, conservative, dark, and angular, echoes English Arts and Crafts sensibilities. The inside, fresh, light, soft, and full of rounded forms, is Viennese in conception but somewhat nationalistic in its motifs. How delightful so unexpectedly to find oneself standing in this pale-blue and white nave with its understated elliptical concrete arches.

Stockholm/Lidingö S-21
** **Millesgården** (sculpture garden) 1906–60
Carl Milles Väg
Carl Milles (sculptor)
Evert Milles (architect)
Jugendstil/Scandinavian Neo-Classicism
Map S-2
Carl Milles designed no buildings. But a sculptor, like an architect, manipulates space. Of all the artists affected by Scandinavia's twentieth-century revival of archaic Neo-Classicism, Milles was among the most creative.

What is truly fascinating here is not just the massed assemblage of Milles's works but rather the way they interact with their setting. Milles and his brother, Evert, blasted, built up and paved this dramatically rugged, fiord-side site until it became the one great sculpture which encompasses all the others. This most manipulated space cascades with stairs and terraces; it bristles with sculpture-capped columns of granite, marble and porphyry – some made especially for the garden, others salvaged from demolished buildings, both ancient and modern.

A more totally created environment than Sert and Miró's garden at St Paul-de-Vence (F-61a), and infinitely subtler than Gustav Vigeland's ponderous *magnum opus* at Oslo (N-2a), the underlying surrealism here is all the greater for having been embodied in such traditional conventional elements.

Örebro S-22
Örebro is, more or less, Sweden's equivalent to Tapiola (SF-19) or Columbus, Indiana, i.e., a small city with a large reputation as an architectural and planning showplace. Örebro's particular speciality is housing.

S-22a Backstrom & Reinius's romantic **Rosta housing area**, 1947–52, is one of the most characteristic and convincing of its time in Sweden. *SW from Örebro ctr (Vasatorget) on Hagagatan / abt $\frac{1}{2}$ mi (1 km) on R*

S-21a Further out on the island of Lidingö is Carl Nyrén's diminutive **Svenska Missionsförbundets kapell** (seminary chapel), 1959–64. It contains not a single unnecessary complication, no polemic or discordant note: proof that simplicity need not mean simple-mindedness. *E on Vasavägen (Map S-2 →) → STOCKBY, abt 3 mi (5 km) / L at TEOLOG SEMINARIET (small sign) / on R at Kattiavägen 116*

S-22b The **Oxhagen area**, 1965–7, by Joran Curman, is notable for its semi-underground central parking street – one of the too few serious attempts to cope with traffic circulation and storage in a project of such low density. *W from Örebro ctr (Vasatorget) on Karlslundgatan / abt 1$\frac{1}{4}$ mi (2 km) on R*

Örebro   **S-23**

Medborgarhuset (civic hall and
theatre) 1965
Drottninggatan 42
Erik & Tore Ahlsén
*S from E3–18 in Örebro ctr on Drottning-
gatan / one blk on R*

The architecture of the twentieth
century is so susceptible to fads that future
chroniclers should be able, on first sight, to
date many of its buildings to within ten
years. Very evident here, despite the
Ahlséns' overlying idiosyncrasies, is an
enthusiasm for low, square-ish, often
hollow buildings with overhanging upper
stories – a building form whose original
source of inspiration was undoubtedly Le
Corbusier's La Tourette monastery (F-55).

In this case the articulation of the upper
floors is accentuated, for better or worse, by

a typical Ahlsén conceit: spandrels of two
different materials, teakwood, and a rosy
brown sandstone, on the two different
stories. Either material by itself would be
acceptable, although wood is unusual in
an urban building and here suffers from
bad detailing and/or poor maintenance.
But together they add confusion to what,
with greater restraint, might have been a
more convincing façade.

Inside, the Ahlséns' unconventionality
becomes even more evident. Ceilings hang
in taut shallow curves from the tops of
windows, while part of the ground floor
slopes disconcertingly in response to the
exterior gradient. This is a clever device
(eliminating the need for steps leading into
the public spaces), of which other modern
examples do not readily come to mind.

Örebro   **S-24**

* Krämaren (department store, shops,
offices and flats) 1954–63
Drottninggatan 27–29
Erik & Tore Ahlsén
Diagonally across rd from S-23

The Ahlséns' logic can be as discon-
certing as it is unique. Often they experiment with a greater number of unusual,
if not always successful, ideas in a single
building than some architects might try in
a lifetime. This large shopping centre, for
instance, has an unexpected natural-
istically landscapped park on its roof.
Standing comfortably if improbably among
the trees of that park are two apartment
towers whose lowest floors are given over
to offices and other appropriate non-
residential uses.

Each of this building's major components
acts almost as if the others did not exist: the
shop façades are sparkling insubstantial
prisms of glass; the park's planting struc-
ture-cum-parapet wall is a superscale out-
ward-leaning concrete window box; the
apartment buildings are of coolly smooth,
and very understated, enamelled steel
sheathing. It sounds at best like picturesque
anarchy, and at worst like New Jersey. But,
with the possible exception of the over-
crude concrete, it does work, because the

individual parts make sense within their
own frames of reference and because the
basic urbanistic idea has merit.

S-24a In the **Kringlan Block,** 1965, in
the centre of Södertälje, the Ahlséns had
an even less restrained go at this same
programme – but with results much closer
in spirit to Örebro's civic centre (S-23).

Tibro   **S-25**
Brittgården (housing area) 1959–64
Hjovägen and Österlanggatan
Ralph Erskine
Scandinavian Empiricism
S from Rt 49 on Rt 201 through Tibro / on L

It would be hard to imagine anything apparently more divergent from the usual highly standardized Swedish housing practices. Brittgården presents playful roofscapes, sensitive landscaping, a variety of dwelling types, and many small, thoughtful gestures and details. Yet the detailing is rational and standardized; and there are only a few house and apartment plans, albeit in right- and left-hand variations.

Göteborg   **S-26**
* **Stadsteatern** (municipal theatre)
1924–35
Götaplatsen
Carl Bergsten
Mannered (Neo-Classical) Moderne
Götaplatsen (culture centre) is at S end of Kungsportsavenyn (Göteborg's main street) / on NE side of square

The façade of Bergsten's theatre is more overtly Neo-Classical than that of Eriksson's once well-known concert hall (S-26d) which it faces. Presumably Bergsten acted out of respect for the Neo-Classical façade of the art museum (S-26b) which dominates the square. But Bergsten's asymmetrically placed Ionic columns – a parody of the International Style's beloved corner window detail – once scandalized Classicists and Functionalists alike, just as twenty-five years earlier Bergsten had also dared to build one of the few even mildly Art Nouveau buildings in Sweden (S-20). However, within the theatre, where there was no further need to defer to the Art Museum, Bergsten's ultimate allegiance to a kind of modernity is made manifest. Perversely this is nowhere more evident than in the main staircases: they attempt spectacularly to reinterpret those *grands escaliers* that were so much a part of the traditional theatre-going experience. Nor was that Bergsten's only dramatic gesture. The upper lobby, to which the stairs lead, is connected to the lounge by a low, broad arch of a gigantic radius – a device that reappears in almost diagrammatic form on the terse brick rear façade.

S-26a The central focus of the **Götaplatsen** is Carl Milles's marvellously Scandinavian Poseidon, who observes all that passes with a slightly twisted Etruscan smile. There is a comparison begging to be made between this provincial fine arts agora of the Depression era and New York's Lincoln Center. It would prove too embarrassing to New York, however.

S-26b The adjacent **Konstmuseet** (art museum), 1916–22, is by Bjerke & Ericson. Almost literally a theatrical backdrop to the Götaplatsen group, it contains only about a quarter of the volume suggested by its façade. At the east end of its topmost floor is a room decorated for the 1889 Paris Exposition by Carl Larsson.

S-26c The museum's spatially ambitious **addition**, 1968, by White Arkitektkontor A. B., suffers from not knowing whether it wants to be Brutalist or 'curtain-wall' slick. Nor is it a suitable place to hang paintings.

S-26d Directly across Götaplatsen is the **Konserthuset** (concert hall), 1931–5, by Nils Einar Eriksson. Philosophically Eriksson may have been no more rigorous a modernist than Bergsten (S-26), but he does reflect a more serious – should one say stuffy? – attitude towards a basically similar problem. This is nowhere more evident than in the mean, too practical low space, bordered by two enormous cloakroom counters and running under the entire length of the auditorium, which one must traverse before arriving at an unexciting, almost *pro forma*, monumental bifurcated staircase. These stairs in turn lead to a lobby space that entirely encircles the hall: a configuration which was to become a cliché of the 60s culture centre boom. The auditorium itself – the presumed jewel in this casket – is remarkably austere, as if 'serious' music demanded a suitably 'serious' setting.

Göteborg   **S-27**
** **Rådhuset** (law court addition)
1934–7
Gustav Adolfs Torg
Gunnar Asplund
Scandinavian Empiricism
N from Götaplatsen (S-26) on Kungsports-
avenyn ⇨ Östra Hamngatan / on L on far
side of square just past second canal

Of Asplund's two late masterpieces one, the Forest Crematorium (S-14), had no real contemporary imitators, while this, the other, had too many (DK-19).

Asplund was too personal, complex and sophisticated to be copied successfully. Consider only the graceful deference of his new façade to the existing Neo-Classical rhythms and patterns, or how the uncompromisingly original new interior none the less harmonizes across an open courtyard with the older building. And then there is the way various programmatic requirements have been united to generate a space which separately none could have warranted: a three-storey hall, with one entire glazed wall facing on to the courtyard and the other three sides encased in honey-coloured panelling, behind which are offices and courtrooms. The lower level serves as a gathering place for lawyers, while the galleries contain waiting areas, foyers for the courtrooms, and even several alcoves for conducting minor judicial procedures. What finally sets Asplund apart here is his ability to marry the humane with the technical and the abstract, as can be seen in any number of elegant and inventive fittings, such as the glass-bowled drinking fountain or the glazed skeletal elevator.

Hälsingborg   **S-28**
* **Konserthuset** (concert hall)
1925–32
Drottninggatan
Sven Markelius
International Style
N on Järnvägsgatan (main rd along water) ⇨
Drottninggatan / abt four blks N of
Stortorget on L

There is something in most of us that delights in disciplined irrationality or ambiguity, or even just in the unexpected – and perhaps all the more so when, as here in the grand staircase, it comes in the guise of simple, straightforward functionality. Immediately upon entering the Konserthuset, one is confronted by a long straight run of stairs containing no fewer than four landings. Instinctively one anticipates a direct progression through this space – or, at least, one is led to do so by its prismatic purity, by the linearity of the twin rows of light globes that float upwards through it like streams of air bubbles rising in water, and by the implied continuity of the lengthy run of the stairs themselves. But one finds that the first landing abruptly becomes a previously hidden half-flight of stairs leading *down* to a glass wall (whose doors once gave access to a restaurant). The wall in turn is surmounted by the second landing, beyond which one can see the continuation of the staircase.

What to do? One must in fact leave the main run of the stairs as well as the main circulation space, and ascend either of two lateral flights, passing around a pair of semicircular cloakrooms, leading on up to the second landing. From there the stairs continue less eventfully to the auditorium.

Thus one is oriented, disoriented and reoriented through a series of clever manipulations whose impact is out of all proportion to the minimal means employed.

The auditorium, unfortunately, is anti-climactic: another of those unadorned, almost claustrophobic, wood-veneered Swedish music boxes (S-26d). Under it is a cinema with its own separate entrance from the side street.

Klippan [near Hälsingborg] S-29
** **St Petri kyrka** (church) 1963–6
Vedbyvägen
Sigurd Lewerentz
Romantic Brutalism
E of Klippan ctr between Rts 21 and 19, at their junction

This church, sheltered behind artificial earth banks in a densely planted landscape, is one of Sweden's most intriguing modern buildings. With the exception of the skylights, there is no sense of gratuitous invention here. But neither has anything been taken for granted. Bricks are only used whole, with none of the usual cutting or breaking, and yet they perform well in a wide variety of roles. The steelwork has been treated with the same Brutalist sense of expediency that one usually finds only in poured-in-place concrete. The exterior lamp standards, by the simple device of offset and slightly bent poles, have been given a sense of orientation missing from conventional symmetrical fixtures, so that they relate more strongly to their non-symmetrical context. And the tinted, double-glazed windows, held in place by locating clips, are simply glued to the brick wall with a weatherproof caulking mastic.

But materials and details alone do not make architecture. Just as essential is the sure handling of form and space. Lew-erentz's asymmetrical space for worship achieves the intimacy of a small arena theatre through flexible seating, slight variations in floor level and subtle manipulation of textures in the brickwork. At the same time it provides adequate space for a larger Holy Day congregation. How different from the usual Swedish axial nave with its elaborately contrived, inevitably compromising accommodation for Holy Day expansion. It is all the more unfortunate, then, that Lewerentz almost destroyed this sense of integrity, intimacy and repose through an arrangement of interior lighting fixtures reminiscent, unfortunately, of airport landing lights – with the altar as runway.

Borgafjäll S-30
** **Högfjällshotellet** (ski resort hotel) 1948–54
Ralph Erskine
Scandinavian Empiricism
W from Rt 343 abt ½ mi (1 km) S of Dorotea → BORGA / 70 mi (108 km) on R

[A major determinant of the overall form of this ski resort was the way in which wind-driven snow would accumulate on and around it, one of the intentions then being that the main roof should serve as a teaching slope. Unfortunately ski poles can pierce the best of roofing materials and so now the snow rests undisturbed on the roof throughout the winter. There have been sympathetic additions by other architects.]

Sheltering under its great ski-slope roof – and tied together by a romantic yet rational structural system that only Erskine could have devised – is an interconnected series of public areas on several levels where structure, space, colours and furnishings all evoke the immediate postwar mood of romantic optimism. The individual guest rooms present another, almost nautical Erskine, whose attention could be given over to the most efficient use of each square foot. There is, then, a three-way romantic tension here between the rational, the functional and the overtly symbolic. In its extreme intensity and balance, this tension is almost unique to Erskine. And it runs through all his work.

Kiruna   S-31
* **Kiruna kyrka** (church) 1903–12
Kyrkogatan
Gustav Wickman
National Romantic/Jugendstil
*NE on Rt 98 / R on first st before Stadshuset
(town hall) / at top of hill*

[The more traditional free-standing bell-tower is of an earlier date.]

It is said that this church was inspired by the traditional Lapp hut – assuming one can envisage a 10,000-square-foot Lapp hut designed by a sophisticated Stockholm architect and harbouring an altarpiece painted by a prince. But Lapp hut or no, it *is* made entirely of wood – from the huge timber frame with its forged iron connections that nimbly spans the entire nave to the vast expanses of shingling that completely cover its exterior. Admittedly the first impression is of a monstrous version of that miserable modern cliché, the A-frame.

But as one approaches the differences appear: the huge buttresses projecting from its sides; the attached, almost Shingle style rectory; the row of vigorously carved gilt wooden statues with their strong intimations of the Jugendstil; and then, within, a space which has few modern equals in the realm of wooden construction.

Kiruna   S-32
* **Kvartert Ortdrivaren** (housing for
mining technicians) 1959–65
H. Lundbohmsvägen and Hantverkaregatan
Ralph Erskine
Romantic Rationalism
*N on Rt 98 / on R one blk past Stadshuset
(town hall, see S-32a below)*

The more unusual aspects of these buildings are all said to result directly from an interplay between various programmatic, constructional and environmental requirements. Thus the modular dimensioning is determined by a system of pre-cast concrete panels, prefabricated windows, and pre-cast concrete balconies – these latter being especially designed with the least possible connection to the buildings so as to minimize heat loss. Similarly the rounded external corners are intended to prevent spalling owing to high winds and extreme cold. Reportedly the overall design was tested and refined in a wind tunnel, the sloped roofs even being shaped to shed snow in a predetermined manner under blizzard conditions.

Each change in the pattern of fenestration also has its causes: perhaps in varying programmatic requirements, or in the special possibilities inherent in ground-floor locations, or because as roofs slope inwards floor plans must be reduced and modified. Nor are the balconies an ornamental embellishment – although economic considerations did reduce their size by half from that originally intended. In the summer, with the sun shining for as long as twenty-four hours a day, there is considerable opportunity for their use, while in the winter they permit, among other things, the freeze-drying of clothes in the desiccating Arctic air.

The effect of all this rationality is remarkably picturesque – but, one is meant to

presume, not deliberately so.

S-32a Just down the street is the **Kiruna Stadshuset** (town hall), 1963, by Artur von Schmalensee.

S-32b In Svappavaara there is another **Erskine apartment block,** 1961–5, also purportedly shaped to counter Arctic conditions. A long yellow building designed to catch and reflect the low northern sun, it was originally to have been part of a very large new town which never happened. It would also seem to illustrate how easy it must be to rethink even the (apparently) most rational of design precepts within just thirty miles and two short years. *E of Rt 98 abt 30 mi (50 km) S of Kiruna*

S-32c In Luleå, about 200 miles (345 km) south of Kiruna, is Erskine's **shopping centre,** 1954–60. The intent was not just a shopping centre but a kind of indoor agora that would bring people together and help maintain a sense of community during the cold, dark Arctic winter. Unfortunately, there appears to have been a lack of understanding of the building's possibilities. *From E4 → centrum / R on Storgatan / half blk before Kungsgatan*

FINLAND

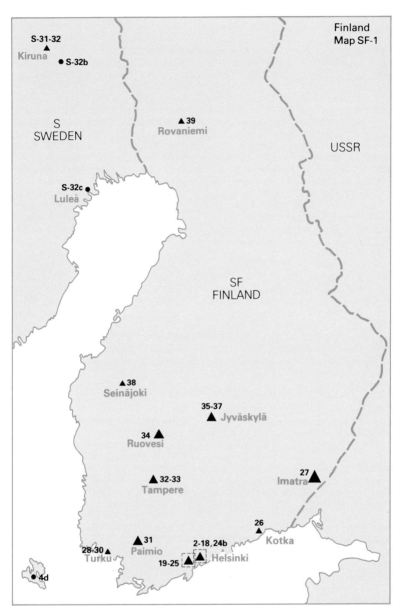

Finland
Map SF-1

S-31-32
Kiruna
● S-32b

S
SWEDEN

▲ 39
Rovaniemi

USSR

S-32c ●
Luleå

SF
FINLAND

▲ 38
Seinäjoki

35-37
▲ Jyväskylä

34 ▲
Ruovesi

▲ 32-33
Tampere

27
Imatra ▲

26
▲ Kotka

28-30 ▲
Turku

▲ 31
Paimio

2-18,24b
▲ ▲ Helsinki

19-25

● 4d

Finland/Suomi SF-1

During the 1950s Finland gained, and has since nurtured, a reputation as one of Europe's more architecturally sophisticated countries, a reputation that rests heavily upon the work of Alvar Aalto. Undeniably postwar Finland has adopted some quite deliberate social, and in a sense political, policies favouring 'good design'. This can be seen in planning decisions that tend to encourage small individually designed developments; in the high value placed on the successful integration of the built and natural environments; and in the practice of holding design competitions for all major building and planning projects.

The question of how Finland, a relatively poor and peripheral country, came to have such a deep concern for the quality of its built environment seems never to have been investigated systematically. Perhaps the roots of this national attitude lie in modern Finland's struggle to gain and keep its independence, because Finland's periods of greatest architectural creativity have also been times of crisis or change. The first of these periods came in the aftermath of the Napoleonic Wars. In 1809 Finland, until then a Swedish province, had been ceded to the Russian Tsar Alexander I as an autonomous grand duchy. The Tsar set about rebuilding Helsinki in a Neo-Classical style (SF-2) – echoing that of his other capital, St Petersburg – to symbolize both Helsinki's new role as the capital of a semi-independent Finland and the Tsar's benevolence towards the Finns.

The next creative period, that of National Romanticism during the twenty years prior to the First World War, was a response to the climax of the Pan-Slavic movement, under whose influence Tsar Nicholas II attempted to 'Russify' Finland. Finnish National Romanticism shares Arts and Crafts roots – and, some would say, a lack of restraint – with the Art Nouveau/Jugendstil then sweeping Europe. Ironically one of its most immediate conceptual and stylistic sources of inspiration would seem to have been the folkloric, artistic revival which accompanied Pan-Slavism itself. (Many of the National Romantic motifs were gathered from Karelia, the region bordering Russia which would later be the major Finnish territory lost to the USSR in the Second World War.)

Finland's most recent architectural efflorescence began as a reaction to its experiences during and after the Second World War, when it had simultaneously to pay huge reparations to Russia; to repair massive war damage throughout the country, caused by both the Germans and the Russians; to accept the loss of large areas that included both important natural resources and the traditional 'homeland' of the Finns; to resettle the entire population of those lost territories – ten per cent of the national total; and to accept a precariously balanced position *vis-à-vis* the USSR. It is easy to understand how a people who had already begun to develop a strong sense of the potential interdependence of the national, the natural and the architectural would, under such circumstances, employ a romantic, 'organic' architecture – typically of red brick with varnished birch

windows and doors, and copper-clad roofs – as an expression of their national identity and as a means of strengthening the social fabric. Certainly the Finns are far from being the first people to have turned in troubled times to architecture as a means of reinforcing cultural bonds.

If this analysis is essentially correct, one might expect to find that there was a lessening of the proportion of Finland's national energy expended upon architecture and a change in the philosophy and style of Finnish architecture as these crises became resolved. And that seems to be just what happened. For example, the sort of showcase new town development that made Tapiola (SF-19) famous has never been repeated.

The philosophical or stylistic nature of Finnish architecture has also changed. Here, as elsewhere in Northern Europe, there is beginning to emerge a kind of modernist vernacular combined with an increasing tendency to make 'architecture' of it, as opposed to mere 'building', by selectively incorporating non-vernacular details or 'gestures' as the circumstances require (S-11, SF-23a). In all of this Aalto played his part. Indeed he contributed as much as anyone to the establishment of the new Scandinavian vernacular. But a majority of Finland's avant-garde seems to be moving in a very different direction, towards a strict Miesian minimalism (SF-4d). At root this is, perhaps, an assertion of impatience in the face of too much Aalto-inspired 'sensitivity'.

Today Finland's architecture is at a point of transition. While Aalto's romantic genius dominates the past and to some extent the present, it is not at all certain who or what will dominate the future. The choice, as now presented, is between the practitioners of a Miesian aesthetic and those who would out-Aalto Aalto. Finns would also have mentioned Viljo Revell as if, had he lived, he would have led the way out of the impasse. Judging from his built work (SF-3a), including Toronto's city hall, that seems like wishful thinking.

Language note Although Finland is officially bilingual, Swedish being spoken by about ten per cent of the population, only Finnish names have been given here, except for those of Swedish institutions or in the few places where Swedish is the dominant language.

Helsinki   SF-2

The legacy of Tsar Alexander I's efforts to win over his new autonomous grand duchy of Finland can be seen in the Neo-Classical Helsinki that arose after it had been devastated by fire in 1808. A new city plan with boulevards and open spaces was prepared by Johan Albert Ehrenström, who also brought the German architect Carl Ludwig Engel, a classmate of Karl Friedrich Schinkel (D-26), to Helsinki. It was Engel who gave Helsinki what the Finns call the 'Empire Style' appearance that today still characterizes its oldest parts, especially

along the Pohjoinen Esplanaadikatu facing the harbour (SF-2a).

In the late 1960s a new plan for central Helsinki was adopted. It includes extensive transportation improvements and major development of the city core centred around the railway station (SF-3). Since the 60s multi-level shopping arcades have also been incorporated into many of the newer buildings. Curiously, there seems to have been little effort to connect these arcades (SF-3a), even where they are in adjacent buildings. It is ironic that this opportunity for sheltered pedestrian links has been

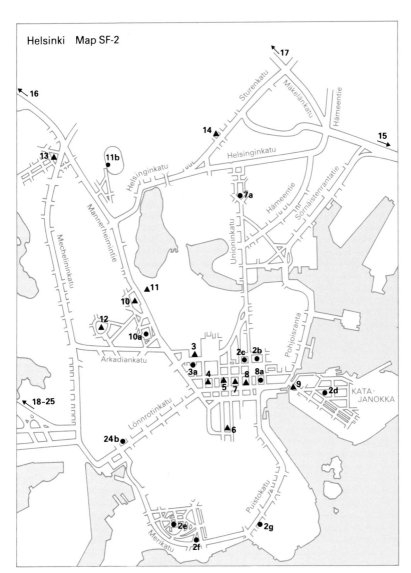

Helsinki   Map SF-2

ignored when many other northern European cities are struggling to create just such separate pedestrian networks.

In addition to the Neo-Classical area, there are several neighbourhoods in Helsinki of architectural interest. These include the following:

SF-2a The Neo-Classical or **Empire Style area** north of the harbour, which was once far more extensive and included a large number of wooden houses. Among the surviving buildings there by Engel are:

SF-2b The **Cathedral,** 1830–52, and

SF-2c The **University,** 1832 – especially the interior of its library.

SF-2d The **Katajanokka Peninsula** is the more urban of two residential areas that consist primarily of National Romantic and

Jugendstil buildings, *c.* 1890–1910. They are interesting, even in their present tired condition, because they reflect such a wide range of influences – rather more than one would have anticipated in this then minor appendage of the Russian Empire.

SF-2e The other National Romantic/Jugendstil area is the **Eira District.**

SF-2f A Jugendstil building of interest in Eira is a former **Gynæcological Clinic,** 1911, by Selim Lindqvist, at Merikatu 23.

SF-2g Of particular importance to scholars is the **Finnish Architecture Museum,** at Puistokatu 4. This is the first and most extensive of a rapidly growing breed. It publishes, mounts exhibitions, maintains a library, fosters historical research, and has photographic files of new and historical Finnish architecture.

Helsinki   SF-3
* **Rautatieasema** (railway station)
1904–14
Rautatientori
Eliel Saarinen
Jugendstil (Art Nouveau)
Map SF-2

The success of Saarinen, Gesellius and Lindgren's 1901 competition-winning National Museum design (SF-10) had signalled public acceptance of National Romanticism. Less than a decade later, Saarinen's final design for Helsinki's railway station indicated its demise.

The original 1904 station competition entry, designed in collaboration with Saarinen's two museum partners, had been National Romantic in spirit. But by 1906 the partnership had broken up, leaving the commission to Saarinen, who was clearly the most sophisticated and internationally minded architect to practise in Finland during the century that elapsed between the time of Engel and that of Aalto. Saarinen soon redesigned the station in the Germanic Jugendstil, even incorporating hints of the Neo-Classicism which in Germany was then already succeeding Jugendstil. Eventually the only remaining vestiges of National Romanticism were the four gigantic figures by Emil Wikstrom.

As finally realized, the station was Finland's first major building of international stature. It has also proved so successful as an urban nexus that since the 60s the city has reinforced its original role by focusing its transportation system upon it and by encouraging the development of a new,

denser city core (SF-11) around it.

SF-3a Facing the railway station, and linked to it by a below-the-street shopping concourse, is the aptly named **City-kortteli** (city centre), 1967, by Viljo Revell & Heikki Castrén, A street-level-arcade at present connects the City-kortteli with a much earlier arcade building designed by Eliel Saarinen, which may eventually be demolished to make way for expansion of the City-kortteli. But for some strange reason the City-kortteli is not connected to its other neighbour, the Kaivotalo building, 1956, by Pauli Salomaa, an earlier postwar example of Helsinki's multi-level arcades. Nor does the City-kortteli respond visually to its surroundings. While parts are only inept, the bulbous edge-beam of the cantilevered parking level makes it a disagreeable neighbour, particularly to the railway station. However, the side street elevation, with its powerful vehicle ramps, is undeniably dramatic in its very confined setting.

Helsinki   SF-4
Rautatalo (Steel Federation building)
1951–5
Keskuskatu 3
Alvar Aalto
Meisian/Late International Style
Map SF-2

It is interesting to note that as early as 1952 Aalto, the arch-romantic, could employ a Miesian curtain wall when he thought it appropriate. Nor is that the only reminder here of the Chicago architecture, which, presumably. Aalto had recently experienced at first hand while teaching in America at the Massachusetts Institute of Technology. The way the curtain wall hangs above the minimally detailed street-level shops and the use of mezzanine levels are both remarkably like practices favoured by Louis Sullivan, while the interior sky-lighted court is conceptually similar to the one in Burnham & Root's Rookery Building. There are also echoes of the late 30s work of Frank Lloyd Wright in this space – and even more so in Aalto's original presentation drawing of it. But only the ideas are similar. The interior built forms are Aalto's alone and refer both forwards (the ceramics around the elevators) and backwards (the skylights with lamps suspended above) to many others of his own works.

SF-4a Aalto and his first wife Aino were founding partners of **Artek,** the company that manufactures and sells his furniture,

lamps and glassware. Its shop is on the street level of the Rautatalo.

SF-4b The **adjacent building** to the right, to which Aalto obviously referred when determining the layout of his façade, is by Eliel Saarinen, 1921.

SF-4c The next building beyond that, at the intersection of Keskuskatu and Esplanaadikatu, is also by Aalto, 1962–9, and is again externally Mieisian. But here Aalto did something Mies never could have.

Responding to the more monumental nature of Esplanaadikatu, Aalto differentiated the design of the curtain walls facing the two streets – and then allowed them to abut at the corner without any mediating gesture. The major interior space, the **Academic Bookshop,** shows just how restrained his handling of the

Helsinki   **SF-5**
* Vakuutusyhtiö Pohjola (insurance company) 1899–1901
Aleksanterinkatu 44
Gesellius, Lindgren & Saarinen
National Romantic
Map SF-2

Seen from outside it is a not very distinguished provincial hodgepodge of bits and pieces. Certainly the best of the National Romantic stone masonry was yet to come (SF-6). But there is an intriguing little door at street level which is in fact the main entrance, opening on to a short corridor which ends in a flight of stairs that curves up and out of sight. There is only the slightest hint of anything more until, on ascending, one finds oneself emerging into the bottom of a large, skylit, organically shaped stairhall which rises with slightly changing contours through the entire height of the building.

The effect of this space is not so much the refined vegetal sinuousness of Art Nouveau, but rather a primitive animism. The ornamental folk motifs – ferns, trolls, forest creatures – are drawn largely from the *Kalevala,* Finland's national epic, and are executed with a crude vigour. Although

Helsinki   **SF-6**
Puhelinyhdistys (telephone exchange) 1905
Korkeavuorenkatu 35
Lars Sonck
National Romantic
Map SF-2

[Other than the vestibule, no decorated interior spaces remain. The copper roof, although suitably detailed, is new and of a much coarser texture than the original red tiles.]

This, it is generally agreed, is the best National Romantic façade in Finland. One's first temptation is to compare it with the work of the mid-nineteenth-century American architect H. H. Richardson. Certainly the feeling for material and ornament, although different, is as original, but the sense of scale and functional appropriateness is missing. Here Sonck fell into a familiar trap. He had such control over his material and its ornamental potential that

similar multi-storey lobby down the street had been.

SF-4d Another small but elegant example of Finnish Miesianism is the **Ferry Terminal,** 1965, by Bengt Lundsten, at Långnäs on the Åland Islands – a stop for some of the Finland–Sweden ferries.

most of the arched doorways lining the landings lead into conventional offices, one somewhat more elaborate door on the first floor opens into a large, almost rustic, banking room.

he seems to have composed the façade without sufficient concern for the realities of the programme. The result is interesting, but it would have been more convincing as a telephone magnate's mansion – if scaled down – than as a telephone exchange.

Helsinki   **SF-7**
Porssi (stock exchange) 1911–12
Fabianinkatu 14
Lars Sonck
National Romantic
Map SF-2

Here, even as he moved towards Neo-Classicism, Sonck's self-assured granite façade showed a marked, if conservative, inventiveness. The same cannot be said of the large courtyard-like lobby space within. This is derivative, a bit confused about what it wants to be, and generally far more interesting. Its inspiration seems to have come primarily from Vienna and Chicago. While a marriage between these two lineages is not unreasonable (A-18a, I-19), one doubts whether this offspring would have been recognized by either parent. The Viennese sense of cool orthogonal abstraction is somewhat at odds with the tactile brickwork of the two middle floors; and the ornament, which so strongly invokes Chicago's Louis Sullivan, looks as it if were – and probably was – the result of Sonck's having seen the original only in fuzzy photographs. Consequently the arched doorways and attenuated columns look reasonable from a distance, while closer inspection reveals their ornamental detail to be crude and clumsy. This example of a design source being weakened or misunderstood is by no means unique. The history of architecture abounds with such transformations and mutations caused by inadequate illustrations, be they engravings, lithographs, drawings or photographs.

The actual exchange hall lies behind the bronze door at the head of the stairs.

SF-7a Despite Sonck's Sullivan-esque ornament, his American connections, if any, are unclear. Yet his pre-First World War exteriors tantalizingly anticipate by a decade or more the work of Bertram Goodhue and other similarly 'advanced' American Beaux-Arts architects who, like Sonck, worked for an essentially 'Establishment' clientele. Sonck's **Kallion kirkko** (church), 1906–12, sited on top of a hill at the northern end of Unionkatu-Siltasaarenkatu, prefigures the work of architects like Goodhue particularly.

SF-7b The **SYP Bank**, 1962–4, across from the stock exchange, is by Aalto.

Helsinki   **SF-8**
Ent. Privatbankenintalo (banking hall, now municipal banqueting hall)
1906
Pohjoinen Esplanaadikatu 19
Lars Sonck & Bertel Jung
National Romantic
Map SF-2

[Located in the Uschakoff Building, 1815–16, designed by Pehr Granstedt. Restored with adaptations in 1968 by Aarno Ruusuvuori, who removed some of Sonck and Jung's interior fittings. Can be viewed by appointment only.]

There is in the history of this room a valuable lesson about the way culturally important works of architecture can evolve over long periods of time. The original building that housed it is an integral part of Engel's Neo-Classical town (SF-2a). When, ninety years later, the new banking hall was to be built, its architects left the old Neo-Classical façade intact even though they were employing a rigorously National Romantic style – one moderated only by a certain deference to the exterior in the palette of colours and in the softness of the plaster ornament.

Eventually the city acquired the building and, this being Finland where architecture is almost venerated, it was decided

to preserve the interior for civic ceremonial uses. Aarno Ruusuvuori, who made the necessary modifications, usually designs in a hard-edged, almost Miesian mode. Yet here he worked with a minimum of intrusion. His only questionable decision concerns the square unfinished column bases which had previously been hidden by banking counters. These flat-sided stone blocks generate a strongly perceived barrier-plane which resists the integration of the side areas with the central space.

SF-8a Ruusuvuori has since completed a similar but more extensive renovation/restoration of C.L. Engel's Neo-Classical **City Hall**, 1823, which stands just to the east on Esplanaadikatu.

Helsinki   SF-9
** Enso-Gutzeit Pääkonttori
(offices) 1960–2
Kanavaranta 1
Alvar Aalto
Romantic Rationalism
Map SF-2

Aalto always argued that his principal concerns here were contextual. His façade had to be designed in sympathy with the colour, rhythm and massing of a line of Neo-Classical buildings facing the harbour along Esplanaadikatu. He indicated this relationship pointedly in a widely published elevation drawing that shows his building terminating that line – with Engel's cathedral looming in the background.

Of course, Aalto could not be obsequious. He knew full well that it was possible to be harmonious and still produce a striking coda to the composition; especially as his building is seen in three dimensions, while the others are seen in only two. He achieved this sense of harmony by covering the building almost entirely with a skin of elegant, white marble window-frame units, or sections thereof. Substantial, square and scaleless, these units are used without concession to either Neo-Classicist or Functionalist scruples concerning the changes to be imposed upon architectonic elements by their relative positions and roles. Thus there is no differentiation between units which actually enclose columns and those which do not. In fact, the very existence of the structural skeleton, to say nothing of the specific grid module, is in no way explicitly recognized, except where Aalto deliberately chose to expose certain columns – like so many bones from which the marble skin has been cut away. The effect is devastatingly sophisticated and quite dominates the buildings to which Aalto was purportedly deferring. It is so subtly skilful, in fact, that no one seems yet to have noticed how neatly he upstaged the Russian Orthodox Cathedral.

Helsinki   SF-10
Kansallismuseo (national museum)
1901–12
Mannerheimintie 34
Gesellius, Lindgren & Saarinen
National Romantic
Map SF-2

This is the National Romantic manifesto of Finland. Ironically, in the four years between the design competition in 1901 and the beginning of construction in 1905, the movement had shed much of its earlier reliance upon archaeological sources (SF-34) – however fitting they may have seemed for an archaeologically oriented institution. By 1912, when the building was completed, the line between Finnish National Romanticism and German Jugendstil had become blurred (SF-3), and some anticipations of Scandinavia's Neo-Classical 1920s were already beginning to appear (SF-7).

The interior of the museum, like the exterior, is comparatively restrained. Only the entrance hall with its staircase and its frescoes by Akseli Gallen-Kallela is of any architectural interest.

SF-10a South on Mannerheimintie is J. S. Sirén's **Parliament Building,** 1927–31, the high point in Finland of Scandinavia's Neo-Classical revival. Except for the chandeliers in the main foyer, it lacks the mannered elegance of its Swedish or Danish counterparts (DK-5, S-7b).

Helsinki   SF-11
Finlandia-talo (Finlandia Hall: concert
hall and conference centre) 1962–71
Mannerheimintie
Alvar Aalto
Neo-Expressionism
Map SF-2

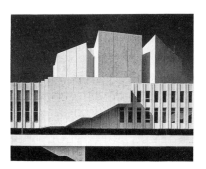

There have been several schemes, going
back to Eliel Saarinen's 1918 Greater Helsinki Plan, for the development of an urban
core around Helsinki's railway terminus.
Aalto's contribution primarily concerned
the area to the north of the station. He
proposed bringing in a motorway along
the eastern edge of Lake Töölö, above the
already elevated railway line; placing a
parking garage, capped by an enormous
plaza, over the railway yards on the south
shore of the lake; and replacing the present
park along the western lakeshore with an
embankment lined with civic buildings.

Although the railway tracks are indeed
rather messy, the lake is so wide that they
do not really disturb the tranquillity of the
park. Aalto's proposal would have substituted a thirty-foot-high wall topped with
roaring traffic on that side of the lake and
would have ruthlessly destroyed valuable
urban parkland on the other side in order to
create an isolated 'civic centre'. Arguments
might be made for the appropriateness of
the location, but not for the solution.
Apparently the citizens of Helsinki have
thought so as well, because this concert
hall, which was to have been the first
element of the civic centre, may now stand
bereft of its intended companions, or even
of adequate parking, for some time to come.

Aalto's forms here may have been as
much his own as ever, but something vital
was lost. Once he would not have been
able to accept lifelessly piled white Italian
marble as an adequate substitute for a lakeside glade of white Finnish birches.

SF-11a Finlandia Hall was not the first
monumental building in this parkland. Not
far beyond the north end of the lake stands

Helsinki's **Olympiastadion** (Olympic
stadium), 1933–52, by Yrjö Lindegren &
Toivo Jäntti. There were only a few successful attempts at creating an International Style monumentality – only a few
International Style architects who were
able to suggest traditional civic virtues
without drifting towards the stripped Neo-
Classicism favoured by Fascist (and some
non-Fascist) governments in the late 30s.
One of those successes is to be seen in the
original central section of this stadium,
where the architects never lost sight of its
functional needs, even if, as in the 230-
foot-high observation tower, those needs
were largely symbolic.

The two end sections have a less happy
history. They were first built in wood for the
1952 Olympics, incorporating some rather
romantic, but visually and functionally
effective, wooden screens. Eventually those
stands gave way to permanent concrete
successors containing offices, which should
have constituted an entirely different design
problem: permanent rather than temporary, concrete rather than wood, solid rather
than void. Regrettably, the new structures
were built, as it were, behind the old
wooden screens. Although appropriate for
their original temporary role, the screens
had never related particularly well to the
central section of the stadium. Now they
no longer even have a sense of purpose.

Helsinki   SF-12
* Temppeliaukion kirkko
(underground church) 1961–9
Lutherinkatu
Timo & Tuomo Suomalainen
Neo-Expressionism
Map SF-2

At the turn of the century, when this
area was first planned, it was a common
Scandinavian practice (S-8, SF-7a) to
reserve the inevitably rocky top of such an
area's most prominent hill for a church,
which often also became the axial focus of
the principal street. Here, happily, the first
competition-winning church design of
1936 – by J. S. Sirén, architect of the Parliament Building (SF-10a) – was never
erected. After the war the neighbourhood
came to feel that even this bare rock was
too valuable an open space to be occupied
by an ecclesiastical 'monument'. There was
a new competition which stressed that the
exposed rock was to be preserved.

The Suomalainens' solution could not be
simpler in conception: a more or less round

hole dug into the rock and covered by a flat
concrete dome. It is neither over-romantic
nor over-simplified – even if, at times, it
approaches being both. It is at its most
successful in the rough-quarried, curving
interior 'wall' of the church which carefully
follows natural cleavage planes in the rock.
It is least successful in its dome. Although
a practical structural solution to a difficult
problem, the copper-sheathed underside is
somewhat distracting and oppressive.

Helsinki
** **Kansaneläkelaitos** (National
Pensions Institute) 1948–56
Minna Canthinkatu 15
Alvar Aalto
Scandinavian Empiricism
Map SF-2
[The interior may be seen by appoint-
ment only after office hours.]

Something here does not quite work. In
his attempt to demonumentalize and break
up the mass of this building, Aalto seems
to have lost control of its organization. One
has the feeling that new employees and
clients – and not just tourists – must be
led about this maze by guides. Even the
important and sensitive conferences
between pensioners and bureaucrats are
squeezed into a mass of tiny, if thoughtfully designed, cubicles that crowd the floor
of a large skylighted and balconied hall –
a symbolic juncture between 'public servants' and those served that can hardly
seem reassuring to an aged pensioner.

Why, then, should one want to see this
building? Mostly for its detailing: for the
above-mentioned skylight, for various
lighting fixtures, for ceiling systems, for a
whole repertoire of special Aalto details,
many of which were first developed here.
There are also some interesting spaces. The
library, although much smaller, is reminiscent of its better-known predecessor,
1927–35, at Viipuri (now in the USSR).
And the garden, which forms a visual
extension to a small neighbouring park and
helps decrease the effect of the building's
mass in happy opposition to the intent of
the original town plan which set aside the
site for a 'civic building'. Unfortunately this
garden is inaccessible to the neighbourhood
even after working hours. Its only concession to the local community is that the
diminutive canal-like stream meandering
through it eventually passes out through
the exterior wall and empties into a small
public fountain.

Helsinki
* **Kulttuuritalo** (political, social and
cultural centre) 1954–8
Sturenkatu 4
Alvar Aalto
Scandinavian Empiricism/
Neo-Expressionism
Map SF-2

When he was on good form, as here,
Aalto took nothing for granted. Each detail
or concept was carefully thought out. It
may then have been treated conventionally, or quite unconventionally, but not
unthinkingly. (Originality alone in architecture is never enough – the world is filled

with unique architectural horrors.) Aalto's
sense of form rarely let him down. It
allowed him to use the plan form from
which this auditorium evolved – an irregular fan expanding from a rectangular core –
repeatedly in various types of buildings
(D-30, SF-38, 39), few of which ever
seemed forced. In spite of having been
designed at the height of Aalto's 'voluptuous' period – his response to the 'delightful' architecture of the late 50s – this
building, happily, has no truly dys-
functional forms. And the simple but pleasant courtyard and no-nonsense office block
are perfect foils to the auditorium.

Helsinki/Vuosaari   **SF-15**
Tilapäiskirkko (demountable
prefabricated church) 1969
Merikorttitie 7
Ola Laiho & Bengt-Vilhelm Levón
Miesian
*E on Rt 6–7 (Map SF-2→) abt 7 mi
(11.5 km) / R on Meripellontie, 1¼ mi
(2 km) / L on Kallvikintie / L on Merikorttitie / follow to R / on R in cul-de-sac*
[If the church is no longer there, ask at
the Architecture Museum. A nineteenth-
century Swedish demountable church was
moved three times before finally coming to
rest.]
    The existence of demanding specific tech-
nical or programmatic requirements can
often greatly assist those designers who are
able to respond to their implications. Here
there was not only a requirement that the
church be prefabricated, but also that it
could be disassembled and moved with a
minumum of difficulty – and presumably
even reassembled in a somewhat different
configuration to suit differing programmatic or site requirements.
    The formal language here happens to be
that of Mies van der Rohe. But, as has not
always been true of recent Finnish architecture, it is thoughtfully employed. Mies's
vocabulary is well suited to this type of
construction. And where the church goes
beyond his specific precedents, as it quite
appropriately does with the plywood wall
system, one feels that the solution might
well have appealed to him.

Helsinki/Munkkiniemi   **SF-16**
Ateljee Aalto (Aalto's studio) 1956
Tiilimäki 20
Alvar Aalto
*N on Mannerheimintie (Map SF-2→) /
→ MUNKKINIEMI / continue straight
past end of bridge / L on Kadetintie /
first R on Riihitie (see SF-16a–b) / L on
Laaja Lahdentie / first R on Tiilimäki / on L*
    Here is an ambiguousness rather more
overt than one usually finds in Aalto's
work: a building whose most important
space is outside, and cannot be used, or at
least cannot be occupied, for most of the
year, but can only be looked at or passed
through. This space is an amphitheatre-
garden whose feeling of enclosure and
quietly dynamic sense of focus both result
from the distortion of a major interior room,
a drafting studio, one of whose sides is
drawn far out into a decreasing-radius
curve to form the rear wall of this almost
primitively ceremonial place. Yet the drafting studio, seemingly so maltreated as if it
were but residue or 'poché', as Beaux-Arts
architects would call it, is all the better for
its deformation, because the curved wall
contains a strip of windows which offer a
spectrum of subtly varying views of the
studio's external other self.

SF-16a The **flats at Riihitie 12–14** are
by Aalto, 1954. *See directions above.*

SF-16b Riihitie 20 is **Aalto's own
house,** 1937. *See directions above.*

Järvenpää [near Helsinki]   **SF-17**
* Vesitorni (water tower) 1966
Laaksotie
Arvi Ilonen
Neo-Expressionism
N on Mäkelänkatu (Map SF-2→) ⇨
Tuusulantie abt 22 mi (36 km) / →
JÄRVENPÄÄ / *R at Y beyond concrete
church* / *across RR tracks and*
HELSINKI *rd* / *L on Laaksotie* /
500 yds (m) on R

In most other countries a water tower
is a prosaic necessity – something to be
designed and placed with little attention
or care. Not so in Finland. Here much skill
and ingenuity is expended on these structures which necessarily dominate the
Finns' beloved landscape. Naturally the
prime consideration must still be the
efficiency of the tanks and their supports.
But often they also fill additional roles as
observation galleries, restaurants, even
astronomical observatories, and frequently,
as in this case, as 'place-markers' in the
landscape.

The major difference between this water
tower and most others is that it is not circular. While round concrete towers are easier
to design and more structurally efficient,
they are also more expensive to build. (To
understand why, one need only consider
the inherent difficulties of producing formwork and reinforcement for compound
curved shapes.) With its slip-formed legs,
prismatic, folded-plate tanks and wood-
sheathed insulation, the simplicity of this
structure must have more than justified its
need for a little extra material – as if such
elegance needed justification.

Kirkkonummi (Kyrkslätt)   **SF-18**
[near Helsinki]
** Hvitträsk (houses and studios)
1901–19
Gesellius, Lindgren & Saarinen
National Romantic/Arts and
Crafts/Jugendstil
*W on Rt 1 (Map SF-2→) abt 12½ mi
(20 km)* / *exit S →* KIRKKONUMMI
(KYRKSLÄTT) / *R→*SIUNTIO / *L →*
LUOMA / *first R beyond* KIRKKONUMMI
(KYRKSLÄTT) *boundary marker →*
FASA / *R at first Y* / *L at second Y*
[Hvitträsk was restored, for the second
time, in 1970. One building had earlier
burned and been rebuilt. It is now a
museum and conference centre.]

With surprising frequency, idealistic
young architects feel compelled to drop out
of society, or at least to back away from it,
so that they can create a micro-society of
their own in which to test themselves and
their theories by building solutions to architectural and social problems. Rarely,
however, are they able to withstand the
pressures for re-absorption into the larger
society, while still, like Wright's Taliesen
Fellowship, being able to build for it. More
typically, after the experiment has served
its purpose, the architects return to that
society – either because they have
readjusted to it or, occasionally, as is somewhat the case here, because it has adjusted
to them.

By the time these three young architects
moved into the first log building at Hvitträsk they had already seen the acceptance
of their National Romantic ideal: they had
won the 1901 National Museum competition (SF-10). But still being young, and
still a step ahead of society, they had by
then realized that National Romanticism
was only a transitional phase born of a
mixture of aesthetic and political needs.
And so the later buildings at Hvitträsk,
although romantic, primarily reflect progressive British and German influences.

By 1906 the Hvitträsk experiment was
dissolving, and Saarinen on his own was
recasting the National Romantic design,
with which he and his former partners had
originally won the Helsinki Railway Station
commission (SF-3), into an almost Neo-
Classical version of German Jugendstil.
Eventually Hvitträsk became Saarinen's
own home until 1923, when he too left
and emigrated to America.

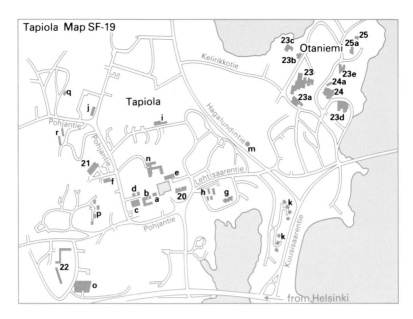

Tapiola Map SF-19

Tapiola [near Helsinki]   **SF-19**
** **Tapiola** (new town) Begun 1952
Aarne Ervi (town plan), *et al.*
W on Rt 1 (Map SF-2→) abt 3¾ mi (6 km)
/ → TAPIOLA
The driving force behind this famous
postwar garden suburb was not a government agency. Rather it was a consortium
of organizations which formed a building
society and held a planning competition for
a model new town. The competition was
won by Aarne Ervi, who had already made
a plan for the same site for a private developer. Originally designed to accommodate
a population of only 17,000, Tapiola's low
density is essentially a result of the anti-
urban attitudes that typified much early
modernist thinking. Unfortunately this did
not mean that there was adequate pro-
vision for the demands of suburban cars
in either street planning or parking. Now
changing needs and ideals make it likely
that there will be a major expansion of
Tapiola's centre to include both housing
and shops, built at high density over a
structure for parking.
Among the more interesting individual
buildings here are:

By Aarne Ervi:
SF-19a **Keskustorni** (office tower
with top-floor restaurant and observation
deck), 1959–61, Keskus (town centre).
SF-19b **Tapiontori** (shops and offices),
1961, Keskus.
SF-19c **Heikintori** (enclosed shopping
centre), 1968, Keskus.
SF-19d **Urheilutalo** and **Terveys-
talo** (offices), 1967, Keskus.
SF-19e **Uimahalli** (swimming hall),
1965–8, Kirkkotie.

SF-19f **Lämpövoimalaitos** (power-
plant), 1957–9, Ahertajantie 4.

By Kaija & Heikki Sirén:
SF-19g **Rivitaloalue 'Otsonpesä'**
(row houses), 1957–9, Otsolahdentie 10.
SF-19h **Rivitaloalue** (row houses),
1955, Kontiontie.
SF-19i **Polar-Tilaelementtitalot**
(prefabricated houses), 1966–8,
Aarnivalkeantie 10.

By Heikki Sirén:
SF-19j **Pohjantori** (neighbourhood
shopping centre), 1962–4, Pohjantie at
Louhentie.

By Alvar Aalto:
SF-19k **Tornitaloja** (apartment
blocks), 1962, Harjuviita 1, 4, 16–18.
SF-19m **Vesitorni** (water tower),
1968–71, Hagalundintie.

By others:
SF-19n **Yhteiskoulu** (school),
1958–60, by Jorma Jarvi, Opintie 1.
SF-19o **Atriumtaloryhmä** (atrium
houses), 1961–4, by Pentti Ahola,
Hakamaankuja.
SF-19p **Kaitiotaloja** (apartment
blocks), 1958, by Viljo Revell,
Kaskenkaatajantie 5, 8, 10.
SF-19q **Kuten Haluatte-
Järjestemä 'Bungalo'** (prefabricated
system-built houses), 1968, by Juhan
Vainio and Pentti Lehtinen, Suokulaisenp
9.
SF-19r **Kaitiotaloja** (apartments),
1965, by Aulis Blomstedt,
Kaskenkaatajantie 16–18.

Tapiola [near Helsinki]   SF-20
* Tapiolan kirkko (church) 1965
Tapionraitti
Aarno Ruusuvuori
Meisian
Map SF-19

The elegantly minimalized detailing of Ruusuvuori's two Tapiola buildings, particularly in their concrete work and glazing systems, reflects a refinement which only comes from having patiently sought the right solution – not just settling for a workable one. But there is also an appropriate difference in the way these buildings respond to their differing programmatic requirements. While the printing plant (SF-21) is exactly the consciously simplified, flexible package that it appears to be,

this church, along with its very specifically prescribed parish social centre, is an assemblage of physically and programmatically discrete interior and exterior spaces lying within, but not completely subsumed by, a unifying perimeter wall.

The nave, the most important of these spaces, is a high, starkly simple grey room. It is the colour of concrete: the concrete of its structure; of its slab ceiling; of its block walls – with their set-in block-sized pre-cast light fixtures; and even of the massive Le Corbusier-inspired *brise-soleil* that shades its only window (in Finland of all places!). Such an ascetic aesthetic is all well and good on a sunny August afternoon, but it might get one down in the darkness of December.

Tapiola [near Helsinki]   SF-21
Weilin & Göös (printing works) 1964
Ahertajantie 5
Aarno Ruusuvuori
Rationalism
Map SF-19

Two of the four projected sections of this highly refined, modular concrete factory have been built. Each section is a cluster of four semi-independent, 81-foot-square structural units, whose upper-floor level is supported by a 27-by-27-foot grid of columns, but whose roof is suspended from four huge cylindrical service columns. Thus the upper floor provides a highly flexible space for the firm's printing presses, while the lower floor accommodates offices and other smaller-scale operations.

All of this is a paraphrase in concrete of one of Mies's favourite themes. But while Mies was essentially a Classicist, and therefore to a degree backward-looking, Ruusuvuori's approach is inherently more

modern. If his work is not always as visually refined, it is often more believable.

Tapiola [near Helsinki]   SF-22
Asuntoalue (apartment blocks)1967–9
Suvikummuntie and Merituulentie
Reima Pietilä & Raili Paatelainen
Neo-Expressionism
Map SF-19

The sensitive siting, romantic façade composition and picturesque massing typify what one would expect from the architects of the nearby Dipoli (SF-24) and the Kalevan Church (SF-33). Happily the apartment plans and detailing are Rational, which is also what one would expect from them – at least when confronted with this sort of prosaic programme.

Otaniemi [near Helsinki]   SF-23
*** Teknillinen Korkeakoulun
päärakennus** (Technical University
main building) 1949, 1960–4
Otaniementie and Kelirikkotie
Alvar Aalto
Scandinavian Empiricism
Map SF-19

The Technical University, whose site
plan follows Aalto's 1949 competition-
winning scheme, lies widely scattered over
a wooded peninsula – too widely scattered,
in fact, to impart any sense of an organic
campus-like unity to the institution as a
whole. Like the adjoining new town,
Tapiola (SF-19), Otaniemi reflects an anti-
urban bias. But here, even more than at
Tapiola, continued prosperity may eventually make the car a major problem.

The basic sensibility of the university's
main building, like that of the site plan,
is poetic: romantic but restrained. It is expressed in a personal vocabulary that had
been refined and had matured over a period
of some fifteen years. But despite the
poetry, there are some problems. Clearly
Aalto felt a strong a need not just to define
one of the university's too few campus-like
spaces – now bordered on its far side by the
Dipoli (SF-24) – but also to create a suitably anonymous setting for the auditorium-
cum-amphitheatre-cum-tower which, if
not for the Dipoli, would undoubtedly be
the school's sole architectural emblem.

What else could justify the singularity of
that one gesture? Other parts of the building house comparably important functions
which could just as logically have been
expressed. (The denial of any such expression is unfortunately apparent in the
lengthy, impersonal internal corridors.)

Otaniemi [near Helsinki]   SF-24
** Dipoli (students' union) 1966
Jämeräntaival
Reima Pietilä & Raili Paatelainen
Neo-Expressionism
Map SF-19

The success of this copper-covered,
boulder-strewn, architectonic explosion
stems from its creators' mastery of an extremely romantic sculptural form language
– one that would have led many other
architects into a morass of undisciplined
theatricals. It may also have been helpful
that there were so few precedents for the
more extreme aspects of this design, hence
that freshness which comes from not
having had recourse to history, modern or
otherwise. Even some of the Dipoli's failures
are interesting, which is more than can be

This entire extensive building is almost
wholly subordinated to a single, elegant,
arbitrary and, one cannot help feeling,
rather soulless symbol. But without it, an
otherwise amorphous campus would be
much the poorer.

SF-23a The immediately adjacent
Library, 1965–9, typifies Aalto's later
work. Here his mannerism, which had
always been an undercurrent, becomes
more overt – as, for example, in the dash of
marble veneer around the side door, which
marks its position and function without
disrupting the building's linear relationship
with the nearby alley of trees.

SF-23b The university's **power-plant,**
1960–3, is also by Aalto.

SF-23c A short distance behind the
power-plant is a poured-in-place **concrete wind tunnel,** the sort of truly technological design problem which architects
are rarely allowed to confront.

SF-23d The **Urheiluhalli** (gymnasium)
was built by Aalto during a time of great
economic stringency, 1949–54, for the
1952 Olympics. It is one of his undeservedly
lesser-known works. The form of the building directly reflects the arrangement of its
main structural elements, a series of 'bent'
wooden plate girders of several different
widths and heights, sized to span economically an oval running track, one of
whose sides overlays the middle portion of
a straight track.

SF-23e On Jämeräntaival are some **dormitories,** 1962–7, by Aalto.

said for most of its imitators.

SF-24a The adjacent example of 'Dipoli'-
style architecture, the **Teknolog-
föreningen Urdsgjaller** (students' club),
1966, is by Kurt Moberg.

SF-24b Before the Dipoli there was the **Poli,** the university's students' union when it was located in Helsinki, at Lönnrotinkatu 29. A sort of National Romantic grotto designed by Walter Tomé and Karl Lindahl in 1903, it remains a student club. Together the Poli and Dipoli may demonstrate either the consistency of student preferences or the cyclical nature of architecture. *Map SF-2*

Otaniemi [near Helsinki] **SF-25**
* **Kappeli** (students' chapel) 1953–7
Jämeräntaival
Kaija & Heikki Sirén
Rustic Meisian
Map SF-19
[Rebuilt in 1978 after a fire.]
Perhaps because it was built by the students themselves, this little sylvan chapel has an air of elegant innocence. In some ways it suggests the spirit of vernacular Japanese architecture. But to talk of architectural inspiration here is misleading. The real inspiration was, as it ought to have been, Finland's own abstract landscape of straight, tall pines standing against the blue northern sky. Seen through the chapel's glazed east wall, nature itself enfolds the celebration at the altar and makes it part of a greater celebration of the changing seasons and the moods of the sky.

SF-25a Near by, and also by the Siréns, is the **Servin Mökki**, 1952, the university's original student restaurant. Once an elegant, highly regarded example of early postwar Finnish design, it is now sadly transformed and neglected.

Kotka/Sunila **SF-26**
* **Sunila Sulfaattiselluloosatehdas** (cellulose factory and employees' housing) 1936–9
Alvar Aalto
Late International Style
N from Kotka on Rt 7 / → SUNILA */ housing on L near end of rd / factory at end of rd*
[1951–4 extension by Aalto. Later additions by others.]
Few architects during the late 1930s were able to build from scratch a project as large as this factory and its attendant housing. Aalto more than rose to the occasion. Although solidly based on International Style aesthetics and precedents, his design includes many of the personal innovations that were eventually to form part of his mature vocabulary. There are some elements and motifs, such as the Expressionistic exterior concrete work, that were never seriously to return. And the conspicuous concrete arch from which part of the factory's roof is suspended may derive from Le Corbusier's influential Palace of the Soviets project. But the romantic massing, the respect with which he treated the site, and the articulation of the foundations in response to the irregularity of the rocky outcrops beneath them all typify the attitude Aalto was to develop in his later work.

Unfortunately much of the overall effect of this composition has been lost over the years – various extensions and modifications having got increasingly out of hand, while an unsympathetic attitude towards the site has caused much of it to be blasted away. Still, the original effect is not entirely lost. The details are all there, if poorly maintained, and the housing area is the best of its time and kind in Finland.

Imatra/Vuoksenniska   **SF-27**
*** Kolmen Ristin kirkko (church)
1958–9
Ruokolahdentie and Temppelikatu
Alvar Aalto
Neo-Expressionism
N on Rt 6 from Imatra / L →
VUOKSENNISKA / *R beyond RR on*
Vuoksenniskantie / abt 1 mi (1.5 km) on R

In this one building Aalto said more about the interdependence of form, function and feeling than most architects could hope to express in a lifetime. The problem was simple enough: a small suburban church with the usual Scandinavian requirement that, in order to accommodate enlarged Holy Day congregations, its nave had to be expandable into an adjoining multi-use space. The standard solution to this problem is a visually and spatially complete nave separated by movable partitions from an independent secular space. And the standard result is a compromise when the partitions are closed and incoherence when they are open.

Aalto avoided this trap by subtracting the secular spaces from the church rather than adding them to it. His two sets of sliding walls – and they are decidedly walls, not partitions – are each composed of one straight and one curved unit. When closed these echo both the arrangement of the seats and the curved planes that occur throughout the interior. Even the lines of closure disappear between pairs of columns, whose primary function may be to reduce the span of the beams carrying the walls, but whose precise location responds to the spatial requirements of the room. These columns, although a minor part of the total composition, illustrate the manner in which Aalto demanded that each element perform a multiplicity of overlapping roles, regardless of whether it was primarily structural, spatial, thermal, acoustic or whatever.

It is hard to imagine a less simple yet still visually coherent built form. As in a complex piece of music, the relationships between the parts may at first be difficult to perceive, but they exist and they operate simultaneously on many levels. And as with such a musical composition, appreciation of these relationships, and hence enjoyment of them, grows in proportion to one's familiarity with them.

Turku (Åbo)   **SF-28**
* Turun Sanomat (newspaper offices
and printing plant) 1928–9
Kauppiaskatu
Alvar Aalto
International Style
Kauppiaskatu is the NE side of Kauppatori (the
market square) / in first blk → river, on L

The façade of this, Finland's first International Style building of importance, shows a marked Corbusian influence – one which was later to be supplemented in Aalto's prewar work by the impact of first German and then Scandinavian ideas.

The interior exhibits a more confident independence: the building's best-known and most original element is a row of semi-mushroom columns in the press room. Despite their almost Mendelsohnian dynamism and spiritual kinship with some of Le Corbusier's later *piloti* (F-63), these columns prefigure, as does nothing else in Aalto's work of this period, his later romantic interplay of geometry and free form.

Turku (Åbo)   SF-29
Mikaelin kirkko (church) 1900
Puistokatu and Puutarhakatu
Lars Sonck
Neo-Gothic (exterior)
Jugendstil/National Romantic (interior)
*Up Aurakatu from market square (away from
river) / L on Puutarhakatu / on L in sixth
block*

Externally it is a more or less conventional Neo-Gothic church, one which
would not seem much out of place in many
older American cities. Only the diminutive
decorative gable arcades and the frescoed
ornament around the doors are out of the
ordinary, the former being an unmodified
restatement of a motif common to medieval
Finnish churches – as can be seen on
Turku's own cathedral – and the latter a
freely adapted, stylized version of a traditional Finnish interior ornamentation.

Within the church, however, the innovative, and especially the nationalistic,
elements dominating the conventional
Gothic ones, such as the windows, seem
out of place. The same National Romantic
painted ornament already encountered on
the exterior is now everywhere. There are
also copper candle-holders and exquisite
lighting fixtures which, although Jugendstil in style, are presumably nationalistic at
least in their choice of material. But it is
the sculpted granite columns, the altar and
particularly the pulpit that best represent
the extraordinary synthetic, folkloric,
'National' style which, in the following
years, would come to full fruition.

Turku (Åbo)   SF-30
* Ylösnousemuskappeli
(Resurrection chapel in municipal
cemetery) 1938–41
Hautausmaantie
Erik Bryggman
Scandinavian Empiricism
*S from Turku ctr on Kaskenkatu / L on
Hautausmaantie / follow cemetery wall to
main entrance / at top of hill*

For a while in the late 1920s and early
30s Bryggman was, in fact and reputation,
Aalto's peer. By the time he designed this,
his best-known work, he and Aalto had
already begun to take separate paths from
the International Style position they had
once shared. Although both participated in
the Scandinavian trend towards romanticism (in Finland, architectural historians
often refer to the 40s as the 'period of
romanticism'), Aalto's appeal tended to be
to the intellect, while Bryggman's was more
to the emotions. Admittedly a funeral
chapel such as this is almost bound to
invoke the non-rational. Still, it is to be
regretted that such a sophisticated building
is marred by an excessively rustic palette
of materials, jarringly combined with tired
Classical allusions – brought forth here, no
doubt, because of the long association of
Classicism with funerary architecture.

SF-30a One of Bryggman's more conventionally modern efforts is the **Sampo
Insurance Building,** 1936–8. *SW from*

*market square on Yliopistonkatu / in second
blk on R*

SF-30b After the Second World War
Bryggman, along with Carin Bryggman
and Olli Kestilä, undertook the difficult
task of restoring **Turku Castle,** a 500-
year-old agglomeration of disparate bits
and pieces. Except for some too quaint
windows, they employed an acceptably
modern idiom while maintaining great
sympathy with the fortress's original forms,
materials, and, especially, its spirit. *SW from
Turku ctr paralleling N side of river on Lin-
nankatu / on L at end of st*

Paimio   **SF-31**
** Sairaala (tuberculosis sanatorium)
1928–33
Alvar Aalto
International Style
E from Turku on E80 abt 18½ mi (30 km) /
N → PAIMIO (at motel) / *R → SAIRAALA*
/ *R at Y into sanatorium grounds*

[Over the years there have been many changes, including the removal of some decorative fins from the top of the smokestack (originally painted black) and the glazing and conversion into additional hospital rooms of the famous fresh-air treatment balcony wing. All of the major work was carried out by Aalto, including the addition of a small wing in his late 50s manner to the left of the entrance.]

With this building, a high point of the International Style, Aalto brought international attention simultaneously to himself and to Finnish architecture. Only a few years after his Neo-Classical workingmen's club in Jyväskylä (SF-35a), he was in undisputed command of this fully modern idiom. His sudden and total acceptance of the modernist cause paralleled Gunnar Asplund's better-known conversion. Indeed, Aalto's thoughtful and truly functional detailing here anticipated the later emergence, in part under Asplund's influence, of a particularly Scandinavian brand of modernism, suffused with the same Arts and Crafts-inspired sensitivity to details that permeates so many of the best early twen-

tieth-century Scandinavian buildings (DK-13, S-3, SF-18). Altogether it is an amazing performance for a man who was not to find his own mature style for another fifteen years. (Only the too stylized form of the entrance canopy strikes a wrong note.)

SF-31a   Aalto-designed housing groups are scattered about the grounds. But the prewar examples, 1933, are not up to the standards of those at Sunila (SF-26), while the postwar ones merely represent good Scandinavian design.

Tampere   **SF-32**
** Tuomiokirkko (Tampere cathedral)
1899–1907
Tuomiokirkonkatu and Satakunnankatu
Lars Sonck
National Romantic/Jugendstil
E from ctr square on Hämeenkatu / *L on*
Tuomiokirkonkatu / *four blks on R*

Often cited as Finland's most important National Romantic monument – and rightly so – this church none the less lacks the assurance of Sonck's later works. He seems still to be trying out new ideas and techniques derived from both Finnish and foreign sources. The interior decor especially reflects his Jugendstil connections – as witness some of the metalwork and Hugo Simberg's curious balcony mural of attenuated youths supporting an enormous swag.

But any lack of mature ornamental coherence is offset by the tectonic vigour and enthusiasm with which Sonck articulated the interior. An almost square space of irregular outline, it is defined on three sides by a balcony which rests on granite piers decorated in the incised style Sonck evolved for that material. Some of the stained glass is as powerfully original as any produced at the time, when that art form was experiencing its last great

flowering. Even the role of the mullion-like tracery is thought out afresh, particularly in the west rose window where from the exterior it modulates the over-large smooth glass surfaces.

Yet despite all of this, there is still not enough consistent innovation: National Romanticism was generally most successful as a style for interior decoration, and that is certainly borne out here.

Tampere SF-33
* Kalevan kirkko (church) 1959–66
Tieskontie and Sammonkatu
Reima Pietilä & Raili Paatelainen
Neo-Expressionism
E from ctr square on Hämeenkatu through
tunnel (see SF-33a below) at end of st

One's first impression is of the power of that dense cluster of upthrust concave blades, all uniformly sliced off and standing like the flutes of some otherwise long-vanished, gigantic deformed column. Then one notices the yellowish square ceramic tiles sheathing the structural slip-formed (continuously cast) concrete wall segments. They are completely at odds with the building's abstract, sculptural nature. Yet, aside from that one questionable decision, the otherwise undeniable power of this church most certainly lies in its architects' comprehension of the implications and limitations of their initial bold design decision. There are no faked elements here, nor any inappropriate uses of materials stemming from some false sense of homogeneity, although there is the feeling of a genuinely harmonious work of art. It is tempting to invoke the Gothic here, not just for the church's obvious verticality, but for its more tough-minded organic unity.

SF-33a On the right just before one reaches the church is an **Adult Education Centre,** 1962, by Timo Penttilä and Kari Virta.

SF-33b Another interesting example of concrete construction here is **Ratina Stadium,** 1966, also by Timo Penttilä. *S from Hämeenkatu, just E of bridge, on Hatanpäänvaltatie / first R past bus station / on R*

Ruovesi SF-34
** Kalela (studio-house, now a museum) 1894–5
Akseli Gallen-Kallela
National Romantic
Ruovesi is abt 47 mi (75 km) N of Tampere / from Rt 66 just S of Ruovesi (and N of junction with rd → VÄÄRINMAJA) →
KALELA

[Open summer only, 1.00–6.00 pm]
Finnish National Romantic architecture began with this sensitively sited log house, designed not by an architect but by a painter-sculptor. Indeed the sculptor's sense of mass and space is everywhere: in the whitewashed living room fireplace-cum-oven; in the porch carved from the building's mass; and especially in the studio/living room with its balcony corridor and great north light. Despite its simple log construction and traditional decorative motifs, Kalela is a surprisingly modern, semi-open-plan house, which must have been, and indeed still would be, a joy to live in.

Undoubtedly it must have been easier for someone who was like Gallen-Kallela outside the architectural profession to initiate this sort of break with conventional ways of ornamenting structure and, to an extent, of organizing space. Although the

sudden appearance of Gallen-Kallela's Arts and Crafts-oriented National Romanticism and the burst of activity it set off seems almost a historical necessity in the Finnish context, in progressive circles throughout Europe there was already a strongly felt need for a style without any traditional precedents: one that, unlike Neo-Classicism, would not be restricted by rigidly defined canons, but would lend itself to the development of new solutions to new problems. In addition, then, to its political role, National Romanticism served this purpose in Finland – much as Art Nouveau did elsewhere.

Jyväskylä SF-35
Although none of Aalto's International Style buildings are here, no other place, including Helsinki, has a more representative sampling of his work, reflecting the full fifty-year span of his career.

Outside the city, in addition to a number of early church restorations and the Säynätsalo community centre (SF-37), Aalto also built his own summer house whose walls incorporate samples of dozens of types and arrangements of materials (not open

to the public).
Within Jyväskylä itself there are, in addition to the University (SF-36), the following works by Aalto:

SF-35a A **working-men's club,** 1923–5. Built in the then ubiquitous Scandinavian Neo-Classical style, it contains a theatre in its windowless upper floor. *Väinönkatu and Kauppakatu in Jyväskylä ctr*

SF-35b The **Police Headquarters,**

1968–70, the first part of a new civic centre, is a good example of Aalto's ability to design 'by exception': on its two street sides it is essentially straightforward Aalto vernacular, while the third façade, which abuts on a lakeside park, is a quietly abstract, sinuous concrete wall whose top edge rolls back at an angle over the building – making it more sculpture than architecture. Since Aalto's death a municipal office building, 1978, and a theatre, 1981, have also been completed. *Hannikaisen-*

katu and Kilpisenkatu, two blks NE of lake steamer dock

SF-35c The rather disappointing **Central Finland Museum,** 1959–62. *On Keskussairaalantie, across from S end of University (SF-36)*

SF-35d The **Alvar Aalto Museum,** 1970–3, a museum devoted to Jyväskylä's most famous son. *Adjacent to the Central Finland Museum*

Jyväskylä   **SF-36**
** **Yliopisto** (University of Jyväskylä)
1950–71
Seminaarinkatu and Keskussairaalantie
Alvar Aalto
Scandinavian Empiricism
S from Jyväskylä ctr on Rt 4 / on W side of rd at edge of town

In his long sequence of designs for this former teachers' training college, Aalto never produced a symbolic gesture comparable to the lecture halls in the central building at Otaniemi (SF-23). But the architecture here abounds with those details and spaces that make his best work at once both strangely abstract and delightfully humane. The most conspicuous example of the former quality is the little, self-consciously temple-like, marble faculty dining hall; while the latter would include the three-and-a-half-storey stairhall next to the

auditorium and its adjacent outdoor arena.

Most of the buildings are constructed in the red-brick, copper-roofed mode Aalto favoured when he won this commission in a competition. Similarly, the site plan and landscaping have remained essentially romantic and may have encouraged the buildings to have a somewhat two-dimensional, almost stage-set-like emphasis on their 'front' sides – i.e., as seen from the sports field or the main entrance to the auditorium.

Aalto's last building here, a 'sports' institute', 1970, partially closes the lower end of the campus. Although still recognizably his work, it is cut from somewhat different cloth. Depending on one's taste, it either disrupts the previous 'sensitive' arrangement or adds a note of vigour to a sometimes limp aggregation.

Säynätsalo [near Jyväskylä]   **SF-37**
** **Kunnantalo** (town hall: including flats, shops, offices and library) 1949–52
Alvar Aalto
Scandinavian Empiricism
E from Rt 4 (S of Jyväskylä) →
SÄYNÄTSALO / *R at Y* / *on island, bear L*

past shops / on L
[The very specialness of this place seems to have kept later development at too respectful a distance. Aalto intended the town hall to be the culmination of a space flanked by two ranks of apartment blocks. Unfortunately, the community's newer

shops and activities are instead all clustered together a few hundred yards away, while the centre's own shopping spaces are given over to governmental functions.]

In the aftermath of the Second World War Aalto's architecture, which tended to reflect the temper of the times, took on a reassuring, almost sheltering, quality. This attitude found its initial and most successful expression in the Säynätsalo Centre.

Because it is built on an island in the region where he had spent his youth and where he had his summer home, Aalto

Seinäjoki   **SF-38**
* Kaupungin Keskustaa (town hall, library and offices) 1959–65
Kirkko (church) 1952–65
Kirkkokatu and Alvar Aallonkatu
Alvar Aalto
Neo-Expressionism (town hall and library)
Just S of town ctr / church tower is visible for miles

Aalto's large church with its tall white tower, a landmark and civic symbol on the flat Ostrobothnian plain, resulted from a 1952 competition. Later, when the town came to need a new civic and cultural centre, a site was chosen opposite the church. In 1959 Aalto won a competition for that also.

In addition to the four buildings already constructed, there is to be a theatre, (designed 1968–9) placed close to the administration wing of the town hall (between the car park and the library), which will eventually plug the worst of the centre's present spatial 'leaks'. That, however, will do nothing about the intrusiveness of the road which bisects the complex, and from which Aalto took such great care to isolate the church, but not the civic buildings.

While Aalto certainly never stood still, and frequently doubled back upon himself to pick up the threads of ideas from years before, it is hard to envisage a group of his buildings which could have as little in common with each other, and in some respects with the general body of his work, as do these.

The most difficult to comprehend are the church buildings. The tower is merely big – nothing else. The forecourt and parish hall might have been interestingly urbane, yet their surroundings could not be less urban. And they deserve to frame something better than this elongated, elephantine box.

If the church is Aalto's clumsiest major building, then the small library must be his most delicately abstract. Possibly in an attempt to make it scaleless, its exterior details have been glossed over. Even the entrance is hidden behind the same strip grill that masks the windows. Its interior peculiarities, however, cannot stem from any such deference. The ceiling of its main

may have been particularly sensitive to the *genius loci* here. But a sense of regional identity alone is not sufficient explanation for the romantic image of the famous flight of grassy steps which lead, if only visually, to the council chamber, or for that room's beautifully organic roof trusses, the logic of which is as much poetic as structural.

Yet, even as Aalto developed this new vocabulary fully, the events that had given rise to it were already receding into history. Never again was he quite able to recapture the lyrical innocence he called forth here.

room, for instance, is an elegantly curved concrete shell which still bears the impression of its formwork. This surface – as distinct from its shape – is about as close as Aalto ever came to Brutalism in his postwar work. Furthermore the ceiling is supported on thin round columns which, bereft of Aalto's ubiquitous postwar sheathing detail, appear startlingly naked.

The cold purplish-blue town hall has, for Aalto, an unusually regular geometry. Again it is abstract. But, unlike the library, it is powerful and self-assured with a street elevation that could almost be a parody of Le Corbusier's Villa Savoye (F-45), a box on stilts with its innards poking out of the top. Unfortunately the council chamber itself, the projecting innard, is anti-climactic.

Altogether Aalto could have done far better here. It is almost as if his heart had not been consistently in the project. Did he recognize that it was built in the wrong place and that, if the community's real centre ever expands sufficiently to incorporate this artificial one, the town will have outgrown it? Meanwhile, some trees would help immensely.

Rovaniemi   SF-39
* **Kaupunginkirjasto** (municipal
library) 1963–8
Hallituskatu 9
Alvar Aalto
*E from Rt 4 roundabout, just S of town ctr,
on Hallituskatu / in first blk on R*

In 1944 the retreating Germans completely destroyed Rovaniemi, the chief city
of Finland's extreme north. Immediately
afterwards a new town plan was drawn up
under Aalto's leadership. This plan, while
it permits the town to function adequately,
does not yet seem superior in layout or in
detail to those of many older Finnish towns.
Its civic centre will eventually include a
town hall and theatre, in addition to the
library and Lappia House (SF-39a). In spite
of being part of the original 1945 scheme,
this project, which should have been the
heart of the town, was placed on a peripheral site, apparently because more
weight was given to its potential as a buffer
to the railway than to its central role in the
life of the community.

The library itself, precisely sculpted but
slightly mechanical and, all white except
for its dark metal roof, porch and column
sheaves, must look its best when seen
against snow in grey Arctic winter light,

with its skylights glowing beckoningly in
the cold. Within is a warm comfortable
space with coloured floors, light-wood trim,
daytime skylights supplemented with
'warm' incandescent lighting and, of
course, the variegated colours of the books
themselves.

Of Aalto's later works, this is the most
appealing. In it he achieved an amalgam
of the humanity he had found during the
difficult postwar years with the earlier self-
assured brashness which had lain repressed
in the 40s and 50s. If it does not have
the fresh vigour of the early modern
movement, nor the 'sensitivity' of Aalto's
red-brick phase, it does reflect a mature
subtlety that only time can bring to those
who have the luck to survive and the per-
severance to continue their artistic growth.

SF-39a The adjacent **Lappia House,**
1975, a provincial museum and cultural
centre, was Aalto's second building for
Rovaniemi's civic centre. It is a dose of 'old-
fashioned' straightforward Functionalism
only partially relieved by the roofs of three
auditoria, which, like a school of corrugated whales briefly surfacing for air,
hump up above the meagre cornices of its
austere and similarly corrugated façades.

Index of Buildings

Index of Building Types

Kindergartens: *see* Schools

Laboratories:
F-61c, 64; NL-18; S-14a; *see also* Universities and colleges
Landscapes, landscape and street 'furniture', fountains, pavilions, etc.:
A-7a, 9a; D-23, 24, 35, 35c, 46c, 53f–h; DK-2c; E-12, 17; F-38c, 53a, 53b; GB-26a, 26b, 38c, 69a; I-14b; N-2a; NL-38a, 51b, 51c, 53; P-3b; S-21, 24, 26a; *see also* Follies *and* Greenhouses
Libraries:
D-14a, 32; DK-4; F-3, 7, 11; GB-12, 48c, 50a, 51a, 75; IRL-2; S-7; SF-23a, 37, 38, 39

Markets:
D-51c; F-6e; NL-23
Military buildings:
A-12; D-71; *see also* Restorations *and* Adaptive re-use
Monasteries and convents:
F-55; I-27; N-6; *see also* Churches
Monuments and tombs:
D-24b, 24c, 26a, 57, 67, 71; DK-13; E-5a, 26c; F-10, 16, 28f; I-14a, 29a
Museums:
A-4; D-13, 26b, 28, 35, 37, 46c, 42b, 47, 51, 51a, 53, 58, 68; DK-2b, 3b, 5b, 18; E-14a; F-6, 6c, 6d, 16b, 16c, 18b, 61; GB-8, 10a, 10b, 49, 55a; I-3a, 3b, 16b, 41a–c, 46, 51b; IRL-2a; N-2b; NL-3a, 32, 53a; P-4; S-12, 22, 26b, 26c; SF-10, 35, 39a, 40c; *see also* Exhibition buildings
Museums and exhibitions of architecture:
A-20; B-6; CH-3; D-12a, 15, 25, 53, 54, 55, 56, 57, 60; E-2b, 12a; F-22, 53; GB-8; I-29b, 47b; NL-21; S-2e; SF-2g; *see also* Architectural drawings and models *and* Exhibits of crafts, etc.

New towns: *see* Urban design
Newspaper offices, radio and TV stations:
A-26; D-20; F-9; GB-22, 31, 67, 81; NL-6

Offices:
A-10; B-8, 18b; CH-2a; D-5a, 9b, 12, 26d, 27, 34, 42a, 43, 51b, 51e, 52, 61a; E-23a, 28; F-9, 9a, 14, 61c; GB-4, 5, 6, 9, 11, 53, 57, 67, 79a, 80; I-21, 22a, 26, 28; N-4; NL-4, 6, 29, 54; P-6; S-2a, 20; SF-4, 5, 7b, 9, 13, 22a, 22d, 28, 30a
Open-air museums: *see* Restorations, etc.

Parking garages:
D-45; GB-8c, 17, 45, 76a; I-18, 26; P-6; SF-2
Pavilions: *see* Landscapes, etc.

Railway stations: *see* Transport buildings
Recreational buildings (gymnasia, swimming pools, etc.):
CH-6, 15; DK-2c; F-32, 39a, 43; GB-38d, 43, 44a, 44b; NL-22d, 25a; SF-19c, 23c
Restaurants and bars:
A-8b; CH-22c; GB-6b, 10, 16, 69, 81; I-34a; NL-10, 55a; S-2d, 13; SF-19a; *see also* Hotels
Restorations, ruins and open-air museums:
F-28a–e; I-54a, 54b; S-12b; *see also* Adaptive re-use
Row, cluster and terraced houses:
A-18c, 20; B-13, 15; CH-12, 21, 21c, 22; D-11a, 60; DK-15a, 17; F-25a, 25b; GB-18,

37, 65, 69, 72; N-7; NL-17a, 37b, 47, 56; SF-19g, 19h, 19o; *see also* Housing

Schools:
CH-1a, 5; D-25m, 39, 59; DK-11, 12, 14; E-11b, 16, 20a; F-11b, 24, 39, 41b, 44; GB-42, 50, 51a, 56, 79, 83, 79a; I-23, 27, 30, 32, 33; NL-16, 17, 23a, 50; P-7; SF-19n, 33a; *see also* Universities and colleges
Shopping centres: *see* Shops and stores
Shops and stores:
A-6, 6a, 8a; CH-9; D-7a, 25h, 28, 32, 42, 59; F-3b–g, 12d, 33, 46i, 50; GB-6a, 6b, 16, 18b, 37b, 38b, 45, 66a, 76a; I-8, 26b; NL-2d, 21k, 26, 27, 42, 51a, 58; P-5b; S-18, 32c; SF-4a, 19c; *see also* Commercial buildings *and* Commercial and residential buildings
Social housing: *see* Housing
Social welfare buildings: *see* Communal and social welfare buildings
Stadia:
A-13a, 13b; CH-7; D-20a–c, 29, 70; E-31; F-54c, 56; I-2a, 5, 50a; SF-10b, 33b; *see also* Auditoria
Stock and commodity exchanges:
F-10c; NL-3; SF-7; *see also* Banks
Stores: *see* Shops and stores
Studios (artists' and architects'):
CH-20; D-53, 69; F-34c; GB-79; N-2a; NL-15; S-1a; SF-16, 18, 34
Swimming pools: *see* Recreational buildings

Technology: *see* Building as Machine *and* Engineering
Telephone exchanges:
F-8; SF-6
Terraced housing: *see* Row, cluster and terraced housing
Theatres: *see* Auditoria
Tombs: *see* Monuments and tombs
Town halls: *see* City halls
Towers: *see* Engineering
Transport buildings (railway stations, etc.):
A-3, 11a; B-14; CH-9b, 18a; D-7a, 58a; DK-2d; F-6d, 17; GB-19, 23, 24; I-9, 21a, 48; NL-55d, 55e; P-1a; SF-3, 4d

Union buildings (Labour): *see* Associations, unions and clubs
Universities and colleges:
CH-11, 14; D-6, 46b, 64, 67a; DK-4, 20; F-34; GB-49a, 50, 51, 51a-c, 52, 55, 58, 58a, 88; I-2b–e, 31, 47c, 52; NL-8, 19a, 55, 55a, 55b; S-9; SF-23, 24, 25, 36; *see also* Dormitories *and* Schools
Urban design (including garden cities):
A-12; B-2, 13, 15; D-10, 22a, 28, 40, 53, 60; DK-2; E-12, 20, 27a; F-3, 4, 27a, 38, 51, 53, 54, 54e, 62; GB-9b, 25, 30, 36, 37, 48, 60, 65, 69, 72, 76a, 86; I-1a, 1b, 2a, 13, 47c; NL-2a, 2b, 2c, 5, 57; S-1, 2, 8a, 18, 22b; SF-2a, 2d, 2e, 11, 19, 23, 39
Utilities (heating and power plants, etc.):
CH-20; F-38c; GB-10e; SF-19f, 23b

Warehouses:
CH-13b; GB-54, 63; N-4a

Youth centres: *see* Communal and social welfare buildings

Zoo buildings: GB-20, 21

Index of Architects

Photographic Acknowledgements

All photographs are by the authors except: page 19 Mary Evans Picture Library; page 25 Rollin la France; D-6 Landesbildstelle Berlin; D-68 Alte Pinakothek, Munich; DK-15 Foto/C, Arkitektensredaktion; F-6, NL-56 Donald Grinberg; GB-22, 34, 42, 46, 76, I-24, 33, N-3, NL-20, 45 Architectural Association; GB-11 Martin Charles; GB-53 John Donat; GB-81 Gillander & Mack; NL-9 Ger van der Vlugt; NL-32 Helen Lewis; S-5 Swedish Museum of Architecture, photo Peter Celsing; S-10 Swedish Museum of Architecture, photo Per Bonde; S-13 Stockholms Stadsmuseum; S-21 Foto Millesgården; SF-11 Kari Hakli, Museum of Finnish Architecture; SF-28 T. Rory Spence